MIGRATION AND ECONOMIC GROWTH

(Second edition)

MIGRATION
AND
ECONOMIC GROWTH

A STUDY OF
GREAT BRITAIN AND THE
ATLANTIC ECONOMY
(Second edition)

BY

BRINLEY THOMAS

CAMBRIDGE
AT THE UNIVERSITY PRESS
1973

Published by the Syndics of the Cambridge University Press
Bentley House, 200 Euston Road, London NW1 2DB
American Branch: 32 East 57th Street, New York, N.Y.10022

This edition © Cambridge University Press 1973
First published 1954
Second edition 1973
Library of Congress Catalogue Card Number: 79–171684

ISBN: 0 521 08566 7

Printed by offset in Great Britain
by Alden & Mowbray Ltd
at the Alden Press, Oxford

CONTENTS

PART I.   HYPOTHESES

PART II.   DESCRIPTION

Part IV. REAPPRAISAL

LIST OF TABLES IN TEXT AND APPENDICES

LIST OF FIGURES

PREFACE

Since the first edition of this book appeared, the subject has been strongly influenced by important new work in economic growth, international trade, monetary theory and quantitative economic history. An indication of the extent of the literature is given in my *International Migration and Economic Development: a Trend Report and Bibliography* (Paris, Unesco, 1961, pp. 65–85) and 'Migration: Economic Aspects', *International Encyclopaedia of the Social Sciences*, 1968, vol. 10, pp. 292–300. There has been a lively debate about long swings and the Atlantic economy, and empirical work has been facilitated by superior quantitative methods and a marked improvement in the range and quality of historical statistics. I need only mention the numerous contributions of Simon Kuznets, the statistical series on the money stock of the United States since 1867 by Milton Friedman and Anna Schwartz, and D. K. Sheppard's *The Growth and Role of U.K. Financial Institutions 1880–1962* (London, Methuen, 1971). Unfortunately, the latter was not available in time for me to use. Economic and demographic research on migration has been stimulated by public concern about problems of population pressure, urbanization, the environment and the assimilation of non-white migrants; and international movements of educated manpower have been a major object of inquiry in many countries. The time is ripe for a new look at the related controversies over the development of the nineteenth-century Atlantic economy and the nature of contemporary migration.

In this new edition I have reproduced Parts I and II and a large section of Part III (Chapters VII to XII), but where improved statistical sources have become available they have been substituted for the older ones. Many teachers and researchers have indicated that they found it very useful to have all the statistical time series printed in full because it gives the book an added value as a work of reference. The reappraisal in Part IV occupies nearly half the text of this edition. In Chapters XIII to XV I have written my own review of Part III and of its critics; the argument about the growth of the Atlantic economy is elaborated in the light of new findings in Chapter XV, the heart of the book. On the whole the original analysis has stood the test remarkably well. In Chapters XVI to XVIII I examine three contemporary themes—regional growth and non-white immigration in Britain, the rise and fall of trans-

Atlantic brain drain since 1950, and Negro migration and the American urban dilemma. The Epilogue takes a brief glance at the United States and the international economy since 1945—the nineteenth-century story in reverse.

Some critics have shown a surprising tendency to explain the economic growth and fluctuations of particular countries (usually their own) exclusively in terms of internal determinants; these views are summarized in Chapter xiv. It has been fashionable in America to argue that the periodic inflows of immigrants and capital to the United States were caused unilaterally by swings in American aggregate demand, no significance being attached to the process of international interaction. Similarly, one or two British economic historians think that British building fluctuations in the nineteenth century were the result of fortuitous domestic factors and had nothing to do with any systematic relation between British and American long swings. The new evidence presented in Chapter xiii amply confirms the primacy of the demographic determinants of building cycles in Britain and the United States as well as the inverse relation between them. In Chapter xv the treatment is extended to cover Canada, Australia and Argentina. With the aid of a model of the international economy, the analysis demonstrates the part played by demographic and monetary factors in causing long cycles in investment, productivity and real income in new countries to be opposite in timing to British cycles up to 1913. In this edition much more attention has been devoted to the monetary aspects of the interaction process. The role of London as the world's financial centre and the international repercussions of the Bank of England's policy are given due weight. The conclusions of Chapter xv refute the view that the American economy was the unmoved mover in the fluctuations of the international economy between mid-nineteenth century and 1913. In carrying out this reappraisal, I have felt that its technique bears a close relation to that of the new economic history in the United States, as exemplified in the valuable symposium, *The Reinterpretation of American Economic History*, edited by Robert W. Fogel and Stanley L. Engerman (New York, Harper & Row, 1971). The next step will be to construct an econometric model on the basis indicated at the end of Chapter xv.

I see no reason to change the conclusion in the first edition that the decade of the nineties was the end of one epoch and the beginning of another (see pp. 118–22). The profound readjustment which was taking place at the end of the century has been brilliantly analysed by Geoffrey Barraclough in *An Introduction to Contemporary History* (London, Penguin Books, 1967). In the following passage, stressing demographic factors, he strikes a note in tune with the theme of this book. 'Hence, as the twentieth century proceeded, the advantages which had ensured European predominance—namely, the monopoly of machine production and the military strength conferred by industrialization—receded and the underlying demographic factors reasserted their importance. It is no exaggeration to state that the demographic revolution of the half-century between 1890 and 1940 was the basic change marking the transition from one era in history to another. At the same time the period of European political hegemony was drawing to a close and the European balance of power, which for so long had governed the relations between states, was being superseded by the age of world politics.' (Ibid. p. 92.)

The Atlantic economy as we conceive it went through a structural change and did not survive after the 1920s. The slump in the international flow of capital in the nineties was different from previous slumps in one important respect: America, by then so large and rich that she would not need to borrow much more from London, was soon to become the world's leading creditor nation. New forces gave a special character to the last great upswing in Britain's foreign investment from 1900 to 1913. It might be argued that this upsurge was a natural continuation of the rhythm which had been a feature of the country's growth for many decades; it was the turn of the marginal efficiency of foreign investment to take the lead. The answer to this is that the pursuit of private gain along traditional channels had become inconsistent with the long-run economic interest of the nation in a changed environment; both the technical efficiency of British industry and the welfare of the wage-earners would have been improved in the decade ending in 1913 if the propensity to lend abroad and the large-scale emigration which it entailed had been curbed and the domestic rate of interest reduced to the level necessary for full employment of home resources. Countries such as Germany and Sweden took full advantage of the technological revolution of that time; home investment and the physical productivity of their industries rose rapidly between 1900 and 1913; and net emigration from both countries was comparatively small. The growth of their productive capacity in that period was akin to what was happening in the United States, while by comparison Great Britain was stagnating. Our analysis of British long swings in productivity and real income (Chapter xv, pp. 283-7) brings out the fact that in the 1900s the mechanism of export-led growth was running down because important parameters had changed to Britain's detriment.

The outstanding difference between recent and nineteenth-century international migration is the prominence of migrants in the professional and technical grades. Chapter xvii surveys the international circulation of professional manpower between 1950 and 1970 and uses the concept of dynamic shortage to explain the phenomenon of brain drain. This diagnosis was first put forward in a lecture at the London School of Economics in March 1967 when I argued that the key explanatory variable was Federal expenditure on Research and Development in the United States. Chapter XVII shows that subsequent events confirmed this variable as an accurate predictor of the course of brain drain.

Fortunate indeed is the author who can say without fear of contradiction that he made no mistakes in his first edition. I cannot claim this. In Chapter VIII dealing with internal and international mobility, I thought I had demonstrated that the hypothesis of an inverse relation between internal and external migration applied to countries of immigration as well as those of emigration (see pp. 130–4). Critics rightly pointed out that this is refuted by the experience of the United States where swings in internal migration corresponded to those in immigration. But perhaps I was lucky after all, for that error turned out to be a blessing in disguise. What happened was that I took the migration of black people from the South to the North of the United States as a proxy for internal migration in general, and I found that its fluctuations were inverse to those of immigration. I thought I had detected symmetry, but the key was really to be found in asymmetry. I had stumbled across a fact of far-reaching significance. There was a clear inverse correlation between the proportion of Negroes and the proportion of foreign white stock in the population of the various States (see pp. 133–4). The black worker was in keen competition not only with poor whites in the South but also with unskilled whites from Europe; his chance of getting a job in the North depended very much on whether immigration was booming or dwindling. Kuznets extended the analysis to other variables and discovered long swings in black mortality and fertility rates, the former corresponding to and the latter inverse to the swings in immigration. (See 'Long Swings in the Growth of Population and in Related Economic Variables', *Proceedings of the American Philosophical Society*, Philadelphia, vol. 102, no. 1, February 1958, p. 31.) If by a miracle there had been racial tolerance, the black workers from the South could have played their full part, in common with immigrants from Europe, in meeting the labour requirements of the rapidly growing cities of the North after the Civil War. The economic and demographic significance of Negro internal migration from 1870 to 1970 is explored in Chapter XVIII.

The peopling of America by the 'huddled masses' of the Old World was a boon to the whites and a curse to the blacks. One would expect the black migrant to come into his own after the ending of free immigration in 1924, and this tendency has gathered considerable strength. Net out-migration of Negroes from the South increased from 454,000 in

1910–20 to 1,400,000 in 1960–70; nearly half of the 22,672,570 black people enumerated in America in 1970 lived outside the South as compared with just over one-fifth of 12,860,000 in 1940. However, the sombre fact is that the cities which the Negroes are at last entering in large numbers are being evacuated by the descendants of the immigrants who founded them; hence the agonizing problems of a shrinking tax base, seething ghettos, mounting welfare rolls, and fierce racial conflict. The social ladder which made the 'American dream' a reality for the European immigrant, whatever his ethnic group, appears to the Negro to be just a pipe-dream.

The migration scene in America and Britain is now overshadowed by the sinister legacy of racial discrimination. Chapter XVII shows how the one big influx of migrants from the West Indies, India and Pakistan into England has tended to produce a segregation pattern in some urban areas. The ghost of the first Atlantic economy, whose mainstay was the horrible traffic in African slaves, is now haunting the Anglo-Saxon world; but the present generation cannot be held responsible for what their forbears did. We all live in glass houses, even though some are more stone-proof than others. If the present generation of young whites retain their idealism and practise non-discrimination when they become middle-aged heads of families and if the blacks meet them half-way, the future will be bright.

This book is mainly about the rhythm of economic growth. In the Preface to the first edition I acknowledged the inspiration I had derived from Schumpeter's great work, *Business Cycles: a Theoretical, Historical and Statistical Analysis of the Capitalist Process*. Working on this second edition made me realize how much I owe to Simon Kuznets's outstanding contributions to the analysis of economic growth. In the Epilogue I pose the question whether long swings were a phenomenon peculiar to the Atlantic economy of the nineteenth century and ceased to exist when the underlying conditions changed. The answer lies in Kuznets's demonstration that the long swing is a fundamental component of the long-term movement. Abramovitz may be right to mourn the passing of the Kuznets cycle if he means the pre-1913 embodiment of that cycle; but, as I point out in the Epilogue, there is still some doubt about the identification of the deceased. As far as the long swing is concerned, this book ends not with a wreath but a bouquet.

June 1972

BRINLEY THOMAS

ACKNOWLEDGEMENTS

When I was writing the first edition several friends were kind enough to comment on some of the chapters and I wish to record my appreciation: Ernest Rubin (Chapter IV), Johan Åkerman (Chapter VII), R. S. Sayers (Chapter XI), and Sir Roy Allen (Appendix 2). My thanks are also due to David Caplin who carried out the analysis embodied in Appendix 1. I was greatly indebted to John Parry Lewis, then Assistant Lecturer in Statistics at University College, Cardiff, for contributing Appendices 2 and 3 and giving valuable research assistance. I wish to record my gratitude to the National Institute of Economic and Social Research for the help I received in writing the first edition and, in particular, to its then Secretary, the late Mrs F. S. Stone, whose unfailing encouragement and close interest meant so much to the progress of the work. I benefited considerably from the critical reading of early drafts of Parts I, II and III by the Institute's Advisory Committee, the members of which were H. S. Frankel, D. V. Glass, Brian Reddaway, E. A. G. Robinson, R. M. Titmuss and the late Sir Frederick Ogilvie. I recall with gratitude the valuable assistance given by the late Julius Isaac, at that time a member of the research staff of the National Institute, Miss H. M. Rogers, the then Librarian, and Miss Joan Ayling who was responsible for most of the computing and drawing of charts for Part III.

In preparing this new edition I was fortunate to be able to enjoy two periods of comparative freedom from teaching and administrative responsibilities. I am grateful to the Principal and Council of University College, Cardiff, for giving me leave to accept a visiting Professorship at Johns Hopkins University for a term in 1968 and at Brown University for a term in 1971 as a National Science Foundation Fellow. Thanks to the generosity of my hosts in these universities and the privilege of using their excellent libraries, I was able to pursue my research in a most congenial environment. I wish in particular to express my thanks to Carl Christ at Johns Hopkins and George Borts and Jerome Stein at Brown for the stimulating experience of working with them and their colleagues and for the interest they took in my work.

Chapter XIII was given as a paper to the Mathematical Social Science Board Conference on the New Economic History of Britain, 1840–1930, held at Eliot House, Harvard University, in September 1970. Early versions of Chapter XV were read as papers to seminars at the Economics and Sociology Departments at Brown University, to the Economic History Workshop at Chicago University, to a seminar organized by J. J. Spengler at Duke University, and to an economics colloquium at the University of Wales. The critical probing which took place on those various occasions was of immense value to me. It has been my good fortune to participate in several of the American conferences on the new economic history, and I profited considerably from lively discussions on long swings with Moses Abramovitz, Douglass North, Richard Easterlin and Jeffrey Williamson. On the demographic side I am greatly indebted to Dorothy Thomas, Hope Eldridge and their colleagues at the University of Pennsylvania Population Studies Center.

When I was writing the first edition of this book the friendly encouragement I received from Simon Kuznets meant a great deal to me; his works have continued to be a rich source of inspiration. Several friends have been kind enough to comment in detail on early drafts of some chapters in Part IV. I wish to record my deep appreciation of the help I received from Conrad Blyth, Henry Phelps Brown and John Parry Lewis, especially in setting out rigorously the ideas of Chapter xv. On some methodological problems arising in Chapter xiii I had the benefit of expert comment by Bernard Benjamin. I learnt a great deal about the statistics of professional manpower and brain drain from discussions with Mrs Joan Cox of the Department of Trade and Industry in London, Dr Milton Levine of the National Science Foundation in Washington, and John D. Alden, Executive Secretary of the Engineering Manpower Commission of the Engineers Joint Council, New York. Any errors that may have crept in are entirely my responsibility.

Part IV of this edition incorporates the contents of chapters 1–2 and 4–7 of my *Migration and Urban Development* (Methuen and Co. Ltd, 1972).

I am grateful to the following for permission to base diagrams and tables on existing material: Sir Alec Cairncross and the Cambridge University Press for Table 147; J. H. Adler, the Macmillan Press Ltd, St Martin's Press Inc. and the International Economic Association for Figs. 50 and 54; H. D. Mitchell and R. Ash, the editor and the *British Medical Journal* for Table 154; Professor Reynolds Farley and the Markham Publishing Company for Fig. 63; the National Science Foundation for Table 151; Allen C. Kelley and the Kent State University Press for Table 57; and Professor Arthur Bloomfield and the International Finance Section, Department of Economics, Princeton University, for Fig. 51.

I thank the following for permission to reproduce sections of work of mine which they have published: the editor of *The Manchester School of*

Economic and Social Studies ('Migration and the Rhythm of Economic Growth, 1830–1913', vol. XIX, no. 3, September 1951, pp. 215–71); Donald N. McCloskey, Methuen and Co. Ltd and Princeton University Press (*Essays on a Mature Economy: Britain after 1840*, copyright Methuen and Co. Ltd 1971, Chapter 2); J. H. Adler, the Macmillan Press Ltd, St Martin's Press Inc. and the International Economic Association (*Capital Movements and Economic Development*, 1967, Chapter 1); the editor of *Erhvervshistorisk Årbog*, Denmark (*The Changing Pattern of Anglo-Danish Trade, 1913–1963*, 1966, Chapter VI); the University of Wales Press (*The Welsh Economy: Studies in Expansion*, 1962, Chapter 1); the editor of *Minerva* ('The International Circulation of Human Capital', vol. V, Summer 1967, pp. 479–506).

I am particularly grateful to Mrs Margaret Evans, a former research assistant, for her expert handling of original data which she collected at the Public Record Office; much of the credit for the charts in Chapter XIII and the methodology underlying them belongs to her. My thanks are due to the social sciences section of the library of University College, Cardiff, for excellent service and to my secretary, Mrs Vida Turner, who not only saw each draft of the new chapters through to their final stage with superb accuracy but was also responsible for drawing some of the charts. The organizing of this new edition has been an exacting task, and I am much indebted to Cambridge University Press and Miss Gillian Little for the splendid way in which they handled it. Once again, it is a pleasure to record my gratitude to my publisher and printer for their enthusiastic cooperation.

B.T.

PART I

HYPOTHESES

CHAPTER I

THE CLASSICAL VIEW OF EMIGRATION

Emigration was the subject of lively debate in England during the forty years after the Napoleonic Wars, and the general approach to the problem was in sharp contrast to the philosophy of the mercantilist era. The intellectual revolution wrought by Adam Smith, coinciding with a rapid increase in population, sounded the death-knell of traditional ideas. In the second half of the seventeenth century the prevailing view was that the nation's interests were best served by encouraging the growth of numbers. In the words of Sir Josiah Child: 'For much want of People would procure greater Wages, and greater Wages, if our Laws gave encouragement, would procure us a supply of People without the charge of breeding them. The Riches of a City, as of a Nation, consisting in the multitude of inhabitants....'[1] Although the mercantilists were prone to worry about lack of sufficient employment, they did not allow this concern to weaken their efforts to achieve a large number of people.

With certain exceptions, emigration was regarded as harmful. Child's analysis of this question drew a distinction between colonies such as Jamaica and Barbados, where every English settler furnished employment for four of his fellow-countrymen at home, and New England where it would need ten settlers to provide a job for one more person in the mother country. Oversea migration would thus have to be carefully controlled so that it would tend to maximize employment at home, and every effort was to be made to attract skilled immigrants from other countries. It was a frankly nationalist creed, and its exponents saw no reason to deny that the successes of one country were won at the expense of others.

By the end of the eighteenth century this system of thought had already been undermined; a fatal blow was delivered by Malthus in his *Essay on Population* which appeared in 1798. Steeped in the philosophy of individualism and possessing a new method of thinking about

---

[1] Quoted in Eli F. Heckscher, *Mercantilism*, English ed., London, Allen and Unwin, 1934, vol. II, pp. 158–9.

economic affairs, the theorists of the early nineteenth century reached conclusions sharply opposed to those of their predecessors. But in one respect there was no difference. The classical economists, like the mercantilists, believed that migration should be regulated by the State. It was one of the few exceptions to the general rule of *laissez-faire*.

I. A DUALISM IN CLASSICAL THINKING

A careful reading of John Stuart Mill's *Principles* shows that he regarded the transactions between Britain and members of her economic empire as different from those between Britain and other sovereign states. To quote his words:

> There is a class of trading and exporting communities, on which a few words of explanation seem to be required. These are hardly to be looked upon as countries, carrying on an exchange of commodities with other countries, but more properly as outlying agricultural or manufacturing establishments belonging to a larger community...The West Indies...are the place where England finds it convenient to carry on the production of sugar, coffee, and a few other tropical commodities. All the capital employed is English capital; almost all the industry is carried on for English uses; there is little production of anything except the staple commodities, and these are sent to England, not to be exchanged for things exported to the colony and consumed by its inhabitants, but to be sold in England for the benefit of the proprietors there. The trade with the West Indies is therefore hardly to be considered as external trade, but more resembles the traffic between town and country, and is amenable to the principles of home trade.[1]

This quotation suggests that classical writers theorized on two different planes. When they discussed international trade, they had nothing to say about migration between countries; their doctrine was usually illustrated by exchanges of British goods for the produce of other sovereign countries like Portugal, Sweden or Poland—cases where, if only for reasons of language, it was perfectly reasonable to assume that inter-

---

[1] J. S. Mill, *Principles of Political Economy*, 6th ed., London, Longmans, 1909, bk. III, ch. XXV, pp. 414–15. Professor J. H. Williams, commenting on the above quotation in his important article, 'The Theory of International Trade Reconsidered' (*Economic Journal*, vol. XXXIX, no. 154, June 1929, p. 208), makes the following point: 'In attempting to ascertain the precise range of application of this suggestion of Mill's, so strikingly in contrast with his general theory of international trade, I find it a matter of the utmost difficulty where to draw the line. Though he mentions several peculiarities of the case of these colonies, the decisive ones, clearly, are that England finds it convenient to produce certain goods there (as is indeed true of all international trade), and that this convenience actuates the movement of English production factors, tending to produce an equality of profit "after allowance is made for the disadvantages" of distance and risks. This applies certainly to very much of English trade in the nineteenth century.'

national mobility of labour would be negligible. But when they considered the 'larger community' of countries referred to by Mill, they had a great deal to say about emigration. A study of the contributions of Torrens, Merivale and Bastable provides ample evidence of this dualism. On the one hand, there was the static theory of international trade, based on the law of comparative costs, which gave scientific justification for the policy of free trade. On the other hand, there was the dynamic theory of colonization, based on the law of diminishing returns and the tendency of profits to fall to a minimum. The art of colonization was listed as one of the few exceptions to the general rule that there must be no State interference with private enterprise: it was held to be not only desirable but indispensable that the Government should spend money on promoting the emigration of labour and capital from the mother country to the oversea territories.

2. SAY'S LAW AND EMIGRATION

The debate on the economic consequences of emigration and capital exports was in some respects a part of the great controversy about the possibility of 'a general glut of commodities'. On one side was Ricardo, echoing Say's Law, declaring that

...there is no amount of capital which may not be employed in a country, because demand is only limited by production. No man produces, but with a view to consume or sell, and he never sells, but with an intention to purchase some other commodity, which may be immediately useful to him, or which may contribute to future production.... There cannot, then, be accumulated in a country any amount of capital which cannot be employed productively, until wages rise so high in consequence of the rise of necessaries, and so little consequently remains for the profits of stock, that the motive for accumulation ceases.[1]

According to this reasoning real wages depended upon the proportion between capital and labour. If labour and capital emigrated in equal proportions, the wages of the workers left in the home country would remain constant. If, however, proportionately more capital than labour flowed out, the demand for labour would be reduced relatively more than the supply, and wages in England would fall. This led to the pessimistic conclusion that colonization would probably worsen the condition of the working classes at home.

This crude doctrine, as depressing as it was fallacious, was strongly attacked, particularly by Edward Gibbon Wakefield, the outstanding figure in the literature of emigration in the nineteenth century. His

[1] Ricardo, *Principles of Political Economy*, Gonner's ed.; London, Bell, 1913, pp. 273-4.

Letter from Sydney, written in 1829 while he was serving a sentence in Newgate, set the keynote of discussion for the next thirty years. Not only did this remarkable man convert the leading economists of the day, but he even captured the allegiance of cabinet ministers and wielded a direct influence on the policy of successive British Governments. In *The Art of Colonization* (1833) Wakefield urged that colonization would confer three advantages on an old society: it would increase the market for its products, give relief from over-population, and promote foreign investment.[1] He was quite unable to take the apostles of Say's Law seriously. Their argument, he pointed out, rested on a false postulate.

If it were true that every increase of capital necessarily gave employment to more labour; if it were true, as Professor M'Culloch has said, that 'there is plainly only one way of effectually improving the condition of the great majority of the community or of the labouring class, and that is *by increasing the ratio of capital to population*', then it might be assumed that colonization would, on account of its expense, do more harm than good. But it is not true that all capital employs labour. To say so is to say that which a thousand facts prove to be untrue. Capital frequently increases without providing any more employment for labour.[2]

He then went on to enumerate the various types of capital export in previous years, from loans to the Emperors of Austria and Russia to investments of British funds in the iron and cotton works of France, the Low Countries and Germany.

If all the capital removed from England in all these ways during the last seventeen years, amounting to some hundreds of millions, had been lost in conducting emigration, employment for labour in England would not have been less than it is at present.[3]

Another powerful exponent of this point of view was Torrens, the gist of whose thesis is given in the following quotation:

In a manufacturing and commercial country, importing raw produce, the field of employment, and the demand for labour, cannot be determined by the amount of capital ready to be invested in manufactures and commerce. In a country thus circumstanced, employment and wages will depend, not so much upon the amount of commercial and manufacturing capital, as upon the extent of the foreign market. If the foreign market does not extend, no increase of manufacturing capital can cause a beneficial increase of production, or a permanent advance of wages. Indeed, an increase of manufacturing and commercial capital, unaccompanied by a proportionate

---

[1] *The Art of Colonization* appeared as a part of his book, *England and America*, in 1833. See Edward Gibbon Wakefield, *A Letter from Sydney and Other Writings*, Everyman ed., London, Dent, 1929, pp. 109–200.

[2] Ibid. pp. 120–1.   [3] Ibid. p. 121.

extension of the foreign market, instead of proving beneficial, might have a necessary tendency to lower the profits of trade, and to reduce the wages of labour.[1]

In another passage he concludes:

In all, manufacturing capital may increase faster than the foreign capital, which raises the materials of manufacture; and thus, in all the departments of industry supplying goods to the foreign markets, there may be contemporaneous overtrading, or a contemporaneous 'home competition', occasioning a general fall of prices, of profits, and of wages, want of employment, and distress.[2]

Torrens was a staunch advocate of colonization on the ground that it was 'merely the application of the redundant capital and population of the United Kingdom to the redundant land of the colonies'.[3]

A writer who specialized on this subject was Herman Merivale, Drummond Professor of Political Economy at Oxford, whose *Lectures on Colonization and Colonies*, delivered before the University, 1839–41, though not particularly original, give a clear account of most matters in dispute at the time.[4] One of the things which exercised people's minds was whether mass emigration from Ireland would be desirable, and Torrens had proposed a planned migration of one million cottiers to America. Merivale was sceptical and referred to the experience of the Isle of Skye where 8,000 out of 11,000 inhabitants emigrated in a few years beginning in 1755, and by the end of the next generation the population had again reached its original size. He thought Ireland would repeat the history of Skye on a much larger scale. In the 1861 edition of his *Lectures*, Merivale had to admit that the mass emigration from Ireland after 1846—the population fell by 1,600,000 between 1841 and 1851—had disproved his earlier argument.

In the debate on the economic consequences of exports of labour and capital, Merivale agreed with Torrens that to send capital out of the country would in certain circumstances be an effective way of preventing a fall in profit. He was impressed by Malthus's attack on Ricardo's position. As he put it, 'however paradoxical the doctrine may at first sight appear, it cannot but be thought that a change from saving to spending—from productive to unproductive expenditure—may

[1] Torrens, *Colonization of South Australia*, London, Longmans, 1835, p. 232.
[2] Ibid. p. 243.
[3] Colonel Torrens, *Speech in the House of Commons on the Motion for a Reappointment of a Select Committee on Emigration, February 15, 1827*, London, Longman, Rees, Orme, Brown and Green, 1828.
[4] H. Merivale, *Lectures on Colonization and Colonies, delivered before the University of Oxford in 1839, 1840 and 1841 and reprinted in 1861* (new ed., Oxford University Press, 1928).

sometimes operate to relieve national industry from temporary plethora or oppression'.[1] Echoing Wakefield and Torrens, he asked: 'Let the whole of the capital which was expended by England in the foundation of the North American colonies be estimated at its fullest amount: is it credible that the total annual increase of that capital, from their first settlement to the era of American independence, would amount to the income which England has derived in the last twenty years from the American cotton trade?'[2]

3. JOHN STUART MILL'S VERSION

The theory of emigration which had won wide approval by mid-century may be found scattered about in John Stuart Mill's *Principles of Political Economy*. His first important reference to it is in dealing with ways in which a nation can defeat the tendency to diminishing returns from land. An effective expedient was to send people overseas to cultivate the open spaces: but he was doubtful whether emigration would ever be extensive enough to dispense with the necessity of checks to population. Secondly, he advocated colonization as a remedy for low wages and gave his blessing to Wakefield's schemes. He wanted 'a grant of public money, sufficient to remove at once, and establish in the colonies, a considerable fraction of the youthful agricultural population'.[3] The third reference comes in the famous chapters on 'the tendency of profits to a minimum', in which he attacks those who opposed emigration on the ground that it involved a leakage of capital from the country. To Mill such an argument was the opposite of the truth for the reason that 'if one-tenth of the labouring people of England were transferred to the colonies, and along with them one-tenth of the circulating capital of the country, either wages, or profits, or both, would be greatly benefited, by the diminished pressure of capital and population upon the fertility of the land'.[4] Finally, we have the most interesting section of all at the end of the last chapter of the book, 'Of the Grounds and Limits of the *Laisser-faire* or Non-interference Principle', where he argues that colonization should be a Government undertaking. He had no hesitation in saying that settlement of emigrants in the colonies was 'the best affair of business in which the capital of an old and wealthy country can engage',[5] but that it was equally obvious that it could not be left to private enterprise. The heart of the matter was the need to make sure that the emigrants remained landless labourers for a long time after arriving in the colonies.

[1] H. Merivale, *Lectures on Colonization and Colonies*, p. 183.   [2] Ibid. p. 185.

[3] J. S. Mill, *Principles of Political Economy*, 6th ed., bk. II, ch. XIII, p. 231.

[4] Ibid. bk. IV, ch. V, p. 450.   [5] Ibid. bk. V, ch. XI, p. 586.

As to the capitalist in the colonies paying the costs, there was no guarantee that he would be the one to derive benefit. Furthermore, to quote Mill: 'If all the capitalists of the colony were to combine, and bear the expense by subscription, *they would still have no security that the labourers, when there, would continue to work for them. After working for a short time, and earning a few pounds, they always, unless prevented by the government, squat in unoccupied land, and work only for themselves.*'[1] Mill was an enthusiastic believer in Wakefield's idea of 'the sufficient price' of land. He wanted to create and maintain in the colonies the system of 'non-competing groups' which prevailed at home; the emigrant labourers must be prevented from becoming peasant proprietors. There was another big advantage in view of the ever-present tendency of profits in the home country to fall to a minimum. 'The knowledge that a large amount of hired labour would be available, in so productive a field of employment, would insure a large emigration of capital from a country, like England, of low profits and rapid accumulation: and it would only be necessary not to send out a greater number of labourers at one time than this capital could absorb and employ at high wages.'[2] He believed that the flow of capital to the colonies and foreign countries had been one of the chief reasons why the decline of profits in England had been arrested and that, up to a certain point, 'the more capital we send away, the more we shall possess and be able to retain at home'.[3]

4. MARX ON OVER-POPULATION AND COLONIZATION

The classical theory of colonization furnished Karl Marx with a most congenial text, of which he took full advantage. In his view the sole merit of Wakefield was not that he had anything new to say about colonies but that his doctrine of the 'sufficient price' threw into relief the real nature of capitalist production in the old world.

The part of Marx's system which bore most directly on this theme was the doctrine of relative surplus population. It will be recalled that in his *Capital* he distinguished between three types of surplus population—floating, latent and stagnant. The first of these exists because the number of employed tends to increase at a lower rate than the scale of production; some of the redundant workers escape abroad in the wake of exported capital.

It is an inherent contradiction of the movement of capital that the natural increase in the working masses is inadequate to satisfy the requirements of the accumulation of capital, and yet is always in excess of those requirements.

---

[1] Ibid. bk. v, ch. xi, p. 586 (italics mine).   [2] Ibid. bk. v, ch. xi, p. 588.
[3] Ibid. bk. iv, ch. iv, p. 448.

Capital needs growing quantities of young male workers and diminishing quantities of adult male workers. This contradiction is not a more glaring one than the contradiction that there should be a complaint of a lack of hands at the very time when thousands are unemployed because the division of labour has chained them to some specific branch of industry.[1]

Secondly, the application of capitalist methods to agriculture results in a latent surplus population because the demand for farm labour diminishes relatively to capital accumulation. The third component of the reserve army is recruited from the mass of the poorest workers in casual employment, a stagnant surplus which 'forms a self-reproducing and self-perpetuating element of the working class'.[2] Marx believed that for each system of production in the course of history there was a law governing population; and here, as elsewhere in his system, he declared that Ricardo had seen the light, if only dimly, in the famous proposition that 'the same cause which may increase the net revenue of the country may at the same time render the population redundant and deteriorate the condition of the labourer'.[3] The law of population valid for the system of capitalist production was based on the central Marxist hypothesis that, as accumulation increases, the ratio of variable to constant capital falls, and that, therefore, the demand for labour, which is governed by the amount of variable capital, declines relatively to the quantity of total capital. This variable capital function was conceived in such a way that the demand diminished relatively to total capital, at an accelerated rate, as total capital increased. Marx had in mind a dynamic process in which there would be interludes during which accumulation would proceed on a given technical basis, that is to say, with the ratio between variable and constant capital stable, and employment increasing in the same proportion as capital. But, as time went on, these interludes were assumed to become shorter: hence an accelerated decline in the variable component of total capital.

Thus, an expanding capitalist economy creates of necessity a reserve army of labour which undergoes a regular fluctuation, which is not the same thing as changes in the rate of growth of the working class. Marx regarded the industrial cycle as an expression of periodical increases and decreases in the reserve army of labour. Since accumulation is the independent variable and wages are the dependent variable, a marked growth of capital in relation to labour raises real wages, diminishes the unused part of the labour force, and eats into the capitalist's surplus.

[1] Karl Marx, *Capital*, 4th German ed., 1890; rev. by Engels, tr. by Eden and Cedar Paul; London, Allen and Unwin, 1928, pp. 708–9.

[2] Ibid. p. 711.

[3] David Ricardo, *Principles of Political Economy and Taxation*, Gonner's edition, London, Bell, 1913, p. 379; quoted in Marx, op. cit. p. 697.

To this the capitalist reacts by accumulating less, with the result that the unused part of the labour force expands and real wages decline. In Marx's words,

the characteristic course of modern industry, its decennial cycles (interrupted by intercurrent oscillations) of periods of average activity, production at high pressure, crisis and stagnation, depends on the continuous formation, the greater or less absorption, and the reconstitution, of the industrial reserve army, composed of the surplus population.... A sudden and fitful expansion in the scale of production is a prelude to equally sudden and fitful contractions. The latter, in turn, evoke the former; but the former, the expansions, are impossible unless there is available human material, unless there has been an increase in the number of available workers irrespective of the absolute growth in population. This supply of available human material is dependent upon the simple fact that some of the workers are being 'set at liberty' by methods which reduce the number of employed workers relatively to the increase in the amount of production.[1]

In his account of the process of expansion Marx recognizes the impetus deriving from the fact of technical complementarity—the need, for example, to build a new railway network in order to fulfil the productive power of existing real investment. Such an extension of activity requires new supplies of labour which can be deployed without disturbing the flow of output in the old areas; the entry of capitalist enterprise into new countries as well as the introduction of labour-saving inventions is a powerful means of recruiting new battalions for the reserve army.

It was in this context that Marx turned his attention to what he called the 'modern theory of colonization'. The writings of Wakefield and his followers provided him with plenty of grist for his mill: he was not likely to overlook Merivale's statement that, owing to the high wages ruling in the colonies, there is an 'urgent desire for cheaper and more subservient labourers—for a class to whom the capitalist might dictate terms instead of being dictated to by them.... In the ancient civilized countries, the labourer, though free, is by law of nature dependent on capitalists; in the colonies this dependence must be created by artificial means.'[2] The Wakefield theory of colonization was

---

[1] Marx, op. cit. pp. 698–9. It is necessary to correct what appears to be a fallacy in Marx's notion of cycles. As Professor Joan Robinson has pointed out, the type of fluctuation inherent in the Marxian model is not the ten-year cycle in the level of income and employment but an undulation with a longer span which is conceivable in a system conforming to Say's Law. 'The difference arises because, in Marx's scheme, the decline in the rate of accumulation is due to a decline in the fund from which savings are made, not from a slackening of the inducement to invest.' Joan Robinson, *An Essay on Marxian Economics*, London, Macmillan, 1942, p. 85.

[2] Marx, op. cit. p. 854.

held to be the clearest possible demonstration of the tenet that capitalist production and private property based on the producer's own labour are mutually exclusive.

In later Marxist literature the overflow of capital from mature industrial countries to colonies became the main part of an explanation why the system is able to postpone the nemesis of a breakdown. Rosa Luxemburg, unlike Marx, faced up to the problem of the inducement to invest and argued that, as long as there are new territories to be opened up, the older capitalist countries can succeed in avoiding the crisis threatened by a chronic excess of saving.[1]

Marx's *Capital* first appeared in 1867, just a few years before classical political economy changed its course under the influence of the 'marginal revolution'. Its importance lies not in its theory of value, the weaknesses of which have often been exposed, but in its attempt to formulate a theory of economic development. From the seventies onward the energies of the leading economists were devoted to the problem of the allocation of resources under static assumptions and the refinement of the theory of value. While no one would wish to underestimate the intellectual achievements of Victorian theorists in this field, it was unfortunate that some of the fundamental questions which had interested the classical school, questions about the nature of economic evolution, were no longer being asked. The territory of economic dynamics was abandoned and the vacuum was filled by the Marxists, who have been highly skilled in extracting the maximum of surplus value from their intellectual monopoly.

5. THE CLASSICAL APPROACH RECONSIDERED

We are now in a position to appreciate more fully the nature of the dualism referred to at the beginning of this chapter. By the word 'colony' Wakefield did not mean a political satellite of Britain: he meant a new country, sparsely populated, which imported labour from an old country and re-exported it to the unoccupied hinterland. He pointed out that,

the United States are still colonies, according to the sense in which the word is used here. They receive people from old states, and send out a much greater number of people to settle in new places....The old country wants an enlargement of its field for employing capital and labour: the colonies want more capital and labour for cultivating an unlimited field.[2]

---

[1] See Joan Robinson, Introduction to Rosa Luxemburg, *The Accumulation of Capital*, tr. by Agnes Schwarzschild; London, Routledge and Kegan Paul, 1951, pp. 26–8.

[2] Wakefield, op. cit. p. 125. Marx took over this idea and expressed it in almost the

Arising out of their very nature, there was a community of interest between old and new countries.

Thus, we may infer that the 'larger community' of which Mill spoke was the Anglo-Saxon economic empire, comprising the colonial settlements overseas and the United States of America.[1] Within this wide domain migration of factors was a necessary expression of the community of interest between the old country and the new ones. It would therefore appear that when the classical writers dealt with the theory of international trade what they really had in mind was the commerce between England and 'old' countries outside the British economic empire, and in such cases it was realistic to assume the absence of international movement of population. A progressive increase in physical productivity was to be achieved on two fronts, first, by free trade with countries outside Britain's economic orbit, and, second, by planned mobility of labour and capital within Britain's economic empire. This seems to have been in J. S. Mill's mind when he wrote:

> To appreciate the benefits of colonization, it should be considered in its relation, not to a single country, but to the collective economical interests of the human race.... If to carry consumable goods from the places where they are superabundant to those where they are scarce, is a good pecuniary speculation, is it not an equally good speculation to do the same thing with regard to labour and instruments? The exportation of labourers and capital from old to new countries, from a place where their productive power is less, to a place where it is greater, increases by so much the aggregate produce of the labour and capital of the world. It adds to the joint wealth of the old and the new country, what amounts in a short period to many times the mere cost of effecting the transport.[2]

Given this way of looking at things, it is easy to see why classical writers did not develop a theory of the dynamic interrelations of international trade and the movement of factors. Their static doctrine of comparative costs proved that universal free trade was the best of all possible worlds: international movements of capital and labour were

---

same words. 'We are speaking here of colonies in the strict sense of the term, of countries with virgin soil, colonized by free immigrants. Economically considered, the United States is still nothing more than a colony of Europe.' Karl Marx, op. cit. p. 848 n.

[1] Cf. L. H. Jenks, *The Migration of British Capital to 1875*, London, Cape, 1938, pp. 196–7: 'A great many areas of the world had been in a vital economic dependence upon Great Britain before the fifties for markets and supplies. They had been dependent for capital in the quantity immediately desired, and they were in turn involved in the correlative obligations of debtor. The American "cotton kingdom" was such an area. In this case the dependence was mutual between Lancashire and the South.'

[2] J. S. Mill, op. cit. bk. v, ch. xi, p. 586.

regarded largely as a domestic affair within the bounds of Britain's economic empire. Since the increase of wealth in this sphere meant also an increase in the wealth of the world, there was no need to ask whether imperial prosperity might be due less to free trade than to political control. The classical theory had little relevance to the sort of 'international trade' that was going on between Britain and her colonies in the third quarter of the century;[1] there is strong historical evidence that the rapid material advance of Britain in that period was due in no small measure to the monopolistic nexus which held together the varied parts of her wide economic domain.

Let us recall some of the relevant facts. The policy, of which the Repeal of the Corn Laws was the symbol, was never intended to weaken the hold which England had on her oversea possessions. Earl Grey satisfied any sceptics by pointing out bluntly that, in embracing the principles of free trade, the British Government 'did not abdicate the duty and power of regulating the commercial policy not only of the United Kingdom but of the British Empire'.[2] And this commercial policy had an important bearing on the course of Britain's economic development after 1846. British foreign investments rose from £300 million at the beginning of the fifties to £1,300 million in 1875, and about two-fifths of this increase was made up of investment in the Empire, with a good deal of it protected by a Government guarantee of interest. *The Cambridge History of the British Empire* gives the following picture of the period under review:

If the risks of investment seemed smaller in the colonies than outside the Empire it was because the political control was retained by the Home Government, and the uses to which capital was put was determined by British engineers, British managers and the requirements of British law.... [Moreover,] English investors in the colonies were in the position of debenture-holders in a first-class concern, and the colonists were in the position of ordinary shareholders....Discussion of the extent to which English capital accumulation was the result of the profits of colonial exploitation concentrates usually on the profits of colonial trade. An element equally important

---

[1] Some later writers classified trade with the colonies as 'international'. J. E. Cairnes stated: 'In the case of colonies, however, the political causes tending to facilitate the movements of capital and labour are, on the whole, overborne by the geographical, climatic and physical circumstances which obstruct those movements; and, therefore, for the purposes of economic theory, we must include colonial under "international" trade.' (*Some Leading Principles of Political Economy*, 1874, p. 367.) See also C. F. Bastable, *The Theory of International Trade*, 4th ed. 1903, p. 12. Neither of these economists seems to have appreciated the point of the distinction drawn by Mill.

[2] Quoted in H. J. Habakkuk, 'Free Trade and Commercial Expansion, 1853–1870', *Cambridge History of the British Empire*, vol. II, 1940, p. 753.

is the extent to which in the second half of the nineteenth century English rentier fortunes were built up ultimately out of the proceeds of colonial taxation. For the debenture-holder not only had the first claim on the profits of the capital construction in the colonies: he had also the right to tax the ordinary share-holder to provide such part of his prescribed share as was not forthcoming from the profits of the concern. The greater part of the guaranteed interest on the Indian railway loans was paid out of taxation.[1]

In the 'fifties and 'sixties political circumstances combined with technical improvements to give English shipping a monopoly of colonial, and indeed of other, shipping, more effective than the Navigation Laws had maintained.[2] In the mid-nineteenth century the United Kingdom had still an actual monopoly of the trade of the Empire; there were only two important streams of trade between colonies and foreign countries: the country trade between India and China, which was an integral part of the Anglo-Indian trade, and the growing trade between Canada and the United States.[3]

Many of the entrepreneurs interested in Britain's oversea investments directed their business from headquarters located in England, and a large fraction of Empire loans was spent on British goods. The habit of consigning British export cargoes to agents in the colonies was widespread, and this made it difficult for a local class of independent merchants to develop overseas. To a notable degree this also applied to the United States, where no less than 60 % of the imported cotton goods were consigned even as late as 1869. It is indeed not surprising that, although free trade hardly affected the price of wheat for a generation after the Repeal, the United Kingdom was enjoying favourable terms of trade in the period 1850–75—particularly with the colonies.[4]

Thus, some of the more striking of contemporary facts found no place in the classical scheme of things. Free trade theorists did not see any need to examine the role of power in the process of trade between the mother country and her dependencies. Nor did they recognize that it was as much to the interest of new countries as of the old to be in a position to benefit from 'external economies'. Their attitude was not free from inconsistency. They argued that the Government should finance the settlement of British labour in the colonies, on the ground that the capitalist overseas could not be expected to incur the cost himself because there was no guarantee that the immigrants would continue to work for him. In other words, it paid to give protection in the form of a subsidy to tide over the difficult pioneering phase, in the expectation that when the colonies had enough labourers, the mother country would reap substantial benefits. If this was true, then surely

---

[1] H. J. Habakkuk, op. cit. p. 798.　　[2] Ibid. p. 764.
[3] Ibid. p. 780.　　[4] Ibid. p. 804.

the colonies, once they had the power, would be equally justified in giving protection to their own industries in order to secure advantages for themselves. There was a glaring failure to look at the exchange relation from the point of view of new and undeveloped countries.

The orthodox classical school saw nothing incongruous in Britannia holding the bible of free trade in one hand and the sword of monopoly power in the other, and they were shocked when their kinsmen overseas paid more attention to the sword than to the bible.

CHAPTER II

FREE TRADE AND DISPLACEMENT OF POPULATION

The classical doctrine of free trade, one of the great intellectual achievements of the nineteenth century, focused attention on comparative costs and the gain from trade; the analysis necessarily abstracted from movements of factors between countries. It was natural, however, that experience of the disturbing force of industrialization and international division of labour would lead people to ask questions about the *long-run* consequences of free trade and the national specialization which it entailed. Toward the end of the century some of the best minds in England were becoming sceptical and turned away from the generalizations of Victorian political economy, because they could not get convincing answers to their questions. Part of the reason was that, after the revolution in economic theory in the early seventies, there was not much interest in problems of economic change or long-term development. The marginal principle dominated the scene.

It will be instructive to glance at what the economists of the late Victorian era had to say about the effect of free trade on international population movements. We have seen in Chapter 1 that tradition had not encouraged discussions of such a topic, since the theory of trade and the theory of international migration had been kept in separate compartments. After re-examining the mobility postulates of Ricardian theory, we shall show how some of those who inherited this method of thinking failed to realize its limitations as an instrument for analysing the secular effects of innovations such as free trade.

1. NON-COMPETING GROUPS

In a note on the scope and method of the classical theory of international trade, Professor Viner wrote:

What underlay their analysis was the assumption of international *place* immobility of the factors of production, irrespective of occupation, and the assumption of internal *occupational* mobility of the factors of production, irrespective of location, and for a large part of their analysis only the former assumption was significant. Much of the criticism of the mobility assumptions of the classical theory of international trade as unrealistic is irrelevant because it fails to note this distinction between types of mobility.[1]

[1] Jacob Viner, *Studies in the Theory of International Trade*, London, Allen and Unwin, 1937, p. 597. (Italics in the original.)

This statement raises two interesting questions. First, is the distinction between types of mobility made by Professor Viner the really important one, and is it true that what was postulated about internal mobility had no significance for a large part of classical analysis?

According to Professor Viner classical theory was merely concerned with internal *occupational* mobility. Now it is evident that the crossing of occupational frontiers is not the only type of mobility conceivable. People are divided not only into occupations but into *classes*, that is to say, groups sharply distinguished according to *source* of income. The familiar division is between those whose livelihood depends exclusively on wages and those who live on income from the ownership of property. A theory of international trade, and particularly the part of it which is welfare economics, must state clearly what it assumes not only about internal mobility of labour between occupations but also about mobility between classes.

An important step away from the ideal world of free competition was taken by Cairnes when he developed the idea of 'non-competing groups'.[1] He regarded the working population as divided into a series of industrial layers; representative of these were unskilled labourers at the bottom, then artisans and skilled workers, higher still the more educated producers and dealers, and at the top the learned professions and higher executive grades. Perfect competition was envisaged within each stratum but not between them. This concession to realism merely recognized immobility as between different sections of the labour force. Cairnes' concept of 'non-competing groups' was incorporated in the theory of international trade by Taussig who argued that 'if the groups are in the same relative positions in the exchanging countries as regards wages...trade takes place exactly as if it were governed by the strict and simple principle of comparative costs'.[2] Taussig's conclusion, however, was not warranted. This change of assumptions did make a difference, for, even with his qualifications, the terms of exchange would be affected. As Professor Ohlin pointed out,

The existence of more or less non-competing groups of labour strengthens the case for temporary, not for permanent duties, and only in very special situations, e.g. in agricultural countries which have facilities for certain manufacturing industries, like the textile industry, but because of small labour mobility are unable to get a sufficient supply of labour for such work unless a substantially higher real wage is paid than in agriculture.[3]

[1] J. E. Cairnes, *Some Leading Principles of Political Economy*, London, Macmillan, 1874, pp. 66–8.

[2] F. W. Taussig, *International Trade*, New York, 1928, p. 48.

[3] B. Ohlin, 'Protection and Non-competing Groups', *Weltwirtschaftliches Archiv*, XXXIII, p. 45.

2. MOBILITY POSTULATES OF FREE TRADE THEORY

Modern work on welfare economics has served as a welcome reminder of the pioneering contributions of Henry Sidgwick. In the present context it is of particular interest to note that one of the arguments used in his chapter on Protection started a controversy which threw an important light on the tacit assumptions of classical theory.[1] Sidgwick was interested in the bearing of free trade on movements of population between trading communities. His case may be summarized as follows. Imagine a thickly populated country, *A*, in which one-third of its agricultural produce is consumed by the people engaged in making manufactured produce protected by a tariff. The country adopts free trade and thereby obtains its manufactures at half the previous price from country *B* in exchange for corn, the elasticity of demand being taken to be unity. Since more output can only be got from agriculture at rapidly increasing cost, what are the displaced industrial workers to do? Some of them will have to emigrate: and as a result of free trade *A* will have a smaller, though richer, population—'the economic gain resulting from it to the community as a whole being a gain which it would require violent governmental interference to distribute so as to retain the labourers thrown out of work'.[2]

The particular example used by Sidgwick is not very satisfactory. The doctrine of free trade was based on an approximation, the assumptions of which excluded international migration of labour. Within the strict confines of that reasoning, it was irrelevant to ask whether a change from protection to free trade would lead to emigration. Moreover, even on his own postulate of international mobility, Sidgwick seemed tacitly to assume that emigration was ruled out in the protected country before free trade was introduced. The importance of the example lies not in itself but in the controversy to which it gave rise and particularly in what Edgeworth had to say in the debate.[3]

It was Bastable's attack on Sidgwick's position in his *Theory of International Trade* (2nd ed. 1897) which brought Edgeworth into the fray. After remarking that Bastable was reasoning on a very abstract plane, Edgeworth said:

We know so little how in any particular case the strains and stresses between the different parts of an economic body will be affected by external forces, that we must often be content with the general reasoning that free exchange

[1] Henry Sidgwick, *The Principles of Political Economy*, London, Macmillan, 1883, bk. III, ch. v.

[2] Ibid. p. 495.

[3] See *Economic Journal*, 1897, vol. VII, pp. 401 *et seq.*; 1899, IX, pp. 126 *et seq.*; 1900, X, pp. 390 *et seq.*; 1901, XI, pp. 228 *et seq.* and pp. 583 *et seq.*

tends to increase of production, and therefore to the benefit of the community as a whole, probably, and in the absence of any presumption that the benefit of some is likely to be attended with a more than compensating detriment to others. It is in this general reasoning that the ordinary free-trader shows his common sense: it is here that the triumphs of a Bastiat are won.[1]

Coming to his own version of Sidgwick's case, he continued:

...the social organisation which I contemplated was exactly that which Professor Bastable, after Ricardo, postulates—'a society composed of landlords, capitalists and labourers'....There is postulated just that degree of mobility which the classical theory assumes, that is, freedom to move across the vertical planes which separate one employment from another, but not freedom to move across the horizontal plane which separates the labouring classes from the owners of the industrial factors. Professor Bastable is silent about this latter species of immobility, but he will surely not deny its existence.... *The fundamental premiss on which the reasoning rests is the fact that labourers and capitalist-employers form 'non-competing groups', exchanging with each other services for finished products in a quasi-international trade.... The country to which as a first approximation the free trader legitimately ascribes solidarity, proves on a closer view to be not a continent, but an archipelago intersected with gulfs more or less impassable.*[2]

With the aid of this construction Edgeworth set out to show that free trade, in certain circumstances, must lead to an outflow of population. The key point in Bastable's case was that, with the expansion of food-growing in country A, costs would eventually rise so high that it would no longer be possible to go on exporting agricultural produce to B, and at that point A would again become an importer of food and an exporter of manufactures. But he could not explain why so much more food would be grown in A that its price would rise above the point at which it just paid to exchange it for the manufactures of B. If, of course, the surplus workers became capitalists overnight, the total demand in A for agricultural produce might well increase considerably, with the result that imports of food would be resumed and manufactured goods exported to pay for it. Only by making such an unreal assumption could Bastable conclude that things would right themselves without any pressure on anyone to emigrate. As soon as we adopt the hypothesis of two closed sectors, there is every reason why the capitalist-employers should go on importing B's manufactures. As Edgeworth put it, 'Why should it be assumed that the working classes should live as well as before? The capitalist, like Talleyrand, "will not see the necessity".'[3]

---

[1] 'Disputed Points in the Theory of International Trade', *Economic Journal*, 1901, pp. 585–6.

[2] Ibid. pp. 586–7 (italics mine).   [3] Ibid. p. 590.

Edgeworth's argument was rounded off in the following words:

To affirm that agricultural products will become so costly as to afford no profit to exporters is to affirm that the part of A (a_1), which is not affected by foreign competition, will have derived no advantage from the opening of trade, and to affirm that a 'nation' (or 'non-competing group') derives no advantages from a removal of international barriers unattended by foreign competition, is to deny a first principle which is at the foundation of the argument for Free Trade.[1]

In his replies Bastable tried to sustain the position that even in the extreme case postulated by Sidgwick and Edgeworth it was impossible to prove theoretically that free trade would lead to a loss of population to country A.[2] On the crucial question of a conflict of interest between classes he was not convincing. He criticized Edgeworth for lumping landlords and capitalists together when every good Ricardian knew that their interests might be sharply opposed; and perhaps his most revealing statement was that 'the Ricardian point of view regards the labourers as independent producers, and therefore as not dependent on the "custom" of the landowners or in need of charity'.[3]

The central point emerging from this controversy was that the issue turned on what was being assumed about internal mobility. Bastable, in common with the dogmatic free trade school, was imagining a society with perfect mobility not only as between occupations but also as between classes. He dwelt in 'one of Mr Owen's parallelograms' (to use Ricardo's phrase) and fondly thought it to be a replica of Victorian England. His reasoning was based on a first approximation in which there was *one nation* with each citizen owning means of production or, alternatively, with no barriers preventing workers from turning themselves easily into capitalists. Edgeworth, on the other hand, had moved on to a second approximation which conceived society as being composed of *two nations*: in the true scientific spirit he had brought the assumptions nearer to reality. Here was the notion of 'non-competing groups' being used in its most relevant sense, to denote class immobility instead of occupational immobility. Both sides claimed the authority of Ricardo, but there can be little doubt as to whom the master would have regarded as his genuine disciple.

3. WICKSELL ON NEW COUNTRIES

It is interesting to recall that, a few years before the controversy between Edgeworth and Bastable, the fundamental point had already been made by Wicksell. In his *Finanztheoretische Untersuchungen* (1896)

[1] Ibid. p. 588.
[2] See C. F. Bastable, *The Theory of International Trade*, 4th ed., London, 1903, App. c.
[3] Ibid. p. 197.

Wicksell observed that free trade theory 'assumes that each member of society is equipped with the various productive factors (land, capital, etc.) in proportion to his requirements: it postulates a uniform distribution of national wealth'.[1] This thesis is illustrated by an examination of the position of colonial countries under free trade. Wicksell takes a simple case of a colony consisting of two classes, landlords and workers, with the product divided between them according to the Ricardo-Thünen law of rent. No account is taken of the complications of capital. Under free trade this colony devotes itself entirely to agriculture and obtains its manufactured goods from abroad in exchange for wheat. It is assumed that the workers can satisfy their demand for manufactures by allocating one-quarter of their income for the purpose, while, let us say, one-third of the labour force would be needed to produce these imported goods at home. Now suppose that a tariff is imposed which makes it profitable to manufacture the industrial goods in the colony. What is the result? According to the assumed law of distribution, the use of a part of the labour supply for industrial production will lead to an increase in wages at the expense of rent. Let us suppose that wages in terms of wheat rise by a little over one-eighth. It then follows that, while somewhat more than a third of the workers are engaged in manufacturing, the remainder—nearly two-thirds— receive more than three-quarters of the previous wages bill, that is to say, more foodstuffs than all the workers together retained under free trade after importing foreign manufactured goods. The workers have obviously gained: they receive more agricultural produce as well as manufactured goods than they did before the tariff was imposed, and the more the landowners demand domestic manufactures the greater will this advantage be.

Wicksell summed up the implications of the argument as follows:

> I cannot help thinking that it has been largely considerations of this kind which have, consciously or unconsciously, inspired the protectionist policy of highly democratic colonial countries. The urge to protect domestic industries will make itself felt as soon as the country has a population large enough to lead to the emergence of rent on a significant scale, with the wage level still appreciably higher than in the old countries.[2]

If land in the colony belongs to absentee owners, the case is even stronger. If the colony, as it became more thickly populated, were to continue to concentrate, according to free trade policy, on producing foodstuffs to be exported to the mother country for manufactured goods, the share of the national income going to rent would increase and

[1] Knut Wicksell, *Finanztheoretische Untersuchungen*, Jena, Gustav Fischer, 1896, pp. 62–3.
[2] Ibid. p. 64.

a proportion of it, varying with the extent of absentee ownership, would be taken out of the colony. Free trade would entail a mounting annual tribute payable abroad.

Wicksell emphasized that, where there is a stratified class structure, circumstances are easily conceivable in which an economic change which otherwise would bring general benefit to the community will enrich one class exclusively and react detrimentally on the mass of the people. He blamed the 'liberal school' for not paying enough attention to this matter and regretted that Marxist writers had been allowed to exaggerate and distort the case—a fact which had hindered a general understanding of what was involved.[1]

The above review shows that Edgeworth and Wicksell regarded the unequivocal policy recommendations of the free trade school as resting on a first approximation in which it is assumed that within each independent trading country there is perfect mobility as between classes as well as occupations. We must note, however, that Edgeworth's views underwent a change and he did not reproduce his earlier argument in his *Papers relating to Political Economy* (1925). While continuing to regard the transactions between the labouring and employing classes as a species of international trade, he warned that 'we must not forget that the exports and imports in this trade are of a very peculiar character'.[2] He meant by this that the elasticity of the aggregate

---

[1] Professor Haberler (*Theory of International Trade*, London, Hodge, 1936, p. 195) tries to refute Wicksell's argument by referring, among other things, to what Wicksell himself said about the effect of technical invention on wages in *Lectures on Political Economy* where he proved, as against Ricardo, that 'a diminution in the gross product, or in its value (assuming, as before, that prices of commodities are given and constant), is scarcely conceivable as a result of technical improvements—under free competition' (Knut Wicksell, *Lectures on Political Economy*, ed. by Lionel Robbins, London, Routledge, 1934, vol. I, p. 137). Professor Haberler has overlooked the fact that Wicksell added an important qualification to the generalization quoted from the *Lectures*. In an article, 'Frihandel och Utvandring' Wicksell wrote: 'If technical and economic changes can bring about a re-grouping of population inside countries, why not, given factor mobility, a re-grouping as between countries too? My thoughts on this subject are closely related to my earlier criticism of Ricardo. I showed that the effect in Ricardo's case can only be partial not general. The total result will be an increase in gross output. But this is true only of a closed system. Given two separate economies, with free mobility, the proposition is true of both together but not of each separately.' (*Ekonomisk Tidskrift*, 1920, pp. 124–5.) Professor Haberler seems to have ignored the main point of the argument in *Finanztheoretische Untersuchungen* (pp. 63–6). The central thesis which Wicksell was at pains to hammer home was that free trade theory rests on the fundamental assumption that the population of a country is a kind of property-owning democracy with capital and land fairly uniformly distributed among the members. On this essential assumption about class structure Professor Haberler is silent.

[2] F. Y. Edgeworth, 'Application of the Differential Calculus to Economics', *Papers relating to Political Economy*, London, Macmillan, 1925, vol. II, p. 376.

demand for labour is high, and he accordingly concluded that 'the supposed case, though possible, is rendered improbable by the probability of finding employment for labour in general, in the long run....'[1] In saying this, Edgeworth was relying on one of the erroneous postulates of classical economics.[2]

4. STATIC MODELS: THEIR USES AND LIMITATIONS

The whole discussion affords a good example of the limitations of static models. It is first necessary to distinguish sharply between the case where international movements of factors are excluded and the case where such movements are assumed. Postulating immobility between countries, we may ask what is the bearing of international trade on the distribution of income in a country which is split into two non-competing class groups. Imagine a trading community A, divided into two classes, Labour (L) and Owners of capital (C), engaged in a quasi-international trade. Static analysis could be usefully applied here to the conditions for the maximizing of group C's gain. In other words, the 'nation' in whose welfare we are interested is one of the non-competing groups within country A. With the aid of community indifference curves one can set up a model in which there are two species of group trade going on simultaneously: (a) there is commodity trade between countries A and B; (b) inside country A Labour and Owners of capital exchange manpower for wage goods and the terms of this exchange determine the distribution of the social product. Group C can be conceived as operating on two fronts: on the home front it makes the best bargain possible with the L group, and on the foreign front it seeks to maximize the gain from commodity trade.

One or two possible cases may be imagined which, though highly abstract, serve to illuminate certain features of historical development neglected by classical theory. First, suppose group C is in the position of a monopsonist internally with respect to group L and a monopolist externally with respect to another country which is a colony. The problem of the conditions under which group C's gain is maximized is then solved by applying the principles of equilibrium under monopoly and monopsony. No account would have to be taken of possible retaliation by the other country, since that is ruled out by the assumption of colonial status. In the second case group C is a monopsonist internally with respect to group L; but the international trade takes

[1] F. Y. Edgeworth, *Papers Relating to Political Economy*, London, Macmillan, 1925, vol. I, p. viii.

[2] See J. M. Keynes, *The General Theory of Employment, Interest and Money*, London, Macmillan, 1936, App. to ch. XIX.

place between two independent parties, countries A and B, the terms of exchange being governed by relative elasticities of demand and not distorted by any power elements. If we further assume that there will be no retaliation from abroad, group C can, by imposing appropriate import duties, put itself in an optimum monopoly position, the extent of the gain at the expense of the other country being determined by the elasticity of the latter's demand for country A's output. Again the theory of monopoly is applicable.

In case III we assume that groups L and C are in a situation of bilateral monopoly. The internal 'terms of trade' are now indeterminate: the point reached on the contract curve depends on relative bargaining power. Given a certain labour price for its wage goods at home, group C will endeavour by import duties to reap the optimum gain through foreign trade with the limits set by the elasticity of B's demand for A's goods and B's disposition to retaliate.

Questions of a different order must be faced as soon as we admit the possibility of factors moving between countries. This was the basis of the example used by Sidgwick. It is very difficult to understand why some of the leading exponents of free trade were so anxious to reject the idea that it may lead to an outflow of population from a country. A labour-saving innovation may well cause a transfer of labour from one region to another; in the same way free trade tends to set in motion a redistribution of population as between countries. One would have thought that the history of Ireland since 1846 had been a sufficiently convincing object lesson. And yet it was Bastable, while holding the Chair of Political Economy in Dublin, who was responsible for the following extraordinary proposition.

The idea that freedom of trade may lead to depopulation rests on a confusion between two different branches of economic action, viz. the unrestricted exchange of commodities, which is all that free trade prescribes, and the mobility of the industrial factors. The latter obviously depends on entirely different causes, and has little connection with the particular fiscal policy pursued.[1]

This statement, which purports to expose a confusion, is itself rooted in fallacy. Free trade, like every other innovation, cannot increase wealth without inflicting losses on minorities. It creates greater economic space through the movement of factors from the scene of loss to areas where opportunity is widening, both within and beyond the frontiers of the country in question.

[1] *The Theory of International Trade*, 4th ed., p. 162.

5. INTERNAL MOBILITY AND INTERNATIONAL MIGRATION

The surprising thing about the controversy arising out of Sidgwick's case was the apparent failure of both sides to appreciate the real significance of emigration of labour from an old country. Even Edgeworth let slip the remark that 'it is not a very popular argument in favour of free trade that it tends to replace part of the native population by foreigners'.[1] There was a strange air of isolationism about the whole discussion. The course of economic development since the eighteen-forties should have made it perfectly clear that an innovation such as free trade implied by its very nature a movement of labour and capital from England to the undeveloped countries. The United Kingdom was a member of a wider community of nations which was undergoing a dynamic transformation under the impact of technical progress, and this entailed an interregional redistribution of factors of production. The process called for a theory of economic development embracing the mutual relationship between national specialization, internal mobility, international migration and the course of trade. Bastable, however, was at great pains to show that free trade would not lead to any emigration. He might just as well have argued that agricultural counties in England suffered no loss of population when neighbouring coalfields were being opened up.

An analysis of the process of emigration is not complete unless the assumptions about internal mobility are made clear. Once we abandon the classical first approximation in which there is perfect internal mobility, we are led to the question: What is the bearing of internal immobility on external mobility? Is there an interaction between these two? The scheme of analysis which suggests itself is as follows. We regard the United Kingdom as an area which is a part of a wider community, the Atlantic economy. Under the influence of driving forces, for example technical inventions or free trade, population and capital flow from the United Kingdom to other regions, and this emigration proceeds unevenly through time. An innovation necessarily leaves a trail of victims in its wake. The welfare economist points out that, from the access of wealth arising from it, there would be a surplus left after the State had compensated the victims out of taxes levied on the beneficiaries. Historically, however, we have to deal with situations where no compensation was in fact paid. Indeed, the peopling of the open spaces of the world was made possible on such a grand scale precisely because the 'gainers' in the old countries did not compensate the 'losers'. Theoretically, the enactment of the principle of compensation comes to the same thing as the classical postulate of perfect internal mobility (between

[1] *Economic Journal*, 1897, p. 403.

classes as well as occupations). If, therefore, nineteenth-century England had been anything like the society postulated by the free trade purists, the outflow of population would have been less than it was. The actual volume of emigration was governed not only by the driving force of the innovations but also by the degree of internal immobility in the 'old' country.

This brings us to an interesting hypothesis. The degree of internal mobility in a country may undergo secular change, the consequences of which may be far-reaching. In the nineteenth century, the major stream of migration flowed from a highly stratified society, the United Kingdom, to a country which offered rough equality of opportunity, the United States. From this condition of fluidity the United States evolved during the second half of the nineteenth century towards a state of stratification. Exactly when the major turning-point was reached is a matter for factual analysis. Our hypothesis suggests that the transition from a relatively high degree of mobility to stratification had a decisive effect on the volume and direction of international migration. If it can be verified by empirical analysis, it will form an essential part of an interpretation of the phases through which inter-national migration passed during the last century.

The conclusions may be summarized as follows:

(1) The pure theory of free trade rests on the assumption of perfect internal mobility as between classes as well as occupations.

(2) A second approximation, in which immobility between classes is postulated, brings the analysis nearer to the facts of the free trade period.

(3) The English free trade purists often failed to distinguish between gain to their own country and gain to the whole world; and they did not understand the real nature of the trend to protection in new countries.

(4) Static models have a limited usefulness in interpreting the consequences of free trade. Once the second approximation is adopted, it is no longer sensible to continue to assume international immobility of factors, since there is an interaction between the degree of internal immobility and the rate of external migration.

(5) What is required is a third approximation which would explore the dynamic inter-relationships between national specialization, internal mobility, international migration and the structure of international trade.

CHAPTER III

MIGRATION AND AN EXPANDING ECONOMY

All sorts of promptings may lie behind the decision of an individual or a family to·leave one country in order to live in another. History shows the influence of the threat of starvation, political oppression, religious persecution, eviction, avoidance of military service, a sense of adventure, an urge to make a fortune, a desire to join relatives abroad or to get away from those at home, or perhaps just a flight from boredom. It is not by making a catalogue of such 'reasons' that one can hope to understand the phenomenon of migration any more than an attempt to describe the manifold motives leading people to want to buy a commodity would constitute analysis of demand. Nothing is easier than to draw up a list of factors labelled 'push' and 'pull' and then write a descriptive account in terms of these two sets of influences. Such an approach, however, will not throw much light on the deeper problems posed by migration as part of the process of economic expansion. Transfers from one country to another are the results of individual acts of choice by a number of people; and over a period of time the statistical record of this movement (assuming it is reasonably accurate) will reveal a certain pattern. In seeking to interpret this picture we must look at the patterns traced by other series reflecting activities bearing some relation to migration. When we have brought together the relevant series, we then proceed to put some questions to this material. Statistical 'facts' do not speak for themselves: their story has to be coaxed out of them. In approaching the subject, one has certain hunches as to the best way of wheedling out the truth. I propose in this chapter to set out briefly some of the ideas which serve as groundwork for the analysis in Part III.

I. INNOVATIONS AS A DYNAMIC AGENT

The theories discussed in the previous chapter stressed the disruptive side of technical change; but the other side of the picture—the constructive achievements of enterprise—is not less important. When the scientist unearths nature's secrets and when men of action go forth to subdue new territories or discover new riches, endless opportunities are brought within the reach of millions who would otherwise be content to continue a dull and uneventful existence. Pioneers are always very few in number, but the range of their influence is incalculable.

No one can approach this theme without being under the influence of Schumpeter's great work. In tracing out the implications of innovations (in the wide sense of that term), he accustomed us to think of the twofold aspect of economic progress—the conflict between the new and the old, the life-giving forces which can assert themselves only by passing a death sentence on the obsolete. Schumpeter also made it clear that the essential features of dynamic change are apt to vanish from sight if we rely on aggregate quantities to indicate how the economic system moves through time. In dealing with the effect of innovations on 'old' firms, he emphasized that

these vital parts of the mechanism of economic evolution, which are readily seen to dominate many business situations and to produce results of fundamental importance, can never be revealed statistically by measuring variation in an index of production, or analyzed theoretically in terms of total output. Such an index would display nothing except increase. But mere increase in total output would not produce those effects. It is disharmonious or one-sided increase and shifts *within* the aggregative quantity which matter. Aggregative analysis, here, as elsewhere, not only does not tell the whole tale but necessarily obliterates the main (and the only interesting) point of the tale.[1]

Experience in using Keynesian models in recent years bears out the relevance of this point.

Another valuable feature of Schumpeter's system is the emphasis on the multiplicity of fluctuations arising from unequal periods of gestation in different lines of investment as well as the differing speeds of reaction of various sectors of the economy to changes occasioned by innovations. While it is difficult to accept his intriguing picture of 'six Juglars to a Kondratieff and three Kitchins to a Juglar',[2] the idea of simultaneous cycles of different order interacting on one another must be regarded as a fruitful hypothesis for the analysis of economic growth. But there are good reasons for thinking that Schumpeter attached far too much significance to the sixty-year cycle.

The system is open to at least two general criticisms. At certain points in his review of the statistical evidence, one cannot help feeling that the failure of fact to conform to theory is explained away in a manner not altogether convincing. For example, in examining the course of wages in the United States, Schumpeter points out that 'Behavior of corrected wage rates is according to expectation, but the strong increase in corrected wage bill, 1895 to 1908, is not, and must be explained by peculiarities of the American environment,

[1] Joseph A. Schumpeter, *Business Cycles*, New York and London, McGraw-Hill, 1939, vol. I, p. 134.
[2] Ibid. p. 173.

immigration among them'.[1] In this case the massive flow of labour into the United States is invoked as an 'outside' factor to account for the divergence between what actually happened and what was supposed to happen according to the model. But surely this must arouse suspicion. There can be no justification for treating international migration in this way, for it is itself part of the process of fluctuation which the model must explain. I suggest that, if the Atlantic economy were taken as the whole and the United States, Great Britain, and Germany as the parts, we should not then be surprised if the three parts did not pass through identical and simultaneous phases according to a theory of a closed system. Internal shifts within the aggregate, which Schumpeter was so careful to emphasize, would take place in the form of international movements of labour and capital; and the expansion in the level of activity of the entire Atlantic economy might well entail salient differences in the economic experience of the component parts.

The other weakness in Schumpeter's construction is its lack of a theory of employment. The whole work contains only one or two references to Keynes's *General Theory* and they are, significantly enough, confined to the theory of interest. Schumpeter's model, which is mainly concerned with movements of output and prices, traces the impact of an innovation as follows. In the prosperity phase (when the innovation is being introduced) the output of consumers' goods declines because factors are attracted away from that sector; in the subsequent recession the fruits of the innovation are garnered in the form of an increase in the output of consumers' goods. Real income in terms of wage goods is higher during recession than during prosperity; but this is true only of those who remain in work the whole time. If Schumpeter had brought in fluctuations in the level of employment he would have had to recognize that consumption in real terms increases during prosperity and declines during recession.[2] The model needed to be reformulated in the light of the Keynesian theory of employment.

Any attempt to interpret time-series over a long period runs into the difficulty that the characteristics of society may change fundamentally so that the behaviour of the series cannot possibly be summed up in one single 'explanation'. Schumpeter was well aware of this, and in an interesting passage he gave the following assessment of his own work.

Our argument rests on [abstractions from] historical facts which may turn out to belong to an epoch that is rapidly passing. In this sense the analysis presented has, in fact, itself been called historical. There is no objection to

[1] Op. cit. vol. II, p. 574. Corrected wage rates mean wage rates divided by an index of wholesale prices.

[2] See Oscar Lange's review of Schumpeter's *Business Cycles*, *Review of Economic Statistics*, vol. XXIII, pt. 4, November 1941, pp. 190–3.

this.... We assume not only private property and private initiative but a definite type of both: not only money, banks and banking credit but also a certain attitude, moral code, business tradition, and 'usage' of the banking community; above all, a spirit of the industrial *bourgeoisie* and a scheme of motivation which within the world of giant concerns—the pattern which we have called Trustified Capitalism—and within modern attitudes of the public mind is rapidly losing both its scope and its meaning. This is why in our discussion of postwar events we shall put the question whether and how far the process still persists. But the writer is quite content to shed light, such as it is, on a piece of economic history and to leave to the reader the decision whether or not he will consider it relevant to practical problems.[1]

We shall be concerned in this book with fluctuations in international migration over a period of a century, and we must recognize that changes in the social ends governing the strivings of human beings may make it necessary to alter the behaviour assumptions.

At this point reference may be made to Professor Johan Åkerman's major study, *Ekonomisk Teori*, particularly vol. II, *Kausalanalys av det Ekonomiska Skeendet*, which appeared in 1944.[2] He denies that the 'atomistic' hypotheses of equilibrium theory are applicable to the interpretation of the business cycle, the inner significance of which, he argues, cannot be appreciated unless we examine the interaction of the groups which make up society. In an elaborate investigation of time-series for the United States, Great Britain, Germany and France over the period 1815–1940, Professor Åkerman propounds a method of indicating fundamental changes in 'structure'. He examines the mutual relations of strategic variables during upswings and downswings, and the 'structure' of the economy is regarded as constant so long as these relations remain the same. The method enables him to identify turning-points separating major phases in the evolution of each country, and he emphasizes the relativity of the explanation of fluctuations according to the structural phase in which they occur. His method indicates two climacterics in the history of both England and the United States, one in the mid-seventies and the other in the world depression of the early nineteen-thirties. The former was a technical transformation which ushered in the era of advanced private capitalism; the latter was dominated by a change in political data—the emergence of State planning.

Professor Åkerman's method of identifying phases of unchanged structure, while it yields suggestive results, is open to the criticism which we have already levelled at Schumpeter's system: it tends to overlook those variables which bring about changes in the balance of economic

---

[1] Schumpeter, op. cit. vol. I, pp. 144–5.
[2] Published by Gleerup, Lund.

power within the international community. It is not enough to assemble a set of hypotheses for a closed system and then look for verification in the time-series of each separate country. We shall adopt a different approach in this book. We begin by regarding movements of population and capital from one country to another as an expression of growth in the international economy; the latter is looked upon as a whole. By approaching the time-series of each country with this hypothesis in mind, we shall not expect them all to tell the same story and we may come across structural turning-points which Professor Åkerman's technique is not able to detect.

2. THE ATLANTIC ECONOMY AS AN EVOLVING UNIT

From the review of classical literature in previous chapters it emerged that the dichotomy of a static theory of international trade and a long-period theory of emigration was unsatisfactory. What is needed is a concept of economic development which stresses the widening of markets, the dynamic of increasing returns,[1] and the international mobility of labour and capital as a medium through which an international economy grows and changes its character. Viewed as an essential part of the process of economic expansion, migration not only induces but is itself partly determined by changes in the structure of the international community.

There was much that was suggestive in John Stuart Mill's idea of 'the larger community' of countries to which, he argued, the theory of *international* trade did not apply. Most of the oversea migration in the nineteenth century was from Europe across the Atlantic, and it was accompanied by a considerable flow of capital in the same direction. To investigate the process of growth, of which this migration was a part, it is instructive to regard the Atlantic community of nations as one economy. The long-period rise in the total real income generated in this economy necessitated various changes in the countries of which it was composed. By looking upon the international movements of labour, capital and commodities as if they were interregional, we shall gain a better insight into the nature and implications of economic growth; it will also have the advantage of making us see the course of Empire settlement in its proper perspective. In the long run changes may be expected in the balance of power as between the old and the new countries. The latter gain in relative strength through periodic injections of labour, the cost of whose upbringing has been borne by the Old

---

[1] See Allyn Young, 'Increasing Returns and Economic Progress', *Economic Journal*, vol. xxxviii, no. 152, December 1928, p. 527, and J. H. Williams, 'The Theory of International Trade Reconsidered', *Economic Journal*, vol. xxxix, no. 154, June 1929, p. 195.

World; ultimately migration dwindles, the direction of capital flow changes, and the international economy has to adjust itself to a new set of conditions.

3. SECULAR CHANGES IN SOCIAL STRUCTURE

Starting from the controversy summarized in Chapter II, we shall now develop a line of argument designed to elucidate the long-run interaction between social immobility and international migration. We take an old country (A) and a new country (B): the former we assume to be split into two classes, workers and entrepreneurs, with an impassable barrier between them, whereas the new country has complete social mobility and equality of opportunity. A is thickly populated, with a well-established industrial sector and a high propensity to save. B is large in area, rich in fertile land and natural resources, but short of labour and capital. Free trade is assumed, so that A tends to specialize in manufactured goods and B in food and raw materials.

It is natural that labour and capital should flow from A to B; a wave of technical progress in A will accentuate emigration, for the workers displaced are uncompensated and there is no means by which the ablest of them can cross over into the capitalist camp and displace the weaker entrepreneurs. Of course, not all the emigration is of this kind; some of it is an outflow which is complementary to capital exports. Indeed there is a sense in which the whole of the migration is an indispensable accompaniment of expanding trade. The rapid development of country B brings about a rise in the price of land, much of which, as a result of previous borrowings, will belong to absentee owners in A. Now, if country B continues its free trade policy and concentrates on producing agricultural produce to sell to A in exchange for manufactured goods, the share of the national income going to rent will increase and much of it will leave the country as annual tribute payable to A. Obviously it is in the national interest of country B to impose a tariff on A's manufactures so as to reduce the scope of agriculture, encourage resources to flow into home industry and thus cut down the slice of the social product taken by landlords.

Nor is this the only sound reason for abandoning free trade in B. The argument based on the concept of external economies is also relevant. The first industrial firms to be established in an agricultural country are under a considerable disadvantage because, although by coming into existence they are conferring benefits on the future, they themselves can receive no help from such facilities as research, technical education, a transport network and a tradition of industrial management. Unless someone makes a start, the community will be deprived of a cumulative flow of benefits; but according to the criterion of private marginal productivity no one is justified in making a start. In such circumstances the State is fully entitled to protect the infant industries. Two powerful considerations, therefore, point to the introduction of tariffs in country B; this leads to intensive industrialization which in turn brings a tendency to social stratification.

A stage will be reached in the evolution of country B when its population will have appropriated all the good land and natural resources. With growing competition for scarce land, its value rises rapidly and complete social mobility is no longer possible. More and more workers in the new country remain permanently in the ranks of the wage-earners; the social structure begins to become rigid; no longer are immigrants welcomed as co-operant factors in the conquest of new space. The last frontier has disappeared. This turning-point in the evolution of B may be marked also by the achievement of a rate of saving high enough to release the country from further dependence on A's capital market and to reverse the direction of the flow of loanable funds. Moreover, with the transition to industrialism in B, the trade between A and B will no longer be merely an exchange of manufactured goods for foodstuffs and raw materials.

A point worth emphasizing is that the degree of social mobility has causal significance. Suppose, for instance, that the Government of country A, anxious to counteract the effects of class immobility, had compensated displaced workers by grants-in-aid to enable them to be trained in new skills or to set up on their own account as small entrepreneurs, then the gain to A as a whole would have been more evenly distributed and the propensity to emigrate correspondingly reduced. On the other hand, if country B could have evolved into an industrial state without losing its original social mobility, it would have continued to absorb immigrants over a longer period. This latter assumption, however, would be highly unrealistic, for industrialization in the circumstances here postulated inevitably entails a stratified society.

The example just outlined is far too simple and one-sided to be a picture of the evolution of Great Britain and America in the nineteenth century. All that is claimed for it is that it provides a clue which, when considered in conjunction with several others, may help towards an interpretation of the problems before us.

4. LONG SWINGS

It is a well-known characteristic of economic growth that industrial countries, needing more labour in times of boom, drew on the surplus population in agriculture; in this way each upswing was more pronounced than would otherwise have been possible. Gustav Cassel argued that cyclical fluctuations were for the most part a feature of the transition from older forms of economic organization to the modern form and that, when the agricultural surplus had disappeared, booms and slumps would become less severe and economic growth would proceed at a more even rate.[1] While it is true that migration varies with the business cycle, there are also prominent fluctuations with a span nearly twice that of the decennial cycle.

These minor secular swings, showing an average interval of about eighteen years from peak to peak, suggest two hypotheses. First, it is possible that agricultural society has experienced a Malthusian cycle involving a regular recurrence of extreme population pressure; Scandinavian vital statistics, which are unbroken from the early part of the eighteenth century, lend colour to this view. As soon as the development of transport had made it physically possible for large numbers of people to cross the ocean, it would be natural to expect heavy emigration to occur in those phases of the demographic cycle when there was relative over-population. Secondly, a considerable inflow of migrants into a new country must exercise an important influence on methods of production. Since these inflows occur in periodic waves, they might be the cause of minor secular changes in manufacturing technique. For example, the growth of mass production in the United States may have passed through qualitative phases induced by the long fluctuations in immigration.

Building is a branch of investment which reacts directly to changes in population. If we postulate an autonomous fluctuation in the outflow of surplus population from an old country, we may expect induced waves of building activity in the receiving country. Just as a large volume of immigration promotes investment in the new country, so does a slump in emigration from an old country, by reinforcing the growth of population, tend to increase the demand for houses. Perhaps a fuller understanding of the nature of the building cycle could be achieved by examining the interaction between migration and construction in a two-country model.

Up to the time when the oversea territory reaches maturity as an industrial nation, the influx of immigrants is accompanied by imports of capital, and there is, therefore, a tendency for periods of relatively rapid increase in population to be associated with upswings in imports of capital and merchandise. On the other hand, the old country experiences its own cycle of booms in emigration and foreign investment followed by booms in home construction. A model of an international economy might be set up consisting of an old country (A) and a new country (B), each divided into two sectors, home construction and export. When emigration and the export of capital from A are booming,

[1] Cassel, *Theoretische Sozialökonomie*, 4th ed., Leipzig, Werner Scholl, 1927, pp. 500-8.

the level of activity in that country is governed mainly by the inducement to invest in the export sector, that is, by the marginal efficiency
of investment in country B; during this phase the volume of A's exports
rises and that of A's imports falls relatively to trend. Modern cycle
theory in 'real' terms may be invoked to explain why the investment
boom in B must result in a crisis and a downturn. This leads immediately
to a sharp fall in immigration and inflow of capital; income generated
by home investment in B declines and factors tend to move into the
export trades. Meanwhile, the rate of growth of population and the
supply of loanable funds in A rise, resources move from the export
sector to home construction, and the level of activity responds to the
marginal efficiency of internal investment. The volume of imports
(i.e. B's exports) now rises and that of exports (i.e. B's imports) falls
relatively to trend; a part of these imports constitutes income on
previous loans to B. If we assume a gold standard, it is clear that this
upswing in home construction in A may well be brought to an end by
a crisis in the balance of payments before full employment is reached.
In any case, the 'real' determinants make a downturn inevitable; it is
the signal for the beginning of another round of foreign investment and
emigration. This brief outline of a process of interaction between cycles
of domestic construction in a lending and a borrowing country provides
a point of departure in examining the economic growth of Great Britain
and the United States up to the First World War.

The main theme of the analysis will be the economic development of
the Atlantic economy as manifested in long swings in international
migration and investment. What determined the time-shape of oversea
emigration from Europe? Did British settlement in the Empire and in
the United States show similar fluctuations? What was the relation
between emigration and the rate of growth of real income a head in
Great Britain? Can it be shown from economic time series that foreign
investment alternated with home investment as the governor of the
level of activity in Great Britain? What was the bearing of periodic
mass immigration into the United States on the major upswings in
investment and the evolution of the technique of production in that
country? Is there evidence that migration is partly caused by the
rigidity of the social structure in an old society and in the long run
helps to create the same rigidity in the receiving country? Did international migration necessarily entail a considerable shift in the balance
of economic power within the Atlantic economy? What were the consequences of the drastic restrictions imposed by the United States in
1924? These are some of the questions which will occupy us in Part III
of this book.

PART II

DESCRIPTION

CHAPTER IV

STATISTICAL SOURCES

The era of free international migration was nearly over before the countries concerned began to give serious attention to their statistical records. The information for the century ending in 1914 is a by-product of legislation which had other purposes in view, and it was not until migration itself became the object of national planning that this branch of statistics was developed for its own sake. Here was a field where Governments had much to gain and hardly anything to lose by forgetting national sovereignty and agreeing on a uniform set of definitions; but instead each State adopted a method of counting which was most likely to help it achieve the aims of its own policy. The result was a jungle of conflicting classifications. The International Labour Office has done a great deal to produce order out of this chaos; its international tables of migration were a valuable attempt to bring various sets of national statistics into line. Recently a fresh attack on the problem has been made by the Population Commission of the United Nations.[1] But as long as the methods of collecting and presenting the information remain so different the task of drawing up an accurate balance sheet of international migration will continue to be full of difficulty.

This chapter will give a brief account of the statistics of the United Kingdom and the United States and an attempt will be made to check their accuracy in the light of calculations based on the number of British-born enumerated in the Population Censuses of the United States. Empirical analysis of British emigration and of its fluctuations and distribution by sex, age, occupation and destination must obviously be based on the data available, imperfect as they are. It is all the more necessary, before using them, to be clear as to how they were collected, whether they are less trustworthy in one period than in another, and why there should be marked discrepancies between British and American records of 'migration' from the United Kingdom to the United States in a given period.

[1] Cf. *Problems of Migration Statistics*, United Nations, Lake Success, New York, November 1949.

I. BRITISH MIGRATION STATISTICS

From 1815 to 1912 the figures of 'emigration' published in the United Kingdom show the movement of passengers sailing to countries outside Europe and the Mediterranean; on April 1, 1912, the authorities adopted a list enabling them to find out how many of those moving into or out of the country were changing their permanent residence. Statistics began to be collected under an Act passed in 1803 'for regulating the vessels carrying passengers from the United Kingdom to His Majesty's plantations and settlements abroad, or to foreign parts, with respect to the number of such passengers'. British ships were allowed only one person for every two tons and foreign ships one person for every five tons. Before granting clearance papers, the Customs officials were to receive lists of passengers from masters of ships and make certain that the law was being observed. The statistics were thus a by-product of legislation introduced to cope with the appalling conditions then prevalent in the vessels carrying emigrants overseas. These controls proved ineffective, as it was easy for vessels to evade inspection by sailing from out-of-the-way parts of the coast: thus in the early years the figures underestimate the number of persons who actually sailed from the United Kingdom.

As long as the business of transporting emigrants remained in the hands of numerous small sailing-ship companies, the restrictions were largely ignored and the wretched steerage passengers continued to be the helpless victims of a corrupt and brutal system of exploitation.[1] It was a technical invention and not Acts of Parliament that led to an improvement of conditions: the first Cunard steamships, which were put into service in 1840, soon revolutionized ocean transport and put an end to the worst of the old evils. Moreover, in 1840 came the establishment of the Colonial Land and Emigration Commissioners whose task, among other things, was to promote oversea settlement through the sale of land in the colonies and to see that the provisions of the Passenger Acts were enforced. This body published annual statistics based on the returns furnished by masters of ships; in 1872, under the terms of the Merchant Shipping Act of that year, responsibility was transferred to the Board of Trade. The *Thirty-third General Report of the Emigration Commissioners*, published in 1873, conveniently summarized the returns on outward movement of passengers from 1815 to 1872.[2]

Though the basis of the information remained the same, some

---

[1] For a well-documented account of these horrors see S. C. Johnson, *A History of Emigration from the United Kingdom to North America, 1763–1912*, London, Routledge, 1913, ch. v, pp. 101–20.

[2] British Parliamentary Papers, 1873, XVIII, C. 768, App. 1.

improvements and extensions were introduced by the Board of Trade. Already in 1853 the published data had begun to distinguish British citizens from aliens. The year 1870 saw the beginning of a series on immigration, based on a requirement that the masters of ships arriving in the United Kingdom must supply a list of steerage passengers. In practice the authorities usually received particulars of cabin passengers as well, though this was not a legal obligation. From 1876 the lists distinguished British citizens from aliens, so that it became possible to estimate fairly accurately the net outward movement of British subjects. The particulars required about age have varied from time to time. Before 1856 persons aged 14 and over were classified as adults; from 1857 to 1908 persons of 12 and over were regarded as adults. For the years 1853–76 the number of children under one year of age was recorded. When the new passenger list was introduced in April 1912 the age composition became more detailed with the introduction of groups 12–17, 18–30, 31–45, and 46 and over. In 1876 an analysis by occupation became available, and this was elaborated when the reform of the statistics took place.

With the adoption of the modern list in 1912, it became possible to measure the volume of genuine migration. The Board of Trade defines a migrant as a passenger who declares that he has lived for a year or more in one country and intends to remain for a year or more in another. The document used in recent times contains a column headed ' Countries of Last Permanent Residence', enumerating England, Wales, Scotland, Northern Ireland, Irish Free State, Other Parts of the British Empire, Foreign Countries, and another column headed 'Country of Intended Future Permanent Residence'. Northern Ireland and the Irish Free State are regarded as separate countries. These declarations by passengers of their intention to change their *permanent* residence form the basis of the Board of Trade's modern statistics of emigration and immigration. Even this information, however, suffers from two serious limitations. In the first place, it covers only persons travelling between the United Kingdom and ports outside Europe and the Mediterranean; migration between Great Britain and the continent of Europe is not taken into account. Secondly, there is no record of traffic by air, and in recent years this gap has been by no means insignificant. For alien as distinct from British migrants, the first of these deficiencies can be partially filled by using other sources, for example the number of foreigners entering the country as a result of an application by a British employer for a permit under Article 1 (3) *b* of the Aliens Order, 1920, and, since 1945, the records kept by the Ministry of Labour and National Service of the number of European Volunteer Workers placed in employment under official schemes for the recruitment of foreigners.

2. THE LIMITATIONS OF PASSENGER FIGURES

As we depend on passenger figures for our knowledge of external migration up to 1912, it is desirable to note some of their weaknesses.

(a) As long as transport was mainly by sailing-ships, there must have been a great deal of evasion of the restrictions laid down by Parliament. Even where there was inspection, the master of a vessel carrying an excessive number of passengers was not likely to include them all in the lists which he submitted. Up to the fifties the returns are undoubtedly incomplete, particularly as ships not clearing with the Customs were all probably overloaded.

(b) When the steamship had come into its own, evasion became rare; but another complication appeared. Since Britain was the pioneer in this faster and more comfortable form of transport, a tendency grew up for emigrants from the continent of Europe to embark from a British port. These were mostly Germans, Norwegians or Swedes passing through this country from one of the Eastern ports to Liverpool on their way to the United States or Canada. This traffic was more than the seriously understaffed port authorities could handle properly.[1] The returns for the first years during which passengers were divided into citizens and aliens included a relatively large number headed 'not distinguished', as shown in Table 1. The number returned as 'not distinguished' for the eleven years 1853–63 was fairly steady at an average of about 20,000 a year and in no way followed the sharp fluctuation in the number of citizens and aliens. In 1860 this nondescript group made up over a fifth of the total who sailed; and then after 1863 it fell abruptly to a few thousand and remained low for the rest of the century.

It is easy to explain this sharp break in 1864. The category described as 'not distinguished' consisted, ironically enough, chiefly of cabin passengers in mail steamships. The Passengers Amendment Act of 1863 (26 & 27 Vict. c. 51) brought vessels carrying mails under the same regulations as ordinary passenger ships, with the result that persons sailing in mail steamships could be more carefully classified than previously.[2] It is reasonable to infer that the existence of this large indeterminate group casts doubt on the accuracy of the numbers

---

[1] 'In 1850 the staff of emigration officials at Liverpool consisted of an officer with a salary of £150 per annum, two assistant officers with salaries of £100, a clerk at £80, and three medical inspectors who were paid on a *per capita* basis, but whose pay averaged between £400 and £500 annually. In the year stated, this staff was called upon to superintend the departure of 174,188 people, and to examine as many as 568 ships.' S. C. Johnson, op. cit. p. 118.

[2] See *25th General Report of the Emigration Commissioners*, British Parliamentary Papers, 1865, XVIII, p. 16.

Table 1. *Passengers from the United Kingdom to extra-European countries, 1853–72*

Year	Total	Citizens	Foreigners	'Not distinguished'
1853	329,937	278,129	31,459	20,349
1854	323,429	267,047	37,704	18,678
1855	176,807	150,023	10,554	16,230
1856	176,554	148,284	9,474	18,796
1857	212,875	181,051	12,624	19,200
1858	113,972	95,067	4,560	14,345
1859	120,432	97,093	4,442	18,897
1860	128,469	95,989	4,536	27,944
1861	91,770	65,197	3,619	22,954
1862	121,214	97,763	3,311	20,140
1863	223,758	192,864	7,833	23,061
1864	208,900	187,081	16,942	4,877
1865	209,801	165,891	28,619	6,291
1866	204,882	170,053	26,691	8,138
1867	195,953	156,982	31,193	7,778
1868	196,325	138,187	51,956	6,182
1869	258,027	186,300	65,752	5,975
1870	256,940	202,511	48,396	6,033
1871	252,435	192,751	53,246	6,438
1872	295,213	210,494	79,023	5,696

SOURCES: Annual *General Report of the Colonial Land and Emigration Commissioners* (British Parliamentary Papers) to 1855. *Report of the Emigration Commissioners*, 1856–73.

recorded as citizens and foreigners up to 1863. Two things are worth noting about the years 1863–72. The proportion of the total number of passengers to the United States and Canada travelling in steam vessels increased as follows: 1863, 45·9%; 1865, 73·5%; 1867, 92·9%; 1872, 98·0%. In the mid-sixties three out of every four emigrants went by steamship even though the average price was from 30 to 50% higher than in sailing vessels, a fact which suggests that the majority of those leaving the country were far from being poor. Moreover, these years saw a marked increase in oversea migration from Germany and Scandinavia. It is, therefore, not surprising that the number of foreigners departing from British ports should have risen so much between 1864 and 1872. Whether the laxity of the steamship companies about distinguishing British subjects from foreigners in their lists introduced a bias into the recorded totals in the second half of the century it is impossible to say. It can be stated on reliable authority that 'the distinction of British from other nationalities in the passenger lists was noticeably imperfect in the first half of the decade (1901–11) and that the inward lists of passengers during that period may have been incomplete as regards cabin passengers'.[1]

(c) With the rapid growth of facilities for international travel—after the sixties—the number of people going abroad on business or pleasure increased considerably and, therefore, the figures included a rising proportion of persons who were not genuine migrants. At first glance this appears to be a very serious weakness. But it would be wrong to jump to the conclusion that it necessarily affects the validity of the outward *balance* of passengers as a measure of net emigration. It depends whether one is thinking of the *aggregate* volume of net migration or of the balance as between Great Britain and a particular foreign country. If we examine the years when the two series are available, we find a marked disparity between the net movement of passengers and the net movement of migrants from the United Kingdom to the United States. Relevant figures are set out in Table 2.

Table 2. *Net outward movement of British passengers and migrants to the United States and to extra-European countries, 1913–30*

Year	To all countries outside Europe		To United States	
	British passengers	British migrants	British passengers	British migrants
1913	241,997	303,685	52,155	78,072
1919	27,002	53,912	−6,971	3,296
1920	172,747	199,047	49,783	60,067
1921	118,938	128,110	33,756	42,468
1922	99,882	106,070	27,689	37,291
1923	197,817	208,695	78,088	95,213
1924	95,584	107,822	10,646	16,964
1925	106,893	112,288	37,718	46,660
1926	142,648	143,776	40,634	47,505
1927	120,949	123,024	35,299	41,538
1928	98,193	100,267	30,149	35,935
1929	103,707	106,183	34,261	41,536
1930	31,902	39,380	23,448	32,017

SOURCE: H. Leak and T. Priday, 'Migration from and to the United Kingdom', *Journal of the Royal Statistical Society*, vol. XCVI, 1933, pt. II, p. 185.

The fairest test will be obtained by avoiding the aftermath of the war when there were complicating conditions and taking 1924–9 as a fairly normal period. In these years the net outflow to the United States shown by statistics of passengers was about 17 % less than the net

[1] H. Leak and T. Priday, 'Migration from and to the United Kingdom', *Journal of the Royal Statistical Society*, vol. XCVI, 1933, pt. II, p. 187.

loss recorded by the migration figures, whereas the aggregate outward balance of passengers (to all countries outside Europe) was only about 2 % less than that of migrants. We must also allow for the fact that persons from Eire emigrating to the United States via a British port were included among passengers leaving the United Kingdom but not in the total of emigrants. If an adjustment could be made for this, the disparity revealed above would be greater than 17 %.

There are other reasons why the net movement of passengers to the United States is an uncertain index of net emigration to that country. First, some of the people counted as outward passengers are British citizens who have their homes in the United States or Canada, and it is probable that the number of these who arrive in the United Kingdom and go home via the continent of Europe is greater than the number who arrive in a continental port and go home via the United Kingdom. Secondly, the form in use since 1912 asks for 'the port at which passengers have contracted to land' (information required for the statistics of passenger citizens by country of destination) and 'country of intended future permanent residence' (information required for the statistics of emigration). British passengers who land in Canada and then cross the border into the United States appear in the returns as citizen passengers to Canada; while some of the people who have declared their intention to live in Canada (and are therefore classed as emigrants to that country) are in fact on their way to the United States. There is plenty of evidence that, in the nineteenth century as well as in recent times, the United States received a good proportion of its British immigrants via Canada. Thirdly, it is possible that a number of mistakes are made when the column 'country of intended future permanent residence' is being filled up. For example, persons domiciled in America may be described as having a permanent residence in the United Kingdom when they are merely returning to their homes, or someone going to the United States to do a job lasting about a year may be classified as an emigrant.

This review suggests that in the first half of the century ending in 1912 the number of British passengers recorded as leaving the United Kingdom is too low and in the second half it is too high. As a measure of aggregate net emigration the total outward balance of passengers is a good approximation for the entire period. In the ten years 1920–9 the passenger figures gave a net outward movement which on the average was 95 % of the net emigration shown by the new Board of Trade statistics. The real difficulty about the statistics up to the First World War is that they excluded travellers between the United Kingdom and the continent of Europe. In a later section of this chapter an attempt will be made to estimate the extent of this gap on the basis of the birthplaces figures of the English and Scottish Population Censuses.

3. AMERICAN SOURCES

Records of immigration in the United States began as in England with legislation to regulate the condition of passenger vessels. The Act of March 2, 1819, provided that lists of passengers arriving from foreign ports should be lodged with the local collectors of customs. The subsequent history of these statistics is a complicated story of changes in source, definitions and classification.[1]

From the fiscal year ending September 30, 1820, until 1874, the responsible authority was the Department of State. Between 1867 and 1895 information was compiled in an improved form by the Bureau of Statistics of the Treasury Department, based as before largely on the returns supplied by the collectors of customs. An important change took place in 1892 with the setting up of the Bureau of Immigration which had its own officials at the ports; this body published annual reports until 1932. Its work has been assimilated into the Immigration and Naturalization Service, particulars of which for the years 1933–40 are given in the Annual Reports of the Secretary of Labor. Since 1943 the information is available in Annual Reports of the Immigration and Naturalization Service presented by the Commissioner to the Attorney-General.

There has been no consistency in the unit of time for which the figures were collected. The 'year' has varied as follows: 1820–31, the twelve months ending September 30; 1832, the fifteen months ending December 31; 1833–42, calendar years; 1843, the nine months ending September 30; 1844–9, the twelve months ending September 30; 1850, the fifteen months ending December 31; 1851–67 calendar years; 1868, the six months ending June 30. Since 1869 it has been the 'fiscal year' ending June 30. All this must be borne in mind in relating the American figures to the British, which are based on calendar years.

The category of persons regarded as immigrants has varied from time to time. Between 1820 and 1867 the returns cover alien passengers, from 1868 to 1891 immigrant aliens arriving, from 1892 to 1894 aliens declaring their intention to reside permanently in the United States, from 1895 to 1897 immigrant aliens arriving, 1898 onwards immigrant aliens intending to reside permanently in the United States.[2] It is

---

[1] An important source book for the early period is William J. Bromwell, *History of Immigration to the United States, 1819–1855*, New York, Redfield, 1856. This volume may be regarded as a quasi-official document, as the author was a civil servant in the U.S. Department of State. It gives the annual number of passengers arriving in the United States in the period 1819–55, with particulars of port of entry, age, sex, occupation and country of birth.

[2] Bureau of Statistics, Treasury Department, *Monthly Summary of Commerce and Finance of the United States*, no. 12, series 1902–3, p. 4336.

fairly certain that up to 1903 the term 'immigrant' applied only to steerage or third-class passengers, so that aliens travelling first or second class were not counted. Not until 1906 do we find a distinction between *immigrant* and *non-immigrant* aliens, the latter being persons of foreign nationality arriving for the first time and declaring that they do not intend to make their home in the United States, or persons of foreign nationality who have entered once before and are returning to resume residence in the United States.[1] Before 1907 aliens who had already been recorded as immigrants on their first arrival were again registered as immigrants each time they returned to the United States. From 1908 the term 'permanent residence' was interpreted as meaning residence for one year or over. An important alteration had been made in 1868 when the Bureau of Statistics of the Treasury Department took over and began the practice of excluding American citizens and foreigners not intending to reside in the United States before estimating the number of immigrants. An indication of how many of the latter category had come in before 1868 is given in the State Department reports from 1854. It appears that these transients numbered about $1\frac{1}{2}\%$ of the 'immigrants' arriving in the period 1856–67 and about 2 % in the period 1820–55.[2]

Emigration from the United States was not recorded until the passing of the Immigration Act of February 20, 1907, which extended to vessels taking alien passengers out of the country rules similar to those applying to incoming traffic. However, there are statistics of the number of passengers leaving by sea for foreign countries outside North America for the period 1868–1907 based on returns furnished voluntarily by the shipping companies; and, according to the Commissioner General of Immigration, 'it is probable that the departures given embrace nearly the entire passenger movement from the United States to foreign countries from our sea-ports'.[3]

The classification in force in the years 1908–32 is explained in the following quotation:

Arriving aliens whose permanent domicile has been outside the United States who intend to reside permanently in the United States were classed as *immigrant aliens*; departing aliens whose permanent residence has been in the United States who intend to reside permanently abroad were classed as *emigrant aliens*; all alien residents of the United States making a temporary trip abroad and all aliens residing abroad making a temporary trip to the

[1] *Annual Report of the Commissioner General of Immigration*, 1906, p. 45.

[2] Marian Rubins Davis, 'Critique of Official United States Immigration Statistics', App. ii of *International Migrations*, vol. ii, ed. Walter F. Willcox, New York, National Bureau of Economic Research, 1931, pp. 647–8.

[3] *Report*, 1907, p. 50.

United States were classed as *non-immigrant aliens* on the inward journey and *non-emigrant aliens* on the outward. The preponderance of non-emigrant over non-immigrant aliens is due largely to the fact that many on arrival who intend to reside permanently change their minds and leave after a temporary residence.[1]

It is curious that during the first half-century no reliable record was kept of the distribution by sex. The totals of males and females for the period 1820–67 are an approximation provided by the Immigration Commission in 1911, and as they are given for fiscal years ending June 30, they are not comparable with the immigration returns for that period. Particulars of age composition have passed through various phases. Up to 1898 there were three groups: under 15 years, 15–40, and 41 and over; between 1899 and 1917 there was a different classification, namely, under 14 years, 15–44, 45 and over. Then from 1918 to 1924 the limit of the lowest group was altered to 16 years. Since 1925 more and more detail has been published, until by 1945 an analysis into five-year age groups was compiled.

As the 'old' immigration gradually gave way to the 'new', it was natural that the legislators should wish to know more about the origin of the newcomers. Up to 1898 aliens are classified by nationality or country of birth;[2] in 1899 a new analysis by 'race' was introduced, in which, for example, English, Welsh, Scots and Irish appear as separate races. From 1899 onward the tables give the number in each racial group admitted by country of last residence. The returns for the nineteenth century suffer from inaccuracies due to the ignorance of port inspectors of the complex political divisions of the Old World, the dishonesty of many immigrants, and the practice sometimes adopted of regarding the port of embarkation as a criterion of the nationality of the passenger. The ports of Liverpool and Hamburg were major points of departure for people of several nationalities. As in England, the officials employed in the United States to cope with immigrants were notoriously few and ill-paid; and when one considers the hundreds of thousands who swarmed through the port of New York, it is no wonder that some of the returns were just guess-work.[3]

---

[1] United States Department of Commerce, *Historical Statistics of the United States, 1789–1945*, Washington, Government Printing Office, 1949, p. 20.

[2] See Treasury Department, *Arrivals of Alien Passengers and Immigrants in the United States from 1820 to 1892* (Washington, 1893); *Monthly Summary of Commerce and Finance of the United States*, June 1903 [Immigration into the United States showing number, nationality, sex, age, occupation, destination, etc., from 1820 to 1903], Washington, 1903.

[3] An official who had been Commissioner of Immigration at the port of New York, March 1893 to August 1897, made the following statement to the Industrial Commission on October 12, 1899: 'I assumed charge of Ellis Island on the 1st of April 1893, just during the time when, in view of the new law about to take effect, there was

Exaggerated criticisms have been levelled against the classification by occupation. It is no doubt true that many who called themselves farmers were in fact labourers and that sometimes it was impossible to distinguish skilled from unskilled. We shall find, however, when we use the data on British immigrants that, despite their inevitable short-comings, they furnish a useful complement to the United Kingdom sources. Not only can we trace the efflux from England, Wales, Scotland and Ireland separately, with distribution by occupation from 1875, but also there are monthly figures from July 1888.

4. PUZZLING FEATURES OF AMERICAN STATISTICS

For reasons already given the immigration statistics of the United States are not strictly comparable over a long period of time. Before considering their usefulness in supplementing the information published in the United Kingdom, we shall glance at some of the peculiar diffi-culties inherent in American sources.

(a) The Leakage through Canada

The Report of the Industrial Commission (1902) described the immigration of Europeans and Asians through Canada as 'the most serious loophole in the law'.[1] The unguarded frontier of 3,000 miles between the two North American nations is an object-lesson in civilized demeanour, but it has not been an unmixed blessing.[2] As the control

an immense immigration into our country...I had an opportunity during this time of acting under the old law...and I found, especially in looking up the old records which were all kept on Ellis Island, that while the few registry clerks in the office were supposed under the old law to take a statement from the immigrants about their nationality, destination and ages, as a matter of fact whole pages did not contain any reply to any of these points. They were nothing more than an index of names of people arriving at the port. It was, as a matter of fact, physically impossible for these people—the port officers—to do more. There were but a few of them who had to register sometimes 4000 or 5000 in a day. Now, under no circumstances could it be expected from them that they could examine the immigrants as to all these specific points, and put them down, and then expect that when through with the day's work they would make up the statistics.' *Reports of the Industrial Commission*, vol. xv, Washington, 1901, p. 179.

For an account of the machinery for admitting and counting immigrants at the Port of New York in the period 1845–69, see Frederick Kapp, *Immigration and the Commissioners of Emigration of the State of New York*, New York, The Nation Press, 1870.

[1] *Final Report of the Industrial Commission*, vol. xix, Washington, 1902, p. 978.

[2] An account of the problem in the period 1790–1840 may be found in George Tucker, *Progress of the United States in Population and Wealth in Fifty Years as exhibited by the Decennial Census from 1790 to 1840*, New York, Press of Hunt's Merchant's Magazine, 1855, ch. x, pp. 80–8. Tucker deals with British migration to the United States via Canada as well as British migration to Canada by way of New York. See also Jesse Chickering, *Immigration into the United States*, Boston, Little and Brown, 1848.

at the ports of the United States became stricter and more efficient, European emigrants, bent on reaching America but fearing the increasing rigour of the law, resorted more and more to the back door from Canada. On the other hand, as the sense of nationhood grew in the Dominion, the leaders of both the British and the French elements began to feel alarm lest the flood of immigrants from Europe should force the best of the indigenous population into the United States. Whether there was any real ground for this feeling will be discussed in a later chapter when it will be suggested that the interchange of population between Canada and the United States was dominated by periodic waves of internal migration encompassing the whole of the North American continent.

The annual estimates of the inflow of immigrants from Canada incorporated in the American totals must be written off as completely untrustworthy, and it cannot even be claimed that the error was always in one direction. For example, in 1881, of the recorded total of 669,431 aliens admitted to the United States 125,450 (or nearly one-fifth) were shown as coming from 'British North American Possessions'. It was pointed out at the time that 'at Huron there has been no attempt whatever at accuracy...American statistics are wholly guess-work... instead of 111,170 emigrants from Canada at this point, the whole residue that cannot be satisfactorily accounted for otherwise is only 4,259 persons'.[1] In 1888 the number officially recorded as immigrants from British North America was precisely 15! And a Committee of the House of Representatives declared that in the six months ending July 30, 1888, probably 50,000 aliens entered the United States after having landed in Canada.[2]

Up to 1893 no record was kept of the number of transients arriving from the north. In October 1893 the Superintendent of Immigration in the United States made an agreement with the railway and shipping companies whereby American inspectors were to examine immigrants arriving at Canadian ports and only those receiving certificates of acceptance would be allowed in at the points of entry on the American side. The railway companies undertook not to sell tickets to any migrants who did not possess such a certificate—a type of control which made no difference as third parties could always obtain the tickets. The situation continued to be unsatisfactory, so much so that in June 1898 the Commissioner General of Immigration sent special agents to Europe to find out how undesirable aliens were being diverted to the Canadian route and the extent to which foreign charities were

---

[1] Letter from the High Commissioner for Canada printed in *The Times*, March 29, 1883.

[2] *Report of the Ford Committee*, 1889, p. 3.

being used to promote the shipment of paupers and criminals. The Report on the United Kingdom included the following statement:

It is the popular belief in provincial England that those who are not beyond doubt outside of the prohibited classes can pass muster by evasion and reservation when being examined by the United States immigration inspectors; and when evasion and reservation are not considered quite effective there is always a way open via Canada. Indeed, one energetic agent boldly declared that anyone who really wanted to go to America could scarcely be kept out, no matter how vigilant the United States authorities may be.[1]

There was a Canadian estimate (probably too high) that, in the year ending in October 1893, between 40,000 and 50,000 aliens from Europe who had arrived in Halifax and Quebec had crossed the border into the United States.[2] For the seven years following the 1893 Agreement the recorded number of alien immigrants entering the United States by way of Canada is given in Table 3.

Table 3. *Immigration to the United States through Canada, 1894–1901*

| Year | Ports of entry into Canada | | | Total |
	Quebec and Port Lewis	St John and Halifax	Vancouver and Victoria	
1894–5	3,889	817	1,282	5,988
1895–6	5,395	1,508	2,018	8,921
1896–7	4,946	1,596	4,104	10,646
1897–8	5,126	2,218	3,393	10,737
1898–9	8,196	2,354	2,303	13,853
1899–1900	14,556	5,455	3,189	23,200
1900–1	16,771	4,894	3,546	25,211

SOURCE: *Reports of the Industrial Commission*, vol. xv, p. 682. Washington, Government Printing Office, 1901.

These statistics were better than nothing but unfortunately they left the picture almost as obscure as before, since they took no account of the aliens who went by rail to the interior of Canada and then slipped over the border. The problem proved insoluble and the record remained inscrutable. So great was the demand for manpower during the First World War that the Bureau of Immigration threw its scruples to the winds and practically invited more than 70,000 aliens over the frontier although they were people who in peace time would have been fair game for the border patrol.

[1] *Report of the Commissioner General of Immigration*, 1898, p. 39.
[2] United States Treasury Department, *Annual Report of the Superintendent of Immigration*, 1894, p. 19.

We must distinguish between two streams of settlers entering the United States—transmigrants from Europe and Canadian citizens. The inevitable gap in the statistical data can be bridged to some extent by turning to the Population Censuses. By applying appropriate death rates to the number of British-born enumerated in successive Canadian censuses, we shall estimate the net flow of immigrants from the United Kingdom in each decade. The American Censuses give particulars of the number of Canadian-born at ten-year intervals together with the year of their immigration; and from these a rough calculation can be made of the net influx of native Canadians into the United States. The results are given in Tables 71 and 72.

(b) Contradictory Laws

In the eighties Congress passed two sets of laws to regulate immigration, and they were essentially at variance with one another. The object of the Act of 1882 was to keep out parasites, criminals and paupers; the contract labour laws of 1885, 1887 and 1888 aimed at excluding aliens arriving 'under contract or agreement...express or implied, made previous to the importation or migration of such aliens...to perform labor or service of any kind in the United States, its Territories, or the District of Columbia'. The left hand knew not what the right hand was doing. The inspectors were being asked to apply two mutually contradictory rules. 'They must discover, first, whether the immigrant is sound in body and mind—that is, whether he can compete successfully for a living with American workmen. If so, they admit him. They must discover, secondly, whether he really has a prospect of finding work, and thereby of competing with American workmen. If so, they exclude him.'[1] For the immigrant it was a test of 'ingenuity and subterfuge to dodge the two extremes. He strives to show that he can support himself, and he strives to show that he does not know of any job by which he can support himself.'[1]

This dualism was a symptom of a powerful force with far-reaching implications. At this point we are interested only in its bearing on immigration statistics. The contract labour laws had their origin in the determination of organized labour to prevent employers from importing alien workers as strike-breakers, and it is interesting that Congress heeded the views of the unions even in the eighties when immigrants from Southern and Eastern Europe were still relatively few. Why the dykes then erected were later overwhelmed by a flood of cheap labour is a question which will need careful examination at a later stage.

[1] J. R. Commons, 'Immigration and its Economic Effects', *Reports of the Industrial Commission*, vol. xv, Washington, 1901, p. 647.

Several exceptions were sanctioned by the decisions of the courts, for example personal or domestic servants, relatives and friends, ministers and college professors, skilled labour, workers required for new industries, and recognized professions. But unskilled labourers on landing had to face the contract labour inspectors after they had been examined by the immigration inspectors. The former class of officials were separately recruited and more intelligent and were paid higher salaries than the immigration inspectors; their job was to discover contract labourers and extract affidavits from them. Even though the number thus excluded was less than 1 % of the immigrants, the existence of this control was a source of anxiety to many thousands of labourers as well as to those agencies interested in bringing them in. There is evidence that many aliens evaded this barrier by travelling first or second class.[1] The cabin passage, like the northern route through Canada, was an effective method of circumventing restrictions; and the error introduced into the official estimates of immigration from the United Kingdom no less than from the continent of Europe was probably considerable in certain years. In 1901, in addition to 487,918 recorded as immigrants, there were 74,950 foreigners who entered as cabin passengers. The total of 562,868 is no less than 15 % higher than the official estimate. The *Report of the Commissioner General for 1899* stated that there were 25,000 aliens who came as cabin passengers in that year 'who intended to remain here and who would have been classified as immigrants had they travelled in the steerage'.[2] One authority has suggested that in the period 1892 to 1903 this particular gap in the statistics amounted to between 6 and 12 % of the recorded volume of immigration.[3]

Another serious deficiency up to 1906 arose out of the failure to inquire whether the alien had been in the United States before. It is difficult to understand why the authorities allowed this omission to go on for so long, since it had such an obvious bearing on the problem of enforcing the laws passed by Congress. A rough idea of the degree of error may be inferred from the following calculation.

If we add to the immigration totals for the years 1906–20 the number of aliens resuming domicile according to the classification of non-immigrants,

[1] An Immigration Bureau Inspector at the port of New York testified before the Industrial Commission in 1899 that 'in recent years a great many who desire to escape the rigid examination at the Barge Office that they would now have to undergo if they came in the steerage, pay the difference and come in cabin expecting to escape that examination. In my opinion a great many contract labourers come through the Cabin. Of course we find some, and some we do not find. We can only take their statements, and have to land them, having no other evidence.' *Reports of the Industrial Commission*, vol. xv, Washington, 1901, p. 149.

[2] Marian Rubins Davis, loc. cit. p. 650.

[3] Ibid. p. 651.

and work out the relation of the number of aliens resuming domicile to that sum, percentages are reached varying from less than one to more than 18, with an average of 10 per cent.[1]

Even allowing for the fact that the habit among the foreign-born in the United States of visiting their relatives in Europe must have been less widespread before 1906 than it was in subsequent years (except for the war period), double-counting must still have been appreciable—perhaps between 5 and 10 % on the average.

5. BOARD OF TRADE FIGURES AS A MEASURE OF AGGREGATE NET EMIGRATION

We have already noticed that the British figures of aggregate net movement of passenger citizens, when tested in the light of the Board of Trade's migration statistics since 1913, are found to be a reasonably accurate estimate of net emigration, whereas that source may give a distorted account of the net transfer of genuine migrants to any one country. It is instructive to compare the total outward balance of British passengers in each of the four decades, 1871–1911, with the most reliable estimate of net loss by migration, namely, the excess of births over deaths minus the decennial increase in the population. The two series are set out in Table 4, where the figures relate to the United Kingdom.

Table 4. *United Kingdom: decennial net loss by migration, and outward balance of passenger citizens, 1871–1911*

Census decade	Net loss by migration* (natural increase minus population growth)	Outward balance of passenger citizens† (Board of Trade statistics)
1871–81	918,000	1,030,000
1881–91	1,557,000	1,650,000
1891–1901	586,000	680,000
1901–11	1,083,000	1,500,000

* *Statistical Abstract for the United Kingdom*, 1928, Cmd. 3084, p. 6.
† H. Leak and T. Priday, 'Migration from and to the United Kingdom', *Journal of the Royal Statistical Society*, vol. XCVI, 1933, pt. II, p. 187.

The passenger series is bound to diverge from the census estimate since the former records only the movement of British subjects to and from places outside Europe and the Mediterranean. It is possible, however, to fill in some of this gap. The Population Censuses of England and Wales, Scotland and Ireland show for the years 1871, 1881, 1891, 1901 and 1911 the number of foreign-born; and these data can be made to yield a rough measure of the migration balance of aliens from one

[1] Marian Rubins Davis, loc. cit. p. 656.

census to the next. The changes in the number of foreign-born in the United Kingdom between 1871 and 1911 are shown in Table 5.

Table 5. *United Kingdom: foreign-born population at each census, 1871–1911*

Census year	Total population of United Kingdom	Born in foreign countries (other than British Empire countries)
1871	31,484,661	157,237
1881	34,884,848	198,450
1891	37,732,922	261,995
1901	41,458,721	385,835
1911	45,221,615	428,030

SOURCE: Cmd. 3084, p. 16.

To estimate the inward balance of aliens in each decennial period, we shall apply appropriate death rates to the numbers of foreign-born. This way of calculating the number of survivors from decade to decade is accurate enough for the purpose in hand:[1] a refined method will be

[1] We take the average male death rates for the United Kingdom in the years 1870–2, 1880–2, 1890–2, 1900–2 and 1910–12, for ten-year age groups. Let the mean of the death rates at 1870–2 and 1880–2 for a given age group be regarded as the mean decennial death rate for that age group for the census decade 1871–81. In this way average death rates for every decade are calculated for each relevant age group. At the beginning of the period, in 1871, there were 157,237 aliens enumerated in the United Kingdom: in order to estimate the proportion of these who were alive in 1881, we apply the decennial death rate of the age group 35–45 for the years 1871–81, namely, 13%. (This is taken to be justified in view of the probable age composition of the alien population.) Subtracting the 136,800 survivors from the total of foreign-born found in 1881, we obtain a round figure of 62,000 as the net inflow in the decade 1871–81. The next step is to apply the 1881–91 death rate of the age group 45–55 (19·5%) to the 136,800 survivors at 1881, and that of the age group 25–35 (8·0%) to the 62,000 immigrants of the previous decade; the sum of the two lots of survivors (164,842) is then deducted from the number of foreign-born enumerated in 1891 (261,995), giving an inward balance of 95,000 for 1881–91. The inflow for 1891–1901 is equal to the alien population in 1901 minus three lots of survivors and so on. The death rates used are as follows:

United Kingdom: estimated decennial death rates for males (%)

Age group	1871–81	1881–91	1891–1901	1901–11
25–35	—	8·0	7·5	6·0
35–45	13·0	13·0	12·0	9·5
45–55	—	19·5	19·5	16·0
55–65	—	—	35·5	32·0
65–75	—	—	—	65·0

SOURCE: Cmd. 3084, p. 31.

For further details of the method see article, 'The Migration of Labour into the Glamorganshire Coalfield (1861–1911)', *Economica*, vol. x, no. 30, November, 1930, pp. 276–80.

developed later for the more important problem of adjusting the figures of net passenger movement to particular countries.

The effect of the operation is given in columns 3 and 4 of the following table.

Table 6. *United Kingdom: corrected balance of migration, 1871–1911*

Census decade	Net loss by migration (Census figures) (1)	Outward balance of citizens (Board of Trade passenger figures) (2)	Estimated inward balance of aliens (3)	Corrected outward balance of citizens and aliens (column 2 minus column 3) (4)
1871–81	918,000	1,030,000	62,000	968,000
1881–91	1,557,000	1,650,000	95,000	1,555,000
1891–1901	586,000	680,000	177,000	513,000
1901–11	1,083,000	1,500,000	116,000	1,384,000

The outward balance of passengers, allowing for the net inflow of foreigners, is pretty near to the net loss by migration based on the Population Censuses except for the decade 1901–11. Part of the remaining discrepancy is due to the fact that column (2) takes no account of British subjects moving to and from the continent of Europe. The marked excess of our adjusted estimate of net outflow over the net loss by migration in the decade 1901–11 is probably explained by two factors—a number of alien transmigrants were counted as British in the first half of that decade and the record of cabin passengers arriving in that period was not complete.[1] On the whole, however, it is reasonable to conclude that the Board of Trade statistics of aggregate net passenger movement are a surprisingly good measure of the course of total net emigration from the United Kingdom in the period ending in 1912.

6. ESTIMATES OF NET EMIGRATION OF BRITISH-BORN TO THE UNITED STATES

It is as a record of emigration from the United Kingdom to any one country, for example the United States, that the passenger figures are apt to go astray. Fig. 1 shows the movement of British passengers to the United States and the American record of net immigration from the United Kingdom in the period 1870–1930. There are considerable discrepancies especially in the nineties and the first decade of this century. Fig. 2 sets out the United Kingdom estimate of immigration of British

[1] Leak and Priday, loc. cit. p. 187.

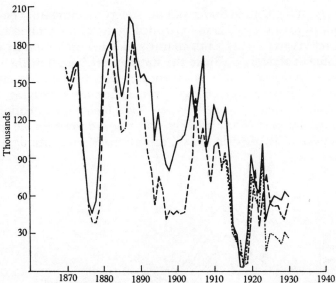

Fig. 1. British and American records of the number of British migrants from the United Kingdom to the United States, 1870–1930. - - - - American figures of immigration from the United Kingdom (fiscal years). ——— British figures of passenger citizens travelling from the United Kingdom to the United States. ...... British figures of emigration to the United States. Source: Table 78.

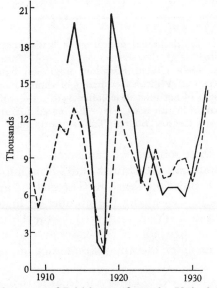

Fig. 2. Migration of persons of British race from the United States to the United Kingdom, 1908–32. ——— United Kingdom sources (calendar years). - - - - United States sources (fiscal years). Source: Table 79.

subjects from the United States and the American estimate of emigration
of people of British race from the United States to the United Kingdom
during recent years when both countries defined migration as a change
of permanent residence. Since the statistics are based on the declared
intentions of passengers, it is not surprising that they can sometimes be
misleading. People can change their minds after arriving at their
destination or they may deliberately hide their real intentions when
questioned by port officials. Then there is the appreciable source of
error, already discussed in detail, arising from the transmigration via
Canada.

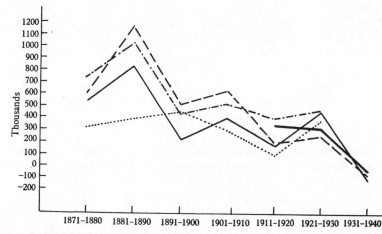

Fig. 3. Estimates of net decennial migration of British-born and Canadian-born
persons into the United States, 1871–80 to 1931–40. - - - - United Kingdom passenger
citizen movements. —— United Kingdom migration figures. - - - - - - United
States official sources and Willcox's estimates of return migration (before 1910);
United States statistics of net migration (after 1910). —— Estimates from United
States Census Returns of British-born. · · · · · Estimated migration of Canadian-born
based on United States Census. Source: Tables 71 and 73.

As a check on these sources, we can calculate the decennial inflow of
British-born persons into the United States from information contained
in the American Population Censuses. The method applied is explained
in full in Appendix 1. We take the number of British-born (English,
Welsh, Scottish and Irish) enumerated in the United States at each
census from 1870 to 1940: for each decade survival rates are calculated,
from which we can infer the approximate net immigration of British-
born.

Fig. 3 indicates for each of the seven decades 1870–80 to 1930–40 the
deviations of the two time series from the estimates derived from American
census sources. The figures of both countries seem to have exaggerated

the net flow of British immigrants into the United States between 1870 and 1914; the American returns are nearer the mark than the British. For the last two decades the Board of Trade figures appear to be a fairly reliable guide; the spread between the estimates for the years 1910–20 is perhaps partly due to the disturbance of the First World War. The movements shown by the American migration figures and the census estimates are not seriously inconsistent as to trend at any point: both display a similar time-shape from one decade to another. The Board of Trade series, however, registers a fall between 1910–20 and 1920–30, whereas the census estimate shows a rise.

The result of this experiment is on the whole encouraging. It suggests, first, that in dealing with time series it is wise to make a break at the First World War and, secondly, that over the entire period the original data, whether British or American, are not likely to be misleading as a measure of *changes* in the migratory stream over time.

CHAPTER V

THE OUTFLOW FROM THE
UNITED KINGDOM

This chapter will give a brief factual survey of emigration from the British Isles during the century 1840–1940. Up to 1923 the statistics published in London cover Great Britain and Ireland and from 1924 they exclude Eire. The story can best be told in two parts: emigration overseas from the British Isles as a whole up to 1923 and from Great Britain and Northern Ireland since 1924, and emigration from Ireland since 1840 both to oversea countries and to Great Britain. The latter will be dealt with in the next chapter, and the long-run effects on the population structure of Ireland will be examined.

I. COUNTRIES OF DESTINATION

The direction of the outflow is given in Table 7.

From the sixties to 1911–13 the proportion taken by the United States fell from 72 to 27 % and the share of the Empire rose from 26 to 65 %. The number going to America reached its zenith at the end of the eighties; it will be one of the tasks of later chapters to offer an explanation of the secular decline which set in. At the beginning of the period one in five of the emigrants (most of them from Ireland) went to Canada and for the rest of the nineteenth century the proportion was about one in ten. On the eve of the First World War Canada was absorbing nearly 190,000 a year, or 40 % of all emigrants from the United Kingdom. As a result of the gold discoveries in the fifties Australasia received 28 % of the outflow in that decade, the proportion falling to 8 % in 1891–1901 and recovering to 18 % in 1911–13. A clearer view of tendencies in the early part of the century is given by the fact that *net* emigration to the United States, after rising from 50,000 in 1900 to 100,000 in 1907, dropped again to 50,000, whereas the *net* outflow to the Empire grew from 25,000 in 1900 to nearly 250,000 in 1912.

2. SEX AND AGE COMPOSITION

Table 8 sets out for the period 1877–80 to 1911–12 the distribution by sex together with the number of children up to 12 years of age. Throughout this period the sex ratio was fairly constant at about four females to every six males. In the late seventies and the eighties when emigration was relatively heavy there were about twenty children to every hundred

Table 7. *Emigration from the United Kingdom to the United States, to the Empire and to other countries, 1843–1913*

Period	Annual averages (nearest thousand)						
	Total	Country of destination					
		United States	British North America	Australia and New Zealand	South Africa	Total Empire	All other countries*
	(1)	(2)	(3)	(4)	(5)	(6)	(7)
1843–52†	214	150	41	20	1	62	2
1853–60	164	100	15	46	2	63	1
1861–70	157	113	13	27	1	41	3
1871–80	168	109	18	30	5	53	6
1881–90	256	172	30	37	8	75	9
1891–1900	174	114	19	13	17	49	11
1901–10	284	126	85	23	28	136	22
1911–13	464	123	189	85	28	302	39
	Percentages						
1843–52	100·0	70·1	19·2	9·3	0·5	29·0	0·9
1853–60	100·0	61·0	9·1	28·1	1·2	38·4	0·6
1861–70	100·0	72·0	8·3	17·2	0·6	26·1	1·9
1871–80	100·0	64·9	10·7	17·8	3·0	31·5	3·6
1881–90	100·0	67·2	11·7	14·5	3·1	29·3	3·5
1891–1900	100·0	65·5	10·9	7·5	9·8	28·2	6·3
1901–10	100·0	44·4	29·9	8·1	9·9	47·9	7·7
1911–13	100·0	26·5	40·7	18·3	6·1	65·1	8·4

* Column 7 includes the relatively few passengers travelling to Empire countries other than those enumerated in columns 3, 4 and 5.

† With the exception of the years 1843–52 and, in the case of South Africa, 1843–76, the statistics for which comprise passengers irrespective of nationality, the table shows the movement of passengers recorded as British citizens.

SOURCE: Official figures taken from I. Ferenczi and W. F. Willcox, *International Migrations*, vol. I, New York, National Bureau of Economic Research, 1929, pp. 627–8, 636–7.

adults; but in the nineties when the outflow slackened the ratio of children to adults fell to 13 % and in the following decade began to rise again. It was when emigration was booming that whole families transferred themselves abroad in large numbers.

The age-composition of immigrants arriving in the United States from the United Kingdom in various years between 1875 and 1914 is set out in Table 9. The great majority were young men and women, and it is interesting to note that in the two decades beginning with 1875 the proportion aged 40 and over was tending to fall.

Table 8. *United Kingdom: outward passenger citizens by sex and age, 1877–1912*

| Period | Adult passenger citizens | | | Children up to 12 years |
| | Annual averages to nearest thousand | | | |
	Total	Male	Female	Annual averages (nearest thousand)
1877–80	125	77	48	25
1881–90	211	128	83	44
1891–1900	154	90	64	20
1901–10	246	147	98	39
1911–12	386	223	162	75
	Percentages			Children as percentage of adults
1877–80	100·0	61·6	38·4	20
1881–90	100·0	60·7	39·3	21
1891–1900	100·0	58·4	41·6	13
1901–10	100·0	60·0	40·0	16
1911–12	100·0	57·8	42·2	19

SOURCE: Annual *Statistical Tables relating to Emigration and Immigration from and into the United Kingdom*, issued by the Board of Trade.

Table 9. *Percentage age distribution of British immigrants to the United States, 1875–1914*

Year	Total	Under 15	15–39	40 and over
1875	100·0	19·6	67·1	13·3
1879	100·0	16·8	69·9	13·3
1884	100·0	22·2	67·8	10·0
1889	100·0	19·0	71·0	10·0
1893	100·0	9·4	86·3	4·3
		Under 14	14–44	45 and over
1904	100·0	10·9	78·9	10·2
1909	100·0	11·8	80·7	7·5
1914	100·0	13·0	77·1	9·9

SOURCE: United States Treasury Department, Bureau of Statistics, and the Bureau of Immigration.

3. OCCUPATION AND DESTINATION

We shall now examine the occupational distribution of male citizens who sailed from the United Kingdom to various oversea countries from 1876 to 1900. The details are given in Tables 10 and 11.

The United States took twice as many British emigrants as Canada and Australasia; but the strength of the pull varied considerably as between occupations and social strata. Farmers did not show much enthusiasm for settling in the Empire; two out of every three of them went to America. In the decade 1876–85 the majority of the farm labourers chose to go to Australia and New Zealand, but for the rest of the period the United States took practically all of them. Merchants and professional men were relatively prominent among emigrants to the Empire. For the first two decades 'all other countries' (comprising mainly South Africa and the colonial dependencies), while absorbing only about a tenth of the total flow of emigrants, were the destination of over a quarter of the merchants and professional group. How many of these were genuine migrants it is impossible to say.

In the years 1876–85 skilled workers found Australia and New Zealand an attractive destination, but the proportion of them going there during the following fifteen years slumped badly. The United States absorbed something over 60 % of the skilled labour—about the same as its share of the total number of emigrants. An interesting pointer in the last quinquennium, 1896–1900, is that a third of the skilled men leaving Britain went to 'other foreign countries'. There can be little doubt as to where unskilled labourers and servants found it profitable to settle. Steadily, throughout the last quarter of the century, about 75 % of them sailed to the United States and nearly 20 % to Canada. No other part of the world could compare with North America as a haven for the poor.

Table 10 throws light on the change in the relative demand for different grades of British labour overseas during the last quarter of the nineteenth century, induced partly by fluctuations in the rate of growth and partly by slow-moving secular changes in economic structure. It is not easy to disentangle these two factors; indeed the story of oversea settlement over the last century may be said to be a commentary on their interaction. If we take the latter half of the seventies and the latter half of the nineties, we shall be comparing two periods falling in roughly similar phases of the cycle of emigration to the United States. The number of emigrants in the two quinquennia were about the same and considerably lower than in the eighties. Interesting changes took place in the types of manpower imported by America from Britain in this quarter of a century. The unskilled element was reduced from

Table 10. *Destination of adult male citizens leaving the United Kingdom, by occupation, quinquennially, 1876–1900*

Period and destination	Merchants and professional men No.	%	Agriculture Farmers and graziers No.	%	Agriculture Labourers No.	%	Skilled workers No.	%	Labourers and domestic servants No.	%	Miscellaneous No.	%	Total with occupations No.	%	Occupations not stated No.	%	Grand total No.	%
1876–1880																		
United States	22,228	42·64	14,588	66·34	1,375	6·36	45,228	58·12	89,820	72·65	5,599	36·64	178,838	57·23	40,099	60·35	218,937	57·78
British North America	10,183	19·53	1,579	7·18	1,451	6·71	5,568	7·16	16,476	13·33	1,194	7·81	36,451	11·67	1,798	2·71	38,249	10·10
Australasia	7,315	14·03	4,526	20·58	18,729	86·62	18,309	23·53	14,025	11·34	3,945	25·81	66,849	21·39	14,747	22·19	81,596	21·53
Other	12,407	23·80	1,297	5·90	68	0·31	8,708	11·19	3,311	2·68	4,545	29·74	30,336	9·71	9,801	14·75	40,137	10·59
Total	52,133	100·00	21,990	100·00	21,623	100·00	77,813	100·00	123,632	100·00	15,283	100·00	312,474	100·00	66,445	100·00	378,919	100·00
1881–1885																		
United States	31,448	51·43	17,654	68·84	12,159	35·55	61,415	59·04	213,103	75·35	6,303	39·97	342,082	65·33	62,348	56·02	404,430	63·70
British North America	9,805	16·03	2,050	7·99	1,692	4·95	3,233	3·11	54,918	19·42	1,519	9·64	73,217	13·98	10,305	9·26	83,522	13·16
Australasia	7,563	12·37	5,134	20·02	20,238	59·17	30,206	29·04	12,718	4·50	4,635	29·39	80,494	15·38	23,208	20·85	103,702	16·33
Other	12,337	20·17	809	3·15	115	0·33	9,167	8·81	2,075	0·73	3,312	21·00	27,815	5·31	15,435	13·87	43,250	6·81
Total	61,153	100·00	25,647	100·00	34,204	100·00	104,021	100·00	282,814	100·00	15,769	100·00	523,608	100·00	111,296	100·00	634,904	100·00
1886–1890																		
United States	26,187	43·29	19,022	58·98	61,934	71·60	97,193	68·12	152,218	77·42	4,201	45·50	360,755	68·35	74,669	61·63	435,424	67·10
British North America	10,809	17·87	6,387	19·80	12,261	14·18	10,343	7·25	29,442	14·97	528	5·72	69,770	13·22	7,251	5·99	77,021	11·87
Australasia	8,266	13·66	5,357	16·61	11,956	13·82	20,395	14·29	12,202	6·21	1,823	19·74	59,999	11·37	20,625	17·02	80,624	12·42
Other	15,232	25·18	1,485	4·61	348	0·40	14,755	10·34	2,746	1·40	2,681	29·04	37,247	7·06	18,607	15·36	55,854	8·61
Total	60,494	100·00	32,251	100·00	86,499	100·00	142,686	100·00	196,608	100·00	9,233	100·00	527,771	100·00	121,152	100·00	648,923	100·00
1891–1895																		
United States	19,111	35·44	11,813	67·51	44,564	92·30	74,404	66·63	104,296	75·00	6,984	54·30	261,172	68·14	76,036	64·33	337,208	67·24
British North America	6,578	12·20	2,003	11·45	1,847	3·82	6,470	5·79	27,973	20·11	930	7·23	45,801	11·95	10,612	8·98	56,413	11·25
Australasia	8,252	15·30	3,136	17·92	1,409	2·92	6,875	6·16	4,553	3·27	1,104	8·58	25,329	6·61	10,216	8·64	35,545	7·09
Other	19,980	37·06	546	3·12	463	0·96	23,917	21·42	2,246	1·62	3,844	29·89	50,996	13·30	21,342	18·05	72,338	14·42
Total	53,921	100·00	17,498	100·00	48,283	100·00	111,666	100·00	139,068	100·00	12,862	100·00	383,298	100·00	118,206	100·00	501,504	100·00
1896–1900																		
United States	13,794	23·91	7,939	48·42	21,907	90·18	57,670	54·34	63,592	72·92	4,889	35·93	169,791	55·62	51,466	57·63	221,257	56·07
British North America	7,951	13·79	3,317	20·23	620	2·55	6,046	5·70	17,308	19·85	1,674	12·30	36,916	12·09	8,412	9·42	45,328	11·49
Australasia	10,617	18·41	3,169	19·33	1,347	5·55	7,916	7·46	3,600	4·13	1,108	8·14	27,757	9·09	3,985	4·46	31,742	8·04
Other	25,315	43·89	1,970	12·02	417	1·72	34,493	32·50	2,703	3·10	5,937	43·63	70,835	23·20	25,448	28·49	96,283	24·40
Total	57,677	100·00	16,395	100·00	24,291	100·00	106,125	100·00	87,203	100·00	13,608	100·00	305,299	100·00	89,311	100·00	394,610	100·00

SOURCE: *Annual Statistical Tables relating to Emigration and Immigration from and into the United Kingdom*, issued by the Board of Trade.

Table 11. *Occupations of adult male citizens leaving the United Kingdom, by destination, quinquennially, 1876–1900*

Period and destination	Total with stated occupation		Merchants and professional men		Agriculture				Skilled workers		Labourers and domestic servants		Miscellaneous	
					Farmers and graziers		Labourers							
	No.	%	No.	%	No.	%	No.	%	No.	%	No.	%	No.	%
1876–1880														
United States	178,838	100·0	22,228	12·4	14,588	8·2	1,375	0·8	45,228	25·3	89,820	50·2	5,599	3·1
British North America	36,451	100·0	10,183	27·9	1,579	4·3	1,451	4·0	5,568	15·3	16,476	45·2	1,194	3·3
Australasia	66,849	100·0	7,315	10·9	4,526	6·8	18,729	28·0	18,309	27·4	14,025	21·0	3,945	5·9
Other	30,336	100·0	12,407	40·9	1,297	4·3	68	0·2	8,708	28·7	3,311	10·9	4,545	15·0
Total	312,474	100·0	52,133	16·7	21,990	7·0	21,623	6·9	77,813	24·9	123,632	39·6	15,283	4·9
1881–1885														
United States	342,082	100·0	31,448	9·2	17,654	5·2	12,159	3·5	61,415	18·0	213,103	62·3	6,303	1·8
British North America	73,217	100·0	9,805	13·4	2,050	2·8	1,692	2·3	3,233	4·4	54,918	75·0	1,519	2·1
Australasia	80,494	100·0	7,563	9·4	5,134	6·4	20,238	25·1	30,206	37·5	12,718	15·8	4,635	5·8
Other	27,815	100·0	12,337	44·4	809	2·9	115	0·4	9,167	32·9	2,075	7·5	3,312	11·9
Total	523,608	100·0	61,153	11·7	25,647	4·9	34,204	6·5	104,021	19·9	282,814	54·0	15,769	3·0
1886–1890														
United States	360,755	100·0	26,187	7·3	19,022	5·2	61,934	17·2	97,193	26·9	152,218	42·2	4,201	1·2
British North America	69,770	100·0	10,809	15·5	6,387	9·2	12,261	17·6	10,343	14·8	29,442	42·2	528	0·7
Australasia	59,999	100·0	8,266	13·8	5,357	8·9	11,956	19·9	20,395	34·0	12,202	20·4	1,823	3·0
Other	37,247	100·0	15,232	40·9	1,485	4·0	348	0·9	14,755	39·6	2,746	7·4	2,681	7·2
Total	527,771	100·0	60,494	11·5	32,251	6·1	86,499	16·4	142,686	27·0	196,608	37·3	9,233	1·7
1891–1895														
United States	261,172	100·0	19,111	7·3	11,813	4·5	44,564	17·1	74,404	28·5	104,296	39·9	6,984	2·7
British North America	45,801	100·0	6,578	14·4	2,003	4·4	1,847	4·0	6,470	14·1	27,973	61·1	930	2·0
Australasia	25,329	100·0	8,252	32·6	3,136	12·4	1,409	5·6	6,875	27·1	4,553	18·0	1,104	4·3
Other	59,996	100·0	19,980	39·2	546	1·1	463	0·9	23,917	46·9	2,246	4·4	3,844	7·5
Total	383,298	100·0	53,921	14·1	17,498	4·6	48,283	12·6	111,666	29·1	139,068	36·3	12,862	3·3
1896–1900														
United States	169,791	100·0	13,794	8·1	7,939	4·7	21,907	12·9	57,670	34·0	63,592	37·4	4,889	2·9
British North America	36,916	100·0	7,951	21·5	3,317	9·0	620	1·7	6,046	16·4	17,308	46·9	1,674	4·5
Australasia	27,757	100·0	10,617	38·2	3,169	11·4	1,347	4·9	7,916	28·5	3,600	13·0	1,108	4·0
Other	70,835	100·0	25,315	35·7	1,970	2·8	417	0·6	34,493	48·7	2,703	3·8	5,937	8·4
Total	305,299	100·0	57,677	18·9	16,395	5·4	24,291	7·9	106,125	34·8	87,203	28·6	13,608	4·4

Source: See Table 10.

a half to a little over a third, while the skilled grew from a quarter to a third. The significance of this tendency can be fully appreciated only after more intensive analysis; it may be a key to an understanding of the deeper forces determining the course of British emigration.

There was little change in the relative importance of different grades of British labour migrating to Canada. The unskilled portion remained constant at about 45 %, and the skilled at about 15 %. There was one difference, however, which foreshadowed a transformation in Canada's economy: the proportion of farmers rose from 4 to 9 %. The total number of emigrants to Australia and New Zealand fell between the first and the last quinquennium from 67,000 to 28,000, and we must therefore be careful in interpreting the difference in occupational composition. A striking feature is the rise in the proportion of merchants and professional men from 11 to 38 %, and the decline in the relative number of agricultural labourers from 28 to 5 %. In contrast emigration to 'other countries' grew from 30,000 to 71,000, and nearly half the manpower absorbed by them in the nineties was skilled as compared with well under a third in the late seventies, a result of the increasing importance of South Africa and the colonial empire as a sphere for British enterprise towards the end of the century.

A different occupational classification was introduced in 1903, and on this basis the particulars for the years 1903–13 are presented in Table 12. In this phase of spontaneous expansion oversea settlement was rapidly changing its direction. In 1911–13 Canada was absorbing annually 65 % of the labourers leaving the British Isles, 46 % of the agriculturists, 40 % of the skilled workers, and 39 % of the commercial and professional group; Australia and New Zealand were taking 30 % of the agriculturists, 20 % of the skilled workers, 15 % of the commercial and professional group and only 10 % of the labourers. The United States, which received in 1903–5 52 % of the skilled and 43 % of the labourers, was attracting only 30 and 25 % respectively in 1911–13.

4. EMIGRANTS FROM THE UNITED KINGDOM TO THE UNITED STATES BY NATIONAL ORIGIN

Some significant facts about emigration are lost from view when we confine ourselves to the aggregate flow. By using American statistics we can map the course of the separate streams to the United States from England, Ireland, Scotland and Wales; the story of Irish emigration will be continued in more detail in the next chapter. The occupations into which the American authorities classified immigrants have been combined into four categories for this analysis: unskilled labourers (including servants and farm workers); farmers; skilled workers;

Table 12. *Destination of adult male citizens leaving the United Kingdom, by occupation, 1903–13.* (*Annual averages*)

Period and destination	Commercial and professional		Agricultural		Skilled		Labourers		Miscellaneous or not stated		Total adult males	
	Number	%	Number	%	Number	%	Number	%	Number	%	Number	%
1903–1905												
United States	6,598	47·3	9,859	50·7	16,153	51·9	16,963	42·5	14,249	40·3	63,822	45·7
British North America	1,975	14·2	8,028	41·3	5,993	19·3	22,003	55·2	5,126	14·5	43,125	30·9
Australasia	1,376	9·9	1,053	5·4	1,772	5·7	399	1·0	2,400	6·9	7,000	5·0
British South Africa	2,817	20·2	330	1·7	6,968	22·4	501	1·3	7,388	20·9	18,004	12·9
Other British	410	2·9	33	0·2	80	0·3	10	0·03	3,854	10·9	4,387	3·1
Other foreign	765	5·5	135	0·7	129	0·4	15	0·04	2,302	6·5	3,346	2·4
Total	13,941	100·0	19,438	100·0	31,095	100·0	39,891	100·0	35,319	100·0	139,684	100·0
1906–1910												
United States	7,296	40·8	8,814	39·2	20,102	51·5	14,507	31·6	14,176	30·2	64,895	37·7
British North America	4,117	23·0	8,551	38·0	10,983	28·1	29,459	64·2	10,174	21·7	63,284	36·7
Australasia	2,289	12·8	4,408	19·6	3,756	9·6	1,847	4·0	4,213	9·0	16,513	9·6
British South Africa	1,910	10·7	213	1·0	3,119	8·0	42	0·1	5,121	10·9	10,405	6·0
Other British	1,002	5·6	139	0·6	434	1·1	25	0·05	7,631	16·2	9,231	5·4
Other foreign	1,276	7·1	356	1·6	672	1·7	31	0·1	5,665	12·0	8,000	4·6
Total	17,890	100·0	22,481	100·0	39,066	100·0	45,911	100·0	46,980	100·0	172,328	100·0
1911–1913												
United States	6,455	25·4	6,603	21·9	13,904	30·1	9,488	24·8	7,256	23·1	43,706	25·5
British North America	9,811	38·7	13,736	45·6	18,656	40·3	24,805	64·8	9,950	31·7	76,958	44·9
Australasia	3,757	14·8	8,973	29·8	9,169	19·8	3,822	10·0	5,814	18·5	31,535	18·4
British South Africa	1,732	6·8	249	0·9	2,421	5·2	39	0·1	2,687	8·5	7,128	4·1
Other British	1,997	7·9	221	0·7	1,142	2·5	29	0·1	3,076	9·8	6,465	3·8
Other foreign	1,614	6·4	330	1·1	980	2·1	96	0·2	2,629	8·4	5,649	3·3
Total	25,366	100·0	30,112	100·0	46,272	100·0	38,279	100·0	31,412	100·0	171,441	100·0

SOURCE: See Table 10.

professional and entrepreneurial grades.[1] Figs. 4–8 show for the period 1875–1930 the occupational distribution of emigrants from the four countries, and from the United Kingdom as a whole.

The first striking fact is that nearly every year up to the First World War well over 80 % of Irish emigrants were unskilled labourers and hardly any of them professional or entrepreneurial. In contrast about 50 % of those who came from Scotland and Wales were skilled workers, and after the early nineties this is also true of the English. An interesting feature of Scottish emigration is its fairly substantial proportion of professional and entrepreneurial grades throughout the period; and after the turn of the century nearly a fifth of English emigration was of this class. There was an unmistakable change in the composition of the Irish outflow after 1900, the proportion of skilled and professional persons steadily increasing to about 25 %. On the whole farmers were slightly less prominent among the Irish than among the other three national groups.

Is there a pattern to be discerned in the changing occupational distribution over time? In the late seventies, when the American economy was in a very severe slump and immigration was low, the proportion of unskilled among British emigrants was comparatively small; in the eighties, when America was enjoying business prosperity and was absorbing population at a high rate, the proportion of unskilled among British emigrants increased. When conditions were unfavourable in the receiving country, a relatively large number of those who did emigrate belonged to the skilled, professional and entrepreneurial group. It is significant, however, that there was a break in this tendency in the mid-nineties, as is clearly brought out in the chart for the United Kingdom. The late nineties were a time of depression in America and we should expect the unskilled portion of the emigration to shrink; moreover, in the first decade of the century when American business was booming we should expect the unskilled portion to expand. But instead of this, the reverse happened; the proportion of skilled, professional and entre-preneurial grades among British emigrants rose from below 20 % in 1900 to over 60 % in 1910. The pattern which had ruled in the seventies and eighties had now ceased to apply.

This phenomenon may be seen from another angle in Fig. 9 showing the proportions of immigrants to America drawn from the four British countries each year from 1875 to 1930. The non-Irish component comprised three-fifths of the total in the American depression of the late seventies but only one-fifth in the depression of the late nineties. The proportion of Irish diminished from 80 % in 1900 to 40 % on the

---

[1] The statistical material is given in Appendix 4, Tables 80–4.

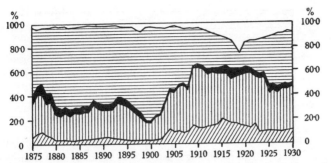

Fig. 4. The United States: percentage distribution of immigrants from the United Kingdom, by occupational group, annually, 1875–1930. ▨▨▨ Professional and entrepreneurial. ▥▥▥ Skilled. ▮▮▮ Farmers. ▭▭▭ Common labourers, farm labourers and servants. ▭ Miscellaneous. Source: Table 80.

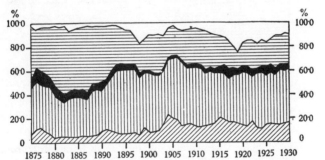

Fig. 5. The United States: percentage distribution of immigrants from England by occupational group, annually, 1875–1930. ▨▨▨ Professional and entrepreneurial. ▥▥▥ Skilled. ▮▮▮ Farmers. ▭▭▭ Common labourers, farm labourers and servants. ▭ Miscellaneous. Source: Table 81.

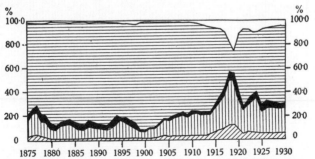

Fig. 6. The United States: percentage distribution of immigrants from Ireland by occupational group, annually, 1875–1930. ▨▨▨ Professional and entrepreneurial. ▥▥▥ Skilled. ▮▮▮ Farmers. ▭▭▭ Common labourers, farm labourers and servants. ▭ Miscellaneous. Source: Table 82.

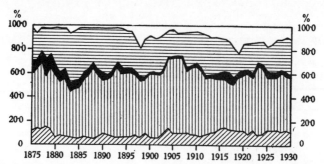

Fig. 7. The United States: percentage distribution of immigrants from Scotland by occupational group, annually, 1875–1930. ▨▨▨ Professional and entrepreneurial. ▥▥▥ Skilled. ■■■ Farmers. ▱▱▱ Common labourers, farm labourers and servants. ▭ Miscellaneous. Source: Table 83.

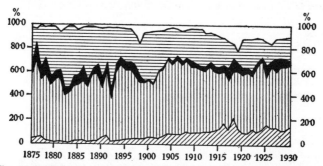

Fig. 8. The United States: percentage distribution of immigrants from Wales by occupational group, annually, 1875–1930. ▨▨▨ Professional and entrepreneurial. ▥▥▥ Skilled. ■■■ Farmers. ▱▱▱ Common labourers, farm labourers and servants. ▭ Miscellaneous. Source: Table 84.

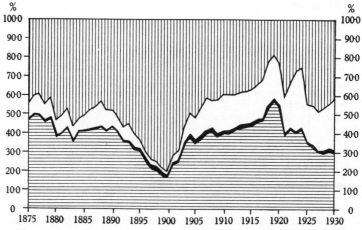

Fig. 9. The United States: percentage distribution of immigrants to the United States from the United Kingdom by national origin, annually, 1875–1930 (total reporting occupation). ▥▥▥ Ireland, ▭ Scotland, ■■■ Wales, ▱▱▱ England. Source: Tables 81–84.

eve of the First World War; and in those years the Scottish component grew to 20 % of the total; by 1930 it was no less than 26 %. From these figures one may infer that about the turn of the century there occurred a fundamental change in the factors determining British emigration to

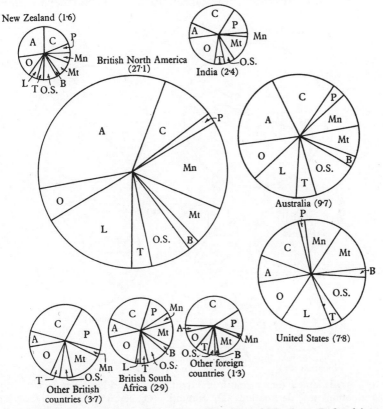

Fig. 10. Adult male emigration from Great Britain and Northern Ireland in 1928, by occupation and destination. A, agriculture; C, commerce; P, professions; Mn, mining; Mt, metals and engineering; B, building; O.S., other skilled; T, transport; L, labourers; O, others. The areas of the circles are proportional to the gross adult male emigration from Great Britain and Northern Ireland to the places named. The sectors subtend angles that are proportional to the percentages of emigrants of the indicated occupations. Source: Table 85.

the United States. No longer did a rapid economic advance in America draw in a relatively large volume of unskilled British labour; on the contrary between 1905 and 1913 the majority of those absorbed were skilled, while *net* immigration from the United Kingdom had ceased to expand. In later chapters we shall investigate the reasons for this change.

5. TENDENCIES BETWEEN THE WARS

In 1920 285,102 emigrant citizens left the British Isles, 70 % of whom went to countries within the Empire and 27 % to the United States. Of the 630,000 who migrated from Great Britain and Northern Ireland to

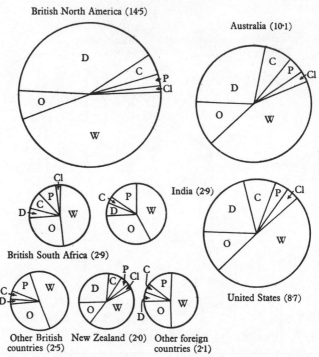

Fig. 11. Adult female emigration from Great Britain and Northern Ireland in 1928, by occupation and destination. D, domestic; C, commerce; P, professions; Cl, clothing; W, housewife; O, other. Where clothing is not shown emigrants in this occupation made less than 2 % of the total adult female emigration concerned. The areas of the circles are proportional to the gross adult female emigration from Great Britain and Northern Ireland to the places named. The sectors subtend angles that are proportional to the percentages of emigrants of the indicated occupations. Source: Table 85.

the four Dominions in the years 1924–9, Canada received just over 50 %, Australia 33 %, New Zealand 9 %, and South Africa 7 %. Statistics for the inter-war period are summarized in Table 13.

As a sample of the structure of emigration while it flourished after the First World War we shall take the figures for the years 1928. Figs. 10 and 11 give an analysis of adult male and female emigration from Great Britain and Northern Ireland by destination and occupa-

Table 13. *United Kingdom: emigrant citizens by destination, and immigrant citizens by country of origin, quinquennially, 1913–38.* (*Annual averages to nearest thousand*)

Period	Destination							
	Total	United States	British North America	Australia and New Zealand	British South Africa	Other British countries	Total Empire	Other foreign countries
1913	389	95	191	71	11	12	285	10
1920–24	214	59	77	47	10	15	149	7
1925–29	148	27	52	43	7	13	115	6
1930–34	42	7	9	7	3	10	30	5
1935–38	31	2	3	6	5	12	26	4
	Percentages							
1913	100·0	24·4	49·0	18·2	2·8	3·1	73·1	2·5
1920–24	100·0	27·4	35·9	21·8	4·9	6·9	69·5	3·1
1925–29	100·0	18·5	35·3	28·8	4·8	8·8	77·7	3·8
1930–34	100·0	16·5	22·1	17·5	7·9	25·0	72·5	11·0
1935–38	100·0	6·1	8·5	20·3	17·2	36·7	82·7	11·2

From April 1, 1923, the figures exclude passengers departing from ports in the Irish Free State.

	Country of origin							
1913	86	17	26	15	11	10	61	8
1920–24	69	12	18	12	7	15	51	6
1925–29	56	7	13	11	5	14	43	6
1930–34	64	10	17	12	5	15	48	6
1935–38	44	4	9	7	4	15	35	5
	Percentages							
1913	100·0	19·4	30·7	17·3	12·3	11·5	71·8	8·8
1920–24	100·0	17·7	25·9	16·6	10·0	21·8	74·3	8·0
1925–29	100·0	12·1	23·4	19·3	9·6	24·5	76·9	11·1
1930–34	100·0	15·3	25·9	18·2	7·4	23·7	75·2	9·5
1935–38	100·0	8·9	20·4	15·2	8·6	34·7	78·9	12·2

From April 1, 1923, the figures exclude passengers arriving at ports in the Irish Free State.

SOURCE: *Board of Trade Journal.*

tion.[1] Easily the most important destination was Canada, and over a half of the male settlers were classified as agricultural and labourers (other than in agriculture and transport). Next came Australia, the prominent occupations being agriculture, commerce and unskilled labour. Ranking third, the United States attracted a high proportion

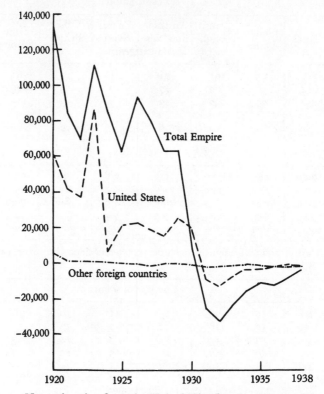

Fig. 12. Net emigration from the United Kingdom by country of future permanent residence, 1920–38. Source: Tables 88 and 89.

of skilled men. As compared with these three countries, the other destinations were negligible. The pattern for women migrants was about the same; about 50 % of those who went to Canada, Australia and the United States were housewives and most of the others domestic servants.

The world depression was a significant turning-point. After 1930 Britain ceased to be a country of emigration and received an inward balance from the Dominions as well as the United States, as shown in

[1] I am indebted to the Board of Trade for allowing me to extract the data on which these charts are based.

Fig. 12. More than 25 % of the men and women returning to the United Kingdom in 1937 were over 44 years of age. Such was the severity of the slump in the primary producing countries that thousands of settlers were uprooted and had to make a new start in the country which they had left years before. In the years 1931–9 Britain's population increased by 507,000 through immigration[1] and to every appearance a century-old tradition of oversea settlement had come to an end.

[1] See *Annual Abstract of Statistics, No. 87, 1938–1949,* 1951, p. 36.

CHAPTER VI

IRISH EMIGRATION, 1846–1946

The flight from Ireland which began with the famine went on at a varying rate for decades and is an almost unparalleled example of mass emigration. Beginning in May 1851, the Emigration Statistics of Ireland give the number of citizens and aliens leaving Irish ports for other countries (including Great Britain), a source to be distinguished from the Board of Trade Tables showing the number of Irish sailing from the United Kingdom (including Ireland) to extra-European countries. Valuable data—in some ways much more detailed than the corresponding information for Great Britain—are to be found in the Reports of the Population Census of Ireland.

I. THE DIRECTION OF THE OUTFLOW

The population of Ireland in 1788 is estimated to have been 4,389,000; in 1841 it reached 8,175,000 and by 1911 it had fallen to 4,390,000. In the latter half of the nineteenth century (1853–1900) about 3,294,000 persons of Irish stock emigrated from the United Kingdom to places other than Europe, 84 % of them to the United States, 9 % to Australia and New Zealand, 6 % to Canada and 1 % to other countries. Nor does this give a complete picture for it omits the stream of emigrants to England, Scotland and Wales. Where the censuses of the receiving countries record the number of Irish-born, we can infer the volume and timing of the immigration. The information is set out in Table 14.

According to the Population Census there were 806,000 Irish-born people in Britain in 1861 as compared with 415,000 twenty years before. The estimated mean annual death rate for persons aged 35–55 in England and Wales in the decade 1841–51 was 15·1 per thousand, and we may thus assume that 15 % of the Irish-born enumerated in Britain in 1841 died during the next ten years. The number of Irish migrating to England and Wales in the decade 1841–51 would accordingly be about 274,000, while Scotland must have received about 100,000. Applying to these immigrants the 20–35 death rate for 1851–60 (9 %) and to the older component the 55–65 death rate for 1851–60 (29 %), we calculate an inflow in the decade 1851–61 of 178,000 Irish-born into England and Wales and 37,000 into Scotland. The number who crossed the Irish Channel in the twenty years 1841–61 could not have been much less than 589,000; at the same time an enormous exodus took

Table 14. *Number of Irish-born persons enumerated
in various countries, 1841–1931*

Census year	Population of Ireland (thousands)	Irish-born persons (in thousands) enumerated in				
		England and Wales	Scotland	U.S.A.*	Canada	Australia
1841	8175	289	126	†	122	†
1851	6552	520	207	962	227	†
1861	5799	602	204	1615	286	†
1871	5412	567	208	1856	223	†
1881	5175	562	219	1855	186	213
1891	4705	458	195	1872	149	227
1901	4457	427	205	1615	102	184
1911	4390	375	175	1352	93	139
1921	4354‡	365	159	1037	93	105
1931	4184‡	381	124	924	108	79

* The year previous to the dates in column 1.
† Not available.
‡ Estimated.
SOURCE: Ireland, *Census of Population, 1936*, vol. IX, *General Report*, Dublin, 1942, p. 20.

place to the United States and Canada. In 1861 Irish-born people comprised 3 % of the population in England and Wales (9 % in Lancashire), 7 % in Scotland, and 5 % in the United States.

2. SEX AND AGE COMPOSITION

The sex distribution of passengers departing from Irish ports from 1851 to 1911 is set out in Table 15. Emigration between 1851 and 1861 was no less than one-sixth of the population at the beginning of that decade; and the corresponding proportion in the years 1901–11 was one-twelfth. The fall in the mean annual rate of outflow after the eighties may have been a sign that the relative number who could emigrate out of a weakened population was declining. There was a striking change in the sex ratio after the eighties. In the sixties and seventies 45 % of the Irish emigrants were females, but in the nineties the proportion went up to 53 %. The significance of this will be examined later.

The age distribution is shown in Table 16.

Irish emigrants were predominantly young people between the ages of 15 and 34; the proportion in this age group grew from 70 % in 1861–71 to 83 % in 1901–11, while the proportion of children under 15 fell from 15 to 9 %. After 1890 three out of every five leaving the country were between 15 and 24 years of age, and only eight out of every hundred were over 34 years of age. This raises the question whether the rate of loss of young people increased or decreased as time went on. Table 90 in Appendix 4 gives the annual number of male and female emigrants in five-year age groups from 1861 to 1910. A glance at

Table 15. *Sex distribution of emigrants from Ireland, decennially, 1851–1911*

Decennial period (ending March 31)	Males	Females	Total	Annual rate per thousand of mean population	Sex ratio	
					Males (%)	Females (%)
1851–61*	601,852	576,034	1,177,886	19·1	51	49
1861–71	469,772	376,951	846,723	15·0	55	45
1871–81	340,928	281,758	622,686	11·9	55	45
1881–91	393,744	374,361	768,105	15·5	51	49
1891–1901	200,125	230,868	430,993	9·4	47	53
1901–11	171,875	173,284	345,159	7·8	50	50
1851–1911	2,178,296	2,013,256	4,191,552	13·4	52	48

* From May 1851.

SOURCE: Sir William J. Thompson, 'The Census of Ireland, 1911', *Journal of the Royal Statistical Society*, vol. LXXVI, 1913, p. 642.

Table 16. *Age distribution of emigrants from Ireland, decennially, 1861–1911*

Decennial period	Age groups				
	Under 15 (%)	15–24 (%)	25–34 (%)	35 and over (%)	All ages (%)
1861–71	14·8	44·4	25·1	15·7	100
1871–81	14·4	46·3	26·8	12·5	100
1881–91	13·7	57·2	18·5	10·6	100
1891–1901	7·8	60·0	23·7	8·5	100
1901–1911	8·9	59·2	24·1	7·8	100

SOURCE: *Population Census of Ireland, 1871–1911.*

Table 17 shows that the relative outflow of men aged 15 to 34 in the eighties was greater than in the previous decade (3·7 % a year as against 3·1 %); but in the twenty years ending in 1910 the proportion of young men leaving the country fell to about 2 % a year.

The rate at which Ireland was losing population as compared with the United Kingdom as a whole is shown in Table 18.

Although the rate of Irish emigration just before the First World War was two-thirds less than it was in the early fifties, the series of high losses over such a long period had had profound demographic and economic consequences.

Table 17. *Percentage of mean male population aged 15–34 years emigrating from Ireland each decade, 1871–1910*

1871–80	1881–90	1891–1900	1901–10
3·1	3·7	2·1	1·9

SOURCE: see Table 91.

Table 18. *Average annual oversea emigration per 10,000 population from the United Kingdom and from Ireland, 1853–1910*

Period	United Kingdom	Ireland
1853–55	84	222
1856–60	43	141
1861–65	48	163
1866–70	56	138
1871–75	60	138
1876–80	42	98
1881–85	73	166
1886–90	69	150
1891–95	51	107
1896–1900	38	85
1901–05	27	84
1906–10	39	73

3. THE OUTFLOW SINCE 1926

A reliable view of trends since the establishment of Eire can be obtained from the results of the Population Censuses of 1926, 1936 and 1946.

Three interesting points emerge from these figures. In the first place, net emigration, which had reached the comparatively low level of 5·6 per thousand of the population in the decade 1926–36, rose to 6·4 per thousand in the decade 1936–46. Secondly, there was a sharp change in sex ratio; the number of females emigrating per thousand males declined from 1,285 in the first decade to 671 in the second. The full significance of this will be brought out in the next section. Thirdly, the British labour market increased its importance in relation to the American as an outlet for Irish workers. Net emigration to Britain from the twenty-six Counties probably averaged 8,000 a year during the period 1901–31; a slump in departures to the United States in 1926–36 coincided with a substantial outflow to Great Britain, in which, it may be noted, there was a much higher proportion of women than there was in the movement to oversea countries. Brisk demand in such occupations as domestic service and nursing in the thirties gave way after 1939 to the call for male labour for the war effort.

Table 19. *Eire: changes in population due to natural increase and migration, decennially, 1926–46*

Eire	Males	Females	Total
Change in population, 1926–36	+ 13,565	− 17,137	− 3,572
Natural increase	86,128	77,050	163,179
Net emigration	72,563	94,187	166,751
Overseas	42,789	48,397	91,186
Other (Great Britain, etc.)	29,774	45,790	75,565
Change in population, 1936–46	− 26,070	+ 11,102	− 14,968
Natural increase	87,599	87,375	174,974
Net emigration	113,669	76,273	189,942
Travel permits issued to persons going to employment in Great Britain and Northern Ireland (September 1939– April 1946)	151,660	77,009	228,669

SOURCE: Ireland, *Census of Population, 1936*, vol. IX, *General Report* (1942), p. 19; *Census of Population, 1946*, Preliminary Report (1946), p. 14.

Particulars of the occupations of the persons to whom travel permits were issued in the years 1942–9 indicate that the highest number of permits granted was in 1942, when 37,263 men, of whom 23,830 were unskilled labourers, and 14,448 women, of whom 6,037 went into domestic service, entered Great Britain and Northern Ireland. The movement dwindled to 13,613 in 1944. After the war this migration recovered strongly, with women outnumbering men. Of the 101,000 arriving between 1946 and 1948, 37 % were female domestic servants and 23 % male labourers; no less than seven out of every ten women were between the ages of 16 and 24.[1]

The decennial rate of decrease in the population of Ireland (excluding the six North Eastern Counties) which was 10·3 % as between 1881 and 1891, fell to 0·1 % in the decade 1926–36. After nearly a century of uninterrupted decline, a reversal of the trend seemed to be at hand;

[1] See *Statistical Abstract of Ireland*, Stationery Office, Dublin, 1950, p. 26.

that it did not occur was due to the active demand for labour in Britain during the war. Although the forces promoting net emigration were far less potent than formerly, they had not yet spent themselves.

4. EFFECTS ON POPULATION STRUCTURE

While the crisis heralded by the famine inflicted suffering on the millions who were uprooted, the economic well-being of those who remained improved. Holdings of more than 30 acres in area increased in number from 49,000 in 1841 to 158,000 in 1861; between 1841 and 1851 the proportion of families living in mud cabins with only one room diminished from 44 to 22 %. Nor must we ignore the flow of remittances from settlers in America to their families at home; these were not a negligible item in the Irish balance of payments and they brought to many a needy household a little of the bounty of the New World.

The effect of mass emigration on age-structure is shown in detail in Table 20.

It is clear from the last line of the table that the major cause of the decreases was emigration. There has been a continuous ageing of the population as shown in Table 21.

Table 20. *Eire: persons at each census per 100 of those 10 years* younger at the previous census, 1851–1936*

	Males Age at beginning of period					Females Age at beginning of period				
	10–14	15–19	20–24	25–29	30–34	10–14	15–19	20–24	25–29	30–34
1841–51	59	46	50	49	67	65	47	54	50	71
1851–61	65	49	53	57	80	68	48	52	58	82
1861–71	70	52	55	59	82	80	56	58	61	85
1871–81	73	61	65	66	85	77	62	67	66	87
1881–91	71	54	56	67	84	68	55	57	68	86
1891–1901	77	61	62	75	86	79	64	65	72	87
1901–11	82	67	68	83	87	78	68	66	76	82
1911–26	69	59	62	73	78	73	61	69	70	77
1926–36	89	78	76	91	91	83	74	77	88	87
Decrease in 10 years (1926–36) due to deaths alone (approx.)	2·7	3·6	4·1	4·6	5·4	2·8	4·0	4·7	5·2	5·8

* 15 years in 1911–26 period.
SOURCE: Ireland, *Census of Population, 1936*, vol. IX, *General Report* (1942), p. 138.

The number of persons aged 65 and over as a percentage of the age group 15–64 in 1936 was 15·4 in Eire, as compared with 13·8 in France, 12·0 in Italy, 11·1 in Scotland, 10·8 in England and Wales, and 8·3 in the United States.[1] It is a striking fact that, despite a fall of 3,560,000 in the population of Eire between 1841 and 1936, there were actually 87,000 more persons aged 65 and over in 1936 than in 1841.

Table 21. *Eire: age distribution of the population, 1841–1946*

Year	0–14	15–44	45–64	65 and over	All ages
1841	38·1	45·9	12·9	3·1	100·0
1861	32·5	45·8	17·1	4·6	100·0
1881	35·4	42·7	15·6	6·3	100·0
1901	30·2	46·0	17·3	6·5	100·0
1926	29·2	42·8	18·9	9·1	100·0
1936	27·6	43·1	19·6	9·7	100·0
1946	27·9	42·4	19·1	10·6	100·0

SOURCE: Ireland, *Census of Population, 1936*, vol. IX, *General Report* (1942), p. 115, and *Preliminary Report of 1946 Census*.

The number of females per thousand males in Ireland (excluding the six Counties) in 1851 was 1,049; by 1936 it had fallen to 952 which compared with 969 in Australia (1933), 970 in New Zealand (1936), 976 in the United States (1930) and 1,088 in England and Wales (1931). Against all expectation the ratio in Ireland was less than anywhere else in Europe and was even lower than in three oversea countries of immigration.

This intriguing result must be due partly to the peculiarities of the migratory stream. In the great evacuation of the early fifties the balance of the sexes was even; from about 1855 there was an excess of males until 1893; after that year there was an excess of females until 1904. Similarly in Sweden we find an excess of males from 1851 to 1893 and an excess of females from 1894 to 1899. In both countries the year 1893–4 marks a change in the sex ratio of emigrants aged 20–24 from a predominance of males to a predominance of females. This break coincided with the onset of a severe slump in America in 1893; the absorption of immigrant labour fell off sharply, but the demand for females was less badly hit than that for males. It is interesting to note that throughout the period 1861–1910 females exceeded males among emigrants aged 15–19 from Ireland. The probable reason is that the demand for domestic servants in the United States and Great Britain did not fluctuate much with general business conditions. It may be

[1] Ireland, *Census of Population, 1936*, vol. IX, *General Report* (1942), p. 117.

recalled that females comprised 60 % of net Irish emigration to Britain between 1926 and 1936; if there had been no emigration in the previous ten years the sex ratio of the population of Eire in 1936 would have been 968 instead of 952. Thus the abnormally low proportion of women in Eire is partly the consequence of the relatively heavy outflow of young women for many decades. Another reason is that, though more boys than girls are born in Ireland as in every country, the expectation of life of females is only very slightly higher than that of males.

Trends in Irish vital statistics up to 1946 are summarized below.

Table 22. *Eire: decennial changes in population, natural increase and net migration, 1871–1946*

Period	Average yearly decline		Average yearly natural increase		Average yearly net emigration		No. of females emigrating per thousand males
	Male	Female	Male	Female	Male	Female	
1871–81	8,003	10,314	16,955	14,900	24,958	25,214	1,010
1881–91	18,384	21,749	10,873	8,727	29,257	30,476	1,042
1891–1901	11,852	12,836	8,463	6,491	20,315	19,327	951
1901–11	2,058	6,156	9,706	8,234	11,764	14,390	1,223
1911–26*	5,508	5,672	8,426	7,396	13,934	13,068	938
1926–36	1,357†	1,714	8,612	7,706	7,255	9,420	1,285
1936–46	2,607	1,110†	8,760	8,737	11,367	7,627	671

* 15 years period.   † Increase.
Source: Ireland, *Census of Population, 1946, Preliminary Report* (1946).

The three periods in which there were fewer females than males among the emigrants were 1891–1901, 1911–26 and 1936–46. In the nineties transatlantic emigration was at a low ebb; and the other two periods were dominated by world war. Of especial significance is the sharp fall in the number of females per 1,000 male emigrants from 1,285 in 1926–36 to 671 in 1936–46, a consequence of the preponderance of women among the return migration and of men among the emigrants to Britain during the Second World War. The table also brings out the considerable excess of females over males in the natural increase in earlier decades, a characteristic which had practically vanished by 1936–46. In that decade the natural increase of females was only 0·3 % less than that of males, whereas in 1926–36 the excess was 12 %. The number of females per 1,000 males in the Irish population in 1946 was 976 as compared with 952 ten years before.

Another exceptional feature is the low marriage rate. The number of married women under the age of 45 per 1,000 of the population in

1930 was 73, compared with 105 in Scotland, 123 in England and Wales, and 145 in the United States; on the other hand, the number of children under five years of age per 100 married women under 45 in Eire was 123, compared with 83 in Scotland, 64 in the United States, and 61 in England and Wales. A relatively large number of women in Ireland remain spinsters, but those who do get married have a high rate of fertility.

The Irish marriage rate did not become exceptionally low until after the first great efflux of emigrants. According to the Population Census of 1871 as many as 48 % of the men and 42 % of the women were unmarried, the corresponding figures for England and Wales being 38 and 36 %, and for Scotland 44 and 43 %. It is noteworthy that at that time there were proportionately even more spinsters in Scotland than in Ireland. The contrast between Ireland on the one hand and England and Wales on the other is most marked in particular age groups; in the age group 25–29, 50 % of the Irish women were spinsters as compared with 36 % of the women in England and Wales.[1] The General Report of the 1871 Census made this comment:

> The Irish as a race, or as a collection of races, are not less attracted to marriage than other people; and they are certainly not more disposed than other people to undervalue the sanctions with which law and religion are emulous to surround the natural relation between the sexes. The Irish beyond all dispute are a nation whose individuals will marry when they can, and be celibates only when they must. Admitting then that they may have grown more provident or more ambitious, or more fastidious, it will still be true to say that the lower marriage rate in Ireland as compared with England and Scotland argues a state of things in the first named country which incapacitates people from marrying who would be willing to marry, if they could be as well started, according to Irish conceptions of well-being, as English people or Scotch would be in England or Scotland, according to English or Scottish ideas.[2]

One would think that a large volume of emigration would tend to raise the marriage rate among those left behind as it would be easier for them to find a good livelihood. That this did not happen is abundantly clear from the statistics of Ireland as well as Sweden and Scotland. The high rate of *net* emigration from these countries reduced the relative size of the population aged 15–35 and thereby lowered the relative number of marriages. When we consider the effect of this factor on fertility there is an interesting difference between Ireland and Sweden. Emigration in Sweden, by removing the poorest from the agricultural communities, took away the most fertile, while the birth

---

[1] *Population Census of Ireland, 1871, General Report*, British Parliamentary Papers, 1876, LXXXI, p. 54.   [2] Ibid.

rate in all classes fell steadily after the eighties. In Ireland, on the other hand, the low number of marriages was partly offset by a relatively large number of children per marriage. Between 1870–2 and 1900–2 the number of births per 1,000 married women in Ireland declined by only 4·7 %, while the corresponding rate in Sweden fell by 9·0 % between 1870–5 and 1896–1900. Since the turn of the century the Irish rate has not fallen as much as in other countries. The rate of natural increase in 1936–46 was over 7 % higher than in the previous decade, a result of the appreciable war-time increase in the marriage rate.

The full demographic consequences of a considerable volume of net emigration are not easy to unravel; but the operative fact is the heavy incidence on the age groups 15–35. What happens may be stated briefly as follows. As a result of the shrinkage of the part of the population aged 15–35, there is a relative decrease in the number of births. This is more than offset by the fact that the propensity to emigrate is lower among children than among young adults, and so the age group 10–15 will become relatively swollen. Thus, fifteen years after the original thinning out of the 15–35 group, the number passing into the 15–20 group is abnormally large in proportion to the total population. This self-generating element is evident in the history of Ireland.[1]

Finally, there is a close connexion between the rate of change in the size of a population and the demand for houses. Table 23 gives the

Table 23. *Ireland: decennial rate of change in population and in number of inhabited houses, 1821–1911*

Year	Number of inhabited houses	Percentage rate of change in population	Percentage increase or decrease in number of inhabited houses
1821	1,142,606		
1831	1,249,816	14·2	9·4
1841	1,328,839	5·3	6·3
1851	1,046,223	− 19·9	− 21·3
1861	995,156	− 11·5	− 4·9
1871	961,380	− 6·7	− 3·4
1881	914,108	− 4·4	− 4·9
1891	870,578	− 9·1	− 4·8
1901	858,162	− 5·2	− 1·4
1911	861,879	− 1·5	0·4

SOURCE: *Population Census of Ireland, 1911, General Report*, British Parliamentary Papers, 1912–13, CXVIII, p. 1.

[1] For an admirable account based on Swedish experience see *Emigrationsutredningen*, Bilaga IV, Stockholm, Kungl. Boktryckeriet, Norstedt, 1910, pp. 40–69.

number of inhabited houses in Ireland at ten-year intervals from 1821 to 1911.

Between 1821 and 1841 there was brisk activity in building to cope with the needs of a rapidly increasing population; then in the decade 1841–51 the number of inhabited houses fell by as much as 21 %, and the decline did not stop until 1901–11. A continuous fall in the population had a paralysing effect on the inducement to invest in fixed capital and this in turn led to further emigration. The experience of Ireland demonstrates that, once such a cumulative process has been going on for some time, it is very difficult to arrest.

PART III

ANALYSIS

CHAPTER VII

MIGRATION AND THE RHYTHM OF ECONOMIC GROWTH

The movement of population from Europe to America comprised the major part of international migration in the nineteenth century; and a great deal is already known about its cyclical character. In his *Migration and Business Cycles*, Harry Jerome, after an exhaustive analysis, concluded that the inflow of population was 'on the whole dominated by conditions in the United States. The "pull" is stronger than the "push".'[1] He found that for the period beginning in 1889,

frequently the turns in the migration movement lag behind the corresponding change in employment, indicating that the passage of some time is required before the full effect of a change in employment is felt upon migration. The extent of this lag varies in different cycles, and is also frequently found to vary on the downturn and the upturn of the same cycle. In a few instances the effect of a change in employment conditions is not seen for almost a year afterward, but in other instances the fluctuations in employment and migration appear to be substantially concurrent. The more common lag in the migration fluctuations is from one to five months.[2]

Another authority, Dr Dorothy Swaine Thomas, in her study of Swedish emigration, came to the conclusion that

of the two factors, industrial 'pull' to America and agricultural 'push' from Sweden, the former played an overwhelmingly important role in respect to annual fluctuation from the 'seventies to the end of the emigration era just before the war.

Dr Thomas added the qualification that

cyclical upswings in Sweden were a far more powerful counter-stimulant than is generally recognized. In prosperous years, Swedish industry was able to compete successfully with the lure of America; and the latent agricultural

---

[1] H. Jerome, *Migration and Business Cycles*, New York, National Bureau of Economic Research, 1926, p. 208.
[2] Ibid. pp. 240–1.

push towards emigration became an active force only when a Swedish industrial depression occurred simultaneously with expanding or prosperous business conditions in the new world.[1]

These conclusions about the dynamics of international migration are based on an intensive analysis of *cyclical* movements. It may be possible to see the course of migration in a new light if we concentrate on another aspect of economic growth—long swings or Kuznets cycles. That this type of undulation calls for study is suggested by a mere glance at Fig. 13 showing annual immigration into the United States from Great Britain and Germany in the period 1831–1913. Four major troughs are clearly visible: 1840, 1860, 1878 and 1897 in the British series, and 1843, 1862, 1878 and 1898 in the German series. A similar impression is given by the course of Irish and Scandinavian migration given in Fig. 14. One cannot, of course, deduce anything by arbitrarily picking out prominent turning-points in a series. There is, however, a presumption that we are here confronted with what Professor Kuznets has called 'secondary secular movements' with a span of about eighteen to twenty years. A study which confines itself to business cycle fluctuations is bound to leave out important features of economic development; it is necessary to pay attention to the long upswings and downswings in international migration and the associated series in a period of unparalleled expansion. This chapter will examine the relation between the flow of transatlantic migration and the rhythm in the economic growth of the United States and Great Britain respectively in the period 1830–1913.

I. THE TREND

The first task is to decide on the most appropriate method of expressing long-run trend. Here it is best to begin by invoking what Schumpeter called 'the Principle of Economic Meaning'. He pointed out that

statistical methods are not general in the sense in which our logic is and that, outside of the range of probability schemata, they must grow out of the theory of the patterns to which they are to apply. From knowledge about the phenomena to be handled, which is of course basically empirical but at the same time a priori with reference to each individual task in hand, we must try to form an idea about the properties of statistical contours and to devise statistical procedure appropriate to expressing those properties.[2]

This analysis is concerned not with short-run oscillations but with minor secular fluctuations in migration over a period of about eighty years

---

[1] Dorothy Swaine Thomas, *Social and Economic Aspects of Swedish Population Movements, 1750–1933*, New York, Macmillan, 1941, pp. 166–9.

[2] Joseph A. Schumpeter, *Business Cycles*, New York, 1939, vol. I, p. 199.

ending in 1913. We know that during this period the population of Western Europe entered a phase of declining rate of growth. We also know that the forward march of industry was made possible by drawing extensively on the agricultural reserve army, and this process was bound in the nature of things to reach its zenith and then become weaker. Given these characteristics of our variable—population—it seems reasonable to ascertain the secular trend by fitting a mathematical curve, for example a parabola. Moreover, thanks to modern statistical research, a great deal is now known about the shape of the trends of economic series for our period. As indices of the economic growth of the United States between 1830 and 1913 we shall use—among others—the annual number of railway miles added and the production of bituminous coal; and here again we have a tendency to a declining rate of growth. Professor Kuznets, in his path-breaking work in this field, indicated that

the most essential hypothetical characteristics were derived from a general survey which suggested the tendency of industries to exhibit a declining rate of growth. This feature limited the choice of curves. From those which express this decline in the rate of percentage increase, we have chosen the simple logistic and the simple Gompertz curves as the most suitable. The statistical analysis of the data revealed that these curves, chiefly the logistic, yielded suitable descriptions of the long-time movements in production or volume of business activity for a number of branches in the five most important industrial countries.[1]

Much of our understanding of this aspect of economic development comes from the researches of Professor Kuznets; the basic statistical technique which I shall employ owes its inspiration to his work.[2]

In this analysis the trend is expressed by fitting to the original data either a second degree parabola or in one or two instances a straight line by the method of least squares, and in most cases this procedure gives a reasonably good fit. The original data are expressed as percentages of the corresponding ordinates of the secular trend; and a nine-year moving average is run through the deviations. This moving average is intended merely as a graphically convenient way of tracing the shape of the minor secular fluctuations.

Some sceptics might argue that this type of analysis is really chasing a mirage, since the so-called 'long cycles' are nothing but bunches of short cycles, the average character of each bunch being a reflexion of

[1] S. Kuznets, *Secular Movements in Production and Prices*, Boston and New York, Houghton Mifflin, 1930, pp. 324–5.
[2] I am grateful to Professor Kuznets for the kind interest he has taken in this chapter.

the eccentricities of the short cycles included in it. Such an objection cannot be taken seriously. The minor secular fluctuation is seen in a wide variety of economic and demographic series, and it would certainly be a remarkable coincidence if in every case the short cycles were bunched appropriately. Moreover, no one will deny the existence of the building cycle, whose duration from peak to peak is about the same as that of the minor secular fluctuation observed in other series. Since investment must entail building activity, it would not be surprising if there were such a phenomenon as an investment cycle with a span of about eighteen years. Professor Kuznets has pointed out that

these swings in rate of secular movement represent a component of the time series that is omitted from view if we confine our attention to the average rate of growth and the average retardation in it, on the one hand; and to changes in the series within the short term cycles (either specific or reference), on the other. Analysis of this component seems definitely worth while, so long as we do not assign to these fluctuations in the secular rate of growth the character of cycles, since their periodic recurrence has not yet been demonstrated or explained.[1]

There is no logical case for regarding the short cycle as the only 'real' one: economic evolution is characterized by a multiplicity of fluctuations. When Schumpeter adopted his three-cycle scheme he made it clear that there was no special reason for his choice and that five would have been better. Even a casual glance at the course of international migration during our period indicates the existence of minor secular fluctuations, and if we sometimes refer to these as 'long cycles' it will simply be because two short words are better than three long ones. The important point is that this particular kind of rhythm seems to have been characteristic of migration and this opens up several interesting problems.

2. TRANSATLANTIC MIGRATION FROM WESTERN EUROPE

In this study the Atlantic community of nations is conceived as being one economy made up of interdependent regions. Between 1830 and 1913 this economy underwent a transformation; and the expansion of the whole entailed a certain rhythm of movement in the parts. Growth required the transfer of labour and capital from east to west (internal migration from the point of view of the Atlantic economy); but this process could not go on indefinitely. One of the chief objects of this analysis is to trace the phases through which this process of migration passed, to throw light on the determinants, and, in particular, to

[1] S. Kuznets, *National Income: a Summary of Findings*, New York, National Bureau of Economic Research, 1946, p. 61.

attempt to unravel the interaction between the pace of development on either side of the Atlantic.

The inflow into the United States from Great Britain, Ireland, Germany and Scandinavia is shown in Figs. 13 and 14. There is a similarity in the long-run trends for Great Britain and Germany; both

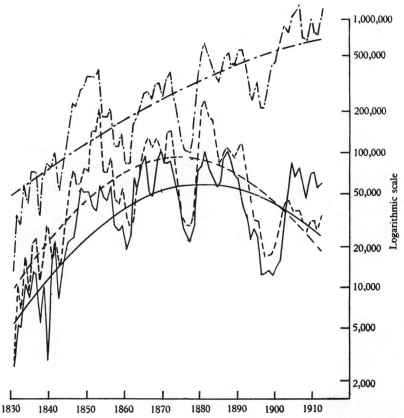

Fig. 13. Immigration to the United States from Great Britain, Germany and Europe, 1831–1913. —— Great Britain. - - - - Germany. —·—·— Europe. Source: Tables 92, 93 and 96.

reach their maximum in the eighties, with German migration then receding somewhat more rapidly than the British. The Irish picture is dominated by the massive influx after 1846 which towers over the rest like an impressive spire. One cannot escape the poignant irony of that peak of Ireland's tragedy in 1851—the year of the Great Exhibition— when 221,000 of her people crossed the Atlantic in a state of indescribable misery. After the first mass evacuation had subsided, the country continued to lose population at a steady rate; the number of Irish

migrants to the United States in 1910 was the same as it had been in
1835. The trend line for Scandinavia rises steeply, with a maximum
point in 1883 and another high peak in 1903; it was not until the
eighties and nineties that the volume of movement became substantial.

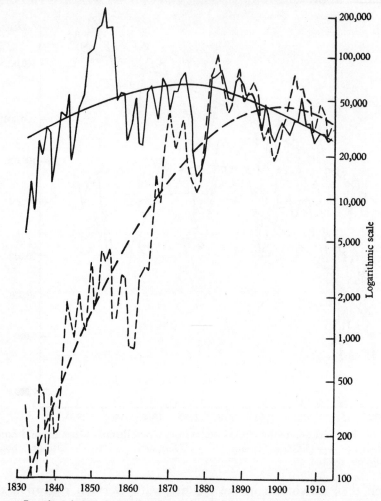

Fig. 14. Immigration to the United States from Ireland and Scandinavia, 1831–1913.
———— Ireland. - - - - Scandinavia. Source: Tables 94 and 95.

In Fig. 15 are plotted the deviations from the trends and the curves
showing the fluctuations. At a glance we note that these four streams
of migration trace out similar minor secular swings. The time-shape is
as follows:

Table 24. *Peaks and troughs of transatlantic migration cycles, 1831–1913*

Troughs	Peaks
1838–43	1849–54
1861–2	1869–73
1877–8	1882–3
1898	1903–7

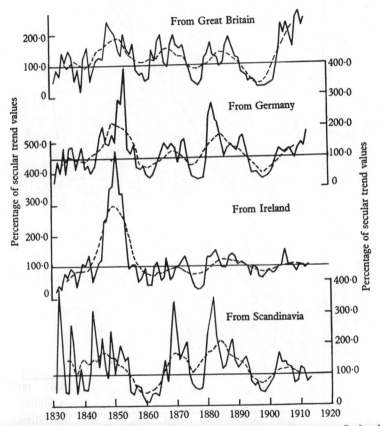

Fig. 15. Immigration to the United States from Great Britain, Germany, Ireland and Scandinavia, 1831–1913 (percentage deviations from trend). Source: Tables 92, 93, 94 and 95.

There are, of course, one or two exceptions: immigration from Britain, unlike that from the other three areas, has a peak at 1888 which is a little more prominent than the one at 1882; after the turn of the century the British and German series suggest a peak at 1913 accentu-

ated by the rapidly falling trend. No importance need be attached to
the erratic behaviour of the Scandinavian series in the thirties and

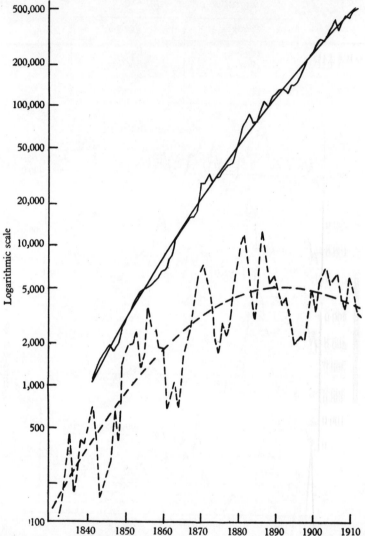

Fig. 16. Bituminous coal output and railway miles added in the United States,
1831–1913. —— United States coal output. - - - - United States railway miles
added. Source: Tables 97 and 98.

forties, as the numbers migrating each year at that time were often
only a few hundred. After a very high point at the beginning of the
fifties, the fluctuations in Irish migration show a relatively low amplitude. The important point is that the span from trough to trough and

from peak to peak is roughly simultaneous and the same length for the four series.

Is this common characteristic a reflexion of the changing rate of advance in the economy of the United States? Figs. 15, 16 and 17 set out

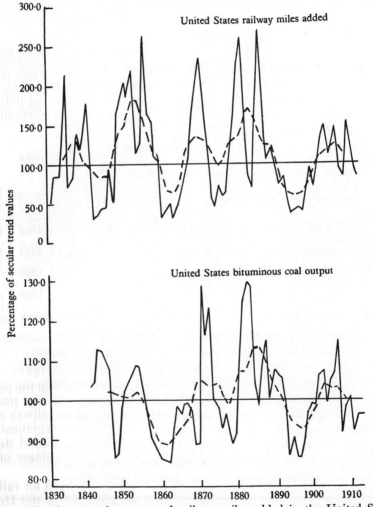

Fig. 17. Bituminous coal output and railway miles added in the United States, 1831–1913 (percentage deviations from trend). Source: Tables 97 and 98.

the course of railway building (mileage added) and immigration in the United States annually from 1831 to 1913. There is clearly a strong resemblance between the minor secular waves in these series. The exact upturns and downturns are worth examining.

A glance at Table 25 indicates that in the first three decades each of the turning-points in immigration precedes that of railway construction by one or more years; at the 1871 peak this appears to be still true of the British and Scandinavian series though not of the Irish and German. In the late seventies, eighties and nineties the three turning-points in immigration occur after that of railway building. Here is a phenomenon which seems to call for more detailed scrutiny.

Table 25. *The United States: peaks and troughs in railway construction and in immigration, 1831–1913*

Series	Trough year	Peak year	Trough year	Peak year	Trough year	Peak year	Trough year	Peak year
Railway miles added	1843, 1844	1856	1861, 1864	1871	1875	1882, 1887	1895	1910
Immigration from Great Britain	1840	1849	1861	1870	1878	1882, 1888	1897	1905, 1911
Immigration from Ireland	1843	1851	1861, 1862	1873	1877	1883, 1888	1898	1905
Immigration from Germany	1843	1854	1862	1873	1878	1882	1898	1907, 1913
Immigration from Scandinavia	1838	1843, 1849	1861	1869	1877	1882, 1888	1898	1903

3. A STRUCTURAL CHANGE IN THE LATE SIXTIES?

Let us take three series of immigration to the United States in the period 1831–1913, i.e. from Great Britain, Ireland and Europe; the pace of American economic development will be represented by railway miles added and bituminous coal mined annually. As already explained, the trend of each series has been ascertained by fitting a second degree parabola, and the original data are expressed as percentages of the corresponding trend ordinate.

A comparison of the graphs of the deviations from trend for railway miles added in the United States and for immigration to the United States from Great Britain (or from Ireland or Europe) reveals a correlation between the two series. But it is no simple correlation. Inspection of the peaks and troughs of the deviations indicates that somewhere round 1870 there is a switch in the direction of lag. It is interesting to note that a similar switch seems to be present, and at about the same time, in several other pairs of data relevant to this analysis.

The idea that suggests itself is that there was an important structural change in the American economy about the beginning of the seventies.

It is tempting to think of the first part of the period as being one in which the pace of investment was set by the inflow of population, whereas in the second part of the period it was the other way about.

Details of the method used to demonstrate the existence of a switch of lag and to locate the 'switch zone' are set out in Appendix 2. The results may be summarized by giving the sub-periods emerging from the analysis. In the years 1849–62 immigration to the United States precedes railway construction in the United States by about two years, and is itself preceded by bituminous coal output by about two years. Then follows an uncertain period, 1863–70, marked by the disturbance caused by the Civil War. The period 1871–85 shows an unmistakable reversal of lags. Railway building precedes immigration by one year and coal output by two years. Between 1886 and 1900 the rail-immigration lag is unchanged but coal tends to precede immigration. After 1901 immigration lags considerably behind railway building (three years) and behind coal output (four years).

The evidence seems to point to a structural change in the American economy just after the Civil War. Before it, immigration preceded railway building and followed coal output. After it, for the rest of the century at least, both immigration and coal output lagged behind railway building. In the light of this result, the generally accepted view that immigration was dominated by the 'pull' of American economic conditions needs to be revised. In the period before the seventies railway construction (which was a major part of current investment) lagged behind the inflow of population. That was the pioneering phase when a comparatively small nation was engaged in subduing a continent and the rate of expansion was conditioned by the arrival of new labour. Stephen A. Douglas, the apostle of 'squatter sovereignty', seems to have had a shrewd insight into the nature of the development of the West when he declared in 1845 that a Pacific railway would have to 'progress gradually, from east to west, keeping up a connected chain of communication, and following the tide of emigration, and the settlement of the country'.[1] Moreover, the railways could not have been built without the gangs of labourers, many of them Irish, recruited in the East and transported to the construction camps.[2]

[1] Atlantic and Pacific Railroad: A Letter from the Hon. S. A. Douglas to A. Whitney, Esq., New York (dated Quincy, Illinois, October 15, 1845). Quoted in Henry Nash Smith, *Virgin Land*, Harvard University Press, 1950, p. 33.

[2] See Oscar Handlin, *Boston's Immigrants, 1790–1865*, Harvard University Press, 1941, ch. III. 'From every part of the United States construction bosses in embankments and water projects, tunnels, canals, and railroads called on Boston for the cheap manpower they knew was always available there. Thus the city's role as labor reservoir assumed national proportions; often the Boston Irish newspapers, in single issues, printed advertisements for more than 2,000 men wanted in widely scattered places.

In the decades after the Civil War, the American economy evolved into a more mature phase, and railway building ceased to be the dominant force which it had previously been. Changes in the rate of inflow of population were now induced by changes in the general level of investment; this is in line with the well-known results of business cycle analysis. But before we can conclude that in this phase the 'pull' was consistently predominant, it will be necessary to examine carefully the pattern revealed by the minor secular fluctuations both before and after the 'switch zone'.

4. THE DRIVING FORCES IN THE OLD WORLD

If, before the seventies, railway building lagged behind population movements, what was it that determined the timing of the latter? A clue to the answer to this question may be obtained by looking at the first cluster of peaks in immigration, Great Britain (1849), Scandinavia (1849), Ireland (1851), Germany (1854), leading up to the peak of railway construction in 1856. One factor was the Californian gold discoveries of 1848 which no doubt explain the sharp jump in the number of immigrants from Britain and even Scandinavia in 1849: many vessels crossing the Atlantic at that time were crowded with speculators fired with visions of untold wealth awaiting them in Sacramento. In ten years from 1850 the population of the State of California increased fourfold from 92,000 to 380,000: and this sudden migration both from within and from outside the United States proved a powerful fillip to railway building in the Far West. But, spectacular though the gold discoveries were, they were certainly not the fundamental reason for the great upswing in immigration between 1849 and 1854. It is to the Old World that we must look for the driving forces. Two of our countries, Ireland and Germany, were passing through a severe Malthusian crisis, the course of which determined the date of their highest emigration.

Between 1781 and 1841 the population of Ireland increased from about 4,048,000 to 8,175,000, while in the same period no less than 1,750,000 had emigrated to Britain and North America.[1] This extraordinary excess of births over deaths was made possible because the potato as the staple diet induced early marriage and a minute subdivision of holdings. By 1841 over 80 % of the 691,000 holdings were

Sooner or later the immigrant in search of employment discovered the labor contractor in search of men' (p. 76). Most of the labourers 'were victimized by rapacious sub-contractors who monopolized supplies in isolated construction camps and took back in exorbitant prices what they paid out in wages'. (Ibid. p. 77.)

[1] K. H. Connell, *The Population of Ireland, 1750–1845*, Oxford University Press, 1950, pp. 25, 29.

less than 15 acres. Thanks to English rule, the Irish economy was deprived of industries and rested on an artificial foundation—the production of cereals for export. This swarming community was existing precariously on borrowed time, and the first unfavourable event was destined to bring calamity. A tremendous crisis in the economic life of Ireland was precipitated by the famine of 1846 and the adoption of free trade by the British Government. A new era had arrived in which an Ireland with eight million people in it was an anachronism. The number of emigrants to America, which had been 20,000 in 1843, reached 220,000 in 1851. To the horrors of the famine the landlords added the unspeakable cruelty of the evictions. Between 1849 and 1856 the recorded number of persons turned out of their holdings was 260,000 which was nearly 18 % of the colossal total of 1,480,000 who emigrated from that tormented island in those seven years. In the words of J. E. Cairnes, 'not far from one in every five of the multitudes who swarmed across the Atlantic had been driven by positive physical violence from his home'.[1]

It used to be thought that the large efflux of people from Germany to the United States in the early fifties was the consequence of the political events of 1848, but modern research does not confirm that view.[2] Close examination of the facts has shown that the districts from which the emigrants came were chiefly in South-west Germany, particularly where the land was tilled as a rule in small holdings. The stress of the early fifties had its roots in an agrarian revolution which had been going on for decades. Pinning their hopes on the new methods of cultivation, many peasants had mortgaged their farms only to find themselves brought to the verge of ruin by the crop failures of the forties. It was not political ostracism but population pressure and the hardship accompanying technical progress which drove out the vast majority of the 726,000 Germans who sailed to America in the six years 1850–5.

Of the 2,093,000 immigrants landing in America from Europe between 1849 and 1854, no less than 1,682,000, or 80 %, came from Ireland and Germany. The time of their arrival in the New World was dictated by the march of events in the Old. Two powerful forces were at work— population pressure and innovations. The former showed itself in a welling up of numbers in the age group 20–30 as a consequence of a peak in fertility about a quarter of a century previously. Technical progress took the form of a transformation of agriculture, free trade, and a revolution in transport. The latter made it possible for the first

[1] J. E. Cairnes, 'Fragments on Ireland' (1866), in *Political Essays*, London, Macmillan, 1873, p. 193.
[2] See Marcus L. Hansen, 'The Revolution of 1848 and German Emigration', *Journal of Economic and Business History*, August 1930, pp. 630 ff.

effective transfer of population within the Atlantic economy to take place. The Cunard Line began to operate its transatlantic steamers in the early forties, and fares soon became quite reasonable. A passage to America had cost £20 in 1825, whereas by 1863 steamships were charging only £4. 15s. 0d. a head and sailing ships £2. 17s. 6d. Without the cheapening of British transport the outflow from Germany in the first half of the fifties could not have been as large as it was. This is confirmed by what the *Sunday Times* of April 4, 1852, had to say about the boom in emigration in that year.

During the forthcoming season, large trans-shipments of continental emigrants via Liverpool to New York are expected, caused by the low fare from that port. From Bremen to New York is about £6, while from Liverpool the charge is only from 50s. to £3; and the expenses from Bremen to the latter port are under 30s. Bodies of emigrants from Coblentz, Hamburg, Leipsic, etc. have arrived at and departed from Liverpool during the past week. Their general appearance and demeanour contrasts strongly with the masses which have previously emigrated in such large numbers from Ireland.

5. THE SUPPLY OF LOANABLE FUNDS

The mass migration helped to furnish the United States with both the manpower and the demand conditions for the great investment boom of the fifties, the spear-head of which was railway development. But the marriage of the displaced labour of Europe to the natural resources of America was not in itself enough to inaugurate that upsurge of economic progress. The level of employment in the early phase of capitalist expansion in the United States was to be conditioned by the supply of loanable funds from outside. We shall now investigate the role of Britain's capital exports as the dynamic which ensured the absorption of Europe's redundant workers into the growing economy of the United States. As the pioneer in the industrial revolution, England had a rich capitalist class with a high propensity to save. Annual estimates of her foreign investment are not available before 1866; by 1851, however, no less than $225 million of American State, Federal, County and City debentures, together with railway bonds (excluding short-term debt) were held in British hands. It may be possible to guess the probable shape of the curve of capital exports in the first three decades of our period by consulting the course of share prices.

An index number of British share prices is available for the period 1840–1913.[1] We shall first examine the minor secular fluctuations in

---

[1] P. Rousseaux, *Les Mouvements de Fond de l'Économie Anglaise, 1800–1913*, Louvain, 1938, p. 272. For the period after 1867 the figures are based on K. C. Smith and G. F. Horne, 'An Index Number of Securities, 1867–1914', *London and Cambridge Economic Service Special Memorandum* No. 37, 1934.

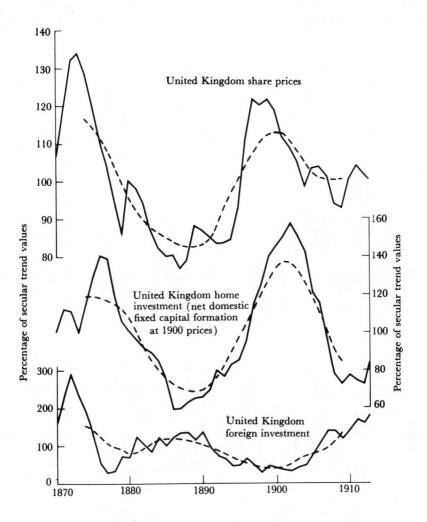

FIG. 18. United Kingdom: share prices, home investment, and foreign investment (percentage deviations from trend), 1870–1913. Source: Tables 99, 100 and 101.

this series in relation to those of British capital exports and home investment in the period 1871–1913. The data are shown in Fig. 18.

There is a striking inverse correlation between the deviations from trend of home and foreign investment. From 1872 home investment rises to a peak in 1877 while capital exports (at constant prices) descend sharply to a trough in the same year. From 1877 to 1888 capital exports rose to a peak, with domestic investment falling to a low point in 1887; the years 1888 to 1901–2 saw a downswing in foreign lending, whereas

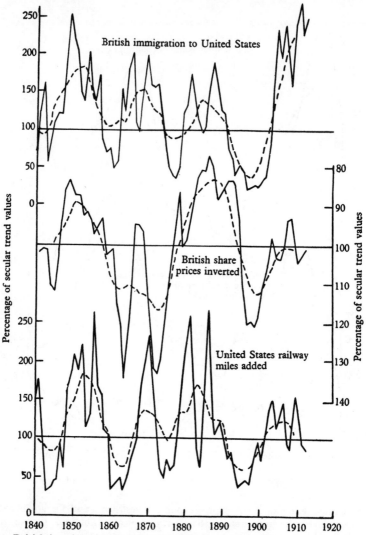

Fig. 19. British immigration to the United States, British share prices, and American railway miles added (percentage deviations from trend), 1840–1913. Source: Tables 92, 98 and 99.

from 1877 to 1899 home investment recovered vigorously. Finally, in the first decade of the century capital exports were rising while capital formation at home was falling off. The index of share prices may be regarded as an indicator of the profitability of investment in the United Kingdom. It is interesting that the swings in this index are approximately in harmony with those of domestic investment and inverse to those of foreign investment. The only exception is seen in the years 1873–7 when security prices were falling rapidly while home investment was rising.[1] It could be argued, however, in the light of the circumstances of those years, that the Stock Exchange as early as 1873–4 was casting the shadow of the slump in real investment, which came in 1877. From 1877 to 1913 the course of the moving average of share prices is a faithful reflexion of the movement of home investment; and if it is inverted it agrees well with the swings of foreign lending.

Assuming that the inverted index of share prices is a guide to the course of foreign investment, we can try the experiment of putting it alongside the deviations from trend of railway construction in the United States and migration from Britain to the United States for the whole period 1840–1913. The result is set out in Fig. 19.

For the first twenty years immigration and our indirect estimate of foreign investment move together from a trough in the early forties to a peak in 1849 and then down to a low point in the early sixties. Railway construction, as already explained, reaches its first peak later—in 1857—and then declines steeply to a deep trough in 1861. The Civil War caused railway development to remain stagnant for five years, but it did not affect immigration, which revived sharply from 1863 to 1866. After a minor break in 1867–8, immigration again swings into line with railway building, which was reviving very rapidly in the late sixties. Fig. 19 is intended simply to fill a gap in the picture of the long cycle from 1840 to 1865; and it is clear that the fluctuation traced out by our derived curve of foreign lending from the trough of 1843–4 to the trough of the early sixties coincides with the wave of immigration and railway building. There seems to have been a sharp increase in capital exports from Great Britain in the late forties with a peak in the same year as emigration. If we take European immigration to the United States, the two peaks which stand out are in the fifties and the eighties, and the same is true of the inverted index of British share prices and American railway construction.

6. MIGRATION, UNITED STATES RAILWAY DEVELOPMENT AND BRITISH EXPORTS

So far the inquiry has brought out a certain relationship between the swings of economic progress in the United States (as shown by railway construction and coal output) and the course of transatlantic migration.

---

[1] For a detailed account of these years, see W. W. Rostow, *British Economy of the Nineteenth Century*, Oxford, 1948, ch. IX, 'The Depression of the Seventies, 1874–9'.

The next step is to relate the above to series reflecting the economic growth of the United Kingdom in the period 1840–1913. Unfortunately

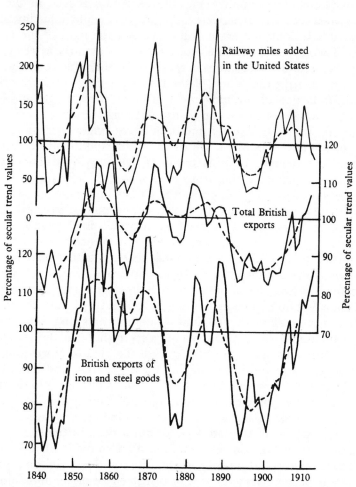

Fig. 20. American railway miles added, volume of total British exports, and volume of British exports of iron and steel goods (percentage deviations from trend), 1841–1913. Source: Tables 98, 102 and 103.

this is not easy owing to the absence of adequate statistical data for the first thirty years of this period. However, we will begin by examining the course of British exports. Fig. 20 shows the minor secular fluctuations in railway building in the United States, total British exports and the exports of finished iron and steel goods in the period 1841–1913. The swings in these three moving averages are in conformity. The time-shape of the long cycles in British exports, and particularly in the part of them consisting of iron and steel goods, corresponds closely to that of railway construction in the United States; and, from what we know

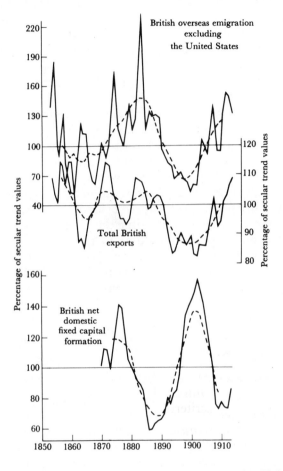

FIG. 21. British oversea emigration to places other than the United States, and volume of total British exports, 1853–1913, and British net domestic fixed capital formation, 1869–1913 (percentage deviations from trend). Source: Tables 100, 102 and 105.

already, the same is true of British emigration and foreign investment. Thus a suggestive pattern of simultaneous long cycles is beginning to emerge.

Up to this point we have dealt only with British emigration to the United States. Fig. 21 shows the long cycles in British emigration to oversea countries other than the United States, total exports and home investment. It is interesting to observe that the cyclical decline in this stream of migration (mainly to the Empire) between 1874 and 1877 was mild compared with the very severe slump in emigration to the United States from 1873 to 1877. For this reason the pattern of Empire migration takes the form of one very long cycle from the trough of the sixties to the trough of the late nineties with a prominent peak in 1883. The moving average for British exports traces out a fairly similar course throughout the period.

There is a striking contrast between the fluctuations in the exports of labour and commodities on the one hand and those in home investment on the other. Capital formation in Britain goes up to a peak in the late seventies while exports and emigration plunge downward. The eighties see exports and emigration well above the norm and domestic investment subnormal; the opposite is true of the nineties. In the first decade of the century exports, emigration (and, we may add, foreign investment) are on the upgrade, whereas capital formation at home slumps badly.

In the very short period one can see evidence of changes in exports carrying with them changes in the same direction in home investment, for example the minor peak and slump in 1871–3 and 1892–3. However, if we confine attention to the long cycle and a half through which the system moved from the late eighties to the eve of the First World War, it is evident that upward deviations of exports from trend were accompanied by downward deviations in home investment and vice versa. A minor secular slump in foreign investment, emigration and commodity exports was associated with a minor secular boom in domestic capital formation.

7. MIGRATION AND THE BUILDING CYCLE

We shall now consider British emigration to the United States in relation to building in the United States and the United Kingdom. It happens that two valuable series are available, Clarence D. Long, Jr.'s index of new building in the United States, 1856–1935,[1] and C. H. Feinstein's estimates of investment in building in Great Britain, 1856–1914.[2] Fig. 22 sets out the minor secular fluctuations in these two series together with those in the emigration of British citizens to the United States, 1857–1913. An explanation of the American statistics is desirable before inferences are drawn from this chart. In the source quoted it is pointed out that turning-points can be located according to one of two criteria, either the index here plotted or the

[1] Clarence D. Long, Jr., *Building Cycles and the Theory of Investment*, Princeton University Press, 1940, pp. 226–7.

[2] Given in B. R. Mitchell and P. Deane, *Abstract of British Historical Statistics*, Cambridge University Press, 1962, pp. 373–4.

medians of the turning points in the various cities comprised in the index.[1] The two usually give the same turning dates, but sometimes they differ by one, two or even three, years. The effect of the great volume of activity and the abnormal size of the unit of building in the city of New York tended to exercise an unfortunate bias on the index. For this reason the turning dates for American building given in the following table are to be regarded as approximate.

Table 26. *Peaks and troughs in building activity in Great Britain and the United States, 1871–1913*

United Kingdom gross residential building		United States new building	
Peak	Trough	Peak	Trough
1876	1869	1871	1880
1899	1886	1886	1900
	1912	1909	

SOURCE: Tables 107 and 109.

There is a remarkable inverse relation between the course of building in the two countries. The top of a boom in America in 1871 coincided with a low point in Britain; corresponding to the British peak in 1876 is a trough in the United States in 1880, and similarly for the next thirty years the two curves are almost exactly reverse in their movement. It is also clear that the long cycles in emigration from the British Isles are in harmony with those of building in the United States and run in the opposite direction to the course of domestic building. Railways and building together make up a large part of current investment. In Fig. 23 they are plotted for the United States alongside of British capital exports in the period 1860–1913; the three sets of long cycles are in unison, with building lagging slightly behind railway construction.

8. MIGRATION, NATIONAL INCOME, WAGES AND EMPLOYMENT

The relation between fluctuations in emigration and those in national income, wages and the level of employment deserves careful scrutiny. We have already noticed that the ups and downs in home investment on the one hand tended to be inverse to those of foreign investment and

[1] See Clarence D. Long, Jr., op. cit. p. 137.

commodity exports on the other. In Fig. 24 we present the following
five series for the period 1870–1913: the deviations of real national
income and real wages from their respective trends, the level of employment (nine-year moving average of the annual percentage of trade
unionists in work), net oversea migration per 10,000 of the population,
capital exports as a percentage of total investment.

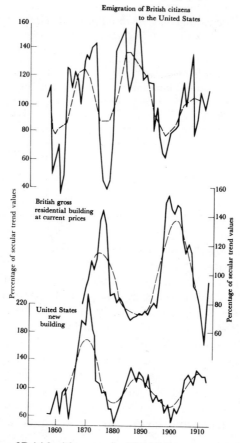

Fɪɢ. 22. Emigration of British citizens to the United States, and American new building, 1857–1913, and British building, 1869–1913. Source: Tables 106, 107 and 109.

We note that income, wages and employment vary together and that
their fluctuations are the opposite of those of net emigration and foreign
investment. From a position of full employment in the early seventies
the three curves sweep down to a low level in mid-eighties, climb to
a peak in the late nineties and then descend to a trough after the middle
of the first decade of the century.

Fig. 25 shows the course of the wages bill and profits respectively as proportions of the national income, net emigration to all parts and to the United States, and capital exports as a fraction of total investment.

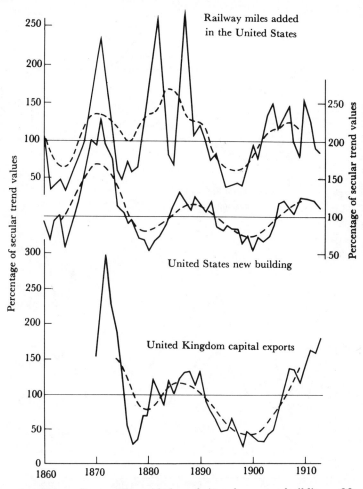

FIG. 23. American railway miles added, and American new building, 1860–1913, and British capital exports, 1870–1913 (percentage deviations from trend). Source: Tables 98, 101 and 109.

At first sight all that the wages bill curve seems to indicate is the well-known fact that the share of the social product received by labour was more or less stable. However, a close inspection brings out some interesting features. In the years 1876–7 to 1886–8 when the rate of growth of real national income was below normal, with a slump in home investment and a steep rise in net emigration and capital exports, the share of income going to labour was declining. From 1886–8 to 1899–1900 a phase of vigorous growth in home investment and national income with a sharp drop in emigration and foreign investment was

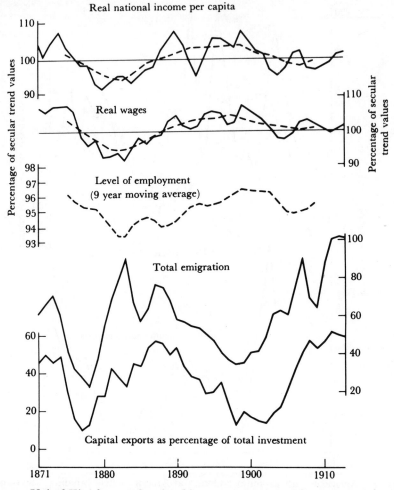

Fig. 24. United Kingdom: real national income per capita, real wages, employment, emigration per 10,000 population, and capital exports as percentage of total investment, 1871–1913. Source: Tables 104, 110, 111, 112 and 113.

accompanied by a marked increase in the relative share of labour up to 1894 which, after a slight setback, was for the most part maintained. Then we come to a striking feature of Fig. 25. From the turn of the century to the eve of the war the rate of growth of income a head slackened significantly, domestic investment was declining and capital

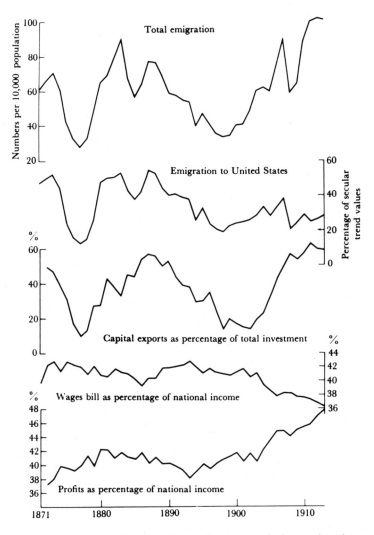

Fig. 25. United Kingdom: total emigration per 10,000 population, emigration to the United States per 10,000 population, capital exports as percentage of total investment, wages bill as percentage of national income, and profits as percentage of national income, 1871–1913. Source: Tables 104, 106, 112 and 113.

exports and total emigration soared to record heights while net emigration to the United States hardly increased at all. In this final phase the part of the national income received by labour fell substantially and the share of profits was correspondingly enlarged.

9. THE INTERACTION OF BRITISH AND AMERICAN
LONG CYCLES

The foregoing analysis suggests a mutual relation between the minor secular fluctuations in the British and American economies. When the United States experienced a strong upsurge of activity, she absorbed

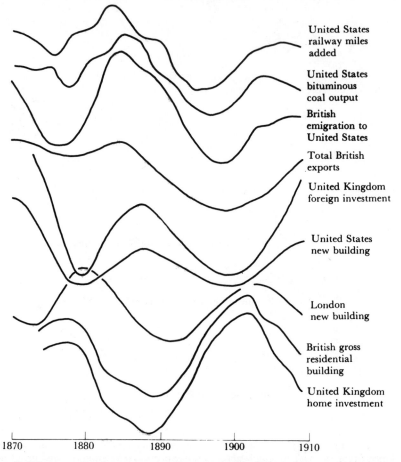

United States
railway miles
added

United States
bituminous
coal output

British
emigration to
United States

Total British
exports

United Kingdom
foreign investment

United States
new building

London
new building

British gross
residential
building

United Kingdom
home investment

1870   1880   1890   1900   1910

FIG. 26. Nine-year moving averages of percentage deviations from trend for various series, 1870–1909. *Note.* Only the turning-points, not the relative amplitudes, of these curves are significant. Source: Tables 97, 98, 100, 101, 102, 106, 107, 109 and 138.

large quantities of labour and capital from Britain and the rate of growth in the latter country slackened. Then, when the American system was digesting what it had swallowed, Britain's appetite for home investment would increase and her real income would grow faster than usual, while her exports of men and money became negligible. There was no such thing as an international long cycle.

Owing to the lack of the requisite time series, one cannot unfortunately obtain a satisfactory picture of the process before 1870. However, since it appears that there was round about that time a structural break after which emigration to America lagged behind railway development in that country, there is perhaps some advantage in concentrating on the period 1870–1913. Fig. 26 sets out for each series the nine-year moving average through the deviations from its trend. These curves are taken to represent the course of the minor secular swings in these series; their relative amplitude has no significance. The pattern that seems to emerge is as follows. From 1870 to the early eighties, British exports of labour, capital and commodities move in the wake of American activity in railway construction and building, which precedes American output of bituminous coal. While British foreign investment and United States building decline and then rise together, British home investment and building rise and then fall together. In the inverse relation between the two building series, the American seems to lag behind the British.

Between the peak of American activity in the early eighties and the structural change of the nineties, the railway index in the United States shows a downswing which is followed by a fall in British emigration to America, in American building and in British foreign lending. The pattern of long cycles persists through the nineties into the first decade of the century, with rather longer lags.[1]

This is perhaps too short a period on which to base any firm generalization. However, so far as the evidence goes, there was a long investment cycle with a span similar to that of the building cycle; and the British investment cycle was inverse to that of the United States.

I now propose to check these results by examining in detail the national income statistics of Britain and the United States over the same period. Fortunately such data are available from 1870 onward. Professor Kuznets has found confirmation of the genuineness of 'secondary secular movements' in his investigation into the rate of growth of the national income of the United States since 1869. He writes:

From an apparent peak in the interval centering on 1876, the rate of change in national income and in income per capita declines to a trough in the interval centering on 1891; rises to another peak in the interval centering on 1901; declines to another trough in the interval centering on 1911.... The average period between troughs is twenty years; that between peaks 22·5 years.[2]

[1] The method and the results of the lag analysis are given in Appendix 2.
[2] S. Kuznets, *National Income: a Summary of Findings*, pp. 63–4.

The figures which led to this conclusion are given for overlapping decades, 1869–78, 1874–83, and so forth. Our first step will be to calculate British national income and income a head for these same decades up to 1929–38. The British series are set out with the American in Tables 27 and 28.

Table 27. *Real national income in the United States and the United Kingdom: annual averages, overlapping decades, 1869–1938*

Decade	United States*		United Kingdom†	
	National income at 1929 prices ($1,000 million)	Per capita ($)	National income at 1900 prices (£ million)	Per capita (£)
1869–78	9·3	215	858·2‡	26·4‡
1874–83	13·6	278	944·6	27·8
1879–88	17·9	326	1,075·6	30·2
1884–93	21·0	344	1,278·3	34·5
1889–98	24·2	357	1,489·6	38·5
1894–1903	29·8	401	1,668·9	41·2
1899–1908	37·3	458	1,799·2	42·4
1904–13	45·0	502	1,930·1	43·6
1909–18	50·6	517	1,975·1	43·4
1914–23	57·3	546	1,981·2	43·7
1919–28	69·0	612	2,082·5	46·3
1924–33	73·3	607	2,229·1	48·8
1929–38	72·0	572	2,486·6	53·3

* From Kuznets, op. cit. p. 32.
† Based on A. R. Prest, 'National Income of the United Kingdom, 1870–1946', *Economic Journal*, vol. LVIII, no. 229, March 1948, pp. 58–9.
‡ These figures are the annual averages during 1870–8.

These figures are not only further evidence of the existence of minor secular fluctuations but they also underline the fact that the rhythm in the growth of Britain was different from that of the United States. While America's rate of expansion of income a head was slowing down in the interval between 1869–78 and 1889–98, the British rate was accelerating up to 1884–93 and was still high in 1889–98. The upswing in the United States from 1889–98 to 1899–1908 is paralleled by a downswing in the United Kingdom. A trough of a long cycle is indicated for both countries in 1908–18; after that the United States goes through a whole cycle ending in a very low trough in the last decade, whereas Britain continues on a fairly steady upswing. The three highest rates of growth for America occur in the fifteen-year periods centring on 1876,

1881 and 1901, and for Britain in the fifteen-year periods centring on 1886, 1891 and 1913. We again reach the conclusion that the rate of economic progress in the United Kingdom tended to be high in those periods when the pace of advance in the United States was low.

Table 28. *Real national income in the United States and the United Kingdom: percentage change from decade to overlapping decade, 1869–1938*

Decade	United States		United Kingdom	
	National income at 1929 prices (%)	Per capita	National income at 1900 prices (%)	Per capita
1869–78	—	—	—	—
1874–83	+45·6	+29·3	+10·1	+ 5·3
1879–88	+31·4	+17·3	+13·9	+ 8·6
1884–93	+17·7	+ 5·5	+18·9	+14·2
1889–98	+14·9	+ 3·8	+16·6	+11·6
1894–1903	+23·1	+12·3	+12·0	+ 7·0
1899–1908	+25·5	+14·2	+ 7·8	+ 2·9
1904–13	+20·5	+ 9·6	+ 7·3	+ 2·8
1909–18	+12·4	+ 3·0	+ 2·3	− 0·5
1914–23	+13·3	+ 5·6	+ 0·3	+ 0·7
1919–28	+20·6	+12·1	+ 5·1	+ 6·0
1924–33	+ 6·1	− 0·8	+ 7·0	+ 5·4
1929–38	− 1·7	− 5·8	+11·6	+ 9·2

Similarly for the period 1870–1913 we can look at the major components of capital formation and compare their time-shape with that of international migration of labour and capital. The data are shown in Table 29.

Table 29 is a shorthand statement of the thesis of this chapter. When the output of producer durables and construction in the United States was increasing rapidly, the United Kingdom experienced a falling rate of real investment at home, a growing surplus in the balance of payments, heavy unemployment and a large net outward flow of migrants. This was evident in the fifteen-year periods centring on 1881 and 1886 and again in the early years of the century. In between the opposite was true; a relatively low rate of capital formation in the United States with Britain going through a phase of unusually high domestic investment, little emigration, slight unemployment and a contracting balance of payments on income account. Columns 5 to 8 of Table 29 yield almost exactly the same result as the curves based on year-to-year data. The long cycle in the United Kingdom—from trough to trough in the case of home investment and from peak to peak in the case of foreign investment and unemployment—runs from the period centring on 1881 to the period centring on 1906.

One peculiarity of the swings of activity in the United States is that the cycle in net construction does not coincide with that in net producer durables (columns 3 and 4 of Table 29). The main reason is the influence on the former index of the part of it which is building. Table 30 enables us to compare the percentage rates of change in residential and non-residential new building with those in real income a head, net producer durables and immigration in the United States.

The building and immigration cycles are equal in length and their amplitude seems to be remarkably similar; the interesting point is that the ups and downs in new building—particularly residential—come one interval after the corresponding change in immigration. This component of American investment appeared to follow in the wake of immigration, which itself lagged behind the movements in real national income and

Table 29. *The United States and the United Kingdom: rates of change in migration and components of investment from decade to overlapping decade, 1869–1913*

Decade (yearly average)	United States				United Kingdom			
	Total immigration	Net immigration from U.K.	Net producer durables	Net construction	Net domestic fixed capital formation	Gross residential capital	Balance of payments on current account	Unemployment
	(%)	(%)	(%)	(%)	(%)	(%)	(%)	(%)
	(1)	(2)	(3)	(4)	(5)	(6)	(7)	(8)
1869–78	—	—	—	—	—	—	—	—
1874–83	+26·4	+104·0	+73·5	+39·0	+ 8·3	− 2·4	−18·8	+32·7
1879–88	+35·1	+ 74·4	+27·7	+53·6	−19·4	−22·6	+54·2	+46·0
1884–93	− 4·4	− 18·7	− 4·2	+56·3	− 6·2	− 1·6	+18·3	− 5·8
1889–98	−19·7	− 37·9	− 7·7	+19·7	+36·7	+70·9	−25·6	−29·2
1894–1903	+ 7·2	− 29·8	+49·2	− 3·1	+55·5	+ 7·5	−26·4	−11·5
1899–1908	+89·3	+ 41·4	+75·3	+15·8	+ 9·9	+ 6·8	+82·4	+10·4
1904–13	+25·2	+ 4·7	+ 9·4	+14·6	−22·6	−28·0	+97·0	+ 9·9

SOURCES:

(1) U.S. Department of Commerce, *Historical Statistics of the United States, 1789–1945*, Washington, 1949, pp. 33–4.

(2) I. Ferenczi and W. F. Willcox, *International Migrations*, vol. 1, p. 641. The first decade is 1871–8.

(3) and (4) S. Kuznets, *National Product since 1869*, New York, National Bureau of Economic Research, 1946, p. 118. At 1929 prices.

(5) Table 100. At 1900 prices. (6) Table 107. At current prices. (7) Table 113.

(8) B. R. Mitchell and P. Deane, *Abstract of British Historical Statistics*, pp. 64–5.

Table 30. *The United States: rates of change from decade to overlapping decade in national income, investment and immigration, 1869–1913*

Decade (yearly average)	Real national income a head	Net producer durables	Residential building*	Non-residential building*	Total immi-gration	Net immi-gration from United Kingdom
	(%)	(%)	(%)	(%)	(%)	(%)
1869–78	—	—	—	—	—	—
1874–83	29·3	73·5	− 38·8	− 47·2	26·4	104·0
1879–88	17·3	27·7	31·6	7·7	35·1	74·4
1884–93	5·5	− 4·2	42·6	21·9	− 4·4	− 18·7
1889–98	3·8	− 7·7	− 6·4	− 3·0	− 19·7	− 37·9
1894–1903	12·3	49·2	− 25·7	− 8·3	7·2	− 29·8
1899–1908	14·2	75·3	16·8	30·9	89·3	41·4
1904–13	9·6	9·4	37·0	44·1	25·2	4·7

* Clarence D. Long, Jr., op. cit. App. B, sect. 3.

the production of durable producers' goods. This inference supports the results given in the previous section based on annual data which permitted a more accurate account of turning-points. Professor Kuznets, after calculating percentage deviations from a straight line or a three-point curve fitted to the rates of percentage change in the national income and population of the United States from decade to overlapping decade, 1869–1938, concluded as follows: 'The troughs and peaks in the population rates of growth lag fairly consistently by one interval behind those in the rates of growth of national income.'[1] Our analysis seems to lead to the conclusion that this lag in the rates of growth of the American population reflected the influence of immigration.

10. FLUCTUATIONS IN EMPIRE SETTLEMENT

So far the analysis has been restricted to population movements across the Atlantic. We shall now inquire whether Empire settlement exhibited a similar pattern. Fig. 27 sets out the course of emigration from the United Kingdom to Canada, Australasia and South Africa from 1853 to 1913. Up to 1900 the movement to Canada is similar to emigration to the United States, but in the first decade of the century there is a sharp divergence when British settlement in the Dominion rose to a very high point. Between 1863 and 1881 the flows to Australasia and Canada are inverse to each other. The former fell and the latter rose markedly

[1] Kuznets, *National Income: a Summary of Findings*, p. 66.

from 1863 to 1871; in the latter half of the seventies the number going to Canada slumped badly in sympathy with the very low level of

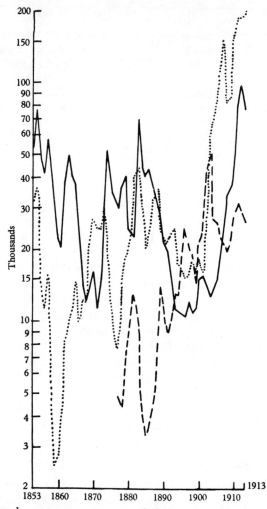

Fig. 27. Outward passenger movement of citizens from the United Kingdom to Canada, Australasia and South Africa, 1853–1913. ····· Canada; —— Australasia; – – – – South Africa. Source: Table 114.

immigration in the United States, whereas the rate of settlement in Australasia was well above normal. Towards the end of the period a strong recovery in emigration to Australasia occurred in 1906, four years later than the beginning of the boom in Canadian immigration. The South African curve pursues an independent course. After a very

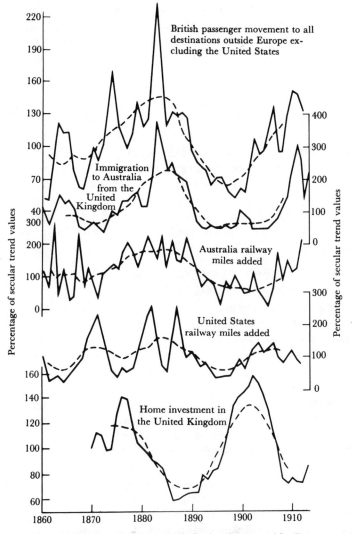

Fig. 28. British passenger movement to all destinations outside Europe excluding the United States, immigration to Australia from the United Kingdom, Australian and American railway miles added, 1860–1913, and United Kingdom home investment, 1870–1913 (percentage deviations from trend). Source: Tables 98, 100, 105, 115 and 116.

pronounced setback from 1882 to 1885, it rises briskly with two minor interruptions to a maximum in 1903; it is inverse to the Australasian series from 1885 to 1896 and from 1903 to 1908.

We have already seen that the best indicator of the pulse of American economic development in the period between 1840 and the First World

War is the annual addition to railway mileage. A similar index for Australia from 1860 is plotted in Fig. 28 together with immigration, British emigration to oversea countries other than the United States, railway miles added in the United States, and British home investment (from 1870). The long-period shape of British settlement in the Empire is similar to that of Australian immigration; and the latter moves in harmony with railway construction. There is a distinct long wave from the sixties to a peak in the eighties, a trough in the nineties and then a revival in the first years of the century. The rhythm of growth differs somewhat from that of America chiefly because Australia avoided a deep depression in the seventies. At a time when American imports of labour and capital slumped heavily, Australia continued to build its railways and attract British settlers. The contrast is clearly demonstrated in the figure which also confirms that fluctuations in British home investment were inverse to those of railway building and absorption of population in Australia.

11. THE 'PUSH' ELEMENT IN THE LONG CYCLES OF MIGRATION

In section 4 reasons were given for the view that the timing of the mass immigration into the United States in the late forties and early fifties was determined by expulsive forces in the Old World. After the structural change of the late sixties it would seem that the 'pull' element is as evident in the long cycles of migration as it is in the short cycles. This question cannot be dealt with fully here; but brief reference must be made to a characteristic of population growth which suggests caution.

According to Eilert Sundt's findings based on Scandinavian vital statistics over an extensive period, there were long cycles in the number of births which led inevitably to periods of ebb and flow in the relative size of the age group 20–35. Swedish statistics reveal that the ebb periods occurred in 1666–80, 1696–1710, 1731–45, 1761–75, 1796–1810, 1826–40 and 1861–75. The flow periods were 1681–95, 1711–30, 1746–60, 1776–95, 1811–25 and 1841–60; it is significant that in the years 1876–90 the flood was channelled away in oversea emigration.[1] Undoubtedly Western Europe in 1841–50 contained a relatively large youthful population—the result of the boom in the birth rate just after the Napoleonic wars; hence the strong propensity to emigrate at that time. It is reasonable to ask what part was played by the same phenomenon later in the century.

A little experiment may be performed on the abundant vital statistics available for Sweden. A graph of the five-year moving averages of

[1] See G. Sundbärg, *Bevölkerungsstatistik Schwedens, 1750–1900*, Stockholm, Norstedt, 1923, p. 11.

Swedish emigration in each quinquennial age group for the period 1860–1908 was plotted and another showing the five-year moving average of Swedish births for the period 1820–1908. Interesting correlations were found between the moving averages of births 1845–88 and emigration 1863–1906 in the 15–20 age group, births 1840–83 and emigration 1863–1906 in the 20–25 age group, and births 1835–78 and emigration 1863–1906 in the 25–30 age group. The correlation coefficients were, respectively, 0·665, 0·732 and 0·556. The correlation coefficient for births 1830–73 and emigration 1863–1906 in the 30–35 age group was 0·242.

The majority of the migrants were between 15 and 30 years of age, and the heaviest outflow usually came from the 20–25 age group. Emigration in these groups, particularly the central one, was evidently related to the level of the birth rate at the time those emigrants were born. That Sweden's greatest loss through emigration took place in the late seventies and the eighties was to some extent predetermined by the births cycle. There can also be little doubt that Ireland was under the Malthusian shadow for many decades after 1850.

A word on Italian emigration is relevant here. The high level of the birth rate in Italy in the seventies and eighties was inevitably followed by a flow period from 1900 onward, and that was when the enormous exodus of Italians across the Atlantic took place. It may well be asked why such mass emigration had not occurred in previous flow periods. There can be no simple answer; but it is pertinent to mention two points. First, emigration from Italy in the nineteenth century was greatest during years in which economic conditions at home were flourishing, and it tended to languish when domestic business was bad. For example, oversea migration as a proportion of the total outflow rose sharply during the comparative prosperity of 1880–7.[1] The 'push' varied in intensity, but people were able to leave the country in substantial numbers only when they could afford the costs of movement.[2] Secondly, after the mid-nineties population pressure reached an unprecedented magnitude; and the new generation, not so illiterate or so desperately poor, were able to find a way of escape, thanks in some measure to the flow of remittances from those who had already gone to America in previous decades.

One cannot ignore the fact that the outstanding minor secular

[1] See Gustaf F. Steffen, 'Utvandringen och de ekonomiska konjunkturerna i Sverige och Italien', *Emigrationsutredningen*, Bilaga xviii, Stockholm, 1910, pp. 48–9.

[2] Cf. Robert F. Foerster, *The Italian Emigration of our Times*, Harvard University Press, 1919, ch. vi. Discussing the heavy emigration from Sicily, this author wrote: 'It is significant that emigration should not have originated where misery was greatest. It began where there was the chance of saving enough for passage fares and has best maintained itself where wages were at a medium level' (p. 104).

upswings in transatlantic emigration from Europe—for example from Ireland and Germany in the forties and fifties, from Sweden in the eighties, and from Italy from the turn of the century to the First World War, occurred at times when the proportion of young people in the population was exceptionally large as a consequence of the births cycle. This factor could be expected to exercise its maximum influence when periods in which the lower age groups were swollen coincided with innovations, for example in agriculture, which made labour redundant. The propensity to emigrate would be further intensified if a demographic flow period accompanied by disturbing innovations took place in a social structure marked by immobility as between occupations and classes. Strong impediments to internal readjustments would make the *external* safety-valve more active. It is arguable that three outstanding contributions of European labour to the American economy—1,187,000 Irish and 919,000 Germans between 1847 and 1855, 418,000 Scandinavians and 1,045,000 Germans between 1880 and 1885, and 1,754,000 Italians between 1898 and 1907—had the character of evacuations. Expelled from Europe, this manpower made for itself a niche in the American system where it exercised a direct formative influence on technical conditions of production and habits of consumption, and thereby set in motion a 'pull' for further immigrants.

12. SECULAR CHANGES IN THE ATLANTIC ECONOMY

Several conditions seem to point to the decade of the nineties as the end of one epoch and the beginning of another. In conducting the analysis of lags (described in Appendix 2) one could not but be struck by the less conclusive results obtained for most pairs after 1900; it looked as if the first part of the new century belonged to a separate period in which the driving forces were undergoing a change. Some of the facts which suggest this conclusion will now be briefly enumerated.

In mid-nineties the 'old' immigration from North West Europe began to be displaced by the increasing mass of 'new' immigration from Southern and Eastern Europe, as shown clearly in Fig. 29. This was not only a symptom of the cumulative spread of population pressure in Europe but was also destined to have profound effects on the social structure and industrial technique of the United States.

By the end of the century the socio-economic structure of the American labour market was passing through a significant phase. The children of previous immigrants from North West Europe had risen in the social scale and were occupying positions superior to those of their parents. For example, whereas in 1890 11 % of the British-born persons in the United States were in 'white-collar' jobs, in 1900 no less than 23 % of the second generation were in jobs of that grade. On the other hand,

12 % of the first generation in 1890 were servants and only 4 % of the second generation in 1900. The process had been going on for some time; but by the nineties this upward movement had become large enough to exercise an important influence on the future of immigration. This secular change will be examined in detail in Chapter IX.

About thirty years after the passing of the Homestead Act of 1862, practically all the good land in America had been appropriated; but not much of it was in the hands of small settlers. By 1890 the railroad companies had taken four times as much land as had been distributed

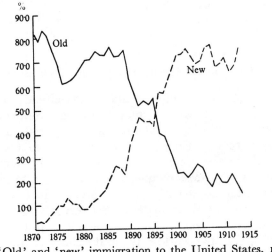

Fig. 29. 'Old' and 'new' immigration to the United States, 1870–1913.
Source: Table 117.

to farmers under the 1862 Act.[1] Of the 8,396,000 persons occupied in agriculture in 1890, 3,004,000 were hired labourers and 1,500,000 tenant workmen, so that less than a half of the people earning a living in the countryside were tilling their own land, including mortgaged farms.[2] 'Only three-eighths of the families of the United States were cultivating the soil as owners, tenants or labourers, and the ratio was declining constantly. Over half of these were on an economic basis scarcely, if any, better than that of the city labourer.'[3] America had emerged as a powerful industrial state bearing the marks of a stratified society.

How strong a member of the Atlantic community the United States had become even by the beginning of the eighties is not always appreciated. The following table speaks for itself.

[1] Fred A. Shannon, 'The Homestead Act and the Labor Surplus', *American Historical Review*, XLI, no. 4, July 1936, p. 638.
[2] *Report of U.S. Industrial Commission*, vol. XI, 1901, p. 77.
[3] Fred A. Shannon, loc. cit. p. 648.

Table 31. *Percentage distribution of the world's manufacturing production by country, 1870–1938*

Period	World	United States	United Kingdom	Germany	France	Russia	Canada	Other countries
1870	100·0	23·3	31·8	13·2	10·3	3·7	1·0	16·7
1881–5	100·0	28·6	26·6	13·9	8·6	3·4	1·3	17·6
1896–1900	100·0	30·1	19·5	16·6	7·1	5·0	1·4	20·3
1906–10	100·0	35·3	14·7	15·9	6·4	5·0	2·0	20·7
1913	100·0	35·8	14·0	15·7	6·4	5·5	2·3	20·3
1926–9	100·0	42·2	9·4	11·6	6·6	4·3*	2·4	23·5
1936–8	100·0	32·2	9·2	10·7	4·5	18·5*	2·0	22·9

* U.S.S.R.

SOURCE: League of Nations, *Industrialisation and Foreign Trade*, Geneva, 1945, p. 13.

In the years 1881–5 the United States was already responsible for a greater share of the world's manufacturing production than the United Kingdom (28·6 % as against 26·6 %), and after 1900 her progress was extremely rapid, her proportion reaching 35·3 % in 1906–10, mainly at the expense of the United Kingdom whose proportion fell to 14·7 %. Meanwhile, Germany, after forging ahead in the latter part of the nineteenth century, had attained a percentage of 15·9 and was stronger than Britain. Between the twenties and the thirties the spectacular fact was the rise of the output of the U.S.S.R. from 4·3 to 18·5 % of the world's, while the share of America declined from 42·2 to 32·2 %. At the end of the period Great Britain was producing less than one-tenth of the world's manufacturing output as compared with nearly one-third in 1870. It was just after the turn of the century that the balance of economic power in the Atlantic community tilted in favour of the United States, when her productive capacity began to exceed that of the United Kingdom and Germany together. Implied in this rate of economic growth was a release from dependence on capital imports.

The turning-point came in the period 1889–1908 when average American indebtedness on international account was only 1 % of net capital formation; the United States was about to emerge as the world's strongest creditor nation.

A noteworthy change, which may have had secular significance, is revealed by an index of the ratio of capital stock to gross national product in the United States from 1879–88 to 1919–28.

There can be little doubt that the American capital structure was going through a rapid process of 'deepening' in the last two decades of the nineteenth century and that this stopped at the end of the nineties.

The implications of these figures will be discussed in a later chapter; the tendency indicated by them will be considered in the context of the fundamental technical innovations which appear in the late nineties, inaugurating the era of electricity, chemistry and the motor car. This phenomenon must form part of any explanation of the change in the composition of immigration to the United States after 1900.

Table 32. *The United States: net changes in claims against foreign countries as a proportion of capital formation, 1868–1928*

Period	Average annual claim in millions of 1929 dollars		
	Dollar total	Percentage of gross capital formation	Percentage of net capital formation
1868–88	− 104	− 3·2	− 5·3
1889–1908	− 48	− 0·6	− 1·1
1909–28	962	6·8	14·1

SOURCE: S. Kuznets, *National Product since 1869*, New York, National Bureau of Economic Research, 1946, p. 84.

Table 33. *The United States: ratio of improvements and equipment to gross national product (per annum), 1929 prices, decennially, 1879–1928*

Decade	Aggregate ratio
1879–88	1·98
1889–98	2·58
1899–1908	2·56
1909–18	2·78
1919–28	2·47

SOURCE: These figures are from an unpublished manuscript belonging to Professor Kuznets. See Table 131 and the accompanying note.

A feature of the growth of an international economy deserving close study is the interaction between movements of factors and the structure of trade. Some interesting facts about the United Kingdom are set out in Table 34.

The decade 1894–1903 marks a deep-seated change in the structure of Britain's trade. Up to 1873 two-thirds of her commerce was of the type usually associated with a great imperial power—the exchange of manufactured goods for food and raw materials; by the end of the century this had dwindled to one-third. Already her supremacy was challenged by powerful industrial rivals, the United States and Germany, witness the fact that a quarter of the total turnover was made up of the

exchange of manufactures for manufactures; whereas imports financed
by the surplus in the invisible account comprised nearly a quarter.
Incidentally this last item (column 1 of Table 34) shows an interesting
undulation from decade to decade; it was comparatively high in periods
when emigration and foreign lending were slack, and when the terms
of trade tended to be in Britain's favour. Such is the alternation in
the economy of a rentier country—first sowing the seed in the form of
capital exports and emigration, then reaping the harvest in imports,
then again sowing more seed and so forth.

Table 34. *Percentage distribution of the foreign trade of the
United Kingdom by types of interchange, 1854–1929*

Period	Commodities against invisible items	Raw materials and food against raw materials and food	Manufactures against manufactures	Manufactures against raw materials and food	Total value (£ million)
1854–63	14·2	11·1	8·8	65·9	2,820
1864–73	12·1	10·9	13·2	63·8	4,553
1874–83	20·1	12·1	17·2	50·4	5,486
1884–93	18·2	14·3	20·1	47·4	5,675
1894–1903	23·9	16·3	25·3	34·5	6,723
1904–13	15·1	20·0	22·7	42·2	9,620
1925–29	23·1	15·8	25·7	35·4	8,880

SOURCE: A. O. Hirschman, *National Power and the Structure of Foreign Trade*, University of California Press, 1945, p. 145.

The figures for the decade 1904–13 bear strong testimony to Britain's
renewed activity as a financier of the international economy; the boom
in exports, foreign investment and Empire settlement entailed a relative
rise in the traditional type of exchange (manufactures for food and raw
materials) and in the export of raw materials (chiefly coal) and a sharp
relative decline in imports on invisible account. London, as the
financial centre of the world, was admirably equipped to give this
mighty impetus to British commerce; but whether the enterprise of
that epoch was inspired by an appreciation of the long-run interests of
British productive efficiency in a world experiencing a technological
revolution is a matter for debate. All that can be said here is that the
triumphs of 1904–13 seem to have been temporary and dearly won;
the secular trend from 1854 to 1903 was not reversed; by 1925–9 the
structure of trade by types of interchange was almost exactly the same
as it had been in 1894–1903.

CHAPTER VIII

INTERNAL AND INTERNATIONAL MOBILITY

The previous chapter showed that during periods when transatlantic emigration was considerable the growth of real income was slow in the United Kingdom and rapid in the United States. The evolution of the international economy was propelled by periodic movements of labour and capital from the Old World to the New, and as this process went on in spurts it must have entailed internal reactions in the supplying and the receiving countries. In this chapter we shall inquire whether there is statistical evidence of an interaction between the rate of external migration and the degree of internal mobility. Perhaps further light can be thrown on the different time-shapes of the long cycles of investment in the United Kingdom and the United States.

By internal migration is meant the movement of people in a given period from one part of a country to take up residence in another part; and this usually implies transfers between occupations. In most countries such movements can be calculated in ten-year intervals from one Population Census to the next; but where local authorities keep annual records of in-migrants and out-migrants—as in Sweden—a more refined analysis is possible. We are not here concerned with internal mobility in the sense of movement between social classes. There is reason to think that this species of mobility has undergone secular change, for example in the United States, and that this helped to bring to an end the flow of international migration. This force acting over the long period will be dealt with in a later chapter. At this stage we are interested in the relation between internal migration as defined above and the minor secular cycles in emigration, income and investment.

I. ENGLAND AND WALES, 1841–1911

It is not easy to devise an index of changes in the volume of internal migration in England and Wales; but, thanks to the pioneering statistical work of T. A. Welton and the extension of it by Professor A. K. Cairncross, it is possible to trace the broad pattern by decade from 1841 to 1911.[1] Welton grouped the registration districts of England

---

[1] T. A. Welton, *England's Recent Progress: an Investigation of the Statistics of Migration, Mortality, etc. in the Twenty Years from 1881 to 1901 as indicating Tendencies towards the Growth or Decay of Particular Communities*, London, Chapman and Hall, 1911, and his 'Note on Urban and Rural Variations according to the English Census of 1911',

and Wales into three classes, Towns, Colliery Districts and Rural Residues. Net gains and losses by migration were calculated from Population Census figures and birth and death rates. I have taken the net inflow of population into the towns and colliery districts in each decade as a measure of internal migration in England and Wales, and it is expressed as a rate per 1,000 of the population of England and Wales at the beginning of the decennial period. The estimates of net emigration have been supplied by the General Register Office and they allow for under-registration of births in the period 1841–71.[1] The internal migration figures are taken from Welton without adjustment.

Table 35. *Decennial internal and external migration in England and Wales, 1841–1911*

Census decade	Population at beginning of decade (thousands)	Internal migration* (thousands)	Net emigration (thousands)	Internal migration	Net emigration	Net efflux from rural residues
				Decennial rate per thousand of population		
	(1)	(2)	(3)	(4)	(5)	(6)
1841–51	15,914	742	− 81	46	− 5	− 27
1851–61	17,928	620	− 327	35	− 18	− 42
1861–71	20,066	624	− 206	31	− 10	− 34
1871–81	22,712	689	− 164	30	− 7	− 37
1881–91	25,974	228	− 601	9	− 23	− 32
1891–1901	29,003	606	− 69	21	− 2	− 23
1901–11	32,528	− 207	− 501	− 6	− 15	− 9

* Net gains of towns and colliery districts. In 1901–11 there was a net loss.
SOURCES: Welton, op. cit., Cairncross, loc. cit. and the General Register Office.

As we are dealing with England and Wales, movement of people to and from Scotland and Ireland is part of external migration. The inverse relationship between internal and external migration is clearly brought out. The rate of industrialization was at its height in the decade 1841–51 when three-quarters of a million people (46 per 1,000 of the population) were absorbed by the urban centres, while net emigration was only 81,000. The contribution from the countryside was barely sufficient to

Journal of the Royal Statistical Society, vol. LXXVI, 1913. A. K. Cairncross, 'Internal Migration in Victorian England', *The Manchester School*, vol. XVII, no. 1, January 1949, pp. 67–87.
[1] See D. V. Glass, 'A Note on the Under-registration of Births in the Nineteenth Century', *Population Studies*, vol. v, no. 1, July 1951.

appease the vast appetite of the growing industrial areas. The next ten years saw a further large gain by the towns, amounting to nearly two-thirds of a million people; but now the flood from the countryside was so great that not even the expanding home industry could cope with it, and one-third of a million people sought a living abroad. During the next two decades, the sixties and seventies, the net gain of the towns

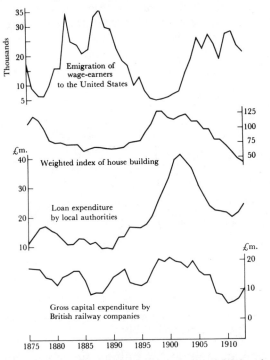

FIG. 30. Emigration and new building for England and Wales; local authority and railway investment for the United Kingdom, 1875–1913. Sources: Tables 81, 84 and 119; J. Parry Lewis, *Building Cycles and Britain's Growth*, London, Macmillan, 1965, p. 317.

totalled one and a third million people representing the same rate of urban growth as in the fifties. Net emigration settled down to a comparatively low level, as industry absorbed three-quarters of the rural exodus. From the seventies to the end of the period the inverse relation from decade to decade is striking. The rate of internal migration in the eighties fell to 9 per 1,000 while the rate of emigration rose to 23 per 1,000; in the nineties internal migration went up to 21 per 1,000 and emigration fell to 2 per 1,000. In marked contrast to the forties, the decade 1910–11 actually registered a net loss for the industrial sector (though the colliery districts by themselves showed a substantial net gain of 114,000), whereas the outward balance of emigration reached 501,000, or 15 per 1,000 of the population.

The ups and downs of internal migration reflect changes in the rate of domestic investment. Unfortunately we can only estimate internal migration from decade to decade; but it is nevertheless instructive to examine the figures against the background of certain indices of economic activity for the period 1875–1913. In Fig. 30 are plotted annual estimates of the rate of new building and the emigration of wage-earners to the United States (for England and Wales in each case), the loan expenditure of local authorities and the estimated capital expenditure of British railway companies. The rhythm of the long cycle

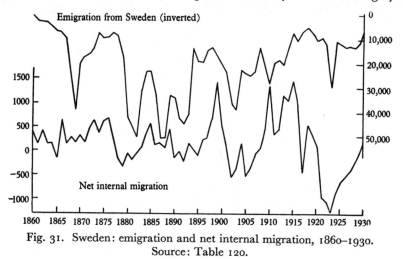

Fig. 31. Sweden: emigration and net internal migration, 1860–1930.
Source: Table 120.

is quite as evident in emigration, railway investment and the loan expenditure of local authorities as it is in the building series. It is interesting to see public investment moving in step with private outlay. The low degree of internal migration in the eighties finds its counterpart in a subnormal rate of investment and a high volume of emigration; and, in the nineties, when internal migration was relatively consider-able, capital outlay showed a sharp upswing, with emigration falling off rapidly to a very low point at the end of the decade. After 1900 the process is reversed: the three investment indices register a marked decline, the urban areas (excluding colliery districts) actually lose population to other districts, and emigration rises steeply.

Despite the shortcomings of the data, there seems clear evidence of an inverse relation between the fluctuations of internal migration and home investment on the one hand and those of emigration (and capital exports) on the other.

2. SWEDEN, 1860–1930

The disadvantage of English statistics of internal migration is that they are available only for decennial periods. In Sweden, however, there is a unique series showing the number of citizens moving into and out of each parish every year, and this makes it possible to study the interaction of internal and external mobility in much more detail.[1] For the period 1860–1930, the annual number of in-migrants moving into the industrial districts of Västmanland County as a percentage of the population of the County are plotted in Fig. 31 with the annual number of emigrants from Sweden. It is relevant to note that Västmanland County is an important industrial area, 70 % of its occupied population being engaged in iron mining and metal manufacturing at the beginning and at the end of the period 1895–1933.[2] The fluctuations of its in-migration are a good index of the pace of economic growth in Sweden. A glance at Fig. 31 reveals interesting divergences between the two series. The first peak of in-migration at the rate of 9·5 % in 1862 coincides with an extremely low level of emigration at about 1 per 1,000. Then the attracting power of industry has a generally falling tendency till it reaches a low trough in 1869, while emigration rises sharply to a peak (10 per 1,000) in that year. From 1869 to 1880 the inverse relation is clearly marked: the upswing and downswing of the rate of recruitment into the metal industry of Sweden are matched by the sweep of the emigration cycle from peak to peak. A similar relation is shown by the two curves from the early eighties to the mid-nineties. From a high point reached in 1902–3 emigration traces a minor secular decline to a low level in the First World War, while internal emigration shows a corresponding increase. After the war there is further evidence of an inverse movement. A curve for in-migration to all industrial communities in the period 1895–1930 would confirm the inferences drawn from the Västmanland series.

Dr Dorothy Swaine Thomas, after a thorough examination of the

---

[1] The reason why Sweden has such excellent data on internal movements of population is that the pastors of the Church of Sweden have the duty of keeping a register in each parish giving details of persons who take up or relinquish residence. The complete record covers births, deaths, in-migrants and out-migrants. A person is listed as an out-migrant after information has been received that he has settled elsewhere. The terms 'in-migrant' and 'out-migrant' are restricted to persons changing their domicile within Sweden: a separate record is kept of immigrants and emigrants. For further particulars see Dorothy Swaine Thomas, *Social and Economic Aspects of Swedish Population Movements 1750–1933*, New York, Macmillan, 1941, pp. 201–20.

[2] The Västmanland figures are the only ones which seem to have been published for the years 1860–94.

interaction of Swedish internal migration and business cycles, reached the following conclusion.

Correlation analysis of the deviations of net internal migration from secular trends in relation to business cycles for the period 1895–1933 confirms the expected relationship for agricultural communities and towns in general.... The negative correlation between net internal migration for agricultural communities and business cycles was −0·74 for males and −0·68 for females; and the positive correlation for towns was 0·60 for males and 0·46 for females.[1]

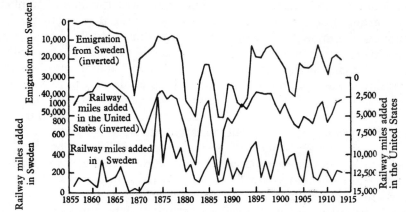

Fig. 32. Swedish emigration and Swedish and American railway miles added, 1856–1913. Source: Tables 98 and 120.

We are concerned with a different aspect of this process. Looking at the entire period 1860–1930 it is possible to discern a minor secular fluctuation in emigration with a corresponding inverse wave-like movement in internal migration. The latter synchronizes with variations in domestic investment. Most interesting is the fact that up to the beginning of the century the long swings in the building of new railway track in Sweden are inverse to the long cycles in emigration and in railway miles added in the United States.[2] This is shown in Fig. 32. Moreover, a long cycle in the rate of investment per worker ran from a trough in 1868 to a trough in 1893, whereas emigration moved from a peak in 1869 to another peak in 1892, as is clear from Fig. 33. For most of the seventies there was rapid economic growth in Sweden and the outflow of labour was at a minimum. The boom in emigration in the eighties and early nineties was associated with a setback in investment per worker; but after the turn of the century investment per worker increased sharply while emigration receded.

[1] Dorothy Swaine Thomas, op. cit. pp. 307–8.
[2] Cf. J. Åkerman, *Ekonomisk Teori*, Lund, 1944, vol. II, p. 89.

The pattern is broadly similar to that of Britain, though Sweden did not become industrialized until late in the nineteenth century. Periods of relatively rapid economic growth in Sweden occurred when the pace

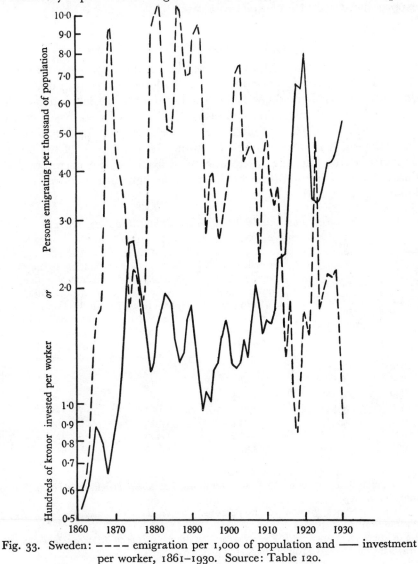

Fig. 33. Sweden: – – – – emigration per 1,000 of population and ——— investment per worker, 1861–1930. Source: Table 120.

of expansion in the United States was relatively slow; and the long cycles in Swedish investment were accompanied by buoyant internal migration and a decline in emigration. In one important respect Sweden's history diverges from that of Britain. During the decade before the First World War the formation of capital in Sweden was proceeding very fast while emigration dwindled; but in Britain, as we have seen, home investment lagged while emigration and capital exports increased at a considerable rate.

3. THE UNITED STATES, 1870–1930

For a country which is absorbing population the hypothesis that long swings in internal migration are inverse to long swings in immigration does not necessarily hold good. For the United States there is no annual record of internal migration and even the decennial data based on the census statistics of State of birth are not well adapted for our purpose. Nevertheless, it is worth while examining the movement of the Negro population from decade to decade in relation to the corresponding fluctuations in immigration of aliens. The figures are shown in the following table and in Table 37:

Table 36. *The United States: alien immigration and internal migration of Negroes, 1870–1930*

Year	Total foreign-born (all races)* (thousands)	Growth of U.S. population by immigration (from one census to the next)† (thousands)	Number of Negroes enumerated in the North‡ (thousands)	Net loss by migration of native Negro population in the South East (from one census to the next)§ (thousands)
1870	5,567	—	453	—
1880	6,680	2,580	615	—
1890	9,250	4,964	701	—
1900	10,341	3,689	881	129
1910	13,516	6,243	1,028	99
1920	13,921	2,225	1,472	323
1930	14,204	3,335	2,409	615

* *Statistical Abstract of the United States.*

† Warren S. Thompson and P. K. Whelpton, *Population Trends in the United States,* 1933, Table 85.

‡ United States Bureau of the Census, *Negroes in the United States, 1926–32,* Washington, 1935, p. 5.

§ Rupert B. Vance, *All These People: the Nation's Human Resources in the South,* University of North Carolina Press, 1945, p. 119.

It may be inferred from Table 37 that when the rate of immigration slackened the number of Negroes moving to the Northern States increased and that when immigration was in full spate the tide of Negro internal migrants was at a low ebb. Comparing the nineties with the first decade of the century we find the rate of increase in the total foreign-born population of the United States rising sharply from 12 to 31%, whereas the net loss by migration of the native Negro population in the South-East fell from 2 to 1 % and the rate of increase of Negroes enumerated in the North from 26 to 17 %. In the period 1910–30 when the inflow of aliens was much diminished, first by the World War, and then by the Immigration Restriction Act of 1924, an extraordinary increase took place in the mobility of the Negroes.

Table 37. *The United States: decennial rates of change in alien immigration and internal migration of Negroes, 1870–1930*

Decade	Rate of increase in foreign-born population (%)	Immigration as % of population growth (%)	Rate of increase in number of Negroes enumerated in the North (%)	Net loss by migration of native Negro population in the South-east (%)
1870–80	20	29	36	—
1880–90	39	43	14	—
1890–1900	12	32	26	2
1900–10	31	42	17	1
1910–20	3	17	44	5
1920–30	3	22	67	8

A detailed analysis of this phenomenon would bring out some puzzling features. Dr Myrdal, in his classic study, comments on the tendency of the Negroes to concentrate in a few of the centres of the North. He pointed out that

there is enough industrial activity, and there could be opportunity for anonymity, as well as a low level of race prejudice, in many of the smaller centres of the North to permit a significant immigration of Negroes. That Negroes have not migrated to these places is as much of a mystery as the relative absence of migration to the West.[1]

Dr Myrdal concluded that

much in the Great Migration after 1915 is left unexplained if we do not assume that there was before 1915 *an existing and widening difference in living conditions between South and North which did not express itself in a mass migration simply because the latter did not get a start and become a pattern.*[2]

Perhaps a convincing explanation would be possible if an annual index of internal migration were available. Even taking our decennial figures,

[1] Gunnar Myrdal, *An American Dilemma: the Negro Problem and Modern Democracy,* Harper, 1944, vol. 1, pp. 189–90.
[2] Ibid. p. 193.

we do observe a pattern in Negro mobility in the forty years before 1910: it seems to have been conditioned by what was happening to alien immigration. The non-white workers of the South found more scope elsewhere at times when their keenest competitors—the European labourers—were less in evidence. This fact became most obvious after 1915 because the First World War drastically reduced the inflow from Europe, but the same tendency had been at work in the previous period. One cannot prove this conclusively with the data at hand. We may suggest, however, that the best way of interpreting the timing and destination of Negro migrants is in the light of the current number of alien immigrants arriving in the country and their contribution to the working population of various industries and cities.

In the decade 1901-10, America absorbed over six million people from Southern and Eastern Europe. They were mostly unskilled labourers who found employment chiefly in the heavy industries of New York, New Jersey and Pennsylvania. This rate of immigration amounting to over 600,000 a year was reduced to an average of only 34,000 between 1925 and 1928, as a result of the restrictions introduced in 1924. An enormous vacuum was created; the iron and steel plants, mines, stockyards and mass production factories, which had been geared to a large supply of cheap foreign labour, were obliged to look for substitutes. The industrialists turned to the reserves of Negro labour in the South. The number of Negroes enumerated in the North-Centre and North-East of the United States increased by a million between 1920 and 1930.

There has been a great deal of research into inter-State and rural-urban migration in the United States in the last thirty years, and some significant facts about the redistribution of population in the twenties and thirties have been brought out. In this context it is sufficient to refer to one interesting point. Between 1920 and 1930, despite the mobility of Negroes and the foreign-born, the majority of the internal migrants were native white Americans. In the six States which had the highest gain by migration during that decade (New York, New Jersey, Illinois, Ohio, Michigan, California), the Negroes and the foreign-born among the newcomers were only half as numerous as the native whites.[1] With immigration kept at a low level, it was essential for the native-born American to be more mobile.[2]

---

[1] Rupert B. Vance, *Research Memorandum on Population Redistribution in the United States*, New York, Social Science Research Council, 1938, p. 99.

[2] In the depression of the thirties, when the Administration had to improvise a relief organization to cope with the sufferings of migrant workers, no less than 94% of those who received assistance from the Federal Transient Scheme were native-born Americans. Ibid. p. 98.

Foreign immigrants distributed themselves over the United States very unevenly, and the degree of concentration in various States varied strikingly over the period 1850 to 1920. At the beginning of this period the Pacific States were outstanding in having a foreign-born element of 21·6% while in New England alien settlers comprised only 11·2% of the population. In 1920 New England ranked highest with a proportion of 25·5% and the Pacific States were third with 20·3%. The Mountain States began in 1850 with a very modest foreign-born element of 5·8%; in 1870 it had risen to 27·6%, and in 1920 it had declined to 13·6%. These changes over time in the relative prominence of the foreign-born in the populations of different sections of the United States are a reflexion of important phases in the economic development of the country. Let us take the pattern as shown in the Census of 1920 and compare it with the proportion of Negroes in the populations of the various regions. The data are set out in Table 38.

Table 38. *The United States: population of geographic divisions by colour and nativity, 1920.* (*Percentages*)

| Geographic division | Percentage of total population | | | | | |
| | White | Negro | Native white of native parentage | Foreign white stock | | |
				Total	Foreign-born white	Native white of foreign or mixed parentage
United States	89·7	9·9	55·3	34·4	13·0	21·5
New England	98·9	1·1	37·9	61·0	25·3	35·7
Middle Atlantic	97·2	2·7	43·3	54·0	22·1	31·9
East N. Central	97·5	2·4	54·9	42·6	15·0	27·6
West N. Central	97·5	2·2	59·6	37·9	10·9	26·9
S. Atlantic	69·0	30·9	62·8	6·2	2·3	4·0
East S. Atlantic	71·6	28·4	68·5	3·1	0·8	2·3
West S. Atlantic	79·2	20·1	68·0	11·3	4·5	6·8
Mountain	96·3	0·9	60·0	36·3	13·6	22·7
Pacific	96·2	0·9	51·9	44·3	18·6	25·7

Source: Niles Carpenter, *Immigrants and their Children*, U.S. Population Census, 1920, Monograph VII, Washington, 1927, p. 34.

Table 38 brings out a clear inverse relation between the proportion of Negroes and the proportion of foreign white stock in the populations of the divisions of the United States. The correlation would be even more evident if we were to present the figures for each of the forty-eight

States.[1] In the words of Niles Carpenter, 'a large Negro population seems to act as a barrier to the immigrant and his children'.[2] The phenomenon cannot be dismissed with a reference to the slow growth of industry in the South or the lack of transport facilities; both these factors were true of the North Western States which nevertheless absorbed large numbers of immigrants. The explanation must be sought in the relation of rivalry between Negroes and unskilled immigrant workers. The latter were more likely to achieve situations of strength and stability in the labour market where Negroes were absent or insignificant; but at times when the inflow of foreign workers slackened the Negroes found the market more favourable and were able to push further afield. When the 'new' immigration was in full swing and the economy of the United States was expanding rapidly, the foreign-born and the black American workers forming one large mass of cheap labour on the one hand, and the managerial and skilled grades on the other, were non-competing groups: they were complementary. But within the unskilled sector there was a high degree of competition between the Negro and the immigrant from South Eastern Europe.

4. CANADA AND THE AMERICAN VORTEX

By immigration into the United States we have meant the inflow from overseas, mainly from Europe. The numbers arriving over the northern and southern land frontiers of the United States did not always react to the same forces as the flow of migrants across the Atlantic. The readjustment which led to the northward trek of the Negroes seems also to have encouraged a considerable immigration of Mexicans. Between 1910 and 1930, parallel to the increase from 437,000 to 1,399,000 in the number of Southern-born black persons living in the North, the number of Mexicans enumerated in the United States grew from 368,000 to 1,423,000. The tendency of Canadians to settle south of the border has varied in strength from time to time; and it would be interesting to study the fluctuations in this inflow in relation to population movements within the United States. Unfortunately it is not possible to pursue this far owing to the lack of reliable statistics.

The limitations of the data on Canadian immigration into the United States have already been pointed out. To obtain an approximate estimate it is necessary to confine the analysis to the birthplaces-figures given in the decennial census.[3] Despite the difficulties it is worth examining the statistics for the twenties in the light of what has been said in this chapter about the interaction between internal and external migration. Dr R. H. Coats has argued that Canadian-born went south because

---

[1] See Niles Carpenter, op. cit. Table 145.   [2] Ibid. p. 34.   [3] See Table 71.

they were pushed out by European immigrants who settled in the Dominion: he has stressed 'the pregnant fact that a big exodus of the Candian-born comes after, rather than before, a big immigration movement'.[1] He has elaborated this thesis in the following passage:

...we can read the individualist, the fortune-seeker, in the enormous scatter which characterizes the Canadian in the U.S.; a scatter which is much greater relatively than the American scatter over Canada, i.e., much larger proportionately to the despatching country. But the fact is that the scattered element is, to repeat, only a fraction and a small one—5 per cent at most—of the Canadian movement as a whole. When we review the residue, we encounter the earmarks, not of an individualistic but of a mass movement, *a movement which must find its explanation in the economic circumstances not of the receiving but of the sending country.* Thirty per cent of it represents what is left of the movement which began sporadically but culminated in that great overflow from rural Ontario and Quebec six or seven decades ago, and which halted at the nearest spot it could, i.e., in border states, where a new home was made under circumstances as like the old home as possible. Once set up, these spots became nuclei for subsequent movements essentially of a social nature—that is, Canadians have kept on going to these places in the States whither Canadian friends and relatives had preceded: sixty per cent of them are in this latter category. *These Canadians have not gone to the parts of the U.S. which were expanding most rapidly, unless by accident: they have not been straws sucked into a vortex.* And the same can be said of the children of Canadians in the States: they have moved about less than the Americans.[2]

The interpretation given by Dr Coats deserves the closest attention, based as it is on an expert examination of the subject. I propose to start from the central fact which explains why the year-to-year figures of migration between Canada and the United States are so poor—the unguarded frontier between the two North American nations. This suggests that an illuminating way of studying the interchange of population is to regard the whole North American continent as one vast network of labour markets. The question is then whether Canadian 'emigration' to the United States is best explained as part of the fluctuating pattern of internal migration in North America rather than as an effect of European immigration into the Dominion. It does not seem meaningful to discuss the absorptive capacity of Canada as if it were an economy separated from the United States by a sea frontier. The historical fact is that geographical mobility over the land border

[1] R. H. Coats, *Canadian Journal of Economics and Political Science*, August 1936, p. 280.
[2] R. H. Coats, 'Two Good Neighbours: a Study of the Exchange of Populations', Canadian-American Affairs Conference at Queen's University, Kingston, Ontario, 1937, *Proceedings*, pp. 116–17. (My italic.) See also R. H. Coats and M. C. MacLean, *The American Born in Canada*, Yale University Press, 1943, p. 27.

was about as easy as it was from east to west within the Dominion. Moreover, it is important to distinguish between the English and the French Canadians.

What is the evidence from census statistics for the decade 1920–30? Table 39 lists the American States in order of rank according to the rate of in-migration of native white persons in that decade. They were California, Florida, Arizona, Michigan, New Jersey, Nevada, Ohio, Oregon, New York, New Mexico, Maryland, Illinois, North Carolina, Indiana, Connecticut, Vermont.

Table 39. *Selected States of the United States, 1920–30: native white in-migration and number of Canadian-born persons enumerated*

State	Net native-white in-migration 1920–30 as percentage of population in 1920*	Number of Canadian-born enumerated†	
		1930	1920
California	43·4	*101,677*	59,686
Florida	33·9	*8,189*	4,141
Arizona	17·5	*2,037*	1,964
Michigan	9·1	*203,783*	165,902
New Jersey	8·3	*16,665*	10,396
Nevada	7·2	955	1,181
Ohio	5·2	*27,345*	24,670
Oregon	5·1	*17,946*	13,800
New York	4·3	*149,148*	112,804
New Mexico	4·1	618	738
Maryland	2·7	*2,307*	1,894
Illinois	2·6	43,988	38,773
North Carolina	2·4	*948*	663
Indiana	1·3	*6,267*	5,147
Connecticut	0·8	*37,863*	24,679
Vermont	0·3	27,194	24,885

* J. J. Spengler, 'Migration within the United States', *The Journal of Heredity*, January 1936, Table III, col. 4.

† Leon Truesdell, *The Canadian Born in the United States*, Yale University Press, 1943, p. 26.

The figures italicized are the maximum recorded at any census up to 1930.

In-migration as a percentage of the population in 1920 ranged from 43·4 % in California to 0·3 % in Vermont. The first point to note is that in twelve of these sixteen States the number of Canadian-born enumerated in 1930 was the maximum ever recorded. This suggests that in the ten years under review Canadians were attracted into the parts of the United States where the rate of expansion was highest. A closer view may be obtained by concentrating on the seven States which head the list (excluding Arizona and Nevada which are too small to have much influence). California, Florida, Michigan, New Jersey, Ohio, Oregon and New York had the largest net gains by internal migration of native white persons. The estimated net immigration of Canadian-born into these States between 1920 and 1930 was 202,000 which was 57 % of the total net immigration of Canadians into the United States. It is clear that in the decade 1920–30 the majority of Canadian emigrants did go to those parts of the United States which were expanding most rapidly: they *were* straws sucked into the American vortex.[1]

What is true of Canadian emigrants as a whole, however, does not apply to the French Canadians. At the American Census of 1930, 366,007 Canadian-born persons reported that they had arrived between January 1, 1920, and April 1, 1930. Of these, 274,559 were English Canadians and 91,448 French Canadians. No less than 59 % of the English Canadians and only 28 % of the French Canadians were in the seven States where expansion was greatest in the decade 1920–30. It is significant that nearly 50 % of the French Canadians settled in Massachusetts, New Hampshire, Rhode Island and Maine—four States which registered a net loss by migration during the decade. While the English element went for the most part to the booming centres, the French Canadians tended to go to places which were losing population. Nor was this a feature peculiar to the years 1920–30. The United States Census of 1920 revealed the fact that in the rural areas of the Middle Atlantic and New England which had been losing population there was a surprisingly large proportion of immigrants who had arrived since 1900. 'Wherever in the rural foreign-born population of these States there is an unusually large number of immigrants who have been here twenty years or less, they are either Canadians or Southern or Eastern Europeans. Apparently, in New England, as the native American farmer "sells out", he is replaced by a recently arrived foreigner.'[2] Most of these Canadians were French-speaking. Not all the 'new' immigrants into the United States flocked into the factories, mills and stockyards: some of them were eager to settle on the land and New England was one of the last areas where farms could still be obtained by men without much means. In this respect French Canadian immigration appears to have more in common with the influx from the continent of Europe than with the movement of the English Canadians.

---

[1] To estimate net immigration of Canadian-born into the seven States I have followed Dr Leon Truesdell by applying a decennial death rate of 17·5 % to the number enumerated in 1920. This rate was derived by applying the 1920–9 life table for the United States Registration States of 1920 to the estimated 1920 age composition of Canadian-born in the United States. See Truesdell, op. cit. p. 99.

[2] Niles Carpenter, op. cit. p. 54.

During the decade 1921–31 a new trend in internal migration was experienced within Canada. For the first time the agricultural west ceased to have an inward balance and began exporting population back to the east. The prairie provinces lost 66,000 native-born persons by migration to the East and British Columbia. Quebec and Ontario registered a net gain of 44,000. There was a significant shift of native-born Canadians from west to east, while the total net efflux of native-born from rural Canada was as much as 550,000 during the decade.[1] The immigrants to Canada went mainly to urban areas. Commenting on the statistics for 1921–31, Professor W. B. Hurd wrote:

> ...despite continuous efforts on the part of the authorities to stimulate rural rather than urban settlement, the proportion of the current net immigration domiciled in towns and cities at the close of the decade was three times greater than that found in the country. Whereas in 1921 only 56 per cent of the foreign-born population in Canada was resident in urban centres, over 75 per cent of the net foreign immigration during 1921–31 found its way to towns and cities. In only two provinces did rural immigration exceed urban, viz., Alberta where occupied farm acreage increased by some 33 per cent, and New Brunswick where the figures reflect a return movement from the United States of second generation French Canadians.[2]

In that decade, the net gain to urban population over natural increase consisted of 67·5 % foreign-born and 32·5 % Canadian-born.[3]

The estimated net emigration of native-born from Canada to all other countries in 1921–31 was 430,000. The net absorption of Canadian-born by the United States in the years 1920–30 was 356,000. From the foregoing analysis we may conclude that North America was in the throes of a tremendous process of internal readjustment. The English Canadians who went south were responding to the same economic forces as the Americans who settled in such large numbers in California. The fact that European immigrants bulked so large in the increase in Canada's urban population does not mean that they pushed Canadians out. In a vast area like North America with no restrictions on geographical and occupational mobility, it was natural that the American vortex should exercise a powerful influence on Canadian labour; this is confirmed by estimates of the net decennial migration of Canadian-born persons to the United States shown in Table 71. The efflux to the United States would have taken place irrespective of what was happening to European immigration into Canada.

[1] W. B. Hurd, 'Population Movements in Canada, 1921–31', *Proceedings of the Canadian Political Science Association*, 1934, pp. 223 and 225.

[2] W. B. Hurd and J. C. Cameron, 'Population Movements in Canada, 1921–31: Some Further Considerations', *Canadian Journal of Economics and Political Science*, May 1935, pp. 237, 238.   [3] Ibid. Table v, p. 237.

CHAPTER IX

THE SOCIAL LADDER IN THE UNITED STATES

Chapter II gave theoretical reasons for thinking that there is an inter-action between the degree of internal social mobility and the rate of inflow or outflow of labour. It was suggested that the class structure of a country would change in the long run and the balance between different groups might alter in such a way as to influence the course of external migration. This factor is, of course, only one among many, and the part it plays must not be exaggerated. It may, however, furnish a key to the answer to certain questions, for example, why net British immigration to the United States failed to increase between 1900 and 1913, a period when America's absorptive capacity was so great.

With this problem in mind, we shall now examine the changing structure of the American labour market towards the close of the century. From the Population Censuses of the United States, 1870–1910, we can find out what was happening to the British and Irish elements in the population, and this will also have a bearing on the fundamental changes which took place in the technique of production in that period.

I. THE STATISTICAL DATA

The 13th Census of the United States (1910) was the starting-point of a valuable series of labour statistics. The occupations listed in that Census were arranged by Dr Alba M. Edwards into what he called 'social-economic groups'.[1] There had been official interest in this problem for many years. For example, William C. Hunt, Chief Statistician for Population in the Bureau of the Census, published in July 1897 in Bulletin No. 11 of the Department of Labor an article in which he divided gainful workers into four groups: the proprietor class, the clerical class, skilled workers, and the labouring class. Dr Alba M. Edwards, who made the outstanding contribution in this field, developed a more elaborate classification in several important articles published between 1917 and 1938.[2] So successful was this achievement of private

---

[1] Alba M. Edwards, 'Social-economic Groups of the United States', *Journal of the American Statistical Association*, June 1917.

[2] E.g. 'A Social-economic Grouping of the Gainful Workers of the United States', *Journal of the American Statistical Association*, December 1933; 'The White Collar Workers', *Monthly Labor Review*, March 1934; 'Composition of the Nation's Labor Force', *Annals of the American Academy*, March 1936; 'The Negro as a Factor in the

enterprise that it eventually won the crown of official approval and was taken over by the State. In 1938 the Bureau of the Census published a volume called *A Social-Economic Grouping of the Gainful Workers of the United States, 1930*, presenting the results of the 15th Census in terms of Dr Edwards's classifications. As one of the documents of the 1940 Census there appeared in 1943 a volume entitled *Comparative Occupation Statistics for the United States, 1870 to 1940*, which gives a comparable series of occupation statistics, 1870–1930, and a social-economic grouping of the labour force, 1910–1940.

The article written by Dr Edwards in 1917 arranged the occupations listed in the 1910 Census in nine 'social-economic groups' as follows:

    (i)   Proprietors, Managers and Officials.
    (ii)   Clerks and Kindred Workers.
    (iii) Skilled Workers.
    (iv) Semi-skilled Workers.
    (v)   Labourers.
    (vi) Servants.
    (vii) Public Officials.
  (viii) Semi-official Public Employees.
    (ix) Professional Persons.

For the purpose of this chapter it would have been most useful if the native and foreign-born enumerated as gainful workers in the Censuses of 1870–1900 could have been divided into the above nine social-economic groups. This was impossible because the data in those censuses, based mainly on an industrial rather than an occupational grading, could not be used to distinguish between skilled, semi-skilled and unskilled workers. Another handicap was that the list of occupations given in those early censuses is much less detailed than in 1910. Even though the distribution of workers by skill was not available, it seemed worth while to proceed with the analysis since it would be feasible to distinguish such categories as professional persons, manual workers, clerks and servants. The classification adopted here, deriving from that of Dr Edwards, identifies seven groups for the census years 1870–1900.

    (i)   Proprietors, Officials and Managers:
        (*a*) Industry and Personal Service.
        (*b*) Agriculture.
    (ii) Professional Persons.

Nation's Labor Force', *Journal of the American Statistical Association*, September 1936; 'Growth and Significance of the White Collar Class', *American Federationist*, January 1938.

(iii) Clerks and Kindred Workers, Public Officials, Semi-official Public Employees.
(iv) Manual Workers:
    (a) Industry and Personal Service.
    (b) Agriculture.
(v) Servants.

In some cases arbitrary allocations had to be made, for example when details were not given in Dr Edwards's paper or when the criteria which he applied to the total occupied population were not equally valid for the foreign-born; but such adjustments affected only a small percentage of the total. The tables compiled for this section are meant to show how broad groups of occupations varied from census to census, and it is reasonable to expect errors in the statistics for individual occupations to cancel out within a group.[1]

2. SOCIAL STATUS OF BRITISH AND IRISH IMMIGRANTS

Table 40 sets out for the years 1870, 1890 and 1900 the distribution by social-economic group of the total occupied population of the United States and of persons born in Great Britain and Ireland. For 1900 similar information is available for the second generation, persons born in the United States of immigrant parents; and this is included in the table.[2] In 1870 the total number of gainfully employed people aged 10 and over in the United States was 12,506,000, of whom 947,000 were born in Ireland and 374,000 born in England, Wales and Scotland. By 1900 the total occupied population had grown to 29,287,000; the number of Irish-born remained more or less the same at 960,000, while there were as many as 1,478,000 second-generation Irish; on the other hand, the number of British-born had increased to 652,000, and there were 675,000 second-generation British. The boom in Irish immigration had taken place in the late forties and fifties, whereas British immigration did not reach its zenith until the eighties. The Irish-born enumerated in the 1900 Census were, therefore, on the average much older than the

[1] In the volume *Sixteenth Census of the United States, 1940, Population, Comparative Occupation Statistics for the United States, 1870 to 1940*, Dr Edwards went over the occupation statistics for the census years 1870–1910 and introduced slight corrections to allow for undercounting in the earlier years, overcounting in 1910 and anomalies caused by imprecise terminology. The undercounting had occurred mainly in the thirteen Southern States where the number of foreign-born is relatively small. It did not seem necessary to attempt similar refinements in this analysis, since it is concerned mainly with broad groups of occupations.

[2] We shall refer to persons born in England, Wales and Scotland as British-born and their children as second generation British, to distinguish them from the Irish-born and the second generation Irish.

British-born. Such differences in age composition must be borne in mind in interpreting the percentages in Table 40. The more remote the period of greatest influx of a foreign-born group, the higher the proportion of middle aged and elderly in that group and the larger and more mature will its second generation be. Failure to make allowance for this point can lead to serious mistakes in comparing the 'new' immigrants with the 'old'.

About half the occupied population of the United States was engaged in agriculture in 1870; of the British-born there were 27 % and of the Irish-born only 19 %. In that year one in five of the British-born were proprietors in agriculture and only one in ten of the Irish-born, whereas the proportion of the Irish-born classed as agricultural labourers exceeded that of the British-born. This is another factor which helps to explain the percentages for 1900. In the last three decades of the nineteenth century agriculture became a less important part of the American economy and in 1900 it contained only 36 % of the total gainfully employed as against 49 % in 1870. It was, therefore, natural that the proportions of the British- and Irish-born thus occupied should fall, respectively, from 27 to 16·5 % and 19 to 11 %. But when we look at the figures for the second-generation British in 1900 we find the apparently curious fact that the proportions classed as proprietors and labourers in agriculture are higher than for the British-born. However, the second-generation Irish were less prominent as proprietors in agriculture and more prominent as agricultural labourers than the Irish-born in 1900. This result can easily be explained. Where the immigrant parents had gone in fair numbers into agriculture, their children would be likely to inherit farms or settle down in rural jobs. Thus in 1900 22 % of the second-generation British were in agriculture as compared with 16·5 % of the British-born.

We now turn to the other side of the picture revealed by Table 40. The British immigrants were of a higher social-economic status than the Irish and they climbed the social ladder faster. In 1900 only 1·6 % of the Irish-born were professional persons and as many as 15·1 % servants, most of whom were women; the corresponding proportions for the British-born were 4·3 and 4·1 %. But the sons and daughters of the Irish immigrants were not lagging much behind the second-generation British: 4·8 % of them were in the professions, as many as 17·8 % clerks and officials, and only 4·8 % servants. That the Irish tended to settle mainly in urban areas is shown by the fact that 55 % of the second generation were manual workers in industry as compared with 45 % of the second-generation British. The interesting point here is that, though the parents were mainly unskilled and uneducated, the fact that they had settled in towns gave them a distinct advantage in placing their

Table 40. *The United States: percentage distribution by social-economic group of total occupied population and of persons born in Great Britain and Ireland, 1870–1900*

Social economic group	U.S. occupied population			British-born			Second generation British	Irish-born			Second generation Irish
	1870	1890	1900	1870	1890	1900	1900	1870	1890	1900	1900
	(%)	(%)	(%)	(%)	(%)	(%)	(%)	(%)	(%)	(%)	(%)
(i) Proprietors, etc.:											
(a) Industry and service	4·6	4·9	5·2	6·2	5·9	7·7	7·1	4·3	5·2	5·8	5·1
(b) Agriculture	24·2	23·6	19·8	19·2	14·3	12·9	14·5	10·0	10·1	8·1	7·0
(ii) Professional persons	2·6	3·8	4·0	2·2	3·3	4·3	6·6	0·8	1·3	1·6	4·8
(iii) Clerks and public officials	4·8	9·4	10·0	7·0	8·9	11·0	16·0	7·0	9·0	10·2	17·8
(iv) Manual workers:											
(a) Industry and service	31·2	35·8	39·8	55·4	57·1	56·4	45·0	53·1	51·7	56·5	54·9
(b) Agriculture	24·8	16·0	15·9	7·7	5·3	3·6	7·6	9·3	6·6	2·7	5·6
(v) Servants	7·8	6·5	5·3	4·3	5·2	4·1	3·2	15·5	16·1	15·1	4·8
Total	100·0	100·0	100·0	100·0	100·0	100·0	100·0	100·0	100·0	100·0	100·0

SOURCE: U.S. Population Censuses, 1870, 1890 and 1900.

children in 'white collar' jobs as compared with even parents of a higher social status who lived in the country. According to the 1900 Census, the proportion of native Americans of native parentage in clerical jobs (3·4 %) was lower than the proportion of second-generation Americans (5·7 %). This is not surprising when it is realized that, in 1900, 60 % of the second-generation white Americans were living in towns and cities, whereas only 30 % of the native white Americans of native parentage were to be found there, and that no less than 5·7 % of the native whites of native parentage were classified as illiterate, as compared with only 1·6 % of the native whites of foreign parentage.[1] The higher-grade occupations of the professional and clerical type called for educational attainments which could be acquired more easily in the cities than in the rural areas.

3.   MOVEMENTS INTO AND OUT OF PARTICULAR OCCUPATIONS

So far we have necessarily had to restrict attention to broad groups; we shall now turn to an examination of particular occupations. The extent to which the foreign-born advanced into various occupations can be expressed in index numbers. For example, take in a given year the number of English-born clerks as a percentage of the total English-born occupied persons enumerated in the United States; set this against a base proportion, the percentage of clerks in the occupied population of the United States. If the former proportion were equal to the base proportion, the index number would be 100; deviations above and below 100 indicate the relatively greater or less participation of a foreign-born group in the given occupation. We can take as basis the total occupied population including the non-white, the native white or the foreign-born white occupied persons.

In Table 41 the total number of native white males in the United States is taken as base. In 1890 the British-born were very much over-represented as miners and cotton-mill operatives, more so than the Irish-born; but by 1900 the index number for miners (English and Welsh) had fallen to 335 for the second generation from 862 in 1890. In the case of cotton-mill operatives (Scottish) there was a decline from 417 in 1890 to 80 for the second generation in 1900. On the other hand, we note a rise in the index number for English and Welsh clerks from 78 in 1890 to 148 in 1900 (second generation), for physicians and surgeᴏ ns from 47 to 86, and for teachers from 24 to 83. It is particularly interesting to see that by 1900 second-generation Scotsmen had made

[1] See A. Ross Eckler and Jack Zlotnick, 'Immigration and the Labor Force', *Annals of the American Academy of Political and Social Science*, March 1949, pp. 98–9.

Table 41. *The United States: indices of relative participation by British and Irish-born males in certain occupations, 1890 and 1900*

Occupation	Index numbers* for 1890				Index numbers* for 1900					
	Native white	England and Wales	Scotland	Ireland	England and Wales		Scotland		Ireland	
					1st generation	2nd generation	1st generation	2nd generation	1st generation	2nd generation
Cotton mill operatives	100	570	417	263	320	120	140	80	140	100
Miners	100	862	739	232	600	335	441	329	188	153
Servants	100	262	212	358	280	100	200	120	340	180
Tailors	100	257	300	240	250	100	350	100	250	150
Bakers	100	155	400	155	150	100	350	100	150	100
Boot- and shoe-makers	100	141	109	206	150	83	117	83	200	200
Carpenters	100	100	148	57	115	100	196	116	73	69
Clerks	100	78	92	44	95	148	105	155	55	160
Traders and dealers	100	93	89	85	106	120	120	114	89	89
Physicians and surgeons	100	47	53	19	57	86	86	114	29	57
Teachers	100	24	27	17	33	83	33	83	17	50

* For each nativity group the index number expresses the proportion engaged in a given occupation as a percentage of the proportion of the total United States native whites engaged in that occupation.

Source: United States Population Censuses.

relatively more headway in the medical profession than native white Americans. The drift away from manual labour into 'white collar' jobs—especially in the second generation—is clearly brought out.

About one-tenth of the total number of male breadwinners enumerated in the 1900 Census were general labourers. The highest percentage of labourers for any group of immigrants was recorded for first-generation Italians, namely, 33·2 %. Next came Poles, with 29·1 %; and then the Irish and Hungarians, with 22·3 % each. The marked change when we look at the second generation is revealing. The percentages drop as follows: Italians, 33·2 to 12·4; Poles, 29·1 to 15·7; Irish, 22·3 to 10·2; Hungarians, 22·3 to 7·0. Commenting on this subject, the Immigration Commission stated:

In the large cities the native white whose parents were foreigners by birth are employed as general labourers to a much greater extent than the native white whose parents were native Americans; in the smaller cities and country districts there is less difference between these classes in this respect. But everywhere the proportion of labourers is greater among the foreign-born, or immigrants, than among either class of native white; and in general these three classes appear to be more sharply differentiated in the city than in the country.[1]

The enormous influx of immigrants from Southern and Eastern Europe led to a series of racial displacements in the basic industries of the United States. What happened is best described in the words of the Immigration Commission.

In the first place, a larger proportion of native Americans and older immigrant employees from Great Britain and Northern Europe have left certain industries, such as bituminous and anthracite coal mining and iron and steel manufacturing. In the second place, a part of the earlier employees, as already pointed out, who remained in the industries in which they were employed before the advent of the Southern and Eastern Europeans have been able, because of the demand growing out of the general expansion, to attain to the more skilled and responsible technical and executive positions which required employees of training and experience. In the larger number of cases, where the older employees remained in a certain industry after the pressure of the competition of the recent immigrant had begun to be felt, they relinquished their former occupations and segregated themselves in certain occupations. This tendency is best illustrated by the distribution of employees according to race in the bituminous coal mines. In this industry all the so-called 'company' occupations, which are paid on the basis of a daily, weekly or monthly rate, are occupied by native Americans or older immigrants and their children, while the Southern and Eastern Europeans are confined to pick mining and to the unskilled and common labour. The same situation exists in iron and steel and glass manufacturing, the textile manu-

[1] *Abstracts of Reports of the Immigration Commission*, 61st Congress, 3rd Session, Senate Document No. 747, Washington, 1911, p. 780.

facturing industries, and in all divisions of manufacturing enterprise. It is largely the reproach which has become attached to the fact of working in the same occupations as the Southern and Eastern Europeans that in some cases, as in the bituminous coal-mining industry, has led to the segregation of the older class of employees in occupations which, from the standpoint of compensation, are less desirable than those occupied by recent immigrants. In most industries the native Americans and older immigrant workmen who have remained in the same occupations as those in which the recent immigrants are predominant are made up of the thriftless, unprogressive elements of the original operating forces. The third striking feature resulting from the competition of Southern and Eastern Europeans is seen in the fact that in the case of most industries, such as iron and steel, textile and glass manufacturing, and the different forms of mining, the children of native Americans and older immigrants from Great Britain and Northern Europe are not entering the industries in which their fathers have been employed. Manufacturers of all kinds claim that they are unable to secure a sufficient number of native-born employees to insure the development of the necessary number of workmen to fill the positions of skill and responsibility in their establishments. This condition of affairs is attributable to three factors: (1) General or technical education has enabled a considerable number of the children of the industrial workers of the passing generation to command business, professional or technical occupations more desirable than those of their fathers; (2) the conditions of work which the employment of recent immigrants has largely made possible have rendered certain industrial occupations unattractive to the prospective wage-earner of native birth; and (3) occupations other than those in which Southern and Eastern Europeans are engaged are sought for the reason that popular opinion attaches to them a higher degree of respectability.[1]

4. SOCIAL-ECONOMIC GROUPS IN 1910

Figures for 1910 showing occupational distribution of the gainfully employed persons in the United States by country of birth were not included in the Census results. However, thanks to the generous assistance of Dr Leon Truesdell, I received from the Bureau of the Census a return of hitherto unpublished statistics giving a detailed occupational classification of male workers aged 10 years and over in the United States in 1910 born in England, Wales, Scotland, Ireland, Germany, as well as of the total foreign-born white males. In addition, I was supplied with a classification of these foreign-born persons into the social-economic groups which Dr Alba M. Edwards used for the 1910 and subsequent censuses. The latter data are given in Table 42 and percentages in Table 43; to facilitate comparison index numbers are set out in Tables 44 and 45.

[1] Ibid. pp. 502–3.

Table 42. *The United States: occupied male workers by nativity group classified into social-economic grades, 1910*

Group	Foreign white male gainful workers 10 years and over	Male workers born in						Total male gainful workers 10 years and over
		Great Britain and Ireland	England	Scotland	Wales	Ireland	Germany	
Male workers 10 years and over	6,588,711	1,066,221	397,988	123,049	38,359	506,825	1,112,898	30,091,564
1. Professional persons	136,956	31,526	17,537	4,209	1,411	8,369	27,363	913,866
2. Proprietors, managers and officials	1,251,680	166,411	75,736	20,493	6,514	63,668	336,852	8,183,553
2A. Farmers	649,034	78,269	36,064	9,195	3,584	29,426	207,712	5,859,228
2B. Wholesale and retail dealers	367,143	36,559	15,929	4,005	1,195	15,430	76,009	1,178,049
2C. Other proprietors and managers	235,503	51,583	23,743	7,293	1,735	18,812	53,131	1,146,276
3. Clerks and kindred workers	356,742	95,980	41,754	11,661	2,903	39,662	63,909	2,744,459
4. Skilled workers and foremen	1,185,114	247,220	98,508	40,398	8,809	99,505	223,656	4,267,327
5. Semi-skilled workers	1,065,440	181,174	67,181	16,745	3,811	93,437	188,702	3,327,652
5A. Semi-skilled in manufacturing	749,929	104,579	48,437	11,614	2,519	42,009	125,118	2,032,946
5B. Other semi-skilled workers	315,511	76,595	18,744	5,131	1,292	51,428	63,584	1,294,706
6. Unskilled workers	2,592,779	343,910	97,272	29,543	14,911	202,184	272,416	10,654,707
6A. Farm labourers	327,007	43,795	15,937	5,556	1,206	21,096	54,965	4,680,521
6B, C. Labourers, excluding farm	2,101,644	262,057	68,114	21,038	13,080	159,825	188,976	5,373,433
6B. Factory and building construction labourers	985,034	105,947	23,770	6,652	2,972	72,553	103,324	2,567,769
6C. Other labourers	1,116,610	156,110	44,344	14,386	10,108	87,272	85,652	2,805,664
6D. Servant classes	164,128	38,058	13,221	2,949	625	21,263	28,475	600,753

SOURCE: Unpublished tables from the United States Population Census, 1910, kindly supplied to the author by the Bureau of the Census, Washington, through the courtesy of Dr Leon Truesdell.

Table 43. *The United States: percentage distribution of males of each nativity group by social-economic grade, 1910*

Group	Foreign white male gainful workers, 10 years and over	Male workers born in						Total male gainful workers 10 years and over
		Great Britain and Ireland	England	Scotland	Wales	Ireland	Germany	
Male workers, 10 years and over	100·0	100·0	100·0	100·0	100·0	100·0	100·0	100·0
1. Professional persons	2·1	3·0	4·4	3·4	3·7	1·6	2·4	3·0
2. Proprietors, etc.	19·1	15·6	19·0	16·6	17·0	12·6	29·9	27·3
2A. Farmers	9·9	7·4	9·0	7·4	9·4	5·8	18·4	19·5
2B. Wholesale and retail dealers	5·6	3·4	4·0	3·2	3·1	3·0	6·7	3·9
2C. Other proprietors and managers	3·6	4·8	5·9	5·9	4·5	3·7	4·7	3·8
3. Clerks and kindred workers	5·4	9·0	10·4	9·4	7·6	7·8	5·7	9·1
4. Skilled workers and foremen	18·0	23·2	24·7	32·5	23·1	19·6	19·8	14·2
5. Semi-skilled workers	16·2	17·0	16·8	13·6	9·9	18·5	16·9	11·1
5A. Semi-skilled in manufacturing	11·4	9·8	12·2	9·4	6·6	8·3	11·2	6·7
5B. Other semi-skilled	4·8	7·2	4·6	4·2	3·4	10·2	5·7	4·3
6. Unskilled workers	39·4	32·6	24·4	24·0	39·0	39·9	24·5	35·5
6A. Farm labourers	5·0	4·1	4·0	4·5	3·1	4·2	4·9	15·6
6B, C. Labourers, excluding farm	32·0	24·6	17·1	17·0	34·0	31·5	16·9	17·9
6B. Factory and building construction labourers	15·0	9·9	6·0	5·4	7·7	14·3	9·2	8·5
6C. Other labourers	16·9	14·7	11·1	11·7	26·2	17·2	7·7	9·3
6D. Servants	2·5	3·6	3·3	2·5	1·6	4·2	2·6	2·0

SOURCE: As Table 42.

Table 44. *The United States: indices of participation by British-, Irish- and German-born males in various occupations as compared with total foreign-born whites, 1910*

(Base—Foreign-born white)

Social-economic groups	Foreign-born white	Born in Great Britain and Ireland	Born in England	Born in Wales	Born in Ireland	Born in Scotland	Born in Germany
1. Professional persons	100·0	142·9	209·5	176·2	80·9	161·9	119·0
2. Proprietors, managers and officials	100·0	82·1	100·0	88·9	66·3	87·9	159·5
2A. Farmers	100·0	74·5	92·9	94·9	59·2	76·5	190·8
2B. Wholesale and retail dealers	100·0	60·7	71·4	55·4	55·4	58·9	121·4
2C. Other	100·0	136·1	163·9	125·0	102·8	163·9	133·3
3. Clerks and kindred workers	100·0	166·7	194·4	140·7	144·4	175·9	105·6
4. Skilled workers and foremen	100·0	128·9	137·8	127·8	108·9	182·2	111·7
5. Semi-skilled workers	100·0	104·9	104·3	61·7	113·6	84·0	104·9
5A. Semi-skilled in manufacturing	100·0	86·0	107·0	57·9	72·8	82·5	99·1
5B. Other	100·0	150·0	97·9	70·8	210·4	87·5	118·7
6. Unskilled workers	100·0	81·9	62·1	98·7	101·5	61·1	62·1
6A. Farm labourers	100·0	82·0	80·0	62·0	84·0	90·0	98·0
6B, C. Labourers, excluding farm	100·0	77·1	53·6	106·9	98·7	53·6	53·3
6B. Factory and building construction labourers	100·0	66·0	40·0	51·3	95·3	36·0	62·0
6C. Other labourers	100·0	87·0	65·7	156·2	101·8	69·2	45·6
6D. Servant classes	100·0	145·8	137·5	66·7	175·0	100·0	104·2

SOURCE: As Table 42.

Table 45. *The United States: indices of participation by British-, Irish- and German-born males in various occupations as compared with total occupied males, 1910*

(Base—Total males occupied in U.S.A.)

Group	Total males occupied in U.S.A.	Born in Great Britain and Ireland	Born in England	Born in Wales	Born in Ireland	Born in Scotland	Born in Germany
1. Professional persons	100·0	98·7	146·7	123·3	56·7	113·3	83·3
2. Proprietors, managers and officials	100·0	57·1	69·9	62·1	46·3	61·4	111·4
2A. Farmers	100·0	37·6	46·7	47·7	29·7	38·5	95·9
2B. Wholesale and retail dealers	100·0	88·2	102·6	79·5	79·5	84·6	174·4
2C. Other	100·0	126·6	155·3	118·4	97·4	155·3	126·3
3. Clerks and kindred workers	100·0	99·0	115·4	83·5	85·7	104·4	62·6
4. Skilled workers and foremen	100·0	165·7	174·6	162·0	138·0	231·0	141·5
5. Semi-skilled workers	100·0	154·6	152·3	90·1	165·8	122·5	153·2
5A. Semi-skilled in manufacturing	100·0	146·3	179·4	97·1	122·1	138·2	166·2
5B. Other	100·0	167·4	109·3	79·1	234·9	97·7	132·6
6. Unskilled workers	100·0	91·8	68·9	109·6	112·7	67·8	68·9
6A. Farm labourers	100·0	26·3	25·6	19·9	26·9	28·8	31·4
6B, C. Labourers excluding farm	100·0	137·3	96·1	191·6	177·0	96·1	95·5
6B. Factory and building construction labourers	100·0	116·6	70·6	90·6	168·2	63·5	109·4
6C. Other labourers	100·0	158·0	119·4	283·9	184·9	125·8	82·8
6D. Servant classes	100·0	180·0	165·0	80·0	210·0	120·0	125·0

SOURCE: As Table 42.

Some interesting differences are to be observed between those born in England, Scotland, Wales and Ireland. One in three of the Scottish-born but only one in five of the Irish-born was a skilled worker; only 24 % of the Scottish-born and as many as 40 % of the Irish-born were unskilled. The English-born had the highest percentages as professional persons, proprietors, managers, officials, and clerks and kindred workers. The large proportion of the Welsh-born classed as 'other labourers' (26 %) is due to the inclusion of coal mine operatives in that category.

Tables 44 and 45 give some indication of the relative progress which the immigrants from England, Wales, Scotland and Ireland had made in climbing the American social ladder. As compared with the total foreign-born white persons gainfully employed, the English, Welsh and Scottish were heavily represented in the professions, clerical and skilled grades, and 'other' proprietors, managers and officials—the latter being mainly builders and contractors, managers and superintendents, and manufacturers, whereas relatively fewer of them were to be found in the semi-skilled and unskilled jobs, with the exception of one or two grades. Immigrants from Scotland were well to the fore in the movement away from manual labour into jobs of a higher status. On the other hand, compared with the general run of the foreign-born, there were relatively fewer Irish in the professions and especially in the proprietor and managerial class, and relatively more of them in the semi-skilled and unskilled groups.[1] Only in the clerical field were the Irish not far behind the British. The immigrants of German origin had not shown any marked tendency to become either clerks or skilled workmen: a relatively large number of them were farmers and wholesale and retail dealers, and their proportion of unskilled workers was as low as that of the English and Scots.

Of the total number of occupied males in the United States in 1910 nearly 20 % were farmers and just under 16 % farm labourers: the corresponding proportions for the British- and Irish-born were 7 and 4 %. This major difference is brought out in the index numbers in Table 44. Another noteworthy feature is the marked preponderance of the English in professional, managerial, clerical and skilled occupations.

5. SOCIAL STRUCTURE AND IMMIGRATION

The interplay of forces shaping the growth of the Atlantic economy between the nineties and the First World War might be tentatively described as follows. The massive inflow into the United States of cheap

---

[1] The Irish had a strong footing in certain occupations. They comprised 10 % of America's guards, watchmen and doorkeepers, 11 % of the policemen, 11 % of the longshoremen and stevedores, 12 % of the labourers in public service, and 18 % of the coachmen and footmen.

labour from Southern and Eastern Europe coincided with technical innovations calling for a 'widening' of the capital structure. These two developments went hand in hand, and it is not easy to say which was the cause and which the effect. The changing technique in the expanding industries entailed minute subdivision of operations and a wide adoption of automatic machines worked by unskilled and often illiterate men, women and children. After 1900 the new supply of manpower was so abundant that firms using the new technique must have driven out of the market many old firms committed to processes depending more on human skill.

Evidence has been presented in this chapter to show that, by the end of the century, the sons of the immigrants who had formerly come from Britain and North Western Europe were consolidating their hold on the better-class jobs in a society which was gradually becoming more stratified; and any further immigrants from Britain would have to face formidable competition particularly if they were unskilled. The result was a remarkable qualitative change in the inflow from the United Kingdom after the turn of the century: this is brought out clearly in the figure in Chapter v based on the number of British immigrants with occupations and showing the distribution by skill, 1875–1930. From 1880 to 1900 between 60 and 80 % of the immigrants were labourers and servants; but from 1900 to 1910–13 there was a striking change, the proportion of labourers and servants falling sharply from about 80 to 25 % with a corresponding rise in the proportion of skilled workers from 15 to 45 %. The same phenomenon is illustrated by the distribution of immigrants from the United Kingdom by nationality. Fig. 9 indicates very clearly the reversal of trend in 1900, at which date the proportion of Irish among the immigrants from the United Kingdom reaches a peak of 80 %, falling rapidly to 40 % by 1910–13. Labourers from the British Isles were kept out of the American market by the flood from South East Europe.[1]

---

[1] The United States Immigration Commission produced numerous statistical tables to show the difference in character between the 'new' and the 'old' immigration. They compared the immigrants from South East Europe with those from North West Europe in the period 1899–1909 and concluded that the percentage of skilled (excluding Hebrews) was more than twice as great in the old immigration as in the new. See also J. W. Jenks and W. J. Lauck, *The Immigration Problem*, New York, Funk and Wagnalls, 1912, p. 31. This was a misleading comparison to make, for the simple reason that in the period 1899–1909 the percentage of skilled coming from Northern Europe was as high as it was because of the displacement of Northern Europe's unskilled by those from South East Europe. Paul H. Douglas demonstrated that the proper comparison would be between the 'new' immigration in the period 1899–1909 and the 'old' in the period 1871–82. On this basis, comparing the totals with occupations, he found that the 'old' immigration contained only a slightly

What were the factors determining the flow of British skilled migrants to the United States after 1900? On the one hand, the *complementarity* between the manual labourers from South East Europe and the managerial, professional and skilled grades in the United States entailed an increased demand for British skilled labour; on the other hand, the vertical flow of second generation British and North European stock within the United States was a *substitute* for British skilled immigrants. In the early years the invasion from South East Europe was so great that British technicians and foremen migrating to America must have found it easy to find employment but later the underlying relationship of rivalry was bound to assert itself. The change in the direction of British capital exports and the ending of America's dependence on loanable funds from London must also be borne in mind. Canada was now attracting British capital on a considerable scale and this exercised a pull on English skilled labour. The annual net immigration of British citizens to the United States, which had been as high as 150,000 in the early eighties, did not rise much above 50,000 between 1900 and 1913. This was not due to any weakening in the propensity to emigrate, for there was a boom in the early years of the century in British oversea settlement in countries other than the United States. The main part of the explanation is to be found in the transformation of the American social-economic structure and techniques of production associated with the enormous flow of cheap labour from South East Europe.

The long-run consequences in America were to be different from the short-run. The native-born and the second generation Americans, as they ascended to the managerial, professional, skilled and clerical posts, needed a growing mass of common labour to form the base of the social-economic pyramid. Far from being a threat to the upper grades, the 'new' immigrants bestowed prosperity on them. They were in keen competition with the Negroes and the failures among the 'old' immigrants and their children. The scope for direct social mobility—the opportunity for an individual *himself* to climb the ladder—was contracting; but there was still ample possibility for advancement from one generation to another. There were glittering prizes for the enterprising sons of humble immigrants. But when these prizes began to appear illusory and the continuing inflow of 'new' immigrants became a threat to the prospects of the second generation, the representatives of organized labour became fervent advocates of exclusion as the only way of keeping America a land of opportunity for members of their class.

higher proportion of skilled persons than the 'new' (22·9% as against 18·1%). See Paul H. Douglas, 'Is the New Immigration more Unskilled than the Old?', *Publications of the American Statistical Association*, vol. XVI, 1918–19, p. 401.

CHAPTER X

IMMIGRATION AND INVESTMENT

I. THE TIME-SHAPE OF EUROPEAN EMIGRATION

We have already seen that the timing of the four waves of European emigrants cannot be explained simply by fluctuations in the demand for labour in the United States. There is reason to think that the births cycle in Europe was responsible for the periodic emergence of population pressure manifesting itself in unusually large numbers in the lower age groups, and that at such times emigration would provide a means of escape for the surplus. An examination of Swedish data yielded some suggestive results. The five-year moving average of emigration in the 15–20 age group in the years 1863–1906 and the five-year moving average of births for the period 1845–88 gave a correlation coefficient of 0·665; emigration 1863–1906 in the 20–25 age group with births 1840–83 gave a coefficient of 0·732; and emigration 1863–1906 in the 25–30 age group with births 1835–78 gave a coefficient of 0·556. Thus, the highest correlation coefficient was for emigration in the 20–25 age group and the number born 20 to 25 years previously. It is now proposed to examine evidence from a wider sphere. Unfortunately the valuable demographic time series available for Sweden and other Scandinavian countries are unique; for the rest of Europe we have to resort to inferior records. We cannot do better than consult the compilation prepared by Sundbärg in 1910 for the Swedish Royal Commission on Emigration,[1] in which he gives estimates of the course of natural increase in Europe in the nineteenth century.

Fig. 34 sets out for the period 1815–1907 the course of total oversea emigration from Europe per 100,000 inhabitants, together with its two component parts—emigration to the United States and to all other countries. The four periods of upsurge are 1844–54, 1863–73, 1878–88 and 1898–1907. Emigration to destinations other than the United States, while it has sharp short-period peaks and troughs, does not show the violent minor secular fluctuations characteristic of emigration to the United States; at least up to 1880 the series runs a fairly even course, though after that date it moves with a perceptible minor secular swing. These short peaks and troughs are worth examining in relation to the contemporary flow to the United States. In 1847 the sudden increase was mainly to Canada, and was part of the evacuation from Ireland

---

[1] G. Sundbärg, *Den svensk och europeiska folköknings- och omflyttningsstatistiken, Emigrationsutredningen*, Bilaga IV, Stockholm, Kungl. Boktryckeriet, Norstedt, 1910.

after the disaster of 1846; the peaks of 1852 and 1854 reflected the gold discoveries in Australia. Between 1860 and 1863, when immigration to America was at a low level, European emigration to the rest of the

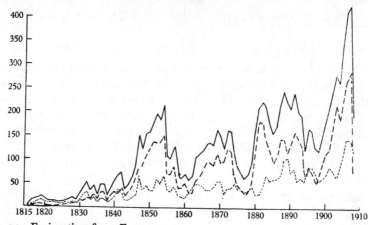

Fig. 34. Emigration from Europe per 100,000 population to all oversea countries, to the United States, and to countries other than the United States, 1815–1908. —— To all countries. - - - - To the United States. ⋯⋯ To all countries except the United States. Source: Tables 121 and 122.

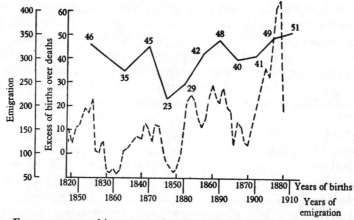

Fig. 35. European natural increase and emigration, 1820–1910. —— Quinquennial excess of births over deaths per 1,000 population (see Table 123). - - - - Annual emigration from Europe per 100,000 population. Source: Tables 122 and 123.

world went up rapidly—to Canada, Australia and Argentina; this latter movement slumped from 1863 to 1867 while the number of European emigrants to the United States rose very rapidly. The high point in 1869 reflected chiefly the settlement of Italians and Spaniards in Argentina. The sharp decline in emigration to America from 1872 to

1874 was accompanied by an increase in departures to Australia; the deep trough of 1875–78 in the movement to America is not to be found in European emigration to the rest of the world. Again the two migratory streams move inversely between 1879 and 1883, 1887 and 1890, 1901 and 1903; but for the last three decades they exhibit similar long fluctuations, with emigration to countries other than the United States expanding vigorously after 1903.

The propensity to emigrate from Europe was higher in the eighties than in the early fifties and it reached its maximum in the first decade of the century; the weakest upswing was in the years 1863–73. We shall now attempt to test the result obtained from Swedish data by examining the available demographic material for Europe as a whole. From statistics collected by Sundbärg it is possible to follow the course of the quinquennial excess of births over deaths in Europe (per 1,000 of the population) from 1820 to 1905.[1] The series, plotted in Fig. 35, indicate a striking fluctuation, with peaks at about 1825, 1840–5, 1860–5 and 1885–90 and troughs at about 1835, 1845–50, 1865–70 and 1890–5. Below this series for 1820–1905 is shown the course of oversea emigration from Europe in the period 1845–1908; it is apparent that corresponding to each peak and trough in natural increase is a peak and trough in emigration a quarter of a century later. The migration waves of 1844–54, 1863–73, 1878–88 and 1898–1907 must be in some way related to the four peaks in the excess of births over deaths in the 1820's, 1840–5, 1860–5 and 1885–90. Although the data leave much to be desired, the analysis suggests that the cycle in the rate of natural increase played a part in determining the timing of the major waves of oversea emigration from Europe. The following figures have a bearing on the biggest efflux of all—from Southern and Eastern Europe in the early years of this century.

Table 46. *Eastern Europe: natural increase and emigration, 1861–1915*

Period	Eastern Europe. Average annual rate of natural increase* (per thousand)	Average annual oversea emigration from Eastern Europe†	
		Period	Thousands
1861–80	10·6	1891–95	400·9
		1896–1900	405·7
1881–90	13·5	1901–5	785·9
		1906–10	1,114·3
1891–1900	13·8	1911–15	1,039·5

* Sundbärg, op. cit. p. 88.
† Dudley Kirk, *Europe's Population in the Interwar Years*, Geneva, League of Nations, 1946, p. 279.

[1] Sundbärg, op. cit. p. 76.

The considerable rise in the rate of natural increase in Eastern Europe in the eighties made it inevitable that population pressure would be acute after the turn of the century, and it was partially relieved by a mass exodus to the United States and South America. There can be little doubt that this would have continued in full spate had it not been for the First World War and the American Immigration Restriction Act of 1924.

2. IMMIGRATION AND INVESTMENT: A HYPOTHESIS

Given the validity of the 'push' element in the long cycles of migration, it is desirable to look more closely at the relation between these waves of immigration and fluctuations in investment. A purely speculative statement will first be put forward.

(a) There were four big expulsions of population from Europe: 1844–54, 1863–73, 1878–88, 1898–1907. The timing was determined by the cycle of births in the Old World and the impact of innovations and/or calamity.

(b) During each of these periods, the strategic component of investment in the United States lags behind immigration (or is simultaneous with it); then there is a switch in the order of lag lasting until the next big expulsion from Europe when immigration again assumes a formative role. Thus the 'push' and the 'pull' alternate.

(c) Each inflow of labour into America, accompanied by a rise in the import of capital, transforms the production functions, inducing a widespread adoption of automatic machines, interchangeable parts, standardized output and dilution of labour.

(d) Each inflow of labour coincides with an upswing of the long investment cycle in the United States; and corresponding to each of these upswings there is a downswing of the investment cycle in the United Kingdom, and vice versa.

(e) Each inflow of labour entails a 'widening' of the capital structure (i.e. declining or constant ratio of capital stock to gross national product); the subsequent downswing in the long investment cycle involves a 'deepening' of the capital structure (i.e. an increase in the ratio of capital stock to gross national product). Given the inverse relation between the two investment cycles, periods of 'widening' in the United States were periods of 'deepening' in the United Kingdom and vice versa.

In this chapter we shall deal only with what this hypothesis suggests about reactions in the United States.

3. THE VERDICT OF LAG ANALYSIS

The indices of the growth of the United States used in this analysis are railway construction, new building, bituminous coal output, production of pig iron, railway freight ton-miles, and merchandise imports at constant prices. Each of these series has been paired with immigration from Europe and from particular European countries, and the technique described in Appendix 2 for locating a switch in the direction of lag has been applied. The results reached will now be consulted to see what light they throw on the relationships hypothetically set out in the previous section.

It will be recalled that the sub-periods obtained by our method determine themselves in accordance with the principles described in Appendix 2. There can be no doubt about the verdict of the analysis on the first two decades, as revealed in the following figures.

Table 47. *The United States: immigration-investment lags, 1843–67*

Origin of immigration	Order of lag with respect to U.S. investment	Period of lag (immigration dates)	Length of lag (years)	Correlation coefficient
Europe	Before rail	1847–59	2	0·671
Great Britain	Before rail	1847–62	2	0·898
Ireland	Before rail	1848–63	1	0·558
Germany	Before rail	1846–67	3	0·670
Europe	Before building	1845–63	3	0·957
Great Britain	Before building	1844–63	2	0·855
Ireland	Before building	1843–62	2	0·867
Great Britain	Before merchandise imports	1847–61	3	0·800
Great Britain	After bituminous coal	1851–62	2	0·818

The first wave of immigrants into the United States started in 1844, and it rose very steeply to a maximum in 1854. Railway investment was reviving haltingly in 1844–6 and it was only in 1847 that a sharp increase took place which continued with two minor interruptions until the peak in 1856. The volume of merchandise imports moved in sympathy with railway investment, lagging a little after it—a characteristic which is true of the entire period 1845–1913. The lag analysis shows that immigration from Europe preceded railway construction by two years (1847–59, correlation coefficient 0·671) and building by three years (1845–63, 0·957); whereas British immigration preceded merchandise imports by three years (1847–61, 0·800). Immigration appears to have induced investment in fixed equipment, which in turn led to a similar movement in merchandise imports. The only exception is bituminous coal output, which preceded immigration from Great Britain in the years 1851–62 by two years (0·818). One has to remember, however, that the relative importance of coal at that time was small, the output in 1851 being 3·2 million tons and in 1861 6·7 million tons, with the population in the latter year well over 32 million.

A significant feature of this first minor secular fluctuation is that immigration led investment not only in the upswing but also in the reaction, which reached a trough in 1862. The 2,871,000 Europeans who landed in the United States between 1844 and 1854 entered a country whose population in 1844 was only 19½ million; and it is not surprising that this formidable invasion had a profound impact on the labour market and on the progress of investment, an impact which, according to this analysis, continued to be felt until the Civil War. There was no change (as suggested in our hypothesis) in the direction of lag when migration receded.

The second inflow of population began in 1863; it was accompanied by a revival in merchandise imports and followed by an upturn in railway construction and building two years later in 1865. German immigration preceded railway construction by three years (0·670) until 1867. That it took as long as two years for building and railway activity to respond to the beginning of the new boom in migration was partly due to the disturbance of the Civil War.

The next set of sub-periods yielded by the analysis of lags begins just before the downturn of the second wave. The results are as follows.

Table 48. *The United States: immigration-investment lags, 1869–90*

Origin of immigration	Order of lag with respect to U.S. investment	Period of lag (immigration dates)	Length of lag (years)	Correlation coefficient
Europe	After rail	1869–83	1	0·837
Great Britain	After rail	1871–83	1	0·868
Europe	After building	1869–79	1	0·893
Ireland	After building	1871–79	1	0·867
Great Britain	No lag building*	1869–79	0	0·947
Great Britain	No lag imports	1871–91	0	0·749
Germany	After rail	1869–82	1	0·789
	No lag rail	1869–82	0	0·784
Sweden	Before rail	1867–88	1	0·519
All countries (Male: quarterly)	Before rail freight ton-miles	1869 (4)–75 (1)	¾	0·594

* This result is for immigration to the U.S.A. from Great Britain (U.S. source) and Dr John R. Riggleman's index of building permits per capita. See Appendix 4, Table 108.

The most striking characteristic is that immigration lagged after building between 1869 and 1879, the only instance in the whole period. On the downswing of the second minor secular fluctuation the inward flow of population was governed by the course of investment in fixed capital; the reversal of lag postulated in our model did take place. It is interesting to observe that the index of rail freight ton-miles does not tell the same story. Building and railway construction were at a peak in 1871, male immigration in the third quarter of 1872 and rail freight in the second quarter of 1873. The correlation coefficient for German immigration paired with railway investment over the sub-period 1869–82 is 0·784 for no lag and 0·789 for a one-year lag (rail first), so that perhaps it would be safest to say that these two variables moved simultaneously. Swedish immigration, however, preceded railway construction by one year in the years 1867–88.

Table 49. *The United States: immigration-investment lags, 1879–1913*

Origin of immigration	Order of lag with respect to U.S.	Period of lag (immigration dates)	Length of lag (years)	Correlation coefficient
All countries (Male: quarterly)	After freight ton-miles	1879 (4)–85 (1)	$\frac{1}{2}$	0·777
Europe	After rail	1884–1900	1	0·789
Europe	No lag rail	1901–13	0	0·621
Great Britain	After rail	1884–98	1	0·880
Great Britain	After rail	1899–1913	3	0·787
Germany	After rail	1883–1913	2	0·724
Great Britain	No lag coal	1885–98	0	0·864
Great Britain	After coal	1899–1913	4	0·942
Great Britain	Before building*	1879–1902	2	0·800
Ireland	Before building	1887–1902	2	0·804
Europe	Before building	1887–1901	2	0·826
All countries (Male: monthly)	After pig iron	1898 (4)–1900 (11)	$\frac{1}{12}$	0·656
	No lag pig iron	1898 (4)–1900 (11)	0	0·628
All countries (Male: monthly)	After pig iron	1900 (12)–1907 (10)	$\frac{1}{12}$	0·514
	After pig iron	1900 (12)–1907 (10)	$\frac{1}{6}$	0·484

* This result is for immigration to the U.S.A. and Riggleman's index. The result for emigration of British citizens to the U.S.A. and Long's index is 1876–84, emigration ahead by four years, 0·936; 1887–1907, emigration ahead by two years, 0·919.

The third and fourth minor secular swings can best be judged together in the light of the remaining lag results.

A fairly accurate view is obtained from the quarterly figures of total male immigrants and rail freight ton-miles (both series purged of seasonal influences); there was a sharp upturn in the index of freight ton-miles in the last quarter of 1877 followed by a revival in immigration in 1878. We find an average lag of two quarters, migration following freight ton-miles, from 1879 (fourth quarter) to 1885 (first quarter), the correlation coefficient being 0·777. We know from previous results that the inflow of population lagged after railway construction in this third upswing, except in the case of Swedish immigrants. The pace of the boom in migration in the eighties and the recession in the nineties was governed by the course of fixed capital investment (other than building) in the United States. It is evident that the order of lag for building is different from that for other investment. From the eighties to the eve of the First World War immigration followed investment in railways and preceded building.

In the years 1898–1907 we come to the great influx of 'new' immigrants from Southern and Eastern Europe. The ideal method would be to compare monthly figures of Southern European immigrants with a monthly index of the output of net producer durable goods. The nearest practicable test was to pair the monthly numbers of male immigrants from all countries with the monthly output of pig iron in the United States (seasonal influences eliminated), April 1898 to October 1907. It was found that from April 1898 to November 1900 the best coefficient was 0·656 for immigration lagging after pig iron output by one month, while the coefficient for no lag was 0·628. For the rest of the period, December 1900 to October 1907, the best coefficient was 0·514 for a lag of one month of the same order, with the next best of 0·484 for a two-month lag. Thus, at the outset of the final upswing, the evidence for the 'pull' of American investment is a lag of something between one month and zero, and it is not conclusive.

The investigation indicates a difference between the flow of population from Northern and from Southern Europe. For example, German immigration lagged two years after railway investment, 1883–1913, whereas immigration from Europe as a whole, 1901–13, coincided with railway investment. Analysis of monthly data of European immigration puts the lag between one month and zero, and it is reasonable to infer that the disparity between the results for German and European immigration is due to the fact that the latter aggregate was dominated in the years 1900–13 by the invasion from Southern and Eastern Europe. It is possible that if the 'new' immigration were examined in detail as a separate stream, the balance would be tipped in favour of no lag. Such a result is indicated by an eye inspection of the quarterly indices of immigration and freight ton-miles from 1897 to 1903.

The conclusions may now be summarized.

(a) In the first two upswings beginning in 1844 and 1863 incoming population preceded fixed capital investment.

(b) Throughout the period 1845–1913, except for the years 1869–79, immigration preceded American building activity.

(c) The third wave of immigration, 1878–98, was on the whole determined by the course of American investment in railways.

(d) The results for Sweden and Germany in the third wave suggest that the agricultural element in this immigration was governed by the 'push' in Europe rather than the 'pull' in the United States.

(e) From the early seventies to 1913 the industrial element in transatlantic migration (for example, from Great Britain) lagged after American investment in railways and, from 1899 onward, after coal output.

(f) The wave of 'new' immigrants from Southern and Eastern Europe was almost entirely agricultural; it preceded the course of new building and was practically simultaneous with capital investment as represented by pig iron output and railway freight ton-miles.

(g) Relatively to the size of the receiving population the two outstanding waves were the first and the fourth, and the evidence that their timing was strongly under the influence of the births cycle in Europe is fairly convincing. An interesting parallel may be drawn between the two periods. In the years 1844–54 the dominant component of American investment was undoubtedly railway construction, with building a good second; in 1899–1908 the value (at 1929 prices) of improvements and equipment in steam railroads was one-fifth of the total for the United States, while that of residential building was one quarter. Taking into account the difference in the centre of gravity in the two periods, we may claim that in each case the pace of the major component of American investment was governed by mass immigration from the over-populated rural areas of Europe.

4. IMMIGRATION AND CAPITAL STRUCTURE

The full economic significance of immigration cannot be assessed without paying attention to the capital structure. In the model outlined in section 2 of this chapter it was suggested that each major inflow of population was accompanied by (and perhaps induced) a 'widening' of the capital structure in the receiving country. Fortunately it is possible to study this question for the latter part of our period with the aid of statistics which give for each sector of the American economy for the decades 1879–88, 1889–98, 1899–1908, 1909–18 and 1919–28 the value (at 1929 figures) of the Gross National Product and of Improvements and Equipment.[1]

---

[1] I am indebted to Professor Kuznets for his kindness in letting me use these valuable data. They are set out in full in Appendix 4, Table 131.

The ratio of Improvements and Equipment to Gross National Product (to be called the Structure Ratio) for the economy as a whole rose significantly from 1·98 to 2·58 between 1879–88 and 1889–98 and then dropped slightly between the latter decade and 1899–1908, which coincides almost exactly with the fourth great wave of immigrants. Now it happens that the eighties were a period of upswing in investment, for example in railroad construction, building and bituminous coal, as well as in immigration, whereas the nineties saw a downswing in these indices. In the latter decade the capital structure of the United States was going through a process of rapid 'deepening' and this ceased round about the turn of the century. The vigorous boom in investment in the years 1899–1908 was marked by a 'widening' of the capital structure.

Before interpreting this result it is important to look closely at the figures. A change in the aggregate structure ratio is brought about in two ways—movements of the ratio of capital to product *within* each sector of the system, and changes in the relative volume of the output generated in the various sectors. The distribution of the gross national product by industrial sector in 1879–88 and 1898–1908 gives the following results: agriculture, a decline from 21·1 to 15·6%; manufacturing, an increase from 17·0 to 20·0%; steam railways, an increase from 3·0 to 5·0%; residential building, constant at 6·6%. The capital-output ratios are high in branches such as public utilities, transport and residential construction, and low in manufacturing, commerce and services. For example, on the average in the period 1879–1928, street railways contributed 0·6% of the gross national product but had a structure ratio of 13·32; electric light and power, comprising 0·4% of the gross national product, had a ratio of 16·59. At the other extreme, manufacturing was responsible for 20·3% of the national product and had a ratio of 1·39; the miscellaneous group, 'all other industries', constituted 46·5% of the national product, with a ratio of 1·07.

We have seen that the aggregate ratio of capital to product rose from 1·98 to 2·58 between 1879–88 and 1889–98. Professor Kuznets has calculated that +0·53 was due to changes in the ratio *within* each branch and +0·07 to changes in the weights of the branches. Thus the process in those years was almost entirely pure 'deepening'. The story for the decade 1899–1908 compared with 1889–98 is different; a decline of 0·37 reflecting pure 'widening' was accompanied by an increase of 0·24 due to shifts in weight between the sectors, the aggregate change in the index being −0·02. From 1899–1908 to 1909–18 pure 'widening' continued its sway, the change in the ratio on this account being only +0·02; but there was an increase of 0·25 due to the relative expansion of industries with a high ratio.

The nature of the 'deepening' during the nineties may now be illustrated more clearly. Manufacturing increased its share of the national product from 17·0 % in 1879–80 to 19·3 % in 1889–98 and its capital-product ratio rose from 0·83 to 1·25; the share of agriculture in the national product declined from 21·1 to 18·6 % while its ratio increased from 1·37 to 1·61; residential building as a proportion of the national product declined slightly from 6·6 to 5·7 % but its ratio grew from 7·61 to 11·62.

In the decade 1899–1908 as compared with 1889–98, the industries which registered an increase in structure ratio were agriculture (+0·16), the relative size of which fell from 18·6 to 15·6 %, manufacturing (+0·16), its share of the national product rising slightly, street railways (+2·88) comprising 0·7 % of the national product in 1899–1908, and electric light and power (+6·60) comprising 0·2 % of the national product in 1898–1908. The sectors where 'widening' prevailed were mining (−0·16), steam railways (−4·91), residential building (−1·65), telephone (−12·58), telegraph (−0·51), other public utilities (−0·33), and all other industries (−0·05).

There must have been some connexion between this change in the capital structure of the United States and the fact that over eleven million people migrated into the country in the years 1900–13 and the net inward movement in the years 1909–13 averaged no less than 701,000 per annum. At a time when there was a remarkable advance in real investment and income the index number of the full-time real wages of unskilled workers in manufacturing fell from 114 in 1897–9 to 101 in 1910–13.[1] There was a premium on processes needing a relatively large quantity of low-grade labour; industries adopting these processes expanded rapidly, their products fell in price, and a number of them found that they no longer required protective tariffs. The introduction of automatic machines eliminating human skill over a wide field was stimulated by the incursion of such a considerable volume of cheap labour; it was profitable to invest in capital-saving equipment. The upswing in the investment cycle in the early years of the century coincided with the fulfilment of technical innovations, for example in electricity and chemistry; thanks to immigration of cheap labour the United States was able to take full advantage of those innovations by 'widening' her capital structure with enormous benefit to her physical productivity and economic power. The 'deepening' phase had taken place in the nineties when immigration was at a relatively low ebb and the rate of economic growth was below normal. When the findings of this section are taken in conjunction with the results of the lag analysis,

[1] Whitney Coombs, *The Wages of Unskilled Labor in the Manufacturing Industries in the United States, 1890–1924*, Columbia University Press, 1926, p. 119.

there is reason to conclude that the large supply of immigrant labour in the period beginning in 1899 exercised a determining influence on the technical coefficients in American industry and acted as an accelerator in the cumulative process of those years. Whether the same thing happened in previous upswings in investment it is impossible to demonstrate statistically; but there may be indirect evidence from other sources.

5. HISTORICAL EVIDENCE

The argument so far has relied entirely on an examination of statistical data, but important witnesses have yet to be called. The problems under review offer ideal opportunities for co-operation between economists and economic historians. I shall conclude by asking what light historical research has to throw on the effects of migration cycles on investment and the technique of production.

Fortunately, there is an authoritative study of the impact of Irish immigration on the economic life of Boston up to 1865.[1] Dr Handlin found that *'no matter what degree of standardization the technical process of manufacturing reached, the absence of a cheap labor supply precluded conversion to factory methods'*.[2] Howe's sewing machine had been invented in Cambridge, Massachusetts, in 1846, just before disaster overwhelmed Ireland, and the coming of the Irish enabled this invention to be adopted on a large scale, thereby revolutionizing the methods of factory production. In the twenty years after 1845 the massive influx of destitute immigrants meant low labour costs and Boston became the fourth manufacturing city in the United States. A seemingly endless supply of unskilled men, women and children was absorbed by mechanized factories from which the element of craftsmanship had been almost entirely banished. There was a brisk demand for female labour; by 1865 24,000 women were employed in Boston as compared with 19,000 men. It is reasonable to infer that, under the influence of mass immigration, the capital structure of the industries of Boston in that period went through a phase of 'widening' similar to what took place in the Eastern States in the decade 1899-1908.

From Dr Handlin's researches it is also clear that the way in which the 'new' immigration acted upon the social structure after the late nineties (analysed in Chapter IX) was nothing new in the history of the United States. Exactly the same thing was happening earlier in the century in the era of frontier democracy, and it is important to remember that the problem of immobile unemployed in the towns dates back to this first great wave of immigrants. In the words of Dr Handlin,

[1] Oscar Handlin, *Boston's Immigrants, 1790-1865*, Harvard University Press, 1941.
[2] Ibid. p. 81 (my italic).

Those who benefited most from the transition were native Americans. Very few foreigners were manufacturers.... Immigration advanced other classes in the community as well.... The demand for professional and commercial services directly aided the merchants and clerks, the traders and artisans—the bulk of the American population of the city.... The only Americans who suffered permanently from the Irish invasion were the unskilled laborers and domestics, few in number, who competed directly with the newcomers.... The flexibility of the economic organization of the United States enabled the displaced artisans to set up as manufacturers, to enter other trades, or to move west.... From the day they landed the immigrants competed for jobs that were fewer than men. Through all these years unemployment was endemic to the economic system.... Not until the war had drawn thousands of men into the army and stimulated new manufacturing developments did the demand for labor approximate the supply. By that time employers were making hurried efforts to attract new immigrants—new workers to restore the labor surplus.[1]

Thus, the economic history of Boston in the years 1845–65 bears out in a striking manner the results obtained by statistical analysis of time series.

We have already seen that the great efflux of population from Europe in the eighties corresponded to a peak in the births cycle a quarter of a century before; it was in that decade too that the Western World began to reap in their fullness the economic consequences of previous innovations. Writing at the end of the eighties, D. A. Wells declared:

When the historian of the future writes the history of the nineteenth century he will doubtless assign to the period embraced by the life of the generation terminating in 1885, a place of importance, considered in its relations to the interests of humanity, second to but very few, and perhaps to none, of the many similar epochs of time in any of the centuries that have preceded it; inasmuch as all economists who have specially studied this matter are substantially agreed that, within the period named, man in general has attained to such a greater control over the forces of Nature, and has so compassed their use, that he has been able to do far more work in a given time, produce far more product, measured by quantity in ratio to a given amount of labor, and reduce the effort necessary to insure a comfortable subsistence in a far greater measure than it was possible for him to accomplish twenty or thirty years anterior to the time of the present writing [1889].[2]

Statistical inquiry suggests—if only faintly—that in so far as the second and third exodus of migrants came from *agricultural* areas in Europe they were governed by expulsive forces in the same way as the Irish and Germans in 1846–54 and the Southern and Eastern Europeans in 1900–7.

[1] Ibid. pp. 88, 89 and 92.
[2] D. A. Wells, *Recent Economic Changes*, New York, Appleton, 1889, p. 27.

It can be shown that Sweden (where information on the history of emigration is almost embarrassingly abundant) experienced in the late sixties the same kind of Malthusian crisis, though by no means as severe, as Ireland had in the forties and fifties. At the beginning of the sixties agriculture in Sweden was responsible for three-quarters of the population increase, and for many decades the relative number of labourers, cottagers, farmers' sons over 15 and farm servants had been increasing and the proportion of farmers declining.[1] The position of this growing rural proletariat was precarious and an escape to home industries was not yet possible. Then came a conjuncture of events remarkably reminiscent of what had happened in Ireland twenty years before; Sweden adopted free trade in 1865 and calamity struck the countryside, with disastrous crop failures in 1861, 1865, 1866, 1867 and 1868. The figures of net emigration for the decade are as follows:

Table 50. *Net emigration from Sweden, 1861–70*

1861	2,732	1866	8,611
1862	3,029	1867	11,154
1863	3,737	1868	32,295
1864	6,187	1869	46,682
1865	7,996	1870	23,904

SOURCE: *Emigrationsutredningen*, Betänkande, 1913, p. 151.

The timing of this first considerable efflux from Sweden was undoubtedly governed by population pressure accentuated by very bad harvests, the sharp rise as early as 1864 being noteworthy.

The next big outflow—in the eighties—amounting to as much as 60 % of the natural increase, coincided with the impact of technical progress in the New World on the rural economy of Sweden. The country was hit along with most of Western Europe by the agrarian crisis of that time; even in 1880 no less than 68 % of the population of Sweden was in agriculture and subsidiary occupations. The turning point in 1881–5 is clearly seen in the figures in Table 51 of Sweden's foreign trade in farm produce (excluding dairy).

It is important to observe that the farming population of Eastern Europe did not suffer in the eighties; with greater scope for extensive cultivation and with very low wages, the farms in those countries were able to some extent to compete with the American farmers in supplying grain to Western Europe. But the time was to come when Eastern Europe too would be overtaken by the Malthusian Devil; after the turn of the century its unwanted millions swarmed across the Atlantic.

[1] See *Emigrationsutredningen*, Bilaga IX, 1909, p. 26.

Table 51. *Sweden: trade in agricultural produce, 1871–1900*

Annual averages	Imports (thousand kr.)	Exports (thousand kr.)	Export surplus (−) Import surplus (+) (thousand kr.)
1871–75	21,731	36,916	− 15,185
1876–80	34,497	39,370	− 4,873
1881–85	43,670	29,162	+ 14,508
1886–90	31,548	18,591	+ 12,957
1891–95	36,077	15,244	+ 20,833
1896–1900	43,265	4,143	+ 39,122

SOURCE: *Emigrationsutredningen*, Bilaga XIII, 1912, p. 41.

One or two examples may be briefly cited to show how the sweep of technical progress destroyed the obsolete elements of the old order in Europe, where the cumulative effect was especially severe in the early eighties. In the words of D. A. Wells,

the Bessemer rail, the modern steamship, and the Suez Canal have brought the wheatfields of Dakota and India, and the grazing lands of Texas, Colorado and Australia, and the Argentine Republic, nearer to the factory operatives in Manchester, England, than the farms of Illinois were before the war to the spindles and looms of New England.[1]

The harvester was introduced in the United States in 1872 and the binder in 1880. The fall in the cost of transporting wheat by rail in America over a distance of 1,500 miles in 1887 as compared with 1870–2 was equivalent to a reduction of eleven shillings a quarter on the cost of delivering the wheat in England; the acreage of land under wheat in England contracted by 40 % between 1869 and 1887. The average price of wheat in England in 1870–80 was 43 % higher than in 1886.

On the wheat farms of the Northwestern United States it was claimed in 1887 that, with wages at twenty-five dollars per month and board for permanent employés, wheat could be produced for forty cents per bushel; while in Rhenish Prussia, with wages at six dollars per month, the cost of production was reported to be eighty cents per bushel.[2]

The coming of cheap bread dealt a heavy blow to the agrarian economy of Europe; the crop failures of 1879, 1880 and 1881, compensated by record imports from the New World and India, aggravated the crisis and drove tens of thousands to emigrate. Not only was the number of people aged 20 to 30 especially large at that time but the means of subsistence for many of them was being taken away by the inexorable

[1] Op. cit. p. 91.   [2] Ibid. p. 59.

force of human invention. The railways which their ancestors in the fifties and sixties had crossed the Atlantic to build were now undermining the traditional livelihood of a new generation, and the floodgates of emigration were opening once again.

The last considerable influx of population into America beginning late in the nineties led to the most exhaustive investigation of the problem ever undertaken in any country—the Immigration Commission, the results of which were published in forty-two volumes in 1911–12. It found that in the industrial area east of the Mississippi and north of the Ohio and Potomac rivers 60 % of the total number of wage earners were of foreign birth and 39 % had come from Southern and Eastern Europe and Asia. Its conclusions on the subject-matter of this chapter are worth quoting at length.

It is not possible to determine definitely whether the recent rapid and unprecedented expansion of industry has been the cause of the recent influx of immigrants from southern and eastern Europe, or whether the existence of an available supply of cheap labor easily induced to immigrate was the cause of the industrial expansion. It is a possibility that if the demand for labor had not found so large a supply of cheap labor available, increased wages and better working conditions required to attract labor might have induced a continuation of immigration from northern and western Europe and the United Kingdom.... It is undoubtedly true that the expansion in all branches of industry between thirty and forty years ago was primarily responsible for the original entrance of the southern and eastern Europeans into the operating forces of the mines and manufacturing establishments. They were found, from the standpoint of the employer, to be tractable and uncomplaining. Although they were possessed of a low order of industrial efficiency, it was possible to use them in a more or less satisfactory way. Upon the ascertainment of this fact by the employers and with the realization of the existence of this large source of labor supply, a reversal of conditions occurred. The industrial expansion which had originally caused the immigration of southern and eastern Europeans was in turn stimulated by their presence, and new industrial undertakings were doubtless projected on the assumption of the continuing availability of this class of labor. At the same time, the influx of southern and eastern Europeans brought about conditions of employment under which there was no sufficient inducement to the races of Great Britain and northern Europe to continue to seek work in those industries. It may be said, therefore, that industrial expansion was the original reason for the employment of races of recent immigration, but that after the availability of this labor became known further industrial expansion became stimulated by the fact of this availability, the original cause thus becoming largely an effect of the conditions it had created.[1]

[1] United States Immigration Commission, *Abstract of Reports*, vol. I, Senate Document no. 747, 61st Congress, 3rd Session, 1911–12, pp. 493–4.

Having thus suggested that by the turn of the century the motive force was immigration and the effect industrial expansion, the Report goes on to describe the associated changes in the technique of production in those years.

An interesting point in this connection is the fact that it was possible to receive such a large body of employees of foreign birth into the American industrial system. The older immigrant labor supply was composed principally of persons who had had training and experience abroad in the industries which they entered after their arrival in the United States. English, German, Scottish and Irish immigrants in textile factories, iron and steel establishments, or in the coal mines, usually had been skilled workmen in these industries in their native lands and came to the United States in the expectation of higher wages and better working conditions. In the case of the more recent immigrants from southern and eastern Europe this condition of affairs has been reversed. Before coming to the United States the greater proportion were engaged in farming or unskilled labor and had no experience or training in manufacturing industry or mining. *As a consequence their employment in the mines and manufacturing plants of this country has been made possible only by the invention of mechanical devices and processes which have eliminated the skill and experience formerly required in a large number of occupations.* In bituminous coal mining, for example, the pick or hand miner was formerly an employee of skill and experience. He undercut the coal, drilled his own holes, fired his own shots and, together with his helper, loaded the coal which came down upon the cars, and was paid so much per ton for the entire operation. By the invention of the mining machine, however, the occupation of the pick miner has been largely done away with, thereby increasing the proportion of unskilled workmen who load coal on cars after it has been undercut and the holes drilled by machinery, and the coal knocked down by a blast set off by a shot firer specialized for that division of labor. Such work can readily be done, after a few days' apprenticeship, by recent immigrants who, before immigrating to the United States, had never seen a coal mine. The same situation is found in the cotton factories where unskilled and inexperienced immigrants can, after a brief training, operate the automatic looms and ring spinning frames which do the work formerly requiring skilled weavers and mule spinners. In the glass factories, also, which are engaged in the manufacture of bottles and window and plate glass, untrained immigrants, through the assistance of improved machinery, turn out the same products which in past years required the services of highly trained glass blowers. In the iron and steel plants and other branches of manufacturing similar inventions have made it possible to operate the plants with a much smaller proportion of skilled and specialized employees than was formerly the case. It is this condition of industrial affairs, as already stated, which has made it possible to give employment to the untrained, inexperienced, non-English-speaking immigrant of recent arrival in the United States.[1]

[1] Ibid. pp. 494–5 (my italic).

The findings of the Immigration Commission support the conclusions of our statistical analysis. The above quotation, however, is open to correction in one respect. Paul Douglas showed that the Commission was wrong in giving currency to the impression that the 'old' immigrants comprised a considerably larger proportion of skilled artisans than the 'new' immigrants; a comparison of these two streams of migration in the same period 1890–1909 was bound to be misleading.[1] There was a strong agrarian element in the movement from North Western Europe in the nineteenth century, for Ireland and Scandinavia were essentially agricultural countries and the rural exodus from Britain and Germany was not negligible. It is not correct to say that 'the older immigrant labor supply was composed principally of persons who had had training and experience abroad in the industries which they entered after their arrival in the United States', if by 'older immigrant labor supply' we mean people who came during the period ending in the nineties. The mass influx from Southern and Eastern Europe after 1899 was largely agricultural, and the Commission came to the fairly definite conclusion that this new population exercised a formative influence on the technique of production; the 'push' was predominant. The verdict of the lag analysis earlier in this chapter tended to suggest that the same was true of the agricultural element (for example the Irish and the Swedes) in the previous booms in transatlantic migration.

Nothing is more difficult than to find a quantitative measure of the course of invention through time. There can be no doubt that there have been fluctuations in the propensity to invent, and it would be most illuminating if these could be related to cycles in migration and investment. Fig. 36 plots the course of the number of patents granted for inventions in the United States from 1839 to 1913. Despite the obvious shortcomings of a series of this kind stretching over such a long period, the impression it gives is worth noting. There was a very sharp rise from 1864 to 1867 (from 4,638 to 12,301), coinciding with the second wave of immigration; from 1867 to 1881 the number of patents granted was stationary at about 12,000 to 14,000; then in the eighties we find another prominent increase in two steps, 1880–3 and 1888–90, corresponding to the double peak in the third great inflow of population. Again there is a phase of stagnation from 1890 to 1898 (25,322 to 20,404) followed by a marked rise between 1898 and 1903 (20,404 to 31,046) coinciding with the beginning of the invasion of migrants from Southern and Eastern Europe. It seems that the outstanding bursts of invention took place at the same time as the big upswings in immigration.

To conclude this survey of historical evidence we turn to an example from the field of internal migration—the absorption of surplus rural

---

[1] See Chapter IX, p. 153, n. 1.

labour in the rapidly expanding industries of Britain between the early fifties and the mid-seventies. Agriculture was passing through a phase of declining profits, shown by the fact that from 1850 to 1875 money wage rates rose by an annual average of 1·44 % and the price of agricultural produce by only 0·31 %. The index number of manpower in agriculture fell from 100 in 1851 to 75 in 1871. The workers who left the countryside went in large numbers into engineering and ship-building; this ample supply was one reason why between 1852 and 1877 money wage rates in those industries rose by only 27 % whereas in the

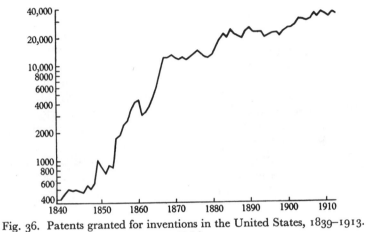

Fig. 36. Patents granted for inventions in the United States, 1839–1913.
Source: Table 130.

cotton industry they went up by 75 %. What was happening to the technique of production during these years? In textiles there was a relative increase in the demand for skilled workers, a factor which pushed up the average money wage rate. On the other hand, in engineering and shipbuilding the methods adopted involved widespread dilution of labour and a corresponding decline in the relative importance of skilled grades.[1] It was, as we have seen, a period which saw a con-siderable amount of internal migration; and it is significant that large detachments of the agricultural reserve army went into those heavy industries which were adopting technical methods entailing a wide use of low grade labour.

[1] For the facts and figures used in this paragraph see Paul Rousseaux, *Les Mouve-ments de Fond de l'Économie Anglaise, 1800–1913*, Louvain, 1938, pp. 129–33.

6. CONCLUSION

The analysis suggests the following tentative propositions.

(1) The outstanding waves of immigration coincided with minor secular upswings in the rate of economic growth of the United States.

(2) The timing of these waves was determined by the births cycle in Europe together with the impact of disturbing innovations (particularly on agriculture).

(3) Building activity in the United States always lagged after inflow of population (except in the seventies).

(4) The great injection of cheap labour from South Eastern Europe after the turn of the century induced a 'widening' of the capital structure of the United States, enabled the country to take maximum advantage of the technical innovations of that time, and established the basis of its modern economic power. It is probable that previous injections (for example those culminating in the fifties and the eighties) also exercised a similar influence on the technical coefficients in the American economy and that 'deepening' of the capital structure occurred in periods when the rate of increase in population was subnormal.

(5) There were minor secular swings in induced investment in fixed capital equipment, and they were propelled by the expansive influence of periodic inflows of population.

CHAPTER XI

MIGRATION AND INVERSE BUILDING CYCLES

I. THE INVERSE RELATION

An examination of time series for the seventy years ending in 1913 shows that spurts in building in the United States were preceded by waves of incoming population, and that in Great Britain upward and downward movements in emigration tended to be accompanied after a short lag respectively by downward and upward movements in building. This inverse relation raises intriguing questions concerning the interaction of the forces governing the level of activity in the United Kingdom and the United States.

Fig. 37 sets out the course of the two building cycles for the period 1830–1948. For the United States I have used Dr J. R. Riggleman's series of Annual Building Permits a head in terms of the 1913 dollar, and New Construction Expenditure (at 1913 prices) a head as from 1924. For the United Kingdom an attempt has been made to trace the fluctuations of building over the period 1830–1948 from the information that could be found.[1]

The inverse relation between the swings of British and American building is clearly marked from 1847 to 1910, but it is not apparent in the years 1830–47 or in the second quarter of the twentieth century. The statistical material for the early years is not very satisfactory, but the two series have a common peak at 1836 and a common trough at 1843. Building in the two countries seems to have moved in unison between 1830 and 1847. From 1847 to 1920 the cycles have the following time-shape.

Table 52. *Peaks and troughs of British and American building cycles, 1847–1920*

British building cycle		American building cycle	
Peak	Trough	Peak	Trough
	1855	1853	
1863			1864
	1869	1871	
1876			1878
	1886	1890	
1899			1900
	1912	1909	
1920			1918

[1] A description of sources and method is given in Appendix 3.

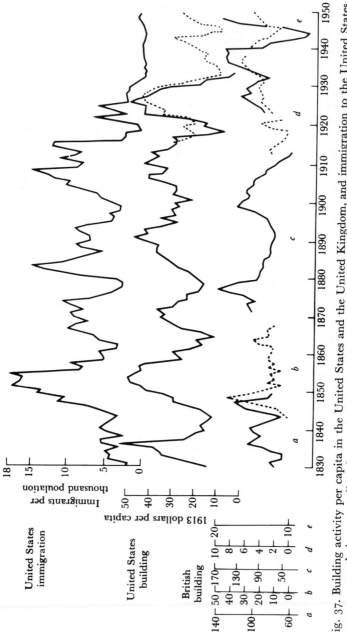
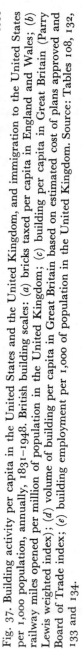

Fig. 37. Building activity per capita in the United States and the United Kingdom, and immigration to the United States per 1,000 population, annually, 1831–1948. British building scales: (*a*) bricks taxed per capita in England and Wales; (*b*) railway miles opened per million of population in the United Kingdom; (*c*) building per capita in Great Britain (Parry Lewis weighted index); (*d*) volume of building per capita in Great Britain based on estimated cost of plans approved and Board of Trade index; (*e*) building employment per 1,000 of population in the United Kingdom. Source: Tables 108, 132, 133 and 134.

The First World War did not affect the economy of the United States as much as it did that of Great Britain. The American building cycle descended sharply from a high point in 1912 and a depression was to be expected even if war had not come; what the war did was to cause a very low point to be reached in 1918. The recovery in British activity between 1912 and 1914 was interrupted by the war, during which building remained at a very low ebb. The significant feature of the period 1923 to 1950 is that building activity in the two countries went up and down together as follows:

Table 53. *Peaks and troughs of British and American building cycles, 1920–44*

British building		American building	
Peak	Trough	Peak	Trough
1927		1925	
	1932		1933
1939		1942	
	1944		1944

The peaks and troughs correspond fairly well; the only serious discrepancy—a peak in 1939 in Great Britain and 1942 in the United States—is due to the fact that America did not enter the Second World War until 1941. We may conclude that the inverse relation which characterized British and American building for over seven decades ceased to hold after the First World War.

A key to the explanation lies in the role of international migration. In the first phase, 1830–46, the United States was an undeveloped agricultural country where British capital was exercising a prominent influence and immigration was still comparatively small. It could almost be described as an oversea extension of the British economy, and the fluctuations of enterprise in both countries were subject to the same impulses.

The second phase begins significantly in 1847, the year in which the first great wave of transatlantic migration started. From then until the eve of the First World War the process of interaction seems to have been as follows. A major influx of population, accompanied by capital imports, induces a boom in construction in the United States; meanwhile the upturn of emigration and foreign investment in Great Britain is accompanied after a short lag by a fall in the volume of building. When a relatively large number of people are leaving the country, internal mobility is low, and there is a tendency for the number of empty houses to increase and for rents to decline. During these periods the expansive impulse coming from the export sector is more than offset by sluggishness in home construction; the net effect is a decline in real income a head relative to trend. The time must come in the United States when the building boom hits the ceiling and a downturn is unavoidable. This is accompanied by a decrease in immigration and capital imports; the centre of activity in Britain now moves from the export sector to domestic capital formation, and it is her turn to receive a fillip from a relative increase in population. The number of empty houses in Great Britain becomes less, rents rise, abundant loanable funds flow into home construction. The inducement to build at home is heightened in such periods by the increase in internal mobility which is associated with a decline in emigration. The expansive force of this induced investment is more potent than the depressing effect of the foreign trade multiplier; hence the rise in real income a head relative to trend. This is a simplified account of the mechanism; in order to be more accurate it will be necessary to take each upswing and downswing separately in the light of a detailed analysis of lags. There is one point which perhaps calls for explanation. It might be objected that when, as a result of the births cycle, a country is in a phase of population pressure, this extra population should induce a rise in building activity in that country, but, according to the above analysis, such phases are characterized by a rise in emigration and a fall in building. It could be argued that, if building is to slump at a time when the number of young adults suddenly rises, emigration must remove more than the excess of young adults over the normal rate of growth in those age groups. This objection may be met as follows. Some of the excess births of twenty years before (the cause of the population pressure) will exert an influence on building in about twelve or fifteen years, when children begin to earn, but cannot have an appreciable effect on emigration until later. It is not unreasonable for high emigration to coincide with low building activity even when the number emigrating is less than that *addition* to the number of people now aged about twenty which arises from the abnormally high births twenty years ago.

The third phase, 1923–50, had one feature in common with the first; immigration into the United States was again negligible. The wheel had turned full circle and America had taken the place of Britain as the dominant power in the Atlantic economy. She had also become the world's leading exporter of capital. No longer was the rhythm of her economic growth to be influenced in the slightest by injections of population from outside. The sequence of economic events in the last thirty-five years has of course been distorted by two world wars and to that extent the time-shape of investment in Great Britain and the United States would necessarily tend to be uniform. Another reason was the change in the balance of economic power within the Atlantic economy. The scale of American investment or disinvestment was such that it dragged Britain in its wake; Britain had become very much the dependent variable. Just as in the early part of the nineteenth century— but for very different reasons—the fluctuations in the volume of construction in the two countries were in unison.

2. FLUCTUATIONS IN FOREIGN TRADE AND BUILDING

The volume of British exports (and of American imports) in the period 1840–1913 shows minor secular fluctuations corresponding to those in

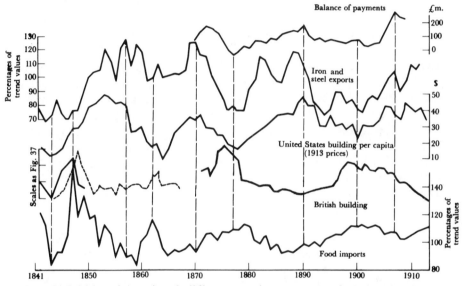

Fig. 38. British and American building per capita, percentage deviations from trend of British food imports and iron and steel exports, 1841–1913, and British balance of payments, 1870–1913. Source: Tables 103, 108, 113, 132 and 135.

railway development in the United States and British and European immigration into the United States. We shall now bring the volume of British imports into the picture.

Fig. 38 sets out the deviations from trend for British imports of food-stuffs and exports of iron and steel goods, and British and American building activity, 1840–1913. In addition, for the years 1870–1910 the course of the British balance of payments on income account is given.

During the entire period there is an inverse relation between the swings in imports and in exports, and there is a marked correspondence between the time-shape of imports and that of home building. From 1843 to 1847 building and imports rise sharply while exports decline; from 1847 to 1855 building and imports fall together, while exports increase steeply from 1846 to 1853. The recovery of building and imports in 1856 was upset by the American crisis of 1857, which had a profound monetary impact; this break in confidence accelerated the descent of American building activity and delayed the revival of British activity until 1859. Building reached a peak in 1863, and imports in 1862 (with exports at a low point); the course of events was disturbed by the American Civil War and the blockade of the South, causing an abnormal fall in imports to 1865. British building proceeded from its peak in 1863 to a low trough in 1871, and imports also register a low point in 1870 which is to be regarded as the minor secular trough corresponding to the minor secular peak in exports in the same year.

From the subnormal level of 1870 imports rose to a peak in 1879, and building reached a maximum three years earlier in 1876; meanwhile, exports reacted violently downwards to a very depressed state in 1876–9. Building and imports both display a long-drawn-out trough in 1885–8, with signs of an upturn in 1889, whereas exports advanced rapidly from the low point in 1879 to a maximum in 1888–9 after a well-marked cyclical interruption. Building and imports reach their next peak together in 1899, and exports, after reacting very sharply to the Baring crisis of 1890, recovered slightly in 1895 and 1896, and then registered a low point in 1901. After the turn of the century building activity receded to a trough in 1912, accompanied by imports until 1908; exports went up strongly from 1901 to 1913.

The time-shape is summarized in Table 54.

Table 54. *United Kingdom: peaks and troughs of cycles in building, food imports and iron and steel exports, 1847–1913*

Building activity		Volume of imports of foodstuffs		Volume of exports of iron and steel goods	
Peak	Trough	Peak	Trough	Peak	Trough
1847		1847			1846
	1855		1855	1857	
1863		1862			1861
	1869		1870	1869–70	
1876		1879			1876–9
	1886		1886	1888–9	
1899		1899–1901			1901
	1912		1908	1910–13	

As one would expect, the balance of payments on income account (estimates of which are available from 1865 onward) displays a clear minor secular swing, with peaks in 1872, 1890 and 1912–13, and troughs in 1877 and 1902. In 1877, when the import curve is near a peak and the export curve at its lowest, the balance of payments is almost negative; at the same time building activity in the United States is in a trough and building activity in Great Britain is at a maximum. At the end of the eighties a maximum for exports, American building and the balance of payments is accompanied by a minimum for British building and imports. Then, about the turn of the century, the relationships characteristic of the late seventies repeat themselves; and the situation just before 1913 resembled the late eighties.

It is of interest to relate the movements of British building and imports to those of gold in one or two early phases of the period under review. In 1847, with a peak in imports and a trough in exports, it is not surprising that there was a crisis. The gold reserve dwindled to £1,606,000 and the bank rate was raised to 8%. In 1852, with low imports and high exports, the reserve was up to £12,000,000 and the bank rate was at 2–2½%. The real export surplus in 1857 looked even more healthy, and yet there was a serious crisis. It was caused by an American collapse at the end of August 1857, the news of which took a fortnight to reach England and had a shattering effect on the financial community. There was a big outflow of gold and a 10% bank rate was reinforced by a Treasury Letter designed to allay panic. Money was being made exceptionally dear at a time when home investment as shown by the construction index was in the depth of depression; the slight recovery which had started in 1856 was nipped in the bud and the slump in investment was intensified in 1857 and 1858. The reserve, which had fallen as low as £581,000 on November 12, 1857, was replenished until it was £13,990,000 on March 9, 1859.

The inquest on the crisis of 1847 brought out a revealing clash of views on the internal implications of Bank of England policy. Cayley, a member of the Commons Committee of Inquiry in 1848, asked James Morris, Governor of the Bank of England, whether he thought that 'under the present system of things, the system is safest under a comparatively small amount of imports'. The Governor replied: 'No, I do not mean to say that; we are speaking of a year (1847) in which there has been a sudden and an enormous import of food.' Cayley continued: 'But when there is a great increase of consumption, which has been produced by an increase of employment of labour, that endangers the condition of the circulation?' Morris replied: 'If there has been a very greatly increased consumption, necessitating a very large importation of foreign commodities, unless we have manufactures or securities to export in payment, the balance must be paid for in the precious metals. The importation of 1847 has been very much larger than the exportation of goods, and therefore the balance has been paid for in bullion.' Again Cayley inquired: 'A diminished power of consumption on the part of the public would have been rather advantageous than otherwise to the system of circulation?' And Morris answered: 'A diminished consumption would have checked importation.' Cayley seized on this and asked: 'Then the more privation the public was subjected to, the safer the system of circulation?' At this point the Governor dropped out of the argument and the Deputy Governor came in with the remark: 'It is necessary sometimes for the public to deny themselves, or for the country to deny itself, the consumption of certain foreign commodities, in order to restore the circulation to a proper state.' One would have thought that Cayley had made his point effectively, but he was determined to hammer it home. He asked, 'Do you think it would be safe, in the present state of European excitement, under the present state of trade, and with a great number of persons unemployed, to very materially thwart the revival of employment?' The Governor's reply, which was hardly a model of clarity, was: 'I do not see how it is to act in that way.' Putting it all in a nutshell, the questioner then said: 'Do you think the system of circulation should be preserved at any cost to the employment of the people?' To this the banker retorted: 'I think it is desirable that the circulation should be placed on such a footing as that it should expand and contract in the same way as a metallic currency would do: I cannot vary from that.'[1]

The essence of the conflict between full employment and solvency was evident in these exchanges of over a century ago; Cayley's concern about the level of employment and the relation to it of the rate of interest had quite a modern ring. Perhaps it is comforting to be reminded that Great Britain has been troubled periodically by her balance of payments ever since she began her career as a great trading nation. Every time home construction and imports reached a peak the country could expect to have a deficit in the balance on income account; with the regularity of what might almost be described as a minor secular cycle, trouble occurred in 1847, 1861, 1878–9 and 1899–1900. These were times of abnormal gold exports and the average bank rate was as follows: 1847, thirty-one weeks between 5 and 8%; 1861, first half, 6%; September 1878 to February 1879, 4·7%; September 1899 to February 1900, 4·4%. But these were not the only occasions when gold was lost and money was made dear. It would be instructive to examine in detail how many times the Bank of England, with its eye on its reserve and on nothing else, compressed effective demand and manufactured unemployment when the economic condition of the country needed quite different treatment. But this is not the place to pursue that interesting theme.

[1] *Report of the Secret Committee of the House of Commons on Commercial Distress*, 1848, questions 3424–7, 3442 and 3445.

The inverse relation between the deviations from trend of British imports and exports and of British and American building activity must be part of the larger phenomenon indicated by the inverse nature of the minor secular fluctuations in the rate of British and American economic growth in the period 1845–1913. Perhaps a closer look at some of the upswings and downswings will yield one or two clues.

3. AN ANALYSIS OF SEQUENCES

An attempt will now be made to see how the two sectors—Export and Home Construction—acted on the general level of activity in the British economy between 1860 and 1910. Without much more detailed research it will not be possible to attain conclusive results, but it seems worth making a preliminary exploration with the aid of the instruments available.

The Export Sector is represented by the following indices: Exports of finished iron and steel goods, emigration of British citizens to the United States, and railway construction and new building in the United States. The Home Construction Sector is represented by share prices up to 1870, home investment after 1870, building, imports of foodstuffs, and an index of empty property in London. The general level of activity is indicated by the volume of employment (inverted percentage of the number of trade unionists recorded as unemployed). The monetary factor is shown by the course of the interior demand for gold. From 1870 onward we have the average rate of real wages, real national income a head, and the wages bill as a proportion of the national income. The statistics used are annual, and the analysis is based on deviations of original data from trend, except where otherwise stated.

The object is to find out in what sequence the variables moved in the course of the minor secular fluctuations in the British economy from 1860 to 1910. Although the moving average through the deviations from trend is for some purposes a good enough representation of this type of fluctuation, it is safer to rely on the deviations themselves. A downturn is located in the year after the highest value and an upturn in the year after the lowest value. There is no question of arbitrarily selecting certain peaks and troughs; the minor secular swing is apparent in all series and the words 'highest' and 'lowest' have a definite meaning in terms of that fluctuation. The series are plotted in Fig. 39 and the downturns and upturns are set out in Fig. 40.

We shall first look at the period 1860 to the early seventies. In 1862 there was a revival in emigration, in 1863 a downturn in imports, and in 1864 a downturn in building and share prices; then in 1865 came

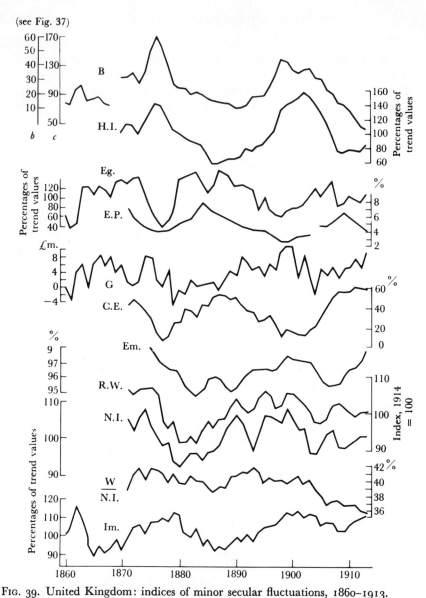

FIG. 39. United Kingdom: indices of minor secular fluctuations, 1860–1913.
  B. Railway miles added per million of population (to 1868) and index of new building per capita (from 1870): Table 132. H.I. British home investment, percentage deviations from trend: Table 100. Eg. Emigration of citizens to U.S.A., percentage deviations from trend: Table 106. E.P. Empty property in London (%): Table 138. G. Interior demand for gold (£ million): Table 138. C.E. Capital exports as % of total investment: Table 113. Em. Level of employment (nine-year moving average): Table 112. R.W. Index of average real wages (1914 = 100): Table 111. N.I. National income per capita at 1900 prices, percentage deviations from trend: Table 110. $\dfrac{W}{N.I.}$ Wages bill as % of national income: Table 112. Im. Volume of imports of foodstuffs, percentage deviations from trend: Table 135.

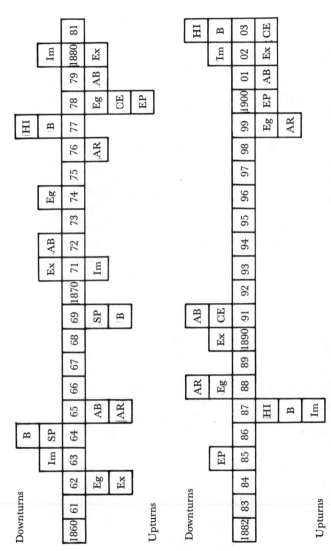

Fig. 40. United Kingdom: minor secular upturns and downturns, 1860–1903.

British Series: See Fig. 39 for definition of **B, H.I., Eg., E.P., C.E., Im.**
Ex. Volume of exports of iron and steel goods, percentage deviations from trend:
Table 103. S.P. Index of share prices, percentage deviations from trend: Table 99.

American Series: A.B. Index of new building, percentage deviations from trend:
Table 109. A.R. Miles of railway track built, percentage deviations from trend:
Table 98.

an upturn in exports and in American building and railway construction. The slump in home investment came to an end with a recovery in share prices in 1869 followed by a rise in imports and a decline in exports in 1871; in the following year American railway and building activity turned down and British building revived. The balance of payments (capital exports) passed its peak in 1874 and emigration in 1875.

The sequences in the fluctuation from the late seventies to the early years of the century were briefly as follows. A revival in railway investment in America in 1876 was followed in 1877 by a fall in building and home investment and a rise in emigration, empty property, foreign investment and the balance of payments. A year later American building recovered and in 1880 there was a downturn of British imports and an upturn in exports. The next phase was inaugurated by a change in the domestic sector—a fall in the index of empty property in 1885; 1888 saw a recovery in home investment, building and the general level of employment, accompanied by a downturn in emigration and American railway construction, after which came changes in imports, exports, foreign investment and American building. The lead in the last phase was taken by an upward movement in emigration and American railway investment in 1899; two years later activity in the domestic sector began to decline; American building revived in 1901 and in 1902 and 1903 came the reactions in foreign trade and capital exports.

Are there any uniformities to be observed? One hesitates to draw any conclusions, if only because of the obvious limitations of annual data. There is, however, a suggestion that in this period upturns in Home Construction preceded downturns in the Export Sector, whereas upturns in the Export Sector (American railway investment and/or emigration) preceded downturns in Home Construction. With one exception turning-points in food imports tended to lag after changes in home investment; and, again with one exception, turning-points in exports tended to accompany or to follow changes in emigration and American railway investment.

The monetary data may now be brought into the picture in a comparison between the course of the interior demand for gold and that of building. The two indices run together from a relatively low point in 1861 to a peak in the mid-sixties, then down to a trough in the early seventies. For six years out of the decade beginning in 1879 there were net gold exports while building languished in a chronic depression and capital exports as a proportion of total investment rose from 28% in 1880 to 56% in 1888.

The movements of the monetary index reflect not only the demand for money for transactions but also the demand for idle balances to satisfy the liquidity motive and for gold as an industrial material. If we look at the index from year to year we are struck by the anomaly that interior demand is sometimes highest when investment activity is low and vice versa. One reason, given by Professor Hawtrey, is that, in the days before modern branch banking and swift communications, '...every country bank had to have an independent reserve of notes and coins, its funds on deposit or at call in London being too remote to be relied on for unexpected demands'.[1] When money was cheap currency would pile up in the provinces; when it was dear there would be a flow to London.[2] Another reason was the influence of financial panics. For example, the aftermath of the collapse of Overend, Gurney and Company in 1866 caused interior demand to soar till 1868 while building activity was slumping. The sharp increase in interior demand in 1878 was due to the failure of the City of Glasgow Bank; on that occasion bank rate went to 6% while building activity was falling precipitously. The Baring crisis of November 1890 was accompanied by a considerable peak in interior demand and a sharp set-back to the strong recovery in home investment which had occurred in 1888 and 1889. Another point to remember is that the rise in money wages in an investment upswing would tend to be followed after the downturn by a short period during which workers' cash balances would show a lag. Despite the short-term consequences of the factors just mentioned, it is interesting to note the harmony between the minor secular swings of home investment and interior demand for gold, as shown by their moving averages.

Finally, we come to the fluctuation in the general level of activity. From a condition of full employment in 1872–3 real national income a head and real wages declined to a trough about 1884, then rose to a high level in the late nineties and fell in the first years of the century. The moving average of the general level of employment pursues a similar course. The wages bill as a proportion of the national income is inverse to capital exports as a proportion of total investment. Capital exports rose from 10% in 1877 to 57% in 1887, while the relative share of wage-earners fell from just under 42% in 1875 to a little over 39% in 1886; capital exports declined from 56% in 1888 to 37% in 1893, and the relative share of labour grew from 39% in 1886 to almost 43% in 1893. The most striking divergence is found in the last years of the period; from 1903 to 1912 capital exports as a proportion of total investment went up from 19 to 60%, whereas the wages bill as a proportion of the national income dropped from 41 to 36%. We conclude that real national income a head, real wages, the level of employment

[1] R. G. Hawtrey, *A Century of Bank Rate*, London, Longmans, 1938, p. 51.
[2] Ibid. pp. 50–5.

and the wage-earners' relative share of the national product exhibited a minor secular fluctuation in unison with that of the Home Construction Sector and inverse to that of the Export Sector.[1]

4. CONCLUSION

This investigation proceeded from the hypothesis that the economic growth of Great Britain and the United States can best be analysed by regarding these countries as parts of the Atlantic economy. The inverse relation between the building cycles in the two countries from 1847 to the First World War is well established, and it is a phenomenon which the theory of fluctuation must explain. The close correspondence between the movements of British building and other strategic series lends support to the view that the building cycle is not a peculiarity to be classified with pig and textile cycles, but is itself an expression of a long cycle in fixed capital equipment. All the recognized estimates of British building and home investment in the period 1870–1913 have a similar shape, whereas American building activity, total construction and real national income a head trace almost an identical pattern in the last half-century.

[1] In the light of the above analysis there is perhaps some reason to be doubtful about one or two of the generalizations on 'The Great Depression' made by Professor W. W. Rostow in his book, *British Economy of the Nineteenth Century*, Oxford, 1948. On pp. 67–8, after quoting various statistical estimates of the amounts of new British enterprise at home and abroad for 1870–5 and 1880–5, Professor Rostow writes: 'However inaccurate these statistics may be, however limited the area of new investment they cover, however dubious any quantitative statements drawn from them, they do attest to a shift away from capital export towards new investment at home.' The qualifying clauses are very strong and perhaps rightly so. I do not think it can be denied that between 1880 and 1887–8 there was a marked expansion in British foreign investment accompanied by a corresponding decline in home investment. Since capital exports in 1888 were 56% of total investment—even higher than the peak of 50% in 1872, it is justifiable to say, as Professor Rostow does, that 'the central causal force in the Great Depression was the relative cessation of foreign lending' (p. 88)? In another passage on the period 1873–86 he writes: 'The picture which emerges, then, is one of a society in which internal investment, devoted to the refinement and increase of the community's capital stock, rose relatively to total new investment, increasing labour's absolute and relative shares in the national income' (p. 107). I find it difficult to reconcile this generalization with the fact that home investment fell from 40% above trend in 1887 to 41% below trend in 1887 and that the wages bill as a proportion of the national income declined from nearly 43% in 1875 to a little over 39% in 1886. There does appear to have been a rise in labour's relative share between 1886 and 1893. Sir Arthur Bowley has warned of the hazards of these statistics, and perhaps it is unwise to base any argument on them. I do suggest, however, that on the major question of what happened to home and foreign investment in the period under review, an analysis of deviations from trend is likely to be less inaccurate than a comparison of absolute figures at various dates.

There has been a tendency to look upon swings in building activity as if they were a kind of weather cycle external to the business cycle; if a downturn in the latter coincides with very bad weather, so much the worse for it. More promising results could be obtained by recognizing that there has been a fluctuation in the production of fixed capital equipment, with a span corresponding to that of the building cycle.[1]

[1] See two important articles by W. Isard, 'Transport Development and Building Cycles', *Quarterly Journal of Economics*, vol. LVII, no. 4, November 1942, pp. 90–112, and 'A Neglected Cycle: the Transport-Building Cycle', *Review of Economic Statistics*, vol. XXIV, no. 4, November 1942, pp. 149–58.

CHAPTER XII

THE ORIGIN AND IMPACT OF
AMERICAN RESTRICTIONS

I. PUBLIC OPINION ON RESTRICTIONS

Whenever the tide of immigration was high, certain elements in American society loudly denounced the alien invader. In the fifties, the 'Order of the Star Spangled Banner' was whipping up public feeling particularly against the Irish and Germans; similar sentiments found expression at the end of the eighties in the American Protective Association, which was fiercely anti-Catholic; then, in 1915, came the Ku Klux Klan in defence of 'hundred per cent Americanism' against Jews, Catholics, Negroes and all foreigners. Spectacular though these outbursts were, they never reflected the bulk of public opinion; the real wishes of the majority are to be seen in the Acts passed by Congress.

It was not until 1882 that the first Federal law on immigration was enacted, introducing the head tax and debarring criminals and feeble-minded persons. This was followed by Acts to keep out other undesirable categories such as polygamists, anarchists and prostitutes. Even when the flood of 'new' immigrants was at its height, the only serious issue before the Congress was whether a literacy test should be imposed, since it was estimated that one-third of the people from Southern and Eastern Europe could not read. The attempt to introduce a reading test was vetoed by the White House three times, and Congress had to wait until 1917 before it was strong enough to override the veto. The great tradition, symbolized by the Statue of Liberty, that America was a haven for the oppressed masses of the Old World, remained dominant even in the early years of the century.

In Chapter IV attention was drawn to the contradictory motives inspiring Federal legislation in the eighties. On the one hand, there were Acts requiring that the new settler must be physically and mentally able to make his own way in competition with Americans; on the other, the Contract Labor Laws made it illegal for a foreigner to come in under an agreement to perform a particular job. The latter legislation, in so far as it would stop the bringing in of strike-breakers, appealed strongly to the trade unions. The inconsistency between the two sets of laws was resolved by an acquiescence in the evasion of the spirit of the Contract Labor legislation, the fundamental reason for which is perhaps to be found in the changes in social structure noted in Chapter IX. The well-organized, relatively skilled workers of Northern European stock were finding that the invasion of low-grade labour from Southern Europe, far from injuring them, was contributing to their own prosperity. The aristocracy of labour could avoid the social disadvantages by living apart in their own communities while enjoying the undoubted economic advantages of being a non-competing group.

If there was a growing conviction on the eve of the First World War that immigration should be curtailed, it was the view of the millions of unskilled labourers who were seeing their real wages falling at a time of unparalleled economic expansion. Even so, there are convincing reasons for thinking that, had it not been for the powerful upsurge of nationalism in the United States as a result of her participation in the First World War, the immigration problem would have been disposed of by the adoption of the literacy test in 1917. What happened was one of those sudden changes in public sentiment motivated by fear. Within a few months of the end of the war Europeans began to arrive in large numbers, and shipping companies were quoted in Congress as saying that no less than ten million passengers were waiting for transport. The vision of this formidable host fleeing from a continent in the throes of political upheaval destroyed the optimistic attitudes of pre-war days. Organizations as powerful as the American Federation of Labor and the representatives of ex-servicemen demanded exclusion; the post-war slump of 1920–1 reinforced the conviction of the American unskilled worker that the only hope of advancement for himself and his children was to close the doors.

Such was the ferment of opinion which led to the Act of May 17, 1921, restricting each country to an annual quota equal to 3 % of the number of persons born in that country enumerated in the United States at the 1910 Census. Under this system the maximum amount of immigration permitted each year would be about 357,000, one-third of the number admitted in 1913. The Quota Act of 1924 altered the formula to 2 % of the number born in each country resident in the United States at the time of the 1890 Census.[1] This was a much more drastic discrimination against people from Southern and Eastern Europe, and reduced the aggregate immigration to be allowed each year to about 162,000. On July 1, 1929, the system was again changed, so that the quota was determined on the basis of the distribution of the white population of the United States in 1920 by national origins, and this made the annual maximum about 153,000. One of the main

---

[1] For the provisions of the 1924 Act see the 1925 Report of the United States Commissioner General of Immigration. The Quota legislation did not apply to native-born citizens of Canada, Newfoundland, Cuba, Mexico and the independent countries of South and Central America.

beliefs underlying this legislation was that the cultural unity of America had to be safeguarded and that the nation could not go on trying to assimilate excessive infusions of alien stock.

2. INTERNAL REPERCUSSIONS

Following on previous analysis, it will be interesting to begin by looking closely at the relation between population and building. Some monthly series for the United States for the period 1919–30 are given in Fig. 41, namely, the value of all construction contracts, the value of residential construction contracts, and net alien immigration. The series have been adjusted for seasonal influences and are plotted so that the construction values for January 1921 are above that of immigration for June 1919 (the latter preceding the former by nineteen months).

There is a marked correspondence between immigration and residential construction nineteen months later. We found that in the years 1887–1901 immigration from Europe preceded American building activity by two years (correlation coefficient 0·826); it is evident that the same lag persisted when population was flowing in again after the war. The rise in immigration from July 1919 to December 1921 is echoed in the upward course of construction (total as well as residential) from January 1921 to August 1923—a lag of nineteen months. The sharp jump in arrivals in October 1920 must have been in anticipation of restrictive action by Congress, and the sudden rise between May and June 1922 was no doubt a result of the extension of the Act of May 1921 beyond June 30, 1922, with an amendment imposing on shipping companies a fine of $200 and a surrender of passage money for each alien brought to the United States in contravention of the Act. Significantly the number arriving between July 1922 and February 1923 was stationary. This flattening out preceded the short downswing in construction by eighteen months. The plans of contractors would be determined partly by recent additions to population and partly by anticipated increases in the near future. The entry into the country at a rising rate in early 1922 induced expansion in building activity in late 1923; but once the flow of population became constant for a few months entrepreneurs would not only have reason to fear an imminent decrease in the rate but would also find that construction already begun was more than adequate to meet the steadied inflow. Hence a decline in new contracts awarded.

Mid-1923 saw a panic-driven rush to enter the country before the second Quota Act came into operation. The corresponding rise in building came sixteen months later and, after a short relapse, it went up to a very high point after a lag of twenty-eight months. The influx in 1923 was so big that a longer time may have been necessary for the building industry to cater for it. Residential building traces a well-marked short cycle from August 1925 to February 1928, the downswing

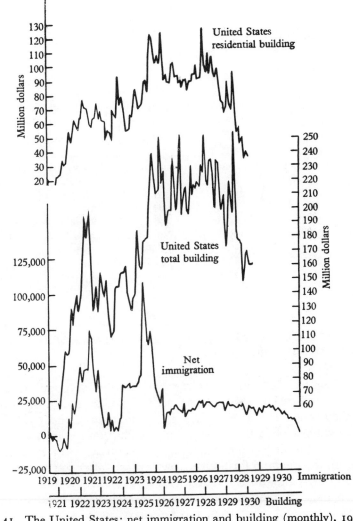

Fig. 41. The United States: net immigration and building (monthly), 1919–30.
Source: Tables 136 and 137.

of which seems to be related to the sharp fall of immigration after the Act of 1924. The recovery during 1927 is probably explained by the considerable increase in internal migration which was one of the consequences of the barriers erected against foreign labour; another factor was the income elasticity of demand for housing during the cyclical boom of the twenties which may well have contributed to the recovery in 1927–8.

The statistics of the migration of farm population within the United States in the years 1920–30 are worth noting.

Table 55. *The United States: internal migration of farm population, 1920–30*

Year	Farm population on Jan. 1	Change through natural increase	Change through migration		
			Arrivals from non-farm areas	Departures for non-farm areas	Net farm to non-farm migration
	(thousands)	(thousands)	(thousands)	(thousands)	(thousands)
1920	31,614	485	560	896	− 336
1921	31,763	550	759	1,323	− 564
1922	31,749	518	1,115	2,252	− 1,137
1923	31,130	494	1,355	2,162	− 807
1924	30,817	500	1,581	2,068	− 487
1925	30,830	491	1,336	2,038	− 702
1926	30,619	458	1,427	2,334	− 907
1927	30,170	475	1,705	2,162	− 457
1928	30,188	454	1,698	2,120	− 422
1929	30,220	426	1,604	2,081	− 477
1930	30,169	377	1,740	2,065	− 325

SOURCE: U.S. Department of Commerce, *Historical Statistics of the United States, 1789–1945*, Washington, 1949, p. 31.

According to these estimates the net transfer of population from farming to industrial areas in the years 1921 to 1929 amounted to nearly 6,000,000. It was especially heavy in 1922–3 and 1925–6, and there is evidence that the majority of the migrants were native-born Americans. This large-scale influx into urban areas was responsible for keeping up the demand for housing particularly after the passing of the Quota Act of 1924, and if it acted with the same lag as immigration it may also help to explain the shape of the curve of residential construction between August 1925 and February 1928.

The extent to which native-born Americans and their families figured among the internal migrants probably led to a demand for better-quality houses. Internal migration differs from net immigration as an inducement to investment in that its expansive effect in certain areas is partly offset by slackness in others. Although residential construction comprised a quarter of total gross investment in the boom of the twenties, the needs of the community were far from being met when the downturn took place. According to George Soule,

no method was devised...by which city dwellers in the lower brackets of income could be enabled to enjoy new housing, and they continued to occupy—or overcrowd—slum tenements and the cast-off dwellings of others. The housing boom tapered off through lack of sufficient effective demand long before decent living quarters were provided for a substantial percentage of the population.[1]

It is arguable that the sudden diminution in new population took the heart out of housing investment and that its early downturn was bound to have an unsettling effect on the general level of activity.

The Quota not only caused a high rate of internal mobility (for example, the movement of large numbers of Negroes to the industrial North) but it also made the United States a very attractive labour market for citizens of Canada and South American countries, for they were not covered by the Restriction Acts. In the period July 1, 1921 to June 30, 1927, it is estimated that net recorded immigration from Canada and Newfoundland exceeded the pre-war rate (1907–14) by 465,000, and the net number of Mexican immigrants exceeded the pre-war rate by 206,000. The number of people emigrating from the United States from 1923 on was well under 100,000 a year, whereas in the years 1912–14 it had been three times as big. It is significant that the net absorption of aliens in the years ended June 1923 and 1924 was at the rate of 536,000 a year which was not very much below the rate of 698,000 in 1912 and 1913. But for the Quota the country would undoubtedly have received during the twenties a wave of immigration comparable to that of the early years of the century.

3. REACTIONS ON INTERNATIONAL MIGRATION

In the years 1900–10 the population of the United States had grown by 6,243,000 through immigration and 8,680,000 through natural increase; in the decade 1920–30 immigration contributed only 3,335,000 and the excess of births over deaths 12,131,000. The sudden change of policy by the world's leading absorber of population set the pace for other countries, and in the thirties there arose a thicket of restrictions which had the paradoxical result of making the crowded nations absorb people from the under-populated.

We shall first examine the effect on various ethnic groups. There is a striking long-period tendency which seems to have been true of most countries of immigration, namely, the predominance, in successive

[1] George Soule, *Prosperity Decade*, London, Pilot Press, 1947, p. 174.

waves, of one racial group after another. Let us, first, take France, the outstanding European example of a country of absorption. It had about three million foreigners in 1931, comprising 7 % of the population, compared with 1,150,000 in 1911, or 2·8 %. Up to the middle of the nineteenth century more than 50 % of the aliens were Germans, Swiss and Belgians, but by 1926 these made up only 20 % of the total. At the end of the century this element was being displaced by the Latin races; and by 1913 three out of every four aliens were Italians or Spaniards. After about 1923 there was a considerable relative increase in the number of Poles, Czechs, Jugoslavs, Greeks and Armenians—a factor which was making the process of assimilation more difficult owing to the sharper differences in culture, language and way of life. The three successive phases are well defined—Germanic, Latin and Slav. And the outlines of a fourth were already visible, for between 1911 and 1926 the number of Africans had risen from 3,000 to 75,000 and Asians from 1,400 to 43,000.

Another interesting example is Brazil, where the first wave of immigrants was composed of Latin peoples. A change became apparent in the years 1916–25 when the number of Italians compared with the previous decade fell from 188,000 to 89,000 and that of Spaniards from 214,000 to 87,000. Comparing the decade 1926–35 with 1916–25, we find further changes in the ethnic character of the immigration. While the number of Portuguese remained stable at just over 200,000 that of Italians and Spaniards continued to decline, people from Poland, Estonia, Latvia, Lithuania and Rumania increased from 27,000 to 85,000, and the Japanese actually rose in number from 26,000 to 133,000. Blocked by the barriers raised by the United States and the British Dominions, Slav and Oriental peoples flocked in the one direction open to them—South America. It is highly significant that no less than 34 % of the Japanese living in foreign countries in 1934 were to be found in Brazil and Peru, with only 17 % in the United States and 3 % in Canada, Australia and New Zealand.

The transition from the 'old' to the 'new' immigration in the history of the United States is well known. Up to the nineties the newcomers had been mostly Irish, English, German and Scandinavian; but afterwards the Southern and Eastern Europeans and the Russians became dominant. Of the 14·7 million people who entered America in the years 1841–90, only 8 % came from the south-eastern countries of Europe; but in the period 1891–1915, 67 % came from that part of the continent. This 'new' immigration was virtually stopped by the 1924 Act, under which twelve out of every fifteen admitted had to be citizens of Britain, Ireland, Germany, the Netherlands and the Scandinavian countries.

From this brief survey of the racial aspect of migration, it is clear that the Anglo-Saxon nations closed their doors just at the time when the surplus populations of the poorest and most crowded countries were beginning to take full advantage of international mobility. The régime of quotas and prohibitions bore most severely on the Southern and Eastern European, the Slav and the Asiatic peoples. A redistribution of labour as between continents was a natural result of the dynamic force of industrialism; but the advanced nations would not allow it to run its course when it meant admitting racial groups regarded as unassimilable.

Not only did restriction hit some races much more than others but, as one would expect, it affected unskilled labour relatively more than skilled. In the years 1911–14, 27 % of the immigrants to the United States were skilled (i.e. the groups called Professional and Business, Mechanics, and Farmers); but in the years 1925–26, the proportion had gone up to 50 %. Another striking feature was the increase in the group labelled 'no occupation' (made up mostly of women, children and persons of advanced age) from 31 % in 1911–14 to 45 % in 1925–6. In the years following the imposition of the Quota there were many more women than men among the immigrants to America; divided families were gradually being united by the arrival of womenfolk who had been left behind in Europe. By 1937, out of a total of 50,000 aliens who entered the United States, no less than 57 % were classed 'no occupation', 16 % were in the professional and commercial group, 12 % skilled workers and only 4 % unskilled workers.

4. AGRICULTURAL PRODUCTION

During the nineteenth century when Europe was pouring its surplus population into the new countries of the world, the terms of trade first went in favour of agricultural products, and then became unfavourable as soon as the large-scale oversea settlement and the accompanying technical progress had fulfilled themselves in an enormous flow of primary produce at a rapidly diminishing price. We have seen how this process brought crisis to the farming communities of the Old World in the eighties. From that decade to the thirties of this century the cheapening of agricultural output in relation to manufactured goods continued, and this was one reason for the economic instability of the inter-war period.

What was the effect of the American immigration barrier on this evolution? In the first place, it encouraged the spread of agricultural protection in Europe. Since the redundant population could not move to America some of it had to be employed in growing subsidized crops at home. As compared with the years 1909–13, the output of grains in Eastern Europe had increased in 1934–8 by 12 % and that of potatoes by 59 %; in Mediterranean Europe the production of grains in 1924–8 was up by 7 % and in 1934–8 by 31 %. The whole of Europe (excluding the U.S.S.R.) was growing 6 % more grains in 1934–8 than before the First World War, and the production of potatoes had risen by 35 %; its net imports of grains were 18·8 million tons as compared with 23·6 million in 1909–13. The increase in Europe's grain output was far from being equal to the 16 % rise in its population between 1913 and 1939;[1] but the significant point is that, but for governmental encouragement, there might well have been an absolute decline.

Secondly, the American Quota deflected the currents of European migration to other oversea countries, for example Canada and South America. With the aid of abundant American funds, the Prairie Provinces over the border developed at a rapid pace; and the expansion of the wheat economy meant a complementary demand for immigrants for the urban sector of Canada. Under the influence of new techniques productivity increased considerably, and in the thirties Canada was responsible for over one-third of the world's total exports of wheat. Those were the years when the Prairie Provinces felt the full force of the economic blizzard. It is relevant here to mention that the policy of Empire migration pursued by British Governments between the wars laid much stress on agricultural settlement; this seems to have been the only way the policy could be made palatable to the Dominions.

Thirdly, technical improvement in American agriculture was so effective that, despite a fall in the number employed, the index of gross farm production (1935–9 = 100) rose from 97 in 1922 to 105 in 1931. The index of gross farm production per worker in these years went up by 12 %.[2] The ban on cheap labour from Europe and the exodus from the farming areas to the cities put a premium on methods of economizing manpower.

For the reasons just indicated, the American Immigration Restrictions may be said to have helped to cause an excess supply of agricultural produce. If immigration on something like the old scale had continued, there would have been no need to extend cultivation artificially in Europe, the majority of the European migrants would have gone into industry in the United States, and consequently a smaller number would probably have gone to the primary producing countries of South America and the British Commonwealth. The world market

---

[1] The statistics in this paragraph are taken from 'Long-term Trends in European Agriculture', *Economic Bulletin for Europe*, vol. III, no. 2 (Second quarter, 1951), pp. 19-39.

[2] *Historical Statistics of the United States, 1789–1945*, p. 97.

in foodstuffs would thus have been firmer and the calamitous fall in prices which made the world depression so severe might have been avoided.[1]

5. INTERNATIONAL CAPITAL MOVEMENTS

Just before the First World War the United States owed other countries a net sum of 3,200 million dollars on long-term account. By 1919 the situation had been reversed and she was on balance a creditor to the extent of 4,000 million dollars. After a century during which her evolution had been marked by absorption of population and capital, she had now become a powerful industrial state with loanable funds to spare for other countries. From mid-1922 to mid-1924, however, American foreign lending was on the decline, partly, no doubt, because of the chaos in Germany and the occupation of the Ruhr but also owing to the considerable revival in net immigration. The entry of new population, as in the past, entailed a demand for capital, and this was now available from internal sources.

From the middle of 1924 to the middle of 1928 there was a great boom in American investment of long-term capital abroad, as shown in Table 56.

Table 56. *American long-term capital invested abroad, 1921–31 (millions of dollars)*

1921	1922	1923	1924	1925	1926	1927	1928	1929	1930	1931
890	957	465	1005	1092	1272	1465	1671	1029	1069	412

SOURCE: *Historical Statistics of the United States, 1789–1945*, p. 243.

Among the factors which promoted this course of events were the re-establishment of the gold standard, the recovery of Europe, and the restoration of a more stable system of international trade. Moreover, it was now cheaper for non-Empire countries to borrow in New York than in London.[2] This striking change in the direction of the flow of capital cannot, however, be fully explained without taking into account the change in the international flow of population; it was not a coincidence that the year 1923–4 was a turning-point.

[1] For a statement of the case for regarding the excessive production of primary produce as a major cause of the world slump, see W. Arthur Lewis, *Economic Survey 1919–1939*, London, Allen and Unwin, 1949, pp. 192–6.

[2] Royal Institute of International Affairs, *The Problem of International Investment*, Oxford University Press, 1937, p. 135.

The Immigration Act of 1924, by practically stopping the inflow, created a vacuum in the American labour market, whereas the pressure of population in Europe was intensified. At the beginning of 1922 the average return on thirty medium-grade United States domestic bonds was 7·1 % compared with 6·8 % on European dollar bonds; in the autumn of 1924 the foreign bond yield began to exceed the domestic and the gap widened until the beginning of 1927 when the rates were 5·7 % (European) and 5·5 % (domestic).[1] Now that the propensity to save in America was so high, the loanable funds which, but for the Quota Act, would have employed European labour in the United States were attracted to cheap labour and high profits in Europe. Between 1924 and 1929 Germany borrowed 6,000,000,000 marks on long-term account and two-thirds of this came from the United States. Meanwhile, the rapid absorption of European labour by Canada in the twenties induced a demand for capital which that country was unable to furnish out of its own resources; America lent Canada no less than $1,261,000,000 in the years 1922–9, to say nothing of a considerable quantity of direct investment funds. Having closed its doors against immigration on the pre-1913 scale, the United States found it necessary and profitable to assume the role of a rentier financing not only the surplus labour which had to stay in Europe but also the employment of immigrants in countries which were still absorbing foreign labour. By 1930 the net creditor strength of the United States on long-term account had reached $9,500,000,000 compared with $4,000,000,000 in 1919, and the dominant role of that country in the Atlantic economy is shown by the fact that the American national income in dollars in 1929 was equal to the combined income of twenty-three countries including the United Kingdom, Germany and France.[2]

The level of activity had become precariously dependent on the continuance of this international flow of capital. Cracks began to appear in the edifice when, in the late stages of the boom, American investors turned from bonds to intensive speculation in equity securities. Even a slight slackening of the supply of dollars had a serious effect in Europe and the severity of the world depression was no doubt in part due to the artificial element in the circumstances which had given birth to the unprecedented movements of capital in the twenties.

An authoritative American Report pointed out that

curtailment in the supply of dollars resulting from our reduced imports and cessation of investment activity presented a readjustment problem of unparalleled dimensions. During the four years from 1926 through 1929

[1] See H. B. Lary, *The United States in the World Economy*, Washington, Government Printing Office, 1943; London, H.M.S.O., 1944, pp. 97 and 205.
[2] Ibid. p. 29.

the amount of dollars supplied ranged between $7,300,000,000 and $7,500,000,000, and foreign incomes and spending habits and the international debt structure were fairly well adjusted to this level. The abrupt fall in the dollar supply by some $5,000,000,000, or 68 per cent, over the short space of 3 years, necessitated vast changes in the foreign use of dollars and in the economic systems from which the demand arose.[1]

The action of the United States in blocking the natural flow of transatlantic migration was only one factor in a complex set of circumstances; but it played an important part in causing the cumulative process which ended in the world depression.

[1] Ibid. p. 5.

PART IV

REAPPRAISAL

CHAPTER XIII

DEMOGRAPHIC DETERMINANTS OF BRITISH AND AMERICAN BUILDING CYCLES, 1870–1913

In the course of the debate on the working of the Atlantic economy no critic has been able to refute the existence of an inverse relation between long swings in construction in Britain and the United States and in British home and foreign investment, at least in the period 1870–1913. There has indeed been ample confirmation.[1] Where disagreement enters is in interpreting the nature of the mechanism by which the economies of the two countries reacted on each other. Contributors to the discussion can be divided into two broad schools—those who accept the reciprocal character of British and American long swings as systematic rather than fortuitous, and those who argue that the operative forces were in the domestic sphere and not in any interacting process. The line taken by this second group is seen in the work of H. J. Habakkuk and S. B. Saul.[2]

Habakkuk is a sceptic not only about systematic influences in the alternation of British and American long swings but even about the

---

[1] An outstanding work is J. Parry Lewis, *Building Cycles and Britain's Growth*, London, Macmillan, 1965. This thorough study confirms the inverse relation between home construction cycles from the eighteen-fifties to 1913, in chapter 7, pp. 164–85. See also A. I. Bloomfield, *Patterns of Fluctuation in International Investment Before 1914*, Princeton University Press, 1968. Bloomfield points out (p. 22) that not only did British home and foreign investment move inversely over the long swing between 1870 and 1913, but they also tended to move inversely *in the short run*. 'The correlation coefficient of the first differences of net capital exports and gross domestic fixed-capital formation from 1860 to 1913 was -0.32, significant at the 5% level. Compare this with Cairncross's assertion (*Home and Foreign Investment 1870–1913*, pp. 187–8) that in the short run home and foreign investment generally moved together.'

[2] H. J. Habakkuk, 'Fluctuations in House-building in Britain and the United States in the Nineteenth Century', *Journal of Economic History*, vol. XXII, no. 2, June 1962, reprinted in A. R. Hall (ed.), *The Export of Capital from Britain 1870–1914*, London, Methuen, 1968, pp. 103–42. The references here are to the latter. S. B. Saul, 'House Building in England 1890–1914', *Economic History Review*, second series, vol. XV, no. 1, August 1962, pp. 119–37.

existence of a British building cycle, as the following quotation indicates.

There has recently been some suggestion that in England after the 1860s the trade cycle was not an independent phenomenon but simply the result of lack of synchronization between the long swings in foreign and domestic investment. [Footnote: Matthews, *A Study in Trade Cycle History*.] The view taken here is the reverse of this: it was the long swings which were the epiphenomena and the trade cycles the reality, in the sense that when the character of the individual cycles has been explained there is no residue which needs to be attributed to the behaviour of a long cycle. The appearance of alternation in British and American long swings is the result of the fact that British trade cycles no longer came to a violent end but the American ones often did.[1]

It is not easy to summarize Habakkuk's paper, but the essence of his thesis can be put as follows. House-building in Britain before the eighteen-sixties did not exhibit long swings but fluctuated with the trade cycle. There were special reasons of domestic origin why the relation between building fluctuations and the trade cycle changed after the sixties. For example, internal migration became more an affair of the middle classes and less connected with changing business conditions, and financial institutions became more stable so that building could be sustained after cyclical downturns. The increasing tendency for building booms to continue after cyclical downturns gave rise to regional long cycles which were not necessarily synchronized. The eighteen-eighties were an exception; even in that decade the volume of emigration was largely the result of domestic influences. 'The alternation of British and American housing activity in the eighties and nineties partly reflects the different rate at which electricity was applied to traction in the two countries. This was, in the present context, almost certainly fortuitous.'[2] With the exception of the later eighties, the effect of emigration and foreign investment on British building fluctuations was '. . . of minor importance compared with domestic factors'.[3] This is a challenging argument deserving attention, although it rests mainly on speculations which are not subjected to rigorous testing. The issue can be decided only by an appeal to the empirical evidence.

S. B. Saul, in his study of local authority records for a large number of English towns in the period 1890–1914, has thrown light on matters such as the relation of building activity to the proportion of empty properties and the effect of changes in the availability of short-term

[1] H. J. Habakkuk, op. cit. p. 120. The footnote reference must be an error: it should be 'Matthews, *The Trade Cycle*'.

[2] Ibid. p. 137.

[3] Ibid. p. 141.

funds.[1] His general conclusion is as follows:

Migration, external and internal, was certainly an important matter and money-market conditions often helped to determine the timing of the upswing of the cycle. But the evidence for a complex interaction of the British and American economies, at least as far as investment in housing in Britain is concerned, is slender. The facts certainly seem to point to an industry whose fate was largely determined internally by the state of demand and by the nature of the operation of the trade itself.[2]

The two contributions mentioned lay stress on so-called fortuitous domestic influences on the course of house-building in Britain: neither has paid enough attention to demographic factors. An adequate interpretation of building fluctuations must give a prominent place to the role of population change.

In preparing this revised edition I have re-examined the course of house-building in England and Wales in the period 1870–1913 on the basis of new data yielding a more comprehensive record of regional cycles. The analysis seeks to attain a more accurate measurement of the demographic determinants of building cycles, regionally as well as in the aggregate. These results are then related to corresponding data on the demographic determinants of the building cycle in the United States in the same period.

I. STATISTICAL SOURCES AND METHODS

The sources used are the Inland Revenue ledgers deposited in the Public Record Office. Inhabited House Duty statistics, available for each county, provide a basis for regional building estimates for the years 1875–1913.[3] The ledgers also contain figures of profit income assessed under Schedule D. The characteristics of these sources and the method used are described in a Note at the end of this chapter.

We have information about the number of dwelling houses assessed and not assessed to house duty as well as 'messuages and tenements' not used as dwelling houses (Appendix Table 139). Sir Josiah Stamp pointed out that the income tax Schedule A figures '. . . undoubtedly represent most closely the real facts but in revaluation years far more closely than at other times'.[4] To test the reliability of these data we

---

[1] S. B. Saul, loc. cit.

[2] Ibid. p. 136. For a critique of Saul's analysis see J. Parry Lewis, op. cit. pp. 203–5.

[3] The series for England and Wales, Scotland and Great Britain are given in B. R. Mitchell and Phyllis Deane, *Abstract of British Historical Statistics*, pp. 236–7.

[4] J. C. Stamp, *British Incomes and Property: the Application of Official Statistics to Economic Problems*, London, P. S. King, 1916, p. 31.

expressed the annual change in the number of premises in Britain shown by the house-duty statistics as an index (1900–9 = 100) and compared it with Weber's estimates of house-building.[1] Fig. 42 indicates clearly that the two series yield virtually the same long swing, and this justifies the use of the Record Office data for our purpose. It also reveals that the house-duty figures were affected by periodic revaluations and cannot be used for year-to-year changes. Both values and numbers were affected by revaluations. To overcome this difficulty we have averaged inter-revaluation years plus the revaluation year

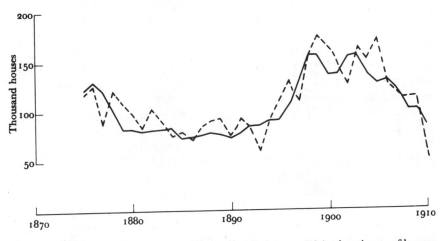

FIG. 42. House-building in Great Britain, 1875–1910. —— Weber's estimate of houses built. ······ Annual increase in number of premises (I.H.D. records). Source: Mitchell and Deane, *Abstract of British Historical Statistics*, pp. 236–9.

following them; this prevents any misleading impression that the series can be used for annual changes and at the same time provides an adequate indication of the time-shape.

The counties of England and Wales have been divided into two broad sectors: urban and rural. The urban counties form seven regions—the Midlands, counties surrounding London, North West England, Yorkshire, Northern England, South Wales and Monmouthshire, and London. The rural regions comprise the Southern agricultural counties, those near the Midlands, and the South West plus rural Wales. We shall deal mainly with the urban regions, defined as predominantly urban in that they contained the greater part of the population of England and Wales at the end of the nineteenth century.

[1] Weber, 'A New Index of Residential Construction, 1838–1950', *Scottish Journal of Political Economy*, vol. II, no. 2, June 1955, pp. 104–32.

The purpose of this analysis is to test the proposition that British building fluctuations in the period 1870–1913 are to be explained mainly by demographic variables and, in particular, by migration. Also, by relating this analysis to recent studies of population change and the building cycle in the United States since the middle of the nineteenth century, we can carry out a new test of the inverse relation between British and American building cycles and the process of interaction between the two economies.

To illuminate the connexion between changes in building and changes in the house-seeking age group we have made estimates of the quinquennial change in the population aged 20–44 in each region, separating the effects of natural increase and migration (Appendix Table 140). Figures on recorded deaths were obtained from the Registrar General's Annual Reports and Decennial Supplements, and these were combined with census population figures in quinary age groups to estimate the quinquennial changes which would have occurred in the absence of migration.

The demographic factors relevant in explaining the volume of house-building in any region in a given period are the natural increase in the 20–44 age group, internal migration, external migration and the headship rate (the ratio of heads of households to the total population in an age group). In this analysis we shall ignore changes in the headship rate: instead we shall refer to changes in the marriage rate. The age group 20–44 is taken as comprising the vast majority of the house-seeking section of the community. We shall concentrate on the first three factors and examine the course of the demographic and building series quinquennially in each region and in the seven regions as a whole. Our method of obtaining regional estimates for both natural increase and migration is explained in the Note at the end of this chapter.

'Natural increase' in the 20–44 age group is an estimate of the population change which would have occurred in this age group in the two quinquennia following each census, if there had been no migration in either of these periods. Changes in natural increase reflect movements in the excess of births over deaths in previous periods. A five-year boom in the birth rate is followed twenty years later by a bulge in the 20–25 age group and, after thirty years, by a bulge in the 30–35 group and, after thirty-five years, by a bulge in the 35–40 group. In any given quinquennium the 20–44 age group is thus a composite of past influences. There is much to be explored under this heading, both nationally and regionally, but we cannot deal adequately here with echo effects.[1]

---

[1] Comprehensive studies of echo effects for the United States are to be found in Richard A. Easterlin, *Population, Labor Force and Long Swings in Economic Growth: The*

The other element to be taken into account is migration, internal and external, affecting the age group 20–44. The estimate is of course a balance of inward and outward movements. There is no means of distinguishing between 'immigrants' who come into a region from one of the other six regions and those who come from outside, i.e. from the rest of the United Kingdom or from abroad; and similarly with 'emigrants' from a region. Despite the limitations of the data, it is possible to make a reasonably firm estimate of the extent to which natural increase in the age group 20–44 in each region was augmented or reduced by migration. Parallel with our aggregate migration series for the seven regions we have plotted from an independent source the quinquennial emigration of occupied persons from England and Wales to the United States.

Having estimated natural increase and the balance of migration in the age group 20–44 in each quinquennium for each region, we derive an estimate of the change in the population in the house-seeking age group.[1] This series is then compared with the course of building in each region and in the seven regions as a whole.

2. REGIONAL BUILDING CYCLES, 1870–1910

Fig. 43 shows the course of the building cycle in each of the urban regions of England and Wales from 1871 to 1910. This series gives the average annual number of houses built in each quinquennium (years between revaluations plus the revaluation year following them being averaged). For brevity I shall refer to the Inhabited House Duty figures as the I.H.D. index. With it we plot for each quinquennium from 1870 to 1910 the average annual increase in the population aged 20–44; this registers the net effect of natural increase and migration which are also shown in the charts.

The picture emerging from these charts dispels the uncertainty over whether regional fluctuations were synchronized or were the result of diverse local circumstances. With the exception of London and South Wales there was a high degree of conformity between regional building swings, although the amplitude varied. London was particularly affected by outward shifts of population to the Home Counties; in the

---

American Experience, New York, Columbia University Press, 1968, and Burnham O. Campbell, *Population Change and Building Cycles*, Bureau of Economic and Business Research, University of Illinois, 1966.

[1] A similar analysis of the potential demand for houses from population aged 20–44 in Great Britain as a whole quinquennially from 1871–5 to 1906–10 was carried out by C. H. Feinstein in his unpublished Ph.D. dissertation, 'Home and Foreign Investment 1870–1913', University of Cambridge, 1959, pp. 291–6. The methods used here, as explained in the Note, are different from Feinstein's.

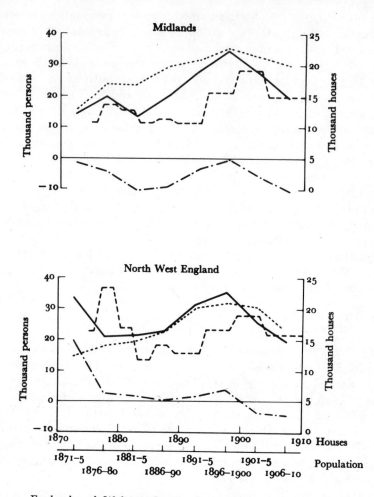

FIG. 43. England and Wales, urban regions: annual population changes (quinquennial averages) in age group 20–44, and building cycles, by region, 1871–1910.
—— Population increase. × × × Natural increase. – · · – Net migration. – – –
Houses built (I.H.D. index). Sources: See 'Note on Sources and Methods', pp.
221–7, and Tables 139 and 140.

Notes: House-building series not charted because distorted by boundary revisions
in 1879 and 1880 for Northern England, and in 1876 and 1877 for the Home Counties.
London population is age group 15–44.

early part of the period, however, there was considerable net in-
migration. The reason why South Wales is an exception is that its
economy was entirely in the export sector.[1]

[1] See Brinley Thomas, 'Wales and the Atlantic Economy', *Scottish Journal of
Political Economy*, vol. VI, no. 3, November 1959, pp. 169–92.

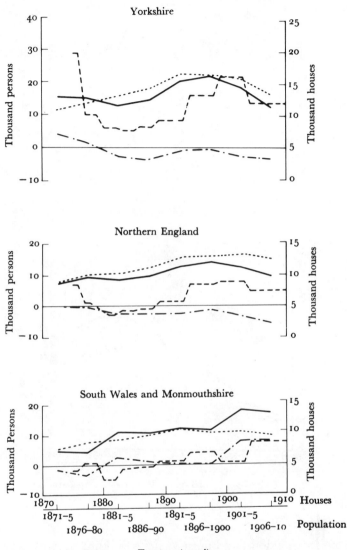

FIG. 43 (contd)

It would be unreasonable to expect the peak of the building cycle to occur in the same year in every region: there is usually a cluster of individual peaks within a neighbourhood of three or four years. Our building series, beginning in 1875, reveals a high level of activity, though often declining, in the late seventies in every region except the counties surrounding London, where the peak came in the early years of the eighties. The downswing lasted until the early nineties in all

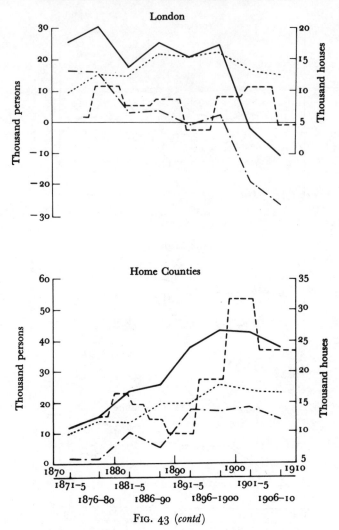

FIG. 43 (contd)

regions except London and South Wales. Building activity was rising during the nineties in all regions, with a peak at the turn of the century everywhere except in South Wales and London.

It might be argued that the averaging technique which has been used to overcome the difficulty of the reassessment years tends to blur the peaks and troughs of the cycle. In order to test the reliability of the new regional indices I shall look at the North West (Lancashire and Cheshire) in more detail and partially disaggregate the I.H.D. index by plotting alongside it annual estimates of building in the Manchester conurbation and Liverpool, based on local authority data.[1] These are shown in Fig. 44 together with the demographic series.

The peak of 1877–9 in our index coincides exactly with the peak in the number of houses erected by private enterprise in Liverpool. The peak in the Manchester conurbation index comes a year earlier, as one would expect since those figures relate to houses for which planning permission had been obtained. The steep descent from the top to a very low trough in 1883–5 shown by the I.H.D. index corresponds exactly to what happened in the Manchester conurbation; in both series building then continues at a very low level until the upturn in 1892–4. The downswing in Liverpool is less steep and there is no early trough in 1883–5; the revival takes place at the same time as is indicated in the other two indices.[2] There is a close resemblance between the final peak and the subsequent decline in the I.H.D. series from 1899 to 1910 and the dominant Manchester component, again allowing for the fact that the latter registers building plans and not houses built. The high average level of activity in the region between 1899 and 1903 recorded by our index reflects a balance between the weakening boom in the Manchester conurbation and a continuation of buoyant conditions in Liverpool. A vigorous boom continued in Liverpool, with another high peak in 1906, whereas the level of activity in the conurbation was midway between the peak of the late seventies and the trough of the eighties. The sharp decline in 1909–13 is the same in both.

The I.H.D. index is the nearest one can get to full coverage of regional building in the period 1875–1910. The comparison with local authority data in two large component parts of the North West region has been reassuring; the close fit with Weber's national index is reproduced regionally. Even before we bring in the population variable, the evidence points strongly against the argument that regional building was shaped largely by diverse local influences. S. B. Saul came near to the main explanation in the following sentence: 'Liverpool followed the national index to the recovery after the Boer War, but then building continued at a high level until as late as 1909, just as it did in South Wales and in the cotton towns.'[3] It is essential to distinguish between

---

[1] The figures for the towns in the Manchester conurbation are the number of houses on approved building plans. For Manchester itself there is a gap from 1871 to 1890 and values for these years were estimated from other sources: see J. Parry Lewis, op. cit. pp. 307–17. The Liverpool series is the number of houses erected by private enterprise. They were supplied to Weber by the Town Clerk of Liverpool: ibid. pp. 335–6.

[2] The kink and sharp rise in the Liverpool index in 1895 is explained by the extension of the boundaries of the city in November of that year, adding 23,263 dwelling houses to the original stock of 106,962: ibid. p. 335.

[3] S. B. Saul, loc. cit. p. 122.

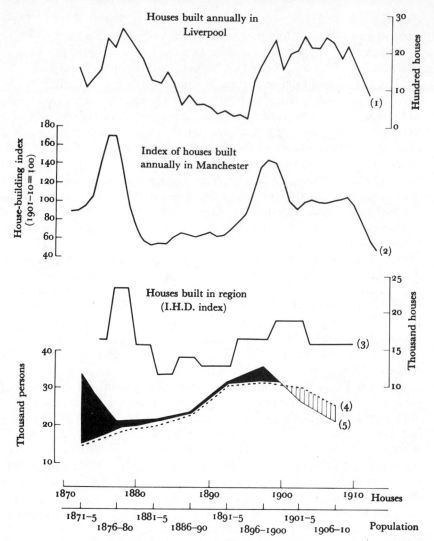

FIG. 44. North West England: migration and annual population changes (quinquennial averages) in age group 20–44, and house-building, 1871–1913. ■■■■■
Net in-migration. ☐☐☐☐☐ Net out-migration. Sources: (1) and (2), J. Parry
Lewis, *Building Cycles and Britain's Growth*, pp. 335–6; (3), (4) Natural increase,
(5) Population increase: as Fig. 43.

the home construction sector and the export sector. Coal-exporting
and cotton-exporting towns belong entirely to the export sector;
building in such areas has a different time-shape from that of the home
construction sector (areas other than purely export areas). There is

always some building going on in the export sector; the regional as well as the national indices are composites of building activity in the two sectors. It is clear from the national index that the high phase of the long swing was the years when the ratio of building in the home construction sector to building in the export sector was high and vice versa in the low phase. The purest case of export sector building is South Wales; the index for that region was rising in the eighties and in the late nineteen-hundreds, contrary to the national swing. The same phenomenon was at work in parts of other regions but it was seldom strong enough to dominate the regional composite.

Saul presents a number of charts showing building in various towns in Cheshire between 1890 and 1913, and finds an upswing in a number of dormitory towns and in Stockport, and a downswing in Crewe.[1] The more it becomes local history, the more variety we are going to see; but this is perfectly consistent with the presence of major ebbs and flows.[2] In the particular case of Cheshire, the boom in building in the dormitory towns was part of a universal tendency in the economic growth of large cities—the overspill (internal migration from the point of view of the region). This is part of the migration variable which, as we shall see, is the major determinant of the ebb and flow of building.

A glance at Fig. 44 shows, for the North West region, the quinquennial course of natural increase and population change in the age group 20–44 from 1871–5 to 1906–10. The excess of population change over natural increase (the shaded area) indicates the volume of net inmigration, and the excess of natural increase over population change (the area with broken lines) indicates the volume of net out-migration. There is a close correspondence between the long swing in housebuilding and the curve of population change in the 20–44 age group, with the former lagging after the latter. The shape of the curve of population change is determined by the swing in the balance of migration.

The period begins with a very heavy net movement of migrants into the region in the years 1871–5, and this leads to a sharp rise in building activity which reaches a high peak in the years 1877–9. There was a

---

[1] S. B. Saul, loc. cit. p. 124.

[2] Analysis is concerned with phenomena which exhibit statistical uniformities. In the words of Sir John Hicks, 'Every historical event has some aspect in which it is unique; but nearly always there are other aspects in which it is a member of a group, often of quite a large group. If it is one of the latter aspects in which we are interested, it will be the group, not the individual, on which we shall fix our attention; it will be the average, or norm, of the group which is what we shall be trying to explain. We shall be able to allow that the individual may diverge from the norm without being deterred from the recognition of a statistical uniformity.' (*A Theory of Economic History*, Oxford University Press, 1969, p. 3.)

marked contraction in in-migration in 1876–80, and it remained negligible through the eighties and beginning of the nineties. This was accompanied by a sharp downswing and a long trough in building activity. Meanwhile, beginning in 1885–90 the curve of natural increase rose sharply until it reached a record level in the nineties. The quinquennium 1896–1900 saw the powerful echo effect of the sharp increase in the birth rate twenty-five to thirty years before and, super-imposed on this very high level of natural increase, was a renewed rise in net migration into the region. There was also a considerable increase in the marriage rate in the nineties. This time the lag relationship is between the natural increase build-up, which attained its maximum in 1891–1900, plus the migration increase with peak marriage rate in 1896–1900 and the upswing in building, which began about 1894–5 and went to a peak at the turn of the century and a few years afterwards. After 1900 net migration was negative until the end of the period and the level of natural increase was falling; this induced, with a lag, a down-swing in the volume of building.

Now that we have taken a preliminary look at the pattern in the North West region, with our I.H.D. index partially disaggregated, we shall examine the evidence for the other regions.

3. DEMOGRAPHIC DETERMINANTS: REGIONAL AND NATIONAL

The time-shape for the North West is repeated in the North, Yorkshire, the Midlands and the counties surrounding London. The dominant influence of the course of migration is clearly brought out in all regions. It is interesting to compare the picture for London with that for the surrounding counties. In the Home Counties building has a long swing corresponding to that of the rest of industrial England, with a very high peak in the early nineteen-hundreds: in London, however, there is only a mild swing. The annual volume of building in the capital in 1902–6 was only slightly above the level of 1877–81, and the troughs in 1892–6 and 1907–10 were relatively shallow. Net migration into London, which was fairly high in the eighteen-seventies, fell to low levels in the eighties and nineties, and became a large net outflow in the nineteen-hundreds. The gross outflows to the Home Counties were an important factor.

Some of these outflows went beyond the periphery of the capital, as can be seen from Fig. 45, which gives the course of building in the predominantly rural areas of England and Wales. In the agricultural Midlands there was a steady low level of activity with hardly any fluctuation; in the Southern counties movements were more erratic and the South West plus rural Wales showed mild peaks in the late eighteen-seventies and early nineteen-hundreds. Putting the three together as a residual rural sector, we find a definite peak in the early nineteen-hundreds, as in the Home Counties, the Midlands, the North West and Yorkshire. This was chiefly the reflexion of the demographic echo effect and the growth of residential and military towns in Southern counties during the nineties.

London displayed a unique pattern because it was a congested capital bursting at the seams. Behind the bare summary of building and demographic change in Fig. 43 is a fascinating story of population mobility, transport innovations and the expansion of suburbs. To do justice to it would need several volumes of the calibre of the admirable study of Camberwell by H. J. Dyos.[1] The following summary of Camberwell's demographic history is in miniature a faithful reflexion of the course of population change in London shown in the chart.

Of the 75,000 persons by which the suburb had grown during its years of maximum development in the 1870s, about 52,000 represented the balance of migration into and out of the district, and 23,000 were the result of natural increase. But the stream of migrants which had been chiefly responsible for the growth of the suburb since the beginning of the century, and which was now in full flood, soon declined, and it had dried up all together by the end of the century. Of the increase of about 49,000 persons recorded between 1881 and 1891, only about 17,000 could be accounted for by net immigration, but in the last ten years of the century the increase of about 24,000 persons was wholly accounted for by natural increase, and would have been higher had not more people—over a thousand—left the suburb than came into it. By 1911, the balance of migration had detached a further 25,000 from Camberwell, and this attrition continued, despite the comparatively low average population density, in the post-war years.[2]

The natural increase component of the population curve rose everywhere to a peak in the late nineties; this was the result of the high level of fertility a quarter of a century earlier (the number of births per 1,000 women aged 15–44 in England and Wales rising from 150·7 in 1863 to 156·7 in 1876). In addition, the marriage rate was at a peak in 1896–1900, 16·1 per 1,000 as against 14·7 per 1,000 in 1886–90.

In all regions, except London and South Wales, population change in the age group 20–44 was at a maximum in the five-year period 1896–

---

[1] H. J. Dyos, *Victorian Suburb. A Study of the Growth of Camberwell*, Leicester University Press, 1961. See also T. A. Welton, *England's Recent Progress*, pp. 188–206; A. L. Bowley, 'Area and Population' and G. Ponsonby and S. K. Ruck, 'Travel and Mobility' in *The New Survey of London Life and Labour*, vol. 1, *Forty Years of Change*, London, P. S. King, 1930; A. K. Cairncross, 'Internal Migration in Victorian England' in *Home and Foreign Investment 1870–1913*, Cambridge University Press, 1953, pp. 65–83.

[2] H. J. Dyos, op. cit. p. 56.

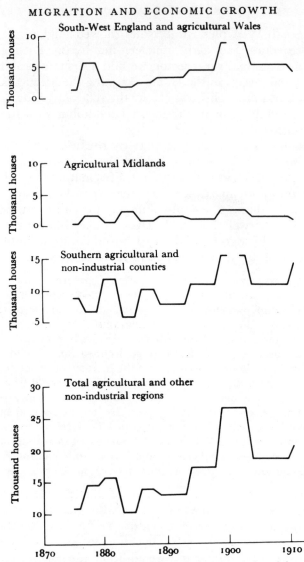

FIG. 45. England and Wales, agricultural and other non-industrial regions: house-building, 1875–1911. Source: Inland Revenue ledgers, Inhabited House Duty records.

Note: Series for South West and Southern agricultural counties distorted by boundary revisions in 1901 and not charted for that year.

1900; there was a combination of a powerful echo effect on natural increase, a deep trough in emigration overseas, and heavy internal migration particularly into the Home Counties and the North West. In each of these five regions the peak in house-building came at the

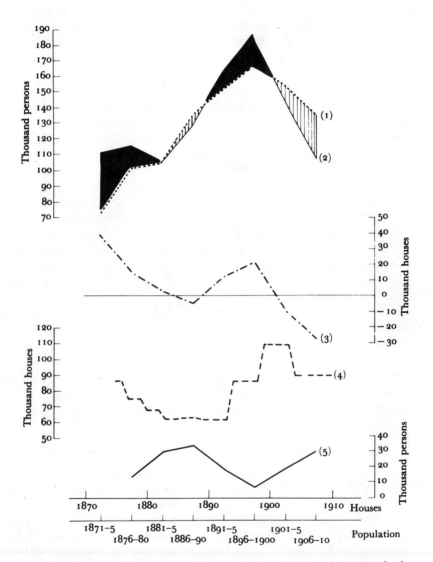

FIG. 46. England and Wales, urban regions: annual population changes and migration (quinquennial averages) in age group 20–44, and building cycles, 1871–1910.
■■■■■ Net in-migration. ☐☐☐☐☐ Net out-migration. (1) Natural increase, (2) Population increase, (3) Net migration, (4) Houses built (I.H.D. index): See 'Note on Sources and Methods', pp. 223–9. (5) Occupied emigrants from England and Wales to the United States: Tables 81 and 84.

turn of the century and there can be no doubt that there was a common demographic determinant. South Wales, which was out of step, had relatively low building activity in 1899–1904 and then came a vigorous boom (in the wake of high in-migration) in the years 1905–10 when every other region was experiencing a decline in house-building.

The building cycle and the demographic variables for the seven urban regions as a whole are shown in Fig. 46. There is a very close similarity between the movements in our I.H.D. building index and those of the Parry Lewis weighted index. Population change in the age group 20–44 is the result of 'natural increase' and current migration. The charts show the quantitative significance of these two components. Fig. 46 indicates the part played by migration in determining the *shape* of the curve of population change in the urban regions of England and Wales taken together. The verdict of the analysis is that nationally and regionally the swing in house-building follows with a lag the swing in the population aged 20–44 as determined by migration. With regard to timing, the divergent fluctuations in London and South Wales did little to modify the major uniform swings in the other five regions which governed the aggregate. The inverse relation between internal and external migration is clearly shown. When internal migration was high, emigration was low; and it was in those years that building, with a lag, expanded; the opposite occurred when internal migration was low and emigration was high. The swings in house-building conform to the swings in the migration-dominated curve of population change. As Cairncross observed in his well-known analysis of fluctuations in the Glasgow building industry, 1860–1914, '. . . the building cycle was little more than a migration cycle in disguise'.[1]

4. THE ALTERNATION OF BRITISH AND AMERICAN CYCLES

Since the first edition of this book appeared, much new work has been done on building fluctuations in the United States. To round off this reappraisal, I shall compare the British pattern with that of the United States in the period 1870–1910, drawing on the valuable researches of Burnham O. Campbell.[2] To take advantage of improvements in earlier building series, I shall use John R. Riggleman's index of the value of building permits as adjusted by Walter Isard, and Clarence D. Long's index of the value of permits as adjusted by Miles L. Colean and Robinson Newcomb.[3]

---

[1] A. K. Cairncross, op. cit. p. 25.
[2] Burnham O. Campbell, *Population Change and Building Cycles*.
[3] For an account of the characteristics of these indices see M. Abramovitz, *Evidences*

Burnham Campbell has conducted a detailed examination of the influence of demographic variables, particularly immigration, on the residential building cycle in the United States. By isolating movements in the headship rate, i.e. the ratio of households to total population in an age group, he has reached illuminating conclusions about the causation of the post-1945 building cycle. In the present context we shall be concerned only with his results for the period ending in 1913. He defines 'required additions' as the population change in each age group during a given period multiplied by the headship rate for the age group at the beginning of the period. He has calculated for the United States the change in population by age group in each quin-quennium from 1850–5 on, and he then estimates the change in required additions by age group due to immigration in each quin-quennium.[1] It is this latter series for the period 1870–5 to 1905–10 which I have reproduced in Fig. 47.

Campbell concludes that:

from the Civil War to the 1890s the rate of change in required additions— and from the 1890s to the 1930s, the direction of change—was controlled by the long swing in immigration. . . . Not only was the long swing in required additions greatly influenced by immigration, but from the 1870s to the 1910s and again in the 1930s there was a close connection between the long swing in immigration and the long swing in household formations and housing starts or residential capital formation. . . . The argument that fluctuations in immigration were the sources of those in residential building can be stated most strongly in terms of quinquennial data. From the 1870s to the 1930s, residential building and required additions due to immigration varied together in all but three half-decades, and the lagged adjustment of residen-tial construction to changes in housing demand could explain all three exceptions. In summary, from the Civil War to World War II the long swing in immigration was the dominant source of the long swing in required additions and so of the residential building cycle in the United States.[2]

In Fig. 47 we plot the British data for the period 1871–1910 with the corresponding American quinquennial data on required additions in the age group 20–44 due to immigration, and three indices of building activity. There is an impressive inverse relation between the quin-quennial increase in population in the age group 20–44 in Britain and the quinquennial change in required additions due to immigration in the age group 20–44 in the United States. The building cycles are inverse and the time-shape of each is governed by the course of migra-

of Long Swings in Aggregate Construction since the Civil War, New York, Columbia Univer-sity Press, 1964, pp. 206–20.
[1] For details of the statistical treatment of immigration see Campbell, op. cit., app. C, pp. 189–94.
[2] Ibid. p. 110.

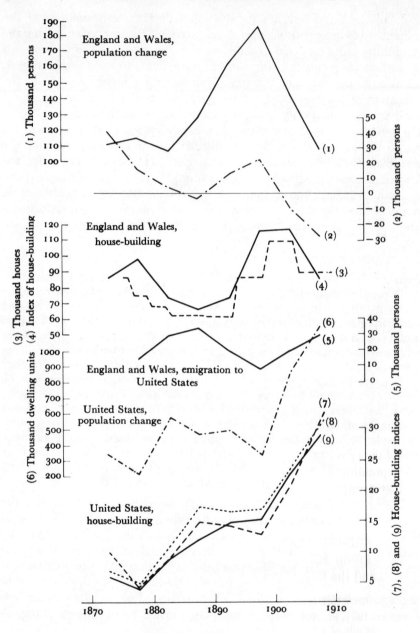

tion. If it were possible to produce quinquennial estimates of internal migration for the United States, this would complete the picture. Kuznets has shown, on the basis of decadal estimates, that changes in internal migration of the native born in the United States were synchronous with changes in additions to total population and that the volume of internal migration in any decade was probably at least equal to the total additions to population.[1]

Fig. 47 amply confirms the conclusions of Chapters VII and XI. The crux of the problem is the mechanism of the migration cycle. House-building is an important part of population-sensitive capital formation, and the fluctuations in the latter are crucial in the process of interaction between the British and American economies in the period under review.

The demographic factor is of course not the sole determinant of the building cycle: there are other factors on the demand and the supply side—for example, income levels, the stickiness of rents, the rate of interest, the quality of houses, the rate of demolitions, and the organization of the building trades. Various elements can be combined to form a satisfactory explanation based on the cobweb theorem. What the empirical evidence demonstrates unequivocally is that migration is a major determinant.

Our analysis refutes the assertions of the writers quoted earlier; for example S. B. Saul's statement about British experience in the period 1890–1914, that it is 'hard to believe that migration of itself could account for more than a small part of the wide fluctuations in house construction'.[2] Habakkuk's speculations about possible lack of synchronization between regional fluctuations in Britain in the period

[1] S. Kuznets, *Capital in the American Economy*, Princeton University Press, 1961, pp. 325–7.

[2] S. B. Saul, 'House Building in England 1890–1914', p. 131.

FIG. 47. England and Wales and the United States: annual population changes (quinquennial averages) in age group 20–44, and building cycles, 1871–1910. England and Wales:
(1) Population increase, (2) Net migration, (3) Houses built (I.H.D. index): as Fig. 46. (4) Weighted house-building index for towns, 1901–10 = 100: J. Parry Lewis, op. cit. p. 317, col. 7. (5) Occupied emigrants to the United States: as Fig. 46.
The United States:
(6) Required additions due to immigration of age group 20–44 (quinquennial changes): B. O. Campbell, op. cit. p. 194. (7) Riggleman's index (adjusted by Isard) of value of building permits per capita, 1920–9 = 100: M. Abramovitz, op. cit. p. 147–9. (8) Long's index of value of residential permits, 1920–30 = 100: ibid. (9) Long's index (adjusted by Colean and Newcomb) of value of all permits, 1920–9 = 100: ibid.

1870–1914 are also wide of the mark. Starting from the notion that the only real cycle is the trade cycle, he suggested that regional trade cycles were behaving in such a way as to produce a bogus long swing in aggregate building which became more moderate in its amplitude. The evidence contradicts any such notion. Statistical analysis confirms that there was a real building cycle determined mainly by migration. The degree of synchronization or lack of it between regional building cycles has very little to do with the trade cycle.[1] Moreover, instead of moderating, the amplitude of the aggregate long swing increased, the high peak of the early nineteen-hundreds reflecting the force of the demographic determinants in the late nineties.

So far as the United States is concerned, Habakkuk says that 'an increase in immigration did not *initiate* a revival of building; the revival was started by changes in migration within the United States which preceded changes in immigration.'[2] There is no statistical support for this assertion; the figures for internal migration cannot be used for this purpose. What we do know about annual time series for immigration and building in the United States refutes the assertion. Lag analysis has demonstrated that throughout the period 1845–1913, except for the years 1869–79, immigration consistently preceded American building activity.[3]

According to Habakkuk, 'the problem posed by the hypothesis of the Atlantic economy is the balance between domestic—and in this context fortuitous—influences on the one hand, and foreign and systematic influences on the other',[4] and he comes down heavily on the side of the former. The empirical evidence presented in this chapter strongly confirms the proposition that migration, internal and external, played a major role in the house-building cycles in Britain and the United States in the period 1870–1913. To those who contemplate the tides of building activity and are impressed only by what seem to be accidental, wayward or local influences, I commend the well-known lines of Arthur Hugh Clough.

> For while the tired waves, vainly breaking,
> Seem here no painful inch to gain,
> Far back, through creeks and inlets making,
> Comes silent, flooding in, the main.

[1] The whole question of house-building and the trade cycle was thoroughly examined by Weber. He concluded that 'taking the period from 1842 to 1913 as a whole, neither an emphatic anti-cyclical movement in building nor the reverse can be established unequivocally': see J. Parry Lewis, *Building Cycles and Britain's Growth*, p. 359.

[2] H. J. Habakkuk, 'Fluctuations in House-building in Britain and the United States in the Nineteenth Century', p. 121. (Italics in the original.)

[3] See pp. 159–63.

[4] Habakkuk, loc. cit. p. 133.

NOTE ON SOURCES AND METHODS

The sources used are Inland Revenue ledgers deposited at the Public Record Office, Ashridge, Hertfordshire.[1] They comprise revenue raised from the Inhabited House Duty and profits assessed under Schedule D. The data are available for each county.

1. Inhabited House Duty Statistics

The Inhabited House Duty was introduced in 1851 and was levied on dwelling houses of £20 annual value and over. There is information about dwelling houses assessed and not assessed to duty as well as 'messuages and tenements' not used as dwelling houses. We took the series showing the total number of houses assessed and not assessed to duty from 1874 to 1912 and obtained a measure of house-building activity from the change in the numbers recorded.

It is important to be clear about the limitations of these data and how we have sought to overcome them. The first difficulty is the effect of the periodic reassessments of properties. In England and Wales with the exception of London, reassessment took place in 1876, 1879, 1882, 1885, 1888, 1893, 1898, 1903 and 1910; the revaluation years for London were 1876, 1881, 1886, 1891, 1896, 1901, 1906 and 1911. In years between revaluations the series tends to be below the true figures. 'The reason is that while effect is given in practice to all *bona fide reductions* in rent wherever they occur, no effect is, or can be, given to *increases* in rents, and the totals are only maintained by new properties and structural alterations. There is a continuous drag downwards, and the "slack" is not taken up until the next revaluation year.'[2] In some areas the figures for revaluation years showed a decline rather than an upward revision; this was likely to happen where a large number of houses were becoming empty or where there was a general fall in rents and the revaluation provided an opportunity for a general revision of assessments. The numbers of houses as well as the values were affected by the reassessments. Another awkward fact about these data is pointed out by B. R. Mitchell and Phyllis Deane, namely, that 'the figures are of net quantities, offsetting much demolition against new building, and it seems probable that demolition was nothing like constant from year to year'.[3]

For the above reasons the Inhabited House Duty figures are not an ac-

[1] Thanks are due to the authorities at the Public Record Office at Ashridge for their courtesy and co-operation in granting facilities for this research. The work was carried out by Mrs Margaret Evans and Mr Kenneth Richards when they were Research Assistants in the Department of Economics at University College, Cardiff. I wish to pay tribute to the substantial contribution which they made in collecting and analysing these data. I am particularly indebted to Mrs Evans for preparing the material for this Note and the charts.
[2] J. C. Stamp, *British Incomes and Property.* (Italics in the original.)
[3] Mitchell and Deane, *Abstract of British Historical Statistics*, p. 233.

curate guide to *year-to-year* changes in house-building, but this does not necessarily rule them out as an indication of the time-shape of house-building. Their reliability for this purpose can be tested by comparing them with Weber's building index. From the house duty records we have taken the annual change in the number of premises in Great Britain[1] and produced an index for the years 1875–1910 (1900–9 = 100). This is shown together with Weber's index of residential construction in Fig. 42.

The chart brings out clearly the effect of the periodic revaluations and the impossibility of using the series for *annual* changes. On the other hand, it also demonstrates that the long swing in building revealed by the Inhabited House Duty statistics follows closely that of the Weber index. It was therefore decided to overcome the reassessment difficulty by averaging the years between revaluations plus the revaluation year following them. The year was the financial year ending April 5; thus, for example, the difference between the number of houses in existence at April 5, 1876 and April 5, 1875 was taken as an estimate of house-building in 1875.

The counties of England and Wales were divided into two sectors, roughly urban and rural. The urban sector had seven regions—North West England, Northern England, the Midlands, London, the Home Counties, South Wales and Monmouthshire, and Yorkshire. The three rural regions were the Southern agricultural counties, the Midlands agricultural counties and the South West plus rural Wales.

In compiling these regional estimates we had to consider the effects of the frequent changes in income tax districts. Since our classification split the country into large sections, most of the district revisions fell within (and not between) regions and could therefore be ignored. Where major revisions distorted our series we noted these on the tables as boundary revisions and left breaks in the charts for the years affected.

For the years 1893 and 1894 two volumes were missing from the Ashridge ledgers: counties are entered alphabetically, and the missing ledgers contained those beginning S–W (including Wales) for 1893 and B–R for 1894. It was therefore necessary to produce estimates, and in most regions, where there were records for one or more counties, we applied the percentage change for available counties in the region to the missing counties. But in two cases where figures for all the counties in a region were missing the percentage change in ledger section totals were used as a guide: the section containing Lancashire, Leicester and Lincoln was used for the North West, and that containing Wiltshire, Worcester and Yorkshire for Yorkshire. A third method seemed preferable for Wales: in view of the slow increase in houses in rural Wales, we assumed no change here between 1892 and 1893, and allocated the whole increase for Wales to the urban section—South Wales and Monmouthshire.

A grouping of this kind is bound to be arbitrary and parts of regions classified as urban were rural; but the seven regions were urban in the sense that they contained the greater part of the population of England and Wales

[1] Ibid. pp. 236–7.

The counties composing the regions were as follows:

North West England
Cheshire
Lancashire

Northern England
Cumberland
Durham
Northumberland
Westmorland

Midlands
Derbyshire
Leicestershire
Northamptonshire
Nottinghamshire
Staffordshire
Warwickshire
Worcestershire

London

Southern agricultural
Bedfordshire
Berkshire
Buckinghamshire
Cambridgeshire
Gloucestershire
Hampshire
Herefordshire
Norfolk
Oxfordshire
Suffolk
Sussex
Wiltshire

Home Counties
Essex
Hertfordshire
Kent (extra-metropolitan)
Middlesex (extra-metropolitan)
Surrey (extra-metropolitan)

South Wales and Monmouthshire
Breconshire
Cardiganshire
Carmarthenshire
Glamorganshire
Monmouthshire
Pembrokeshire
Radnorshire

Yorkshire

Midlands agricultural
Huntingdonshire
Lincolnshire
Rutland
Shropshire

South West and rural Wales
Cornwall
Devon
Dorset
Somerset
Anglesey
Caernarvonshire
Denbighshire
Flintshire
Merionethshire
Montgomeryshire

in the last quarter of the nineteenth century. A great advantage of the Inhabited House Duty data is that they give even coverage of all parts of the country, so that a comprehensive picture of regional cycles can be obtained.

2. Profits Assessed to Schedule D

The Inland Revenue ledgers contain a great deal of information on profit income assessed to Schedule D. They show gross and net profits, with allowances for wear and tear and life assurances, and a table is given of profits arising from foreign and colonial securities and possessions. Stamp approved the use of Schedule D profits as a guide to trade prosperity. 'This test is generally regarded as one of the most reliable and it has been made by many writers. There is no doubt a close correspondence between the assessments and trade. . . . '[1] Breaks affect the gross assessment series in 1876 and 1894, i.e. the financial years ending April 5, 1877 and 1895, and Stamp presents six alternative methods of allowing for these. We have applied a form of the second method (using abatements) described in his appendix I,[2] and the series are linked accordingly.

This is one more break in 1874. From 1866 to 1874 the profit figures described as gross were actually net of life assurance allowances,[3] and to make them comparable with later series some adjustment for this should be made. Also from 1866 to 1873 we have not deducted profits arising from foreign securities and possessions. If we take the North West, for example, we find that in 1874 the allowances for life assurance amounted to £57,900 and the profits from foreign securities were very small, certainly never more than £100,000 and probably in the region of £50,000 annually. Therefore the two adjustments required would seem to be almost entirely offsetting.

The records contain two sets of figures separating 'Trades, Manufactures, Professions and Employments' from 'Public Companies, societies, etc.' Since there would have been transfers over time from one group to the other with the extension of limited liability, we have taken the two groups together, and have used gross profit figures to avoid breaks caused by statutory changes in allowances and abatements. From this total profit income we have deducted (except in 1866–73) profits earned from foreign securities and possessions. We should also have deducted profits on railways outside the United Kingdom, which are listed separately, in order to get a more accurate figure for domestic profits. However, they were negligible in relation to total profit income, so that they were ignored, except in London for which they were deducted.

Before 1874 abatements were not included in profit income but given separately, so that they had to be added to the figures for profits to make them comparable with subsequent years. With regard to London, before 1875 separate figures are not given for the metropolitan and extra-metropolitan parts of the counties of Kent, Middlesex and Surrey. Therefore an assumption was made that the proportionate distribution of profits between the two areas was the same before 1875 as in the years immediately following. For each of the years 1875–8, 94% of the profits were assessed in the metropolis and so this figure formed the basis for our metropolitan estimates of profit income in 1867–74.

Some of the ledgers are missing for the years 1892 (i.e. the year ended April 5, 1893) and 1893, so an estimate had to be made for profit income (as well as building) for those years. Summary totals in ten sections are available and the percentage change in profits recorded in the relevant year in these section totals was applied to the particular county which forms part of the section.

---

[1] Stamp, op. cit. p. 257.   [2] Ibid. pp. 473–90.   [3] Ibid. p. 207.

Space does not allow an analysis of these data on profits, but the figures have been used as part of the method of handling the demographic data, as explained below.

3. Demographic Data

We have concentrated on population change as reflected in the 20–44 age group and have made quinquennial estimates for each region, separating the effect of natural increase and migration. Data on recorded deaths for each region were collected from the Registrar General's Annual Reports and Decennial Supplements, and these were used with census population figures in quinary age groups to estimate the quinquennial changes which would have occurred in the absence of migration.

The method was as follows. We took the population in quinary age groups at each census date, and allocated recorded deaths for the next five years to these groups, thus obtaining an estimate of the survivors from each group (now five years older) at a mid-census point. In the allocation we assumed that the deaths, say, of persons aged 15–19 during the five years could be allocated on a fifty–fifty basis between the persons aged 10–14 at the census date (moving up into the 15–19 group) and those aged 15–19 at the census date (moving up into the 20–24 group). From these estimates of mid-census survivors we then deducted deaths for the following five years in a similar way to produce an estimate of survivors from the previous census population at the subsequent census date. The difference between actual census population and estimated survivors from the previou*r* census indicates the decade's migratory flows.

Where population is flowing into an area, some of the persons dying would be migrants, and to adjust for this we assumed that migrant deaths bore the same proportion to total deaths in their age groups as these migrants' life-years in the decade bore to total life-years of all persons in the area of the relevant ages for the same decade. That is, we applied the following equation:

$$x = d.c(m-x)/[10(i+x)+c(m-x)],$$

where x is migrants' deaths,

d is total deaths in relevant age groups,
c is life-year coefficient for migrants,
m is migratory flow before adjusting for migrant deaths,
and i is the estimate of survivors from the previous census population at the subsequent census date (i.e. the natural increase component of population) before adjusting for migrant deaths. (The life-year coefficient for i is, of course, 10.)

The figure for x thus obtained was deducted from m and added to i, producing final estimates of migration and natural increase which take account of migrant deaths.

Our 'natural increase' in population aged 20–44 is the change in the number of persons within these age groups shown by the survivor estimates five and ten years later. It should be noted that the increase is based in *both* quinquennia on the population of the preceding census. For the second quinquennium it would have been preferable to calculate from a mid-census population. In order to obtain a mid-census population in quinary age groups, however, we must be able to allocate migration quinquennially for each group of persons as they move up through two succeeding age groups. As we cannot do this with the information available, the base for the second quinquennium has been left as the population of the census taken five years earlier. The definition of natural increase in this context must therefore be carefully noted. The natural increase figures are estimates of the population changes which would have occurred in the two quinquennia following each census if there had been no migration in either of these periods. At each census date the population base is changed, but between census reports it remains the same.

Although it was not possible to split the migration figures quinquennially within each age group, we have used the domestic profit income series as the criterion for allocating the total migration. We have already noted that there is a close correspondence between assessments and trade, and it seems reasonable to assume that migration into an area is likely to occur mainly during times of rising local business activity and that this local activity will also influence the amount of any outflow, with perhaps, in each case, a short lag before the effects are transmitted.

We have taken the years where assessed profit income rose as the probable years of migratory inflow, and the Inland Revenue's use of a preceding year basis of assessment has the effect of introducing a short lag. The next step was to compare the number of probable years of inflow in each interdecadal quinquennium, and split the decade's migration in the proportions indicated by this comparison. For example, if migration probably occurred in five years of the first quinquennium of a decade and in one year of the second, the decade's migration would be split between the quinquennia in the proportions of five to one.

Since we wish to compare the demographic features with the other long swing series, it would have been more satisfactory to use some independent indication of migration. Where population is flowing out of an area we have brought in external factors by looking at the Board of Trade figures for external migration, taking an average of the proportions indicated by internal and oversea criteria. Where net decennial flows were very small, we did not attempt any division of numbers, but merely divided the migrants equally between the two periods. A low decennial total could be misleading where a flow in one direction during one quinquennium is offset by a flow in the opposite direction during the next.

We compared our decadal migration figures with those obtained from the census Reports, having first adjusted our totals to take account of any boundary changes which occurred. The best way of doing this was to compare, say, the total population in 1901 of a region with area of 1891, with population in 1901 of the region with area of 1901, the difference being actually due to a change in boundary. Assuming that 35% of the total population is contained in the age groups 20–44, we reduce or increase migration figures by an amount corresponding to 35% of the numbers spuriously gained or lost by a change in boundary. In some areas it was found that migration in our age group was of opposite sign to total migration, implying that the flow of migrants aged under 20 and over 44 was greater and in the opposite direction.

A special note needs to be added about London. As already mentioned, our method produced estimates of natural increase based, in each inter-decadal quinquennium, on the population at the preceding census date. This did not allow for the effects of migration during the first quinquennium on the natural increase in the second quinquennium. In certain circum-stances, this could give misleading results, as in London where the heavy inward movement of young women (under 20) made the method inap-propriate. Since we could find no way of arriving at a reasonably accurate mid-census population, we took the age group 15–44 for the analysis of London. This avoids the distorting effect which a swollen age group can have on the results shown by our usual method.

CHAPTER XIV

AMERICA-CENTRED INTERPRETATIONS OF THE LONG SWING

The central issue in this reappraisal is the significance of the inverse relation between British and American long swings in capital formation and the mechanism by which migration and capital movements influenced the growth process in the two countries.

I. SPECTRAL ANALYSIS OF LONG SWINGS

The long swing hypothesis has attracted the attention of statisticians using the technique of spectral analysis, and one or two have reported unfavourably. The possibility that long swings might be a statistical mirage was discussed in the first edition of this book in Chapter VII, and it was dismissed.[1] The main series used in this analysis exhibit long swings in the original data: for Britain—emigration, building, home investment, and share prices; for the United States—immigration, building, capital imports, incorporations, railway miles added, and bituminous coal output. The same is true for migration, construction and capital flows in many other countries.

Spectral analysis is relevant where smoothing techniques such as a moving average are used to bring out the cycle. Irma Adelman's conclusion was that 'it is likely that the long swings which have been observed in the U.S. economy since 1890 are due in part to the introduction of spurious long cycles by the smoothing process, and in part to the necessity for averaging over a statistically small number of random shocks'.[2] Apart from objections which might be raised against the methodology of this test, the result is unconvincing for two reasons. The series covered a period profoundly disturbed by two World Wars, and the analysis left out two crucial variables, construction and population.

A more comprehensive test was made by Jon P. Harkness on forty-eight time series for Canada, the majority extending over about a hundred years. He concluded that:

---

[1] Pp. 85-6.

[2] Irma Adelman, 'Long Cycles—Fact or Artifact?', *American Economic Review*, vol. LV, no. 3, June 1965, p. 459. See also R. C. Bird, M. J. Desai, J. J. Enzler and P. J. Taubman, 'Kuznets Cycles in Growth Rates: the Meaning', *International Review*, vol. VI, May 1965, pp. 229-39.

we can accept the hypothesis that long swings exist both in rates of growth and in deviations from trend of economic magnitudes in Canada. This is particularly significant in the case of rates of change, which not only give the most favourable results but also represent the currently most popular version of the long-swing hypothesis. In the case of the deviation-from-trend version, acceptance is based on a preference for harmonic over log-linear trend elimination when using spectral analysis.[1]

There is no reason to expect a different result if the methods used in this investigation were applied to the time series of other countries.

2. THE GAP IN SCHUMPETER'S SYSTEM[2]

As a preliminary step, it is instructive to look again at Schumpeter's account of the growth of Britain, the United States and Germany in the nineteenth century. What difference would it have made to Schumpeter's system if he had not treated international movements of population as an 'external' or exogenous factor, i.e. not inherent in the working of the economic organism itself? He admits in the introductory chapter of *Business Cycles* that 'migrations in particular are so obviously conditioned by business fluctuations that no description of the mechanism of cycles can claim to be complete without including them, and including them—at least some of them—as internal factors'.[3] And then he adds: 'However, as we shall not deal with this group of problems in this volume—although the writer is alive to the seriousness of this breach in our wall—it will be convenient to consider migrations

[1] Jon P. Harkness, 'A Spectral-Analytic Test of the Long-Swing Hypothesis in Canada', *Review of Economics and Statistics*, vol. L, no. 4, November 1968, pp. 429–36. The nature of the results is indicated by the following quotations (pp. 434–5): 'In terms of a two-tail test, estimated spectra of the rate-of-change version are extremely favourable to the long-swing hypothesis. If we accept a frequency band centred on 9·6 years as being within the relevant range, then 45 of the 48 spectra estimated demonstrate quite sharp peaks in the long-cycle frequency bands. The estimates indicate an average period for the Kuznets cycle in all series of between 10 and 14 years, which conforms to the results obtained by Daly in Canada and Abramovitz in the United States, using less sophisticated techniques to test the rate-of-change version. . . . The over-all results of the harmonic trend version are generally favourable to the hypothesis. Of the 48 spectra estimated 30 indicate relatively strong peaks within the long-cycle frequency domain. . . . The average cycle length indicated by the 30 definite series appears to be about 20 years. This conforms with results of other investigators who have dealt with deviations from trend using less sophisticated techniques.'

[2] The theme of this section is developed in my article 'The Rhythm of Growth in the Atlantic Economy' in H. Hegeland (ed.), *Money, Growth and Methodology, and Other Essays in Economics in Honor of Johan Åkerman, March 31, 1961*, Lund, Gleerup, 1961, pp. 39–48.

[3] J. A. Schumpeter, *Business Cycles*, vol. I, p. 10.

over the frontiers of the territories to which our statistics refer, provisionally, as *an external factor*, while migration within those territories, which it would be impossible so to consider, will be noticed but incidentally.'[1] This decision had a far more profound effect on his investigation than he seemed to realize.

The method was to build a set of hypotheses for a closed system and then to seek verification in the economic time series of each country— England, United States and Germany—taken separately. It was argued that the rhythm postulated in the system could be observed simultaneously in the history of the three countries. Unfortunately, there was one irritating exception and it could not be brushed aside as peripheral. Schumpeter found that 'England's economic history from 1897 to 1913 cannot, owing to the comparative weakness of the evolution (in our sense) of her domestic industries, be written in terms of our model—the only case of this kind within the epoch covered by our material.'[2] One cannot help wondering why perfidious Albion failed to toe the line in this period. There is a significant clue in *Business Cycles*, where the reader is reminded that 'the cyclical aspects of international relations . . . cannot receive due attention within this book'.[3] Then comes this important admission:

Of all the limitations imposed by the plan and purpose of this book, this is the most serious one. *Not only do cycles in different countries systematically affect each other, so much so that the history of hardly any one of them can be written without reference to simultaneous cyclical phases in other countries*, but cycles really are, especially as regards the great innovations which produced the Kondratieffs' international phenomena. That is to say, such a process as the railroadization or the electrification of the world transcends the boundaries of individual countries in such a way as to be more truly described as one world-wide process than as the sum of distinct national ones. Capitalism itself is, both in the economic and the sociological sense, essentially one process, with the whole earth as its stage.[4]

This is a crucial point. If the phenomena under review were 'one worldwide process' and not 'the sum of distinct national ones', one would have thought that Schumpeter might at least have indicated that his mode of verification, based on the notion that the process *was* the sum of distinct national ones, was to be regarded as merely a first approximation. Instead of that, he went on to say that

Both reasons—interactions and supernational unity of fundamental processes —explain why in our historical survey the cycles in our three countries were found to be so much in step. The fact that they were is not more obvious

[1] J. A. Schumpeter, *Business Cycles*, vol. 1, p. 10. (My italics.)
[2] Ibid. vol. 1, p. 435.   [3] Ibid. vol. 11, p. 666.   [4] Ibid. (My italics.)

than the mechanism that produced it and also—in principle, at least—the manner in which these relations affected the working of pre-war central banks and of the pre-war gold standard.[1]

Schumpeter was bent on having it both ways.

What happens when the basic postulates are changed? First, let us regard international factor movements as endogenous and the countries belonging to the Atlantic community as an entity, the Atlantic economy. Secondly, let us transfer attention from the Kitchin, Juglar and Kondratieff fluctuations to the Kuznets cycle. In other words, we conceive the evolution of capitalism (as Schumpeter said we ought to) as a process transcending national boundaries, and we drop his three cycle scheme. This was the starting-point of the analysis in Part III above. As soon as we regard the individual nations as regions comprising an aggregate and we ask what are the conditions under which the rate of growth of income in this aggregate can be maximized over time, there is no reason to expect each of the parts to pass through identical and simultaneous phases according to a theory of a closed system. Secular growth entails internal shifts within the aggregate via international factor movements; the expansion of the whole may well express itself through disharmonious rates of growth in the parts. This is what happened in the Atlantic economy between the middle of the nineteenth century and the First World War. There was an inverse relation between the long swings in capital formation in the United Kingdom and in countries of new settlement overseas. There were four major outflows of population and capital from Europe: 1845–54, 1863–73, 1881–8 and 1903–13. The upward phase of the long swing in transatlantic migration and foreign lending coincided with an upswing in capital construction in the United States and a downswing in capital construction in the United Kingdom; the downward phase of the long swing in transatlantic migration and foreign lending coincided with a downswing in capital construction in the United States and an upswing in capital construction in the United Kingdom.

It seems to be a condition of this inverse investment cycle that (a) a substantial part of capital formation is sensitive to the rate of population growth, and (b) the rate of population growth is mainly determined by the net migration balance. The mechanism also entails an inverse relation between internal and external migration. For example, when capital exports to the United States were in the upswing phase and British home construction was relatively declining, surplus labour from the rural sector in Britain tended to migrate to America rather than to urban areas at home. In the succeeding phase when the rate of

[1] Ibid.

capital formation in Britain rose rapidly, the workers released from agriculture moved into the flourishing industrial towns and emigration ebbed away. A wave of home construction drew the rural surplus into urban employment at home; a wave of foreign investment drew the rural surplus into urban employment abroad. International movements of labour and capital were thus a pivotal element in determining the time-shape of economic development in the sending and receiving countries. One may summarize the process as an interregional competition for factors of production within the Atlantic economy, with the Old World and the New World alternating in their intensive build-up of resources.[1] This is the essential characteristic which distinguishes these long swings from short business cycles. Long swings are fluctuations in the rate at which resources are developed, whereas the short business cycles are fluctuations in investment in producer durables and inventories.

From this analysis it is clear that Schumpeter was not justified in claiming that 'interactions and supernational unity of fundamental processes' gave added support to his finding that the cycles in his three countries were in step. On the contrary, this particular approach leads to inverse long swings and to the conclusion that the United States economy had fluctuations of a greater amplitude than the United Kingdom because in the latter country movements in home investment were counterbalanced by opposite movements in foreign investment and this was not the case in the United States. The difference between American and British experience could be put as follows. In the United States a wave of prosperity (or depression) in building would usually be transmitted to the rest of the economy; in the United Kingdom (where the export sector and the home construction sector were more evenly balanced) a wave of prosperity (or depression) in building was partially offset by an opposite swing in the export sector.

3 · ONE-SIDED INTERPRETATIONS

An odd feature of some contributions to the literature is a propensity to regard the economic growth of individual countries (usually the author's own) as domestically determined. There is a disposition among some American economists to seek an explanation of every

[1] R. C. O. Matthews, in *The Trade Cycle*, Cambridge University Press, 1959, accepts the reality of the inverse relation and the interpretation suggested above. 'At least as far as building is concerned, migration is perhaps the most plausible explanation, but the other causes have probably had some significance as well, especially competition for finance' (p. 194).

feature of American long swings almost exclusively in terms of forces operating within the United States itself. According to Abramovitz:

a long swing in the volume of additions, perhaps even in the rate of growth of additions, to the stock of capital, that is, in capital formation, is likely to involve a fluctuation in effective demand and thus to generate an alternation between states of relatively full and relatively slack employment. A long swing in unemployment rates in turn appears to have been among the chief causes of Kuznets cycles in the volume of additions to the labor force and, perhaps, in capital formation.[1]

This mechanism interprets swings in immigration to the United States as '...responses to the occurrences of protracted periods of abnormally high unemployment and to the recovery from such periods'.[2] No significance is attached to an interaction between the United States and other economies. Similarly Easterlin's analysis of European migration to the United States concludes that 'on the whole the movements were dominated by conditions in this country'.[3] This stress on unilateral causation finds adherents in O'Leary and Arthur Lewis who assert that 'the U.S. governed its own fortunes in the nineteenth century and if any adjustment had to be made it was made on the other side of the Atlantic'.[4]

This line of thought, at first sight, is not without some degree of credibility when applied to an economy of the stature of America even in the second half of the nineteenth century, but economic self-determination is hardly reasonable in the case of Australia. Net capital inflow from Britain to the Australian colonies in the eighteen-sixties and eighties was about half their gross domestic capital formation in each decade; gross residential construction accounted for one-third of gross capital formation; unassisted immigration was by far the most important single factor governing housing demand; high levels of pastoral investment were increasingly financed in the eighteen-seventies and eighties by Scottish law firms and solicitors advising clients to buy Australian debentures; the ratio of British to Australian-held deposits in Australian banks rose from 10% in 1873-4 to 37% in 1891; and by 1889 nearly 40% of the proceeds of Australian exports were mortgaged for investment income payable to Britain. And yet, despite these

[1] M. Abramovitz, 'The Nature and Significance of Kuznets Cycles', *Economic Development and Cultural Change*, vol. IX, no. 3, April 1961, p. 230.

[2] Ibid. p. 243.

[3] R. A. Easterlin, 'Influences in European Overseas Emigration before World War I', *Economic Development and Cultural Change*, vol. IX, no. 3, April 1961, p. 348.

[4] P. J. O'Leary and W. Arthur Lewis, 'Secular Swings in Production and Trade, 1870–1913', *Manchester School*, vol. XXIII, no. 2, May 1955, p. 126. This statement is very wide of the mark: if anything it was the other way about, as will be apparent in Chapter XV.

significant evidences of the close economic dependence of the colonies on Britain produced by Noel Butlin in his monumental work on the period 1861–1900,[1] this author argues that the decisive influences on events were in Australia. For example, he states that '... the basic determinants of the speed, stability and complexity of Australian growth were in local Australian conditions'[2] and that 'the rate of inflow of British capital and merchandise imports and the allocation of funds and resources between different activities were determined in Australia'.[3]

Is it plausible to think that the nature and time-shape of the economic growth of Australia were domestically determined? Surely what is called for here is an examination of the process of interaction between a small developing country with a population (in 1861) of just over one million and the advanced factor-providing country with a population of twenty-three million. Without giving any convincing reasons, Butlin dismisses the explanation of Britain's capital outflow in terms of inverse long swings in home and foreign investment, although the evidence for it in this period is overwhelming. Nearly all the data for a statistical test of this explanation and of Butlin's hypothesis are in his book.

A similar preoccupation with the dominance of domestic factors in the United Kingdom is to be seen in the work of H. J. Habakkuk and S. B. Saul which we have already discussed. Their contention was that the effect of migration on British building fluctuations, 1870–1913, was of minor significance compared with domestic or fortuitous factors. This has been refuted by the quantitative evidence about the migration determinant presented in Chapter XIII.

The same applies to the views of O'Leary and Arthur Lewis. Intrigued by the inverse relation but sceptical of the influence of migration and capital flows, these authors confess that they 'cannot rule out the possibility that the alternation of the U.S. and U.K. building cycles was a sheer accident, springing perhaps from the different effects which the Napoleonic Wars may have had upon the progress of residential building in the two countries'.[4] An engaging thought but hardly to be taken seriously. The statistical picture presented in Chapter XIII does not look very much like a belated fall-out from the Napoleonic Wars.

Those who interpret the growth and fluctuations of individual countries as domestically determined seem to forget a fundamental truth which Alfred Marshall expressed in a famous analogy relating to

---

[1] Noel G. Butlin, *Investment in Australian Economic Development, 1861–1900*, Cambridge University Press, 1964.

[2] Ibid. p. 31.

[3] Ibid. p. 38.

[4] P. J. O'Leary and W. A. Lewis, loc. cit. p. 127.

the question whether value is governed by utility or cost of production. 'We might as reasonably dispute whether it is the upper or the under blade of a pair of scissors which cuts a piece of paper.... It is true that when one blade is held still, and the cutting is effected by moving the other, we may say with careless brevity that the cutting is done by the second, but the statement is not strictly accurate, and is to be excused only so long as it claims to be merely a popular and not a strictly scientific account of what happens.'[1] This gem of Marshallian wisdom is highly relevant in the present context.

4. LIMITATIONS OF AMERICA-CENTRED MODELS

It was Simon Kuznets who first drew attention to the significance of the long swing as a feature of economic growth; his work has inspired most of the analytical developments in this field. It is fitting that this type of fluctuation should now be known as the Kuznets cycle.

The mechanism of a self-perpetuating long swing in the United States up to the nineteen-twenties which Kuznets tentatively put forward was as follows.

The long swings in additions to per capita flow of goods to consumers resulted, with some lag, in long swings first in the net migration balance and then in the natural increase, yielding swings in total population growth. The latter then induced, again with some lag, similar swings in population-sensitive capital formation, which caused inverted long swings in 'other' capital formation, and in changes in per capita flow of goods to consumers. The swings in the latter then started another long swing in the net migration balance, and so on.[2]

One of Kuznets's path-breaking contributions is the distinction between, on the one hand, population-sensitive capital formation, i.e. non-farm residential construction and capital expenditure by railroads, and, on the other hand, 'other' capital formation, i.e. construction other than non-farm residential or railroad (largely industrial plant, store and office building), producers' durable equipment other than railroad (largely industrial machinery), changes in inventories (largely in distributive channels), and changes in net claims against foreign countries.[3] He found an inverse relation between the swings in these two components of capital formation, and this was explained by the

[1] Alfred Marshall, *Principles of Economics*, 8th ed., London, Macmillan, 1922, bk. v, ch. 3, p. 348.
[2] S. Kuznets, 'Long Swings in the Growth of Population and in Related Economic Variables', *Proceedings of the American Philosophical Society*, vol. cii, no. 1, February 1958, p. 34.
[3] Ibid. p. 33.

savings constraint on total capital formation having the result that
'...acceleration (or deceleration) in the population-sensitive components left so much less (or so much more) room for the growth of other
capital formation. This restraining influence of a limit on total
capital formation appears to have been removed in the nineteen-
twenties, and synchronism has prevailed since.'[1] The inverse relation
between the two capital formation components is essential to the logic
of Kuznets's model. However, the degree to which savings were a
restraining influence depends to a considerable extent on an external
factor—the inflow of funds from abroad, mainly Britain. The use
which his formulation makes of the savings constraint is a tacit admission that the long swing in America was partly determined by demand
and supply conditions in the British capital market. The implications
of this are not worked out.

Moreover, the explanation depends on a suspiciously long 'lag'
between additions to the flow of goods to consumers and additions to
population. The point to notice here is that Kuznets regards changes
in the per capita flow of goods to consumers as an index of the varying
strength of the 'pull' which the American economy exercised on net
immigration: the empirical evidence shows an inverse relation between
swings in immigration, additions to population and population-
sensitive capital formation, on the one hand, and 'other' capital
formation and the per capita flow of goods to consumers on the other.
The argument then runs as follows.

The long swings in additions to flow of consumer goods *per capita* are
inverted to those in additions to population before World War I—and quite
prominent. *Yet they suggest one explanation of the swings in additions to popula-*
tion, if we allow for a long lag that would, in a sense, turn negative into positive
association. . . . Immigration, particularly in its timing, could be assumed to
be responsive to the pull—that is, largely to conditions in this country
rather than in the country of origin. This assumption of the responsiveness
to the pull is clearly indicated by the fact that *net* additions were affected not
only by gross inflow but also by emigration, which clearly reflected conditions
in this country. It is indicated also by the fact that the long swings in
emigration from various countries of origin were fairly similar. One could,
then, argue that a sizable reduction in additions to per capita flow of goods
to consumers (with some lag), all other things being equal, would represent a
discouragement to immigration, while a sizable rise in additions to per
capita flow of goods to consumers would represent an encouragement.[2]

Kuznets emphasizes that this '...is a tentative sketch designed to
indicate lines of further exploration and does not claim even rough

[1] S. Kuznets, *Capital in the American Economy*, p. 333.
[2] Ibid. pp. 347–8. The italics for the sentence are mine.

validity'.[1] The trouble is that to make it work he has to turn the inverse relation between immigration and flow of goods to consumers into a positive one and insert a long lag. This is asking too much. Since these are *long* swings with a span of about twenty years, the implied response interval stretches over so many years that it cannot be meaningful. And what justification can there be for singling out one particular case of inverse relation and calling it a long 'lag'? If it is right to do it in one case, why not in others too? One must reject this linking of swings in immigration to swings in flow of goods to consumers. Nevertheless, Kuznets's distinction between population-sensitive and other capital formation is crucial to an understanding of the international aspects of the long swing mechanism, as we shall see later.

A major contribution to the theory of long swings has been made by Abramovitz.[2] He regards them as 'the outcome of interactions between the pace at which resources were developed, the generation of effective demand, and the intensity of resource use'.[3] The long swing in the inflow of labour from various countries depends on a 'common cause' in the United States, i.e. the long swing in unemployment. Abramovitz does recognize interactions via the foreign balance, international capital movements and the supply of money, but the whole emphasis is on the unilateral swing of demand in the United States. There is only one indirect mention of the inverse relation between American and British long swings when he says that 'the competing pressures for finance of British home investment and of demands in other areas of the world played their parts in determining whether the United States could continue to finance a large deficit'.[4] No attempt is made to quantify these competing pressures or to discuss their implications.

A comprehensive examination of the demographic aspects of Kuznets cycles is to be found in Easterlin's authoritative work.[5] Like Abramovitz, he regards immigration as depending on the swing of unemployment in the United States. He found that he could test this hypothesis adequately only in the period beginning in 1890 when estimates of unemployment began to be recorded. An analysis of reference-cycle averages for the years 1890–1915, covering one long swing, gave a close correspondence between the rate of change of output and that of unemployment and between the average unemployment rate and the gross immigration rate, with the former leading. Extending the test back to 1870 in decennial periods, by using Lebergott's estimates of

[1] S. Kuznets, 'Long Swings in the Growth of Population and Related Economic Variables', p. 34.
[2] Abramovitz, 'The Nature and Significance of Kuznets Cycles'.
[3] Ibid. p. 246.   [4] Ibid.
[5] R. A. Easterlin, *Population, Labor Force, and Long Swings in Economic Growth*.

unemployment, he obtained for 1870–1965 a correspondence between
the first differences of the induced component of labour force growth,
i.e. net migration plus participation rate change, and the first differences
of the average unemployment rate.[1] From these findings, which are
what one would expect, Easterlin concludes that the swings in immigration were determined unilaterally in the receiving country; but
this does not necessarily follow.

There is an extraordinary omission in Easterlin's analysis. At no
point does he pay any attention to long swings in the inflow of capital.
The mechanism of the long swing in the United States cannot be
properly interpreted if this aspect is left out. The United Kingdom
in the eighteen-seventies and eighties carried much more weight in the
international economy than the United States. In 1870 Britain accounted for 31·8% of world manufacturing output as against 23·3% in
the United States and 13·2% in Germany; in 1880–5 the proportions
were 26·6%, 28·6% and 13·9% respectively.[2] In 1880 Britain was
responsible for 63·1% of world exports of capital goods and 41·4% of
world exports of manufactured goods as compared with 19·0% and
19·3% respectively in Germany and 5·7% and 2·8% respectively in the
United States.[3]

Between 1869 and 1876 the net inflow of foreign capital into the
United States was on the average 15·5% of total net capital formation,
and from 1882 to 1893 it was 10·3%. In the period 1870–1914 Britain
was the source of between 55 and 60% of foreign investment in the
American economy.[4] These are significant quantities. By ignoring
them, Easterlin was bound to get a one-sided view of the long swing
mechanism. As Williamson pointed out, 'with this knowledge, surely
we must find that domestic investment opportunities for British capital
had an important impact on the movement of foreign capital into the
United States'.[5] This goes for the parallel movements of immigration
as well.

At one crucial point Easterlin is assailed by doubt. He points out
that 'several studies have indicated that economic activity in the
European countries also shows long swings'.[6] He then makes this

[1] R. A. Easterlin, *Population . . .* , pp. 148–53.   [2] See p. 120.
[3] S. B. Saul, 'The Export Economy 1870–1914' in J. Saville (ed.), *Studies in the
British Economy 1870–1914*, Special Number, *Yorkshire Bulletin of Economic and Social
Research*, vol. XVII, no. 1, May 1965, pp. 12 and 16.
[4] See Jeffrey G. Williamson, *American Growth and the Balance of Payments, 1820–
1913*, University of North Carolina Press, 1964, pp. 142–5 and the sources cited
there.
[5] Ibid. p. 145.
[6] R. A. Easterlin, 'Influences in European Overseas Emigration before World
War I', p. 347.

admission. 'If these were common in timing and *inversely* related to those in the United States, then the view attributing dominant importance to swings in American demand would be weakened.'[1] He discounts this possibility by saying that 'O'Leary and Lewis on the basis of series referring primarily to industrial output and exports in France, Germany, Great Britain and the United States lean towards the view that investment booms in the respective countries were fairly autonomous'.[2] This article by O'Leary and Lewis confirms the inverse relation between swings in capital formation in Britain and the United States. Having said that 'writers have sought to explain why investment in the U.S. and the U.K. should have fluctuated in opposite directions',[3] these authors go on to discuss possible reasons for this phenomenon. They suggest that the Kuznets cycles in these two countries and France and Germany were 'autonomous'; but this does not mean—and on their evidence could not mean—that there was no inverse relation between British and American swings.

Easterlin criticizes the thesis of Part III of this book, and contends that 'Brinley Thomas, in his analysis, appears to suggest that swings in the British economy as *a whole* were inversely related to those in the United States (op. cit. pp. 108–13). His comparison of the movements in the United States and the United Kingdom national product series, however, shows little evidence of systematic inverse movements.'[4] This is a question of fact. The statistics are set out in Fig. 48 and they indicate clear inverse swings in rates of change in real national income per head in the United States and the United Kingdom between 1869 and 1913. The evidence also refutes R. C. O. Matthews's statement, quoted by Easterlin, that 'despite the elements of inversion referred to, fluctuations in *national income* in Great Britain have not generally stood in an inverse relation to those in the United States'.[5] The British long swing in real national income per capita, real wages and the level of employment between 1871 and 1913 is shown in Fig. 24. National income in Britain fluctuated with a smaller amplitude than in the United States because the offsetting effect of the export sector was so much larger in Britain.[6]

---

[1] Ibid. p. 347. (Italics in the original.)   [2] Ibid.
[3] P. J. O'Leary and W. A. Lewis, loc. cit. p. 125.
[4] Easterlin, loc. cit. pp. 347–8. (Italics in the original.)
[5] R. C. O. Matthews, *The Trade Cycle*, p. 194. (Italics in the original.)
[6] The Kuznets–Easterlin theory of unilateral 'pull' has even been applied to United States growth in the eighteen-fifties where it is least plausible. Albert Fishlow, in his *American Railroads and the Transformation of the Ante-Bellum Economy*, Cambridge, Mass., Harvard University Press, 1965, ch. IV, maintains (p. 202) that 'pending further analysis, and more is needed, we should not be quick to overthrow the hypothesis advanced by Kuznets and others that the common response of many European

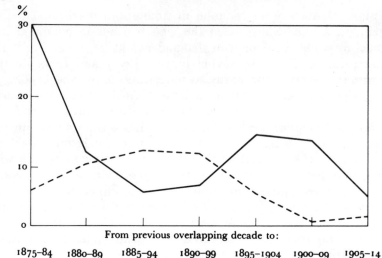

From previous overlapping decade to:

1875–84   1880–89   1885–94   1890–99   1895–1904   1900–09   1905–14

FIG. 48. The United States and the United Kingdom: rate of change (from decade to overlapping decade) in real national income per head, 1869–1913. ——— The United States (1929 prices). – – – The United Kingdom (1913 prices). Sources: S. Kuznets, 'Long Swings in the Growth of Population and in Related Economic Variables', table 15; Brinley Thomas, 'The Dimensions of British Economic Growth, 1688–1959', *Journal of the Royal Statistical Society*, series A, vol. CXXVII, pt. 1, 1964, p. 121, Table 2.

The demonstration of the inverse relation in Part III has been confirmed by later research,[1] including the analysis in Chapter XIII of the demographic determinants of building cycles in Britain and the United States. On Easterlin's own admission, this weakens the view

countries suggests a single external cause, the state of the American economy.... the railroad was an important determinant of that economy in the 1850s.' In his attempt to justify this, he criticizes my analysis in Chapter VII above on the ground that the figures I used led me to locate the peak of railroad construction in 1856, whereas it is now established by Fishlow's more accurate estimates that the peak was in 1853–4 (p. 201). However, this makes no difference to my argument on pp. 92–4 above. The fundamental point is that the peak in immigration from Europe came in 1851 (see Table 96), two to three years before the peak in railway building. Indeed Fishlow's own analysis confirms that settlement preceded railway building; he points out (p. 175) that '... by the time that many prairie railroads were finally completed, even if not in their earliest planning stage, not inconsiderable settlement and economic development had already taken place'. An important element in this process of prior settlement was the arrival of nearly three million immigrants in the decade ending in 1854 (most of them expelled from Ireland by calamity and from Germany by agrarian crisis), an influx which was no less than one-sixth of the population of America in 1844. In the interaction process in that period the supply side had more force than the demand (see the lag analysis on pp. 159–60 above).

[1] See Arthur I. Bloomfield, *Patterns of Fluctuation in International Investment before 1914*, pp. 21–4.

that swings in American demand were dominant. However, the matter cannot rest there. This issue will not be settled by models of the long swing which ignore international interaction and which take no account of the transmission mechanism linking money with other economic variables. The long swing models referred to in this chapter are all deficient in this respect. From 1879, when the United States resumed specie payments at the pre-Civil War parity, to 1913 the leading countries of the Atlantic economy were on the gold standard. The financial dominance of London and the international repercussions of the Bank of England's policy were major factors. In each country there was an interaction between the 'real' economic magnitudes and the changes in the supply of money entailed by the discipline of the gold standard. In the next chapter we shall examine this interaction as part of an attempt to explain the inverse rhythm of growth in the United Kingdom, the leading lender, on the one hand, and the United States and other countries of new settlement, on the other.

CHAPTER XV

THE ATLANTIC ECONOMY:
THE PROCESS OF INTERACTION

The analysis in Part III and the new findings in Chapter XIII can be summarized as follows. The long swing was a fluctuation in the building up of infrastructure. The transfer of factors within the Atlantic economy did not proceed evenly through time. The highly industrialized creditor country was heavily dependent on the underdeveloped debtor countries for food and raw materials. When industrialization was advancing rapidly in the United States and other countries of new settlement, with the aid of capital and immigrants from Europe, Great Britain could not have an upsurge in her own capital formation. In the upswing phase of the migration-lending cycle, the debtor countries pushed ahead with investment in their infrastructure; then in the downswing phase it was the turn of the creditor country to do likewise, aided by a copious flow of imports of food and raw materials from the debtor countries, made possible by the investment boom in the previous period.

Between the eighteen-forties and the nineteen-twenties about fifty million migrants moved into the continent of North and South America; after this great reshuffle one-eleventh of the population of the world was people originating in Europe living outside that continent. By 1913 Great Britain, the world's leading lender, had invested £3,763 million abroad, 70% of which was located in North America, South America and Oceania.[1] In the words of Schumpeter, 'the story of the way in which civilized humanity got and fought cheap bread is the story of American railroads and American machinery'.[2] The part played by agriculture in the economic involvement between America and Europe must not be underestimated. Output per man-hour in the production of wheat and oats in the United States went up fourfold between the eighteen-forties and the early nineteen-hundreds. Even as late as the eighties farming accounted for over half the labour force in the United States, and foodstuffs and crude materials comprised as much as 80% of total exports, the major market being the United Kingdom. There

[1] For an extended treatment of foreign investment see Brinley Thomas, 'The Historical Record of International Capital Movements to 1913', also the comment on this paper by George Borts, both in John H. Adler (ed.), *Capital Movements and Economic Development*, London, Macmillan, 1967, pp. 3–32 and 60–6.

[2] J. A. Schumpeter, *Business Cycles*, vol. I, p. 319.

was a high industrial input (drawing heavily on the metal industries) into agriculture and new settlement. Leontief has estimated that a dollar's worth of agricultural output requires far more iron and steel output and machinery production than does an equivalent dollar volume of output generated by textiles or miscellaneous manufacturing, or even by the iron and steel industry itself.[1] A significant proportion of agricultural investment was devoted to land clearing which entailed substantial demands for breaking ploughs, axes, scythes and hoes.[2]

In a fundamental sense the evolution of American agriculture represented the very heart of the process of interaction between the New World and the Old. In the words of Robert E. Lipsey,

since agricultural exports played so large a role, the development of American trade during this period must be studied against the background of shifting and interacting supply and demand conditions for agricultural production in the United States and her chief market—Europe. These supply and demand changes were interrelated; long-term shifts in supply conditions encouraged and yet depended on the changes in demand.... The Eastern seaboard of the United States played the same role *vis-à-vis* the West that Europe played in relation to the United States, as its population shifted from rural to urban areas and from agriculture into manufacturing.[3]

For some commodities, foreign trade...quickly provided an extensive market which could only have been created much more slowly by the growth of the American economy itself. In this respect American development depended on the willingness of the older industrial nations, particularly the U.K., to permit their domestic resources to be shifted out of agriculture by the influx of cheaper products from the developing areas.[4]

Any interpretation of the interaction between the British and American economies in the pre-1913 period must also account for the fact that all the oversea developing countries—for example, the United States, Canada, Argentina, and Australia—had their investment upswings and downswings at the same time. Those who have attempted a one-sided explanation of the long swing in terms of variations in American aggregate demand see supporting evidence in the fact that there were *simultaneous* swings in migration from a number of European countries to the United States:[5] they never posed the

[1] W. Leontief, 'Factor Proportions and the Structure of American Trade: Further Theoretical and Empirical Analysis', *Review of Economics and Statistics*, vol. xxxviii, no. 4, November 1956, app. iii.

[2] S. Lebergott, 'Labor Force and Employment 1800–1960' in *Output, Employment and Productivity in the United States after 1800*, Columbia University Press, 1966.

[3] R. E. Lipsey, *Price and Quantity Trends in the Foreign Trade of the United States*, Princeton University Press, 1963, p. 45.

[4] Ibid. p. 52.

[5] See Chapter xiv, p. 238.

question why there were *simultaneous* immigration and investment swings in a number of countries of new settlement. This latter phenomenon, which can hardly be explained by swings in United States demand, is an important part of the problem of the causation of the inverse cycles.[1]

The answer is to be sought in two basic features of the period. First, the opening up of new sources of food and raw materials required flows of population and capital funds to be invested in infrastructure overseas, and there was necessarily a long lag between the input phase and the output phase. As Schumpeter said, this was essentially one vast process transcending national boundaries, with the whole earth as its stage. Secondly, the countries were linked together by the gold standard dominated by London, the financial centre of the world. When an infrastructure boom overseas became intense, there was a serious problem of under-effected transfer; and strong action by the Bank of England to protect its reserve had powerful repercussions on the supply of money in all oversea borrowing countries.

I. THE MONETARY FACTOR

In the first edition of this book I argued that an explanation of inverse long swings would be found in the 'real' type of theory then being developed. Monetary influences were not ignored, but they did not form an important part of the mechanism of interaction.[2] In this re-examination it is necessary to take into account recent developments in monetary economics and particularly the new empirical work on the supply of money in the period under review. There have also been

---

[1] Space does not allow an analysis of British fluctuations in investment and trade in relation to those of countries of Europe. That the primary causal forces were within the Atlantic economy is attested by the following comparison between Germany and Britain based on the matrix of world trade in 1887: see P. J. O'Leary and W. A. Lewis, loc. cit. p. 129. Germany was responsible for 11·7% of world exports, about nine-tenths going to Europe including the United Kingdom and under one-tenth to the United States; she took 11·5% of world exports, only 8% of which came from the United States and 88% from Europe including the United Kingdom. The United Kingdom was responsible for 16·5% of world exports, two-thirds going overseas and one-third to Europe; she took 25% of world exports, of which 54% came from overseas (22% from the United States) and 46% from Europe. Since one-fifth of German exports went to the United Kingdom, the German export sector was geared to home construction swings in Britain and not those in the United States, and this would make the German construction cycle coincide with that of America.

[2] See chapter XI, pp. 181–3 and 'Migration and International Investment' in Brinley Thomas (ed.), *The Economics of International Migration*, London, Macmillan, 1958, pp. 3–11, reprinted in A. R. Hall (ed.), *The Export of Capital from Britain 1870–1914*, London, Methuen, 1968, pp. 45–54.

notable advances in the study of long swings; for example, the invaluable contributions of Simon Kuznets, particularly his 'Long Swings in the Growth of Population and in Related Economic Variables' and *Capital in the American Economy*.[1] Another major source of new data on the United States is the work on population redistribution and economic growth, 1870–1950, by Kuznets, A. R. Miller and R. A. Easterlin.[2] Thanks to the monumental work of Milton Friedman and Anna Schwartz, our knowledge of the evolution of the money stock of the United States has been immensely enriched.[3] There is also Phillip Cagan's illuminating book, *Determinants and Effects of Changes in the Stock of Money 1875–1960*.[4]

There is plenty of room for improvement in British monetary statistics. Take, for example, the sources on the rate of growth of bank deposits in Britain over the period 1878–1914. Confident conclusions by several writers, including Pigou, Schumpeter, Tinbergen and Rostow, were based on a series which give the *Economist*'s total for *reporting* banks only, but they are very misleading, particularly in the earlier decades.[5] René P. Higonnet, who unearthed comprehensive estimates from the relevant issues of the *Economist* for the years 1877–1914, revealed the fragile character of arguments founded on the incomplete estimates. 'Econometric research, monetary theory and business cycle theory have been seriously led astray; for it makes little sense to compare the deposits of, say, 60 per cent of the banks with those of 90 per cent of the banks at another time, without any adjustment.'[6] An influential article by J. T. Phinney, using these defective data, purported to show that between 1875 and 1913 there was 'a relatively constant rate of growth of bank reserves and bank currency, quite unaffected by variations in gold production or by trends in prices'.[7] The corrected estimates show that this is not true: there were clear fluctuations in the growth of bank money.[8] Rostow, relying on

[1] See pp. 237 and 238 above.

[2] S. Kuznets, A. R. Miller and R. A. Easterlin, *Population Redistribution and Economic Growth, United States 1870–1950*, vol. II, *Analysis of Economic Change*, Philadelphia, American Philosophical Society, 1960.

[3] Milton Friedman and Anna Jacobson Schwartz, *A Monetary History of the United States 1867–1960*, Princeton University Press, 1963.

[4] Phillip Cagan, *Determinants and Effects of Changes in the Stock of Money 1875–1960*, Columbia University Press, 1965.

[5] These are the figures in Walter T. Layton and Geoffrey Crowther, *An Introduction to the Study of Prices*, London, Macmillan, 1938, app. C, p. 253, table III.

[6] René P. Higonnet, 'Bank Deposits in the United Kingdom 1870–1912', *Quarterly Journal of Economics*, vol. LXXI, no. 3, August 1957, p. 332.

[7] J. T. Phinney, 'Gold Production and the Price Level: the Cassel Three Per Cent Estimate', *Quarterly Journal of Economics*, vol. XLVII, no. 3, August 1933, p. 677.

[8] See Higonnet, loc. cit. pp. 354–8.

Phinney, reached spurious conclusions about the monetary interpretation of the fall in the price level from 1873 to 1896.[1] And so did
Schumpeter.[2] In a penetrating critique of Rostow's views, D. H.
Robertson concluded with the comment: 'Respectfully, I do not
believe the last has been heard of the view that gold had something
more than other kinds of dirt to do with the behaviour of money prices
in the gold-using nineteenth century.'[3]

Friedman and Schwartz, in their summary of the course of the money
supply in the United States in the years 1867–1913, recognize the
existence of long swings; but they are reluctant to regard them as
cyclical in character. They prefer to interpret the period 1873–1913
as 'a relatively stable rate of growth interrupted by two monetary
episodes from which the system rebounded to approximately its initial
path.'[4] However, they do add that:

it is worth emphasizing here that there is an alternative interpretation which
would designate 1879 or thereabouts as the trough of a long cycle, some date
in the 1880s as the peak and in the mid-1890s as a second trough, and something like 1906 as the next peak. And this interpretation is based not alone
on the evidence for these four decades, but also on data that suggest the
existence of swings of roughly the same duration for a much longer period
before and since. On this alternative interpretation, the monetary difficulties
are in part the product of the underlying cyclical process.... We have
described these interpretations as if they were mutually exclusive. Of course,
they are not. One can regard the monetary events partly as shocks that
trigger a cyclical reaction mechanism; partly as consequences of prior
cyclical reactions...for the United States, the movements of capital from
and to the outside world played an important role in monetary changes, and
they too can be regarded as moving in long swings and as reflecting the
fundamental factors giving rise to coordinated long swings in a variety of
economic activities.[5]

This is a scrupulously fair statement of the fundamental issues and it
serves as an excellent starting-point for our reappraisal.

[1] 'Explanations of the Great Depression' in W. W. Rostow, *British Economy of the
Nineteenth Century*, pp. 145–60. Higonnet comments (loc. cit. pp. 353–4): 'Rostow's
differences of opinion with Sir Robert Giffen, whom he criticizes, are not, as he
believes, those of "men observing honestly the same set of data", but those of men
observing honestly different sets of data, and Sir Robert Giffen's set of data is far
superior to Rostow's.' For a refutation of Rostow's thesis regarding a relative cessation
of foreign lending during 'The Great Depression', see p. 188 above.

[2] J. A. Schumpeter, *Business Cycles*, vol. II, p. 473.

[3] D. H. Robertson, 'New Light on an Old Story', *Economica*, new series, vol. xv,
no. 60, November 1948, p. 297.

[4] Friedman and Schwartz, op. cit. p. 187.

[5] Ibid. pp. 187–8.

2. OUTLINES OF AN INTERACTION MODEL

We regard the Atlantic economy of the second half of the nineteenth century as comprising, on the one hand, Great Britain, highly industrialized with growing population pressure on a small land area and, on the other, a periphery of under-populated developing countries with extensive land and natural resources. Britain practised free trade, London was the financial centre of the system and the gold standard was virtually a sterling standard.

The following hypotheses may be put forward about the interaction between the creditor country (C) and the factor-importing 'country' (D) (representing the whole periphery):

(i) Each is divided into two sectors, home construction and export.

(ii) C exports capital goods and D food and raw materials.

(iii) Migration depends on the difference in real wages which can be approximated by the difference in real incomes.

(iv) Export capacity is generated through population-sensitive capital formation, i.e. the building of infrastructure—railways, roads, land clearing, ports, houses, public utilities, etc.—and this investment has a relatively long gestation period. There is an inter-temporal relation between a country's infrastructure investment in one period and its export capacity in the next period.

(v) The level of activity of a country's export sector depends on the expected marginal efficiency of investment in the construction sector of the other country. The marginal efficiency of investment is the marginal physical product of capital multiplied by the ratio of the price of output to the price of capital input. Applied to exported output, this means that the marginal efficiency of investment depends on the expected future purchasing power per unit of factor input, i.e. the 'single factoral terms of trade'.

(vi) A major fraction of total capital formation is population-sensitive, i.e. varying with the rate of change in population growth and internal migration.

(vii) The population growth rate is a function of population structure (i.e. a vector showing proportions of population in various age and sex groups) and the external migration balance.

(viii) The countries are linked by a gold standard with specie currency.

These assumptions imply a complicated see-saw movement in which both 'real' and monetary factors are at work. The population cycle, with migration as a crucial element, determines the time-shape of capital formation in C and D. The demographic variables, through their impact on the course of investment, which in turn is conditioned by the gestation lag, create a state of high sensitivity in which monetary shocks can effectively change the direction of things. A monetary cobweb is superimposed on the real instability inherent in the interplay of the real magnitudes.[1]

The task is to take the basic relationships and build an econometric model. An important constraint on the form of the functions is the long infrastructure gestation period. Another crucial factor is that population structure in each country has a cyclical element in it—at any moment it is a function of an earlier population structure and of intervening migration. The ability of the model to generate long swings would seem to depend very much on population structure and the infrastructure lag. What is required is an experimental simulation of a complete model, to try out various types of functions with different numerical values of the parameters and different lags to discover what effects these different functions have on the simulated values of the endogenous variables.

3. TESTING THE ASSUMPTIONS

We shall now consider the evidence for the basic assumptions of the model.

(a) Export capacity is generated through population-sensitive capital formation; there is an inter-temporal relation between a country's infrastructure investment in one phase of the long swing and its export capacity in the next

For the United States this is amply confirmed in Fig. 49 and Table 141 (short cycle influences being eliminated by plotting average reference standings, peak to peak and trough to trough). The upswing in immigration and construction in the late eighteen-sixties is followed in the seventies by an upswing in exports and a downswing in imports (each as a proportion of gross national product). A similar process is repeated in the eighties and nineties. Finally, in the nineteen-hundreds the steep rise in immigration and construction is accompanied by a sharp fall in exports and a mild rise in imports as a proportion of gross national product. It is interesting to note that imports, unlike exports, show a secular fall between 1870 and 1913 from 8% to 5% of gross national product, but the long swing is clearly marked. Fig. 49 also

---

[1] A formal account of the model is given on pp. 287–9. For a mathematical model of inverse long cycles indicating population as a key variable in their determination, see J. Parry Lewis, 'Growth and Inverse Cycles: a Two-Country Model', *Economic Journal*, vol. LXXIV, no. 293, March 1964, pp. 109–18.

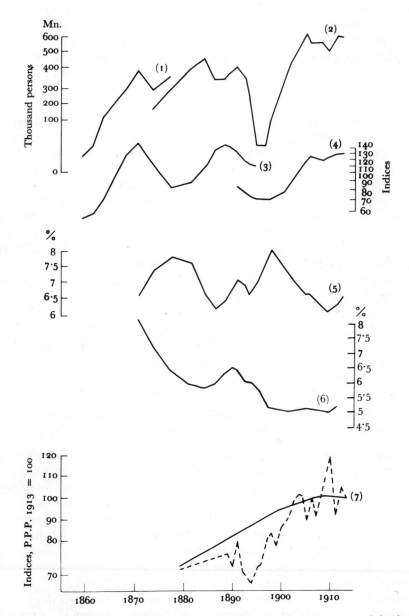

Fig. 49. The United States: long swings in immigration, construction and foreign trade (average reference-cycle standings), 1858–1913. (1) Gross immigration. (2) Net immigration. (3) and (4) Indices of volume of construction. (5) Exports as a percentage of G.N.P. (6) Imports as a percentage of G.N.P.: Table 141. (7) Single factoral terms of trade (indices, 1913 = 100). —— Manufactured exports, – – – Agricultural exports: R. E. Lipsey, *Price and Quantity Trends in the Foreign Trade of the United States*, p. 465, table H-16.

gives an estimate of the single factoral terms of trade for agricultural and manufactured exports for the period 1880–1913. The purchasing power of agricultural factors of production increased slightly in the eighteen-eighties, dipped in the early nineties, and then rose very rapidly in the second half of the nineties and early nineteen-hundreds, when America's export sector was booming.

Another test may be made by using Kuznets's figures of changes in population-sensitive capital formation and net changes in claims on foreign countries over the long swing. The last two columns of Table 142 clearly demonstrate the see-saw movement between the construction and export sectors. An upswing in infrastructure investment in one phase of the long swing was followed by an upswing in the export sector in the next.

Statistics for other countries of the periphery tell the same story. The long swing in immigration and railway building in Australia was shown in Fig. 28. In the years 1881–90, when the net inflow of capital to Australia was £174 million, the value of merchandise exports was £230 million, or two-thirds of the value of merchandise imports. In the downswing of the investment cycle, 1891–1900, net capital inflow was reduced to £48 million, while exports rose to £322 million, practically equal to imports (£326 million). The evidence for Argentina can be seen in A. G. Ford's authoritative work,[1] and for Canada on pages 256–8 below.

(b) *A major fraction of total capital formation is population-sensitive, i.e. varying with the rate of change of population growth and internal migration*

Kuznets has pointed out how difficult it is to get a comprehensive estimate of population-sensitive capital formation. Non-farm residential construction and capital expenditure by railroads in the United States comprised about 40% of total capital formation in the eighteen-seventies but these are not the only items which should be included. For example, the construction of stores, local transport facilities and service establishments are population-sensitive, but these are lumped in Kuznets's 'other' private construction and producer durables.[2] What we need is a measure of total infrastructure investment. If it were statistically possible to bring all the genuinely population-sensitive components together, infrastructure investment would probably comprise well over half the total.

[1] A. G. Ford, *The Gold Standard 1880–1914: Britain and Argentina*, Oxford University Press, 1962, Statistical Appendix, p. 195.
[2] S. Kuznets, *Capital in the American Economy*, p. 340.

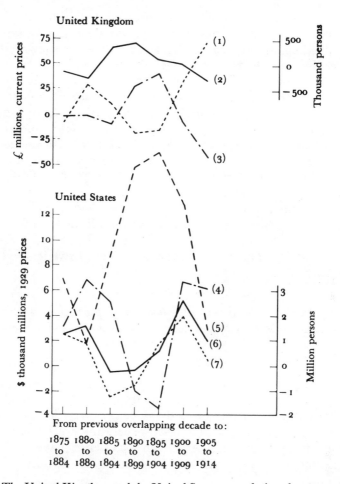

FIG. 50. The United Kingdom and the United States: population changes and capital formation, 1875–1913.

The United Kingdom: J. B. Jefferys and D. Walters, 'National Income and Expenditure of the United Kingdom, 1870–1952' in *Income and Wealth*, series v, Bowes and Bowes, 1955, pp. 1–40. (1) Changes in net oversea lending (yearly averages). (2) Changes in population increase per decade. (3) Changes in net domestic capital formation (yearly averages).

The United States: S. Kuznets, 'Long Swings in the Growth of Population and in Related Economic Variables', Tables 7 and 13. (4) Changes in population-sensitive capital formation. (5) Changes in other capital formation. (6) Changes in total population increase. (7) Changes in net migration.

Fig. 50 shows the parallelism between changes in total population increase and in net domestic capital formation in the United Kingdom, and in population-sensitive capital formation in the United States.

The inverse relation between population-sensitive and 'other' capital formation in the United States and between home investment and oversea lending in the United Kingdom is clearly shown. In both countries internal migration moved in harmony with changes in population additions.[1] In other countries of new settlement—for example, Canada and Australia—the magnitude of investment in infrastructure in relation to total capital formation was considerable.[2] The significance of demographic variables in the economic growth of Australia has been quantified by Allen C. Kelley.[3] He calculated the demand for residential construction in the period 1861–1911 on the basis of the 1881 age distribution, compared it with the actual demand, and concluded that changes in age distribution had a significant influence. He found that if the age-structure had remained constant the demand for residential construction would have been 80% higher in 1865–70, 26% lower in 1880–5, unchanged in 1890–5 and 20% higher in 1900–5. This factor largely explained the wide amplitude of the fluctuations.

(c) *The population growth rate is a function of population structure (i.e. a vector showing proportions of population in various age and sex groups) and external migration*

Evidence for Great Britain and the United States is in Chapter XIII, which concentrates on the growth rate in the household-forming age group, 20–44.[4] In discussing Irish emigration we have already shown how a kinked age distribution and the heavy incidence of emigration among young adults can lead to a self-generating cycle.[5] Kuznets and Easterlin, in their studies of American experience, have explored the demographic factors behind the long swing in fertility. Easterlin found that:

---

[1] See Brinley Thomas, 'Long Swings in Internal Migration and Capital Formation', *Bulletin of the International Statistical Institute*, vol. XL, bk. 1, 1964, pp. 398–412.

[2] For Canada see M. C. Urquhart and K. A. H. Buckley (eds.), *Historical Statistics of Canada*, Cambridge University Press, 1965, pp. 511–15. For Australia see Noel G. Butlin, *Investment in Australian Economic Development, 1861–1900*, pp. 47–8.

[3] Allen C. Kelley, 'Demographic Change and Economic Growth: Australia 1861–1911', *Explorations in Entrepreneurial History*, second series, vol. v, Spring–Summer 1967, pp. 207–77. See also A. R. Hall, 'Some Long-period Effects of the Kinked Age Distribution of the Population of Australia, 1861–1961', *Economic Record*, vol. XXXIX, no. 85, March 1963, pp. 43–52.

[4] On Great Britain see also J. Parry Lewis, *Building Cycles and Britain's Growth*, ch. III, VII and X.

[5] See p. 81.

while the fertility of the total white population declined substantially from the latter part of the nineteenth century to the mid-1930s, there was significant variation in the rate of change over time and among component population groups. Even after averaging data so as to eliminate or substantially reduce variability due to the business cycle, marked fluctuations— Kuznets cycles of fifteen or more years duration—stand out in the patterns for the total, native, and foreign-born white populations.[1]

The analysis is necessarily complicated, comprising the effects of immigration, mortality and fertility rates, labour force participation, the headship rate and echo effects. Easterlin concluded that:

the fertility for the *total* white population has been subject to substantial variation as a result of major fluctuations in the fertility of the foreign-born and rural white components. The fluctuations for these groups in turn appear to have been caused by the impact of the rise and fall of immigration on the age, sex, and nationality composition of the foreign-born, and of major swings in agricultural conditions on the economic conditions of the farm population.[2]

Clear evidence can be seen in the history of Australia, where population cycles originated in the heavy immigration of the eighteen-fifties, and subsequent immigration waves tended to reinforce and accentuate these cycles. This has been demonstrated by Allen C. Kelley by taking the size and the age and sex-composition of the population of Australia in 1861, and then calculating what would have been the shape of population growth if Australia had had no net migration thereafter. Special attention was given to the cohorts 20–24, 25–29 and 30–34. 'In *both* the total (including migration) and the net-of-migration cases the rate of age-specific demographic change occurring within selected cohorts of the Australian population exceeded by three to nine times the rate of change of the respective aggregate population for all ages.'[3]

The timing pattern in the three cohorts results in a remarkably consistent tendency for net-of-migration cycles to precede the population change including the impact of migration....The conclusion thus emerges that with respect to the three most important cohorts of total population change (as measured by their role in key economic activities—labor force entrance, residential demand, and saving), the wave-like movements may be *initiated* by influences deriving from the demographic shock, and subsequent migration follows and lengthens each movement.[4]

Moreover, Kelley's work provides a detailed Australian counterpart to

[1] R. A. Easterlin, *Population, Labor Force and Long Swings in Economic Growth*, pp. 89–90.

[2] Ibid. p. 99.

[3] Allen C. Kelley, loc. cit. p. 250.

[4] Ibid. p. 253.

the analysis in Chapter XIII of the demographic determinants of the long swing in construction in Britain.

4. LONG SWINGS IN CANADA AND AUSTRALIA

In the first edition of this book the main emphasis was on the inverse relation between long swings in the United Kingdom and in the United States; I pointed out in the Preface that it had not been possible to do justice to the flow of migrants and capital into Canada and South America. Much research has since been done on these and other countries of the periphery. We shall now summarize the long swing pattern in Canada and Australia.

(a) Canada

The relevant time series for Canada in the period 1870–1913 are given in Fig. 51.[1] Canadian long swings have the same time-shape as those of the United States, but their amplitude is greater. There is a close correspondence between net capital imports and gross immigration, and the latter leads urban building and transport investment, as in the United States.

Canada had a close economic involvement with Great Britain, and in view of its small size, the interplay of forces had a powerful effect. The hypotheses of our model of the Atlantic economy are well borne out. From a peak in the early eighteen-seventies there was a decline to a trough at the end of the decade. The long swing pattern for the rest of the period was briefly as follows:

> The years 1878–89 saw an upswing in immigration with a promi-
> nent peak in 1883 and a mild one in 1889; capital inflow was similarly
> well above trend. In the early part of the eighties there was a boom
> in railway construction and later on in urban building. Meanwhile,
> the value of exports to Britain fell from $42,600,000 in 1881 to
> $33,500,000 in 1889, whereas imports from Britain rose sharply in
> the early years (from $30,900,000 to $51,700,000) and then settled
> down at about $40 million. In 1881–8 the terms of trade moved in

---

[1] Our understanding of Canadian long swings owes much to the pioneering researches of Kenneth Buckley—'Urban Building and Real Estate Fluctuations in Canada', *Canadian Journal of Economics and Political Science*, vol. XVIII, no. 1, February 1952, pp. 51–62, *Capital Formation in Canada 1896–1930*, Toronto University Press, 1955, and *Population, Labor Force and Economic Growth, 1867–1962*, vol. II, Banff School of Advanced Management, 1964—and the work of Don Daly, 'Long Cycles and Recent Canadian Experience' in *Report of the Royal Commission on Banking and Finance*, appendix vol., Ottawa, 1964, pp. 283–301.

favour of Canada, and real exports per capita fell. In Britain during those years home construction was falling and capital exports rising. From 1889 to the end of the nineties there was a severe downswing

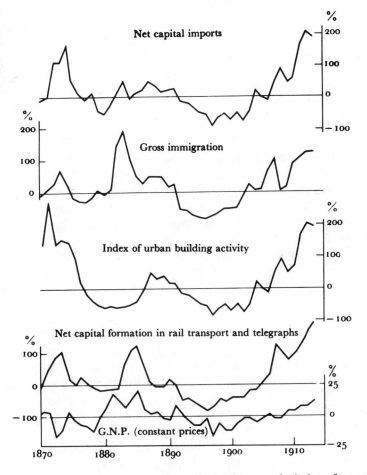

Fig. 51. Long swings in Canada, 1870–1913 (percentage deviations from trend). Source: A. I. Bloomfield, *Patterns of Fluctuation in International Investment Before 1914*, p. 25. I am indebted to Professor Bloomfield for kindly supplying the underlying data.

in Canadian immigration, capital imports and infrastructure investment, whereas Britain experienced a strong construction boom and declining foreign lending. Between 1889 and 1901 Canada's imports from Britain remained stationary, while her exports to Britain increased threefold. The sharp rise in real exports per capita was accompanied by a shift in the terms of trade against Canada in the years 1895–1901.

What happened in the period 1900–13 is a classic case of the growth process during a Kuznets cycle upswing in a new country. It has been well documented.[1] The net capital balance rose from $30 million in 1900 to $542 million in 1913, immigrant arrivals from 42,000 to 401,000, total home investment from $123 million to $628 million. The sectoral price levels moved as follows, 1900–12, domestic +62%, export +39%, import +13%. Real exports per capita tended to fall after 1903. In the decade 1902–12 the value of exports to Britain increased by 35%, while the value of imports from Britain increased by 139%; the terms of trade moved in favour of Canada from 111 to 122.

The evidence amply confirms the inverse relation between long swings in Britain and in the periphery as well as the inter-temporal relation between infrastructure investment in one period and export capacity in the next. Up to the turn of the century exports had very little causal role,[2] but in the last great upswing the shift in the demand curve for Canadian wheat was an important factor. The course of events in Canada in the early nineteen-hundreds reflected a change of direction in the flow of men and money into the periphery, partly induced by the stage of development which the United States had reached by the turn of the century.[3]

(b) Australia

The inverse relation between fluctuations in home investment in Britain and railway investment in Australia from the eighteen-seventies to 1913 was shown in Fig. 28 above. It is true that the span of the upward and downward phases tended to be longer in Australia than in other countries. This can be explained on demographic grounds: it does not mean that the interaction mechanism was essentially different from what it was in the rest of the periphery.

Clear evidence of the alternation between swings in infrastructure investment and in export capacity has already been cited. By ignoring

[1] See J. Viner, *Canada's Balance of International Indebtedness, 1900–13*, Cambridge University Press, 1924; A. K. Cairncross, 'Investment in Canada, 1900–13' in *Home and Foreign Investment 1870–1913*, pp. 37–64. For a critique of Viner's analysis see John A. Stovel, *Canada in the World Economy*, Cambridge, Mass., Harvard University Press, 1959, pp. 127–213.

[2] See Kenneth Buckley, *Capital Formation in Canada 1896–1930*, pp. 48–50.

[3] See p. 154 where the change in the destination and quality of British emigrants to North America after 1900 is analysed.

this basic inter-temporal relationship, Arthur I. Bloomfield has erroneously argued that the Australian economy for most of the period 1861–1913 'appears to have followed a relatively independent orbit'.[1] He is here echoing Noel Butlin's thesis on which we have already expressed doubt. The nature of Bloomfield's argument can be seen in the following quotation. 'Indeed, real exports, when adjusted for trend, appear to have undergone a long-swing contraction from the early 1870s to the mid-1880s, when the other Australian series were in the expansion phase; and the peak in real exports in the mid-1890s

Table 57. *Australia: peaks and troughs of age-composition effects on savings, work-force additions and residential demand, 1861–1911*

Average household savings		Work-force additions		Residential demand	
Peak	Trough	Peak	Trough	Peak	Trough
1872	1862*	1876	1862*	1862*	1870
1906	1888	1905	1892	1883	1900
	1910*		1910*	1910*	

* Determined as the initial or terminal date in the series.
SOURCE: A. C. Kelley, 'Demographic Change and Economic Growth'.

came well after the other series had begun to turn down.'[2] This is exactly what one would expect to happen in a country of new settlement. These facts are evidence of the inverse relation between infrastructure investment and the export sector: far from showing that Australia was in an independent orbit, they confirm that she was in the same orbit as other countries of the periphery. She was involved in the same process of interaction with the British economy.

Further proof is found in the demographic determinants of the Australian long swing, with changes in external migration and population structure as the primary variables. Kelley has broadened the analysis by bringing in the effects on additions to the labour force and household savings. His chronology of peaks and troughs is given in Table 57, indicating changes due *solely* to variations in the age-structure of the population.

[1] A. I. Bloomfield, *Patterns of Fluctuation in International Investment Before 1914*, p. 29.
[2] Ibid. p. 29 n (61).

Like H. J. Habakkuk on English building cycles, Noel Butlin attempted to show that Australia did not experience the usual kind of building cycle.[1] He thinks Australia had a long fifty-year cycle punctuated by short-period disturbances. Kelley's conclusions, based on a rigorous demographic analysis, are as follows.

On the basis of these tests we would propose that each argument in the Butlin thesis is subject to modification. (i) Speculative excesses, as measured by either positive deviations of residential capacity from trends in long-run demand or by the provision of housing ahead of demand are not generally prominent in Australia in the 1880s; (ii) the impact of change in the age-structure of the population has been under-estimated; and (iii) the relative importance of age-compositional effects, vis-à-vis rapid urbanization, points to the former as the more powerful explanatory variable.[2]

The weight of quantitative evidence on the United Kingdom, the United States, Canada and Australia justifies the proposition that, with population structure and international migration as crucial variables, the demographic cycle (and its concomitant, infrastructure investment) in the United Kingdom was inverse to the corresponding cycles in the periphery.

5. THE INTERACTION PROCESS: REAL AND MONETARY FACTORS

We shall now explore the nature of the interaction between the creditor country, C, and the factor-importing 'country', D, representing the whole periphery, paying particular attention to the interplay of real and monetary factors.

(a) The Upswing in Emigration and Lending

Let us assume a large flow of young migrants from C to D, with consequent opposite impacts on the countries' population structure and internal migration. This increases population-sensitive capital formation in the receiving country and reduces it in the sending country. There will be an accompanying flow of lending from C to D attracted by the higher marginal efficiency of investment in D's construction sector. We distinguish between ex ante lending, i.e. the purchase of D securities by C residents, and ex post capital exports, i.e. the balance on current account. This ex ante lending can be considered in terms of

---

[1] N. G. Butlin, *Investment in Australian Economic Development, 1861–1900*, pp. 224–7 and 231.

[2] A. C. Kelley, 'Demographic Change and Economic Growth: Australia 1861–1911', p. 246.

periodic stock adjustments by C investors. The optimal portfolio of diversified home securities held by the 'representative' investor in country C is necessarily subject to the risk of a change in the general level of activity. When he sees the prospect of a construction slump at home coinciding with a boom abroad, he can reduce this risk by substituting foreign securities for some of his domestic securities. In the words of C. H. Lee,

given the expected rates of return, variances and covariances of returns of individual securities, there is a unique optimal composition of the securities in a portfolio, and this portfolio can be considered a composite good. Likewise, an optimal portfolio is derived for foreign securities only and this portfolio forms a second composite good. In the second stage, then, the investor makes a choice concerning the allocation of his total wealth between the two composite goods.[1]

When the actual amount of D securities held by C residents is less than the optimum portfolio of D securities, an outflow of capital takes place, and this can occur even if the rate differential is unchanged.

The increased purchase of D securities (*ex ante* foreign lending) is followed by a rise in the demand for C exports, and the export sector in country C gets a boom at the expense of infrastructure investment. During this upswing the induced investment in C will be in export-sensitive producer durables, such as shipbuilding; but this is more than counterbalanced by the decline in population-sensitive construction.

Thus, in this first phase there is an infrastructure boom in D and an export sector boom in C. In country D there is an internal shift of labour and resources from the export sector to construction, and vice versa in C. The effect of the upswing on D's price structure is seen mainly in a rise in the price level of domestic goods; next come export prices, and the price level of imports rises least. An important determinant of the latter is the fact that country C in the early stage of the upswing can draw factors easily into its export sector owing to declining activity in the construction sector. A rise in measured productivity enables its expansion to proceed for some time without a rise in costs. During this phase the net barter terms of trade (the ratio of export prices to import prices) move against C and in favour of D.

With regard to the course of the upswing in D, it is relevant to note that in an infrastructure boom we have not only *income-induced* accelerator investment but also *investment-induced* investment. The latter is of a complementary nature and is in a fixed relation to the primary

[1] C. H. Lee, 'A Stock-Adjustment Analysis of Capital Movements: the United States–Canadian Case', *Journal of Political Economy*, vol. LXXVII, no. 4, pt. I, July–August 1969, pp. 514–15.

investment.[1] This introduces an additional lag into the process and helps to account for the length of the construction upswing.[2]

There are three main determinants of the duration of the upswing in D: first, the course of the demand for additional infrastructure induced by the change in the population structure and the life-cycle spending decisions taken by the household-forming age groups, secondly, the interaction between the multiplier and the accelerator (with lags), and, thirdly, the transfer problem. The financing of the lending by country C has multiplier effects on the balance of trade. When these are allowed for, the question is whether the financing and use of the transferred funds changes the demands for goods so that the improvement in C's balance of trade equals the amount lent.[3] We must note that the flow of interest payments involves wealth effects which should not be left out, as they usually are in the literature on the transfer problem. As we

[1] For example, for a given increase in residential building, additional investment is required in public utility services, schools, hospitals, etc. For orders of magnitude see John M. Mattila and Wilbur R. Thompson, 'Residential-Service Construction: a Study of Induced Investment', *Review of Economics and Statistics*, vol. XXXVIII, no. 4, November 1956, pp. 465–73. Writing of the United States in the period 1946–54, these authors point out (p. 467) that 'housing, which unassisted accounts for only 37 per cent of all new construction activity, when bundled up with what we intend to show to be complementary construction, has constituted almost 64 per cent of all new construction activity in the postwar period'.

[2] Following Hicks, we could regard the upswing of population-sensitive capital formation as a hump in autonomous investment. In the early phase of the boom in country D the hump in autonomous investment, via the 'super-multiplier', raises the equilibrium line but not above the ceiling. See J. R. Hicks, *A Contribution to the Theory of the Trade Cycle*, Oxford University Press, 1950, pp. 120–3.

[3] Harry G. Johnson's elegant formulation can be summarized as follows:
Let m^1 and s^1 be the changes in demand for imports and saving respectively caused by the financing and use of the transfer, expressed as proportions of the amount lent. Let M be the marginal propensity to import and S the marginal propensity to save. Then, the transfer will be under-effected if $m_c^1 + m_d^1$ (the sum of the proportions of the amount lent by which expenditure on imports is changed by the financing and use of the loan) is less than $1 + (M_c/S_c)s_c^1 + (M_d/S_d)s_d^1$, i.e. one plus the sum of the proportions of the transfer by which saving is changed (with expenditure unchanged) by the financing and use of the loan, each weighted by the ratio of the marginal propensity to import to the marginal propensity to save in the country concerned.

Johnson also shows how the analysis can accommodate the proportions in which changes in saving are divided between holdings of domestic and foreign assets. 'If the transfer is treated as an income change, it will be under-effected or over-effected according as the sum of what may be described as "the marginal foreign investment ratios" is less or greater than unity; in other words, the transfer will be under-effected if there is a bias (at the margin) in each country towards investment in domestic assets—such as would result from additional ignorance and uncertainty about foreign conditions, or from exchange control, but not from difference in yields as such—and vice versa.' See H. G. Johnson, 'The Transfer Problem and Exchange Stability' in *International Trade and Economic Growth*, London, Allen and Unwin, 1958, pp. 179–83.

shall see, the flow of interest and dividends on foreign investment from the periphery to Britain was a very large item.

In the early part of the upswing in D there is not likely to be trouble. To simplify, let us ignore saving and postulate that the lending is entirely at the expense of home investment in C and that the borrowings are entirely spent by D; then the transfer will be effected without price or income adjustments if the marginal propensities to import add up to unity. A moderate degree of under-effected transfer will entail adjustments which will slow down the boom in D, but the infrastructure investment projects already launched are unlikely to be much curtailed.

In the later stage of the boom the situation changes. As the export upswing gathers momentum in C, a turning-point is reached. Investment induced by the growth of exports increases rapidly, and at the higher level of employment marginal costs rise, while demand is running high in construction activity in D. Productivity in C's export sector has ceased to go up and may be falling, and export prices rise relatively to import prices. Meanwhile, C investors are receiving an increasing flow of interest and dividends on their foreign securities. This wealth effect is likely to promote further *ex ante* lending which now reaches a very high level. The population variable, emigration, is also at a high level but its rate of growth is already declining for demographic reasons and after a short lag this entails an upturn in construction from the low point reached in C.

At this stage transfer becomes seriously under-effected; the growth of the current trade balance cannot keep up with the *ex ante* lending. The monetary authority in C is faced with an external drain of gold to D and an internal drain due to a combination of export-induced investment and a revival in construction. This means severe monetary instability. The central bank must take drastic action to replenish its reserves and raises the interest rate to a punitive level. This attracts a large flow of short-term balances and gold from D, and there is a fall in purchases of D securities. The representative investor in C, impressed by the increasing risk attached to D securities and attracted by the marginal efficiency of investment in home construction, will now optimize by increasing his stock of domestic securities at the expense of his foreign portfolio.

The monetary cobweb thus set in motion breaks the infrastructure boom in D. The large loss of gold reduces D's money supply or sharply reduces its rate of growth and this precipitates a downturn.

(b) The Downswing in Emigration and Lending

We now have the reverse process—a decline in emigration and lending, an expansion in C's construction sector and D's export sector. Given absolute confidence in the ability of the creditor country to maintain convertibility, the action taken by C, with its curb on foreign lending, quickly restores C's balance of payments equilibrium through a deflation of effective demand. The incidence of the adjustment, however, is felt mainly in the periphery which gets the full force of the monetary contraction and the reversed accelerator-multiplier process. Prices fall in D much more sharply than in C. The vigorous upswing in construction accompanied by a downswing in the export sector in the borrowing country had made its economy much more vulnerable to monetary contraction than the economy of the creditor country, which had been through a phase of declining construction combined with expanding exports. The degree of credit restriction applied to restore monetary equilibrium in C necessarily overshoots the mark and inflicts on D a steep fall in investment and income.

Under the gold standard D's money supply is a variable dependent on outside forces. The causal sequence runs from the balance of payments and the gold flow to the money stock and then to the level of prices which is consistent with the fixed exchange rate. If the debtor country is to remain on the gold standard, the correction of under-effected transfer by the creditor necessarily entails a reduction in the debtor's money supply and a fall in its price level relative to the creditor's.

Infrastructure investment in D responding to the population variable declines rapidly, and there is a rise in the output of the export sector geared to the expanding activity in C's construction sector. The productivity of D's export sector is directly related to the expansion which took place in infrastructure in the previous period; a substantial supply of primary produce is exported at falling prices. D's net barter terms of trade are declining; but the significant fact is that its 'single factoral terms of trade' (the net barter terms corrected for the rise in physical productivity in the production of exports) are rising. This is similar to what occurred in C during the early stage of the boom in its export sector in the previous period. Each country, debtor as well as creditor, in its infrastructure boom period, lays the foundations for the performance of its export sector in the following period; and during export upswings there is a shift away from home construction to investment in producer durables, the demand for which is a function of the level of activity in the export sector.

In C substantial internal migration takes the place of emigration; and population-sensitive capital formation sets the pace for the economy. *Ex ante* foreign lending falls and the price of domestic stocks rises. With the supply schedules of labour and loanable funds facing the construction sector moving to the right, the multiplier-accelerator process draws in a growing volume of imports of primary produce. Since the export sector is in decline, the balance on current account shrinks.

It is possible for a monetary crisis to occur before the lags in the real process in C dictate a downturn. The rapidly rising current account balance of country D causes a continuing gold outflow from C and an acceleration of the rate of growth of the money supply in D. This means that sooner or later the price of D's exports will begin to rise. This will increase the strain in C, where infrastructure investment has reached a high level and unemployment is at a minimum. The monetary authority in C is now facing a double strain—a continued outflow of gold together with a rapidly increasing interior demand. The representative investor in C, worried by the increasing risk attached to his domestic portfolio and attracted by the expected profitability of investment in construction abroad, will optimize by switching into D securities. This rise in *ex ante* lending adds to the instability. The reserves of the system reach the danger level, and the central bank raises its interest rate enough to replenish its reserves. Gold will then flow in from D with a consequent deceleration of the growth of the money supply in that country, and the stringent credit restriction will precipitate a downturn in C's construction sector. This downturn brings D's export boom to an end. The stage is now set for a new upswing in infrastructure investment and a downswing in exports in D and an emigration-lending upsurge with falling infrastructure investment in C.

In this model, country D stands for the periphery of countries of new settlement in the second half of the nineteenth century. The critical turning points in the long swing are attributable to monetary instability occurring in the lending country, the financial centre of the system. The see-saw movement arises fundamentally out of the inverse demographic cycles and the alternation of infrastructure and export upsurges, but the whole thing is played according to the rules of the gold standard game, with the monetary authority in the creditor country as referee. This mechanism of interaction offers an explanation of the fact that the oversea countries of new settlement in the pre-1913 period experienced *simultaneous* long swings in capital formation which were inverse to those of the United Kingdom.

6. HISTORICAL EVIDENCE

The main phases of the inverse long swing, 1862–1913, will now be examined in the light of historical evidence.

(a) 1862–79

It is necessary to look separately at the period 1862–79, before the United States returned to the gold standard. After the Civil War the upsurge of investment in the United States gathered strength, reached a peak in 1871–2, from which there was a sharp descent to a very low level at the end of the seventies. A major factor in this period was the political objective to resume specie payments at the pre-Civil War parity; this entailed a considerable fall in American prices. The average price level in 1865 was over twice what it had been in 1861; the index (1910–14 = 100) fell from 185 in 1865 to 86 in December 1878.[1]

Friedman and Schwartz, in their account of this period, point out that

for some five or six years after the Civil War, the dollar price of sterling was less than might have been expected from commodity price movements alone. The explanation is a sizable capital inflow from abroad for investment—up to 1870, particularly in U.S. government securities, and after that, in railway bonds. When the capital inflow declined sharply, as it did in 1873–79, the dollar price of sterling first rose by comparison to the ratio of U.S. to British prices, then moved in accord with that ratio.[2]

These authors suggest that, in the decade after the Civil War, America's competitive power in exports increased more than its demand for imports and this favourable shift in comparative advantage raised the value of the dollar in terms of foreign currencies at which trade would balance.[3] This needs to be carefully interpreted.

Fig. 49 shows that it was in the downward phase of the long swing in the seventies that exports rose and imports fell; this was a sequel to the increase in capacity built up in the upward phase culminating in 1871. The rest of the picture can be seen in the series given in Fig. 52. There was a very steep fall in net capital inflow and in the ratio of American to British prices (partly the result of resumption policy); this was accompanied by a marked expansion in the export sector—exports as a proportion of gross national product rising from 6 to 9% and as a proportion of imports from 80 to 140%. This boom in exports was mainly geared to the upswing in home investment in the United Kingdom (see Fig. 53),[4] the upturn of which had led the downturn in capital inflow to the United States. Friedman and Schwartz point to the apparent contradiction between the National Bureau's evidence of a protracted and severe slump from 1873 to 1879 (the longest in the American record) and the fact that physical volume series indicate that output was rising in the last part of the contraction. They see the obvious explanation in '...the behaviour of prices, which unquestion-

---

[1] See Friedman and Schwartz, *A Monetary History of the United States 1867–1960*, pp. 80–1.

[2] Ibid. p. 86.   [3] Ibid. p. 78.

[4] In the period 1861–78 over half America's exports went to Britain, ibid. p. 64.

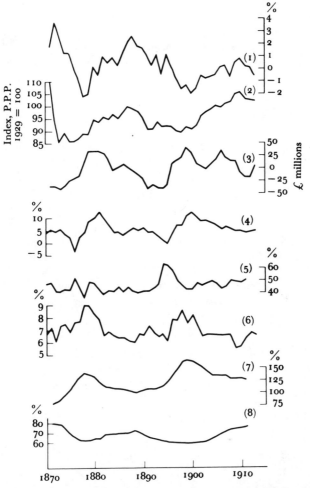

Fig. 52. The United States and the United Kingdom: money stock, capital flows and other indices, 1870–1913. (1) U.S. net international capital flow as a percentage of G.N.P.: Friedman and Schwartz, *A Monetary History of the United States 1867–1960*, pp. 769–70, table A-4, col. 4. (2) Index of U.S. prices/U.K. prices, P.P.P. 1929 = 100, ibid. col. 1. (3) U.S. net international gold flow (5-year moving average): M. Simon, 'The United States Balance of Payments, 1861–1900' in *Trends in the American Economy in the Nineteenth Century*, Princeton University Press, 1962, table 27, line 28, and Friedman and Schwartz, op. cit. table A-4. (4) Change in U.S. money stock (5-year moving average): Friedman and Schwartz, op. cit. pp. 704–7. (5) Bank of England reserve (as a percentage of liabilities): A. C. Pigou, *Industrial Fluctuations*, London, Macmillan, 1927, p. 369. (6) U.S. exports as a percentage of G.N.P. (current prices): Lipsey, *Price and Quantity Trends in the Foreign Trade of the United States*, p. 430. (7) U.S. exports as a percentage of imports (current prices, 5-year moving average): ibid. pp. 154–5. (8) U.K. exports as a percentage of imports (current prices, 5-year moving average): A. H. Imlah, *Economic Elements in the Pax Britannica*, pp. 96–8.

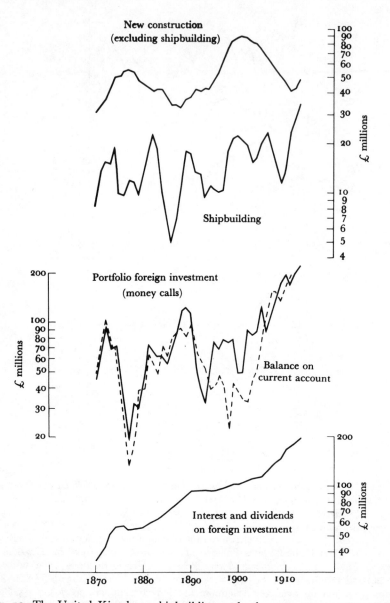

Fig. 53. The United Kingdom: shipbuilding and other new construction, foreign investment and interest and dividends received, balance on current account, 1870–1913. Sources: Cairncross, *Home and Foreign Investment 1870–1913*, p. 169; M. Simon, 'The Pattern of New British Portfolio Foreign Investment, 1865–1914' in J. H. Adler, *Capital Movements and Economic Development*, p. 53; A. H. Imlah, *Economic Elements in the Pax Britannica*, pp. 72–5.

ably fell sharply from 1877 to early 1879, and the continuing state of monetary uncertainty up to the successful achievement of resumption. ...Observers of the business scene then, no less than their modern descendants, took it for granted that sharply declining prices were incompatible with sharply rising output.'[1] There is no contradiction when it is realized that an upswing in the export sector coexisted with a downswing in immigration, capital inflow and infrastructure investment, the long swing peak of the former and the trough of the latter occurring in 1877–8.

We shall now glance at the behaviour of the monetary variables. In Fig. 52 we plot the annual rate of change in the United States money stock (five-year moving average), the net external gold flow (five-year moving average), and the Bank of England reserve as a percentage of liabilities. In the first half of the eighteen-seventies there was a considerable net outflow of gold from America and the curve of the rate of change in money stock was falling, with an absolute decline in 1876; the Bank of England reserve moved inversely and peaked in 1876. Then the United States money stock rose sharply as the Government sold bonds to build up a reserve before resuming specie payments in 1879, and the export boom created a very favourable trade balance. At the same time other countries were absorbing gold. The net imports into France in the five years 1874–9 were £83 million, of which £14·5 million came from Britain; and Germany absorbed £20 million. The result of all this was a steep fall in the Bank of England reserve. The bank rate was raised to 5% and 6% in 1878 and this reversed the flow. The downswing in the construction cycle in Britain was already gathering momentum before the upturn in the export sector had really begun: indeed the shipbuilding cycle reached a low trough in 1879 (Fig. 53). In the words of Hawtrey, 'It was the stringency and crisis of 1878 that at last brought British industry to a sufficient state of prostration to free the Bank of England from anxiety in regard to its reserve. The Bank cheerfully watched its reserve fall from £21,372,000 in July 1879 to £12,578,000 in January 1881 before raising the rate to 3½ per cent.'[2]

An interesting feature of this early period is the severe amplitude of the investment downswing in the United States in the seventies, only partially offset by the export boom pivoted on the construction boom in Britain. Prices fell partly in response to the productivity-raising investment in the previous period but mainly as a result of monetary policy. The exchange rate had to come back within the range determined by the gold points. In the words of Friedman and Schwartz, 'any attempt to return to the pre-war parity before the greenback price of the pound

[1] Friedman and Schwartz, op. cit. pp. 87–8.
[2] R. G. Hawtrey, *A Century of Bank Rate*, p. 102.

sterling had fallen to that level would have meant a "pound shortage" strictly comparable with the post-World War II "dollar shortage" associated with the maintenance by other countries of official exchange rates that overvalued their currencies'.[1] There was a close interaction both in real and monetary terms between the United States and Great Britain.

(b) 1879–1913

Between 1879 and 1913, with the international gold standard established, the money supply of the countries of the periphery was a dependent variable determined by outside influences. Predominant among those influences was the Bank of England's policy as guardian of its reserves. Under these circumstances a one-sided interpretation of the fluctuations in the United States is not valid. As Phillip Cagan has pointed out, '...one might argue—about the pre-1914 period at least— that U.S. cycles frequently stemmed from foreign influences and were not usually transmitted abroad. This country's economy during the nineteenth century could not have counted heavily with most foreign economies, while world trade clearly affected U.S. exports. Their irregular cyclical pattern, as noted, reflected the ups and downs of foreign business activity, which often moved counter to domestic business.'[2]

Fig. 53 shows, for Great Britain, the course of new construction excluding shipbuilding (population-sensitive capital formation), shipbuilding (export-sensitive capital formation), British purchases of foreign securities (*ex ante* foreign lending), the balance on current account minus gold imports (*ex post* capital exports), and interest and dividends received on foreign investment.

With shipbuilding excluded from the construction index, the long swing stands out very clearly in the raw data, and so does the short shipbuilding cycle. The ups and downs in shipbuilding correspond to the minor and major fluctuations in the export sector. For example, in the first phase of the upswing of the eighties there was a minor peak in

[1] Friedman and Schwartz, op. cit. p. 80.

[2] Phillip Cagan, *Determinants and Effects of Changes in the Stock of Money 1875–1960*, p. 110. Friedman and Schwartz have estimated (op. cit. p. 89, n. 2) that 'at the time of resumption the U.S. held just over 5% of the world's monetary gold stock, and perhaps 8% of that part of the gold stock which served as monetary reserves; a year later these percentages were 9 and 13; and for the rest of the century both percentages were probably below 20. This is one rough measure of the relative importance of the U.S. economy in the gold standard world and one that almost surely overstates its importance since both the unit banking system in the U.S. and the absence of a central bank probably worked to make the ratio of the gold stock to the money stock higher than in most other important gold-standard countries.'

foreign lending in 1881 with a peak in shipbuilding in 1882. After a short recession in foreign lending accompanied by a sharp fall in shipbuilding, the upswing proceeded to a long swing peak in 1889, with a matching peak in shipbuilding.

The portfolio investment and current account series give a rough indication of whether there is over- or under-effected transfer. The annual amount of interest and dividends on foreign investment rises from £30 million in 1870 to as much as £200 million in 1913, and, as expected, it traces out a mild long swing corresponding to that of foreign investment. The distribution of British foreign lending by geographical area is given in Fig. 54. There is strong evidence that the upward and downward phases were simultaneous in different parts of the periphery. North and South America clearly swing together, and they dominate the total. The upswing of the early eighteen-seventies is very evident in Europe as well as North and South America. The bulge in investment in Asia in the late nineties and in Africa in the early nineteen-hundreds reflects the activity of colonial powers.

The balance on current account (*ex post* capital exports) lags behind portfolio foreign investment, indicating that the causal sequence ran from the purchase of foreign securities to the trade balance.[1] The money was first raised and then a great deal of it was spent on British goods and services. Fig. 53 shows that when foreign lending was rising the current account balance kept in step with it remarkably well: there was no serious transfer problem until the final stage of the boom. The propensity to spend funds borrowed from Britain on British exports, however high it might be, was by no means the whole story.[2] The cumulative upsurge in infrastructure investment in the periphery, associated with inflowing capital and population, entailed a big shift in demand curves for British goods and services and, in view of Britain's primacy as an exporter of capital goods and manufactures[3] and the fact that the downswing in her home investment had a depressing effect on imports, it was possible to generate a current balance equal to the flow of foreign lending, except in certain critical phases.

In Fig. 55 we plot for Great Britain the external and internal gold flows, the annual rate of change in the reserve, and the average level of bank rate each year. When these data are read in relation to the course

---

[1] See A. G. Ford, 'Overseas Lending and Internal Fluctuations 1870–1914' in J. Saville (ed.), *Studies in the British Economy 1870–1914*, p. 27: 'it is of great interest that deviations in overseas issues exhibited a marked cyclical pattern but *led* fluctuations in exports and in world trade by one to two years'.

[2] See A. J. Brown, 'Britain in the World Economy 1870–1914', ibid. pp. 51–4.

[3] In 1880 she supplied 63% of world exports of capital goods and 41% of world exports of manufactured goods, see p. 240 above.

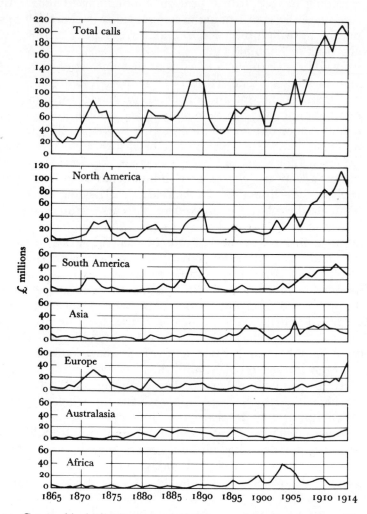

Fig. 54. Geographical distribution of British portfolio investment, 1865–1914.
Source: M. Simon, 'The Pattern of New British Portfolio Foreign Investment,
1865–1914', p. 45.

Fig. 55. The United Kingdom: new construction, portfolio foreign investment,
external and internal gold flows, bank rate and change in reserves, 1870–1913.
Sources: Cairncross, op. cit. p. 169; Simon, 'The Pattern of New British Portfolio
Foreign Investment, 1865–1914', p. 53; R. G. Hawtrey, *A Century of Bank Rate*,
App. II, pp. 297–300; W. E. Beach, *British International Gold Movements and Banking
Policy, 1881–1913*, Harvard University Press, 1935, pp. 52–3 and 66–7.

Note: The figures for gold flows (4-quarter moving averages) are from Hawtrey for
the period 1870–80 and from Beach from 1881 onwards. The former source gives
figures for June and December, the latter for July and January.

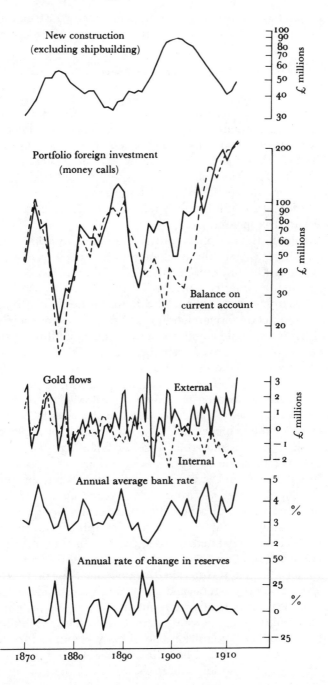

of foreign lending, *ex ante* and *ex post*, and home construction, we can gauge the pressures which built up in the course of each boom.

(c) The Upswing in Oversea Investment, 1879–89

This vigorous upswing was interrupted at an early stage in 1881 when, as shown in Fig. 55, there was already under-effected transfer, with a gold outflow accompanied by an internal drain. By February 1882 the reserve was down to £9,175,000, a loss of £7,856,000 since a year before, intensified by the failure of the Union Générale in Paris in January 1882. The Bank of England raised its rate to 5% in October 1881 and 6% in January 1882. This had the required effect in a sharp reaction in foreign lending and a reflux of gold; by 1884 the transfer difficulty had disappeared.

The impact on the periphery can be illustrated by what happened in the United States, where the stock of gold had risen from $210 million in June 1879 to $439 million in June 1881. This increase in the money supply raised the American price level in relation to the British from 89·1 in 1879 to 96·1 in 1882. The Bank of England's intervention, through its impact on foreign lending and prices, reversed the gold flow. This was the classic gold standard mechanism in action. If the United States was to retain its fixed exchange rate, a fall in her income and price level was unavoidable. British investors, fearing that the United States would not be able to stay on the gold standard, began to sell American securities, leading to a further outflow of gold which helped to cause a panic in May 1884. Because British prices fell 12% between 1882 and 1885, the achievement of a 1% decline in American prices relative to British necessitated an absolute fall of 13% in the American price level over these three years.[1]

The rate of growth in the American money stock fell sharply between 1881 and 1885 (see Fig. 52) from 16% a year to 3%, and that of real output declined from 7% a year to 1%. Severe though the recession was, it was only an interruption in the infrastructure investment upswing which was resumed in 1885, with a further strong inflow of capital from Britain. By 1888, as Fig. 55 clearly indicates, there was serious under-effected transfer in Britain; the flow of *ex ante* foreign lending exceeded the current balance by a large margin. The situation there at the peak of portfolio investment in 1889 was as follows: there was an external and an internal drain of gold; the shipbuilding cycle was at a peak; oversea migration had already begun to turn down; the upturn in home construction had already begun; and a shift in British investment away from the United States to Argentina had started.

[1] On this episode see Friedman and Schwartz, op. cit. pp. 100–1.

The Bank of England alarm bells were ringing loudly; the rate went up to 5% in October 1888 and to 6% at the end of December 1889, in response to which gold began to flow back. At the end of 1890 there was a further spell of dear money. The result was a huge reflux of gold.

The repercussions were felt throughout the periphery. With the shock of the Baring crisis in November 1890, Argentina experienced a severe reaction.[1] The effect in the United States is shown by the parallel movement of net capital imports and the purchasing power parity index (see Fig. 52). The ratio of American to British prices began falling in 1887. Looking at this from the British end, one can interpret the course of events as follows: between 1880 and 1887, the first phase of the lending-export boom, British prices fell by 30% while money wages remained constant; this is a strong suggestion of rising productivity in the export sector which did not lead to higher money wages. There was a high elasticity of supply of factors for the export sector due to the downswing in home construction. As the boom gathered momentum, a turning-point was reached; marginal costs began to rise because of bottlenecks at the higher level of employment in the export trades and export-sensitive investment, while demand was running high in oversea construction activity. The turning-point came in 1887; from that year to 1890 British export prices rose by 18% and money wages by 8%; we may infer that in those years physical productivity fell. After 1887 there was a shift in the supply schedule of capital against the United States. Because of the rise in British prices, the absolute fall required in American prices was moderate.

Nevertheless, this ushered in a phase of great difficulty for the United States, with substantial gold outflows, a fall in the rate of growth of money stock, and a banking panic in 1893. The maintenance of the gold standard once again necessitated a drastic deflation of prices and income. Meanwhile, the gold stock of the Bank of England rose to a record of £49 million in February 1896. Bank rate fell to 2% and was ineffective; for much of the time the market rate of discount was under 1%.[2]

(d) The Upswing in British Home Investment, 1890–1901

The upswing in home construction in Great Britain which began in 1889 was halted in 1891–3 and then developed into an intense boom

---

[1] For a detailed account of the boom and collapse in Argentina see A. G. Ford, *The Gold Standard 1880–1914: Britain and Argentina*, ch. VIII.

[2] For a well-documented account of the London money market during the nineties see W. E. Beach, *British International Gold Movements and Banking Policy, 1881–1913*, Cambridge, Mass., Harvard University Press, 1935, pp. 122–36.

which reached its peak in 1901. In the periphery, conditions in the early part of the decade were bordering on collapse; British portfolio investment dropped sharply from £120 million in 1889 to just over £30 million in 1893, and the current balance receded to a low trough of £22·9 million in 1898.

In the United States the reaction from the investment boom of the eighties was intensified by lack of confidence in the stability of the dollar. The Sherman Silver Purchase Act and the McKinley Tariff Act of 1890 helped to increase the uncertainty, the years 1890–4 saw large outflows of gold (see Fig. 52), and net capital inflows declined to a trickle—foreign investors selling $300 million of American securities. The effect of the gold outflow on the money stock was strengthened by the public tending to hold a higher ratio of currency to deposits. In the first half of the decade there was a steep decline in the rate of growth of the money supply; and, in view of falling prices abroad, America had to experience a severe price and income deflation if convertibility was to be maintained. The long crisis of confidence did not end until the triumph of the Republicans in the election of 1896: from then on there was a dramatic change in the fortunes of the American economy, aided by the powerful effect of the gold discoveries in South Africa, Colorado and Alaska.

Similar depressive influences dominated the rest of the periphery—for example, Argentina, Canada and Australia—in the first half of the nineties. Whereas the export capacity of all these countries had been greatly increased by the infrastructure boom of the eighties, their export sectors did not have a real income expansion until the second half of the decade, when the fall in world prices was reversed and the home construction boom in Britain really got going. Argentina is a good example of the cobweb-type instability to which the periphery was exposed because of the lag between infrastructive investment and the subsequent phase when it matured in increased exports. In the years 1885–9 Argentina absorbed £60 million of British portfolio investment and a net total of 640,000 foreign immigrants, and by 1890 the annual servicing of the foreign debt, which had to be made in gold or sterling at a fixed rate, took 60 million gold pesos, or 60 % of the export proceeds in 1890.[1] According to A. G. Ford, 'the slow maturing of investment projects for which the service charges were immediate was a main cause of the Baring crisis'.[2] The *volume* of exports of wheat and wool increased substantially after 1890, but export *values* did not show a marked rise until 1898. As in the United States, there was a strong export upswing in real terms in the late nineties, pivoted to a large

[1] A. G. Ford, *The Gold Standard 1880–1914*, pp. 140–1.
[2] Ibid. p. 142.

extent on the home investment upsurge in the United Kingdom. Similarly in Canada the index of the value of exports between 1895 and 1900 rose from 114 to 192 and in Australia total exports rose from £36,500,000 to £49,200,000.

Even when full allowance is made for special political and other circumstances in the oversea countries, there was undeniably a basic common factor. Their economies were seriously destabilized in the wake of the corrective measures taken by the Bank of England in 1890; when Britain caught a cold, the periphery caught pneumonia. There is no clearer demonstration of the process of interaction than the monetary series for the nineties (Fig. 52). Gold flowing out of the United States and other countries went into the coffers of the Bank of England. Between June 1892 and June 1896 there was actually an absolute fall of 5% in the United States money stock, the first such decline since the seventies, whereas the Bank of England reserve increased spectacularly from £15 million to no less than £49 million (February 1896). When America was struggling desperately to stay on the gold standard, Britain was enjoying such a surfeit of liquidity that the market rate of discount was below 1%. In the second half of the nineties the reverse happened; the Bank of England reserve as a proportion of liabilities fell almost as rapidly as it had risen, while the money stock of the United States increased by 50%.

The demographic determinants of the inverse construction cycle have been fully demonstrated in Chapter VIII. The upturn of the cycle in Britain preceded the downturn in the export sector. Detailed research has established the primacy of residential construction in the home boom of the nineties.[1] 'This is the major single item of home investment which begins a decade's rise gradually but steadily as early as 1891–2, preceding all other types of home investment by several years.'[2] Its progress was accelerated by two powerful forces—abnormally cheap money and the high peak in internal migration and the natural increase component of the 20–44 population curve in the second half of the decade.[3]

The ability to borrow money at abnormally low rates had been, according to *The Economist*, the most important cause behind the rising prices of Stock Exchange securities, having 'enabled enterprising investors to carry large blocks of securities with loans obtained from the banks. While money could be obtained upon Consols at 1 per cent and under, and while the banks were willing to lend at but little over that figure upon home railway stocks....it

---

[1] The subject has been admirably explored by E. M. Sigsworth and Janet Blackman, 'The Home Boom of the 1890s' in J. Saville (ed.), *Studies in the British Economy 1870–1914*, pp. 75–97.
[2] Ibid. p. 78.   [3] See Fig. 47.

was obviously good business to enter into such transactions.'...The favourable cost structure of the building industry in a period of cheap money and of increasing demand for new and better quality houses made housing a particularly attractive field for speculative investment; and it was this sector which dominated the expansion of the 1890s.[1]

This strong investment upswing in Britain was the foundation of the export sector boom in the periphery. American exports as a proportion of imports rose from 105% early in the decade to 165% at the end. (Fig. 52), and net gold imports to the United States from mid-1896 to mid-1899 amounted to $201 million or 40% of the initial stock. With domestic mines producing at the rate of $60 million a year, the monetary gold stock had reached $859 million by the middle of 1899, a rise of 90% in three years.[2]

In 1898 and 1899 there were signs of strain in the British economy. Construction was at a very high level, and shipbuilding was nearing a peak. The Bank of England up to 1890 had regarded a reserve of about £10 million as a sign that the rate should go up: after 1896 the critical level was held to be about £20 million. In April 1898, when the reserve had fallen to £18·3 million, the rate was raised to 4%; there was a sizeable reflux and then a further loss, so that the rate was again raised to 4% in October 1898, and gold again flowed in. Fig. 55 shows how the internal drain was rising rapidly at the height of the boom; gold imports had to accommodate this demand and so did not strengthen the Bank's stock. The outbreak of the South African War led to the rate being raised to 6% in November 1899. For the second half of 1900 it was at 4%, and it was put up to 5% in January 1901.

The peak of the boom had been reached in 1899, when unemployment was as low as 2%, interior demand for gold was running at over £10 million, and the index of share prices touched its highest point. Meanwhile in the United States the demographic cycle had already turned upwards; net immigration had begun to recover in 1898 and rose from 121,000 in that year to 201,000 in 1899, accompanied by a 20% jump in real construction. This was happening at the very time when the steam had gone out of the demographic cycle in Britain. The London stock market was signalling a downturn in 1900 and unemployment rose to 2·5%; total construction reacted in 1901, unemployment rose to 3·3%, and in 1902 a vigorous upswing in portfolio foreign investment was in progress, with the index of share prices 9% down from the top. The British investment boom of the nineties was over, and the final infrastructure upswing in the periphery was under way.

[1] J. Saville (ed.), op. cit. pp. 96–7.   [2] Friedman and Schwartz, op. cit. p. 141.

Friedman and Schwartz, in their analysis of this period, are baffled by what they regard as the 'puzzle' of 'why should the United States have been a net exporter of capital during 1897–1906, let alone on so large a scale?'[1] They are intrigued by the fact that 'the whole level of the capital movement series for the period after 1896 seems lower compared with the relative price series than the level before 1896 does'[2] (see Fig. 52); and after several attempts they end up by saying that they can find no satisfactory explanation, 'we are inclined to believe that there are either some other important economic factors at work or some errors in the figures that we have been unable to discover'.[3] There *are* indeed some other important factors at work and they have been the main subject matter of this chapter; once these are recognized, the puzzle disappears.[4]

There is a marked parallel between America's export upswing of the late nineties and that of the late seventies (see Fig. 52). In both periods net capital exports were substantial, a large net inflow of gold was accompanied by a sharp rise in money stock, and an upturn in American prices relative to British preceded the reversal in net capital outflow. The slump in investment in America in the nineties coincided with a strong boom in Britain; and it was natural that some of the American-owned foreign balances created by the export upsurge should have been invested abroad. At the long swing turning-point in 1900 net capital outflow declined sharply and by 1906 there was again a net inflow.

When we compare the nineteen-hundreds with the eighteen-eighties the only difference is that the rate of absorption of foreign capital by the American economy had declined; in Fig. 52 the level of the capital flow series with respect to the relative price series in the nineteen-hundreds is much lower than in the eighties.[5] The reasons for this are fairly clear. First, America had become the world's largest manufacturing country, producing 30% of the world's output in 1896–1900 as against Britain's 20%; she was already emerging as an exporter of

---

[1] Ibid. p. 142. [2] Ibid. p. 147.
[3] Ibid. p. 148.
[4] In the treatment of export upswings, Friedman and Schwartz attach far too much significance to episodes such as the bumper harvests in America (coinciding with bad harvests in Europe) in 1880–1 and 1897–8 (pp. 97–9 and 140). Their interest is to see how the gold standard mechanism worked; they found it worked beautifully in 1880–1 but not so well in 1897 and after. Hence the puzzle. A glance at Fig. 52 will show that the moving average of the series of American exports as a percentage of imports, 1870–1913, traces a definite long swing which reduces the quirks of the weather to insignificance.
[5] This reflected the growth in the industrial strength and competitive power of the United States.

capital[1] and was soon to become the world's biggest creditor. Secondly, the nineteen-hundreds saw a change in the direction of British investment in the periphery, with less going to the United States and much more to Canada and South America.

Space does not allow an account of the course of events in the United Kingdom, 1900–13. Figs. 53 and 55 show the similarity between this period and the eighties, with construction falling and capital exports flourishing. It ended with under-effected transfer coinciding with a shipbuilding peak and heavy internal demand for gold; and the high average level of bank rate had the customary corrective effect.

7. CONCLUSIONS

The results of this analysis can now be summarized.

(a) United States experience in the period 1870–1913 can best be interpreted within the ambit of the inverse long-swing relationship between the periphery and Great Britain, with an alternation of infrastructure and export upsurges. An interaction model fits the facts better than the notion of '. . . a relatively stable rate of growth interrupted by two monetary episodes from which the system rebounded to approximately its initial path'.[2] It also has much more explanatory power than the one-sided models based on fluctuations in the 'pull' of the United States economy[3] (see Chapter XIV).

(b) Home investment was dominated by population-sensitive capital

---

[1] See pp. 120–1. For details of the growth of American foreign investment see Cleona Lewis, *America's Stake in International Investments*, Washington, Brookings Institution, 1938, pp. 335–40, and J. H. Dunning, *American Investment in British Manufacturing Industry*, London, Allen and Unwin, 1958, pp. 19–36.

[2] Friedman and Schwartz, op. cit. p. 187.

[3] Regression analysis bears this out. Jeffrey Williamson did a univariate test, with net expenditure on railroads in the United States as a variable to explain net capital imports in the period 1871–1914. 'The best fit occurs when net capital imports $(\dot{K})$ lag Ulmer's net expenditure in the railroads (I_{US}) by one year $(\bar{R}^2 = 0.624)$ where the coefficient is positive and significant:

$$(1871-1914) \quad \dot{K}^t = 6.7487 + 1.0189 I^{t-1}_{US}, \quad \bar{R}^2 = 0.624$$
$$(0.1271)$$

When, however, we add the Cairncross series of British home investment (I_{GB}), an extraordinary thing happens. Not only does the fit improve only slightly, but also the coefficient of I_{US} becomes insignificant.

$$(1871-1914) \quad \dot{K}^t = 914.45 - 0.0303 I^t_{US} - 8.8473 I^t_{GB}, \quad \bar{R}^2 = 0.654$$
$$(0.2000) \quad (0.1556)$$

It would seem that Ulmer's series does not add much to the explanatory power of the Cairncross series. Over the long swing, and statistically, it seems that the rate of British home investment is inversely related to the rate of net capital inflow and that conditions in the American railroad industry are somewhat unimportant. This holds

formation, and inverse long swings in the latter were associated with (and probably attributable to) inverse swings in the demographic variables—population structure and migration—in Great Britain and the periphery.

(*c*) The fact that the United States, Canada, Argentina and Australia had simultaneous swings cannot be fully explained without recognizing the constraints of the gold standard and the effect of the Bank of England's reserve policy. This is not meant to imply that the Old Lady 'managed' the pre-1914 international gold standard system: on the contrary, according to her lights, she minded her own business and on critical occasions this was very much at the expense of all the borrowers.[1]

(*d*) It is very difficult in the present state of knowledge to sort out the parts played by real and monetary elements in the long swing interaction. Fig. 52 suggests some interesting clues. The course of the rate of change in the growth of the United States money stock (five-year moving average) traces out a long swing corresponding to that of net external gold flows (five-year moving average), with the former showing a short lag. The gold stock accounted for most of the large changes in high-powered money in the United States up to 1913.[2] The

true, incidentally, under all reasonable lead-lag conditions.' (*American Growth and the Balance of Payments 1820–1913*, pp. 147–8.)

Reference should also be made to an econometric analysis by Maurice Wilkinson, 'European Migration to the United States: An Econometric Analysis of Aggregate Labor Supply and Demand' (mimeographed), presented to the European Meeting of the Econometric Society, Brussels, in September 1969. His conclusion (p. 19) refutes one-sided interpretations of American long swings. He found that 'European migration to the U.S. prior to World War I was significantly influenced by both employment opportunities in the particular European country (as represented by changes in domestic output) and the gain in real income to be achieved by migration to the U.S.'.

[1] In Jacob Viner's words,

'it may be that the need of the Bank for income for dividend-paying purposes was an adequate justification for the Bank's failure to accumulate larger gold reserves from its own capital resources. But there were many ways in which the Government could have made it possible for the Bank to acquire adequate gold reserves without depletion of its revenues. As far as England as a whole was concerned, it managed to operate its part of the international gold standard throughout the nineteenth century on an investment in gold stocks pitiably small in relation to the benefits which would have accrued to it and to the world if there had been less parsimony in this connection'.

('Clapham on the Bank of England', *Economica*, new series, vol. xii, no. 46, May 1945, p. 63).

See also Arthur I. Bloomfield, *Monetary Policy under the International Gold Standard: 1880–1914*, Federal Reserve Bank of New York, October 1959, pp. 23–6.

[2] See P. Cagan, *Determinants and Effects of Changes in the Stock of Money 1875–1960*, pp. 50–1.

swings in net gold flows correspond to and lag behind the swings in American exports as a percentage of imports. There was an inverse relation between the swings in the rate of change in the growth of the American money stock and the swings in the Bank of England reserve as a percentage of liabilities. Fluctuations in net capital flows were related to those in the ratio of American to British prices (purchasing power parity, 1929 = 100).

It is clear that the American trade balance determined the gold flow, and the latter determined the rate of growth of the money supply. There is no basis for the notion that investment upswings, by generating excess demand, attracted net capital inflows which more than offset the unfavourable trade balance, thereby inducing gold inflows.[1] Gold inflow, and as a consequence the money stock, rose most rapidly in the phases of the long swing when exports were surging upwards and infrastructure investment and imports were declining. Moreover, it was in these periods that upswings in additions to the labour force and to gross national product took place.[2] In these phases Britain was having a home investment boom, her exports as a proportion of imports were falling, and gold flowed from the Bank of England to the periphery. When the United States had its investment upswing, the trade balance deteriorated and gold tended to flow out, with the result that the rate of growth of the money stock tended to fall.

There can be no such thing as a purely monetary theory of the inverse long swing; but it seems to be equally true that no explanation will be satisfactory if it leaves out important monetary forces. First, in the words of Milton Friedman, 'the major source of long-period changes in the quantity of money in the United States has been changes in high-powered money, which, until 1914, reflected mostly changes in the amount of gold.'[3] Secondly, Cagan, after a careful analysis, reached the following conclusion:

Severe contractions are an important exception...to the...statement that fluctuations in business activity seem to produce the cycles in the money series. For severe contractions, this effect may explain the timing, but apparently a deep depression cannot account for the sharp decline in the rate of change in the money stock associated with it....Panics made ordinary business contractions severe when they led to substantial decline in the rate of monetary growth, and not otherwise....The variety of reasons for decline in monetary growth during severe depressions rules out

---

[1] This is the thesis argued by Jeffrey Williamson, op. cit. p. 183: 'The rate of net gold flow over United States borders...is predominantly caused by income movements and excess demands for real-money balances.'

[2] S. Kuznets, *Capital in the American Economy*, pp. 342–6.

[3] P. Cagan, op. cit. foreword, p. xxv.

any single cause and rules out, in particular, a sharp fall in business activity as the main reason for the associated decline in monetary growth. The evidence is therefore consistent with, and, taken as a whole, impressively favors emphasis on the decline in the rate of monetary growth as the main reason some business contractions, regardless of what may have initiated them, became severe.[1]

This conclusion is in line with our analysis of the impact of changes in the money stock when long swing expansions came to their usually severe end. In short, our view of the pre-1913 Atlantic economy is that the inverse cycle was propelled by real determinants but that, in the crucial phases when expansion gave way to contraction, changes in the stock of money played a significant independent part in influencing the course of the economy.

8. LONG SWINGS IN PRODUCTIVITY AND REAL INCOME

With the aid of Fig. 56 we can see what the analysis suggests about the growth and fluctuations of productivity and real income per capita.

(a) Both in the United Kingdom and the United States the rates of change in fixed capital formation are inverse to those in exports as a percentage of imports; in other words, export performance in any one period correlates with the movement of fixed investment in the previous period.

(b) In the United States there is a strong positive correlation between rates of change in 'other' capital formation (which includes producer durables), exports as a percentage of imports, and changes in additions to the real flow of goods to consumers per capita. The course of these three variables is reflected (after a short lag) in the rate of change of real gross national product per capita. In other words, in the upward phase of the long swing in population-sensitive capital formation, the economy is investing in capacity to produce more output per unit of input in the future. *Ex post*, the high rate of growth in real national income per capita is the pay-off on the population-sensitive capital formation of the previous phase; *ex ante*, it is the inducement to a further round of fixed investment in the next phase. It is in the pay-off phase that the balance of payments is strong, the rate of growth of the money supply is high, and the standard of living grows relatively fast; the economy is reaping the increasing returns to scale arising out of the rapid rise in immigration and investment in the previous phase. The above process is a plausible explanation of the long swings ob-

[1] Ibid. p. 267.

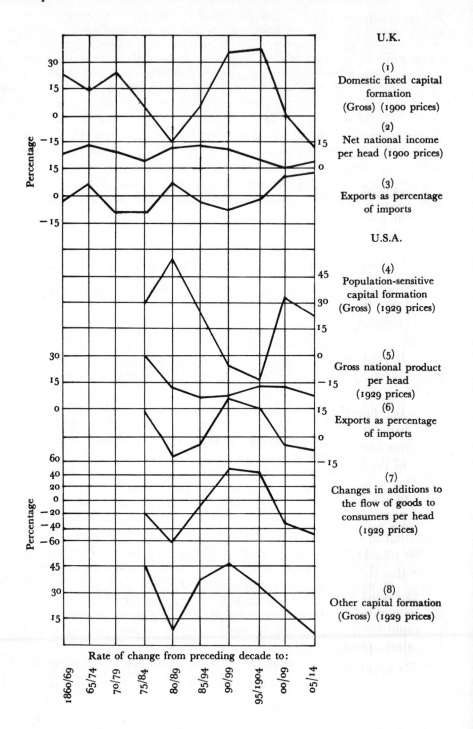

Rate of change from preceding decade to:

1860/69 65/74 70/79 75/84 80/89 85/94 90/99 95/1904 00/09 05/14

U.K.

(1)
Domestic fixed capital
formation
(Gross) (1900 prices)

(2)
Net national income
per head (1900 prices)

(3)
Exports as percentage
of imports

U.S.A.

(4)
Population-sensitive
capital formation
(Gross) (1929 prices)

(5)
Gross national product
per head
(1929 prices)

(6)
Exports as percentage
of imports

(7)
Changes in additions to
the flow of goods to
consumers per head
(1929 prices)

(8)
Other capital formation
(Gross) (1929 prices)

served in productivity in the United States,[1] and it applies to the United Kingdom as well.

(c) The inverse relation between the swings in real income per capita in the United Kingdom and the United States is bound up with the see-saw movement in the population growth rate, changes in population structure (through migration) and in population-sensitive capital formation.

(d) For the United Kingdom we have figures going back to 1855. The positive association between real income per capita and the export sector's performance holds good until the turn of the century; these variables go up together between 1860/69 and 1865/74 and between 1875/84 and 1880/89. One would have expected the same to happen between 1890/99 and 1900/09, but it did not. The sharp upturn in foreign investment and the export-import ratio in those years was accompanied by a relative fall in real income per capita. Here perhaps is further evidence of the validity of the argument that important parameters had changed to Britain's detriment and the high propensity to invest overseas which had suited her so well in the nineteenth century had become inconsistent with a high rate of growth in the standard of living.[2] Meanwhile, parameters affecting the United States had also changed; she had built up a large and highly productive manufacturing sector (accounting for 35% of world output in 1906–8) and had become a net creditor country; the share of manufacturing producer durables in gross domestic capital formation increased from

---

[1] See S. Fabricant, *Basic Facts on Productivity Change*, Occasional Paper 63, New York, N.B.E.R., 1959, pp. 16–17. The productivity estimates are based on John W. Kendrick, *Productivity Trends in the United States*, N.B.E.R., Princeton University Press, 1961. Fabricant points out that '...Kendrick's estimates, and similar data compiled earlier by Kuznets and Abramovitz for the full period following the Civil War, suggest the existence of a long cycle in productivity. High rates of increase in net national product per unit of total input came, it seems, during periods of a decade or more centered in the late 1870s, the late 1890s, the early 1920s, the late 1930s, and the late 1940s or early 1950s. Low rates of increase came during periods centered in the late 1880s, the late 1910s, the early 1930s and the 1940s' (op. cit. p. 17). This confirms our analysis in section 8 and Fig. 56.

[2] See Brinley Thomas, 'The Historical Record of International Capital Movements to 1913' in John H. Adler (ed.), op. cit. pp. 30–1.

Fig. 56. Long swings in real national product and related variables in the United Kingdom, 1855–1914, and the United States, 1870–1914. Sources: (1) C. H. Feinstein, 'Income and Investment in the United Kingdom, 1856–1914', p. 374. (2) B. R. Mitchell and Phyllis Deane, *Abstract of British Historical Statistics*, p. 367. (3) and (6) see Fig. 52. (4), (5), (7) and (8) S. Kuznets, 'Long Swings in the Growth of Population and in Related Economic Variables', Tables 13 and 15.

31% in 1869–78 to 57% in 1899–1908.[1] In 1834–43 American income per capita was probably lower than the British. 'Between 1834–43 and 1944–55 American G.N.P. increased at an exceptionally high rate of 42% per decade, a rate perhaps never equalled elsewhere for such an extended period. G.N.P. per capita also increased at a high rate, compared with British and French growth.'[2]

(e) Our analysis of the mechanism by which productivitá and real income grew in the Atlantic economy has a close affinity with the results obtained by George H. Borts and Jerome L. Stein in their investigation of the causes of differential regional rates of growth in the United States. In order to explain the convergence of per capita personal incomes among states between 1880 and 1950, these authors found it necessary to discard simple aggregative theory and use a model with two sectors, one providing construction of all kinds and the other producing goods traded among regions. Their analysis led to the conclusion that the fastest economic growth occurs in those regions of a free market economy where the supply of labour increases most rapidly; they stress the crucial role of shifts in labour supply functions (via intra- and inter-regional migration) in determining differences in regional growth rates.[3]

Similarly, there is a link with the thesis propounded by Nicholas Kaldor in his analysis of the causes of slow growth in the United Kingdom,[4] in which he stresses the dynamic relationship between rates of change of productivity and output, based on the work of P. J. Verdoorn[5] and others. The following quotation is highly relevant.

The rate of growth of industrialization fundamentally depends on the exogenous components of demand (a set of forces extending far beyond the income elasticities of demand for manufactured goods). The higher the rate of growth of industrial output which these demand conditions permit, the faster will be the rate at which labour is transferred from the surplus-sectors to the high productivity sectors. It is my contention that it is the rate

---

[1] Robert E. Gallman, 'Gross National Product in the United States, 1834–1909' in *Output Employment and Productivity in the United States after 1800*, Studies in Income and Wealth, vol. 30, by the Conference on Research in Income and Wealth, New York, N.B.E.R., Columbia University Press, 1966, p. 15. In this important paper, Gallman has shown that the movements of the real G.N.P. series and the main components conform well to the chronology of long swings as established by Abramovitz (ibid. pp. 21–3).

[2] Ibid. p. 23.

[3] George H. Borts and Jerome L. Stein, *Economic Growth in a Free Market*, New York, Columbia University Press, 1964, especially Chapters 3, 4 and 5, pp. 48–100.

[4] N. Kaldor, *The Causes of the Slow Rate of Growth of the United Kingdom*, Cambridge University Press, 1966.

[5] P. J. Verdoorn, 'Fattori che regolano lo sviluppo della produttivitá del lavoro', *L'Industria*, vol. 1, 1949.

at which this transfer takes place which determines the growth rate of the economy as a whole. The mechanism by which this happens is only to a minor extent dependent on the *absolute* differences in the levels of output per head between the labour-absorbing sectors and the surplus-labour sectors. The major part of the mechanism consists of the fact that the *growth* of productivity is accelerated as a result of the transfer at both ends—both at the gaining-end and at the losing-end; in the first, because, as a result of increasing returns, productivity in industry will increase faster, the faster output expands; in the second because when the surplus-sectors lose labour, the productivity of the remainder of the population is bound to rise.[1]

This passage describes the essence of the growth process in the Atlantic economy which has been explored in this chapter. Kaldor stresses that the relationship between the rate of growth of productivity and of output is a phenomenon peculiar to the secondary rather than the primary and tertiary sectors of the economy. In our analysis we have seen how essential it is to split this secondary sector into construction, public utilities etc., on the one hand, and manufacturing, on the other. In this way one can observe how a high rate of growth of population and construction is a prelude to a high rate of growth of labour supply and manufacturing output, thereby entailing a high rate of growth of productivity through increasing returns and technical change.[2]

FORMAL STATEMENT OF THE MODEL

Notation

Y	real income	h	population structure (vector)
N	population	E	exports (supply)
C	creditor country	M	imports (demand)
D	debtor country	P	home prices
I	investment	P_E	export prices (import prices)
r	population growth rate	g	investment gestation period
m	migration		

We first give a simple version of the model which can later be elaborated.

Investment and population growth functions for each country

In each country, creditor and debtor, investment is a function of population growth rate and population structure, and the population growth rate is a function of migration and population structure, h, which is a vector whose elements are the numbers in various age, sex and marital status groups.

---

[1] N. Kaldor, 'Productivity and Growth in Manufacturing Industry: a Reply', *Economica*, vol. xxxv, no. 140, November 1968, p. 386.

[2] See Chapter x on technical change.

$$(1) \quad I_C = f_1(r_C, h_C),$$
$$(2) \quad I_D = f_2(r_D, h_D),$$
$$(3) \quad r_C = f_3(m, h_C),$$
$$(4) \quad r_D = f_4(m, h_D).$$

This system can be closed if we make assumptions about migration and population structure. We can write migration as a function of relative real income per head and population structure:

$$(5) \quad m = f_5\left(\left[\frac{Y_D}{N_D} - \frac{Y_C}{N_C}\right], h_C, h_D\right)$$

Population structure (h) in each country has a cyclical element in it; at any moment it is a function of an earlier population structure and of intervening migration. Thus,

$$(6) \quad h_C^t = f_6(h_C^{t-\tau}, m_t, m_{t-I}, \ldots, m_{t-\tau}),$$

$$(7) \quad h_D^t = f_7(h_D^{t-\tau}, m_t, m_{t-I}, \ldots, m_{t-\tau}).$$

We can define N in terms of structure. Thus,

$(8) \quad N_C = \Sigma h_C^i$ where h_C^i is the ith element of the vector h_C,

$(9) \quad N_D = \Sigma h_D^i$ where h_D^i is the ith element of the vector h_D.

Let us forget income for the time being. Export supply depends on investment lagged by the infrastructure gestation period (g), while import demand depends on investment in the importing country. We make P home prices and P_E export prices (import prices). We can write exports as an increasing function of the ratio of export prices to home prices. Then,

$$(10) \quad E_D = f_{10}\left(I_D\{t-g_D\}, \frac{P_{ED}}{P_D}\right),$$

$$(11) \quad E_C = f_{11}\left(I_C\{t-g_C\}, \frac{P_{EC}}{P_C}\right).$$

We now make imports (M) an increasing function of real income and a decreasing function of the relevant price ratio.

$$(12) \quad M_D = f_{12}\left(Y_D, \frac{P_{EC}}{P_D}\right),$$

$$(13) \quad M_C = f_{13}\left(Y_C, \frac{P_{ED}}{P_C}\right).$$

Still leaving income aside, we can close this part of the model. We have the identities

$$(14) \quad E_C \equiv M_D,$$

$$(15) \quad E_D \equiv M_C.$$

As a first approximation, home prices can be written simply as a function (possibly a weighted average) of export and import prices:

$$(16) \quad P_D = f_{16}(P_{ED}, P_{EC}),$$

$$(17) \quad P_C = f_{17}(P_{ED}, P_{EC}).$$

This leaves income which can be written as a function of investment and exports. To handle it properly we should include lags, but as a simplification we may write:

$$(18) \quad Y_C = f_{18}(I_C, E_C),$$

$$(19) \quad Y_D = f_{19}(I_D, E_D).$$

This version of the basic relationships can now be taken a little further. We need the accelerator effect which can be introduced by Y or ΔY. The marginal efficiency of investment is the marginal physical product times a price ratio, i.e. P_E/P. Thus, we rewrite the investment functions as:

$$(1a) \quad I_C = f_{1a}\left(r_C, h_C, \Delta Y_C \frac{P_{EC}}{P_C}\right),$$

$$(2a) \quad I_D = f_{2a}\left(r_D, h_D, \Delta Y_D \frac{P_{ED}}{P_D}\right).$$

Then we have to add:

$$(20) \quad \Delta Y_C = f_{20}(Y_C^t, Y_C^{t-1}, \ldots)$$

$$(21) \quad \Delta Y_D = f_{21}(Y_D^t, Y_D^{t-1}, \ldots)$$

In this model capital formation is 'population-sensitive' not just 'migration-sensitive'. Its ability to generate long swings would seem to depend on g and h, the infrastructure lag and population structure. There are a number of different possible forms of the investment function, particularly with respect to lags, which are conceivable, and the best empirical form can be found only by experimenting. It is proposed as a future development of this work to simulate a complete model, to try out various functions with different parameters and lags so as to see what effects they have on the simulated values of the endogenous variables.

CHAPTER XVI

MIGRATION AND REGIONAL GROWTH
IN BRITAIN

Chapter VIII contained a brief analysis of internal and external migration in England and Wales, 1841–1911, and it demonstrated a clear inverse relation between swings in internal migration and home investment on the one hand and swings in emigration and capital exports on the other. The new evidence on regional building cycles presented in Chapter XIII has confirmed these results and has shown that the two regions which did not conform to the national pattern were London and South Wales. It would be interesting to do a separate analysis of London with reference to long swings in the growth of the Atlantic economy, but this would be a major work in itself.

The first part of this chapter deals with the Welsh economy separately, since it was based entirely on coal exports and its fluctuations were a direct index of those of the British export sector in the period 1860–1913. Then I shall examine the southward shift of population in Britain between 1911 and 1966 with particular reference to London and the South East. The chapter will conclude with an analysis of the volume and regional incidence of the immigration from the New Commonwealth, mainly India, Pakistan and the West Indies, in the nineteen-fifties and sixties.

I. WALES AND THE ATLANTIC ECONOMY

Reasonably accurate estimates of regional net losses or gains by migration can be obtained for periods between Population Censuses by taking the increase in the enumerated population from one census to the next and subtracting from it the excess of births over deaths during the inter-censal period. A net gain by migration is registered when the increase in the enumerated population exceeds the excess of births over deaths, and a net loss when the increase in the enumerated population is less than the excess of births over deaths.

Table 143 sets out the record for England, Wales, and Scotland from 1851–61 to 1961–6; the figures are expressed as annual rates per 10,000 mean population. They are illustrated in Fig. 57.

The period 1851–1911, which was not interrupted by major wars, shows some interesting features. The decennial rates of migration exhibit long swings. England and Scotland have a common long swing, with that of Scotland having the greater amplitude: the migration cycle for Wales is inverse to that of England and Scotland. This interesting fact, which could be brought into the open only when the England and Wales total was disaggregated, may throw some light on the mechanism of internal migration.

Let us first look at regional rates of long-term growth. In the forty years, 1871–1911, Scotland had a net loss by migration of 619,000, whereas Wales had a net gain by migration of 20,000. In this period

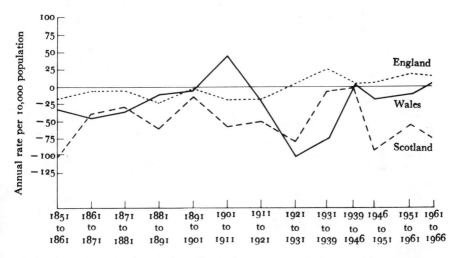

Fig. 57. England, Wales and Scotland: annual rates of net migration, each intercensal period, 1851–1966. Source: Table 143.

Scotland, starting in 1871 with a population of 3,360,000, lost 31 % of its natural increase of 2,019,000 through migration, whereas Wales, starting in 1871 with a population of 1,421,000, kept the whole of her natural increase of 986,000 and added 20,000 through net absorption. In England the net loss by migration in the period 1871–1911 was 1,355,000, which was 10 % of her natural increase. It is clear that the secular rate of economic growth in Wales in the period 1871–1911 was higher than in England and much higher than in Scotland. It was based mainly on the phenomenal expansion of the steam-coal export trade. In the process Cardiff became the world's greatest coal-exporting port, the volume of exports increasing fifteenfold from 708,000 tons in 1851 to 10,577,000 tons in 1913. This phase of secular expansion culminated in the first decade of this century when Wales was a country of new settlement absorbing immigrants at a rate not much less than the United States in the same period (an annual rate of 4·5 per 1,000 as against 6·3).

We shall now examine the inverse relation between the long swings
in the migration experience of England and Scotland on the one hand
and Wales on the other. This can be done most clearly by concentrating
on England and Wales and on the time-shape of coalfield development

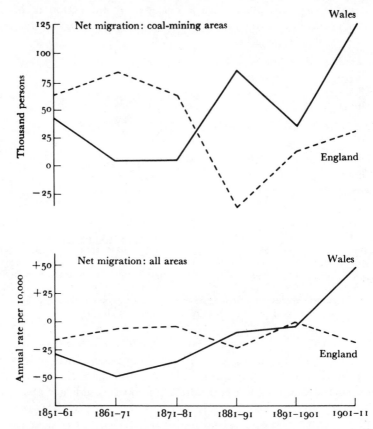

Fig. 58. England and Wales: migration balances in coal-mining areas and all areas,
1851–1911. Source: Table 144.

in the two regions. Table 144 and Fig. 58 set out the annual net
absorption of labour decennially in Welsh and English coalfields
together with the parallel course of net migration in Wales and England
respectively. There is a marked inverse relation between the rate of
growth of the Welsh and English coalfields except in the decade
1901–11. In the sixties and seventies the main expansion was in England; in the eighties Wales took the lead, whereas the bulk of the

advance in the nineties was in England. In the years 1901–11 both were expanding, but the Welsh districts much more than the English.

The interpretation of this inverse relation lies in the fact that Welsh industry was geared almost entirely to the export trade in coal. When we divide Britain into two sectors, home investment and export, the coal-mining areas of Wales fell wholly within the export sector. In the period 1861–1911 long swings in the export sector of Britain were inverse to those in home investment. The rate of output of coal in Wales synchronized with fluctuations in the British export sector, whereas the rate of output of English coal consumed on the home market was sensitive to the long swing in home capital construction. Thus, a phase of decline in the rate of expansion of the export-oriented coalfields of Wales would correspond to a phase of increase in the rate of expansion of the domestically oriented coalfields of England, and vice versa.

We have already seen that Wales experienced a very rapid rate of long-run growth in the period 1851–1911, based on the export multiplier-accelerator effects of the secular expansion of the international demand for steam coal. Wales started with a population of 1,187,000 in 1851, and in the following sixty years the excess of births over deaths was 1,137,000. Only 80,000, or a mere 6%, of this huge natural increase, was lost through migration. The net migration balances for the rural and urban areas of England and of Wales separately for 1871–1911 are set out in Table 145.

Here we find an interesting contrast between the fluctuations in the rural-urban transfers of population in Wales and in England. In the seventies practically the whole of the rural exodus in England was absorbed in the urban sector of that country, whereas only one-fifth of the rural exodus in Wales was absorbed internally. In the eighties, on the other hand, 82% of the rural exodus emigrated out of England, while in Wales it was almost exactly the reverse—83% of the rural exodus being absorbed in the Welsh urban sector. In the nineties the flight from the land in England was counterbalanced by an almost equal net intake of population by the urban areas: in Wales the number of rural migrants taken by the home urban sector was only about half of the number in the previous decade and 16% emigrated. At no time was the contrast more evident than in the decade 1901–11: in England there was a net efflux from the urban as well as the rural sector, giving a net emigration of 597,000, or an annual rate of 19 per 10,000 mean population; in Wales a net rural exodus of 38,000 was overshadowed by a net absorption of no less than 132,000 in the urban sector, giving a net immigration of 94,000, or an annual rate of 45 per 10,000 mean population.

Some light on the destination of emigrants from different parts of

Britain can be obtained by consulting United States figures. The United States was the major destination of British emigrants, accounting for over two-thirds of them in the period under review. Table 58 indicates that the rate of gross outflow from Wales to the United States between 1881 and 1911 was negligible as compared with that of Scotland and England, and it did not fluctuate much.

Table 58. *United States: immigrants from England, Scotland and Wales, 1881–1911*

Period and country of origin	Mean population of country of origin (thousands)	Immigrants to U.S.A.		Annual rate per 10,000 mean population	
		Total	With occupation	Total	With occupation
England					
1881–90	25,812	644,680	319,118	25	12
1891–1900	28,861	224,350	128,107	8	4
1901–10	32,061	387,005	237,227	12	7
Scotland					
1881–90	3,881	149,869	79,342	39	20
1891–1900	4,294	60,046	28,006	14	7
1901–10	4,617	133,333	86,976	29	19
Wales					
1881–90	1,677	12,640	5,682	8	3
1891–1900	1,895	11,219	5,005	6	3
1901–10	2,238	18,631	11,708	8	5

SOURCE: Brinley Thomas, 'Wales and the Atlantic Economy', table III, p. 176.

The popular impression that Welsh workers flocked to the United States in the latter half of the nineteenth century is a myth. In the decade 1881–90 when the absorptive power of the United States was at a peak, the effect on Wales was hardly noticeable. In proportion to population, English emigrants to America (with occupation) were four times as numerous as the Welsh, and the Scots seven times as numerous. Welsh emigrants were not forced out by the impoverishment of the economy as happened in Ireland and Scotland; it was a complementary export of labour on a very minor scale induced by the export-biased nature of the Welsh economy. In the short cycle, however, emigration, as one would expect, was inverse to fluctuations in income in Wales. Sharp and frequent changes occurred in the price of coal; when the price rose there was prosperity and the incentive to emigrate weakened, and vice versa when the price fell. These short cyclical ups and downs are to be distinguished from the long swing.

The interaction of the long swings for the period 1871–1911 (Fig. 58 and Table 145) may be explained in the following terms. Since the Welsh economy was entirely export-oriented, its upswings coincided with upswings in the English export sector: the latter were accompanied by downswings in the home construction sector of England. During such phases (i.e. 1881–90 and 1901–11) Welsh economic growth was strong enough to retain nearly the whole of the country's natural increase or even to attract an appreciable net inflow from the rest of the United Kingdom, whereas in England the relatively slow rate of growth of the home construction sector caused a large part of the rural surplus (and in 1901–10 many people from the urban areas) to emigrate overseas. Thus, low emigration from (or immigration into) Wales coincided with high emigration from England. On the other hand, when the Welsh economy was in a downswing relative to trend, the English home construction sector was simultaneously experiencing a rapid upswing, with the export sector declining relative to trend. In this phase the workers displaced from the land in Wales, facing a weak demand for labour in the urban areas of their own country, migrated over the border to England, where there was a brisk demand for labour in the flourishing home investment sector. Thus, high emigration from Wales coincided with low emigration from England. The surplus agricultural population in Wales was recruited either for the export-geared urban sector within Wales or for the home construction sector in England: there was comparatively little recruitment for overseas.

2. THE SOUTHWARD SHIFT OF POPULATION, 1911–66

It is very difficult to identify the timing and amplitude of long swings for the half-century beginning in 1911, since all time series reflect the profound economic consequences of two World Wars. The internal migration picture is summarized in Fig. 57. The sharpest break took place in the fortunes of Wales, where an annual net population inflow of 4·5 per 1,000 in 1901–11 was converted into an annual net loss of 10·2 per 1,000 in the nineteen-twenties. Between 1921 and 1939 Wales lost on balance 450,000 people by migration; the natural increase in the period was 259,000, and so the population fell by 191,000. Scotland was also hard hit in the twenties, with an annual loss by migration of 8 per 1,000, but in the thirties the rate of outflow was negligible as compared with the exodus from Wales. Most of the migrants from Wales and Scotland settled in England, where there was an average annual inflow of 2·4 per 1,000 between 1931 and 1939. The exceptional circumstances of the Second World War brought a temporary halt in inter-regional population flows.

The outstanding fact about the inter-war period was the heavy incidence of mass unemployment in the coal-mining regions and the redistribution of population in favour of the relatively prosperous areas of Southern England. The extent of the southward shift between 1931 and 1961 is seen in Table 146. Much has been written about the alleged imbalance between the old industrial North and the new industrial South, and it is often inferred that it began during the great depression between the wars. This inference is quite correct in the case of Wales, where the remarkable export-led secular growth in the period 1860–1913 ended in a collapse in the inter-war years. But it would be wrong to generalize.

No explanation of the deeper factors behind the southward shift can be adequate unless it takes into account the tendencies already evident in the years 1881–1911, as shown in Table 147. The data on regional building cycles in Chapter XIII also threw light on this. Fig. 45 revealed a peak in building at the turn of the century in the mainly rural counties of the South and South West. The location of this activity is illustrated in the migration figures for certain towns given in the note to Table 147.

Residential building was the most important element in the upswing in domestic capital formation in the nineties. The composition and geographical distribution of the investment were determined partly by changes in the pattern of consumers' expenditure which favoured the growth of seaside towns and by the location of Government expenditure on the armed forces. Above all were the powerful spin-off effects of the dominance of London, and these were bound to be felt mainly in the South of England. In the period 1881–1911 nearly all towns in Northern England were recording net losses by migration, with the exception of the residential towns which showed moderate gains. On the other hand, in the South the residential towns received large net gains of population, as did the industrial towns, unlike those of the North. The trend in favour of the South which was characteristic of the late Victorian and the Edwardian era continued in the inter-war period, albeit in very different circumstances.

For the period 1939–61 the one exception in the Southern part of Britain is London and the South East, where big net losses by migration were recorded, but this hides some interesting intra-regional flows. The net outflow of 640,000 between 1939 and 1951 was largely the result of the War; the population of Greater London in 1951 was 400,000 fewer than the peak of 8,728,000 in 1939. Between 1951 and 1961 the centrifugal tendency continued, with a net loss of 502,000 in Greater London and a net gain of 319,000 in the rest of the South East region.

3. REGIONAL GROWTH OF MANUFACTURING

Regional migration balances for the period 1951–66 are shown in Table 148, which ranks the regions according to rate of growth of employment in manufacturing.[1] The contrast between the South and the North is again striking. Between 1951 and 1966 the Southern part of Britain absorbed 1,059,000 migrants and the Northern part lost 815,000, with Scotland accounting for nearly half a million. The South West, the South East and East Anglia, and the Midlands rank high in rate of expansion of manufacturing and in rate of net in-migration. The Northern regions and Scotland have a relatively low rate of advance in manufacturing and heavy net out-migration.

Wales is an exception in having a rate of expansion in manufacturing almost as high as the South East but without attracting population. It had been more specialized in coal mining than any other region and, apart from its steel and tinplate industry, a virtually new manufacturing sector has developed since the war. Plenty of labour was available from the huge surplus released by mining and other declining industries and through the recruitment of the hitherto untapped supply of women workers. Between 1959 and 1966 employment in manufacturing grew faster in Wales than in any other region, i.e. by 18% as compared with 12% in the South West, 8% in London and Eastern England, the Midlands and Yorkshire, 6% in the North, 4% in Scotland, and a slight decline in the North West.

The Board of Trade has published information about the movement of manufacturing establishments in the period 1945–65. For this purpose the United Kingdom was divided into fifty areas, and the survey related to the opening of new manufacturing establishments when the development in question had its origin outside the area in which the new establishment was opened. Such 'moves' include not only transfers (a new factory in one area replacing a closure in another area) but also branches (an additional factory opened by a firm in an area where it had not manufactured previously).[2] These statistics throw light on trends in regional economic growth in relation to internal shifts of population. A summary is given in Table 149.

In 1966, 56% of employment in British manufacturing was in the industrial South, i.e. the South East, East Anglia, the South West and the Midlands, and nearly a third was in the South East and East Anglia. Between 1953 and 1966 no less than half the increase in

---

[1] The boundaries of the Economic Planning Regions and of development areas etc. are shown in the map on p. 298.

[2] For precise definitions see R. S. Howard, *The Movement of Manufacturing Industry in the United Kingdom 1945–1965*, Board of Trade, 1968, pp. 48–9.

manufacturing employment in Britain (452,000 out of 879,000) took place in the South East and East Anglia, which had an increase in

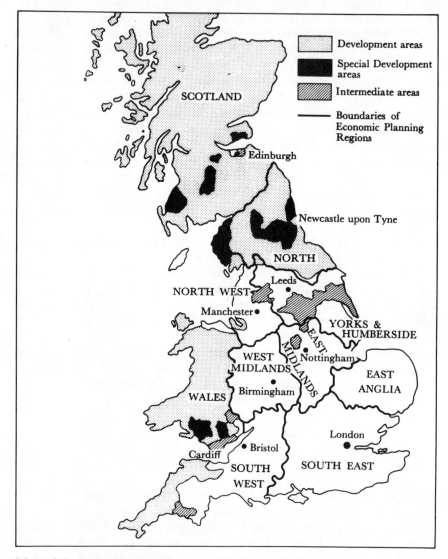

Map of Economic Planning Regions of Great Britain, showing also development areas, special development areas and intermediate areas.

population in this period equal to 47% of the growth in Britain as a whole.

Successive British Governments have pursued policies designed to attract industries into the Development Areas, which are located mainly in regions where coal mining has been rapidly contracting, i.e. Scotland, the North, the North West and Wales. The last two columns of Table 149 give some indication of the extent to which these measures have succeeded. In Scotland and the North West the manufacturing sector, apart from the employment gained through inward moves of factories, underwent a sizeable decrease; Wales and the North fared better. It is clear that, without the incentives in favour of the Development Areas, the growth of manufacturing in the industrial South would have been even more pronounced.

One of the chief causes of the difficulties of the older industrial areas is that the British economy is switching from coal to more economical sources of energy, such as natural gas, nuclear power and oil. The country as a whole will gain considerably from the consequent increase in productivity, but the heavy incidence of the transition falls on particular regions, such as Scotland, Wales and the North. In the nine years 1959–68 the decline in employment in mining and quarrying was 53,200 in Scotland, 86,100 in the North and 55,700 in Wales. The increase in employment in manufacturing was 13,600 in Scotland, 16,600 in the North and 51,800 in Wales. Whereas the growth of manufacturing in Wales came near to offsetting the contraction of mining and quarrying, in Scotland and the North the increase in manufacturing was only one-fifth of what was lost through mining closures.

The main source of migrating establishments was Greater London, accounting for 43% of the employment entailed by internal moves; but it is significant that the overspill of manufacturing from Greater London to the rest of the South East and East Anglia was nearly twice as large as the movement to the old industrial North (194,000 as against 115,000 in terms of employment).[1]

The population of the South East region increased from 15,200,000 in 1951 to 17,100,000 in 1966, i.e. from 34·7 to 35·6% of the population of England and Wales. The growth took place in the outer areas. There was an absolute fall in population in Greater London from 8,200,000 to 7,900,000, a rise in the outer metropolitan area from 3,500,000 to 5,000,000, and a rise in the outer South East from 3,500,000 to 4,100,000. Net in-migration accounted for 68% of the population increase of the outer metropolitan area and 72% of that of the outer South East.[2]

Post-war Government measures to steer manufacturing industry to

[1] R. S. Howard, op. cit., p. 15.
[2] See *A Strategy for the South East: A First Report of the South East Economic Planning Council*, London, H.M.S.O., 1967, p. 70.

regions of high structural unemployment, while they have had a moderate success, have been overshadowed by the powerful effect of the inflow of population into the South, particularly the counties surrounding London. In 1966 the value of construction orders received by contractors in the private and public sectors in the South East region was 36% of the total for England and Wales, which was exactly the region's proportion of the total population. Our analysis has shown that half the increase in manufacturing employment in Britain in 1953–66 took place in the South East and East Anglia, where nearly half the growth in Britain's population occurred. This population upsurge was to a large extent a migration dynamic and, as in similar previous periods, it was associated with a high rate of growth of population-sensitive capital formation, manufacturing, and services.

The components of population change for the South East in 1961–6 are shown in Table 59. The striking feature is the big net inflow of

Table 59. *South East England: components of population change, 1961–6.* (*Thousands*)

| Year ended 30 June | Natural increase | Net migration | | | Home population, total changes* |
		Within England and Wales	Outside England and Wales	Total	
1962	+95	−40	+141	+101	+201
1963	+93	−14	+42	+28	+126
1964	+123	−17	+49	+32	+151
1965	+121	−36	+42	+5	+126
1966	+109	−29	+28	−1	+118

* Including changes in the number of armed forces and minor statistical corrections.
SOURCE: *A Strategy for the South East*, p. 86.

302,000 external immigrants (from outside England and Wales) and the net outflow of 136,000 internal migrants. The abnormal number of immigrants in 1961–2 was followed by a sharp rise in natural increase in 1963–5. To interpret this pattern it is necessary to examine a new phase in Britain's migration history—the entry of immigrants from New Commonwealth countries, particularly the West Indies, India and Pakistan, in the fifties and sixties.

4. THE NEW IMMIGRATION

The middle of the nineteen-fifties saw the beginning of a remarkable inflow into Britain of migrants from the West Indies and Asia. Between 1955 and 1960 net arrivals from the Caribbean, India and Pakistan came to 219,540, of whom 96,180 were from Jamaica and 65,270 from the rest of the Caribbean. Almost as many, 203,470, entered in the year and a half ending in June 1962, 45% from India and Pakistan, an abnormal influx caused in large measure by a rush to come in before the restrictions contained in the Commonwealth Immigrants Act came into force on July 1, 1962. From the middle of 1962 to the end of 1967 there was a net inward movement of 231,830 from the West Indies, India and Pakistan; 60% were from the latter two countries, and over two-thirds of the total were dependants.[1]

(a) Controls

Section 2 of the Commonwealth Immigrants Act of 1962 gave immigration officers power to refuse admission or to admit subject to a condition respecting the period of stay, with or without a condition restricting freedom to take employment. People born in the United Kingdom and certain classes of people holding United Kingdom passports were competely exempt from control. There was no general power to refuse admission to people ordinarily resident in the United Kingdom, to holders of Ministry of Labour vouchers, or to wives and children under sixteen accompanying or joining husbands or parents. Returning residents, wives, and children under sixteen could be refused admission only if they were subject to a deportation order. Voucher holders, students and persons of independent means (including visitors) could be refused admission if they were subject to a deportation order, on medical or security grounds, or on account of criminal record.

 A Commonwealth citizen who wished to work and settle in Britain had to have a Ministry of Labour voucher. There were three categories: category A for applications by employers in the United Kingdom who had a specific job to offer to a particular Commonwealth citizen; category B for applications by Commonwealth citizens without a specific job to come to but with certain special qualifications (for example, nurses, doctors, teachers); category C for all others. Priority was given to the first two categories. The issue of vouchers in category C was subject to the condition that no country received more than a quarter of the vouchers available for issue, and within category C

---

[1] The source of these figures is the Home Office annual statistics issued under the Commonwealth Immigrants Act, 1962. For details see E. J. B. Rose and Associates, *Colour and Citizenship: A Report on British Race Relations*, Oxford University Press, 1969, pp. 82–4.

preference was given to applicants who had served in the British armed forces. Vouchers were issued to other applicants in category C in the order in which their applications were received in London.

In 1962 and the first months of 1963 a high proportion of the vouchers issued were not taken up and the rate of issue was accordingly stepped up. As time went on a much higher proportion of the vouchers issued came to be used, and the rate of issue was reduced until it settled at about four hundred a week, of which about three-quarters were being used. When the scheme was introduced it was thought that most of the vouchers would be for applicants in category C, i.e. mainly unskilled workers. However, between September 1964 and the middle of 1965 the two priority classes of skilled workers, categories A and B, took up the whole issue of four hundred a week, so that there was no room for any applicants in category C. There was soon a waiting list of no less than 300,000 persons in this group.

In 1965 Government policy became much more restrictive. The White Paper of that year[1] abolished category C and fixed the annual issue of A and B vouchers at 8,500 a year (1,000 of which were reserved for Malta). It specified the kind of person who would be favoured: doctors, dentists and trained nurses; teachers eligible for the status of qualified teacher in Britain; graduates in science or technology with at least two years' experience in suitable employment since graduation; and non-graduates with at least two years' experience in suitable employment since qualifying. Applicants in category A, whether skilled or unskilled, are admissible if they have a specific job to come to in Britain. The White Paper stated that 'the Government will continue to welcome people who come from other Commonwealth countries on holiday, social or business visits or to follow a course of study'.

(b) Regional Incidence

There is an extensive literature on many aspects of this new im-immigration.[2] What concerns us particularly in this context is the regional distribution of the newcomers. According to the 1966 Census there were in Britain 2,603,250 persons who were born abroad, including the Irish Republic; 850,600 of these, or nearly a third, came from New

---

[1] *Immigration from the Commonwealth*, Cmnd. 2739, 1965.

[2] For a comprehensive inquiry into the whole problem see Rose *et al.*, op. cit. which contains an excellent bibliography. For an authoritative economic analysis see K. Jones and A. D. Smith, *The Economic Impact of Commonwealth Immigration*, Cambridge University Press, 1970. An illuminating account of immigration from the West Indies is to be found in Ceri Peach, *West Indian Migration to Britain: A Social Geography*, Oxford University Press, 1968.

Commonwealth countries,[1] and 738,790 were from the Irish Republic. As many as 60% of the New Commonwealth immigrants were in the South East and East Anglia and 13% were in the West Midlands.[2] Of those in the South East and East Anglia, 35% were from the Caribbean and 30% from India and Pakistan; the corresponding percentages for the West Midlands were 38 and 50. The majority of the 850,600 New Commonwealth immigrants had settled in large urban areas and no less than 43% were in Greater London.

Table 150 sets out the changes in population and number of immigrants in each region and conurbation between 1961 and 1966. The regions are ranked, as in Table 148, according to rate of growth of manufacturing, 1953–66.

The increase of 381,500 immigrants enumerated in Britain between 1961 and 1966 was dominated by 309,500 from New Commonwealth countries, of whom 40% were in Greater London. If we exclude Greater London from the South East and East Anglia, the three regions with the fastest growth in manufacturing employment received an addition of only 61,700 New Commonwealth immigrants between them. As a national average, people born in New Commonwealth countries were 16·3 per 1,000 of the population in 1966: the proportion in the South West was 10·1, in the South East and East Anglia (excluding Greater London) 13·5, and in Wales 3·8. The one fast growing region which showed a high absorptive capacity was the West Midlands, with an increase of 49,600 and a proportion of 22·8 per 1,000 in 1966. The North and Scotland, like Wales, were hardly in the picture.

The newcomers were a significant input in the labour market, contributing more than a fifth to the increase in the British labour force between 1961 and 1966;[3] but most of this addition took place in areas which were losing indigenous population. Table 150 shows that the six conurbations as a whole absorbed 199,000 immigrants from New Commonwealth countries between 1961 and 1966 while losing 622,000 of their indigenous population. In Greater London there was a decline of 5% in manufacturing employment, a decrease of 452,000 in indigenous population, and an absorption of 125,000 New Commonwealth immigrants: in the rest of the South East and East Anglia employment in manufacturing grew by 11%, the indigenous population increased by

[1] New Commonwealth countries then comprised: Barbados, British Guiana, Jamaica, Trinidad and Tobago, and other countries in the Caribbean; Ceylon, Cyprus, Hong Kong, India, Malaysia, Pakistan and Singapore; British East and Central Africa, Nigeria and other countries in West Africa, Gibraltar, Malta and Gozo.

[2] *Sample Census 1966: Great Britain, Summary Tables*, London, H.M.S.O., 1967, pp. 29–38.

[3] See K. Jones and A. D. Smith, op. cit. pp. 36–7.

675,000, and the number of New Commonwealth immigrants rose by only 49,000.[1]

The census classification by country of birth cannot tell us the exact number of non-white residents; white persons born abroad must be excluded. There is also reason to believe that there was under-enumeration of some groups, particularly Pakistanis. Careful estimates made by the Institute of Race Relations indicate that in 1966 the total of Commonwealth non-white residents in England and Wales who were born abroad was 711,000, and the number born in the United Kingdom 213,000, giving a non-white total of 924,000, or just under 2% of the population. This total comprised 240,000 from India and Ceylon, 120,000 from Pakistan, 274,000 from Jamaica, 180,000 from the rest of the Caribbean, 50,000 from British West Africa, and 60,000 from the Far East.[2]

The evidence for the conurbations suggests that most of these immigrants tend to establish themselves in areas which are losing population. Are the newcomers replacing local people in areas where economic growth is weak? This can only be tested by an analysis covering a large number of small neighbourhoods. Ceri Peach, in his study of the distribution of West Indians between 1951 and 1961, found that 'they have settled most in the large towns, least in the small towns; most in the decreasing towns; most of all in the large decreasing towns and least in the small increasing towns'.[3] He reached the following conclusion.

In spite of the shortcomings of the available statistics, it seems clear that West Indians have acted as a replacement population in this country. Geographically, they have been drawn to those regions which, in spite of demand for labour, have not been able to attract much net population from other parts of the country. In towns they are proportionately twice as numerous in those that lost population between 1951 and 1961 as in those which increased. They have gone to the decreasing urban cores of expanding industrial regions.[4]

The process is in an early phase but it has in it the seeds of the ghetto; there is an ominous similarity with the experience of the American Negro. In Chapter VIII we found a clear inverse relation between the

[1] The figures for manufacturing employment are for 1960 and 1964, years which were at a comparable position in the trade cycle: see *A Strategy for the South East*, pp. 89 and 92.

[2] For details of these estimates see Rose *et al.*, op. cit. pp. 96–103 and app. III. 4.

[3] Ceri Peach, op. cit. p. 81. In 1961, in Birmingham 86% and in London 87% of the West Indians were in local authority areas which had had a net decline in white population (ibid. p. 89).

[4] Ibid. p. 82.

Negroes' success in establishing themselves in the North and the volume of immigration from Europe.[1] The black people did best in areas where white people were not coming in or were moving out, and they were concentrated in the lower paid jobs. Segregation in Britain is by no means as marked as in the United States but the symptoms are the same. However, since the scale of the problem is so much smaller, it should be feasible to conduct active policies to achieve the highest possible degree of equality of opportunity and geographical dispersal.

[1] See pp. 130–4 above and Chapter xviii.

CHAPTER XVII

THE DYNAMICS OF BRAIN DRAIN

A striking feature of the international scene since the Second World War is the high proportion of migrants who can be regarded as human capital, i.e. 'the professional, technical and kindred grades'. Advanced countries are keen to attract qualified manpower and they erect barriers against the entry of the unskilled; the actions of Governments suggest that immigration policy has come to resemble tariff policy as an instrument for the pursuit of national gain, as the following statements show.

At the hearings on the 1965 United States immigration bill, the American Secretary of State said:

The significance of immigration for the United States now depends less on the number than on the quality of the immigrants. The explanation for the high professional and technical quality of present immigration lies in part in the non-quota and preference provisions...that favor the admission of the highly qualified migrants. But still more it depends on world conditions of post-war economic and social dislocations....Under present circumstances, the United States has a rare opportunity to draw migrants of high intelligence and ability from abroad; and immigration, if well administered, can be one of our greatest national resources....We are in the international market of brains.[1]

In a White Paper on immigration in October 1966 the Canadian Minister of Immigration made the following statement.

Canada has become a highly complex industrialized and urbanized society. And such a society is increasingly demanding of the quality of its work force. If those entering the work force, whether native-born or immigrants, do not have the ability and training to do the jobs available, they will be burdens rather than assets. Today, Canada's expanding industrial economy offers most of its employment opportunities to those with education, training, skill....The high cost of training professional and skilled people—engineers, doctors, skilled technicans, etc.—is a measure of the benefit derived upon their arrival in Canada....Other countries are in competition with us for immigrants.[2]

[1] *Hearings, July 2–August 3, 1964*, no. 13, pt. II, Judiciary Committee, House of Representatives, 88th Congress, 1964, pp. 389–90 and 401.
[2] Department of Manpower and Immigration, *Canadian Immigration Policy*, Ottawa, 1966, pp. 8 and 11.

In the Atlantic economy, 1860–1913, as well as within the United States, 1880–1950, migration helped to bring about the convergence of regional (national or State) growth rates.[1] The question arises whether, in the conditions prevailing in 1950–70, the international flows of human capital tended to widen the gap between developed and less developed countries.

I. THE STATISTICAL GROUNDWORK

Research on international movements of highly trained manpower has been based largely on the statistics of the main receiving countries, particularly the United States, Canada and Australia. Such countries have always had good reason to keep reasonably accurate records of the number, quality and origins of immigrants, but they do not have the same interest in measuring outward flows. A word of caution is therefore necessary. When we use statistics showing gross inflows of professional manpower into these countries, we are hampered by a partial eclipse since there are no reliable data on the outward movement of immigrants to their homelands or to other destinations and we cannot satisfactorily measure the emigration of highly trained nationals from these countries. Our knowledge of *net* international flows is incomplete.

In the absence of the required flow data, it is sometimes possible to remedy some of these gaps by using Population Census statistics. For example, according to the United States Census for 1960, only about 50,000 Americans in the professional, technical and kindred grades were living abroad in that year and over 50% of those aged 25 and over had been abroad only for three years or less. Moreover, more than 70% of the American citizens abroad were employees of the Government or dependants of Federal employees. From these figures there can be little doubt that the emigration of highly trained American manpower is an insignificant proportion of the immigration of highly trained foreigners. In fact the *inflow* of foreign immigrants in the professional, technical and kindred grades in the year 1967 alone was 41,652, which was not far short of the total *stock* of Americans in these grades abroad in 1960.

---

[1] The classic source on the United States is the work of George H. Borts and Jerome L. Stein, *Economic Growth in a Free Market*, Columbia University Press, 1964. Their detailed theoretical and empirical analysis has established beyond doubt the crucial part played by shifts in labour-supply functions (via intra-State and inter-State migration) in explaining the convergence of State growth rates in the United States, 1880–1950. See also their article, 'Regional Growth and Maturity in the United States: a Study of Regional Structural Change', *Schweizerische Zeitschrift für Volkswirtschaft und Statistik*, vol. xcviii, no. 3, 1962, pp. 290–321. For further evidence on the Atlantic economy see Brinley Thomas, 'International Factor Movements and Unequal Rates of Growth', *Manchester School*, vol. xxix, no. 1, January 1961, pp. 7–9.

The lack of accurate information on return movements is a serious handicap and not easy to rectify. In the United Kingdom the International Passenger Sample Survey introduced in 1964 cannot yield accurate figures of the inward and outward migration of professionals, since the number of migrants among the sampled passengers is so small as to entail a wide margin of error. Fortunately, the estimates for qualified scientists and engineers have been greatly improved, and we shall be using the new series on the British net balance later in this chapter.

A comprehensive international flow chart should distinguish between the private and public circuits. On the one hand, we have the market-oriented international flow of professional manpower, most of it from poor to rich countries, and, on the other, there is a reverse, publicly financed flow of technical and scientific personnel, national and international, from rich to poor countries. If adequate statistics were available, we could estimate for the private and public circuits the annual inward and outward flows for each country. Given accurate benchmark figures of stocks derived from census enumerations at, say, five-year intervals, we could relate net external flows of each category of professional manpower to the corresponding stocks and annual outputs in each country. We may eventually be able to carry out such an exercise for some countries.

2. THE PATTERN OF INTERNATIONAL FLOWS

A summary view of the pattern of international flows may be obtained by dividing countries into four groups:

(i) Advanced countries with a large net inflow.
(ii) Intermediate advanced countries with a large two-way traffic.
(iii) Advanced countries with a large net outflow.
(iv) Developing countries with a large net outflow.

In the first group, advanced countries with a large net inflow, we have the United States and Australia. The United States is by far the largest and the preferred ultimate destination of professional migrants. In the second group are Canada and the United Kingdom. Many migrants of varying degrees of skill move by stages out of low-income countries via intermediate to more advanced ones, forming currents of migration determined by the magnetic influence of the richest destinations. The third group, advanced countries with a large net outflow, consists mainly of European countries such as Norway, the Netherlands and Switzerland. Finally, there is a heterogeneous fourth group of underdeveloped countries with a relatively large net outflow, such as Greece, Iran and Turkey.

The immigration of workers (excluding dependants and persons with no occupation) into the United States, Canada and Australia in the period, 1947–67, was as follows: 2,490,000 into the United States, of whom 18% were professional; 1,534,000 into Canada, of whom 13% were professional; and 1,099,000 into Australia, of whom 8% were professional.[1]

Table 60. *The United States: immigrants with occupation by skill group, 1907–23 and 1967. (Percentages)*

Skill group	1907–23	1967
	(1)	(2)
Professional and entrepreneurial	3	35
Craftsmen, operatives & clerical	22*	35
Private household and other service workers	24†	19
Labourers	51	11
Total	100	100

* Skilled workers.
† Service and other occupations.
Sources
(1) H. Jerome, *Migration and Business Cycles*, p. 48.
(2) U.S. Department of Justice, *Annual Report of the Immigration and Naturalization Service*, 1967.

In 1967 well over a quarter of the inflow into the United States and Canada was in the professional and technical grades, whereas Australia, where the proportion is about one-tenth, has been relatively more interested in skilled craftsmen.

An analysis by skill group of persons with occupation immigrating into the United States in 1967 is compared with one for 1907–23 in Table 60. The professional and entrepreneurial element in the flow to the United States is now 35% as against 3% in the earlier period, while the proportion of labourers has gone down from 51 to 11%.

3. CANADA: AN INTERMEDIATE COUNTRY

Between 1950 and 1963 Canada received an annual average of 7,790 professional immigrants of whom 1,230 came from the United States;

[1] U.S. Department of Justice, *Annual Reports of the Immigration and Naturalization Service*; Government of Canada, *Annual Reports of the Department of Citizenship and Immigration*; Department of Immigration, *Australian Immigration: Consolidated Statistics*, no. 1, 1966. For Australia the period is 1949–66.

but 4,681 left for the United States and 795 for the United Kingdom. In order to keep 2,314 professional immigrants, Canada had to import 7,790 per annum. The situation in regard to skilled craftsmen is more favourable to Canada, the inflow being 18,384 a year and the outflow 6,210, leaving an annual net gain of 12,074.[1]

The statistics reveal that many scientists and engineers migrated from their country of birth to at least one other foreign country before eventually arriving as immigrants to the United States. For example, in 1962 and 1963 the United States received 2,316 scientists and engineers from Canada as their country of last permanent residence, whereas the number who were Canadian-born was only 1,159. Thus, 50% of the scientists and engineers who crossed the border into the United States as immigrants were non-Canadians who had resided temporarily in Canada.

In the decade 1953–63 the number of architects entering Canada was equal to 141% of the number graduating in Canadian universities; the corresponding percentage for engineers was 73 and for physicians and surgeons 53. The Census of 1961 showed that 25% of the persons qualified as engineers and physical scientists in Canada were post-war immigrants. For other professions the percentages are as follows: architects, 35; computer programmers, 21; physicians and surgeons, 19; professors and college principals, 16; actuaries and statisticians, 15; and biological and agricultural professionals, 14.

The relative gross absorption of human capital by Canada has been phenomenally high. Her intake of professional migrants nearly quadrupled between 1962 and 1967 (from 8,218 to 30,853). With a population one-tenth of that of the United States, Canada's gross absorption in 1967 as a proportion of the gross inflow into the United States was as follows: total professional migrants, 74%; engineers, 42%; natural scientists, 60%; physicians and surgeons, 36%; professional nurses, 88%.

Canada's imports of highly qualified personnel from developing

---

[1] Louis Parai, *Immigration and Emigration of Professional and Skilled Manpower during the Post-War Period*, Ottawa, Queen's Printer, 1965, p. 2. As far as Canadian-born professionals are concerned, the migration balance between Canada and the United States became favourable in 1967 and 1968. In 1961–5 the United States gained about 2,000 a year: in 1967 and 1968 Canada had surpluses of 500 and 1,000 respectively (see T. J. Samuel, Department of Manpower and Immigration, *The Migration of Canadian-born between Canada and United States of America 1955 to 1968*, Ottawa, 1969, p. 42). The main reason for this change must be the arrangements operating under the United States immigration law of 1965, which, from July 1, 1968, limits immigration from all Western Hemisphere countries to 120,000 a year. Mr Samuel's monograph makes no attempt to determine if Canada's newly gained surplus is just a temporary phenomenon.

countries have been rising rapidly, with no less than 37% of her intake of professionals in 1967 coming from countries outside Europe and the United States. In proportion to her population, Canada is easily the largest importer of human capital in the world. Her situation next door to the massive American market explains the big difference between the relative magnitudes of professional immigration to Canada and to Australia (26 as against 10%). Since the United States is the favourite destination of professional immigrants and the whole of North America is one large market, Canada, as a separate sovereign State, has had to work trebly hard in the immigration business in order to keep her end up. It is not a coincidence that the proportion of professional migrants in the total inflow is almost exactly the same in the United States and Canada, 27 and 26% respectively in 1967. Australia, at the other end of the world, loses relatively few immigrants and has no need to over-import in order to ensure an adequate input of human capital, since she is far away from the special influences operating in the United States.

If we examine the flows of skilled craftsmen as distinct from professional personnel, we find there is less difference between Canada and Australia. Between 1950 and 1963 Canada absorbed on the average 18,284 a year, 1,068 of whom came from the United States, while the outward movement was 6,210, with 5,135 going to the United States. Thus, of the gross import of 18,284, Canada kept 12,074 on average each year. Australia between 1949 and 1960 absorbed 185,544 skilled craftsmen, or about 16,860 a year, most of whom stayed as permanent immigrants.[1]

4. IMMIGRANTS TO AMERICA FROM DEVELOPING COUNTRIES

The number of immigrants to the United States in the professional, technical and kindred grades rose from 18,995 in 1956 to 41,652 in 1967, or by 119%; and among them the rate of increase was 215% for engineers (2,804 to 8,822), 189% for scientists (1,002 to 2,893), and 115% for doctors (1,547 to 3,326). The proportion originating in developing countries, which was 25% in 1956, reached no less than 57% in 1967; and in this period immigrant scientists from these countries rose tenfold, engineers sixfold and doctors threefold. The contribution of Asian countries (excluding Japan) to this movement of professional migrants jumped from about 2,000 in 1965 to 13,000 in 1967.

This sudden change in 1966–7 was the result of the Act of October 3,

---

[1] *Australian Immigration: Consolidated Statistics, no. 1, pp. 54–5.*

1965,[1] which abolished the quotas based on national origins and substituted a new system whose philosophy is, within limits, justification by skill instead of by skin. The Act provided for a transition period of three years, July 1, 1965 to July 1, 1968, during which the national-origins system was to be phased out by enabling qualified applicants in the 'third preference' category from countries with over-subscribed quotas to be given quota numbers unused by countries with large quotas, until the limit of 17,000 a year was reached. This led to the sharp increase in the number immigrating from developing countries in 1967 and 1968.[2] Because of the limitations, there was a backlog of many thousands of applicants from developing countries who could not be admitted during the transition period and whose entry was delayed until after July 1, 1968.

As from July 1, 1968, former quota countries were given an overall limit of 170,000 immigrants a year with a maximum of 20,000 for any one country. Members of the professions and people with outstanding ability in the sciences and arts comprise the 'third preference' group which must not exceed 10% of the total of 170,000 in any year. Another 10% is allocated to the 'sixth preference' group covering skilled and unskilled workers, including scientists and engineers, whose immigration has the effect of relieving shortages of labour in the United States. Moreover, as in the past, professional, technical and kindred workers eligible on the basis of, for example, family relationship may enter either within or outside the numerical limitations. The Western Hemisphere, where previously no restrictions applied, is now subject to a limit of 120,000 a year.

The non-return of students plays a significant part in causing the inflow of professional immigrants to be as large as it is. In 1968 as many as 70% of the 4,100 scientists and engineers recorded as immigrants to the United States were students who had entered the country with the declared intention of obtaining education or training and then returning home. They could do this by turning in their 'F' student visa for an immigration visa when they had obtained their degree, provided an immigration quota number was available. The ratio of student to total professional immigration in 1967 was 89% for Taiwan, 80% for Korea, 78% for India, and 71% for Iran. Nearly all the students from developing countries who did not go home were either scientists or engineers.

[1] Immigration and Nationality Act of 1952 (P.L. 414, 82nd Congress, 66 Stat. 163) as amended by the Act of October 3, 1965 (P.L. 89–236, 89th Congress, 79 Stat.). For a detailed account of these revisions of the basic immigration law and their effect on immigration see State Department, *Annual Report of the Visa Office*, 1967.

[2] Many of them were already in the United States as non-immigrants and changed to immigrant status.

A valuable source of information on the stock of professional man-power in the United States is the National Register of Scientific and Technical Personnel, giving particulars of birth, high school, highest degree and citizenship. The data for foreign-born scientists in 1966 have been analysed by Herbert G. Grubel.[1] The foreign-born represent 9·5% of all scientists in the United States and 14·0% of scientists with a Ph.D., the largest contributors being Canada (3,097), China (2,195), United Kingdom (2,041), India (1,382) and Austria (1,099). If we take scientists fully educated in their native country the ranking becomes United Kingdom (1,049), Germany (995), Canada (872), India (378), Austria (296), Japan (282) and Switzerland (264).

In order to gauge the incidence on the countries of origin, Grubel uses the number of scientists in higher education in these countries as a proxy for their stock of scientists, and he finds that the top five are Cyprus, Austria, Canada, Rhodesia and Switzerland. Another set of calculations puts the 1966 stock of foreign-born scientists in relation to general immigration to the United States in the period 1958–67. Viewed in this light India is outstanding, in that the 1966 stock of American scientists fully educated in India equals 32% of Indian im-migrants to the United States in that period. The next in order are Austria (17·3%), New Zealand (15·4%) and Switzerland (14·7%); the figure for the United Kingdom is 4·3%. The Indian figure brings out clearly the influence of the immigration quotas based on national origins which severely restricted immigration from Asian countries and which could be circumvented most easily by highly educated persons. These are samples of the instructive data, hitherto unavailable, which the records of the National Science Foundation make possible.

Details of the country of last permanent residence of the 12,973 engineers and scientists and the 3,060 physicians and surgeons im-migrating into the United States in 1968 are shown in Table 151. Western Europe contributed 4,772 engineers and scientists (nearly half of them from the United Kingdom), Canada 1,940, Asia 4,021 (of whom 1,232 were from India, 752 from the Philippines and 626 from Taiwan), and South America 595. Of the 3,060 physicians and surgeons nearly 40% were from Asia (as many as 639 from the Philippines), 572 from Western Europe, 325 from Canada and 341 from South America.[2]

---

[1] Herbert G. Grubel, 'Characteristics of Foreign Born and Educated Scientists in the United States, 1966' (mimeographed paper prepared under National Science Foundation Grant 1678).

[2] For a guide to the vast literature on the brain drain see S. Dedijer and I. Sven-ningson, *Brain Drain and Brain Gain: A Bibliography on the Migration of Scientists, Engineers, Doctors and Students*, Lund, Research Policy Program, 1967. The most comprehensive assessment of the world situation is the report on an international research project initiated by Education and World Affairs—Committee on Inter-

5. IMMIGRATION IN RELATION TO UNITED STATES
OUTPUT OF EDUCATED MANPOWER

It is of interest to assess the significance of America's imports in relation to her own output of human capital. The information set out in Table 152 leads to the following conclusions for the period 1956–67:

(a) The United States output of scientists more than doubled, while imports nearly trebled until in 1967 they were 2·6% of American output. (In 1967 50% of the immigrants were from developing countries.)

(b) The United States output of engineers rose by 72%, while imports increased more than threefold until in 1967 they were 16% of American output. (In 1967 48% of the immigrants were from developing countries.)

(c) The United States output of physicians remained virtually unchanged, while imports more than doubled until in 1967 they were nearly one-third of American output. (In 1967 two-thirds of the immigrants were from developing countries.)

An official American report summed up the position as follows:

In 1967 U.S. domestic output of 173,210 graduates was an increase of 14,334 over the number graduated in 1966 of 158,876. Thus, the 7,913 scientific immigrants from the developing countries represent a supply equal to more than half of an entire year's growth in the production of U.S. scientific manpower.... These facts do not support a common impression that scientific immigration into the United States is largely a phenomenon affecting a few advanced countries nor the view that the brain drain from the developing countries is insignificant in size.[1]

Finally, it must be noted that the above figures are an underestimate of the true gross inflows of human capital from poor countries, since they omit professional immigrants from developing countries who enter the United States via intermediate developed countries such as Canada, the United Kingdom and Japan. It is estimated that in 1962–4 only 1,844 out of 3,460 scientists immigrating into the United States from Canada were Canadian-born, and there is evidence that a number of students from South East Asia stay in Japan until they can qualify for permanent residence in the United States.

national Migration of Talent, *The International Migration of High-Level Manpower: Its Impact on the Development Process*, New York, Praeger, 1970.

[1] *Scientific Brain Drain from Developing Countries*, 23rd Report, Government Operations Committee, House of Representatives, 90th Congress, 1968, p. 14.

6. BRITAIN'S NET BALANCE

The picture given for the United States, although it rests on figures of gross immigration, is a reasonably good approximation since the outward movement is known to be relatively small. For Britain it is important to be able to measure the two-way traffic.

(a) Engineers, Technologists and Scientists

In the light of new statistics based on the Censuses of 1961 and 1966, it is possible to present firm estimates of the annual outward and inward

Table 61. *The United Kingdom: net changes in numbers of qualified engineers and scientists, 1961–6*

Component of change in numbers	Those qualified in	
	Engineering and technology	Science
Net migration		
Born Great Britain	−5,555	+455
Born Commonwealth or Ireland	+220	+830
Others	+2,460	+2,030
Total	−2,875	+3,315
Natural increase*	+42,315	+39,635
Overall change	+39,440	+42,950

  * New graduates minus deaths.

  SOURCE: Department of Trade and Industry, *Persons with Qualifications in Engineering, Technology and Science 1959 to 1968*, p. 33.

movements of qualified scientists and engineers.[1] What happened between 1961 and 1966 is summarized in Table 61.

In the five years under review the 'natural increase' of engineers was 42,315; a net emigration of 5,555 born in Great Britain was half offset by a net immigration of 2,680 Commonwealth, Irish and foreign-born, giving an overall net loss of 2,875. In the case of scientists there was a net inflow of 455 born in Great Britain in addition to the 2,860 inward balance of persons born outside Britain, so that the 'natural increase' of 39,635 British scientists was augmented by 3,315.

In interpreting these figures, allowance must be made for the differences between the quality of the outward and inward flows. According to an official report, 'the indications are that the immigrants contain a higher proportion of people from the newly-independent

[1] Department of Trade and Industry, *Persons with Qualifications in Engineering, Technology and Science 1959 to 1968*, London, H.M.S.O., 1971.

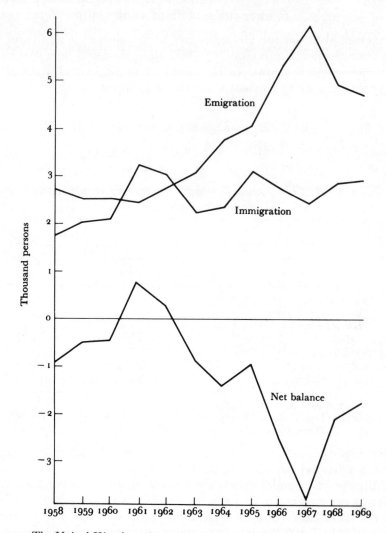

Fig. 59. The United Kingdom: inward and outward migrants with qualifications in engineering and technology, 1958–69. Source: Table 153.

Commonwealth countries than the emigrants, and that they will generally lack the training and experience which is taken out of the country by the emigrants.'[1]

The year-to-year changes from 1958 to 1969 (see Table 153 and Fig. 59) show a substantial rise in the net outflow of engineers to a peak

[1] Department of Education and Science, *The Brain Drain: Report of the Working Group on Migration*, Cmnd. 3417, 1967, p. 13.

of 3,740 in 1967, then a sharp reduction to 1,755 in 1969. The peak net loss of engineers was no less than a third of the output three years earlier. There was a fluctuating net gain of scientists for most of the period, until 1967, when the net loss was relatively large, and in 1969 there was a net gain once more.

(b) Doctors

In a book published in 1964, B. Abel-Smith and Kathleen Gales estimated that, between 1955 and 1962, doctors born and trained in Britain had been leaving the country at the average rate of 392 a year, about a quarter of the annual output of British medical schools.[1] About 30% of British doctors resident abroad were in low-income countries, and the majority of the rest were in the United States, Australia and Canada.

Subsequent analysis has thrown light on the scale and characteristics of inward as well as outward movements, as shown in Table 154.[2]

The results for 1962–4, taking into account adjustments not made in Table 154, can be summed up as follows. Of British or Irish-born doctors 1,678 emigrated from Britain and 1,075 entered or re-entered the country, the net loss being 603 or 300 a year. Of doctors born outside the United Kingdom or the Irish Republic, 2,377 took up residence in Great Britain and 2,034 emigrated, the net gain being 343 oversea doctors or 170 a year. This latter figure, however, is an under-estimate since it does not include foreign-born doctors who decided to stay in Britain after graduating in British medical schools or those who obtain registrable qualified status after coming to Britain. If allowance is made for this omission, the true net gain of oversea doctors was about 300 a year. After extending the analysis to September 1965, the authors reached the following conclusion.

The current estimate of the movement in the three years ended September 1965 of fully or provisionally registered doctors born overseas indicates that the true total net gain to medical manpower in Great Britain of such doctors seems to counterbalance the net loss of doctors born in the United Kingdom and Irish Republic.[3]

In 1965 Great Britain had a stock of 62,700 'economically active' doctors, or 1,181 per million of the population.[4] Of these over 10,000 working in the National Health Service were born outside the British

---

[1] B. Abel-Smith and K. Gales, *British Doctors at Home and Abroad*, London, Bell, 1964.

[2] R. Ash and H. D. Mitchell, 'Doctor Migration 1962–1964', *British Medical Journal*, March 2, 1968, pp. 569–72.

[3] Ibid. p. 572.

[4] *Report of the Royal Commission on Medical Education*, Cmnd. 3569, 1968, p. 133.

Isles (8,000 in the hospital service and 2,600 in general practice in England and Wales),[1] and two out of every three of these non-British doctors had come from developing countries, mainly India and Pakistan. In 1967 the graduates of non-British medical schools who established practice in Britain (2,053) outnumbered those who had qualified at home (1,933).[2]

One effect of the American immigration law of 1965 has been to deflect oversea doctors from Britain. To obtain a licence to practise in America, doctors must pass the examination of the Educational Council for Foreign Medical Graduates, and the number of candidates each year is a good index of the propensity to emigrate. The number rose from 254 in 1964 to 620 in 1965 and 802 in 1966; in 1968 the American Embassy in London revealed that over half the doctors sitting the examination for entry to America were non-British. This new factor has added to the difficulties facing the British National Health Service.

Both Britain and the United States are drawing medical personnel from the developing countries, but there is an important difference. The United States has very little leakage outward; her stocks gain by almost the amount of her imports. The supply of graduates from American medical schools hardly increased at all in the nineteen-sixties. Britain, on the other hand, is very much part of the international circular flow; it is the high rate of emigration to the United States, Canada, Australia and similar countries which makes it necessary to import so many doctors from developing countries.

7. DYNAMIC SHORTAGE AND BRAIN DRAIN

The trends brought out by our statistical survey and the contrast with the nineteenth-century pattern can be summed up in a generalization. The combination of mass unskilled migration, population-sensitive capital formation and portfolio foreign investment has been replaced by professional elite migration, science-based capital formation and direct foreign investment. The question raised by 'brain drain' is whether, in this new setting, there is a tendency for the growth potential of countries of emigration (particularly the less developed) to be reduced in favour of that of countries receiving a large net immigration.[3]

[1] O. Gish, 'The Royal Commission and the Immigrant Doctor', *The Lancet*, June 29, 1968, p. 1423.

[2] Committee on International Migration of Talent, op. cit. p. 602.

[3] Some economists, using the techniques of welfare economics, have tried to show that there is no significant possibility of 'world loss' from the international migration of educated people (e.g. Herbert B. Grubel and Anthony D. Scott, 'The International Flow of Human Capital', *American Economic Review*, vol. LVI, no. 2, May 1966, pp. 268–74). Such reasoning implies a 'world social welfare function', and it is hard to

The diagnosis to be put forward here receives support from developments in growth theory. Of particular interest are models based on the notion of a gap between the discovery of new techniques and the application of them in industry, for example, the one by R. R. Nelson and E. S. Phelps which states that the rate at which the most advanced technology is applied in industrial practice depends on the degree of human capital intensity and the level of technology in practice. The rate of increase of technology in practice is an increasing function of human capital intensity and proportional to the gap. These authors have indicated the bearing of these ideas on human capital and growth.

According to these models, the rate of return to education is greater the more technologically progressive is the economy. This suggests that the progressiveness of the technology has implications for the optimal capital structure in the broad sense. In particular, it may be that society should build more human capital relatively to tangible capital the more dynamic

see what possible meaning could be attached to such a notion. It must be recognized that, since there are strong barriers to the international movement of unskilled labour, we are confronted with a 'second-best' situation. The issue turns on the presence of externalities. Given the maximization of world output as the value criterion, there can be no dispute as to the existence of several theoretical possibilities of world loss through the loss of externalities to sending countries, which are not offset by gains of externalities to receiving countries, and which also more than counterbalance the increase in private income received by the migrants. See Brinley Thomas, 'The International Circulation of Human Capital', *Minerva*, vol. v, no. 4, Summer 1967, pp. 479–506; Harry G. Johnson, 'Some Economic Aspects of Brain Drain', *Pakistan Development Review*, vol. vii, no. 3, Autumn 1967, pp. 388–9; Brinley Thomas, 'The International Circulation of Human Capital: a Reply to Harry G. Johnson', *Minerva*, vol. vi, no. 3, Spring 1968, pp. 423–7.

The main contributions to this controversy have been reprinted in M. Blaug (ed.), *Economics of Education*, vol. ii, Harmondsworth, Penguin Books, 1969, pp. 241–301. The formidable difficulties of operating a 'world social welfare function' have been pointed out by Don Patinkin in his paper, 'A "Nationalist" Model', in W. Adams (ed.), *The Brain Drain*, New York, Macmillan, 1968, pp. 99–108. The point which he makes in the following passage (pp. 105–6) is highly relevant. 'Countries which are concerned with their losses from the "brain drain" have been criticized by some economists as acting in accordance with "anachronistic" concepts of "economic and military power" and national prestige (Grubel and Scott, loc. cit., p. 274.) An implicit assumption of this criticism is that such "nationalistic" actions are interfering with the free flow of manpower resources in an international market which would otherwise reflect the welfare-maximizing behavior of individuals. But this is simply not the case for the "brain drain" as it exists today. For this market already reflects to a highly significant degree a demand for manpower generated by the nationalistic considerations of the U.S. government defense and space programs. Correspondingly, the nationalistic influences which the "brain-losing" countries attempt to exert on the *supply* side of the international manpower market can to a large extent be seen as an offset of the nationalist forces on the *demand* side.' This comment is fully borne out by the evidence on the causes of dynamic shortage presented in this chapter.

is the economy.... If innovations produce externalities, because they show the way to imitators, then education—by its stimulation of innovation—also yields externalities. Hence, the way of viewing the role of education in economic growth set forth here seems to indicate another possible source of divergence between the private and the social rate of return to education.[1]

The importance of science-based capital formation has added greatly to the role of Research and Development. That this is highly relevant to an analysis of the international circulation of professional manpower is borne out by the fact that, in the United States, more than half the foreign-born scientists are in Research and Development compared with 35% of all American scientists and 41% of foreign-born engineers compared with 27% of all American engineers. Promising work has been done on the Research and Development factor as an explanatory variable in international trade and international investment and in inter-State productivity differentials in industry and agriculture.[2] The results suggest interesting hypotheses concerning human capital flows and differentials between growth rates of countries at different levels of development.

The highest grades of professional manpower are expensive to produce and they take a long time to train; they play a far more crucial role in the process of growth than they did in the nineteenth century, as the pace is now set by science-based industries. Human capital is highly mobile internationally and is attracted to areas where real private productivity is highest. Because of the increasing demand for educated manpower in the technologically progressive economies and the externalities yielded by education-intensive investment through the stimulation of innovations, there is keen competition between advanced countries for supplies of top skills.

An important reason for the upward shifts in the demand for scientists and engineers in the United States after 1950 was the prominent part played by the Federal Government in financing Research and Develop-

[1] R. R. Nelson and E. S. Phelps, 'Investment in Humans, Technological Diffusion and Economic Growth', *American Economic Review*, vol. LVI, no. 2, May 1966, pp. 72-5.

[2] For example, W. Gruber, D. Mehta and R. Vernon, 'The R. and D. Factor in International Trade and International Investment of United States Industries', and Donald B. Keesing, 'The Impact of Research and Development on United States Trade', both in *Journal of Political Economy*, vol. LXXV, no. 1, February 1967, pp. 20-48; Z. Griliches, 'Production Functions in Manufacturing: Some Preliminary Results' in M. Brown (ed.), *The Theory and Empirical Analysis of Production*, Columbia University Press, 1967, and 'Research Expenditures, Education and the Aggregate Agricultural Production Function', *American Economic Review*, vol. LIV, no. 6, December 1964, pp. 961-74; Stanley M. Besen, 'Education and Productivity in U.S. Manufacturing: Some Cross-Section Evidence', *Journal of Political Economy*, vol. LXXVI, no. 3, May-June 1968, pp. 494-7.

ment. Expenditure on Research and Development in industry rose from $7,731 million in 1957 to $14,197 million in 1965, and 55% of it came from Federal funds. In 1965 the number of Federally financed R. and D. scientists and engineers totalled 162,900, or nearly half of all such personnel (346,000) in industry. The Department of Defense supported 59% and the National Aeronautics and Space Administration 30% of all R. and D. scientists and engineers engaged in Federal projects. Total expenditure on Research and Development (public and private sectors) rose from $5,210 million in 1953 to $25,000 million in 1968, and $15,500 million of the latter, or over 60%, came from the Federal Government.

The number of R. and D. scientists and engineers in industry rose from 243,800 in January 1958 to 358,900 in January 1966, i.e. by 47%; in the same period industrial R. and D. funds increased by 84%. The expansion of employment of R. and D. scientists and engineers in two industries in this period was outstanding: 43,300 or 90% in electrical equipment and communications and 42,100 or 72% in aircraft and missiles; and it is in these industries that Federal financing is paramount —63 and 88% respectively. It is a striking fact that no less than 74% of the all-industry growth in the employment of R. and D. scientists and engineers between 1957 and 1965 occurred in these two industries, largely governed by the defence and space programmes of the Federal Government. In January 1966 the aircraft and missiles industry alone employed 28% of all R. and D. scientists and engineers.

Fig. 60 and Table 155 show a close relationship between the annual percentage rates of change in Federal expenditure on Research and Development and in immigration of professional manpower over the period 1954–68. There can be little doubt that Federal expenditure was a major determinant and the statistics show that immigrant scientists and engineers were on the average of superior quality and more heavily engaged in Research and Development than their American counterparts.

Let us draw a distinction between skills which are 'general' and those which are 'specific'.[1] General training equips the trainee with a skill which is as useful elsewhere as in the firm providing the training. Consequently the marginal productivity of the trainee is raised equally both outside and inside the firm, and under competitive conditions the costs of training will be borne by the trainee. In the case of purely specific training the marginal productivity is raised only within the firm and not outside, so that the training costs are borne by the firm. The United Kingdom has a large capacity for producing educated

[1] G. S. Becker, *Human Capital: A Theoretical and Empirical Analysis with Special Reference to Education*, New York, National Bureau of Economic Research, 1964.

manpower whose skills are general rather than specific. Scientists and technologists are a good example of human capital which is universally usable, and this is particularly true of British personnel going to other English-speaking countries.

The production of educated manpower in the United Kingdom is heavily subsidized out of public funds. It would not be doing undue violence to the facts to conceive of the United Kingdom as a gigantic

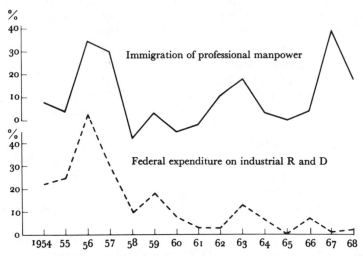

Fig. 60. The United States: immigration of professional manpower and Federal expenditure on industrial Research and Development, 1954–68 (annual rates of change). Source: Table 155.

public firm with a large annual output of general skills, the cost of whose production is borne mainly by the firm itself. In a situation where public investment in general skills is financed in a manner appropriate to specific skills, i.e. the firm paying the costs, not the trainee, it is easy to attract a plentiful supply of trainees but not so easy to keep them when they are qualified.

Following Arrow and Capron[1] we can say that, if there is a steady upward shift in the demand for scientists and engineers over a period of time, and if there continue to be unfilled vacancies in positions where salaries are the same as those being currently paid in others of the same type and quality, there is a dynamic shortage. With every shift in the demand curve the market price tends to rise towards the equilibrium price, but the equilibrium price moves and the market price does not

[1] Kenneth J. Arrow and William M. Capron, 'Dynamic Shortages and Price Rises: the Engineer-Scientist Case', *Quarterly Journal of Economics*, vol. LXXIII, no. 2, May 1959, pp. 292–308.

catch up with it. The magnitude of this dynamic shortage depends on the rate of increase of demand, the reaction speed in the market (i.e. the ratio of the rate of price rise to the excess demand), and the elasticity of supply and demand.

The reaction speed in the market for engineers and scientists in America has been low, because of long-term contracts, the diversity and special requirements within each profession causing an imperfect spread of information, and the dominance of oligopolistic firms in Research and Development. The elasticity of supply of scientists and engineers in the short run is necessarily low because of the time it takes to train new ones, but even over the long period the evidence suggests that the engineering profession in the United States has been becoming relatively less attractive. Engineering students as a proportion of all freshmen declined from 22% in 1957 to 13·5% in 1965. A more significant symptom is the change in the preferences of the most gifted students reported on by the National Merit Scholarship Corporation. The proportion of the Merit Scholars opting for engineering fell from 33·6% in 1957 to 20·2% in 1965, whereas the proportions going in for teaching and law rose from 8 to 15·5% and 6·5 to 11% respectively. Furthermore, whereas 23% of Merit Scholars going to college in 1956 planned to enter engineering, a follow-up study revealed that only 4% of these same students had the same goal in 1964.[1]

To sum up, there were two powerful forces pushing the American demand curve for human capital to the right during the nineteen-fifties and most of the sixties: first, autonomous public investment—the large-scale expansion in the education-intensive space and defence programmes of the Federal Government—and, secondly, the endogenous factor in the economy—the tendency of private investment to require increasing doses of human capital to sustain its rate of growth. The dynamic shortage thus generated coexisted with heavily subsidized production of general skills together with administered salary levels in a large sector of the economy in the United Kingdom and other countries, and this played a crucial part in causing brain drain.

When I put forward this interpretation in a lecture in March 1967 I added the qualification that

we must be careful about prophesying a permanent dynamic shortage in the market for professional manpower in the United States. One recalls how preoccupied people were with the 'dollar shortage' in the 1950s and how that shortage soon gave way to a dollar glut. . . . It is conceivable that changes in the elements governing dynamic shortage in the United States could bring a relaxation in the world market for skills at the very time when the current flow of output of professional manpower in Europe is sharply rising as a

[1] See Engineers Joint Council, *Engineering Manpower Bulletin*, no. 6, April 1967.

result of an increase in investment undertaken a few years earlier in circumstances of extreme scarcity.[1]

As it turned out, this prognosis proved to be justified. By the end of the sixties the motive force governing dynamic shortage had weakened, but the reality was temporarily blurred by the effects of the change in the American immigration law. Although the data do not allow us to measure with any precision some of the operative elements—for example the ratio of the rate of increase in the salaries of engineers and scientists to the excess demand (the reaction speed) and the elasticities of supply and demand—we do know fairly accurately what was happening to our main explanatory variable, Federal expenditure on Research and Development.

We have already noted the clear correlation between annual rates of change in Federal expenditure on industrial Research and Development and in immigration of professional, technical and kindred grades, 1954–68 (Fig. 60). The only exception was the year 1967, and this will need to be looked at in the light of the change in the immigration law.

To get a closer picture we shall examine the market for engineers, the available information for which is given in Fig. 61. First, we can see how steep was the rise in Federal expenditure on Research and Development as a proportion of gross national product—from 0·7% in 1956 to a peak of 2·25% in 1964 and an average of 2·12% in the years 1963–7. In the late fifties the number of students taking first degrees in engineering rose sharply from 22,000 to 38,000, but this was followed by a decade of stagnation, the number graduating in 1968 being no higher than it had been in 1959. Meanwhile, the number of M.S. and Ph.D. degrees awarded in engineering soared from just over 5,000 in 1956 to nearly 18,000 in 1967. The recruitment of immigrants, with year-to-year variations in line with Federal expenditures, had a strong upward trend, and one can infer from the course of the earnings of engineers that the reaction speed was low.

The interesting question is whether the sharp fall in immigration in 1969 indicates a temporary relaxation or a more lasting phase in which dynamic shortage will have lost much of its force. One cannot be certain. The market for professional manpower in the inflationary boom of the late sixties was complicated by the effects of selective service and changes in the immigration law. In the transition, when the national origins system was being phased out, qualified applicants from countries with small quotas were given quota numbers unused by countries with large quotas, and the dramatic consequence of this is quantified in Fig. 62. In the three years 1966–8, no less than 25% of

[1] 'The International Circulation of Human Capital', a lecture delivered at the London School of Economics on March 2, 1967.

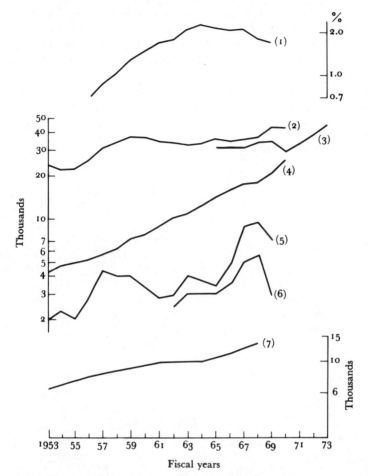

Fig. 61. The United States: internal supply, immigration and earnings of engineers, 1953–70. (1) Federal expenditure on R. and D. as a percentage of G.N.P., (2) first degrees in engineering, (3) total new U.S. engineers available, (4) Masters' and Ph.D. degrees in engineering, (5) immigrant engineers, (6) immigrant engineers and scientists born in Europe, (7) overall adjusted median earnings of engineers. Sources: National Science Foundation, *Science Resources Studies Highlights*, August 14, 1970, p. 2, and *Reviews of Data on Science Resources*, no. 13, March 1968, no. 18, November 1969; Engineers Joint Council, *Prospects of Engineering and Technology Graduates 1968*, p. 29, *Professional Income of Engineers 1968–69*, p. 20, and *Engineering Manpower Bulletin*, no. 17, September 1970, p. 3.

the 32,701 engineers and scientists who 'immigrated' were former students resident in the United States who obtained immigrant visas and 90% of these former students were Asian-born. Admission on a first-come, first-served basis according to skill categories began to operate in the fiscal year 1969, and there was a backlog from the transition period. In that year Asian-born immigrants were the largest group of engineers and scientists admitted—5,300 as compared with 4,400 in 1968. The introduction of a quota for the Western Hemisphere was an additional factor. Persons born in Asia were able to compete more effectively for available immigrant visas.

We can now return to the main question. The major determinant—Federal expenditure on Research and Development as a proportion of

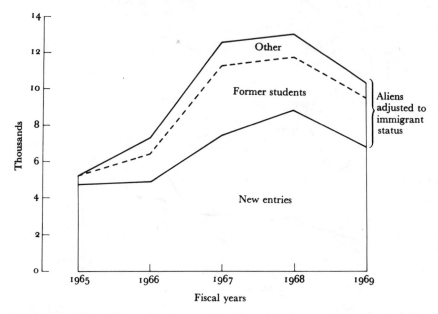

FIG. 62. The United States, immigrant scientists and engineers: new entries and alien residents changing status, 1965-9. Source: Table 156.

gross national product—fell from 2·1% in 1967 to 1·7% in 1969, and total R. and D. outlay (private as well as public), which had levelled off at 3% of gross national product in the mid-sixties, was also sagging. It was estimated that defence spending planned for the year ended June 30, 1971 would be $17,000 million less (in constant dollars) than at the peak of the Vietnam war, and the number of people employed in industries connected with defence declined by 400,000 in 1969-70. There was also a cut-back in the space programme. A new and sombre phenomenon darkened the scene; there was widespread professional unemployment in the industries and areas which had profited so handsomely from the spectacular rise of the Federally supported 'military-industrial complex'.

The number of European-born engineers and scientists immigrating in 1969 was 50% less than in the previous year (Fig. 61). The Engineering Manpower Council's projection for the early seventies of the total new United States engineers who will be available (after allowing for various leakages) gives a decline from 35,600 in 1969 to 29,800 in 1970 followed by a steady rise to 45,500 in 1973. If this proved correct, and the Federal expenditure variable did not change its course (Fig. 61), the relaxation in the market for engineers and scientists would continue; but in the aftermath of the new immigration law this can be quite consistent with a not insignificant absorption of educated people from developing countries.

8. CONCLUSION

Our main purpose has been to identify the determinants of brain drain by concentrating on demand conditions in the United States, the largest market for human capital, and supply conditions in the leading countries of emigration. The quantitative evidence suggests that the model of dynamic shortage helps to explain the course of events in the period 1950–70. The main cause of the excess demand in the international market for skills was an autonomous factor—the huge public investment programme of the United States Government. It is not possible to measure the extent, if any, to which the absorption of human capital by the main net importers restricted the growth of the countries supplying the migrants. The annual real growth rate per capita in developing countries as a whole was 2·5% in 1960–7 compared with 2·3 in 1950–60; the corresponding rates for industrialized countries were 3·6% and 2·8% respectively. This indicates a substantial divergence, due largely to the differential rate of growth of population. Any estimate of the role of brain drain as a factor contributing to this divergence would have to be made by examining each developing country separately, as conditions vary so much.

At the beginning of this chapter attention was drawn to the two international circuits—the movement of professional manpower from poor to rich countries and the reverse flow of publicly financed technical personnel into the poor countries; and we have seen how large a part is played in the brain drain by the non-return of students. The Pearson Commission on International Development concluded that

indiscriminate scholarship awards for study in advanced countries, as well as some training programs, have contributed to acceleration of the 'brain drain' out of poor countries. This problem is of disturbing dimensions. The present flow of skilled and qualified personnel from poor to rich countries actually outnumbers the number of advisory personnel going from rich to poor.

In 1967, the developing countries obtained the temporary services of 16,000 foreign advisers (out of a total of over 100,000 technical assistance personnel), but the U.N. estimates that close to 40,000 of their own national professionals emigrated to the industrialized countries.[1]

Whether this emigration is to be regarded as brain drain in the technical sense, i.e. a brake on growth, depends on conditions in the country concerned. There is abundant evidence that a number of underdeveloped countries have been producing far more graduates than could possibly be gainfully employed at home;[2] stocks of university graduates have been going up at the rate of about 10% a year, whereas gross national product has been rising at about 5% a year.[3] The situation in India has been described as follows.

Expansion acquires a momentum which cannot easily be resisted when altered circumstances require a change of policy. The ultimate limitation of resources dictates a decline in standards, which accelerates the scramble for higher education by further postponing the saturation of labour markets, only to recreate a still more intractable problem later on. The process has probably gone further in India than anywhere else, but India is the mirror in which the developing countries of Africa and Asia can see the problem they will be facing in the decade of the 1970s.[4]

Clearly, the overflow of talent from these countries will continue as long as they maintain an educational system which 'only too easily becomes an instigator of maladjustment and structural unemployment rather than an essential source of growth and development'.[5] Unfortunately, this overflow contains men of exceptional ability, such as leaders of teams, and their departure is a real economic loss, particularly where the infant industry argument applies.

In the case of some of the middle group of countries, including the United Kingdom, as well as some developing countries in the Middle East and East and Central Africa, the incidence of brain drain can be more clearly established, since the growth of the economies presupposed adequate inputs of particular skills and there is less unemployed human capital. Here, for reasons previously referred to, the leakage of talent means an economic loss. When the United States, in pursuit of her national goals, absorbs human capital which other countries have paid for by taxation to promote the achievement of their own goals, there is

---

[1] Commission on International Development, *Partners in Development*, London, Pall Mall Press, 1969, pp. 201–2.
[2] See Committee on International Migration of Talent, op. cit.
[3] Ibid. p. 685.
[4] M. Blaug, P. R. G. Layard and M. A. Woodhall, *The Causes of Graduate Unemployment in India*, London, Allen Lane The Penguin Press, 1969, p. 250.
[5] Commission on International Development, op. cit. p. 68.

brain drain in the true sense. It behoves the United States, Canada and Australia to spend more of their own resources in expanding their capacity to produce expensive skills, particularly medical graduates, so as to reduce their reliance on other countries' public investment. Our model showed that, in the country of emigration, public subsidizing of the production of general skills together with administered salary levels in the public sector tended to increase the outflow; if appropriate policies were applied to change these supply conditions, the incidence of brain drain would be reduced.

As to the future, any projection is bound to be hazardous. The propensity of American professionals to emigrate may increase and the attractiveness of America for Europeans may diminish, thereby enlarging the scope for qualified immigrants from the poorer countries. The method of financing higher education in the United Kingdom and other countries may be changed, for example, by the substitution of loans for grants, so that the costs of training in general skills are borne in greater measure by the beneficiaries. A continued pronounced shift in the interest of American students away from science and technology could have a profound effect on future supplies of engineers and scientists, whereas a combination of a static output of graduates from American medical schools and a high income elasticity of demand for medical service would mean an increasing levy on the supplies of graduates from other countries' medical schools. The revival of public and private demand for human capital in a buoyant American economy could entail another phase of serious dynamic shortage.

Finally, we must remember that the fifties and sixties were unique in that the emergence of the American science giant involved an immense accelerator effect; the steep rate of growth of R. and D. expenditure as a proportion of gross national product was bound to level off. The demand for human capital cannot go on growing faster than the economy, and there has to be a limit to the number of Ph.D.s who can be absorbed by the science establishment.[1] There must be some natural rate at which the growth of demand for human capital will ultimately tend to settle, and the movement towards this equilibrium will bring problems with international repercussions very different from those of dynamic shortage.

[1] For a formal presentation of this line of thought see Joseph P. Martino's valuable paper, 'Science and Society in Equilibrium', *Science*, vol. CLXV, August 22, 1969, pp. 769–72.

CHAPTER XVIII

NEGRO MIGRATION AND THE AMERICAN
URBAN DILEMMA

After the Civil War the best thing that could have happened to the black workers of the United States would have been a fair opportunity to contribute to satisfying the great demand for labour in the rapidly growing cities of the North and West. They could have participated alongside the millions of European immigrants in each upswing of the long cycle in urbanization; this would have materially raised the real income of the black migrants themselves and conferred benefits indirectly (e.g. through remittances) on those left in the South. The Negroes as an ethnic group could have earned their place like the Irish, the Scandinavians, the Germans, the Jews and the Italians in an expanding economy which permitted a continually changing equilibrium between a succession of very different ethnic groups. That this did not happen is part of the tragic history of racial intolerance.

Gunnar Myrdal, in his classic study published in 1944, pointed out that there was '... enough industrial activity, and there could be opportunity for anonymity, as well as a low level of race prejudice, in many of the smaller centres of the North, to permit a significant immigration of Negroes. That Negroes have not migrated to these places is as much of a mystery as the relative absence of migration to the West.'[1] He concluded that '... much in the Great Migration after 1915 is left unexplained if we do not assume that there was before 1915 *an existing and widening difference in living conditions between South and North which did not express itself in a mass migration simply because the latter did not get a start and become a pattern.*'[2] Since Mydral wrote, the findings of research on internal migration have yielded important clues to the solution of the mystery. This chapter presents evidence that in the period between the Civil War and the Immigration Restriction Act of 1924 the ability of the Negro to establish himself in the North was conditioned by the volume of immigration. The outflow of the blacks from the South exhibited a time-pattern which was the opposite of that of the inflow of Europeans and the internal migration of native whites.

[1] Gunnar Myrdal, *An American Dilemma: the Negro Problem and Modern Democracy*, Harper, 1944, Twentieth Anniversary edition, 1962, pp. 189–90.
[2] Ibid. p. 193.

I. THE PATTERN OF NEGRO MIGRATION, 1870–1950

When I examined this subject in the first edition of the book,[1] my object was to test the general hypothesis that swings in external migration were inverse to swings in internal migration in countries of immigration as well as those of emigration. I happened to use the statistics for Negro migration in the United States as a proxy for total internal migration, and I thought I had verified my hypothesis when I found that swings in Negro internal migration were inverse to those in immigration.[2] However, as critics pointed out, in the United States total internal migration (dominated by the movement of whites) moved harmoniously with immigration,[3] and so the hypothesis was refuted. Negro migration, far from being a proxy, was itself inverse to the internal migration of whites. This striking fact opened up a promising area of inquiry.

The inference from Table 37 was that when immigration of foreign workers was in full spate the northward movement of Negroes was at a low ebb and vice versa. The rate of increase in the foreign-born population rose sharply from 20% in 1870–80 to 39% in 1880–90, whereas the growth in the Negro population in the North fell from 36% to 14%. The opposite occurred when we compare 1890–1900 with 1880–90. During the period 1910–30, when immigration was drastically reduced, first by the World War and then by the Immigration Restriction Act of 1924, an extraordinary increase took place in the number of Negroes enumerated in the North, 44% in 1910–20 and 67% in 1920–30. The validity of the original argument can be tested by looking at the results of the major research project on population redistribution and economic growth, 1870–1950, which was carried out at the University of Pennsylvania.[4] Hope T. Eldridge and Dorothy S. Thomas reach the following conclusion about regional rates of urban growth.

The rates for native whites are closely similar to those for the population as a whole. *It is the contrapuntal movement of rates for foreign-born whites and Negroes in the northern regions that is of particular interest. For the North-east, the pattern of fluctuation in the rates of foreign-born whites is inverse to that of Negroes up to 1910–20; there is evidence of some opposition also in the rates of the North Central. It would be difficult to interpret these findings in terms other than a tendency for the*

---

[1] See pp. 130–4. [2] See p. 131.

[3] For a criticism see Dorothy S. Thomas's chapter on international migration in P. Hauser, ed., *Population and World Politics*, Glencoe, Ill., Free Press, 1958, p. 152.

[4] *Population Redistribution and Economic Growth, United States 1870–1950*, Philadelphia, American Philosophical Society, vol. I (1957) by Everett S. Lee, Ann Ratner Miller, Carol P. Brainerd and Richard A. Easterlin; vol. II (1960) by Simon Kuznets, Ann Ratner Miller and Richard A. Easterlin; vol. III (1964) by Hope T. Eldridge and Dorothy S. Thomas.

movement of the foreign born into urban areas to have a repressive effect upon the movement of Negroes into the same areas.[1]

A closer examination reveals that the Negro migrants tended to go to certain specific areas in the North: it was not until the nineteen-forties that the big movement to California took place. The favourite states were New York, New Jersey and Pennsylvania (sub-region N3), Ohio, Indiana, Illinois, Michigan and Wisconsin (sub-region C1) and the District of Columbia. The proportions of all state gains contributed by the migration of blacks to the above destinations were 76% in 1910–20, 79% in 1920–30, 68% in 1930–40 and 70% in 1940–50, the fall in the last two percentages being a reflection of the increasing pull of California. Net migration rates for the native white, the Negroes and the foreign-born white in sub-regions N3 and C1, 1870–1950, are given in Table 157.

In interpreting Table 157 we must bear in mind that the migration rate for Negroes is on a much higher *level* than that for foreign-born white because it is based on the average Negro population whereas the other rate is based on the average *total* population. These figures again demonstrate the inverse relation and the breakthrough of the blacks to the North as from 1910–20. Significant also is the fact that most of these northern states were losing white and gaining black population;[2] this was true of Pennsylvania in every decade between 1870–80 and 1940–50, of Ohio, Indiana, Illinois and Wisconsin in at least six decades and of New York in five decades.[3] In contrast, the southern states of Texas and Virginia had large gains of native whites and large losses of Negroes. There are two factors to be noted here. First, the westward movement was composed largely of native whites. Secondly, immigrants' children born in the United States were an addition to the native population and the size of this element varied from region to region; on the other hand, there was hardly any influx of blacks from abroad. Thus, since the immigrants were to be found mainly in the eastern regions of America and the migration to the west was predominantly native white, the children of the foreign-born tended to reduce the degree of redistribution of native whites below what it would have been otherwise.[4]

Immigration, which had been running at an average of over a million a year between 1910 and 1914, was practically stopped by

[1] Hope T. Eldridge and Dorothy S. Thomas, op. cit. vol. III, *Demographic Analyses and Interrelations*, p. 224. My italics.
[2] Ibid. p. 93.
[3] A similar process can be seen in the conurbations of England, 1961–6. See Chapter XVI, pp. 303–4.
[4] For a detailed analysis of this see Eldridge and Thomas, op. cit. pp. 98–100.

World War I and there was a dramatic rise in the movement of Negroes into the northern states. So severe was the shortage of labour that many recruiting agents were sent to the South; for example, the Pennsylvania Railroad could not have carried out its essential maintenance work without bringing to the North many thousands of Negro workers. In the decade 1910–20 net migration into New York, Pennsylvania and New Jersey was 388 per 1,000 of the black population there as compared with 272 per 1,000 in the previous decade, and in Ohio, Indiana, Illinois, Michigan and Wisconsin the increase was even more spectacular, from 187 per 1,000 to 564 per 1,000 (see Table 157). When the war was over immigration was resumed on a large scale, and in the five years, 1920–4, no less than 2,775,000 arrived. This last great upsurge was brought to an abrupt end by the passing of the Immigration Restriction Act of 1924.

In contrast to 1901–10 when an average of 600,000 Southern and Eastern Europeans came to America every year, the number admitted between 1925 and 1928 was a mere trickle of 34,000 a year. At last there was a vacuum in the mines, steel works, stockyards and factories of the North which only the black workers from the South could fill; the number of Negroes enumerated in the North Centre and North East rose by a million between 1920 and 1930. This tendency has continued ever since and received another powerful impetus during World War II.

What the evidence suggests is that in the sixty years after the end of the Civil War the strong competition of white workers from abroad in a society where the dice were loaded against the Negro set a stern limit to the number of blacks who could obtain employment in the booming urban areas of the North and West, and consequently they suffered relative impoverishment during an era of record advance in the average standard of living of Americans. The invisible hand of the market was no match for the all too visible hand of discrimination. Hemmed in between the poor whites in the South and the poor whites from Europe in the North, the Negroes found that their only chance of making any headway was at times when the immigration tide was going out. It was not until World War I that they got their first real break, and then came the 1924 Immigration Restriction Act which was to prove of lasting benefit to them.

2. FERTILITY AND MORTALITY

Since the migration experience of the blacks differed so much from that of the whites, one wonders whether there was also a significant contrast between the course of the fertility and mortality of the two groups.

Kuznets found it '...particularly noteworthy that additions to the non-white population do not show a rise from the 1890s to the first decade of the twentieth century similar to those in the additions to other sections of the population'.[1] Moreover, '...the long swings in

Ratios

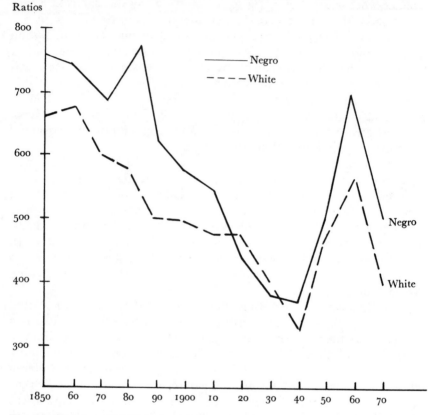

Fig. 63. Number of children 0–4 per 1,000 women 15–44 in the white and Negro population of the United States, decennially, 1850–1970.
Source: Reynolds Farley, *Growth of the Black Population* (Chicago: Markham, 1970), Figure 3-2. U.S. Bureau of the Census, *Census of Population: 1970*, PC(V2)-1, Table 2.

the births of non-white population also show a markedly different pattern from those in white population—the former missing the second swing, viz., the larger additions to births during the first decade to decade and a half of the twentieth century.'[2] Finally, '...fluctuations in the deaths of the non-white population differ substantially from

[1] S. Kuznets, 'Long Swings in the Growth of Population and in Related Economic Variables', p. 26.
[2] Ibid. pp. 26–7.

those of the white, the former declining and the latter rising during the 1890s and the early twentieth century. The difference in the timing pattern is most pronounced after the 1870–1880s and until about World War I.'[1] Kuznets referred to my analysis in Chapter VIII and suggested that it might be a key to the explanation of the deviant movement of non-white births, deaths and net increase during the pre-World War I period, since the upswing of the immigration cycle made life harder for the blacks and the downswing of the cycle was an alleviation. In Kuznets's words '. . . this would explain an *inverse* relation between the long swings in the net increase of non-white population and those in the net increase of both native white and foreign-born. The disappearance of this inverse relation after World War I would then be associated with the marked drop in the flow of immigrants from abroad.'[2]

To understand these intriguing patterns, we must look at the long-run picture. For fertility this is given in Fig. 63 based on the number of children 0–4 per 1,000 women 15–44 at each census. For mortality there is no reliable composite index for the nineteenth century, but various estimates have been made from the partial information which does exist.[3] Intensive research by demographers suggests the following interpretation.[4] In the initial stage, which covered most of the nineteenth century up to the eighteen-seventies, the mortality of the Negroes was very high but their fertility was even higher, and it is estimated that the population grew by well over 2% per annum. The censuses of 1910 and 1940 contain information on the number of live children born to women who had ever been married. On the basis of the information relating to Negroes, Reynolds Farley found that '. . . two-thirds of the women who survived to be enumerated bore at least five children and, on the average, each had seven children. Such high numbers of children support the view that Negro fertility was near a biological maximum during much of the nineteenth century.'[5] Fig. 63 shows that the ratio of children 0–4 to women 15–44 for Negroes fell steeply from a very high level of 750 in 1880 to well under 400 in 1940; the decline in the

---

[1] S. Kuznets, 'Long Swings . . .', p. 27.   [2] Ibid. p. 31.

[3] Life tables for Negroes were not calculated until the beginning of this century, and at first they were confined to people enumerated in the Death Registration Area comprising ten northern cities and the District of Columbia. The Negroes in that area were nearly all urban dwellers, whereas in the United States as a whole in 1910 as many as 77% of Negroes were country dwellers.

[4] I have benefited greatly from the authoritative work of Reynolds Farley, *Growth of the Black Population: a Study of Demographic Trends*, Chicago, Markham Publishing Company, 1970. My thanks are due to the author and publisher for their kind permission to reproduce Figure 3-2.

[5] Ibid. p. 57.

ratio for whites was more gradual, and by the nineteen-twenties and nineteen-thirties there was very little difference between the fertility of the two groups. The evidence about mortality shows that the expectation of life of blacks in the South in 1930 was only slightly higher than it had been in 1860. The annual rate of growth of the black population in the decade of the Great Depression was only 0.79%.

Here we have a demographic cycle different from C. P. Blacker's 'high stationary' phase (high birth rate and high death rate) followed by the 'early expanding' phase (high birth rate and lower, or falling, death rate) and then the 'late stationary' (declining birth rate and death rate, with the latter consistently lower than the former).[1] Why did the Negro population have this unique experience up to the nineteen-forties? Reynolds Farley made a thorough analysis of this fundamental question, and reached significant conclusions. The steep decline in the fertility of the blacks between about 1880 and the nineteen-thirties cannot be attributed to changes in family patterns or to the practice of birth control.[2] It is since the beginning of the nineteen-forties that contraceptives have been widely used by Negroes, and yet between 1940 and 1960 their fertility went up sharply (see Fig. 63). A factor which appears to explain much of the long-period fall in fertility is a change in the physical ability of Negroes to have children, i.e., their fecundity. Farley demonstrates the high incidence of foetal deaths and fertility-inhibiting diseases such as pellagra, gonorrhoea and syphilis in the South up to the nineteen-thirties,[3] and he suggests that the '. . . fluctuations in childlessness reflect changes in fecundity rather than intentional changes in planned family size'.[4]

The demographic cycle which we have outlined cannot be explained except in terms of what was happening to the Southern economy. For several decades after the Civil War the South East of America was seriously overpopulated and the living conditions of many blacks were deteriorating. After the early eighteen-nineties the depredations of the boll weevil had a calamitous effect. In the sixty years before the Great Depression of the nineteen-thirties, the acreage devoted to agriculture in the South East contracted and the yield of cotton and tobacco per acre was stationary, but the labour force on the farms almost doubled. The South was in the grip of a creeping Malthusian crisis,[5] and there was hardly any safety-valve. The inability of blacks in large numbers

[1] C. P. Blacker, 'Stages in Population Growth', *The Eugenics Review*, vol. 39, no. 3, October 1947, pp. 89–94.
[2] See Reynolds Farley, op. cit. Chs. 6 and 8.
[3] Ibid. pp. 208–33.
[4] Ibid. p. 226.
[5] See Gunnar Myrdal, op. cit. pp. 230–50.

to escape to gainful employment in the North, except to some extent when immigration was waning, condemned them to languish in an overpopulated depressed area; this led to intensified population pressure in the South, increasing poverty with consequent high mortality and lower fecundity.[1]

The way it worked out was that, when the safety-valve of out-migration was operating, the forces keeping up the death rate and reducing fecundity in the South were weakened; the fact that the mortality of blacks was greater and their fertility lower in the North than in the South could not have much countervailing effect because the national rates were dominated by the vast majority who were in the rural South.[2]

Migration to the North was a necessary but not sufficient condition for an improvement in the living standard and prospects of Negroes. There also needed to be fair competition in the labour market, adequate welfare provision (including education), and an effective social ladder. It was not likely that these conditions could be fulfilled quickly and so the growing movement of blacks to the cities in the nineteen-forties and nineteen-fifties was accompanied by a big increase in broken families, high unemployment and general disillusionment.[3] Nevertheless, real progress has been achieved, as we shall see in the next section. The Negro infant mortality rate, which was as high as 83 per 1,000 births in 1937, was down to 42 by 1956, and it was further reduced to 35 by 1967. Between 1937 and 1956 the overall Negro death rate, adjusted for age composition, fell from 19 per 1,000 to 10, but there was hardly any change in the nineteen-sixties.

[1] Alan Sweezy, in an interesting paper, has attempted to refute the proposition that fertility varies positively with economic conditions. He argues that changes in fertility have been mainly determined by changes in attitudes. 'The Economic Explanation of Fertility Changes in the United States', *Population Studies*, vol. 25, no. 2, July 1971, pp. 255–67. The evidence for the Negro population runs contrary to his argument.

[2] This is borne out by components of difference in an analysis of the decline in the ratio of children 0–4 to women 15–44 for the black population, 1910–40, from 519 to 368. Farley shows that this total change of −151 was attributable as follows: fertility rates in North and West −3, fertility rates in urban South −11, fertility rates in rural South −80, change in distribution of population −78, and interaction of factors +21 (Reynolds Farley, op. cit. p. 113). Farley comments: 'The decrease in childbearing by rural Southern Negroes played a role every bit as important as urbanisation in bringing down the national fertility rate. Had there been no shift to urban residence, there still would have been a large decline in Negro fertility. This means that the long term decline in Negro fertility must have been the result of the reduced childbearing of those Negro women who remained on the farms of the South' (ibid. p. 114).

[3] See Daniel P. Moynihan, *The Negro Family: the Case for National Action*, Washington D.C., Department of Labor, Office of Policy Planning and Research, 1965.

In the nineteen-fifties the fertility of the blacks rose far more than that of the whites, and their population grew by 2·3% per annum— almost as fast as it did in the eighteen-forties; in the nineteen-sixties, with the widespread use of the pill, the Negro birth rate declined with that of the whites but less sharply (Fig. 63), bringing the annual rate of growth down to 1·7% in 1967–9. A most significant portent in its bearing on the future is that Negro women with four years or more of college education are having fewer children than white women with similar education.[1]

As far as fertility and mortality are concerned, it looks as if the forces making for convergence between the experience of the two groups will become stronger as time goes on.

3. THE IMPACT ON THE CITIES

Between 1940 and 1970 the number of Negroes went up to 77%, making it just over 11% of the population of the United States; in 1970 53·2% of the 22,673,000 Negroes were in the South, 39·4% in the North and 7·5% in the West. The net migration out of the South was 1,599,000 in 1940–50, 1,456,000 in 1950–60, and 1,400,000 in 1960–70; and yet, because of high fertility in the South, its population went up by just over 2 million. The effect on the large cities of the North and West has been considerable. The largest totals of Negroes are in New York (1,500,000), Chicago (1,150,000), Detroit (800,000), Los Angeles (700,000), and Philadelphia (700,000); the highest proportions of the population are in Washington D.C. (68%), Detroit (47%), Baltimore (47%), St Louis (46%) and Chicago and Philadelphia (32%).

Amid the welter of discussion on the crisis of the cities, one is staggered by the complexity of what is happening. I propose merely to refer to one or two findings of expert research which refute some popularly held beliefs. How much and what kind of displacement of population has taken place in the cities? This question can be answered by examining the census results,[2] and this has been thoroughly

[1] *Report of the National Advisory Commission on Civil Disorders*, New York Times Co., Bantam Books, 1968, p. 239. In 1960 the fertility rates were as follows: women with four years of college education, non-white 1·7 and white 2·2; women with five or more years of college education, non-white 1·2 and white 1·6.

[2] Unfortunately, even the census statistics have serious deficiencies. It has been estimated that 10% of the Negroes were not counted in 1960, and in 1950, according to Ansley J. Coale, as many as one in five of the non-white males were not covered (The Population of the United States in 1950 classified by Age, Sex and Color—a Revision of Census Figures', *Journal of the American Statistical Association*, vol. L, March 1955, p. 44). Many of these would have been migrants. There is also the high number of those who failed to answer the questions on socio-economic characteristics.

done by Karl and Alma Taeuber for the period 1955–60.[1] They examined the figures for the Standard Metropolitan Statistical Areas (S.M.S.A.s) which correspond to conurbations in Britain; each of these is divided into the Central City and the Outer Ring. The data are based on the answers to the question regarding place of residence on April 1, 1955 and at the time of the census in April 1960.

According to expectation, there was a massive efflux of whites from central cities to the outer rings; in eight of the cities for every six persons who moved out only one came in. New York City stands out by having a huge influx of immigrants from abroad (e.g. Puerto Ricans). There was also a considerable movement into all outer rings from other metropolitan areas. Among the striking things revealed is that movements of young men joining the armed forces have a considerable influence in exaggerating the outflow to the suburbs in some metropolitan areas. For example, '...one third of men in the labor force among migrants (regardless of origin) to the rings of Philadelphia, Washington and Baltimore were in the armed forces in 1960'.[2] Moreover, the classification of the migrants by socio-economic categories disproved the commonly held notion that those who go from cities to suburbs are people of high status while those who move the other way have a low status. The three basic findings of the authors are important. 'City-to-ring and ring-to-city migrants are highly similar with regard to average measures of educational and occupational status. Migrants of a given origin going to the city tend to resemble those going to the ring. Migrants, whether to city or ring, tend to be of higher educational and occupational status than the non-migrant population'.[3]

We now turn to a similar analysis of the non-white population, and since nearly all these migrants went to the central cities the S.M.S.A. totals will serve the purpose. The important point emerging is that in the northern metropolitan areas half the in-migrants come from other similar areas where they have had urban experience: this is true of only one in three in the South. The picture of the black migrant as the poor oppressed rural proletariat escaping to the city hardly applies any longer to the majority. A special analysis of city-to-ring movements brings out once again the side effect of the military draft in creating a phoney rise in suburbanization; '...about half of the men in the labor force moving from our S.M.S.A.s to the suburban ring of another metropolitan area were in the armed forces. Military-connected migra-

[1] See Karl and Alma Taeuber, 'White Migration and Socio-economic Differences between Cities and Suburbs', *American Sociological Review*, vol. xxix, October 1964, pp. 718–29.
[2] Ibid. p. 725.
[3] Ibid. p. 727.

tion also accounts for much of the movement from metropolitan to non-metropolitan places'.[1]

Most striking are the findings on occupational and educational characteristics; recent non-white migrants from the South living in the North had median educational levels on a par with those of non-whites born in the North. Contrary to what is usually believed, Negro in-migrants in 1955–60 had a much higher average socio-economic status than the Negroes living in a number of the big conurbations. Our authors' general conclusion is worth quoting in full.

Very likely a high-status intermetropolitan stream of Negro migrants always existed, but its relative importance has increased substantially in recent years owing to the rapid urbanization of the Negro population. We have found that it is in-migrants of non-metropolitan origin who most nearly resemble the stereotype of the socioeconomically depressed migrant. It seems reasonable that as this component declines and the intermetropol-itan component increases in relative importance, the status of the total in-migrant group would rise. As the character of the Negro population has changed from that of a disadvantaged rural population to a largely metro-politan population of rising social and economic status, Negro migration should increasingly manifest patterns similar to those found among the white population.[2]

Thus, we may conclude that trends in migration as well as fertility and mortality for the Negro population may be converging towards those for the whites. If this is so, it has important implications for the future.

4. ASSIMILATION OR POLARIZATION?

Chronologically, the wave of Negro in-migrants to the North and West after World War II is the sixth in a succession of immigration waves since the Irish-German in 1845–54. The fundamental question is whether it is so different in kind from its predecessors that the mechanism of absorption can no longer work.

Nathan Glazer and Daniel P. Moynihan, in the introduction to the second edition of their remarkable book, *Beyond the Melting Pot*, found reason for doubt and disappointment when they looked back in 1970 at the basic hypothesis of their first edition (1963). They had assumed that in New York City '... the larger American experience of the Negro, based on slavery and repression in the South, would be overcome, as the

---

[1] Karl and Alma Taeuber, 'The Changing Character of Negro Migration', *American Journal of Sociology*, vol. LXX, January 1965, p. 435.

[2] Ibid. p. 442.

Negroes joined the rest of society, in conflict and accommodation, as an ethnic group.'[1] But they had to admit that it did not happen.

The experience of Negroes in New York since the great migration fifty years ago has had a great deal in it, good and bad. If one compared it with the first fifty years of the Irish, the Italians, and the Jews, we are convinced that there would be enough in that comparison to justify an ethnic rather than a racial or an 'internally colonized' self-image. But the arts of politics, as exercised in the nation and the city, were insufficient to prevent a massive move toward what must be, for the nation and the city, a more damaging entity. The failure is a complex one.[2]

The mills of ethnic absorption, like the mills of God, grind slowly, but they don't grind exceeding small; a long sense of historical perspective is needed to judge their effectiveness. After well over a century of assimilation, the differences between, say, the Irish Americans and the WASPS (the white Anglo Saxon Protestants) are not insignificant, so much so that the analogy of the melting pot seems hardly appropriate. Indeed, before considering the prospects of the Negroes, one might look at the experience of the millions of destitute Irish who came to America after the great famine. Like the Negroes, they were escaping from a caste system and an agricultural economy undergoing a long-drawn-out Malthusian crisis; they knew from bitter experience what it meant to be 'internally colonized'. In their new country these post-1845 immigrants found a big generation gap between themselves and the old stock going back to the Revolution; in New York there had been a long tradition of keeping Irish Catholics out of political life; they had to face their full share of discrimination[3] and, as with all ethnic groups, there was a great deal of residential segregation.

Very few of the Irish-born managed to obtain jobs of high status. The proportion in the professional class was as low as 0·8% in 1870 and 1·3% in 1890, and even by 1900 it was still only 1·6% as compared with 4·3% of the British-born. At the other end of the social scale the proportion of the Irish-born who were servants was 15·1% in 1900 as against 4·1% of the British-born.[4] In some occupations the Irish had a very strong footing; in 1910 they accounted for 18% of America's coachmen and footmen, 12% of the labourers in public service, and 11% of the

---

[1] Nathan Glazer and Daniel P. Moynihan, *Beyond the Melting Pot: The Negroes, Puerto Ricans, Jews, Italians and Irish of New York City*, second edition, 1970. The M.I.T. Press, Cambridge, Mass., p. XIII.

[2] Ibid. p. XIV.

[3] Thomas N. Brown, *Social Discrimination against the Irish in the United States*, The American Jewish Committee, November 1958 (mimeographed).

[4] See pp. 147–52.

policemen.[1] For half a century the progress of the first-generation Irish up the social ladder had been extremely slow: it was their sons and daughters who found the doors of opportunity opening to them. In 1900 4·8% of the second-generation Irish were in the professions, not much lower than the 6·6% of the second-generation British, whereas the proportion in the servant class was down to 4·8%, not much above the 3·2% of the second-generation British. At the turn of the century as the second-generation Irish and other Northern Europeans were occupying the better-class occupations, the great influx of Italians and Eastern Europeans was entering the unskilled sector of the labour market, and in the long run many of their children would rise in the social scale.

The history of successive ethnic groups shows how American society was able to evolve a remarkable social device for maintaining a tolerable equilibrium in situations which often looked impossible; '... there are many groups; coalitions form and re-form; positions in the pecking order shift; there is a rhetoric of civility and celebration'.[2] Is this system going to fail now that the turn of the Negro has come? The overriding threat is the age-old powerful force of racial discrimination, different in kind from ethnic antagonism. W. E. B. Du Bois, describing conditions in Philadelphia in 1899, declared that:

...the industrial condition of the Negro cannot be considered apart from the great fact of race prejudice—infinite and shadowy as that phrase may be. It is certain that, while industrial cooperation among the groups of a great city population is very difficult under ordinary circumstances, here it is rendered more difficult and in some respects almost impossible by the fact that nineteen-twentieths of the population have in many cases refused to cooperate with the other twentieth, even when the cooperation means life to the latter and great advantage to the former. In other words one of the great postulates of the science of economics—that men will seek their economic advantage—is in this case untrue, because in many cases men will not do this if it involves association, even in a casual and business way, with Negroes. And this fact must be taken account of in all judgments as to the Negro's economic progress.[3]

If market forces had been allowed to work, real gains would have accrued both to the middle and high status groups and to the Negroes in the lowest stratum, even though there was marked residential segrega-

[1] In New York City it was recently estimated that 54% of the Catholics in Brooklyn have relatives or close friends in the police force. (Glazer and Moynihan, op. cit. p. LXXIV.)

[2] Daniel P. Moynihan, 'On Ethnicity', *The New York Times*, May 2, 1971.

[3] W. E. Burghardt Du Bois, *The Philadelphia Negro*, 1899, reissued 1967, New York, Benjamin Blom Inc., pp. 145–6.

tion. Race prejudice was in direct conflict with the American creed and the principles of free enterprise, and this forced the Negro to turn in upon himself. In the words of a historian of Negro thought, '... urbanization served as the chief basis of the new group life which Du Bois and others perceived as developing and which formed the basis of the Dream of Black Metropolis in Chicago and elsewhere; which created a new race consciousness, a new racial solidarity and self-reliance, a new middle class that depended for its support upon the Negro community, and ultimately the cultural flowering of the Harlem Renaissance.'[1]

The race factor is important but it is by no means the whole story. Even if it had been absent, the Negroes would still have faced formidable handicaps. By the time their turn came, there was much less demand for unskilled and blue-collar labour than there had been in the pre-1913 era when millions of unskilled European immigrants had built the infrastructure of American cities. There has been a marked shift towards craft and white-collar skills which the vast majority of the Negroes have been unable to acquire. Circumstances had also changed in that there was no longer much scope for economic advancement through political patronage. When the big cities were being built, powerful political machines held out substantial economic prizes to members of the older ethnic groups in exchange for support at the polls. 'By the time the Negroes arrived, the situation had altered dramatically. The great wave of public building had virtually come to an end; reform groups were beginning to attack the political machines; the machines were no longer so powerful or so well equipped to provide jobs and other favors.'[2] In many cities the areas where the blacks are concentrated are dominated by politicians belonging to the older ethnic groups, and this is a cause of bitter conflict.

In these unpromising circumstances, what progress has the Negro been able to make in scaling the socio-economic ladder? The record for the non-white population in the United States outside the South between 1940 and 1960 is shown in Table 158.

One of the snags about these figures is that there is no information on over a tenth of those enumerated in 1960. Nevertheless, they are the best source available and we can draw some firm inferences. Starting at the bottom, we can group private household and service workers, labourers, and the 'unknown'. Non-white females outside the South have been the most successful in moving out of these low-status occupations, even though more than half of them still remained there in

---

[1] August Meier, *Negro Thought in America, 1880–1915*, Ann Arbor, University of Michigan Press, 1963, p. 276.
[2] *Report of the National Advisory Commission on Civil Disorders* (1968), p. 279.

1960; similarly, non-white males have done relatively better than whites outside the South and much better than non-whites in the South. In the North and West the non-white population is clearly involved in the national shift away from unskilled labour, whereas in the South this tendency is much less evident.[1]

The number of non-white males employed in skilled jobs as craftsmen went up three-fold, bringing the percentage up to 11·2 as compared with 20·5 for the whites, and the increase in the middle class white collar occupations (mainly clerical) was as much as seven-fold, the percentage for non-white males reaching 9·4 with that of whites being 14·6. At the top of the pyramid, in the professional, technical and kindred grades, the proportion of non-white males rose from 3·1% to 4·8% and that of females from 3·7% to 7·2%. Undeniably there *was* vertical mobility between 1940 and 1960, but it was only a beginning; it is consistent with the observed rise in the average socio-economic status of Negro migrants. In the North and West in this period the amount of total new employment was 14·5 million, of which non-whites accounted for 13·8%; 5·3 million of these new jobs were in the unskilled category and a quarter of these were occupied by non-white workers; additional employment in the professional grades amounted to 8·3 million, of which non-whites accounted for only 6·2%.

It must be noted that the extent to which Negroes have been able to enter professions where they are competing with whites is more apparent than real. In examining the situation revealed in the 1930 census, Myrdal observed that '...the poverty of the Negro people represents a general limitation of opportunity for Negro businessmen and professionals. Since they are excluded from the white market, it becomes important for them to hold the Negro market as a monopoly. The monopoly over the Negro market of teachers, preachers, undertakers, beauticians and others is generally respected.'[2] In 1960 the picture had not changed very much.[3] Of the 115,683 Negro males classified as professionals, 30% were teachers in schools or colleges, 11% clergymen, 5% musicians or music teachers, and just under 3% funeral directors: only 3·6% were engineers as against 19·4% of the white professionals and 15·7% of those of Japanese origin. In the case of Negro females classified as professionals, as many as 60% were teachers in schools or colleges as compared with 44% of white female

---

[1] C. Horace Hamilton, 'The Negro leaves the South', *Demography*, vol. 1, 1964, p. 293.

[2] Myrdal, op. cit. pp. 304–5.

[3] See U.S. Bureau of the Census, *U.S. Census of Population 1960. Special Reports. Characteristics of Professional Workers*, Final Report P.C.(2)7E, U.S. Government Printing Office, Washington D.C., 1964, pp. 9 and 10.

professionals. Of the latter, it is interesting to find that 21% were professional nurses, the corresponding proportion for Negro females being 18%. As the black population has grown relatively to the white and its average standard of living has risen, the scope for inside employment of certain classes of professionals has become comparatively larger: a significant breakthrough into the white economy has yet to take place.

The distribution of the American population by race and socio-economic status, on the basis of the new socio-economic measures used in the 1960 census, can be summarized as follows.[1] In the top quartile are 20% of the whites, 3·2% of the blacks, and 13·8% of other races: in the bottom quartile are 12·9% of the whites, 45·4% of the blacks and 25·2% of other races.

No one who has read the Report of the National Advisory Commission on Civil Disorders (the Kerner Report) can have any illusions about the plight of the cities, with their eroding tax base, mounting cost of welfare, and the increase in crime and racial conflict. At the same time there can be no doubt that a growing number of Negro migrants made a real advance during the nineteen-sixties. The Kerner Report found that:

...the Negro 'upper-income' group is expanding rapidly and achieving sizeable income gains. In 1966, 28 per cent of all Negro families received incomes of $7,000 or more, compared with 55 per cent of white families. This was double the proportion of Negroes receiving comparable incomes in 1960 and four times greater than the proportion receiving such incomes in 1947. *Moreover, the proportion of Negroes employed in high-skill, high-status and well-paying jobs rose faster than comparable proportions among whites from 1960 to 1966.*[2]

According to a sample survey of New York adults in 1963,[3] the proportions engaged in professional employment in various groups were as follows: Negroes 9·5%; Puerto Ricans 3%; Italians (first and second generation) 9%; Irish (first and second generation) 9%; foreign-born Jews 10·5%; native-born Jews 21·5%; and white Protestants 22%. The dark side of all this is that the increasing Negro middle class widens the gap between the haves and the have-nots; about two-thirds of the lowest income group—or about a fifth of all Negroes—remain in dire poverty, many of them in the worst parts of the central cities.

It took many decades for the Irish immigrants of the nineteenth

[1] See U.S. Bureau of the Census, *U.S. Census of Population 1960, Special Reports, Socioeconomic Status*, Final Report, P.C.(2)5C, Washington D.C., 1967, p. XIII.

[2] *Report of National Advisory Commission on Civil Disorders* (1968), p. 251. (My italics.)

[3] Glazer and Moynihan, op. cit. p. lvi.

century to escape from poverty, and it is only after three or four generations that Eastern and Southern European immigrants from rural backgrounds have been able to make their way out of the lowest occupations. What the Negroes in the North and West have achieved in two or three decades is not to be underrated when we consider the long haul which was the lot of previous ethnic groups.

The evidence reviewed in this chapter suggests that the mass migration of Negroes has begun to bring about a convergence of the trends in their fertility, mortality, internal migration, and occupational distribution towards the white pattern. The black population is much younger than the white; in 1969 the median age of Negroes was 21·1 years as against 29·3 for whites. It is estimated that by 1985 less than a third of the expected increase of 8·7 million in the black population of central cities will have been due to in-migration: from now on the main dynamic will be natural increase. The stage is set in the northern cities for high growth and strong demographic echo effects in the future. American society, facing human problems of the most appalling complexity, has the resilience to overcome them in the long run. Assimilation according to the ethnic model must triumph over the ideological and other forces making for racial polarization. In Myrdal's phrase, 'separate can never be equal'.

EPILOGUE

The experience of Britain since World War II is in marked contrast to the alternation of capital formation and export upsurges characteristic of her growth up to 1913. Because of the balance of payments constraint, increases in home investment have been frequently nipped in the bud by deflationary measures; there were many balance of payments crises and the pound was devalued twice. If Britain's international margin had been wide enough, and the labour supply elastic enough, to allow her to have one or two sustained upswings in capital formation as a basis for a major breakthrough in exports, her average growth rate since 1945 would have been higher. Successive governments concentrated on the regulation of internal demand, entailing 'consumption-led' rather than 'export-led' growth.[1] Ironically enough, 'export-led' growth was precisely what West Germany and Japan, with copious aid from the victors, were able to achieve after the war.

AMERICA AND HER PERIPHERY, 1946–71

The course of events since World War II can be regarded as the nineteenth-century story in reverse, with the United States in the role of financial centre providing funds (though not, of course, migrants) for her periphery and presiding over an international 'dollar standard' with fixed exchange rates. There have been three long swing phases and the beginning of a fourth. The first, between 1946 and the early nineteen-fifties, was marked by an enormous flow of government loans and grants from the United States to Europe—exports of public capital to enable the Old World to recover from the impact of the war. During these years the American economy advanced vigorously, while European countries suffered balance of payments difficulties at a time of 'dollar scarcity'. From the mid-nineteen-fifties to the beginning of the nineteen-sixties there was a tremendous economic upsurge in the periphery with a retardation in the United States, and a 'dollar glut' appeared. In the second half of the nineteen-sixties America was in an upward phase of the long swing, whereas the rate of advance in Western Europe and Japan was less than in the previous phase. Mean-

[1] See N. Kaldor, ed., *Conflicts in Policy Objectives*, London, Basil Blackwell, 1971, pp. 1–19.

while, fundamental changes had taken place in the economic balance of power, culminating in the suspension of the dollar's convertibility in August 1971.

Post-war Reconstruction

In the first phase the United States was in a particularly strong economic situation. The Federal Government had absorbed no less than 40% of the gross national product during the years of all-out war effort, 1942–4; personal consumption had been restricted to 75% of disposable personal incomes in this period. Only an insignificant amount of residential construction had been carried out, and gross business investment was only two-fifths of gross business savings. The productive capacity of the economy had expanded to an unprecedented extent; the real gross national product in 1946 was double that of 1940; and this enormous productive potential was ready for the transition to peace-time demands to be exercised by a population holding very large liquid balances. Moreover, since the productive capacity of several of the other major industrial countries, particularly in Europe, had been seriously reduced by the ravages of war, there was bound to be an abnormally high demand for American products for some years. In these circumstances it was natural that the United States should be poised for a phase of rapid economic growth in the immediate post-war period. Between 1947 and 1955 gross national product in real terms increased by 39%, an average annual rate of growth of 4·2%. Industrial production rose by 47%, an annual growth of nearly 5%. Residential construction in real terms went up by 90%, and real expenditure on fixed investment in durable goods manufacturing (to 1957) by 58%.

The key to the reconstruction of the international economy after the war is to be found in the massive export of *public* capital from the United States. Between 1946 and 1952 total *gross* movements of public capital and grants amounted to $75,500 million, 58% of which came from the United States and Canada in 1948; these transfers were equal to 20% of the aggregate value of world imports in that year.[1] The net amount of public funds supplied by the United States was $33,800 million, of which $22,800 million went to Europe. The latter was five times larger than the entire net volume of $4,400 million of American

---

[1] See M. L. Weiner and R. Dalla-Chiesa, 'International Movement of Public Long-term Capital and Grants, 1946–50', International Monetary Fund, *Staff Papers*, vol. IV, no. 1, September 1954, p. 116; and J. Barnénas, 'International Movement of Public Long-term Capital and Grants, 1951–2', ibid. vol. V, no. 1, February 1956, p. 110.

private direct investment (i.e. investment by United States companies in their subsidiaries and branches abroad) throughout the world in the same period. Thanks to this generous aid the exhausted economies of Europe were able not only to cover their large trade deficits but also to operate a considerable measure of multilateral trade and resume capital exports and emigration to oversea countries within their orbit. There was very little American *private* investment in Western Europe in this period: it comprised only 8% of total United States direct foreign investment in 1946–52. However, there was a large flow of American private capital to Canada and Latin America, and this helped the resumption of European emigration to these countries while the outer Sterling Area was strengthened. Such was the triangular mechanism which in the early post-war years put new life into the world economy; it was based on the European Recovery Programme, and it made possible a rapid revival of commercial relations between North America, Europe and the developing countries overseas. The beneficiaries have been too apt to forget what they owe to the unparalleled statesmanship which inspired the Marshall Plan, with which the name of its chief architect, the late Dean Acheson, will always be associated.

Economic Resurgence of Western Europe

The nineteen-fifties saw a remarkable economic revival in Western Europe. Between 1953 and 1961 industrial production in the European Common Market countries went up by 82% as against an increase of 20% in the United States and 30% in the United Kingdom. One is reminded of the nineteenth-century pattern of development when Great Britain was the world's leading creditor; phases of heavy British investment in countries of new settlement overseas were followed by phases in which the production and export capacities of these countries showed a rapid increase. The extraordinary upsurge in production and export capacities in Western Europe and Japan in the nineteen-fifties would not have been possible without the basic capital formation and renewal of resources brought about by the inflow of public capital in the years 1946–52.

Between 1953 and 1961 the volume of industrial production in Germany rose by 90% and productivity per manhour by 63%, the labour force increased by no less than 5,000,000 i.e. by one-third, the volume of exports expanded by 169%, and the Central Bank's gold reserve grew from 1,368 million to 14,427 million D.marks. One of the necessary conditions of this 'economic miracle' was the absorption of immigrants on a unique scale. The population of the Federal Republic increased by one-third in twelve years. Between May 1945 and July

1959 Western Germany absorbed 3·2 million refugees from the Soviet zone and 9·4 million from beyond the Oder–Neisse, from the Sudeten area and from South Eastern Europe. These newcomers included a high proportion of skilled manpower and qualified personnel; they spoke the same language and had the same background as the people of the host country. Highly adaptable and mobile, these immigrants found little difficulty in being assimilated. At a later stage a large number of workers were recruited from Southern Europe, particularly Italy, Spain, Greece and Turkey. This massive inflow of labour into an economy with an advanced industrial technique provided the basis for a rapid increase in productivity; and government policy concentrated on the promotion of a high rate of capital accumulation and the introduction of the most modern methods of production.

Retardation of Growth in the United States, 1955–61

Between the middle of the nineteen-fifties and 1961/62 the rate of growth in the United States was much slower than in the previous high phase, 1947–55; and it was in sharp contrast to what was happening in continental Europe. For example, real expenditure on automobiles and parts in the years 1956–61 averaged 16% below the peak of the previous upward phase. Even in 1962 real expenditures on plant and equipment in manufacturing and public utilities were 15% below the previous peak. In the years 1955–62 expenditures on residential construction rose on an average by about 1% per annum, which was far less than the rate of advance before 1955. The relative stagnation shown by these strategic economic variables was reflected in the movement of the gross national product in real terms which showed an average annual increase of only 2·7% between 1955 and 1962.

The emergence of Western Europe as a strong power in the world's market was bound to lead to a redistribution of monetary reserves. Between 1953 and the end of 1961 the official gold and foreign exchange holdings of the European countries belonging to O.E.C.D. rose from $11,200 million to $26,800 million whereas those of the United States fell from $22,000 million to $17,000 million. From the point of view of the working of the international economy this was a salutary development and it was not necessarily harmful to the United States. As an American writer pointed out in 1960:

...Whatever difficulty the United States may be having in maintaining its previous relative position in world trade is not due to the higher relative prices of our export goods, but to the ability of the Western European countries to offer far larger supplies than formerly at the same relative prices as the United States. Even so, the payments position of the United States would not be adversely affected by the greater increase in production and exports in Western Europe, if these countries would increase their imports and foreign investments to an equivalent extent. This balance of payments difficulty apart, and for which an appropriate remedy can be found, the United States clearly benefits from the growth in European productivity and would benefit from the growth in output in the underdeveloped countries.[1]

The continental European countries which absorbed monetary reserves on such a large scale did not, however, increase their imports and foreign investment to anything like an adequate extent. Meanwhile, in addition to a very considerable outflow of United States government funds for defence purposes, there was an appreciable increase in private foreign investment, both direct and portfolio. In 1958 American military *expenditure* abroad amounted to $3,416 million of which $1,852 million was incurred in Western Europe. The fact that the latter was the equivalent of over half the exports of Western Europe to the United States is an indication of its size in relation to the balance of payments. About three-quarters of these military expenditures were incurred by the Defence Department for supplies, services and construction in the countries where American forces were located. The total of United States military *grants* to foreign countries in 1958 was $2,522 million, of which $1,514 million went to Western Europe. The aggregate of all foreign transfers and payments by the United States Government in 1958 was equal to 45% of aggregate private outlay on imports of goods and services plus the net outflow of American private capital.[2]

With the sharp change in relative growth rates in America and Western Europe in the period 1955–62, 'dollar shortage' gave way to 'dollar glut'. The deficit in the overall payments of the United States amounted to $3,400 million in 1958 and $4,000 million in 1959. An important factor in this situation was the growth in American private foreign investment superimposed on the politically determined outflow of government loans and grants. The value of United States direct investment in Europe in 1962 was more than double what it was in 1957 ($8,843 million as against $4,151 million). The increase in the European Common Market countries was from $1,680 million to $3,671 million, and in the United Kingdom from $1,974 million to $3,805 million. There was also a considerable growth in American private investment other than direct investment, i.e. purchases of

[1] Edward M. Bernstein, *International Effects of U.S. Economic Policy*, Study Paper No. 16, prepared for the Joint Economic Committee, Congress of the United States, January 25, 1960, Washington D.C., 1960, p. 35.

[2] See Brinley Thomas, 'Recent Trends in American Investment in Western Europe', *The Three Banks Review*, No. 47, September 1960, p. 19.

foreign dollar bonds, other foreign securities and short-term assets; this category of private investment in Western Europe increased from $3,386 million in 1957 to $5,617 million in 1962. American policy to reduce the payments deficit included an investment equalization tax designed to discourage portfolio investment abroad, and some reductions were made in foreign aid and military expenditures overseas. The weakness of the dollar and the high price of gold on the London market prompted the American authorities to bring into existence in 1961 the gold pool agreement between leading central banks; concerted buying and selling by this official consortium helped to stabilize the gold market.

The End of an Epoch

In the third phase, beginning in the early nineteen-sixties, the pace of activity was strong in the United States, and the deficit in her balance of payments, aggravated by the effect of the Vietnam War on the capital account, became much worse. Meanwhile, the receiving countries, particularly Germany and Japan, went on expanding their share of world exports and adding to their already huge stock of dollar assets. Between 1959 and 1969 the combined gross national product of the European Economic Community and Japan grew from 49% of that of the United States to 61%. By the first half of 1971 the gold and foreign exchange reserves of Germany ($16,900 million) and Japan ($10,400 million) were together well over double those of the United States ($12,500 million). The periphery's performance had been too much of a good thing. On August 15, 1971, President Nixon made his historic announcement: 'I have directed Secretary Connolly to suspend temporarily the convertibility of the dollar into gold and other reserve assets', and he levied a temporary surcharge of 10% on imports. This momentous change of policy ushered in a new era.

It had been evident for some time that the United States dollar was overvalued in terms of other currencies and that the fundamental disequilibrium was due in part to the piling up of excessive payments surpluses by the periphery, particularly Germany and Japan. It was a glaring example of the basic truth emphasized by Lord Keynes when he presented his plan for an International Clearing Union in 1943. He pointed out that:

...the world's trading difficulties in the past have not always been due to the improvidence of debtor countries. They may be caused in most acute form if a creditor country is constantly withdrawing international money from circulation and hoarding it, instead of putting it back into circulation, thus refusing to spend its income from abroad either on goods for home consumption or on investment overseas.[1]

The drastic action by the United States on August 15, 1971, led to an upward revaluation of the major currencies of Europe and that of Japan, and the American dollar was devalued in terms of gold. This introduced a new phase in which it was expected that the huge deficit of at least $9,000 million in the American balance of payments would be substantially reduced and the rate of economic growth in the United States would tend to be higher and that of the periphery lower than in the previous phase.

THE PASSING OF THE KUZNETS CYCLE?

We conclude with the solemn question whether we should say farewell to the Kuznets cycle. Abramovitz, as chief mourner, has written a moving epitaph.

The Kuznets cycle in America lived, it flourished, it had its day, but its day is past. Departed, it leaves to us who survive to study its works many insights into the kinds of connections and responses which go together to make for spurts and retardations in development. We are the wiser for its life, but it is gone. *Requiescat in pace*. Gone but not forgotten.[2]

For my own part, I am inclined to repeat Mark Twain's remark when he read an obituary of himself in the papers; he said that the news was somewhat exaggerated.

What Abramovitz is saying is that the old Kuznets cycle was '...a form of growth which belonged to a particular period in history and that the economic structure and institutions which imposed that form on the growth process have evolved, or been changed, into something different'.[3] He is anxious '...to guard the integrity and usefulness of the Kuznets-cycle hypothesis for interpreting development in the United States, Canada and Western Europe from about the 1840s to 1914 by shielding it from an inappropriate confrontation with the different form which the growth process is taking, and is likely to take, in the contemporary world.'[4] He is not saying that *long swings* have had their day. This he makes clear in the following sentence. 'What I do wish to argue is that the specific set of relations and response mechanisms which were characteristic of pre-1914 "long swings" in growth are

---

[1] Lord Keynes, speech delivered in the House of Lords, May 18, 1943, quoted in *The New Economics: Keynes' Influence on Theory and Public Policy*, edited by S. E. Harris, London, Dennis Dobson, 1947, p. 362.

[2] M. Abramovitz, 'The Passing of the Kuznets Cycle', *Economica*, vol. xxxv, no. 140, November 1968, p. 367.

[3] Ibid. p. 349.   [4] Ibid.

unlikely to be characteristic of future long swings. These will be of a different sort and may, indeed, not have much in common with one another in, say, their durations, amplitudes or internal structure.'[1] It would appear, then, that the deceased mourned by Abramovitz was that well-known member of the family, the American Kuznets Cycle, Born 1840: Departed this Life 1914.

One feature of the modern world weighing heavily in the argument is the ending of mass immigration; it is held to be a matter of chance whether long swings produced merely by the echo effects of past fluctuations in births will generate the pre-1914 type of Kuznets cycle. Then there is the point that governments now know how to prevent serious depressions. Another factor is the greatly increased volume of Federal, State and local government expenditures in the United States and the prominence of government grants and loans in the out-flow of capital. However, Abramovitz admits that '...the adaptive variation in the flows of capital funds which, before 1914, made possible regular divergent fluctuations in the growth rates of Europe and the United States, may well continue to operate in the future. But it will probably be called on to operate only sporadically; not regularly. For with the disappearance of the migration link, the chief cause of regular divergent fluctuations between the two halves of the Atlantic Community has been removed.'[2] This emphasis on the migration link as the basic cause of the inverse rates of growth in the pre-1914 period is in line with the main thesis of this book; but as to the future one should keep an open mind despite the disappearance of trans-Atlantic mass migration. Much more research needs to be done on long swings in the post-1945 period.[3]

Changes in population structure and their echo effects on both sides of the Atlantic must continue to be reckoned with, and the demographic determinants of construction cycles will not disappear, particularly in an age in which problems of population and urbanization are going to be crucial. Waves of internal or intra-continental migration can be a potent generator of long swings and in the United States even the demographic force of immigration is by no means a thing of the past. As we saw in the last chapter, the North and West between 1950 and 1970 received a massive influx of 3 million young blacks, the echo effects of which are bound to entail demographic cycles with a powerful

---

[1] M. Abramovitz, op. cit., pp. 349–50.   [2] Ibid. p. 366.

[3] For an instructive pioneering study see Edward M. Bernstein, 'The Post war Trend Cycle in the United States', New York, Model Roland and Co., *Quarterly Review*, First Quarter 1963, pp. 1–10. See also Bert G. Hickman, 'The Post war Retardation: Another Long Swing in the Rate of Growth?', *American Economic Review*, vol. LIII, May 1963, no. 2, pp. 490–507.

social and economic impact. If we add the 5 million immigrants from abroad, we get a decennial rate of over 4 million for 1950–70 which is half the record inflow into the United States in 1901–10. Since the future demographic and economic consequences in America are likely to conform to well-established patterns, the old American Kuznets cycle may yet show that it is not half as dead as it looks. Finally, the ending of the Bretton Woods international monetary regime in 1971 may be the beginning of a new process of interaction which could entail systematic long swing divergencies between growth rates in the United States and an enlarged European Community of comparable magnitude.

APPENDIX 1

A METHOD OF ESTIMATING NET MIGRATION FROM POPULATION CENSUS DATA

The numbers of British-born enumerated in the United States at each census beginning in 1870 were divided into age groups, and, from age specific death rates, the numbers of survivors were calculated decennially. Net immigration may be estimated by subtracting the survivors at the end of a given decade from the British-born enumerated at that date. The details of the method are set out below.

Age distribution

As the American Census returns did not classify the British-born by age group, we took the age composition of foreign-born persons and applied it to the British-born for the years 1870, 1880 and 1890. This is a reasonable thing to do, since most of the immigrants up to 1890 had come from the United Kingdom and other countries of North Western Europe. The procedure could not be applied after 1890 owing to the predominance of immigrants from Southern and Eastern Europe in that period. Table 62 shows median ages of foreign-born and English- and Welsh-born respectively from 1890 to 1930.

Table 62. *Median ages of foreign- and English- and Welsh-born persons in the United States, 1890–1930*

	1890	1900	1910	1920	1930
Foreign-born	36·9	38·0	37·1	40·0	44·4
Born in England and Wales	37·2	40·2	48·0	45·2	48·1

In a supplement to the 1930 Census of the United States, there is an analysis of the British-born by age for twelve selected states in 1910 and 1930, and this has been assumed to hold for all forty-eight states. By linear interpolation between the percentage age distribution of foreign-born in 1890 and of British-born in 1910, and between the percentage distributions of British-born in 1910 and 1930, estimates for 1900 and 1920 were obtained. Extrapolation also yielded an age distribution for 1940.

Unfortunately, in the only reliable statistics of age distribution of British-born (1930 Census Supplement figures), the first age group is

0–20. Although this is too large a group we have had to use it throughout
the period after 1890.

From these estimates of percentage distribution, absolute age
distributions have been calculated separately for England and Wales,
Scotland and Ireland (Tables 63, 64 and 65).

Table 63. *The United States: age distribution of persons born in England
and Wales enumerated in census years, 1870–1940.* (*Thousands*)

Age	1870	1880	1890	1900	1910	1920	1930	1940
0–19	90·0	91·9	137·2	103·7	83·4	57·2	37·4	19·7
20–24	70·5	60·5	101·9	74·7	57·5	48·4	40·8	25·0
25–34	161·1	162·9	223·0	192·4	183·2	150·5	130·3	84·8
35–44	144·8	171·2	190·7	186·8	203·3	175·1	162·5	114·4
45–54	93·7	137·5	165·5	163·5	177·4	177·7	190·3	154·5
55–64	43·9	77·7	111·0	114·0	128·5	138·1	156·4	132·1
65–74	16·9	33·1	56·5	67·3	84·4	90·6	101·7	85·5
75 plus	6·3	9·7	19·7	29·0	40·3	44·0	49·5	41·4

Table 64. *The United States: age distribution of persons born in
Scotland enumerated in census years, 1870–1940.* (*Thousands*)

Age	1870	1880	1890	1900	1910	1920	1930	1940
0–19	20·1	20·9	32·9	24·8	19·8	21·1	31·9	27·1
20–24	15·8	13·8	24·5	20·1	18·8	18·6	25·9	20·4
25–34	36·1	37·1	53·5	51·1	56·6	53·2	71·6	54·5
35–44	32·4	39·0	45·8	46·2	53·8	51·4	70·2	54·2
45–54	21·0	31·3	39·7	40·4	47·8	47·6	67·7	54·5
55–64	9·9	17·7	26·6	27·8	33·2	32·3	45·4	36·0
65–74	3·8	7·7	13·6	15·4	20·3	20·4	29·1	23·5
75 plus	1·4	2·2	4·6	7·0	10·4	9·7	12·8	9·5

Table 65. *The United States: age distribution of persons born in Ireland
enumerated in census years, 1870–1940.* (*Thousands*)

Age	1870	1880	1890	1900	1910	1920	1930	1940
0–19	265·4	228·1	254·5	126·0	28·4	23·9	24·0	19·7
20–24	207·9	150·2	189·0	135·7	89·2	69·5	61·9	45·5
25–34	475·1	404·3	413·6	336·0	263·7	179·4	139·5	87·5
35–44	426·8	424·7	353·7	332·8	302·9	212·6	172·7	114·7
45–54	276·5	341·2	306·9	276·2	240·7	205·4	200·4	160·1
55–64	129·9	192·9	205·9	205·2	193·4	172·2	175·5	145·2
65–74	50·1	83·5	104·8	142·2	160·9	119·3	102·5	72·6
75 plus	18·6	24·1	35·6	56·5	70·3	52·9	45·3	31·9

Death rates

To calculate the decennial rates of survival we require the mean annual specific death rates for the periods 1871–80, 1881–90... 1931–40 for British-born persons residing in the United States. Unfortunately the only relevant mortality rates in existence are for foreign-born persons for 1896–1905, 1906–15... etc. and for the State of Massachusetts over an earlier period. We estimated the death rates of the foreign-born for decades previous to 1896–1905 by applying conversion factors to each age specific rate in the Massachusetts figures. Table 66 shows a comparison of the two death rates for 1900 and 1910 (both per 1,000 in that age group).

Table 66. *Age specific death rates for Massachusetts and for foreign-born whites in the United States, 1900 and 1906–15.* (*Per thousand*)

Age	1900 death rates		1906–15 death rates	
	Massachusetts	Foreign-born white	Massachusetts	Foreign-born white
0– 1	175·8	166·7	148·7	124·7
1– 4	18·7	29·7	14·0	18·9
5–14	3·7	3·8	2·9	3·0
15–24	5·5	5·5	4·1	4·5
25–34	7·5	7·8	6·1	5·9
35–44	9·9	11·2	8·7	9·5
45–54	15·3	18·2	14·3	16·2
55–64	28·9	33·8	29·7	33·8
65–74	58·4	65·3	60·1	67·6
75–84	121·2	132·0	123·0	133·6
85 plus	263·7	272·0	248·5	263·3

Table 67 shows the ratio

$$\frac{\text{Foreign-born white death rate}}{\text{Massachusetts death rate}}$$

for the two periods considered and, in the third column, the conversion factor used to convert Massachusetts death rates to foreign-born death rates for early years.

The rates thus obtained were subjected to interpolation to express them in terms of 1871–85, 1886–95, etc.

The rates finally obtained are shown in Table 68.

For the period after 1890, it is probable that these estimates are too high, since it is fairly certain that 'new' immigrants had a higher age specific death rate than those who came from Western Europe. This might mean that our first estimates slightly overestimate net immigration into the United States.

Table 67. *Conversion factors for deriving death rates of foreign-born in the United States from Massachusetts death rates*

Age	1896–1905	1905–15	Factor
0– 1	0·95	0·84	0·90
1– 4	1·59	1·35	1·47
5–14	1·03	1·03	1·03
15–24	1·00	1·10	1·05
25–34	1·04	0·97	1·01
35–44	1·13	1·09	1·11
45–54	1·19	1·13	1·16
55–64	1·17	1·14	1·15
65–74	1·12	1·12	1·12
75–84	1·03	1·06	1·04
85 plus	1·03	1·06	1·04

Table 68. *The United States: estimated annual death rates by age group for foreign-born persons, 1871–80 to 1931–40. (Per thousand)*

Age	1871–80	1881–90	1891–1900	1901–10	1911–20	1921–30	1931–40
0–20	10·7	8·6	6·8	5·1	4·5	3·5	2·0
20–24	9·4	8·1	6·5	5·0	4·6	3·7	2·2
25–34	10·2	9·9	8·7	6·9	6·0	4·9	2·9
35–44	12·1	12·6	12·1	10·4	8·6	6·9	5·1
45–54	16·0	17·4	18·2	17·2	14·8	12·8	11·3
55–64	26·1	25·8	28·7	33·8	30·8	27·6	25·9
65–74	52·2	59·1	63·7	66·5	65·2	59·5	55·5
75 plus	147·0	167·3	173·0	178·0	175·0	168·0	156·0

Calculation of decennial survival rates from the annual death rates

The survival rate for the ten-year period is calculated by constructing a life table using the mean death rates for each decade. Using Reed and Merrell's tables[1] the values of $_n m_x$ (death rate in the age group x to $x+n$) are transformed into the corresponding values of $_n q_x$ (probability of dying in the age group x to $x+n$). Values of $_n L_x$ (the total number of years lived by those in the age group x to $x+n$ in the ten years considered) are then calculated. The decennial survival factors are then equivalent to $\dfrac{_{10}L_x}{_{10}L_{x-10}}$, i.e. the ratio of the number of years lived

[1] U.S. Bureau of the Census, *Vital Statistics, Special Reports*, vol. IX, no. 54, June 1940, Lowell J. Reed and Margaret Merrell, 'A Short Method for Constructing an Abridged Life Table, being a reprint of Paper No. 212 from the Department of Biostatics, School of Hygiene and Public Health, The Johns Hopkins University, Baltimore'.

by those in a ten-year age group to the number of years lived by those in the last ten-year age group.

If S_{10} is the decennial survival factor for a particular age group at time T, then the number of survivors of that age group ten years later is given by AS_{10}, where A is the original number in that age group at time T. These survivors are then subtracted from the appropriate age group of British-born in the United States at date $T+10$. (The survivors, of course, are now ten years older than at the beginning of the period.) The difference between estimated survivors and residents gives net immigrant survivors for the decade. Two cases now arise, (a) where there is net immigration into America; (b) where there is net emigration out of America.

(a) Let I = true immigration,

  I' = immigrant survivors,

  $S_5 = \dfrac{10 L_{x-5}}{10 L_x}$ = reciprocal of quinquennial survival rate.

Then, assuming all immigration occurs at the middle of the period considered (i.e. in the years 1875, 1885, 1895... 1935), $I'S_5 = I$, and net immigration for the period is found.

(b) In the case of net emigration,

  Let E = true emigration,

  E' = emigrant survivors.

Assuming that as before all emigration occurs in the fifth year of each period, then it appears that we have overestimated the number of deaths occurring in the United States amongst the original cohort, since, as emigration occurs in the fifth year of the decade, these groups would not have been present in America to be subjected to the risk of death in the remaining years of the decade. I.e. $E(1 - 1/S_5)$ is the amount by which we have overestimated the deaths in the original cohort.

$$\therefore\ E' + E\left(1 - \frac{1}{S_5}\right) = E;$$

$$\therefore\ E' = E - E\left(1 - \frac{1}{S_5}\right) = \left[1 - \left(1 - \frac{1}{S_5}\right)\right] = \frac{E}{S_5};$$

$\therefore\ E = E'S_5$ giving a symmetrical result with the case of net immigration.

An example of the calculation is shown below.

1891–1900

Age in 1890	Mean death rate per thousand in decade	$_nm_x$	$_nq_x$	$_np_x$	x	$_nL_x$
0– 1	185·0	·1850	·145823	·854177	100,000	89,443
1– 4	35·5	·0355	·120817	·879183	85,418	313,459
5–14	4·7	·0047	·046073	·953927	75,098	733,680
15–24	6·5	·0065	·063240	·936760	71,638	693,730
25–34	8·7	·0087	·083870	·916130	67,108	642,940
35–44	12·1	·0121	·115000	·885000	61,480	579,450
45–54	18·3	·0183	·169452	·830548	54,410	498,000
55–64	28·7	·0287	·254410	·745590	45,190	394,415
65–74	63·8	·0638	·488575	·511425	33,693	254,620
75–84	128·5	·1285	·757580	·242420	17,231	107,040
85 plus	261·6	·2616	·957721	·042279	4,177	21,770

$$\frac{_{15}L_{10}}{_{15}L_0} = \frac{1,056,771}{1,136,581} = ·92978$$

$$\frac{_{10}L_{25}}{_{10}L_{15}} = \frac{642,940}{693,730} = ·92679$$

$$\frac{_{10}L_{35}}{_{10}L_{25}} = \frac{579,450}{642,940} = ·90125$$

$$\frac{_{10}L_{45}}{_{10}L_{35}} = \frac{498,000}{579,450} = ·85944$$

$$\frac{_{10}L_{55}}{_{10}L_{45}} = \frac{394,415}{498,000} = ·79200$$

$$\frac{_{10}L_{65}}{_{10}L_{55}} = \frac{254,620}{394,415} = ·64556$$

$$\frac{_{10}L_{75}}{_{10}L_{65}} = \frac{107,040}{254,620} = ·42039$$

$$\frac{_{10}L_{85}}{_{10}L_{75}} = \frac{21,770}{107,040} = ·20338$$

$$\frac{_{10}L_{95}}{_{10}L_{85}} = \frac{885}{21,770} = ·04065$$

Age group	$_nm_x$	$_nq_x$	$_np_x$	$_nl_x$	$_nL_x$
10–20	·0056	·054689	·945311	75,368	713,620
20–30	·0076	·073602	·926398	69,356	668,035
30–40	·0104	·099545	·900455	64,251	610,530
40–50	·0152	·142592	·857408	57,855	537,300
50–60	·0235	·212906	·787094	49,605	443,245
60–70	·0463	·381303	·618697	39,044	316,000
70–80	·0962	·645138	·354862	24,156	163,640
80 +	·1951	·895180	·104820	8,592	47,355

$$\frac{{}_{20}L_0}{{}_{20}L_5} = \frac{1{,}487{,}160}{1{,}427{,}410} = 1{\cdot}04186$$

$$\frac{{}_{10}L_{20}}{{}_{10}L_{25}} = \frac{668{,}035}{642{,}940} = 1{\cdot}03903$$

$$\frac{{}_{10}L_{30}}{{}_{10}L_{35}} = \frac{610{,}530}{579{,}450} = 1{\cdot}05364$$

$$\frac{{}_{10}L_{40}}{{}_{10}L_{45}} = \frac{537{,}300}{498{,}000} = 1{\cdot}07892$$

$$\frac{{}_{10}L_{50}}{{}_{10}L_{55}} = \frac{443{,}245}{394{,}415} = 1{\cdot}12380$$

$$\frac{{}_{10}L_{60}}{{}_{10}L_{65}} = \frac{316{,}000}{254{,}415} = 1{\cdot}24107$$

$$\frac{L_{70}}{L_{75}} = \frac{210{,}995}{128{,}810} = 1{\cdot}63803$$

The results yielded by the method for the decade 1890–1900 are shown in Table 69.

The following points should be borne in mind in assessing the accuracy of the method.

1. There is no doubt that some under-registration of births, etc., occurred during certain periods, thus affecting the death rates for the early years of life.

2. Foreign-born death rates are probably higher than those of British-born persons.

3. The correction applied to derive the number of immigrants from the number of immigrant survivors assumes a one-way movement of persons. Actually, the figure of net immigrants is a residue of the inward and outward movement, each with a different age structure. In the interests of accuracy the death rates should be applied to both series and the results compounded, but this is impossible by the nature of the problem.

4. The method assumes, in effect, an even flow of migrants over the decade. This, of course, seldom occurs in practice.

Net immigration into the United States of Canadian-born

The above technique was applied with slight modifications to determine the net migration of Canadian-born persons into the United States.

As no better figures appeared to be available, it was assumed that the death rates used in the previous analysis were also valid in this case.

Table 69. *Estimate from census sources of net immigration of British-born to the United States, 1890–1900.* (*Thousands*)

Age	British-born resident in U.S.A. in 1890 (thousands)	Survivor rate	Survivors 1900 (thousands)	Age 1900	British-born resident in 1900	Immigrant survivors	Factor	Net immigration
—	—	—	—	0– 5	(28·0)	(28·0)	—	—
0–15	246·7	·92978	229·4	5–24	457·0	+227·6	1·04186	+237·1
15–24	493·4	·92679	457·3	25–34	579·5	+122·2	1·03903	+127·0
25–34	690·1	·90125	622·0	35–44	565·8	− 56·2	1·05364	− 59·2
35–44	590·2	·85944	507·2	45–54	480·1	− 27·1	1·07892	− 29·2
45–54	512·1	·79200	405·6	55–64	347·0	+ 58·6	1·12380	+ 65·9
55–64	343·5	·64556	221·7	65–74	224·9	+ 3·2	1·24107	+ 4·0
65–74	174·9	·42039	73·5	75–84	92·5	+ 6·9	1·63803	+ 11·3
75 plus	59·4	·20338	12·1	85 plus	—	—	Total	+225·1

The percentage age distribution of Canadian-born living in the United States was assumed to be the same as that of foreign-born whites in the United States in 1870, 1880 and 1890. Truesdell[1] gives the proper Canadian-born figures for 1910 and 1930. The figures for 1900 and 1920 were obtained by linear interpolation of the 1890, 1910 and 1930 figures.

The numbers of Canadian-born living in the United States are given by Truesdell decennially from 1870 to 1930.[2]

Our estimates are certainly not free from error, but they should provide a useful indication of the direction and approximate size of the net migration. It is interesting to note that Truesdell computes, by a different method, a value for net migration during 1920–30 of 356,000 which may be compared with our value of 382,000.

Net immigration into Canada of British-born

In this case life-table analysis was impossible before 1900. For the subsequent decades the age specific death rates used were those for all Canadian residents. Before 1920 they were obtained from data in Canadian Year Books. For the later years the figures were taken from Vital Statistics reports. The age distribution of British-born was obtained from census estimates, and the general procedure was unchanged.

The final estimates are given in Tables 70, 71 and 72.

Table 73 contrasts these results with other migration data.

Table 70. *Net decennial migration of British-born persons to the United States estimated from American census returns, 1871–80 to 1930–40.* (*Thousands*)

Mean age	1871–80	1881–90	1891–1900	1901–10	1911–20	1920–30	1930–40
0– 4	+ 61·5	+ 93·2	+ 237·1	+ 338·5	+ 342·3	+ 335·4	+ 169·2
5–19	+ 300·4	+ 478·7					
20–29	+ 204·5	+ 353·8	+ 127·0				
30–39	+ 34·7	+ 53·2	− 59·2	+ 29·6	− 29·7	+ 45·5	− 45·6
40–49	− 16·0	− 37·1	− 29·2	− 29·3	− 71·8	+ 63·2	− 4·7
50–59	− 32·5	− 75·5	− 65·9	− 21·5	− 33·7	+ 27·6	− 75·0
60–69	− 2·2	− 23·4	+ 4·0	+ 64·1	+ 6·4	+ 8·8	− 89·3
70–	− 3·6	− 6·1	+ 11·3	+ 18·6	− 44·4	− 24·8	− 74·1
Total	+ 546·8	+ 836·9	+ 225·1	+ 400·0	+ 169·1	+ 454·7	− 119·5

[1] L. Truesdell, *The Canadian Born in the United States*, p. 125, Table 51.
[2] Ibid. p. 26, Table 9.

Table 71. *Net decennial migration of Canadian-born persons to the United States estimated from American census returns, 1871–80 to 1920–30. (Thousands)*

Mean age	1871–80	1881–90	1891–1900	1901–10	1911–20	1921–30
0–19	106·9	223·0	179·4	143·3	146·9	170·3
20–29	88·5	120·2	125·7	100·1	59·8	71·7
30–39	59·6	38·5	56·9	24·9	−26·4	16·2
40–49	40·4	12·2	58·0	19·7	−23·9	42·8
50–59	14·3	−5·7	9·4	−29·9	−37·8	24·7
60–69	7·7	3·7	3·0	83·8	8·9	46·6
70 plus	2·5	2·2	−3·2	−46·1	0·1	9·5
Total	319·9	394·1	429·2	295·8	127·6	381·8

Table 72. *Net decennial migration of British-born persons to Canada estimated from Canadian census returns, 1901–10 to 1931–40. (Thousands)*

Mean age	1901–10	1911–20	1921–30	1931–40
0– 9 ⎱ 10–19 ⎰	170·1	140·5	40·7 67·3	4·2 −3·1
20–29	152·2	103·6	69·5	−12·0
30–39	34·4	51·9	38·6	−14·7
40–49	21·4	24·4	13·2	−12·6
50–59	22·1	8·7	−2·2	−9·9
60–69	24·8	3·4	5·8 ⎱	6·1
70 plus	22·5	0·0	−4·2 ⎰	
Total	447·5	332·5	228·7	−42·0

Table 73. *Net British migration to the United States, 1870–1940: decennial estimates from different sources. (Thousands)*

Period	Census estimates	Board of Trade passenger citizens	Board of Trade net migration	U.S. migration estimates	Willcox's estimates
1871–80	546·8	610*	—	—	739
1881–90	836·9	1169	—	—	1024
1891–1900	225·1	520	—	—	437
1901–10	400·0	638	—	—	528
1911–20	169·1	191	346·6†	399	—
1921–30	454·7	251	319·4	468	—
1931–40	−119·5	−67	−40	—	—

* No figure for 1872.   † Partly estimated.

Table 74. *Net British migration to Canada, 1870–1940: decennial estimates from different sources.* (*Thousands*)

Period	Census estimates	Board of Trade passenger citizens	Board of Trade net migration
1871–80	—	123·7	—
1881–90	—	223·9	—
1891–1900	—	90·3	—
1901–10	447·5	600·1	—
1911–20	332·5	520·8	512·1
1921–30	228·7	418·3	401·5
1931–40	−42·0	−65·3	−63·1

Note. The death rates for the United States used in the above analysis were taken from the following sources:

39th Registration Report of the State of Massachusetts, 1880;
63rd Registration Report of the State of Massachusetts, 1904;
U.S. Bureau of the Census, *Vital Statistics Rates in the United States, 1900–1940,* Washington, 1943.

APPENDIX 2

TIME-SERIES ANALYSIS OF IMMIGRATION AND INVESTMENT: A METHOD OF LOCATING REVERSALS IN DIRECTION OF LAG, AND A SUMMARY OF RESULTS

This note describes the method used to demonstrate the existence of a reversal of lag, and the results achieved.

I. THE ORIGINAL METHOD

We may begin by considering a simple and hypothetical case in which, up to 1870, data A lag one year behind B, while after 1870 data B lag one year behind A.

If our data extend from 1840 to 1900 then the maximum correlation coefficient for 1840–70 will be for a lag (defined to be positive) of one year, while for 1870–1900 it will be for a lag (negative) of one year. If we now calculate the correlation coefficient for 1840–71 with a one-year positive lag, we may expect the coefficient to be lower than that for 1840–70, for while in the latter case the one-year positive lag existed throughout the whole series, in the former case it definitely does not exist in the last year. For 1840–75, the coefficient should be much lower than that for 1840–70, since the one-year positive lag has become a less good description of the relationship between these series. Similarly the coefficient for 1865–1900 with a one-year negative lag should be lower than that for 1870–1900. The switch-year 1870 would thus be a year after which the correlation coefficient for a one-year positive lag for the period 1840–T would markedly decrease as T moved from 1870, while that for a one-year negative lag for the period T–1900 would increase as T approached 1870. Graphically the coefficients could be represented roughly as below.

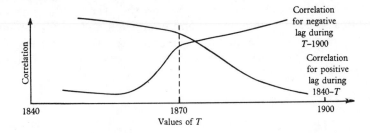

In the more complicated, and also more real, case where the switch-year is replaced by a switch-range, say 1860–80, during which the lagging progressively changes from one year positive to one year negative, the above figure could reasonably be expected to appear rather more like the one below, where the beginning of the switch-range is marked by the maximum value of the positive lag 1840–T coefficient, and the end of the switch-range by the maximum value of the negative lag T–1900 coefficient.

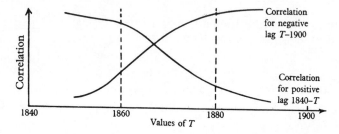

Returning to the graphs of deviations from trend we see that the lags—as far as we can determine them—are of not more than three years. In order to be on the safe side, however, the possibility of lags up to six years either way was admitted. The squares, products, and sums necessary to determine the correlation coefficients for the periods 1831–60, 1831–62, 1831–63..., 1831–99 and 1861–1913..., 1900–13 with lags, for each period, ranging from +6 years to −6 years were then tabulated.

Careful examination of the table revealed that, for the pre-switch period, the coefficients for Railways lagging behind Immigration by one year and by two years would be higher for the periods beginning in 1831 than would the coefficients for other lags for the same periods. Accordingly, only these were calculated. Similarly only lags of one and two years (Immigration now behind Railways) were calculated for the post-switch period.

The resulting coefficients are shown on the accompanying graphs (Figs. 64 and 65) which appear to indicate that a switch commences in 1864 and is completed by 1890. However, the peculiar fluctuations of the graphs could not be ignored, and compelled a closer examination of the figures appearing in the table. The ensuing investigation suggested a modified form of analysis which would be more accurate and entail rather less work.

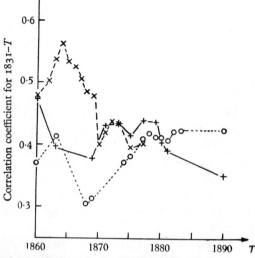

Fig. 64. Correlation coefficients for various lags for periods $1831-T$ for railway miles added in the United States *following* immigration from Great Britain. ××× Lag of 2 years. +++ Lag of 1 year. ooo No lag.

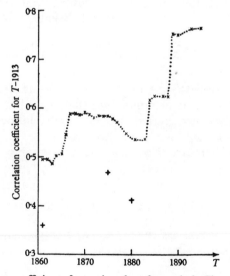

Fig. 65. Correlation coefficients for various lags for periods $T-1913$ for railway miles added in the United States *preceding* immigration from Great Britain. ××× Lag of 1 year. + No lag.

Note. In the above diagrams the lines joining the marked points have no significance: they serve merely to aid the eye.

Consider the formula

$$r = \frac{N\Sigma xy - \Sigma x . \Sigma y}{[\{N\Sigma x^2 - (\Sigma x)^2\}\{N\Sigma y^2 - (\Sigma y)^2\}]^{\frac{1}{2}}}.$$

If we use this to calculate for no lag and then for a one-year positive lag, there is going to be comparatively little change in the values of Σx, Σy, $(\Sigma x)^2$, $(\Sigma y)^2$, Σx^2 and Σy^2. The largest difference is likely to be in the term Σxy for $\Sigma x_t y_t$ has to be replaced by $\Sigma x_t y_{t-1}$.

This suggests that if a column of totals for Σxy for a certain lag gives consistently higher values than the totals of some other column, while the changes in the values of Σx, Σy, Σx^2, Σy^2, etc. that are necessitated by the use of this particular lag are clearly of less consequence than the change in Σxy, then the column that gives the highest Σxy corresponds to the lag that gives the highest coefficient.

Consider Table 75, which is an extract from the worksheet drawn up for the original method, for railway miles added annually in the United States and immigration from Great Britain to the United States.

For a lag of one year, the period 1849–63 is positively correlated (for the values of Σx, Σy, etc. were found to be, in fact, comparatively unimportant, although they were never allowed to go out of sight). The period for the one-year lag is defined thus because:

(1) the years immediately before 1849 have negative values for xy and thus lower the coefficient noticeably if the period is extended before 1849;

(2) the years before 1846 (not shown) alternate in small groups of three or four years negative, and then a similar positive period;

(3) there is only a short period of negative correlation within 1849–63 and then the negative values are small;

(4) after 1863 there are large negative values for xy;

(5) while 1868 marks the beginning of a fairly long period of positive xy this period is described better by a lag in a different direction.

Similarly for a two-year lag, the period as 1849–64 is positively correlated.

For a three-year lag, we define the period as 1849–65. The single negative xy in 1848 is held to mark the beginning of a period because

(1) it is high;

(2) the preceding positive values are much lower;

(3) earlier years behave as described above.

We have thus isolated a definite period of positive correlation that begins in 1849 and ends between 1863 and 1865. That there are similar

Table 75. *The United States: values of xy and of Σxy for various periods and lags for immigration and railway construction*

Year	Immigration one year before railway construction			Immigration two years before railway construction			Immigration three years before railway construction		
	+	−	Σ	+	−	Σ	+	−	Σ
1846	.	*	− 3,037	483	.	− 7,364	*	.	− 1,403
1847	.	*	− 3,106	.	41	− 7,405	*	.	− 1,376
1848	.	*	− 4,077	.	1,061	− 8,467	.	*	− 2,012
1849	*	.	745	1,407	.	− 7,059	*	.	− 474
1850	*	.	14,057	6,210	.	− 849	*	.	1,338
1851	*	.	26,700	16,018	.	15,169	*	.	8,811
1852	*	.	36,170	10,398	.	25,569	*	.	21,984
1853	*	.	42,922	13,172	.	38,739	*	.	36,447
1854	*	.	43,477	774	.	39,513	*	.	37,946
1855	*	.	46,427	1,058	.	40,571	*	.	39,567
1856	*	.	55,682	16,874	.	57,444	*	.	45,620
1857	*	.	58,412	3,871	.	61,315	*	.	52,677
1858	*	.	62,646	2,253	.	63,568	*	.	55,866
1859	.	*	62,499	632	.	64,200	*	.	56,203
1860	.	*	62,418	.	49	64,151	*	.	56,417
1861	*	.	63,848	1,853	.	66,004	*	.	57,544
1862	*	.	66,795	1,284	.	67,288	*	.	59,208
1863	*	.	68,827	2,551	.	69,839	*	.	60,319
1864	.	*	65,004	2,694	.	72,533	*	.	63,701
1865	.	*	63,938	.	2,865	69,668	*	.	65,721
1866	.	*	61,406	.	661	69,008	.	*	63,944
1867	.	*	59,954	.	1,151	67,856	.	*	63,644
1868	*	.	60,029	856	.	68,712	*	.	64,323

Note. Except in the central column the values of *xy* have been replaced by an asterisk in the properly signed column.

Σ for a particular year denotes the sum of the values of *xy* from the year 1831 (or if a one-year lag, from 1832, etc.).

periods earlier or later is of no consequence; here is a period whose correlation is made less good if it be extended either way. Having isolated it, we may investigate its lag.

To determine the lag we note that the respective totals for these periods are 68,827−(−4,077) = 72,904; 72,533−(−8,467) = 81,000; 65,721−(−2,012) = 67,733.

Clearly the biggest total Σ*xy* is for a two-year lag. However, this is for 1849–64, while the smaller value for a one-year lag is for 1849–63. Despite this, the two-year lag seems best, as for the identical periods 1849–63 the total is higher for two years than for one year. Furthermore, with very few exceptions, the totals for sub-periods within 1849–63 are higher for a two-year lag than for a one-year or three-year lag.

We conclude that probably a two-year lag best describes this period. All the time, of course, the other terms involved in computing *r* were borne in mind. It is, however, quite safe to say that even if some peculiarity of the other terms has escaped attention, the best lag is of one or two years—probably two.

Accordingly the values of *r* were computed for the probable best lag (two years) and for the probable second best lag (one). The results were:

   1849–64   two-year lag   Immigration first *r* = 0·898.
   1849–63   one-year lag   Immigration first *r* = 0·700.

The period 1865–70 was difficult. For any short lag, of say up to three or four years, it gave a negative correlation and that not very high. Greater lags were shown, by examining the graphs, to have the effect of omitting peaks that were obviously important. And for the time being this short period of disorder was omitted.

The rest of the period was examined in a similar manner. The disorderly period before 1849 was omitted as a period about which it was not possible to make any definite statement.

1869–83 gave Σxy higher for no lag; second highest for a lag of one year rail first. 1871–83, 1872–83, etc., gave Σxy higher for the one-year lag than for no lag. The beginning of the period was thus put at 1871. The end of the period, 1885, was chosen because of the tendency of the totals to suggest a higher correlation, but for the same lag, for the period beginning 1884 and ending around 1900. The date 1883 is thus a division of the value of correlation rather than lag. The lag period, in full, is 1871 to about 1900. The totals of Σxy for 1901–13 for lags of one, two, or three years were fairly close. The highest totals were for 1899–1913.

The actual procedure was aided by the device shown below. The numbers give Σxy for the period mentioned. Highest totals for the pre-determined periods are boxed. Others to be calculated are marked with an asterisk. That a total has not been put down means simply that it would obviously give a much lower value of *r*.

In the whole of the analysis, reference was constantly made to the graphs of the percentage deviations from trend in order to check the plausibility of particular results. At the same time, an eye was kept on values of Σx^2 etc.

An analysis of this kind, involving yearly data, is complicated by a series of changes in the statistical years. The year of the Riggleman building index ends on June 30 throughout. The Long building index is for calendar years. American rail figures are for calendar years up to 1889, six months in 1890, and for years ending on June 30 thereafter.

Table 76. *The United States: values of Σxy for various periods and lags for immigration and railway construction*

Lag of immigration first by		No lag	Lag of rail first by			
Two years	One year		One year	Two years	Three years	Four years
1849–62 75,754	1849–62 70,872	1849–62 60,735	1850–62 52,919			
1849–59 72,667*	1849–58 66,723	1850–62 50,398	1850–57 53,431*			
1849–64 81,000*	1849–63 72,904*	1849–57 46,389*				
		1869–83 53,528	1868–83 51,798*			
		1871–83 39,357*	1871–83 45,235	1871–83 35,440*		
		1884–88 14,812*	1884–88 19,963			
		1884–98 32,933	1884–98 37,953			
		1901–13 22,957	1901–13 29,395	1901–13 27,630	1901–13 30,427	
		1899–1913 25,074	1899–1913 35,459	1899–1913 35,693	1899–1913 39,489	1899–1913 33,248

Immigration figures taken from the United States sources are subjected to several changes, as mentioned in Chapter IV; the main change in our period is from calendar year up to 1867 to six months in 1868 and thereafter to years ending on June 30. The other series are for calendar years. Unless otherwise stated, the figures used for immigration to the United States from Britain are taken from the American source, and the Riggleman building index is used.

It is possible to allow for a difference in the years of two series. For instance, if series A is for years ending on June 30 and series B for calendar years, then if the analysis reveals a lag of two years, A preceding B, over the period (say) 1870–80, we could interpret the result as implying that on June 30, 1870, the value of A corresponds to a value of B on December 31, 1872, giving a lag of two and a half years.

Similarly if series *B* were first by two years, the result would imply a lag of one and a half years. This device was used in the paper based on this chapter which appeared in *The Manchester School*, September 1951. Further reflexion, however, has led to a reluctance to introduce lags of half a year into an analysis based on yearly data. Not only does it tend to give a wrong impression about the time unit employed, but it might also stretch the result beyond the limits of the data and the method. Consequently, in this book the minimum time unit has been taken as a year, and lags are expressed in terms of this unit, unless quarterly or monthly data are employed. In the paper just mentioned the allowance for the half-year was inadvertently made in the wrong direction in some cases, without substantial effect on the argument. The result for United Kingdom capital exports and United States railway miles for 1885–1901 suffered from an arithmetical slip and should read as given below for a modified period.

The main results are summarized in Table 77.

Table 77. *Main results of the analysis of reversal of lags*

1. Immigration to the United States from Great Britain and railway miles added in the United States

1849–64	Two-year lag	Immigration first	$r=0.898$
1871–83	One-year lag	Rail first	$r=0.868$
1884–98	One-year lag	Rail first	$r=0.880$
1889–1913	Three-year lag	Rail first	$r=0.787$

2. Immigration to the United States from Great Britain and bituminous coal output in the United States

1851–62	Two-year lag	Coal first	$r=0.818$
1870–83	One-year lag	Immigration first	$r=0.830$
1885–98	No lag		$r=0.864$
1899–1913	Four-year lag	Coal first	$r=0.942$

3. Railway miles added in the United States and bituminous coal output in the United States (done as a check)

1853–67	Three-year lag	Coal first	$r=0.849$
1870–82	One-year lag	Rail first	$r=0.896$
1884–	One-year lag	Rail first	$r=0.771$
1901–13	No lag		$r=0.496$

4. Immigration to the United States from Ireland and railway miles added in the United States

1849–64	One-year lag	Immigration first	$r=0.558$
1871–84	One-year lag	Rail first	$r=0.856$
1885–1907	One-year lag	Rail first	$r=0.799$

(*Note.* The period 1871–1907 was divided at 1884 for curiosity, the periods for the previous pairs suggesting such a division. This is the only case in which the periods of one pair have been used in the analysis of another pair.)

5. Immigration to the United States from Europe
and railway miles added in the United States

1847–59	Two-year lag	Immigration first	$r = 0.671$
1871–83	One-year lag	Rail first	$r = 0.868$
1884–1900	One-year lag	Rail first	$r = 0.789$
1901–13	No lag		$r = 0.621$

6. Immigration into the United States from Great Britain
and merchandise imports into the United States

| 1850–64 | Three-year lag | Immigration first | $r = 0.800$ |
| 1871–91 | No lag | | $r = 0.749$ |

The above results show a general agreement which speaks well of the consistency of the method, especially when the limitations of yearly data are borne in mind. The lags given are, of course, average lags over the period concerned. Were quarterly or monthly information available, further variation might possibly be observed. The results suggest a sub-division of the period 1831–1913 into the following approximate sub-periods: 1831–48, 1849–62, 1863–70, 1871–85, 1886–1900 and 1901–13.

Other coefficients, used in Chapters vii and xi, are listed below.

Immigration from Britain during 1871–1883 and American railway miles added: (a) no lag 0.776, (b) immigration one year behind 0.868.

Immigration from Britain during 1870–1883 and American bituminous coal output: (a) immigration behind by one year 0.649, (b) no lag 0.763, (c) ahead by one year 0.830, (d) ahead by two years 0.669.

United Kingdom total exports during 1862–1890 and American railway miles added: (a) no lag 0.784, (b) exports behind by one year 0.861, (c) exports behind by two years 0.678.

American railway miles added during 1868–1878 and United Kingdom capital exports: (a) no lag 0.721, (b) capital exports behind by one year 0.948, (c) capital exports behind by two years 0.903.

Emigration of British citizens to the United States during 1869–79 and new building in the United States (Long): (a) emigration ahead by two years 0.743, (b) ahead by one year 0.776, (c) no lag 0.894, (d) behind by one year 0.904, (e) behind by two years 0.868.

Immigration from Britain during 1869–79 and annual building permits per capita in the United States (Riggleman): (a) immigration ahead by one year 0.904, (b) no lag 0.947, (c) behind by one year 0.929, (d) behind by two years 0.992. Volume of investment in building in Great Britain during 1871–80 and volume of new building in the United States: (a) Britain behind by one year 0.496, (b) no lag 0.556, (c) ahead by one year 0.576, (d) ahead by two years 0.699.

United States merchandise imports during 1871–91 and immigration from Britain: (a) immigration ahead by one year 0.402, (b) no lag 0.749, (c) behind by one year 0.720.

Immigration from Britain during 1884–98 and American railway miles added: (*a*) no lag 0·745, (*b*) immigration behind by one year 0·880.

Immigration from Britain during 1885–98 and American bituminous coal output: (*a*) immigration behind by one year 0·801, (*b*) no lag 0·864, (*c*) ahead by one year 0·581.

American railway miles added during 1886–1907 and United Kingdom exports: (*a*) rail ahead by four years 0·616, (*b*) ahead by three years 0·833, (*c*) ahead by two years 0·737.

New building in the United States during 1885–1903 and emigration of British citizens to the United States: (*a*) immigration ahead by one year 0·777, (*b*) ahead by two years 0·841, (*c*) ahead by three years 0·816.

Immigration from Britain during 1879–1902 and annual building permits per capita in the United States: (*a*) immigration ahead by one year 0·692, (*b*) ahead by two years 0·800, (*c*) ahead by three years 0·737.

Volume of new building in the United States 1884–1904 and volume of investment in building in Great Britain: (*a*) Britain ahead by one year 0·784, (*b*) no lag 0·816, (*c*) behind by one year 0·852, (*d*) behind by two years 0·866.

APPENDIX 3

A BRITISH BUILDING INDEX, 1911–50: METHOD OF CONSTRUCTION

This index is based on the estimated cost of building plans approved in various towns up to 1933 and on the Board of Trade index of activity in building and building materials for 1934–8 and 1946–50. The war years will be mentioned later.

Annual figures of the estimated cost of building plans approved are based on returns made by selected local authorities. The separate figures for each authority are not readily available but a total figure is published in Statistical Abstracts. This figure relates to a varying number of towns: to 80 towns for 1911–12 and 1923–5; to 78 towns for 1911–13 and 1919–21, 1923–30; and to 146 towns for 1924–38. No figures exist for 1922.

The 78-town figures for 1911–13 and 1919–21 were expressed as percentages of the figures for 80 towns in these years. The mean percentage was 99·42 and this was used to adjust the 80-town figures for 1914–18 to 78-town values. With the exception of 1922, there was thus obtained a series of 78 towns for 1911–30. This series and the one for 146 towns for 1924–38 were adjusted for constant costs by using the index described below.

The new series were then used to calculate an index of building at constant costs. To do this the means and standard deviations of both series were calculated for the common period 1924–30. If we denote the mean and standard deviation for 1924–30 by $\bar{x}$ and s for 78 towns and $\bar{X}$ and S for 146 towns, then the annual values X for 146 towns for 1924–38 were converted into values x for 78 towns from the formula:

$$\frac{(X - \bar{X})}{S} = \frac{(x - \bar{x})}{s}.$$

The means of the values of x thus obtained for 1924–30 and the original 78-town values were then taken. Thus an index was obtained comprising the original 78-town figures for 1911–21 and 1923, the means just mentioned for 1924–30 and the adjusted 146-town figures for 1931–8.

The Board of Trade index of building and building materials, based on 1930 = 100, exists for 1934–8 and 1946–50. By the procedure outlined above, taking 1930 and 1934–8 as common years, these figures were converted successively into 146-town and then into 78-town figures. These last values were used in the final index for 1934–8 and 1946–50.

The period 1939–45 was not easy to complete. The estimated value of work done on air-raid damage was subtracted from the estimated value of total construction activity in Great Britain for 1940–6. These net figures were then divided by the level of July weekly wages to obtain an estimate of work done at constant wage rates. The 1946 figure so obtained was divided into the 1946 figure derived from the Board of Trade index and the new war-time figures were then multiplied by this quotient. This may not be a very satisfactory procedure, but, as it does not influence the values for either pre-war or post-war years, it is not open to serious objection.

Finally, the series was divided by the population of England, Wales and Scotland. A constant population equal to the 1946 value was assumed for the years 1940–6.

The final series is thus based on the following figures:

1911–13   Estimated cost of plans approved in 78 towns.
1914–18   Estimated cost of plans approved in 80 towns.
1919–21   Estimated cost of plans approved in 78 towns.
1922   No value.
1923   Estimated cost of plans approved in 78 towns.
1924–30   Estimated cost of plans approved in 78 and 146 towns.
1931–3   Estimated cost of plans approved in 146 towns.
1934–8   Board of Trade index of building and building materials.
1939   No value.
1946–50   Board of Trade index of building and building materials.
1940–5   Ministry of Works: value of construction activity.

Note on building costs

The estimated value of building approved 1911–38 was deflated by the use of a cost index. This was based on the following indices.

1911–22   G. T. Jones's index of building costs (*Increasing Return*, Cambridge University Press, 1933).
1921–32   Colin Clark's index given in the *London and Cambridge Economic Service Special Memorandum* No. 38 (1934).
1924–38   *The Economist* index.

These indices were spliced by the method described above.

APPENDIX 4

STATISTICAL MATERIAL

Table 78. *Immigration of British-born persons to the United States,*
1870–1930

Year	Board of Trade estimates of passenger citizens from U.K. to U.S.A. (thousands)	Board of Trade estimates of emigration from U.K. to U.S.A. (thousands)	U.S.A. estimates of immigration (fiscal years) (thousands)	Year	Board of Trade estimates of passenger citizens from U.K. to U.S.A. (thousands)	Board of Trade estimates of emigration from U.K. to U.S.A. (thousands)	U.S.A. estimates of immigration (fiscal years) (thousands)
1870	153	—	161	1901	104	—	46
1871	151	—	143	1902	108	—	46
1872	162	—	154	1903	124	—	69
1873	167	—	167	1904	146	—	88
1874	114	—	116	1905	122	—	137
1875	81	—	86	1906	145	—	102
1876	55	—	49	1907	170	—	114
1877	46	—	38	1908	97	—	93
1878	55	—	38	1909	110	—	72
1879	92	—	50	1910	132	—	99
1880	167	—	145	1911	122	—	102
1881	176	—	154	1912	117	80*	83
1882	182	—	179	1913	129	95	88
1883	192	—	158	1914	93	70	73
1884	155	—	129	1915	38	29	41
1885	138	—	110	1916	29	23	25
1886	153	—	113	1917	4	2	16
1887	202	—	162	1918	3	2	3
1888	196	—	182	1919	33	24	7
1889	169	—	154	1920	91	77	48
1890	152	—	123	1921	67	56	80
1891	156	—	122	1922	62	50	36
1892	150	—	94	1923	101†	93	61
1893	149	—	79	1924	39	17(2)‡	78§
1894	104	—	53	1925	55	30(5)	54§
1895	127	—	75	1926	60	29(5)	50§
1896	99	—	66	1927	58	26(5)	52§
1897	85	—	41	1928	57	22(4)	45§
1898	80	—	38	1929	64	31(4)	41§
1899	92	—	45	1930	59	27(3)	54§
1900	103	—	48				

* Nine months.

† From 1 April 1923 figures exclude passengers departing from ports in the Irish Free State.

‡ The figures in brackets represent emigrant British citizens from the Irish Free State.

§ Includes Irish Free State.

SOURCES

British: *Statistical Tables relating to Emigration and Immigration from and into the United Kingdom,* issued by the Board of Trade to 1913, and *Board of Trade Journal* for later years.

American: United States Department of Commerce, *Historical Statistics of the United States, 1789–1945,* Washington, 1949, series B 306 and 307, and Ferenczi and Willcox, *International Migrations,* vol. 1, New York, National Bureau of Economic Research, 1929, pp. 384 ff.

Table 79. *Migration of British-born persons from the United States to the United Kingdom, 1908–32*

Year	Board of Trade estimates of migration from U.S.A. to U.K.	Immigrant British citizens, U.S.A. to Irish Free State	U.S. estimates of migration from U.S.A. to U.K. (fiscal years)
1908	—	—	8,196
1909	—	—	4,979
1910	—	—	7,063
1911	—	—	8,681
1912	14,726*	—	11,651
1913	16,619	—	10,774
1914	20,444	—	13,122
1915	16,138	—	11,670
1916	11,044	—	7,715
1917	2,163	—	4,478
1918	1,302	—	1,639
1919	20,571	—	5,898
1920	17,084	—	13,159
1921	13,925	—	10,661
1922	12,611	—	9,184
1923	7,042	—	7,421
1924	10,880	332	6,410
1925	8,045	268	9,670
1926	6,261	197	7,128
1927	6,765	222	7,548
1928	6,775	243	8,753
1929	6,012	277	9,043
1930	7,931	369	7,097
1931	11,501	435	9,534
1932	14,907	542	14,407

* Nine months.

SOURCES
British: *Board of Trade Journal.*
American: *Annual Report of the Commissioner General of Immigration.*

Table 80. *Percentage distribution of immigrants to the United States from the United Kingdom, by occupation, 1875–1930*

Year ended June 30	Professional	Skilled	Farm labourers	Farmers	Common labourers	Servants	Entre- preneurial group	Miscel- laneous	Occupation not stated	TOTAL occupied (%)	TOTAL occupied (number)
1875	1·6	28·2	0·4	6·7	39·8	17·4	3·7	2·0	0·2	100·0	43,815
1876	2·4	32·0	1·0	8·6	30·0	15·7	6·2	3·9	0·2	100·0	24,841
1877	2·7	30·8	1·5	10·1	31·6	13·6	7·0	2·5	0·2	100·0	19,234
1878	1·9	25·9	1·7	10·0	36·3	15·6	5·8	2·4	0·4	100·0	18,507
1879	1·7	28·8	1·2	8·0	39·0	13·7	4·9	2·4	0·3	100·0	26,009
1880	0·6	21·7	0·4	7·2	50·3	16·3	2·3	0·9	0·3	100·0	78,680
1881	0·9	20·1	0·5	6·1	54·2	13·5	2·8	1·4	0·5	100·0	77,656
1882	0·8	22·2	0·1	5·8	54·3	12·7	2·7	1·1	0·3	100·0	93,296
1883	0·7	20·5	—	5·3	49·4	18·9	2·0	1·2	2·0	100·0	83,113
1884	0·8	22·6	—	5·5	46·5	19·6	2·0	1·3	1·7	100·0	69,344
1885	1·0	21·8	—	5·4	46·8	20·5	2·3	1·6	0·6	100·0	59,766
1886	1·2	21·8	—	6·3	46·6	19·2	2·8	1·9	0·2	100·0	63,002
1887	1·0	22·4	—	5·3	50·0	17·5	2·6	1·1	0·1	100·0	90,545
1888	1·5	27·8	—	5·7	45·7	14·4	2·7	2·1	0·1	100·0	96,410
1889	1·4	25·4	—	5·5	43·6	19·6	2·9	1·5	0·1	100·0	83,811
1890	1·9	22·4	—	6·3	43·2	20·5	3·8	1·8	0·1	100·0	69,567
1891	1·9	22·6	—	4·7	42·7	21·9	4·5	1·6	0·1	100·0	68,488
1892	1·7	23·7	—	5·5	38·5	26·2	3·1	1·2	0·1	100·0	61,849
1893	1·5	28·7	—	6·0	30·3	29·1	2·8	1·5	0·1	100·0	54,892
1894	1·5	28·3	—	6·6	23·1	35·6	2·5	2·4	0·02	100·0	36,414
1895	1·5	27·2	—	5·3	21·7	38·9	2·2	3·2	—	100·0	48,283
1896	1·3	24·4	—	5·4	22·8	41·3	1·9	2·9	—	100·0	36,452
1897	1·3	20·7	—	5·5	22·4	43·0	1·9	4·9	0·3	100·0	29,672
1898	1·2	18·3	—	5·3	24·7	42·1	1·5	6·9	0·02	100·0	29,104
1899	1·7	15·0	3·5	1·3	27·7	45·4	1·6	3·8	—	100·0	36,754
1900	1·3	14·9	4·2	1·3	33·1	41·5	1·1	2·6	—	100·0	39,262
1901	1·8	19·2	2·8	1·2	28·9	41·1	1·5	3·5	—	100·0	33,905
1902	2·0	20·2	3·9	1·0	27·3	40·5	1·6	3·5	—	100·0	36,930
1903	4·0	25·9	3·3	1·7	24·0	33·1	3·0	5·0	—	100·0	54,815
1904	6·3	31·3	3·3	1·6	17·3	31·5	5·8	2·9	—	100·0	65,247
1905	4·8	32·8	3·1	2·2	18·3	32·0	4·9	1·9	—	100·0	92,203
1906	5·7	36·5	4·0	2·4	17·6	25·5	4·6	3·7	—	100·0	76,482
1907	5·1	39·9	3·8	2·0	20·2	21·3	3·4	4·3	—	100·0	80,455
1908	5·7	35·3	3·9	2·6	18·6	25·9	3·9	4·1	—	100·0	70,976
1909	9·4	46·7	3·2	3·3	12·5	14·2	6·3	4·4	—	100·0	59,422
1910	7·7	49·6	4·2	3·4	12·7	13·0	5·3	4·1	—	100·0	81,816
1911	8·1	49·0	3·7	3·5	10·6	14·9	4·6	5·6	—	100·0	85,444
1912	9·0	43·5	3·9	3·8	9·6	17·6	5·3	7·3	—	100·0	71,562
1913	9·4	44·5	3·3	3·9	9·4	15·4	5·1	9·0	—	100·0	79,474
1914	10·4	42·6	3·4	4·0	9·1	15·3	5·2	10·0	—	100·0	72,675
1915	14·5	37·7	3·2	5·6	6·8	15·2	5·9	11·1	—	100·0	50,112
1916	12·3	38·8	3·4	6·5	7·2	12·7	7·0	12·1	—	100·0	43,622
1917	11·0	36·5	3·8	8·7	7·8	11·8	6·1	14·3	—	100·0	37,304
1918	13·0	38·7	1·5	6·9	6·3	10·2	3·9	19·5	—	100 0	12,640
1919	10·9	40·8	1·6	5·7	5·4	6·2	4·5	24·9	—	100·0	27,124
1920	10·5	43·7	2·2	5·6	6·7	10·8	4·2	16·3	—	100·0	59,938
1921	9·3	45·7	1·8	4·7	8·1	12·1	3·6	14·7	—	100·0	77,498
1922	11·9	39·2	1·7	5·9	6·4	15·6	4·3	15·0	—	100·0	38,091
1923	6·9	44·6	3·7	4·1	11·8	12·4	2·6	13·9	—	100·0	80,741
1924	6·8	45·6	4·3	4·7	13·3	9·8	2·6	12·9	—	100·0	118,933
1925	7·1	31·6	7·3	6·8	13·2	18·6	3·0	12·4	—	100·0	75,448
1926	6·8	33·9	8·3	5·8	12·3	18·5	3·3	11·1	—	100·0	72,886
1927	6·7	32·9	9·5	5·2	13·3	21·0	3·0	8·4	—	100·0	72,896
1928	7·1	35·5	8·2	4·6	12·3	21·6	2·3	8·4	—	100·0	63,801
1929	7·8	34·2	7·4	4·9	12·2	24·0	2·7	6·8	—	100·0	53,872
1930	7·5	35·5	5·9	3·7	11·1	25·3	3·2	7·8	—	100·0	70,029

SOURCE: Original data taken from returns issued by the United States Bureau of Statistics of the Treasury Department and the *Annual Report of the Commissioner General of Immigration*.

Table 81. *Percentage distribution of immigrants to the United States from England, by occupation, 1875–1930*

Year ended June 30	Professional	Skilled	Farm labourers	Farmers	Common labourers	Servants	Entre-preneurial group	Miscel-laneous	Occupation not stated	TOTAL occupied (%)	TOTAL occupied (number)
1875	2·1	38·8	0·5	7·4	33·7	9·5	5·1	2·5	0·4	100·0	20,541
1876	2·9	40·4	1·4	11·4	23·1	7·0	8·5	5·1	0·2	100·0	12,216
1877	3·8	35·0	1·4	12·7	28·5	5·6	9·5	3·1	0·4	100·0	9,365
1878	2·6	37·0	2·4	11·5	29·1	6·6	7·5	2·6	0·7	100·0	8,466
1879	2·2	38·0	1·1	9·1	33·9	6·2	6·0	2·9	0·6	100·0	12,247
1880	1·0	34·7	0·3	8·9	42·9	6·5	3·5	1·3	0·9	100·0	29,767
1881	1·5	30·6	1·0	8·1	45·9	5·7	4·1	2·1	1·0	100·0	30,355
1882	1·4	28·6	0·03	7·3	51·6	5·1	4·0	1·5	0·5	100·0	39,360
1883	1·4	32·1	—	6·9	41·7	8·4	3·3	2·1	4·1	100·0	29,023
1884	1·4	33·7	—	6·7	40·5	9·8	3·2	1·9	2·8	100·0	28,016
1885	1·6	33·0	—	5·9	41·8	10·3	3·7	2·4	1·3	100·0	23,948
1886	2·0	31·4	—	6·9	43·3	9·1	4·4	2·5	0·4	100·0	25,798
1887	1·7	30·8	—	6·0	47·9	8·1	3·9	1·4	0·2	100·0	37,580
1888	2·5	36·3	—	6·1	40·2	8·3	3·9	2·6	0·1	100·0	41,184
1889	2·2	37·9	—	5·8	37·3	9·9	4·6	2·0	0·3	100·0	33,955
1890	3·2	34·1	—	8·2	35·3	10·2	6·1	2·8	0·1	100·0	29,899
1891	3·4	36·8	—	4·8	32·4	11·3	8·4	2·7	0·2	100·0	27,452
1892	3·4	45·0	—	5·7	24·3	13·3	6·1	2·1	0·1	100·0	21,780
1893	3·1	51·5	—	5·6	16·7	15·5	5·3	2·1	0·2	100·0	19,242
1894	2·8	52·9	—	6·2	11·7	18·0	4·5	3·8	0·1	100·0	11,324
1895	3·3	52·7	—	5·1	12·9	16·0	4·6	5·4	—	100·0	14,677
1896	3·3	52·7	—	5·1	12·9	16·0	4·6	5·4	—	100·0	8,947
1897	4·1	52·1	—	4·9	11·4	12·8	4·4	9·4	0·9	100·0	6,150
1898	3·3	47·8	—	4·6	10·9	13·0	3·6	16·7	0·1	100·0	5,764
1899	6·7	45·6	3·1	2·3	11·6	11·7	5·9	13·1	—	100·0	6,280
1900	5·4	48·6	2·1	3·0	15·7	11·8	4·0	9·4	—	100·0	6,491
1901	5·5	46·9	1·8	2·4	17·2	12·5	3·8	9·9	—	100·0	8,099
1902	6·2	45·9	2·5	2·1	18·2	12·3	4·0	8·8	—	100·0	9,105
1903	8·6	45·9	2·0	2·0	14·0	11·8	6·6	10·4	—	100·0	18,600
1904	11·8	45·9	1·8	2·0	7·7	14·7	11·5	4·6	—	100·0	24,682
1905	10·1	50·2	1·9	2·4	8·8	13·9	10·0	2·7	—	100·0	32,175
1906	10·8	51·2	1·8	2·1	8·9	11·2	8·8	5·2	—	100·0	28,249
1907	8·4	53·5	2·1	1·6	11·8	11·0	5·5	6·1	—	100·0	32,078
1908	9·1	47·1	3·0	2·5	12·6	13·8	6·2	5·7	—	100·0	28,997
1909	9·4	46·7	3·2	3·3	12·5	14·2	6·3	4·4	—	100·0	22,698
1910	7·7	49·6	4·2	3·4	12·7	13·0	5·3	4·1	—	100·0	32,544
1911	8·1	49·0	3·7	3·5	10·6	14·9	4·6	5·6	—	100·0	33,962
1912	9·0	43·5	3·9	3·8	9·6	17·6	5·3	7·3	—	100·0	29,201
1913	9·4	44·5	3·3	3·9	9·4	15·4	5·1	9·0	—	100·0	33,345
1914	10·4	42·6	3·4	4·0	9·1	15·3	5·2	10·0	—	100·0	31,087
1915	14·5	37·7	3·2	5·6	6·8	15·2	5·9	11·1	—	100·0	21,945
1916	12·3	38·8	3·4	6·5	7·2	12·7	7·0	12·1	—	100·0	20,013
1917	11·0	36·5	3·8	8·7	7·8	11·8	6·1	14·3	—	100·0	17,360
1918	13·0	38·7	1·5	6·9	6·3	10·2	3·9	19·5	—	100·0	6,753
1919	10·9	40·8	1·6	5·7	5·4	6·2	4·5	24·9	—	100·0	15,551
1920	10·5	43·7	2·2	5·6	6·7	10·8	4·2	16·3	—	100·0	31,964
1921	9·3	45·7	1·8	4·7	8·1	12·1	3·6	14·7	—	100·0	30,454
1922	11·9	39·2	1·7	5·9	6·4	15·6	4·3	15·0	—	100·0	16,086
1923	8·2	45·6	2·5	4·6	10·3	7·9	3·5	17·4	—	100·0	32,719
1924	7·4	47·6	3·3	5·3	12·0	6·3	3·3	14·8	—	100·0	50,076
1925	10·0	41·5	4·5	7·8	8·8	6·8	4·4	16·2	—	100·0	26,593
1926	10·1	43·3	4·4	6·4	8·9	8·0	4·9	14·0	—	100·0	24,125
1927	10·0	41·7	4·8	6·0	10·4	11·4	4·4	11·3	—	100·0	22,060
1928	10·7	46·3	3·7	5·4	8·7	10·7	3·3	11·2	—	100·0	19,064
1929	11·4	43·7	3·6	6·0	9·1	13·0	4·2	9·0	—	100·0	16,398
1930	11·6	44·8	2·8	4·1	7·5	14·8	4·7	9·7	—	100·0	20,948

SOURCE: See Table 80.

Table 82. *Percentage distribution of immigrants to the United States from Ireland, by occupation, 1875–1930*

Year ended June 30	Professional	Skilled	Farm labourers	Farmers	Common labourers	Servants	Entre-preneurial group	Miscel-laneous	Occupation not stated	TOTAL occupied (%)	TOTAL occupied (number)
1875	0·7	13·3	0·3	5·1	50·9	27·1	1·3	1·1	0·2	100·0	19,446
1876	1·4	16·7	0·8	5·2	43·3	28·1	2·5	1·8	0·2	100·0	9,933
1877	1·2	17·7	0·5	7·0	42·5	25·9	3·2	1·9	0·1	100·0	7,492
1878	1·3	11·2	1·2	7·1	48·5	26·1	2·6	2·0	0·01	100·0	8,222
1879	1·2	11·4	0·9	6·0	52·3	24·2	2·1	1·9	0·03	100·0	10,646
1880	0·3	7·6	0·2	5·7	60·4	24·4	1·0	0·4	0·002	100·0	41,900
1881	0·3	6·9	0·1	4·2	66·5	20·3	1·0	0·6	0·1	100·0	39,232
1882	0·3	10·3	—	3·7	63·9	20·4	0·9	0·5	0·04	100·0	43,503
1883	0·3	10·8	—	4·1	57·1	25·9	0·8	0·5	0·5	100·0	47,040
1884	0·3	11·5	—	4·2	54·3	27·6	0·8	0·6	0·7	100·0	36,293
1885	0·4	9·5	—	4·8	53·8	29·6	0·9	0·9	0·1	100·0	30,497
1886	0·4	7·3	—	5·6	55·3	29·2	1·0	1·2	0·02	100·0	29,916
1887	0·4	7·1	—	4·5	59·2	27·3	0·8	0·7	0·02	100·0	41,680
1888	0·5	8·8	—	5·7	60·5	21·9	1·1	1·5	0·002	100·0	41,002
1889	0·5	8·5	—	5·4	55·0	28·7	1·0	0·9	—	100·0	40,053
1890	0·6	7·6	—	4·6	54·9	30·5	1·2	0·6	0·02	100·0	33,152
1891	0·7	6·9	—	4·5	54·8	31·3	1·1	0·7	—	100·0	34,621
1892	0·5	6·7	—	5·4	50·4	35·6	0·9	0·5	0·01	100·0	34,827
1893	0·5	8·7	—	6·6	42·2	40·1	1·0	0·9	—	100·0	30,075
1894	0·7	11·4	—	6·9	31·2	46·9	1·3	1·6	—	100·0	21,757
1895	0·5	11·7	—	5·5	27·2	52·4	0·8	1·9	—	100·0	30,145
1896	0·5	11·7	—	5·5	27·2	52·4	0·8	1·9	—	100·0	25,285
1897	0·5	9·5	—	5·6	26·3	53·8	1·0	3·2	0·1	100·0	21,815
1898	0·5	8·1	—	5·5	29·4	52·2	0·8	3·5	—	100·0	21,601
1899	0·4	6·3	3·6	1·0	32·1	54·7	0·6	1·3	—	100·0	28,610
1900	0·3	6·2	4·6	0·9	37·7	48·9	0·5	0·9	—	100·0	31,318
1901	0·5	7·8	3·2	0·8	33·7	52·3	0·7	1·0	—	100·0	24,192
1902	0·5	8·4	4·4	0·6	31·5	52·7	0·7	1·2	—	100·0	25,751
1903	0·9	10·5	4·0	1·5	31·7	49·0	0·9	1·5	—	100·0	31,079
1904	1·8	13·2	4·7	1·0	27·7	48·9	1·3	1·4	—	100·0	32,260
1905	1·3	13·4	4·0	2·1	27·8	48·9	1·3	1·2	—	100·0	47,496
1906	1·7	15·1	6·2	2·8	28·7	42·4	1·3	1·8	—	100·0	35,387
1907	1·6	16·3	5·9	2·7	33·9	36·7	1·2	1·7	—	100·0	33,077
1908	2·4	17·0	4·8	2·7	27·3	42·4	1·4	2·0	—	100·0	30,092
1909	2·0	15·8	4·3	2·7	30·6	41·9	1·3	1·4	—	100·0	25,047
1910	1·9	18·1	9·2	3·6	26·5	37·7	1·2	1·8	—	100·0	31,959
1911	2·1	18·6	8·7	2·5	26·3	38·1	1·4	2·3	—	100·0	33,575
1912	2·5	17·0	8·3	2·6	24·9	40·2	1·2	3·3	—	100·0	28,269
1913	2·6	17·0	9·9	3·5	23·4	38·2	1·2	4·2	—	100·0	30,775
1914	3·3	16·0	9·3	3·2	22·5	39·9	1·4	4·4	—	100·0	27,782
1915	4·7	19·4	9·0	4·4	25·1	29·7	1·9	5·8	—	100·0	18,510
1916	5·4	24·4	7·9	5·8	20·1	26·4	2·7	7·3	—	100·0	15,012
1917	5·9	27·8	3·5	7·1	9·2	33·7	3·2	9·6	—	100·0	11,740
1918	9·2	37·9	1·8	8·1	6·5	14·1	2·7	19·7	—	100·0	2,765
1919	8·8	37·1	1·9	7·1	9·4	7·1	3·4	25·2	—	100·0	4,896
1920	6·2	27·5	5·3	5·9	12·6	29·1	2·1	11·3	—	100·0	14,578
1921	3·4	20·2	6·9	3·7	17·3	40·9	1·1	6·5	—	100·0	31,229
1922	5·6	22·0	4·8	4·7	12·1	42·2	1·5	7·1	—	100·0	12,469
1923	4·7	26·9	7·9	4·7	19·2	24·8	1·8	10·0	—	100·0	21,778
1924	4·3	29·4	8·5	5·3	20·5	20·6	1·8	9·6	—	100·0	29,622
1925	3·8	18·7	10·8	5·9	19·4	32·4	1·5	7·5	—	100·0	33,602
1926	3·5	21·7	13·3	5·6	16·9	29·9	1·9	7·2	—	100·0	33,170
1927	3·5	21·9	14·6	4·7	17·1	30·6	1·9	5·7	—	100·0	35,104
1928	3·7	21·5	14·0	4·7	16·7	32·7	1·4	5·3	—	100·0	29,615
1929	4·3	20·6	12·8	4·5	15·9	36·0	1·5	4·4	—	100·0	23,758
1930	3·8	21·0	11·0	4·4	16·1	36·8	1·9	5·0	—	100·0	28,447

SOURCE: See Table 80.

Table 83. *Percentage distribution of immigrants to the United States from Scotland, by occupation, 1875–1930*

Year ended June 30	Professional	Skilled	Farm labourers	Farmers	Common labourers	Servants	Entre-preneurial group	Miscel-laneous	Occupation not stated	TOTAL occupied (%)	TOTAL occupied (number)
1875	3·6	47·0	0·3	11·8	15·7	10·1	8·1	3·3	0·1	100·0	3,596
1876	4·0	49·2	0·3	8·5	11·9	9·4	9·8	6·7	0·2	100·0	2,534
1877	3·0	56·1	5·0	9·8	8·4	6·4	9·3	1·9	0·1	100·0	2,255
1878	2·3	40·2	0·6	16·5	14·2	9·9	13·3	2·8	0·2	100·0	1,716
1879	1·6	53·0	2·5	10·7	11·2	7·2	11·1	2·4	0·3	100·0	2,858
1880	0·9	50·1	2·1	9·3	20·4	10·3	5·3	1·6	—	100·0	6,512
1881	1·2	44·3	0·7	8·6	26·4	9·6	6·7	2·1	0·4	100·0	7,637
1882	1·0	47·8	0·6	9·1	22·5	10·2	5·9	2·2	0·7	100·0	9,747
1883	0·9	37·3	—	6·8	27·2	15·9	5·3	2·6	4·0	100·0	6,276
1884	1·3	40·2	—	7·6	23·7	18·0	4·6	2·2	2·4	100·0	4,692
1885	1·5	41·2	—	7·1	28·6	14·6	4·1	2·1	0·8	100·0	4,840
1886	1·9	47·0	—	7·2	22·8	13·9	4·9	2·3	—	100·0	6,785
1887	1·3	51·6	—	6·2	21·6	12·8	4·7	1·7	0·1	100·0	10,448
1888	1·8	58·0	—	4·7	18·6	10·6	3·8	2·5	0·01	100·0	13,484
1889	2·3	50·9	—	5·1	19·0	16·2	4·3	2·2	—	100·0	9,218
1890	3·1	44·4	—	6·5	19·8	17·0	6·3	2·9	0·03	100·0	6,215
1891	2·1	45·9	—	4·9	21·4	16·9	6·3	2·3	0·2	100·0	6,190
1892	2·4	48·7	—	5·3	18·4	17·6	5·3	2·3	0·02	100·0	4,928
1893	2·2	58·5	—	3·9	12·0	17·0	4·3	2·1	0·02	100·0	5,148
1894	2·2	52·9	—	5·4	8·2	23·5	4·5	3·3	0·03	100·0	2,914
1895	2·4	53·2	—	4·5	8·9	21·9	4·3	4·8	—	100·0	2,732
1896	2·4	53·2	—	4·5	8·9	21·9	4·3	4·8	—	100·0	1,616
1897	2·5	50·2	—	4·2	11·9	14·3	5·5	10·7	0·7	100·0	1,159
1898	2·5	47·2	—	4·5	10·2	13·7	3·4	18·5	—	100·0	1,087
1899	5·7	44·9	3·5	2·0	10·3	18·2	4·0	11·4	—	100·0	1,157
1900	3·9	52·6	4·1	1·0	12·1	14·7	2·7	8·9	—	100·0	1,075
1901	3·8	53·9	1·7	1·2	12·6	14·4	1·8	10·6	—	100·0	1,218
1902	3·8	52·5	2·0	1·1	16·0	12·5	2·3	9·8	—	100·0	1,586
1903	6·7	50·4	3·2	2·1	13·2	14·2	3·2	7·0	—	100·0	4,395
1904	7·5	57·7	2·1	2·0	5·4	14·1	7·2	4·0	—	100·0	7,157
1905	4·9	61·9	2·4	2·1	6·6	13·8	5·8	2·5	—	100·0	10,938
1906	5·6	62·8	2·4	1·7	6·0	10·5	4·9	6·1	—	100·0	11,207
1907	5·8	63·1	2·9	1·4	7·5	9·4	3·8	6·1	—	100·0	13,574
1908	6·4	51·7	4·1	2·6	11·5	13·6	4·4	5·7	—	100·0	10,287
1909	5·3	56·0	4·3	2·8	10·6	13·0	3·3	4·7	—	100·0	10,701
1910	5·5	57·0	3·8	3·4	9·7	12·8	3·1	4·7	—	100·0	15,913
1911	4·8	54·6	3·8	2·7	8·9	16·6	3·0	5·6	—	100·0	16,356
1912	5·6	46·7	4·1	3·1	8·2	21·5	3·3	7·5	—	100·0	12,595
1913	7·4	45·7	3·9	3·3	8·3	18·5	3·4	9·5	—	100·0	13,494
1914	7·9	44·4	3·5	3·9	9·4	18·2	3·4	9·3	—	100·0	12,122
1915	10·5	41·3	3·1	5·8	6·8	18·8	3·5	10·2	—	100·0	8,783
1916	9·4	40·2	3·8	7·0	6·9	16·5	5·6	10·6	—	100·0	7,986
1917	8·5	39·4	3·6	9·1	7·1	15·2	4·6	12·5	—	100·0	7,712
1918	10·2	37·4	1·3	6·5	4·5	18·6	2·5	19·0	—	100·0	2,962
1919	9·0	44·2	1·4	5·5	5·3	8·7	3·1	22·8	—	100·0	6,276
1920	9·4	45·9	2·3	5·1	7·1	12·4	3·2	14·6	—	100·0	12,538
1921	7·4	49·2	1·9	3·9	7·2	14·0	2·5	13·9	—	100·0	14,742
1922	9·9	43·7	1·7	4·7	6·1	17·1	3·1	13·7	—	100·0	8,999
1923	7·1	58·1	1·6	2·9	7·7	7·6	2·2	12·8	—	100·0	25,267
1924	8·0	55·1	2·4	3·5	9·5	6·2	2·4	12·9	—	100·0	37,625
1925	9·3	43·1	4·1	7·1	7·5	8·9	3·7	16·3	—	100·0	14,707
1926	8·8	44·8	4·1	5·2	8·2	10·5	3·7	14·7	—	100·0	14,775
1927	9·4	44·9	4·5	4·8	9·2	13·4	3·5	10·3	—	100·0	14,992
1928	9·2	48·9	2·7	3·4	8·4	14·0	2·7	10·7	—	100·0	14,165
1929	9·7	45·8	2·6	4·1	9·7	16·6	3·0	8·5	—	100·0	12,757
1930	8·4	45·5	1·8	2·2	8·0	20·7	3·5	9·9	—	100·0	19,447

SOURCE: See Table 80.

Table 84. *Percentage distribution of immigrants to the United States from Wales, by occupation, 1875–1930*

Year ended June 30	Professional	Skilled	Farm labourers	Farmers	Common labourers	Servants	Entrepreneurial group	Miscellaneous	Occupation not stated	TOTAL occupied (%)	TOTAL occupied (number)
1875	—	51·7	—	6·5	20·7	14·2	4·3	2·2	0·4	100·0	232
1876	2·5	67·1	0·6	12·7	8·9	1·9	2·5	3·8	—	100·0	158
1877	0·8	48·4	0·8	9·0	31·2	4·9	4·9	—	—	100·0	122
1878	1·9	55·3	—	14·6	20·4	4·9	1·0	1·9	—	100·0	103
1879	0·4	45·3	—	6·6	41·1	3·9	2·3	0·4	—	100·0	258
1880	0·4	52·5	—	6·8	34·1	3·4	1·0	1·8	—	100·0	501
1881	0·7	52·5	—	6·7	28·7	3·7	1·9	5·8	—	100·0	432
1882	0·3	37·7	—	7·9	47·7	2·3	1·5	2·6	—	100·0	686
1883	0·1	42·5	—	4·6	46·8	4·8	0·3	0·9	—	100·0	774
1884	0·6	46·3	—	7·6	34·1	8·2	2·0	1·2	—	100·0	343
1885	1·9	46·4	—	8·5	31·8	6·0	1·4	4·0	—	100·0	481
1886	1·2	49·9	—	11·9	25·6	7·4	2·2	1·8	—	100·0	503
1887	0·5	45·4	—	4·6	43·0	4·2	1·3	1·0	—	100·0	837
1888	1·2	55·4	—	4·3	32·9	3·5	1·6	1·1	—	100·0	740
1889	0·5	57·4	—	7·2	24·1	6·0	1·7	3·1	—	100·0	585
1890	1·7	41·9	—	7·3	32·5	9·6	3·3	2·0	1·7	100·0	301
1891	3·6	55·5	—	5·3	24·9	4·9	3·6	2·2	—	100·0	225
1892	0·3	35·4	—	9·2	38·2	12·1	2·2	2·6	—	100·0	314
1893	0·7	56·0	—	8·0	27·1	4·0	2·3	1·9	—	100·0	427
1894	1·4	63·3	—	7·4	14·8	9·5	1·2	2·4	—	100·0	419
1895	1·8	58·1	—	7·4	19·4	7·5	2·5	3·3	—	100·0	731
1896	1·8	58·1	—	7·4	19·4	7·5	2·5	3·3	—	100·0	604
1897	2·7	53·1	—	9·3	11·3	13·7	2·2	7·7	—	100·0	548
1898	1·7	46·8	—	6·7	15·9	10·6	2·5	15·8	—	100·0	652
1899	2·8	47·4	5·5	1·3	23·3	11·5	1·7	6·5	—	100·0	707
1900	4·5	47·6	10·6	0·5	15·1	14·0	1·9	5·8	—	100·0	378
1901	4·0	43·7	6·8	1·5	18·4	18·7	2·3	4·6	—	100·0	396
1902	2·9	55·1	7·6	1·0	12·9	13·3	2·5	4·7	—	100·0	488
1903	5·0	55·5	5·4	2·1	13·1	12·1	2·3	4·5	—	100·0	741
1904	6·7	61·4	2·9	2·2	8·2	13·0	3·1	2·5	—	100·0	1,148
1905	4·9	57·7	3·1	2·9	7·3	17·6	4·7	1·8	—	100·0	1,594
1906	4·9	62·4	3·1	4·1	8·4	10·0	4·0	3·1	—	100·0	1,639
1907	5·0	58·4	2·3	2·9	12·4	11·1	3·5	4·4	—	100·0	1,726
1908	5·9	59·3	2·8	3·0	8·9	11·4	5·1	3·6	—	100·0	1,600
1909	6·6	55·8	4·1	5·8	11·9	9·8	3·1	2·9	—	100·0	976
1910	6·7	54·4	5·5	4·2	11·1	11·2	3·6	3·3	—	100·0	1,400
1911	6·6	53·3	5·2	3·4	10·9	14·6	3·0	3·0	—	100·0	1,551
1912	7·5	50·7	5·6	5·1	7·1	14·5	3·1	6·4	—	100·0	1,497
1913	7·2	54·3	3·9	4·7	6·6	14·1	3·4	5·8	—	100·0	1,860
1914	7·7	50·5	4·5	4·4	7·7	14·7	3·8	6·7	—	100·0	1,684
1915	10·3	47·5	4·9	6·1	5·3	14·6	2·6	8·7	—	100·0	874
1916	12·9	42·1	2·3	7·0	5·9	14·6	5·9	9·3	—	100·0	611
1917	9·1	40·2	2·9	11·4	5·5	14·0	4·3	12·6	—	100·0	492
1918	18·1	40·0	1·2	10·6	6·3	5·0	4·4	14·4	—	100·0	160
1919	8·7	48·9	1·7	7·5	4·2	4·5	4·0	20·5	—	100·0	401
1920	6·5	48·5	2·3	6·4	6·3	14·9	3·9	11·2	—	100·0	858
1921	7·7	50·7	2·9	4·0	6·9	14·6	2·1	11·1	—	100·0	1,073
1922	10·2	45·4	1·5	5·2	4·9	18·4	3·2	11·2	—	100·0	537
1923	8·1	55·0	3·5	4·4	6·2	10·3	3·1	9·4	—	100·0	977
1924	9·5	57·8	2·0	4·4	7·9	5·0	3·0	10·4	—	100·0	1,610
1925	12·6	39·4	4·6	10·6	7·0	7·7	4·9	13·2	—	100·0	546
1926	10·3	52·4	1·6	4·5	4·7	7·4	3·9	15·2	—	100·0	816
1927	11·4	47·7	4·2	11·2	5·9	5·4	3·3	10·9	—	100·0	740
1928	9·9	54·2	2·8	7·0	5·4	7·5	2·6	10·6	—	100·0	957
1929	9·2	53·8	1·1	7·3	5·3	10·2	3·1	10·0	—	100·0	959
1930	11·5	51·4	1·6	4·8	5·8	11·6	4·1	9·2	—	100·0	1,187

SOURCE: See Table 80.

Table 85. *Adult males and females emigrating from the United Kingdom, by destination and occupation, 1928*

MALE

Destination	Over 17 years of age											12–17 years	Children
	Agricultural	Commercial	Professional	Mining	Metal	Building	Other	Transport	Labourers	Other	Total		
British North America	8,850	2,408	328	4,205	1,825	425	1,961	844	4,730	1,483	27,059	4,492	3,622
New Zealand	415	305	75	109	137	18	166	43	79	212	1,559	479	375
Australia	1,881	1,733	265	914	884	210	1,124	444	930	1,233	9,718	2,789	2,614
South America*	56	578	142	20	202	5	68	54	3	113	1,241	48	128
U.S.A.	594	1,216	157	888	1,126	205	1,181	258	1,162	1,031	7,818	979	2,004
British South Africa	233	728	291	107	422	53	322	89	20	600	2,865	210	492
India	202	680	364	26	398	3	107	112	5	518	2,419	53	492
Other foreign countries	19	442	238	4	242	5	61	67	—	174	1,252	37	247
Other British countries	228	1,097	793	78	570	20	204	139	13	579	3,921	77	332

FEMALE

Destination	Over 17 years of age							12–17 years	Children
	Domestic	Commercial	Professional	Clothing	Wife or housewife	Other	Total		
British North America	5,724	672	377	197	6,615	924	14,509	1,606	3,418
New Zealand	569	131	103	38	929	273	2,043	162	357
Australia	2,714	758	454	232	4,650	1,272	10,080	1,332	2,281
South America*	42	50	93	3	395	214	797	52	137
U.S.A.	1,771	829	310	335	4,360	1,091	8,696	1,018	1,830
British South Africa	136	244	317	44	1,405	769	2,915	174	442
India	196	53	464	8	1,233	941	2,895	112	531
Other foreign countries	55	56	241	3	611	316	1,282	52	234
Other British countries	57	74	343	11	1,213	763	2,461	79	317

* Excluding British territories.

Based on material kindly supplied by the Board of Trade.

Table 86. Occupational distribution of adult male and female emigrants of British nationality from the United Kingdom to extra-European countries, 1921–38

	Great Britain and Ireland				Great Britain and Northern Ireland														
	1921	1922	1923	1924	1924	1925	1926	1927	1928	1929	1930	1931	1932	1933	1934	1935	1936	1937	1938
MALES:																			
Agricultural	13,454	12,937	26,223	18,984	12,222	9,912	14,238	14,460	12,478	12,314	6,174	1,169	840	763	864	811	726	895	1,033
Commercial, finance and insurance	12,404	9,706	12,960	9,438	8,922	8,574	9,798	10,205	9,187	9,822	7,848	2,799	2,208	2,050	2,462	2,668	2,465	3,001	3,283
Professional	5,583	4,404	4,387	3,761	3,483	3,543	3,492	2,934	2,653	2,369	2,635	1,917	1,441	1,716	1,551	1,740	1,690	1,964	2,052
Skilled trades:																			
Mining and quarrying	3,577	4,836	7,300	2,774	2,745	3,612	5,558	3,802	6,351	3,903	1,329	187	130	177	321	291	229	350	254
Metal and engineering	8,016	10,536	24,724	7,742	7,487	7,515	8,676	7,806	5,806	6,561	3,587	1,040	1,279	1,500	1,644	1,568	1,535	1,686	1,623
Building	1,345	1,525	3,642	1,507	1,397	1,008	1,189	1,394	944	1,224	656	140	93	112	123	97	118	255	197
Other	8,151	7,835	16,867	6,906	6,630	5,030	6,711	5,543	5,194	6,238	4,121	709	427	480	601	661	599	1,075	1,031
Transport and communications	3,096	3,009	4,573	2,745	2,664	2,198	2,584	2,398	2,050	2,267	1,137	364	247	214	244	278	301	355	387
Labourers not in agriculture or transport	9,661	7,022	19,017	6,834	5,505	4,224	4,989	5,057	6,942	5,842	2,548	161	110	140	147	88	103	127	151
Other and ill-defined occupations	7,918	8,462	10,495	8,240	7,908	6,183	7,401	7,142	5,947	6,561	4,496	2,379	2,264	2,279	2,789	2,643	2,863	2,477	2,326
Total*	73,205	70,272	130,188	68,931	58,903	51,799	64,636	60,741	57,552	57,101	34,531	10,865	9,039	9,431	10,746	10,845	10,629	12,185	12,337
FEMALES:																			
Domestic, hotel, etc., service	21,986	18,025	23,580	18,797	13,125	11,789	13,422	13,219	11,264	13,633	8,532	1,972	931	960	980	924	696	854	960
Commercial, finance and insurance	4,471	3,099	4,289	3,079	2,901	3,399	3,644	3,341	2,867	3,541	3,267	777	500	425	598	694	631	851	1,059
Professional	4,999	4,180	3,674	2,720	2,483	2,747	2,917	2,987	2,702	3,040	3,023	1,635	1,537	1,417	1,687	1,540	1,765	1,837	2,042
Clothing trades	2,148	1,809	2,365	1,502	1,407	1,593	1,551	1,094	874	1,106	851	159	90	126	126	97	122	136	138
Wife or housewife	38,904	30,884	39,106	29,537	28,365	24,958	28,365	25,502	21,411	21,966	15,512	7,356	6,653	5,969	6,397	7,073	7,388	7,833	8,519
Other and ill-defined occupations	9,014	7,816	9,707	7,298	7,010	6,756	7,279	6,775	6,560	7,427	6,132	3,715	2,777	3,281	3,055	3,408	3,577	2,952	3,118
Total*	81,522	65,753	82,721	62,933	55,493	51,242	57,178	52,918	45,678	50,713	37,317	15,614	12,488	12,178	13,443	13,736	14,179	14,463	15,836

* Including a small number of migrants of 12 years of age and over whose ages were not specified. Residence for a year or more is treated as permanent residence for the purpose of this table.

SOURCE: *Board of Trade Journal.*

Table 87. *Occupational distribution of adult male and female immigrants of British nationality to the United Kingdom from extra-European countries, 1921–38*

	Great Britain and Ireland				Great Britain and Northern Ireland														
	1921	1922	1923	1924	1924	1925	1926	1927	1928	1929	1930	1931	1932	1933	1934	1935	1936	1937	1938
MALES:																			
Agricultural	2,884	2,373	2,243	2,649	2,510	2,403	2,202	2,581	2,789	3,022	3,698	3,955	3,402	2,451	1,943	1,583	1,430	1,413	1,253
Commercial, finance and insurance	5,810	5,151	4,348	4,693	4,581	4,217	3,738	4,454	4,350	4,208	4,588	5,042	5,387	4,549	3,785	3,422	3,467	2,990	3,284
Professional	3,467	3,622	2,807	2,814	2,702	2,568	2,346	2,497	2,358	2,502	2,735	2,816	2,866	2,611	2,471	2,314	2,382	2,247	2,247
Skilled trades: Mining and quarrying	1,249	737	779	1,355	1,331	856	562	693	2,166	712	876	993	1,027	636	298	390	356	360	283
Metal and engineering	2,881	2,557	2,893	4,118	4,065	3,019	2,459	2,732	3,064	2,634	3,159	3,679	3,959	2,585	1,983	1,901	2,056	1,851	2,066
Building	614	408	482	687	677	387	322	351	396	392	456	625	1,236	457	204	109	113	118	88
Other	3,495	2,546	2,130	3,317	3,244	1,955	1,854	2,305	2,662	2,519	4,130	4,446	4,033	2,134	1,335	1,128	1,141	1,116	922
Transport and communications	1,257	1,190	1,026	1,147	1,102	830	780	955	1,207	1,097	1,042	1,114	1,263	745	530	546	642	605	599
Labourers not in agriculture or transport	2,287	1,545	1,262	1,945	1,638	1,401	1,094	1,190	3,165	1,812	2,722	3,509	3,252	1,663	1,094	737	637	566	516
Other and ill-defined occupations	4,848	4,613	4,156	4,697	4,492	3,662	3,653	4,085	3,812	3,527	3,959	4,554	4,840	4,592	3,858	3,899	4,054	3,229	2,878
Total	28,792	24,742	22,126	27,422	26,342	21,298	19,010	21,843	25,969	22,425	27,365	30,733	31,265	22,423	17,501	16,029	16,278	14,495	14,136
FEMALES:																			
Domestic, hotel, etc., service	2,932	3,531	2,797	3,590	3,028	2,793	2,909	2,423	2,926	3,483	4,497	4,046	4,272	2,119	1,265	998	935	881	602
Commercial, finance and insurance	959	952	880	1,130	1,078	1,025	803	856	812	984	931	931	1,109	1,023	715	727	811	840	798
Professional	1,989	2,296	1,967	1,686	1,637	1,660	1,640	2,026	1,877	1,997	2,132	2,115	1,776	2,046	2,226	2,055	1,996	1,988	2,115
Clothing trades	499	493	344	380	361	306	227	214	276	244	288	278	347	235	211	137	128	139	103
Wife or housewife	15,676	15,066	12,399	13,286	12,957	12,903	11,223	12,366	11,884	11,773	12,939	14,109	16,097	14,947	14,305	13,544	13,006	12,171	11,581
Other and ill-defined occupations	5,268	5,823	5,420	5,349	5,221	3,781	3,997	4,211	3,797	3,488	3,724	3,681	4,082	3,171	2,157	2,677	3,642	2,685	2,544
Total	27,323	28,161	23,807	25,421	24,282	22,468	20,799	22,096	21,572	21,969	24,511	25,160	27,683	23,541	20,879	20,138	20,518	18,704	17,743

SOURCE: *Board of Trade Journal.*

Table 88. *Persons of British nationality emigrating from the United Kingdom to extra-European countries by country of future permanent residence, 1913 and 1920–38*

Year	Total	British North America	Australia	New Zealand	South Africa	India including Ceylon	Other British possessions	Total Empire	U.S.A.	Other foreign countries	Total foreign
1913	389,394	190,854	56,779	14,255	10,916	6,810	5,432	285,046	94,691	9,657	104,348
1920	285,102	118,837	28,974	14,853	15,157	12,188	8,585	198,594	77,151	9,357	86,508
1921	199,477	67,907	27,751	11,513	12,903	9,830	6,873	136,777	56,393	6,307	62,700
1922	174,096	45,818	39,099	12,259	8,772	7,054	5,408	118,410	49,902	5,784	55,686
1923*	256,284	88,290	39,967	9,392	7,629	6,344	5,440	157,062	93,076	6,146	99,222
1924	155,374	63,016	38,599	11,061	7,568	6,630	5,343	132,217	17,315	5,842	23,157
1925	140,594	38,662	35,006	11,730	7,004	6,584	6,239	105,225	29,549	5,820	35,369
1926	166,601	49,632	44,513	16,565	8,295	6,799	6,502	132,306	28,740	5,555	34,295
1927	153,505	52,916	40,991	7,841	7,572	6,476	6,937	122,733	25,662	5,110	30,772
1928	136,834	54,709	28,714	4,975	7,095	6,502	6,987	108,982	22,345	5,507	27,852
1929	143,686	65,558	18,377	4,700	5,766	6,265	6,234	106,900	30,709	6,077	36,786
1930	92,158	31,074	8,517	3,981	4,559	5,636	5,474	59,241	27,336	5,581	32,917
1931	34,310	7,620	4,459	2,266	3,441	5,081	4,284	27,151	2,593	4,566	7,159
1932	26,988	3,104	4,595	1,554	2,453	5,403	4,140	21,249	1,285	4,454	5,739
1933	26,256	2,243	4,200	1,233	2,587	5,890	4,607	20,760	1,331	4,165	5,496
1934	29,230	2,167	4,572	1,191	3,392	6,096	5,548	22,966	2,028	4,236	6,264
1935	29,781	2,175	4,552	1,440	4,994	5,940	5,155	24,256	1,590	3,935	5,525
1936	29,836	2,281	4,096	1,462	5,010	6,160	5,476	24,485	1,639	3,712	5,351
1937	31,764	2,850	4,122	1,981	5,577	5,632	5,949	26,111	2,423	3,230	5,653
1938	34,144	3,367	5,472	2,425	6,003	5,540	6,201	29,008	1,992	3,144	5,136

* From April 1, 1923, the figures exclude passengers departing from ports in the Irish Free State.
Source: *Board of Trade Journal.*

Table 89. *Persons of British nationality migrating to the United Kingdom from extra-European countries by country of last permanent residence, 1913 and 1920–38*

Year	Total	British North America	Australia	New Zealand	South Africa	India including Ceylon	Other British possessions	Total Empire	U.S.A.	Other foreign countries	Total foreign
1913	85,709	26,288	12,351	2,446	10,541	5,928	3,971	61,525	16,619	7,565	24,184
1920	86,055	24,341	12,854	2,568	7,313	11,999	4,802	63,877	17,084	5,094	22,178
1921	71,367	21,055	8,861	1,568	5,894	9,393	5,776	52,547	13,925	4,895	18,820
1922	68,026	16,197	8,310	2,223	7,509	9,809	5,639	49,687	12,611	5,728	18,339
1923*	57,606	12,424	8,384	2,204	7,103	8,750	5,573	44,438	7,042	6,126	13,168
1924	64,112	15,822	8,295	2,321	6,919	8,734	5,265	47,356	10,880	5,876	16,756
1925	56,335	13,939	7,737	1,964	5,412	8,188	5,099	42,339	8,045	5,951	13,996
1926	51,063	10,481	7,599	2,172	5,575	8,087	5,165	39,079	6,261	5,723	11,984
1927	55,715	12,570	8,032	2,511	5,433	7,821	5,817	42,184	6,765	6,766	13,531
1928	59,105	15,804	8,395	2,911	5,558	7,604	5,898	46,170	6,775	6,160	12,935
1929	56,217	12,294	9,516	2,704	4,872	8,152	6,411	43,949	6,012	6,256	12,268
1930	66,203	15,820	12,808	3,144	4,416	8,581	6,673	51,442	7,931	6,830	14,761
1931	71,382	17,864	11,747	3,623	4,666	8,448	6,833	53,181	11,501	6,700	18,201
1932	75,595	21,187	7,700	3,327	6,060	8,401	7,594*	54,269	14,907	6,419	21,326
1933	59,324	16,371	6,417	2,112	4,781	8,084	6,877	44,642	9,144	5,538	14,682
1934	49,843	12,128	6,022	1,925	3,978	7,748	7,045	38,846	5,919	5,078	10,997
1935	46,244	9,712	5,228	2,206	3,752	8,027	6,860	35,785	5,042	5,417	10,459
1936	47,242	10,107	5,362	1,966	3,594	9,022	7,273	37,324	4,166	5,752	9,918
1937	42,628	8,970	4,649	1,864	3,973	7,713	6,998	34,167	3,057	5,404	8,461
1938	40,611	7,341	3,892	1,801	3,966	8,273	7,325	32,598	3,484	4,529	8,013

* From April 1, 1923, the figures exclude passengers arriving at ports in the Irish Free State.
SOURCE: *Board of Trade Journal.*

Table 90. Male and female emigrants from Ireland classified into five-year age groups, annually, 1861–1910

Years		Under 1 year	1 and under 5	5 and under 10	10 and under 15	15 and under 20	20 and under 25	25 and under 30	30 and under 35	35 and under 40	40 and under 45	45 and under 50	50 and under 55	55 and under 60	60 and upwards	Ages not specified	Total males and females	Total
		(1)	(2)	(3)	(4)	(5)	(6)	(7)	(8)	(9)	(10)	(11)	(12)	(13)	(14)	(15)	(16)	(17)
1861	Males	445	2,079	1,830	1,449	3,035	9,481	6,246	2,272	1,343	1,282	561	374	113	124	1,739	32,373	64,292
	Females	478	1,960	1,675	1,362	4,521	9,184	4,659	1,958	1,370	1,612	694	571	149	175	1,587	31,919	
1862	Males	320	2,331	2,069	1,362	3,264	11,108	6,717	2,366	1,283	1,237	748	507	179	128	2,927	36,546	70,117
	Females	311	2,222	1,895	1,368	4,692	10,256	3,948	2,066	1,233	1,223	634	619	169	203	2,732	33,571	
1863	Males	403	3,641	3,266	2,656	5,354	19,739	10,993	4,288	2,031	2,103	1,212	1,048	315	308	3,949	61,306	117,229
	Females	506	3,536	3,277	2,559	7,669	18,094	6,624	3,414	1,756	1,933	1,161	1,161	292	354	3,587	55,923	
1864	Males	417	3,908	3,183	2,351	4,097	17,700	12,539	4,615	1,818	1,895	1,234	1,282	324	270	5,059	60,692	114,169
	Females	509	3,956	3,004	2,321	5,071	17,074	7,140	3,568	1,722	1,933	1,300	1,522	297	385	3,675	53,477	
1865	Males	320	2,901	2,670	2,192	4,128	17,943	10,708	3,990	1,535	1,906	832	906	209	278	4,696	55,214	101,497
	Females	360	2,826	2,482	1,848	4,589	15,438	6,222	2,814	1,334	1,790	911	1,067	229	367	4,006	46,283	
1866	Males	157	2,486	2,487	1,966	4,902	22,873	12,411	6,014	2,237	1,951	600	659	243	249	326	59,561	99,467
	Females	196	2,321	2,188	1,668	5,819	14,869	5,224	2,800	1,153	1,415	591	814	229	278	341	39,906	
1867	Males	182	1,593	1,946	1,752	4,509	16,676	8,056	4,920	1,803	1,354	717	652	308	244	503	45,215	80,624
	Females	176	1,662	1,895	1,656	5,868	12,942	4,020	2,657	1,004	1,133	728	778	281	222	387	35,409	
1868	Males	121	1,196	1,327	1,055	2,765	13,099	8,966	3,199	1,116	1,004	424	450	187	147	356	35,412	61,018
	Females	147	1,103	1,154	1,055	3,762	9,857	3,952	1,659	594	899	414	449	172	131	258	25,606	
1869	Males	136	1,179	1,187	1,209	3,197	14,797	9,154	4,306	1,498	1,284	430	517	195	156	369	39,614	66,568
	Females	134	1,066	1,159	1,023	3,612	10,596	4,388	1,896	671	1,001	369	463	173	136	267	26,954	
1870	Males	187	1,445	1,544	1,357	4,041	15,116	8,536	6,397	1,882	1,599	466	493	250	204	367	43,884	74,855
	Females	166	1,210	1,423	1,284	4,308	10,883	4,422	3,377	1,117	1,087	414	564	189	150	377	30,971	
1871	Males	150	1,327	1,636	1,326	3,851	14,510	7,747	5,719	1,340	2,116	484	483	202	179	328	41,398	71,240
	Females	159	1,284	1,456	1,176	4,487	11,114	3,956	3,028	775	1,028	377	502	140	124	236	29,842	
1872	Males	147	1,332	1,678	1,633	4,516	15,889	11,480	4,793	1,802	1,403	530	551	228	207	23	46,212	78,102
	Females	143	1,311	1,495	1,501	4,801	11,548	5,278	2,437	1,029	980	421	564	214	159	9	31,890	
1873	Males	201	1,808	1,947	1,855	5,231	18,079	12,935	4,635	1,880	1,585	586	729	210	245	4	51,930	90,149
	Females	192	1,954	1,797	2,028	6,345	14,265	5,648	2,077	1,114	1,162	500	723	181	227	6	38,219	
1874	Males	264	1,978	2,076	1,825	3,681	11,246	8,450	3,763	1,963	1,711	836	723	281	297	2	39,096	73,184
	Females	237	2,024	1,990	1,817	5,421	11,022	4,815	2,385	1,361	1,245	578	683	219	290	1	34,088	
1875	Males	249	1,585	1,491	1,163	2,537	6,483	5,361	2,826	1,589	1,127	661	543	212	254	16	26,097	51,462
	Females	225	1,591	1,423	1,265	4,328	7,387	3,640	2,085	1,091	895	466	563	147	246	13	25,365	
1876	Males	184	1,016	1,000	757	1,730	4,885	3,816	2,700	1,719	1,029	475	415	164	184	3	20,077	37,587
	Females	190	978	950	802	2,844	5,002	2,315	1,740	923	768	355	377	114	146	6	17,510	

Year	Sex	(1)	(2)	(3)	(4)	(5)	(6)	(7)	(8)	(9)	(10)	(11)	(12)	(13)	(14)	(15)	(16)	Total
1877	Males	259	1,080	996	851	2,022	5,429	4,221	2,368	1,239	1,014	439	470	172	272	15	20,847	38,503
	Females	237	1,065	1,003	828	2,870	5,211	2,424	1,552	676	683	287	392	155	269	4	17,656	
1878	Males	229	1,275	1,240	795	2,099	5,944	3,952	2,122	1,042	974	398	443	158	217	—	20,916	41,124
	Females	209		1,138	829	3,715	6,093	2,752	1,600	761	644	365	389	148	290	—	20,208	
1879	Males	243	1,355	1,354	923	2,541	8,103	5,046	2,502	1,280	1,164	505	439	135	217	—	25,807	47,065
	Females	159	894	890	768	4,208	7,529	2,796	1,709	682	669	277	376	110	191	—	21,258	
1880	Males	388	2,271	2,484	1,682	6,696	16,041	8,636	4,271	1,616	1,812	696	736	280	304	24	49,937	95,517
	Females	358	2,183	2,376	1,922	11,251	16,089	4,828	2,501	1,090		531	691	265	255	5	45,580	
1881	Males	304	1,896	1,949	1,587	5,747	15,516	6,321	2,928	1,178	1,118	567	516	215	215	49	40,106	78,417
	Females	331	1,789	1,905	1,767	9,994	13,502	3,793	1,861	879	962	477	554	231	217	49	38,311	
1882	Males	390	2,240	2,324	1,966	6,686	18,008	7,186	3,249	1,512	1,520	740	580	243	304	30	46,978	89,136
	Females	425	2,084	2,135	2,086	10,478	14,802	4,159	2,159	1,086	1,154	526	597	206	238	23	42,158	
1883	Males	508	3,321	3,849	3,526	8,835	17,890	7,041	3,347	1,697	2,139	1,174	1,067	359	435	76	55,264	108,724
	Females	506	3,123	3,434	3,438	13,560	15,987	4,603	2,534	1,600	1,935	1,027	955	324	355	79	53,460	
1884	Males	297	2,066	2,231	1,965	5,838	12,261	5,714	2,591	1,327	1,494	847	809	312	302	—	38,054	75,863
	Females	296	1,959	2,084	1,923	9,483	11,761	3,822	2,003	1,170	1,295	743	697	237	261	—	37,809	
1885	Males	225	1,382	1,414	1,171	4,640	10,885	4,821	2,273	1,062	1,211	719	595	190	232	6	30,873	62,034
	Females	238	1,254	1,248	1,137	8,391	10,829	3,248	1,637	825	944	527	483	181	208	2	31,161	
1886	Males	243	1,166	1,175	978	4,566	12,389	5,292	2,491	943	1,135	615	506	178	249	21	31,950	63,135
	Females	233	1,143	1,066	1,058	7,974	11,687	3,363	1,641	765	893	485	467	253	177	55	31,185	
1887	Males	287	1,464	1,489	1,268	6,493	18,123	7,047	2,748	1,154	1,216	679	602	258	249	104	43,176	82,923
	Females	301	1,370	1,344	1,315	10,398	15,471	3,946	1,872	956	984	601	624	184	216	91	39,747	
1888	Males	288	1,383	1,324	1,232	6,543	17,457	6,627	2,650	1,081	1,102	568	526	203	229	116	41,310	78,684
	Females	276	1,338	1,236	1,143	9,943	14,516	3,696	1,742	961	935	503	545	201	215	122	37,374	
1889	Males	312	1,304	1,308	1,064	5,491	15,219	6,005	2,052	1,083	881	528	442	187	247	89	36,226	70,477
	Females	287	1,252	1,221	994	9,078	13,253	3,658	1,450	954	729	443	449	188	212	84	34,251	
1890	Males	209	1,102	1,041	835	4,683	13,646	5,365	1,592	839	815	426	417	130	184	28	31,361	61,313
	Females	212	961	990	910	8,352	11,493	3,288	1,260	756	613	390	353	143	173	13	29,952	
1891	Males	201	939	901	817	4,888	13,242	5,124	1,434	710	740	400	354	113	164	2	30,046	59,623
	Females	191	890	890	790	8,700	11,750	2,996	1,137	640	586	358	375	148	131	—	29,577	
1892	Males	189	747	789	638	3,983	11,304	4,538	1,322	594	559	342	262	113	110	11	25,495	50,867
	Females	188	747	754	579	6,827	10,298	2,934	1,137	575	485	310	295	99	91	4	25,372	
1893	Males	136	556	653	580	3,765	10,091	4,223	1,301	493	511	258	246	129	105	3	23,044	48,147
	Females	156	595	566	590	7,085	10,231	3,211	1,058	483	409	260	272	111	86	2	25,103	
1894	Males	164	444	456	347	1,891	5,420	3,897	1,065	541	314	248	261	153	140	1	15,318	35,895
	Females	164	409	469	390	4,574	8,840	3,232	936	502	355	258	221	165	110	6	20,577	
1895	Males	103	532	521	435	1,981	8,322	5,954	1,389	665	468	341	349	144	185	—	21,398	48,703
	Females	137	550	505	414	5,974	12,188	4,277	1,256	602	416	345	355	146	119	—	27,305	
1896	Males	111	407	440	350	1,272	6,875	5,269	1,216	545	419	259	301		138	2	17,751	38,995
	Females	126	419	429	422	3,432	10,122	3,481	1,038	615	365	225	307		112	5	21,244	

Table 90 (continued)

Years		Under 1 year	1 and under 5	5 and under 10	10 and under 15	15 and under 20	20 and under 25	25 and under 30	30 and under 35	35 and under 40	40 and under 45	45 and under 50	50 and under 55	55 and under 60	60 and upwards	Ages not specified	Total males and females	Total
		(1)	(2)	(3)	(4)	(5)	(6)	(7)	(8)	(9)	(10)	(11)	(12)	(13)	(14)	(15)	(16)	(17)
1897	Males	105	350	362	321	1,056	5,366	3,883	977	547	303	199	217	130	148	2	13,966	32,535
	Females	119	338	332	346	3,488	8,609	2,799	906	521	339	223	271	150	125	3	18,569	
1898	Males	98	389	331	306	816	5,386	4,078	1,033	565	311	235	209	132	140	1	14,030	32,241
	Females	106	384	365	315	3,036	8,998	2,710	791	537	317	207	234	114	95	2	18,211	
1899	Males	137	531	470	375	969	7,813	5,285	1,263	662	403	237	214	124	138	—	18,621	41,232
	Females	141	483	459	372	3,832	11,006	3,502	1,038	710	330	192	292	155	98	1	22,611	
1900	Males	151	678	598	475	1,639	10,042	4,951	1,413	716	428	229	257	155	169	—	21,901	45,288
	Females	186	655	550	447	4,317	10,331	3,582	1,279	820	376	252	301	167	124	—	23,387	
1901	Males	150	703	601	398	1,568	7,533	3,921	1,346	706	509	219	224	119	130	—	18,127	39,613
	Females	158	679	595	457	3,951	9,334	3,084	1,159	850	456	221	256	170	116	—	21,486	
1902	Males	123	600	589	384	1,710	7,793	4,223	1,386	693	477	233	229	144	176	5	18,765	40,190
	Females	156	576	538	433	4,175	8,794	3,507	1,218	881	390	202	230	203	106	16	21,425	
1903	Males	157	637	634	441	1,532	7,603	4,256	1,515	720	433	198	229	157	158	1	18,671	39,789
	Females	146	615	610	492	4,190	8,369	3,643	1,275	699	375	202	212	175	113	2	21,118	
1904	Males	148	498	541	445	2,247	7,387	3,376	1,186	447	343	190	153	107	86	11	17,165	36,902
	Females	125	536	505	498	6,170	7,520	2,288	806	373	247	185	228	139	103	14	19,737	
1905	Males	109	502	454	345	2,179	7,173	3,157	1,035	431	276	126	128	83	71	13	16,082	30,676
	Females	110	419	370	386	4,112	5,810	1,767	628	285	205	142	180	93	85	2	14,594	
1906	Males	121	648	565	435	2,624	8,363	3,728	1,392	567	364	166	110	94	53	—	19,230	35,344
	Females	113	615	502	465	4,451	5,997	2,060	827	370	262	129	148	101	74	—	16,114	
1907	Males	142	638	587	501	2,789	9,073	4,391	1,594	614	370	168	135	64	57	1	21,124	39,082
	Females	116	637	574	485	4,817	7,012	2,194	954	372	297	163	163	93	80	1	17,958	
1908	Males	72	487	449	309	1,282	3,776	2,135	1,051	392	234	116	85	53	39	—	10,480	23,295
	Females	58	443	394	335	3,553	4,750	1,728	701	308	196	105	109	69	66	—	12,815	
1909	Males	64	381	341	276	1,835	6,174	3,459	1,340	462	285	141	83	31	44	—	14,916	28,676
	Females	52	345	341	324	4,013	5,438	1,882	626	252	182	100	90	57	55	3	13,760	
1910	Males	63	414	365	290	2,170	7,604	4,106	1,523	582	314	126	90	44	46	—	17,737	32,457
	Females	57	388	288	337	4,301	5,652	2,192	713	300	189	101	93	51	58	—	14,720	

NOTE: This table does not include the persons returned in the publications of the Registrar General as 'Residents of other Countries', who emigrated from Irish ports.

SOURCE: *Population Census of Ireland*, 1871 to 1911. British Parliamentary Papers, 1876, LXXXI, *General Report*, Table LXXXVI, p. 192; 1882, LXXVI, *General Report*, Table 159, p. 377; 1892, xc, *General Report*, Table 157, p. 527; 1902, cxxIx, *General Report*, Table 167, p. 577; 1912–13, cxvIII, *General Report*, Table 143.

Table 91. *Male and female emigrants from Ireland classified into five-year age groups, decade totals, 1861–70 to 1901–10*

Decade		Under 1 year	1 and under 5	5 and under 10	10 and under 15	15 and under 20	20 and under 25	25 and under 30	30 and under 35	35 and under 40	40 and under 45	45 and under 50	50 and under 55	55 and under 60	60 and upwards	Ages not specified	Total males and females
1861–70	Males	2,688	22,759	21,509	17,349	39,292	158,532	94,336	42,367	16,546	15,615	7,224	6,888	2,323	2,108	20,291	469,817
	Females	2,983	21,882	20,152	16,108	49,911	129,193	50,599	26,209	11,954	14,026	7,216	8,008	2,180	2,401	17,217	380,019
	Total	5,671	44,621	41,661	33,457	89,203	287,725	144,925	68,576	28,500	29,641	14,440	14,896	4,503	4,509	37,508	849,836
1871–80	Males	2,314	15,055	15,902	12,810	34,994	108,609	71,644	35,699	15,470	13,935	5,610	5,532	2,042	2,376	415	342,317
	Females	2,109	14,559	14,518	12,936	50,270	95,260	38,452	21,114	9,502	9,309	4,157	5,260	1,693	2,197	280	281,616
	Total	4,423	29,614	30,420	25,746	85,174	203,869	110,096	56,813	24,972	23,244	9,767	10,792	3,735	4,573	695	623,933
1881–90	Males	3,063	17,324	18,104	15,592	59,522	151,394	61,419	25,921	11,876	12,631	6,863	6,060	2,364	2,646	519	395,298
	Females	3,105	16,273	16,663	15,771	97,651	133,301	37,576	18,159	9,952	10,444	5,722	5,724	2,277	2,272	518	375,408
	Total	6,168	33,597	34,767	31,363	157,173	284,695	98,995	44,080	21,828	23,075	12,585	11,784	4,641	4,918	1,037	770,706
1891–1900	Males	1,395	5,567	5,521	4,644	22,260	83,861	47,202	12,413	6,038	4,456	2,748	2,670	1,323	1,437	35	201,570
	Females	1,514	5,470	5,319	4,665	51,265	102,373	32,724	10,576	6,005	3,978	2,630	2,923	1,398	1,091	25	231,956
	Total	2,909	11,037	10,840	9,309	73,525	186,234	79,926	22,989	12,043	8,434	5,378	5,593	2,721	2,528	60	433,526
1901–10	Males	1,149	5,508	5,126	3,824	19,936	72,479	36,752	13,368	5,614	3,605	1,683	1,466	896	860	31	172,297
	Females	1,091	5,253	4,717	4,212	43,733	68,676	24,345	8,907	4,690	2,799	1,550	1,709	1,151	856	38	173,727
	Total	2,240	10,761	9,843	8,036	63,669	141,155	61,097	22,275	10,304	6,404	3,233	3,175	2,047	1,716	69	346,024

NOTE: This table does not include persons returned in the publications of the Registrar General as 'Residents of other Countries', who emigrated from Irish ports.

SOURCE: See Table 90.

Table 92. *Immigration to the United States from Great Britain, 1831–1913: original data as percentage of trend*

Year	Original data	Original data as percentage of trend	Year	Original data	Original data as percentage of trend
1831	2,475	45·36	1873	89,500	162·60
1832	5,331	89·04	1874	62,021	110·95
1833	4,916	74·97	1875	47,905	84·54
1834	10,490	146·34	1876	29,291	51·09
1835	8,970	114·67	1877	23,581	40·73
1836	13,106	153·84	1878	22,150	37·95
1837	12,218	131·91	1879	29,955	51·00
1838	5,420	53·92	1880	73,273	124·21
1839	10,271	94·34	1881	81,376	137·59
1840	2,613	22·20	1882	102,991	174·02
1841	16,188	127·43	1883	76,606	129·59
1842	22,005	160·82	1884	65,950	111·89
1843	8,430	57·30	1885	57,713	98·40
1844	14,353	90·89	1886	62,929	108·01
1845	19,210	113·56	1887	93,378	161·64
1846	22,180	122·62	1888	108,692	190·11
1847	23,302	120·70	1889	87,992	155·79
1848	35,159	170·94	1890	69,730	125·20
1849	55,132	252·06	1891	66,605	121·51
1850	51,085	220·03	1892	42,215	78·39
1851	51,487	209·31	1893	35,189	66·64
1852	40,699	156·45	1894	22,520	43·57
1853	37,576	136·84	1895	28,833	57·09
1854	58,647	202·70	1896	24,565	49·88
1855	47,572	156·33	1897	12,752	26·60
1856	44,658	139·80	1898	12,894	27·68
1857	58,479	174·70	1899	13,456	29·79
1858	28,956	82·71	1900	12,509	28·60
1859	26,163	71·58	1901	14,985	35·46
1860	29,737	78·07	1902	16,898	41·46
1861	19,675	49·66	1903	33,637	85·73
1862	24,639	59·90	1904	51,448	136·45
1863	66,882	156·90	1905	84,189	232·78
1864	53,428	121·16	1906	67,198	194·07
1865	82,465	181·12	1907	79,037	238·85
1866	94,924	202·29	1908	62,824	199·03
1867	52,641	109·05	1909	46,793	155·70
1868	24,127	48·67	1910	68,941	241·36
1869	84,438	166·20	1911	73,384	270·83
1870	103,677	199·47	1912	57,148	222·74
1871	85,455	161·00	1913	60,328	243·79
1872	84,912	156·95			

SOURCE: *Historical Statistics of the United States, 1789–1945*, series B 306.

TREND LINE: $\log Y_c = 1·7332 + 0·0079X - 0·0004X^2$ centred on $X = 0 = 1872$.

NOTE (years):

1831	Twelve months ending Sept. 30.	1844–9	Twelve months ending Sept. 30.
1832	Fifteen months ending Dec. 31	1850	Fifteen months ending Dec. 31.
1833–42	Calendar years.	1851–67	Calendar years.
1843	Nine months ending Sept. 30.	1868	Six months ending June 30.

1869–1913 Twelve months ending June 30.

Table 93. *Immigration to the United States from Germany, 1831–1913:
original data as percentage of trend*

Year	Original data	Original data as percentage of trend	Year	Original data	Original data as percentage of trend
1831	2,413	25·24	1873	149,671	161·30
1832	10,194	96·35	1874	87,291	93·64
1833	6,988	59·82	1875	47,769	51·13
1834	17,686	137·44	1876	31,937	34·18
1835	8,311	58·77	1877	29,298	31·43
1836	20,707	133·54	1878	29,313	31·59
1837	23,740	139·95	1879	34,602	37·55
1838	11,683	63·10	1880	84,638	92·70
1839	21,028	104·31	1881	210,485	233·19
1840	29,704	135·62	1882	250,630	281·53
1841	15,291	64·41	1883	194,786	222·36
1842	20,370	79·34	1884	179,676	208·92
1843	14,441	52·13	1885	124,443	147·73
1844	20,731	69·52	1886	84,403	102·53
1845	34,355	107·27	1887	106,865	133·14
1846	57,561	167·74	1888	109,717	140·53
1847	74,281	202·48	1889	99,538	131·37
1848	58,465	149·42	1890	92,427	125·98
1849	60,235	144·66	1891	113,554	160·21
1850	78,896	178·47	1892	119,168	174·44
1851	72,482	154·79	1893	78,756	119·89
1852	145,918	294·85	1894	53,989	85·67
1853	141,946	272·03	1895	32,173	53·33
1854	215,009	391·70	1896	31,885	55·35
1855	71,918	124·84	1897	22,533	41·05
1856	71,028	117·74	1898	17,111	32·79
1857	91,781	145·63	1899	17,476	35·31
1858	45,310	68·98	1900	18,507	39·52
1859	41,784	61·17	1901	21,651	48·98
1860	54,491	76·88	1902	28,304	67·97
1861	31,661	43·15	1903	40,086	102·45
1862	27,529	36·33	1904	46,380	126·42
1863	33,162	42·48	1905	40,574	118·24
1864	57,276	71·36	1906	37,564	117·29
1865	83,424	101·34	1907	37,807	126·78
1866	115,892	137·58	1908	32,309	116·63
1867	133,426	155·14	1909	25,540	99·48
1868	55,831	63·73	1910	31,283	131·77
1869	131,042	147·20	1911	32,061	146·38
1870	118,225	130·98	1912	27,788	137·84
1871	82,554	90·41	1913	34,329	185·42
1872	141,109	153·12			

SOURCE: *Historical Statistics of the United States, 1789–1945*, series B 310.
TREND LINE: $\log Y_c = 1 \cdot 9645 + 0 \cdot 0035X - 0 \cdot 0005X^2$. Centred on $X = 0 = 1872$.
NOTE (years): See note to Table 92.

Table 94. *Immigration to the United States from Ireland, 1831–1913:*
original data as percentage of trend

Year	Original data	Original data as percentage of trend	Year	Original data	Original data as percentage of trend
1831	5,772	21·99	1873	77,344	134·63
1832	12,436	45·63	1874	53,707	93·59
1833	8,648	30·59	1875	37,957	66·28
1834	24,474	83·54	1876	19,575	34·28
1835	20,927	68·99	1877	14,569	25·62
1836	30,578	97·46	1878	15,932	28·15
1837	28,508	87·91	1879	20,013	35·56
1838	12,645	37·77	1880	71,603	128·10
1839	23,963	69·38	1881	72,342	130·40
1840	39,430	110·77	1882	76,432	138·95
1841	37,772	103·06	1883	31,486	149·55
1842	51,342	136·17	1884	63,344	117·46
1843	19,670	50·76	1885	51,795	97·14
1844	33,490	84·16	1886	49,619	94·20
1845	44,821	109·79	1887	68,370	131·51
1846	51,752	123·69	1888	73,513	143·40
1847	105,536	246·32	1889	65,557	129·81
1848	112,934	257·65	1890	53,024	106·68
1849	159,398	355·78	1891	55,706	113·97
1850	164,004	358·47	1892	51,383	107·01
1851	221,253	474·02	1893	43,578	92·46
1852	159,548	335·35	1894	30,231	65·41
1853	162,649	335·70	1895	46,304	102·26
1854	101,606	206·12	1896	40,262	90·84
1855	49,627	99·05	1897	28,421	65·58
1856	54,349	106·81	1898	25,128	59·34
1857	54,361	105·29	1899	31,673	76·63
1858	26,873	51·35	1900	35,730	88·64
1859	35,216	66·44	1901	30,561	77·81
1860	48,637	90·69	1902	29,138	76·22
1861	23,797	43·90	1903	35,310	94·97
1862	23,351	42·65	1904	36,142	100·05
1863	55,916	101·21	1905	52,945	150·98
1864	63,523	114·06	1906	34,995	102·90
1865	29,772	53·08	1907	34,530	104·79
1866	36,690	65·00	1908	30,556	95·78
1867	72,879	128·44	1909	25,033	81·14
1868	32,068	56·27	1910	29,855	100·14
1869	40,786	71·32	1911	29,112	101·15
1870	56,996	99·41	1912	25,879	93·23
1871	57,439	100·02	1913	27,876	104·21
1872	68,732	119·61			

SOURCE: *Historical Statistics of the United States, 1789–1945*, series B 307.

TREND LINE: $\log Y_c = 1\cdot7594 + 0\cdot0001X - 0\cdot0002X^2$, centred on $X = 0 = 1872$.

NOTE (years): See note to Table 92.

Table 95. *Immigration to the United States from Scandinavia, 1831–1913: original data as percentage of trend*

Year	Original data	Original data as percentage of trend	Year	Original data	Original data as percentage of trend
1831	36	50·00	1873	35,481	203·84
1832	334	388·37	1874	19,178	102·59
1833	189	181·73	1875	14,322	71·54
1834	66	52·80	1876	12,323	57·62
1835	68	45·64	1877	11,274	49·50
1836	473	265·73	1878	12,254	50·65
1837	399	188·21	1879	21,820	85·14
1838	112	44·62	1880	65,657	242·54
1839	380	127·95	1881	81,582	286·08
1840	207	59·14	1882	105,326	351·59
1841	226	54·85	1883	71,994	229·40
1842	588	121·49	1884	52,728	160·82
1843	1,777	313·95	1885	40,704	119·16
1844	1,336	202·42	1886	46,735	131·68
1845	982	127·86	1887	67,629	183·92
1846	2,030	227·83	1888	81,924	215·63
1847	1,320	127·91	1889	57,504	146·89
1848	1,113	93·53	1890	50,368	125·22
1849	3,481	254·09	1891	60,107	145·82
1850	1,589	101·08	1892	66,295	157·39
1851	2,438	135·52	1893	58,945	137·32
1852	4,106	200·00	1894	32,400	74·28
1853	3,396	145·31	1895	26,852	60·74
1854	4,222	159·14	1896	33,199	74·31
1855	1,349	44·92	1897	21,089	46·83
1856	1,330	39·24	1898	19,282	42·60
1857	2,747	72·00	1899	22,192	48·92
1858	2,662	62·15	1900	31,151	68·70
1859	1,590	33·17	1901	39,234	86·81
1860	840	15·70	1902	54,038	120·28
1861	850	14·27	1903	77,647	174·35
1862	2,550	38·55	1904	60,096	136·50
1863	3,119	42·59	1905	60,625	139·69
1864	2,961	36·62	1906	52,781	123·70
1865	7,258	81·53	1907	49,965	119·44
1866	14,495	148·30	1908	30,175	73·78
1867	8,491	79·33	1909	32,496	81·49
1868	11,985	102·55	1910	48,267	124·49
1869	43,941	345·29	1911	42,285	112·48
1870	30,742	222·45	1912	27,554	75·80
1871	22,132	147·88	1913	32,267	92·06
1872	28,575	176·80			

SOURCE: *Historical Statistics of the United States, 1789–1945*, series B 308.

TREND LINE: $\log Y_c = 3\cdot2085 + 0\cdot0328X - 0\cdot0006X^2$, centred on $X = 0 = 1872$.

NOTE (years): See note to Table 92.

Table 96. *Immigration to the United States from Europe, 1831–1913:
original data as percentage of trend*

Year	Original data	Original data as percentage of trend	Year	Original data	Original data as percentage of trend
1831	13,039	26·97	1873	397,541	145·64
1832	34,193	67·24	1874	262,783	93·30
1833	29,111	54·44	1875	182,961	62·99
1834	57,510	102·34	1876	120,920	40·38
1835	41,987	71·12	1877	106,195	34·42
1836	70,465	113·68	1878	101,612	31·98
1837	71,039	109·19	1879	134,259	41·04
1838	34,070	49·92	1880	348,691	103·60
1839	64,148	89·64	1881	528,545	152·68
1840	80,126	106·82	1882	648,186	182·14
1841	76,216	96·99	1883	522,587	142·91
1842	99,945	121·47	1884	453,686	120·52
1843	49,013	56·91	1885	353,083	91·58
1844	74,745	82·96	1886	329,529	83·29
1845	109,301	116·02	1887	482,829	118·99
1846	146,315	148·59	1888	538,131	129·36
1847	229,117	222·72	1889	434,790	102·00
1848	218,025	202·96	1890	445,680	102·08
1849	286,501	255·52	1891	546,085	122·17
1850	308,323	263·58	1892	570,876	124·81
1851	369,510	302·92	1893	429,324	91·77
1852	362,484	285·09	1894	277,052	57·92
1853	361,576	272·96	1895	250,342	51·22
1854	405,542	293·99	1896	329,067	65·91
1855	187,729	130·75	1897	216,397	42·46
1856	186,083	124·57	1898	217,786	41·87
1857	216,224	139·19	1899	297,349	56·05
1858	111,354	68·96	1900	424,700	78·52
1859	110,949	66·13	1901	469,237	85·13
1860	141,209	81·05	1902	619,068	110·27
1861	81,200	44·90	1903	814,507	142·49
1862	83,710	44·61	1904	767,933	132·02
1863	163,733	84·15	1905	974,273	164·66
1864	185,233	91·84	1906	1,018,365	169·28
1865	214,048	102·43	1907	1,199,566	196·21
1866	278,916	128·88	1908	691,901	111·42
1867	283,751	126·66	1909	654,875	103·86
1868	130,090	56·12	1910	926,291	144·76
1869	315,963	131·81	1911	764,757	117·82
1870	328,626	132·62	1912	718,875	109·23
1871	265,145	103·56	1913	1,055,855	158·31
1872	352,155	133·18			

SOURCE: *Historical Statistics of the United States, 1789–1945*, pp. 33–4, series B 305.
TREND LINE: $\log Y_c = 1·4223 + 0·0139X - 0·0001X^2$, centred on $X = 0 = 1872$.
NOTE (years): See note to Table 92.

Table 97. *Bituminous coal output in the United States, 1841–1913:*
original data as percentage of trend

Year	Thousand net tons of 2000 pounds	Original data as percentage of trend	Year	Thousand net tons of 2000 pounds	Original data as percentage of trend
1841	1,109	103·84	1878	36,246	92·36
1842	1,244	104·36	1879	37,898	88·76
1843	1,504	113·08	1880	42,832	92·27
1844	1,672	112·82	1881	53,961	107·00
1845	1,830	110·84	1882	68,430	124·98
1846	1,978	107·68	1883	77,251	130·05
1847	1,735	84·88	1884	82,999	128·88
1848	1,968	86·66	1885	72,824	104·37
1849	2,453	97·23	1886	74,645	98·81
1850	2,880	102·86	1887	88,562	108·36
1851	3,253	104·73	1888	102,040	115·47
1852	3,665	106·45	1889	95,683	100·22
1853	4,170	109·36	1890	111,302	107·97
1854	4,582	108·58	1891	117,901	106·01
1855	4,785	102·48	1892	126,857	105·78
1856	5,012	97·11	1893	128,385	99·36
1857	5,154	90·42	1894	118,820	85·41
1858	5,548	88·18	1895	135,118	90·26
1859	6,013	86·63	1896	137,640	85·52
1860	6,494	84·88	1897	147,618	85·36
1861	6,688	79·35	1898	166,594	89·71
1862	7,791	83·98	1899	193,323	97·02
1863	9,534	93·42	1900	212,316	99·38
1864	11,067	98·65	1901	225,828	98·67
1865	11,900	96·57	1902	260,217	106·15
1866	13,352	98·71	1903	282,749	107·80
1867	14,722	99·21	1904	278,660	99·35
1868	15,859	97·49	1905	315,063	105·12
1869	15,821	88·78	1906	342,875	107·14
1870	17,371	89·05	1907	394,759	115·59
1871	27,543	129·07	1908	332,574	91·32
1872	27,220	116·68	1909	379,744	97·86
1873	31,450	123·40	1910	417,111	100·94
1874	27,787	99·87	1911	405,907	92·30
1875	29,863	98·39	1912	450,105	96·25
1876	30,487	92·13	1913	478,435	96·28
1877	34,841	96·65			

Source: *Historical Statistics of the United States, 1789–1945*, series G 13.
Trend line: $\log Y_c = 1·55694 + 0·03705X - 0·00015X^2$, centred on $X = 0 = 1877$.

Table 98. *Miles of railway track added in the United States,
1831–1913: original data as percentage of trend*

Year	Original data	Original data as percentage of trend	Year	Original data	Original data as percentage of trend
1831	72	51·80	1873	4,097	120·89
1832	134	85·90	1874	2,117	60·23
1833	151	86·29	1875	1,711	47·03
1834	253	129·74	1876	2,712	72·14
1835	465	214·29	1877	2,274	58·65
1836	175	72·31	1878	2,665	66·78
1837	224	83·58	1879	4,809	117·26
1838	416	140·07	1880	6,711	159·56
1839	389	118·24	1881	9,846	228·66
1840	516	142·15	1882	11,569	262·87
1841	717	179·25	1883	6,745	150·26
1842	491	111·59	1884	3,923	85·84
1843	159	32·92	1885	2,975	64·06
1844	192	36·29	1886	8,018	170·20
1845	256	44·21	1887	12,876	269·94
1846	297	46·92	1888	6,900	143·12
1847	668	96·95	1889	5,162	106·15
1848	398	53·07	1890	5,915	120·79
1849	1,369	167·98	1891	4,844	98·42
1850	1,656	187·54	1892	3,656	74·04
1851	1,961	205·34	1893	4,143	83·80
1852	1,926	186·63	1894	2,899	58·66
1853	2,452	220·50	1895	1,895	38·43
1854	1,360	113·71	1896	2,053	41·81
1855	1,654	128·72	1897	2,163	44·31
1856	3,642	264·30	1898	2,026	41·83
1857	2,487	168·72	1899	3,466	72·27
1858	2,465	156·61	1900	4,628	97·62
1859	1,821	108·46	1901	3,324	71·06
1860	1,837	102·86	1902	4,965	107·75
1861	660	34·79	1903	6,169	136·18
1862	834	41·47	1904	6,690	150·51
1863	1,050	49·32	1905	5,084	116·77
1864	738	32·81	1906	5,565	130·73
1865	1,177	49·64	1907	6,188	148·96
1866	1,716	68·78	1908	3,897	96·29
1867	2,249	85·81	1909	3,238	82·29
1868	2,979	108·37	1910	5,908	154·70
1869	4,615	160·41	1911	4,740	128·14
1870	6,078	202·26	1912	3,301	92·28
1871	7,379	235·45	1913	3,003	86·99
1872	5,870	179·95			

SOURCE: S. Kuznets: *Secular Movements in Production and Prices* (1930), pp. 526–7.
TREND LINE: $\log Y_c = 2\cdot5135 + 0\cdot0170X - 0\cdot0004X^2$, centred on $X = 0 = 1872$.

Table 99. *Index of share prices in the United Kingdom, 1841–1913: original data as percentage of trend*

Year	Original data	Original data as percentage of trend	Year	Original data	Original data as percentage of trend
1841	56	102·56	1878	85	94·97
1842	56	101·08	1879	78	86·19
1843	57	101·24	1880	92	100·55
1844	63	110·33	1881	91	98·27
1845	65	112·26	1882	88	94·02
1846	62	105·44	1883	83	87·65
1847	56	93·80	1884	79	82·55
1848	52	85·95	1885	78	80·58
1849	51	83·06	1886	79	80·69
1850	53	84·94	1887	76	76·85
1851	55	87·03	1888	79	79·00
1852	56	87·36	1889	89	88·12
1853	60	92·31	1890	89	87·08
1854	60	91·05	1891	88	85·27
1855	62	92·81	1892	87	83·41
1856	66	97·49	1893	88	83·57
1857	65	94·61	1894	90	84·51
1858	65	93·39	1895	100	93·02
1859	72	102·13	1896	121	111·31
1860	73	102·10	1897	133	121·24
1861	73	100·83	1898	133	120·04
1862	85	115·80	1899	136	121·54
1863	90	121·13	1900	134	118·58
1864	102	135·45	1901	127	111·31
1865	94	123·20	1902	125	108·60
1866	87	112·55	1903	122	104·99
1867	74	94·51	1904	115	98·04
1868	75	94·58	1905	122	103·04
1869	78	97·14	1906	124	103·77
1870	87	107·01	1907	122	101·16
1871	98	119·08	1908	114	93·75
1872	110	132·05	1909	114	92·91
1873	113	134·05	1910	124	100·16
1874	110	128·96	1911	130	104·17
1875	104	120·51	1912	129	102·46
1876	97	110·98	1913	128	100·79
1877	92	104·07			

SOURCE: P. Rousseaux, *Les Mouvements de Fond de l'Économie Anglaise, 1800–1913* (Louvain, 1938), p. 272. K. C. Smith and G. F. Horne, 'An Index Number of Securities, 1867–1914', *London and Cambridge Economic Service Special Memorandum No. 37*, June 1934.

TREND LINE: $\log Y_c = 0.94649 + 0.00509X - 0.00002X^2$, centred on $X = 0 = 1877$.

NOTE: Average of 1884 and 1896 taken as 100.

Table 100. *The United Kingdom: net domestic fixed capital formation (at 1900 prices), 1869–1913: original data as percentage of trend*

Year	Original data (£ millions)	Original data as percentage of trend	Year	Original data (£ millions)	Original data as percentage of trend
1869	40	74·1	1892	69	80·0
1870	56	101·1	1893	67	76·5
1871	64	112·7	1894	74	83·1
1872	65	111·7	1895	77	85·2
1873	59	99·0	1896	88	95·9
1874	70	114·8	1897	108	115·9
1875	81	129·8	1898	127	134·3
1876	90	141·1	1899	135	140·6
1877	91	139·6	1900	141	144·8
1878	80	120·1	1901	148	149·8
1879	72	105·9	1902	158	157·7
1880	70	100·9	1903	154	151·6
1881	68	96·0	1904	147	142·7
1882	66	91·4	1905	136	130·3
1883	66	89·7	1906	122	115·3
1884	64	85·3	1907	105	97·9
1885	57	74·6	1908	83	76·4
1886	46	59·1	1909	81	73·6
1887	47	59·3	1910	86	77·2
1888	51	63·3	1911	84	74·5
1889	54	65·8	1912	84	73·6
1890	55	65·9	1913	100	86·5
1891	59	69·5			

SOURCE: C. H. Feinstein, 'Income and Investment in the United Kingdom, 1856–1914', *Economic Journal*, vol. LXXI, no. 282, June 1961, p. 374.

TREND LINE: $Y_c = 52·6 + 1·4X$, with $X = 0 = 1868$.

Table 101. *The United Kingdom: balance of payments on current account,
1870–1913: original data as percentage of trend*

Year	Original data (£ millions)	Original data as percentage of trend	Year	Original data (£ millions)	Original data as percentage of trend
1870	44·1	155·28	1892	59·1	76·75
1871	71·3	233·01	1893	53·0	66·83
1872	98·0	298·78	1894	38·7	47·48
1873	81·3	231·62	1895	40·0	47·79
1874	70·9	190·08	1896	56·8	66·12
1875	51·3	129·87	1897	41·6	47·22
1876	23·2	55·64	1898	22·9	25·36
1877	13·1	29·84	1899	42·4	45·84
1878	16·9	36·66	1900	37·9	40·02
1879	35·5	73·50	1901	33·9	34·98
1880	35·6	70·50	1902	33·3	33·60
1881	65·7	124·67	1903	44·8	44·18
1882	58·7	106·92	1904	51·7	49·90
1883	48·8	85·31	1905	81·5	77·03
1884	72·3	121·72	1906	117·5	108·80
1885	62·3	101·14	1907	154·1	139·84
1886	78·9	123·67	1908	154·7	137·63
1887	87·7	132·88	1909	135·6	118·32
1888	91·9	134·75	1910	167·3	143·24
1889	80·9	114·91	1911	196·9	165·46
1890	98·5	135·67	1912	197·1	162·62
1891	69·4	92·78	1913	224·3	181·62

SOURCE: A. M. Imlah, *Economic Elements in the Pax Britannica*, Table 4,
pp. 72–5.
TREND LINE: $Y_c = 74 \cdot 8359 + 2 \cdot 2101 X$, centred on $X = 0 = 1891$.

Table 102. *Volume of total exports from the United Kingdom, 1841–1913:*
£ thousand (at constant prices) and original data as percentage of trend

Year	Original data	Original data as percentage of trend	Year	Original data	Original data as percentage of trend
1841	49,061	85·02	1878	215,754	93·25
1842	48,834	80·84	1879	226,287	95·03
1843	55,573	87·91	1880	252,557	103·10
1844	60,698	91·81	1881	276,589	109·81
1845	60,938	88·46	1882	282,581	109·15
1846	59,594	82·51	1883	286,823	107·85
1847	58,676	77·78	1884	288,534	105·66
1848	59,848	75·99	1885	275,474	98·28
1849	75,304	91·63	1886	286,595	99·67
1850	83,312	97·19	1887	301,624	102·30
1851	89,339	99·96	1888	312,570	103·43
1852	93,215	100·09	1889	319,724	103·27
1853	106,494	109·78	1890	319,855	100·89
1854	104,636	103·60	1891	301,065	92·78
1855	105,696	100·47	1892	290,924	87·64
1856	125,605	114·90	1893	283,686	83·57
1857	128,940	113·45	1894	291,977	84·15
1858	127,141	107·64	1895	315,988	89·14
1859	140,441	114·47	1896	331,101	91·47
1860	145,875	114·52	1897	324,958	87·95
1861	136,085	102·95	1898	325,243	86·28
1862	120,326	87·75	1899	345,190	89·80
1863	125,901	88·56	1900	328,277	83·78
1864	125,658	85·29	1901	329,619	82·57
1865	136,630	89·53	1902	351,100	86·36
1866	152,075	96·24	1903	355,491	85·91
1867	159,285	97·40	1904	361,986	85·98
1868	169,133	99·98	1905	393,871	91·99
1869	178,036	101·79	1906	424,160	97·46
1870	192,409	106·45	1907	453,161	102·48
1871	213,949	114·58	1908	413,311	92·04
1872	218,715	113·44	1909	428,687	94·05
1873	210,851	105·97	1910	469,028	101·41
1874	211,597	103·09	1911	483,242	103·03
1875	211,411	99·89	1912	507,966	106·84
1876	207,232	95·01	1913	525,245	109·03
1877	213,229	94·90			

SOURCE: W. Schlote, *Entwicklung und Strukturwandlungen des englischen Aussenhandels von 1700 bis zur Gegenwart*, Jena, 1938, p. 138.

TREND LINE: $\log Y_c = 1\cdot3516 + 0\cdot0128X - 0\cdot0001X^2$, centred on $X = 0 = 1877$.

Table 103. *Volume of exports of finished iron and steel goods from the United Kingdom, 1841–1913: £ thousand (at constant prices) and original data as percentage of trend*

Year	Original data	Original data as percentage of trend	Year	Original data	Original data as percentage of trend
1841	4,286	75·19	1878	16,914	74·00
1842	4,062	68·06	1879	17,616	74·89
1843	4,459	71·40	1880	21,998	90·90
1844	5,476	83·85	1881	24,328	97·77
1845	4,909	71·89	1882	29,323	114·66
1846	4,862	68·14	1883	29,521	112·36
1847	5,673	76·13	1884	27,645	102·48
1848	5,819	74·79	1885	26,953	97·34
1849	7,342	90·43	1886	27,420	96·53
1850	8,505	100·44	1887	31,742	108·98
1851	9,345	105·84	1888	35,324	118·32
1852	9,794	106·46	1889	36,121	118·10
1853	11,529	120·31	1890	34,756	110·98
1854	11,224	112·50	1891	30,740	95·90
1855	9,856	94·93	1892	26,416	80·55
1856	13,112	121·41	1893	25,952	77·39
1857	14,229	126·73	1894	24,407	71·21
1858	12,741	109·20	1895	26,573	75·88
1859	15,066	124·31	1896	32,005	89·50
1860	14,973	118·98	1897	32,341	88·60
1861	12,686	97·14	1898	30,020	80·61
1862	13,563	100·13	1899	31,712	83·51
1863	15,464	110·11	1900	29,700	76·73
1864	14,442	99·22	1901	28,957	73·43
1865	15,186	100·73	1902	33,561	83·57
1866	16,145	103·43	1903	35,161	86·01
1867	16,692	103·32	1904	34,940	84·01
1868	17,458	104·47	1905	38,566	91·18
1869	21,574	124·86	1906	42,954	99·91
1870	22,385	125·36	1907	45,345	103·81
1871	21,362	115·81	1908	40,135	90·47
1872	21,913	115·05	1909	43,386	96·35
1873	20,241	102·98	1910	49,728	108·84
1874	18,932	93·37	1911	49,289	106·38
1875	18,174	86·93	1912	52,531	111·84
1876	16,096	74·70	1913	55,328	116·26
1877	17,411	78·44			

SOURCE: See Table 102.

TREND LINE: $\log Y_c = 1\cdot3463 + 0\cdot0128X - 0\cdot0001X^2$, centred on $X = 0 = 1877$.

Table 104. *Persons of British nationality sailing from the United Kingdom to all destinations outside Europe, 1853–1913: original data as percentage of trend*

Year	Original data	Original data as percentage of trend	Year	Original data	Original data as percentage of trend
1853	278,129	189·90	1884	242,179	133·48
1854	267,047	182·34	1885	207,644	112·83
1855	150,023	102·39	1886	232,900	124·70
1856	148,284	101·11	1887	281,487	148·44
1857	181,051	123·28	1888	279,928	145·33
1858	95,067	64·61	1889	253,795	129·65
1859	97,093	65·84	1890	218,116	109·59
1860	95,989	64·91	1891	218,507	107·94
1861	65,197	43·95	1892	210,042	101·95
1862	97,763	65·66	1893	208,814	99·55
1863	192,864	128·99	1894	156,030	73·03
1864	187,081	124·55	1895	185,181	85·05
1865	174,891	115·84	1896	161,925	72·95
1866	170,053	112·02	1897	146,460	64·69
1867	156,982	102·79	1898	140,644	60·87
1868	138,187	89·90	1899	146,362	62·05
1869	186,300	120·37	1900	168,825	70·07
1870	202,511	129·88	1901	171,715	69·74
1871	192,751	122·66	1902	205,662	81·71
1872	210,494	132·84	1903	259,950	100·97
1873	228,345	142·85	1904	271,435	103·03
1874	197,272	122·28	1905	262,077	97·17
1875	140,675	86·36	1906	325,137	117·70
1876	109,469	66·53	1907	395,680	139·78
1877	95,195	57·24	1908	263,199	90·69
1878	112,902	67·14	1909	288,761	97·01
1879	164,274	96·58	1910	397,848	130·26
1880	227,542	132·18	1911	454,527	144·96
1881	243,002	139·41	1912	467,666	145·22
1882	279,366	158·22	1913	469,640	141·93
1883	320,118	178·89			

SOURCE: I. Ferenczi and W. F. Willcox, *International Migrations*, vol. I, New York, National Bureau of Economic Research, 1929, pp. 636–7.

TREND LINE: $\log Y_c = 1\cdot2527 + 0\cdot0059X + 0\cdot0001X^2$, centred on $X = 0 = 1883$.

NOTE: In Figs. 24 and 25 the above data are plotted per 10,000 of the population as given in Mitchell and Deane, *Abstract of British Historical Statistics*, pp. 9–10.

Table 105. *Persons of British nationality sailing from the United Kingdom to destinations outside Europe excluding the United States, 1853–1913: original data as percentage of trend*

Year	Original data	Original data as percentage of trend	Year	Original data	Original data as percentage of trend
1853	87,177	136·33	1884	86,899	152·34
1854	113,420	183·02	1885	69,957	119·52
1855	63,784	106·00	1886	80,190	133·27
1856	53,353	91·15	1887	79,961	129·03
1857	75,535	132·39	1888	83,942	131·27
1858	45,711	82·08	1889	85,024	128·63
1859	39,997	73·42	1890	65,703	95·98
1860	28,110	52·66	1891	62,112	87·45
1861	27,037	51·59	1892	60,003	81·28
1862	49,037	95·13	1893	59,865	77·87
1863	62,336	122·73	1894	52,029	64·87
1864	56,916	113·51	1895	58,679	70·00
1865	56,428	113·79	1896	63,004	71·77
1866	38,213	77·77	1897	61,136	66·39
1867	30,931	63·42	1898	60,150	62·15
1868	29,697	61·22	1899	53,880	52·87
1869	39,563	81·86	1900	66,028	61·42
1870	49,045	101·67	1901	67,520	59·43
1871	41,963	86·99	1902	97,164	80·78
1872	48,712	100·79	1903	136,287	106·82
1873	61,615	127·02	1904	124,990	92·19
1874	83,498	171·19	1905	139,707	96·79
1875	59,482	121·06	1906	180,320	117·12
1876	54,915	110·74	1907	225,416	137·02
1877	49,714	99·15	1908	166,330	94·44
1878	58,208	114·60	1909	179,061	94·80
1879	72,468	140·59	1910	265,656	130·89
1880	60,972	116·34	1911	332,713	152·29
1881	66,898	125·32	1912	350,356	148·70
1882	97,463	178·91	1913	340,471	133·71
1883	128,545	230·81			

SOURCE: See Table 104.

TREND LINE: $\log Y_c = 0\cdot7458 + 0\cdot0100X + 0\cdot0004X^2$, centred on $X = 0 = 1883$.

Table 106. *Persons of British nationality sailing from the United Kingdom to the United States, 1853–1913: original data as percentage of trend*

Year	Original data	Original data as percentage of trend	Year	Original data	Original data as percentage of trend
1853	190,952	221·42	1884	155,280	124·22
1854	153,627	174·81	1885	137,687	109·65
1855	86,239	96·34	1886	152,710	121·11
1856	94,931	104·16	1887	201,526	159·23
1857	105,516	113·77	1888	195,986	154·36
1858	49,356	52·32	1889	168,771	132·55
1859	57,096	59·53	1890	152,413	119·43
1860	67,879	69·64	1891	156,395	122·33
1861	38,160	38·54	1892	150,039	117·19
1862	48,726	48·47	1893	148,949	116·24
1863	130,528	127·94	1894	104,001	81·12
1864	130,165	125·77	1895	126,502	98·67
1865	118,463	112·90	1896	98,921	77·19
1866	131,840	123·98	1897	85,324	66·64
1867	126,051	117·01	1898	80,494	62·96
1868	108,490	99·47	1899	92,482	72·47
1869	146,737	132·94	1900	102,797	80·74
1870	153,466	137·44	1901	104,195	82·06
1871	150,788	133·56	1902	108,498	85·73
1872	161,782	141·78	1903	123,663	98·07
1873	166,730	144·65	1904	146,445	116·62
1874	113,774	97·75	1905	122,370	97·90
1875	81,193	69·12	1906	144,817	116·44
1876	54,554	46·04	1907	170,264	137·66
1877	45,481	38·07	1908	96,869	78·79
1878	54,694	45·42	1909	109,700	89·81
1879	91,806	75·68	1910	132,192	108·97
1880	166,570	136·36	1911	121,814	101·15
1881	176,104	143·24	1912	117,310	98·18
1882	181,903	147·08	1913	129,169	109·01
1883	191,573	154·04			

SOURCE: See Table 104.

TREND LINE: $\log Y_c = 1\cdot0947 + 0\cdot0023X - 0\cdot0001X^2$, centred on $X = 0 = 1883$.

NOTE: In Fig. 25 the above data are plotted per 10,000 of the population as given in Mitchell and Deane, *Abstract of British Historical Statistics*, pp. 9–10.

Table 107. *The United Kingdom: gross residential building (at current prices), 1869–1913: original data as percentage of trend*

Year	Original data (£ millions)	Original data as percentage of trend	Year	Original data (£ millions)	Original data as percentage of trend
1869	14·5	80·6	1892	16·8	73·1
1870	16·5	91·2	1893	17·0	78·0
1871	17·7	96·7	1894	17·9	81·4
1872	20·2	109·8	1895	17·5	79·2
1873	19·4	104·3	1896	21·2	95·1
1874	20·9	111·2	1897	26·6	118·8
1875	26·1	138·1	1898	33·9	150·0
1876	27·8	145·5	1899	35·4	155·3
1877	26·1	135·9	1900	33·6	146·7
1878	21·4	110·3	1901	33·1	143·3
1879	16·9	86·2	1902	34·6	149·1
1880	17·3	87·8	1903	34·4	147·0
1881	16·1	80·9	1904	29·5	125·0 ·
1882	16·9	84·5	1905	27·5	116·0
1883	16·6	82·2	1906	29·0	121·3
1884	16·1	78·9	1907	28·0	116·6
1885	15·0	73·2	1908	22·5	93·0
1886	14·4	69·6	1909	21·9	89·8
1887	14·9	71·3	1910	19·7	80·0
1888	15·3	72·9	1911	16·1	65·2
1889	15·7	74·1	1912	13·3	53·6
1890	15·6	73·2	1913	14·0	95·6
1891	16·2	75·3			

SOURCE: B. R. Mitchell and P. Deane, *Abstract of British Historical Statistics*, pp. 373–4.

TREND LINE: $Y_c = 17 \cdot 8 + 0 \cdot 16X$, with $X = 0 = 1868$.

Table 108. *Index of annual building permits in the United States, 1831–1913 (dollars of 1913 purchasing power per capita): original data as percentage of trend*

Year	Original data	Original data as percentage of trend	Year	Original data	Original data as percentage of trend
1831	19	64·30	1873	29	96·93
1832	28	95·01	1874	24·5	81·61
1833	35	119·05	1875	24·5	81·31
1834	37	126·19	1876	20	66·14
1835	39	133·33	1877	18	59·29
1836	52	178·14	1878	17	55·77
1837	25	85·82	1879	20	65·36
1838	22	75·65	1880	21·5	69·96
1839	19	65·45	1881	25	81·01
1840	16·5	56·94	1882	28	90·32
1841	17·5	60·47	1883	30	96·31
1842	14·5	50·17	1884	32	102·27
1843	13	45·03	1885	36	114·50
1844	14·5	50·28	1886	37·5	118·67
1845	17·5	60·74	1887	38·5	121·22
1846	24	83·36	1888	37	115·88
1847	30	104·24	1889	44·5	138·63
1848	30	104·28	1890	48	148·74
1849	34	118·22	1891	42·5	130·97
1850	42	146·04	1892	43	131·78
1851	44	152·99	1893	31·5	95·98
1852	48·5	168·58	1894	29	87·85
1853	50·5	175·47	1895	35·5	106·93
1854	47·5	164·99	1896	30	89·82
1855	44·5	154·46	1897	31·5	93·72
1856	45	156·09	1898	27	79·83
1857	42	145·53	1899	31	91·10
1858	27	93·43	1900	22·5	65·69
1859	28	96·79	1901	30·5	88·48
1860	30·5	105·28	1902	30	86·46
1861	20	68·92	1903	29·5	84·45
1862	18	61·92	1904	33·5	95·28
1863	20·5	70·37	1905	42	118·64
1864	13·5	46·25	1906	42	117·85
1865	17·5	59·83	1907	35·5	98·91
1866	25	85·27	1908	33	91·29
1867	29·5	100·37	1909	43·5	119·51
1868	33	111·98	1910	39·5	107·75
1869	35·5	120·14	1911	38	102·90
1870	35·5	119·81	1912	40·5	108·87
1871	37·5	126·18	1913	33	88·05
1872	30	100·60			

Source: J. R. Riggleman, 'Building Cycles in the United States, 1830–1935' (unpublished thesis in the Library of the Johns Hopkins University, Baltimore). I am grateful to the Librarian of the University for sending me a microfilm of part of this dissertation. The figures are taken from Chart 3 on p. 32 of the work cited.

Trend line: $Y_c = 29·8172 + 0·0966X + 0·0022X^2$, centred on $X = 0 = 1872$.

Note: Year ending July 1.

Table 109. *Index of new building in the United States, 1857–1913:*
original data as percentage of trend

Year	Original data	Original data as percentage of trend	Year	Original data	Original data as percentage of trend
1857	18	63·38	1886	37	132·62
1858	18	63·83	1887	34	121·43
1859	22	78·57	1888	30	106·38
1860	27	96·78	1889	36	126·76
1861	18	64·98	1890	34	118·47
1862	26	94·20	1891	30	103·81
1863	28	102·19	1892	35	120·27
1864	16	58·61	1893	26	88·44
1865	22	80·88	1894	24	80·81
1866	29	107·01	1895	27	90·00
1867	38	140·74	1896	25	82·51
1868	47	174·72	1897	26	84·97
1869	54	200·74	1898	20	64·52
1870	52	193·31	1899	24	76·68
1871	62	231·34	1900	17	53·63
1872	52	194·03	1901	23	71·65
1873	47	175·37	1902	22	67·69
1874	30	111·94	1903	24	72·73
1875	29	108·21	1904	29	86·83
1876	25	92·94	1905	39	115·04
1877	26	96·65	1906	42	121·74
1878	19	70·63	1907	39	111·43
1879	19	70·37	1908	37	103·93
1880	14	51·66	1909	46	127·42
1881	18	66·18	1910	46	125·00
1882	20	73·26	1911	46	122·99
1883	24	87·59	1912	46	120·73
1884	27	97·83	1913	43	110·82
1885	33	119·13			

SOURCE: Clarence D. Long, Jr., *Building Cycles and the Theory of Investment*, Princeton University Press, 1940, pp. 226–7.

TREND LINE: $\log Y_c = 0.4428 + 0.0024X + 0.0001X^2$, centred on $X = 0 = 1885$.

NOTE: 1920–1930 taken as 100.

Table 110. *National income per head (at 1900 prices) in the United Kingdom,*
1871–1913: original data as percentage of trend

Year	Original data £	Original data as percentage of trend	Year	Original data £	Original data as percentage of trend
1871	25·22	105·66	1893	35·38	95·39
1872	24·79	101·31	1894	38·02	101·01
1873	26·30	104·91	1895	40·42	105·87
1874	27·64	107·63	1896	40·84	105·50
1875	27·15	103·27	1897	40·84	104·10
1876	27·19	101·08	1898	41·00	103·17
1877	27·03	98·22	1899	43·39	107·83
1878	27·72	98·54	1900	42·67	104·79
1879	26·90	93·57	1901	41·97	101·89
1880	26·97	91·86	1902	41·95	100·72
1881	28·15	93·89	1903	40·57	96·39
1882	29·22	95·52	1904	40·44	95·11
1883	29·66	95·06	1905	41·84	97·46
1884	29·85	93·84	1906	43·76	100·99
1885	31·05	95·77	1907	44·57	101·97
1886	31·96	96·79	1908	42·71	96·89
1887	32·89	97·83	1909	42·90	96·58
1888	34·94	102·13	1910	43·54	97·30
1889	36·66	105·34	1911	44·32	98·36
1890	38·16	107·86	1912	45·42	100·15
1891	37·50	104·28	1913	46·28	101·45
1892	36·11	98·85			

SOURCE: A. R. Prest, 'National Income of the United Kingdom, 1870–1946', *Economic Journal*, March 1948, pp. 58–9.

TREND LINE: $\log Y_c = 0.5626 + 0.0067X - 0.0001X^2$, centred on $X = 0 = 1892$.

Table 111. *Index of real wages in the United Kingdom, 1871–1913:*
original data as percentage of trend

Year	Original data	Original data as percentage of trend	Year	Original data	Original data as percentage of trend
1871	62	106·53	1893	94	101·40
1872	63	105·00	1894	98	104·59
1873	66	106·80	1895	100	105·71
1874	68	106·92	1896	100	104·82
1875	70	107·03	1897	98	101·87
1876	71	105·50	1898	99	102·17
1877	68	98·55	1899	104	106·78
1878	68	96·05	1900	103	105·21
1879	71	97·80	1901	102	103·76
1880	69	92·87	1902	101	102·33
1881	71	93·42	1903	99	100·10
1882	73	94·07	1904	97	97·98
1883	73	92·06	1905	97	97·88
1884	77	95·18	1906	98	98·99
1885	81	98·30	1907	101	102·12
1886	81	96·54	1908	101	102·33
1887	84	98·48	1909	100	101·73
1888	86	99·19	1910	98	100·10
1889	90	102·27	1911	97	99·59
1890	93	104·14	1912	97	100·10
1891	92	101·66	1913	97	100·83
1892	92	100·44			

SOURCE: For 1871–9: G. H. Wood, 'Real Wages and the Standard of Comfort since 1850', *Journal of the Royal Statistical Society*, March 1909. For 1880–1913: A. L. Bowley, *Wages and Income in the United Kingdom since 1860*, Cambridge University Press, 1937, pp. 30 and 34.

TREND LINE: $\log Y_c = 0.9621 + 0.0052X - 0.0002X^2$, centred on $X = 0 = 1892$.

NOTE: 1914 = 100.

Table 112. *Profits and the wages bill as percentage of the national income in the United Kingdom; and the level of employment in the United Kingdom, 1871–1913*

Year	Profits as percentage of national income*	Wages bill as percentage of national income†	Level of employment in Great Britain (nine-year moving average)‡	Year	Profits as percentage of national income*	Wages bill as percentage of national income†	Level of employment in Great Britain (nine-year moving average)‡
1871	38·60	39·51	—	1893	38·12	42·93	95·47
1872	37·37	42·27	—	1894	39·07	42·05	95·39
1873	38·13	42·81	—	1895	40·22	41·05	95·40
1874	39·81	41·48	—	1896	39·59	41·77	95·51
1875	39·08	42·86	96·18	1897	40·29	41·21	95·84
1876	39·71	42·28	95·74	1898	40·85	41·10	96·23
1877	39·98	42·09	95·46	1899	41·15	40·97	96·48
1878	41·55	41·08	95·33	1900	41·34	41·34	96·46
1879	39·80	42·16	95·23	1901	40·55	41·71	96·27
1880	42·31	40·91	94·60	1902	41·60	40·56	96·23
1881	42·23	40·70	93·98	1903	40·49	41·19	96·13
1882	41·00	41·87	93·37	1904	42·37	39·38	95·49
1883	41·89	41·05	93·28	1905	43·51	38·50	94·91
1884	41·11	41·02	94·00	1906	44·92	37·75	94·76
1885	40·97	40·43	94·38	1907	44·96	38·28	94·87
1886	41·76	39·30	94·53	1908	44·18	38·21	95·03
1887	40·55	40·46	94·40	1909	45·01	37·61	95·47
1888	41·17	40·45	93·99	1910	45·52	37·52	—
1889	40·14	41·86	94·06	1911	45·98	37·48	—
1890	40·39	41·89	94·32	1912	47·05	36·68	—
1891	39·83	42·06	94·81	1913	47·89	36·19	—
1892	39·38	42·10	95·29				

SOURCES

  * Prest, loc. cit.

  † Prest, loc. cit.

  ‡ Inverted percentages of trade unionists unemployed. A. C. Pigou, *Industrial Fluctuations*, London, Macmillan, 1927, pp. 353–4.

Table 113. *The United Kingdom: balance of payments, domestic fixed capital formation, and capital exports as percentage of total investment, 1870–1913*

Year	Balance of payments on current account	Portfolio foreign investment (money calls)	Gross domestic fixed capital formation (current prices)	Total invest-ment (1)+(3)	Capital exports (1) as percentage of total investment (4)
	£ millions				(%)
	(1)	(2)	(3)	(4)	(5)
1870	44·1	44·7	74	118	34
1871	71·3	70·2	86	157	45
1872	98·0	93·9	98	196	50
1873	81·3	69·3	96	177	46
1874	70·9	74·5	110	181	39
1875	51·3	46·1	114	165	31
1876	23·2	30·4	121	144	16
1877	13·1	19·4	120	133	10
1878	16·9	31·7	108	125	14
1879	35·5	30·5	91	127	28
1880	35·6	41·7	94	130	28
1881	65·7	74·2	91	157	42
1882	58·7	67·5	95	154	38
1883	48·8	61·2	98	147	33
1884	72·3	63·0	88	160	45
1885	62·3	55·3	79	141	44
1886	78·9	69·8	66	145	54
1887	87·7	84·4	65	153	57
1888	91·9	119·1	72	164	56
1889	80·9	122·9	82	163	50
1890	98·5	116·6	86	185	53
1891	69·4	57·6	91	160	43
1892	59·1	39·8	98	157	38
1893	53·0	32·1	91	144	37
1894	38·7	48·3	96	135	29
1895	40·0	77·7	93	133	30
1896	56·8	68·5	105	162	35
1897	41·6	78·4	131	173	24
1898	22·9	76·6	156	179	13
1899	42·4	78·2	173	216	20
1900	37·9	49·6	190	229	17
1901	33·9	49·5	191	225	15
1902	33·3	89·3	196	229	14
1903	44·8	82·9	192	237	19
1904	51·7	88·0	185	237	22
1905	81·5	128·9	173	255	32
1906	117·5	85·0	164	282	42
1907	154·1	116·3	150	304	51

Table 113. (*contd.*)

Year	Balance of payments on current account	Portfolio foreign investment (money calls)	Gross domestic fixed capital formation (current prices)	Total investment (1) + (3)	Capital export (1) as percentage of total investment (4) (%)
	£ millions				
	(1)	(2)	(3)	(4)	(5)
1908	154·7	147·4	120	275	57
1909	135·6	175·7	121	257	53
1910	167·3	198·0	124	291	57
1911	196·9	169·2	120	317	62
1912	197·1	200·7	129	326	60
1913	224·3	217·4	157	381	59

SOURCES

(1) A. H. Imlah, *Economic Elements in the Pax Britannica*, Cambridge, Mass., Harvard University Press, 1958, pp. 72–5.

(2) M. Simon, 'The Pattern of New British Portfolio Foreign Investment, 1865–1914' in J. H. Adler (ed.), *Capital Movements and Economic Development*, pp. 52–3, Table 2, col. 4.

(3) C. H. Feinstein 'Income and Investment in the United Kingdom, 1856–1914', *Economic Journal*, vol. LXXI, no. 282, June 1961, p. 374.

Table 114. *Movement of passenger citizens from the United Kingdom to Canada, Australasia and South Africa, 1853–1913*

Year	British North America	Australia and New Zealand	Cape of Good Hope and Natal	Year	British North America	Australia and New Zealand	Cape of Good Hope and Natal
1853	31,779	54,818	—	1884	31,134	44,255	3,954
1854	35,679	77,526	—	1885	19,838	39,395	3,268
1855	16,110	47,284	—	1886	24,745	43,076	3,897
1856	11,299	41,329	—	1887	32,025	34,183	4,909
1857	16,803	57,858	—	1888	34,853	31,127	6,466
1858	6,504	36,454	—	1889	28,269	28,294	13,884
1859	2,469	28,604	—	1890	22,520	21,179	10,321
1860	2,765	21,434	—	1891	21,578	19,547	9,090
1861	3,953	20,597	—	1892	23,254	15,950	9,891
1862	8,328	38,828	—	1893	24,732	11,203	13,097
1863	9,665	50,157	—	1894	17,459	10,917	13,177
1864	11,371	40,073	—	1895	16,622	10,567	20,234
1865	14,424	36,683	—	1896	15,267	10,354	24,594
1866	9,988	23,682	—	1897	15,571	12,061	21,109
1867	12,160	14,023	—	1898	17,640	10,693	19,756
1868	12,332	12,332	—	1899	16,410	11,467	14,432
1869	20,921	14,457	—	1900	18,443	14,922	20,815
1870	27,168	16,526	—	1901	15,757	15,350	23,143
1871	24,954	11,695	—	1902	26,293	14,345	43,206
1872	24,382	15,248	—	1903	59,652	12,375	50,206
1873	29,045	25,137	—	1904	69,681	13,910	26,818
1874	20,728	52,581	—	1905	82,437	15,139	26,307
1875	12,306	34,750	—	1906	114,859	19,331	22,804
1876	9,335	32,196	—	1907	151,216	24,767	20,925
1877	7,720	30,138	4,834	1908	81,321	33,569	19,568
1878	10,652	36,479	4,337	1909	85,887	37,620	22,017
1879	17,952	40,959	6,895	1910	156,990	45,701	27,297
1880	20,902	24,184	9,059	1911	184,860	80,770	30,767
1881	23,912	22,682	12,905	1912	186,147	96,800	28,216
1882	40,441	37,289	12,063	1913	196,278	77,934	25,855
1883	44,185	71,264	5,742				

SOURCE: Ferenczi and Willcox, op. cit. p. 636.

Table 115. *Immigration to Australia from the United Kingdom, 1861–1913: original data as percentage of trend*

Year	Original data	Original data as percentage of trend	Year	Original data	Original data as percentage of trend
1861	17,191	63·93	1888	31,092	201·07
1862	29,163	113·38	1889	29,981	192·87
1863	38,910	157·86	1890	18,146	115·90
1864	29,179	123·30	1891	11,511	72·86
1865	30,853	135·55	1892	8,092	50·67
1866	23,381	106·60	1893	7,899	48·84
1867	11,246	53·11	1894	9,050	55·15
1868	9,394	45·87	1895	8,303	49·78
1869	11,888	59·91	1896	8,265	48·66
1870	13,113	68·08	1897	9,685	55·89
1871	10,250	54·72	1898	8,756	49·43
1872	7,277	39·87	1899	10,078	55·56
1873	12,791	71·80	1900	18,986	102·03
1874	17,657	101·35	1901	18,369	96·05
1875	15,741	92·22	1902	15,774	80·10
1876	21,691	129·48	1903	9,367	46·11
1877	22,332	135·56	1904	9,928	47·29
1878	24,120	148·72	1905	10,279	47·29
1879	25,656	160·17	1906	11,671	51·76
1880	18,818	118·82	1907	15,586	66·52
1881	18,484	117·82	1908	20,491	84·00
1882	31,501	202·32	1909	28,620	112·48
1883	59,231	382·60	1910	38,200	143·67
1884	45,907	297·69	1911	68,913	247·57
1885	34,672	225·32	1912	88,551	303·32
1886	38,370	249·40	1913	75,649	246·61
1887	32,559	211·28			

SOURCE: These figures were kindly supplied by Dr F. Crowley who based them on official British source material.

TREND LINE: $\log Y_c = 1\cdot1878 + 0\cdot0011X + 0\cdot0004X^2$, centred on $X = 0 = 1887$.

Table 116. *Australia: miles of railway track added, 1855–1919:*
original data as percentage of trend

Year	Original data	Original data as percentage of trend	Year	Original data	Original data as percentage of trend
1855	14	70·00	1888	569	148·95
1856	16	69·57	1889	888	222·56
1857	85	326·92	1890	766	184·58
1858	15	51·72	1891	590	136·89
1859	39	118·18	1892	310	69·51
1860	44	115·79	1893	449	97·61
1861	28	66·67	1894	418	88·19
1862	130	270·83	1895	292	60·08
1863	22	41·51	1896	68	13·65
1864	74	123·33	1897	424	83·46
1865	21	31·34	1898	316	61·00
1866	29	39·19	1899	534	101·52
1867	192	234·15	1900	421	79·14
1868	71	78·02	1901	252	46·93
1869	129	129·00	1902	278	51·39
1870	83	75·45	1903	611	112·52
1871	36	29·75	1904	265	48·71
1872	138	104·55	1905	171	31·49
1873	182	126·39	1906	12	2·22
1874	222	141·40	1907	302	56·24
1875	209	122·94	1908	957	179·89
1876	328	178·26	1909	440	83·65
1877	409	205·53	1910	768	148·26
1878	389	181·78	1911	591	116·34
1879	290	126·64	1912	665	133·53
1880	425	173·47	1913	1,057	217·49
1881	592	225·95	1914	795	167·72
1882	555	198·92	1915	1,734	376·96
1883	473	159·80	1916	1,511	338·79
1884	710	226·84	1917	995	230·86
1885	447	135·45	1918	495	119·28
1886	738	212·07	1919	393	98·50
1887	566	155·07			

TREND LINE: $\log Y_c = 1·5622 + 0·0204X - 0·0006X^2$.

SOURCE: These figures are based on information kindly supplied to me by Dr F. Crowley, who also prepared the following note.

Note to Table 116

The figures given in the table refer to the additional length of railway line, exclusive of sidings and cross-overs, open for traffic on the last day of the working year, which has been taken as December 31 from 1854 to 1889 and as June 30 thereafter. The figure given for 1890 was obtained by doubling the figure for the six months ending June 30. The following are the actual years during which the change of date was made in each state, and which should be taken into account if the figures are to be used for graphing:

Victoria 1885.
New South Wales 1889.
Queensland 1890.
South Australia 1890.
Western Australia 1893.
Tasmania—all years used were for December 31 up to 1906.

The length of privately owned lines was never very great. For example on June 30, 1891 it amounted to 600 miles out of 10,133, and on June 30, 1898 to 837 out of 12,410. The increase in the years 1907–8 was not significant, as more particulars were furnished at that time about private railways in small undertakings, e.g. timber cuttings, mining, etc.

The sources used were as follows:

For 1854–72: T. A. Coghlan (ed.), *The Seven Colonies of Australasia, 1901–2* (1903).
For 1873–1905: *Victorian Year Book 1905* (Australasian Statistics).
For 1906–19: *Commonwealth Year Book*, nos. 1–13.

Table 117. *'Old' and 'new' immigration to the United States,
1870–1924*

Year ending June 30	'Old'	'New'	'Other'	Year ending June 30	'Old'	'New'	'Other'
1870	82·3	2·5	15·1	1898	34·5	62·4	3·2
1871	79·3	3·2	17·5	1899	28·9	68·0	3·1
1872	83·8	3·3	13·0	1900	23·1	72·4	4·4
1873	81·6	4·9	13·5	1901	23·7	73·6	2·6
1874	76·0	7·8	16·1	1902	21·4	75·0	3·6
1875	70·4	10·0	19·6	1903	23·8	72·1	4·1
1876	61·2	9·9	28·8	1904	26·8	68·4	4·9
1877	61·6	13·3	25·1	1905	25·6	69·9	4·5
1878	62·6	10·8	26·6	1906	20·2	75·7	4·0
1879	65·1	10·5	24·5	1907	17·7	76·2	6·0
1880	67·9	8·3	23·7	1908	22·8	66·9	10·4
1881	70·6	8·3	21·0	1909	19·6	68·5	11·9
1882	71·4	10·8	17·8	1910	19·4	70·9	9·6
1883	74·5	12·2	13·4	1911	23·0	65·2	11·8
1884	73·4	14·1	12·5	1912	19·2	68·1	12·7
1885	73·0	16·4	10·7	1913	15·3	74·9	9·9
1886	76·5	22·1	1·3	1914	13·5	75·2	11·3
1887	72·1	26·4	1·4	1915	24·2	37·4	38·3
1888	72·6	25·8	1·5	1916	17·1	32·2	50·7
1889	74·9	23·1	2·0	1917	13·0	32·2	54·8
1890	62·8	35·3	1·8	1918	11·7	16·4	71·9
1891	56·7	41·2	2·1	1919	12·8	4·7	82·5
1892	51·9	46·6	1·5	1920	20·3	38·3	41·5
1893	53·9	44·9	1·2	1921	17·2	65·3	17·5
1894	52·1	44·9	3·0	1922	25·7	44·9	29·4
1895	54·7	43·2	2·1	1923	29·9	29·4	40·7
1896	40·0	57·0	2·9	1924	28·8	23·2	48·0
1897	39·0	56·8	4·2				

100 % = the total number of immigrants for whom country of origin is known.

SOURCES: For 1870–1910, from United States Immigration Commission, *Statistical Review of Immigration, 1820–1910*; for 1911–24, from returns published by U.S. Bureau of Immigration.

The 'old' countries include those of Northern and Western Europe: Belgium, Denmark, France, Germany, the Netherlands, Norway, Sweden, Switzerland and Great Britain and Ireland.

Under 'new' are listed countries of Eastern and Southern Europe: Austria, Hungary, Czechoslovakia, Bulgaria, Finland, Greece, Italy, Poland, Portugal, Rumania, Russia, Spain and Turkey. See also Harry Jerome, *Migration and Business Cycles*, New York, National Bureau of Economic Research, 1926, p. 42.

Table 118. *Immigrant wage-earners (skilled, farm labourers, common labourers, and servants) entering the United States from England and Wales, 1875–1913*

Year	Number of immigrants	Year	Number of immigrants	Year	Number of immigrants	Year	Number of immigrants
1875	17,150	1885	20,787	1895	12,588	1905	25,450
1876	8,916	1886	22,044	1896	7,805	1906	22,032
1877	6,702	1887	33,375	1897	5,124	1907	26,599
1878	6,440	1888	35,602	1898	4,609	1908	23,513
1879	9,929	1889	29,418	1899	5,142	1909	18,180
1880	25,558	1890	24,047	1900	5,405	1910	27,016
1881	25,627	1891	22,304	1901	6,696	1911	27,846
1882	34,222	1892	18,247	1902	7,619	1912	22,936
1883	24,579	1893	16,491	1903	14,117	1913	25,686
1884	23,843	1894	9,728	1904	18,295		

SOURCE: See Tables 81 and 84.

Table 119. *The United Kingdom: loan expenditure by local authorities and gross capital expenditure by railways, 1875–1913. (£ millions at current prices)*

Year	Loan expenditure by local authorities	Gross capital expenditure by railways	Year	Loan expenditure by local authorities	Gross capital expenditure by railways
1875	10·8	17·8	1895	16·2	11·5
1876	13·4	17·5	1896	17·5	12·7
1877	16·1	17·4	1897	20·3	17·3
1878	17·0	14·6	1898	25·2	20·5
1879	15·4	14·0	1899	29·1	19·8
1880	14·8	12·0	1900	33·4	21·2
1881	12·8	14·6	1901	39·5	19·7
1882	10·7	15·5	1902	41·2	19·1
1883	10·9	16·9	1903	35·9	17·3
1884	12·8	16·6	1904	36·4	19·8
1885	12·4	13·7	1905	30·7	16·3
1886	10·8	8·6	1906	27·3	15·0
1887	11·6	9·3	1907	23·6	15·0
1888	9·2	9·1	1908	22·1	8·7
1889	9·0	11·5	1909	21·9	8·1
1890	9·5	14·5	1910	21·3	5·3
1891	13·1	15·7	1911	19·9	5·9
1892	13·3	17·1	1912	21·2	7·0
1893	16·7	12·8	1913	24·1	10·2
1894	16·4	12·0			

SOURCE: C. H. Feinstein's estimates given in Mitchell and Deane, *Abstract of British Historical Statistics*, pp. 373–4.

Table 120. *Sweden: total emigration, emigration per 1,000 population, net internal migration, railway track built, and investment per worker, 1857–1930*

Year	Emigration from Sweden	Emigration from Sweden per thousand of population	Net internal migration	Railway track built in Sweden (kilometres)	Investment per worker (kronor)
	(1)	(2)	(3)	(4)	(5)
1857	1,831	0·50	—	143	—
1858	571	0·15	—	117	—
1859	276	0·07	—	121	—
1860	348	0·09	393	80	—
1861	2,286	0·59	123	44	53
1862	2,535	0·64	395	337	57
1863	3,127	0·78	135	106	61
1864	5,177	1·28	157	129	74
1865	6,691	1·64	− 160	162	87
1866	7,206	1·74	643	262	84
1867	9,334	2·23	120	120	78
1868	27,024	6·46	272	0	66
1869	39,064	9·38	175	40	75
1870	20,003	4·80	302	0	87
1871	17,450	4·17	189	90	102
1872	15,915	3·76	484	118	144
1873	13,580	3·18	622	386	197
1874	7,791	1·80	387	1,040	262
1875	9,727	2·23	614	318	264
1876	9,418	2·14	692	619	225
1877	7,610	1·71	275	539	186
1878	9,032	2·00	− 144	356	148
1879	17,637	3·87	− 316	484	119
1880	42,109	9·21	− 46	199	128
1881	45,992	10·07	− 183	294	158
1882	50,178	10·97	− 40	135	174
1883	31,605	6·88	56	95	190
1884	23,560	5·10	357	200	190
1885	23,493	5·04	542	290	180
1886	32,889	7·00	116	387	146
1887	50,786	10·75	181	111	128
1888	50,323	10·61	61	139	135
1889	33,363	7·01	452	361	167
1890	34,212	7·16	− 164	130	179
1891	42,776	8·92	− 13	261	146
1892	45,504	9·47	− 222	182	114
1893	40,869	8·49	145	321	95
1894	13,358	2·76	22	452	108
1895	18,955	3·87	− 96	522	101

Table 120 (*continued*)

Year	Emigration from Sweden	Emigration from Sweden per thousand of population	Net internal migration	Railway track built in Sweden (kilometres)	Investment per worker (kronor)
	(1)	(2)	(3)	(4)	(5)
1896	19,551	3·96	220	140	121
1897	14,559	2·92	279	330	128
1898	13,663	2·71	672	134	152
1899	16,876	3·32	1,407	348	165
1900	20,661	4·04	553	595	147
1901	24,616	4·77	134	271	125
1902	37,107	7·15	− 563	377	123
1903	39,525	7·59	− 386	411	128
1904	22,384	4·27	153	181	147
1905	24,046	4·56	− 535	104	130
1906	24,704	4·65	− 357	441	168
1907	22,978	4·29	− 62	160	206
1908	12,499	2·31	11	116	182
1909	21,992	4·03	429	240	153
1910	27,816	5·06	1,341	225	164
1911	19,997	3·61	329	113	161
1912	18,117	3·25	458	229	173
1913	20,346	3·62	1,156	206	233
1914	12,960	2·29	1,029	267	239
1915	7,512	1·32	1,469	219	242
1916	10,571	1·84	1,013	90	341
1917	6,440	1·11	− 436	108	497
1918	4,853	0·84	509	91	676
1919	7,337	1·26	302	2	643
1920	10,242	1·74	40	6	800
1921	8,950	1·51	− 933	26	583
1922	11,797	1·98	− 1,060	214	340
1923	29,238	4·88	− 1,270	102	329
1924	10,671	1·77	− 894	213	340
1925	11,948	1·98	− 650	266	379
1926	13,043	2·15	− 544	98	415
1927	12,847	2·11	− 421	192	419
1928	13,450	2·21	− 271	430	434
1929	11,019	1·80	− 70	21	480
1930	5,682	0·93	213	88	531

SOURCES
Columns (1) and (2). *Statistik Årsbok för Sverige, 1950*, Stockholm, Statistika Centralbyrån, table 39.
Column (3). T. Widstam, 'Industriella konjunkturer, skördar och omflyttning', *Statsvetenskaplig Tidskrift*, 1934, I, pp. 24–5. Net movement into or out of (−) the industrial communities of Västmanland.
Column (4). Sveriges officiella statistik, *Allmän järnvägsstatistik*.
Column (5). Svennilson, *Wages in Sweden, 1860–1930*, London, King, 1935, p. 263.

Table 121. *Europe: estimated population and emigration to the United States, 1815–1908*

Year	Population (thousands)	Emigration to U.S.A. (thousands)	Year	Population (thousands)	Emigration to U.S.A. (thousands)
1815	202,000	1	1862	286,428	84
1816	204,000	11	1863	288,995	164
1817	206,000	12	1864	291,561	185
1818	208,000	15	1865	294,060	221
1819	210,000	13	1866	295,867	282
1820	212,000	8	1867	297,708	286
1821	214,100	8	1868	299,721	266
1822	216,200	6	1869	301,773	335
1823	218,300	5	1870	304,162	289
1824	220,400	7	1871	305,891	297
1825	222,500	9	1872	307,511	381
1826	224,500	11	1873	309,546	369
1827	226,500	19	1874	311,989	208
1828	228,500	24	1875	314,986	144
1829	230,500	17	1876	318,211	115
1830	232,600	27	1877	321,439	95
1831	234,500	26	1878	324,228	111
1832	236,200	43	1879	327,048	184
1833	238,000	43	1880	329,984	442
1834	239,700	62	1881	332,999	600
1835	241,400	42	1882	335,947	603
1836	243,100	71	1883	338,770	498
1837	244,800	75	1884	342,014	408
1838	246,600	36	1885	345,418	327
1839	248,200	64	1886	348,601	385
1840	249,900	80	1887	351,746	508
1841	251,455	77	1888	354,943	513
1842	253,294	100	1889	358,230	420
1843	255,297	57	1890	361,286	481
1844	257,765	78	1891	364,246	579
1845	260,308	113	1892	366,706	533
1846	262,627	157	1893	369,346	479
1847	263,668	228	1894	372,854	241
1848	263,466	225	1895	376,531	315
1849	263,717	284	1896	380,391	285
1850	265,068	320	1897	384,820	209
1851	266,698	370	1898	389,244	254
1852	268,457	363	1899	393,766	335
1853	269,998	362	1900	398,074	446
1854	271,365	406	1901	402,600	500
1855	272,035	188	1902	406,700	702
1856	272,894	186	1903	411,000	894
1857	274,830	237	1904	415,400	759
1858	277,070	112	1905	419,300	986
1859	279,363	112	1906	422,700	1,136
1860	281,572	141	1907	426,400	1,220
1861	283,837	81	1908	430,600	331

SOURCE: *Emigrationsutredningen*, Bilaga IV, *Utvandringsstatistik*, Stockholm, 1910, pp. 102–3.

Table 122. *European emigration to all oversea countries and to the United States, per 100,000 of the population, 1815–1908*

Year	To all countries	To U.S.A.	To all other countries	Year	To all countries	To U.S.A.	To all other countries	Year	To all countries	To U.S.A.	To all other countries
1815	2	0·6	1·4	1847	151	86·5	64·5	1879	100	56·3	43·7
1816	10	5·2	4·8	1848	121	85·4	35·6	1880	162	134·0	28·0
1817	14	5·9	8·1	1849	154	107·7	46·3	1881	210	180·3	29·7
1818	17	7·1	9·9	1850	158	120·7	37·3	1882	224	179·5	44·5
1819	20	6·0	14·0	1851	176	138·7	37·3	1883	216	147·1	68·9
1820	15	3·8	11·2	1852	196	135·2	60·8	1884	177	119·2	57·8
1821	12	3·5	8·5	1853	184	134·1	49·9	1885	155	94·7	60·3
1822	13	2·6	10·4	1854	215	149·6	65·4	1886	172	110·6	61·4
1823	11	2·5	8·5	1855	107	69·1	37·9	1887	215	144·5	70·5
1824	10	3·0	7·0	1856	102	68·2	33·8	1888	247	144·7	102·3
1825	11	4·2	6·8	1857	129	86·2	42·8	1889	222	117·3	104·7
1826	14	4·9	9·1	1858	66	40·4	25·6	1890	208	133·2	74·8
1827	17	8·4	8·6	1859	62	40·1	21·9	1891	241	159·1	81·9
1828	19	10·5	8·5	1860	70	50·1	19·9	1892	203	145·2	57·8
1829	16	7·4	8·6	1861	58	28·5	29·5	1893	192	129·7	62·3
1830	28	11·6	16·4	1862	68	29·3	38·7	1894	121	64·6	56·4
1831	39	11·1	27·9	1863	107	56·7	50·3	1895	169	83·7	85·3
1832	51	18·2	32·8	1864	112	63·5	48·5	1896	161	75·0	86·0
1833	34	18·1	15·9	1865	120	75·2	44·8	1897	128	54·2	73·8
1834	46	25·9	20·1	1866	134	95·3	38·7	1898	121	65·2	55·8
1835	27	17·4	9·6	1867	135	96·1	38·9	1899	148	85·2	62·8
1836	48	29·2	18·8	1868	132	88·7	43·3	1900	179	112·2	66·8
1837	48	30·6	17·4	1869	167	111·0	56·0	1901	210	124·3	85·7
1838	25	14·6	10·4	1870	149	95·0	54·0	1902	250	172·7	77·3
1839	40	25·8	14·2	1871	125	97·0	28·0	1903	281	217·6	63·4
1840	54	32·0	22·0	1872	163	124·0	39·0	1904	263	182·6	80·4
1841	66	30·6	35·4	1873	159	119·4	39·6	1905	343	235·3	107·7
1842	73	39·5	33·5	1874	116	66·7	49·3	1906	413	268·6	144·4
1843	38	22·3	15·7	1875	85	45·8	39·2	1907	429	286·1	142·9
1844	45	30·3	14·7	1876	73	36·0	37·0	1908	194	76·9	117·1
1845	63	43·4	19·6	1877	63	29·5	33·5				
1846	87	59·8	27·2	1878	71	34·4	36·6				

SOURCE: See Table 121.

Table 123. *Europe: quinquennial excess of births over deaths per thousand of population, 1821–85*

Average quinquennial excess during 1821–30	46
Average quinquennial excess during 1831–40	35
Quinquennial excess during 1841–5	45
Quinquennial excess during 1846–50	23
Quinquennial excess during 1851–5	29
Quinquennial excess during 1856–60	42
Quinquennial excess during 1861–5	48
Quinquennial excess during 1866–70	40
Quinquennial excess during 1871–5	41
Quinquennial excess during 1876–80	49
Quinquennial excess during 1881–5	51

These figures are based on Sundbärg, *Emigrationsutredningen*, Bilaga IV, p. 76. The source gives quinquennial figures for 1841–5 onwards and decennial figures for 1821–30 onwards. The values above for 1821–30 and 1831–40 are half of the decennial values.

In Fig. 35 the values are plotted at the mid-points of the decades 1821–30 and 1831–40, and thereafter at the mid-points of the quinquennia.

Table 124. *Merchandise imports into the United States at constant prices (in million dollars), 1831–1913: original data as percentage of trend*

Year	Original data	Original data as percentage of trend	Year	Original data	Original data as percentage of trend
1831	103	108·42	1873	477	114·94
1832	100	102·04	1874	438	101·86
1833	106	103·92	1875	437	97·98
1834	119	113·33	1876	404	87·26
1835	141	129·36	1877	418	87·08
1836	175	154·87	1878	444	89·16
1837	114	97·44	1879	493	95·54
1838	86	71·07	1880	703	131·40
1839	140	112·00	1881	633	114·05
1840	99	76·74	1882	687	119·27
1841	133	99·25	1883	692	115·91
1842	114	82·01	1884	688	111·15
1843	73	50·69	1885	649	101·09
1844	135	90·60	1886	761	114·26
1845	141	91·56	1887	829	119·97
1846	142	89·31	1888	847	118·13
1847	142	86·06	1889	892	119·89
1848	173	101·17	1890	968	125·39
1849	172	97·18	1891	1,030	128·59
1850	209	114·21	1892	1,047	125·99
1851	252	132·63	1893	1,125	130·51
1852	243	123·35	1894	885	98·88
1853	285	139·71	1895	1,038	111·73
1854	291	137·91	1896	1,122	116·39
1855	237	108·72	1897	1,125	112·50
1856	289	127·88	1898	886	85·36
1857	323	138·03	1899	942	87·38
1858	258	106·17	1900	1,069	95·62
1859	352	139·68	1901	1,010	86·99
1860	376	144·06	1902	1,082	89·79
1861	318	117·78	1903	1,186	94·80
1862	196	70·00	1904	1,139	87·68
1863	205	70·69	1905	1,277	94·66
1864	194	64·45	1906	1,378	98·36
1865	126	40·38	1907	1,551	106·67
1866	242	74·92	1908	1,298	85·96
1867	236	70·45	1909	1,374	87·63
1868	223	64·27	1910	1,542	94·72
1869	270	75·00	1911	1,543	91·25
1870	305	81·77	1912	1,687	96·07
1871	393	101·81	1913	1,786	97·92
1872	471	117·46			

SOURCE: *Historical Statistics of the United States, 1789–1945*, series L 2 and M 54.
TREND LINE: $\log Y_c = 1 \cdot 60259 + 0 \cdot 01565 X + 0 \cdot 00001 X^2$, centred on $X = 0 = 1872$.

Table 125. *Volume of total imports into the United Kingdom, 1841–1913: £ thousand (at constant prices) and original data as percentage of trend*

Year	Original data	Original data as percentage of trend	Year	Original data	Original data as percentage of trend
1841	74,164	99·93	1878	346,499	102·47
1842	71,314	91·47	1879	354,948	101·64
1843	76,995	94·05	1880	383,995	106·52
1844	83,817	97·55	1881	373,136	100·32
1845	93,389	103·61	1882	392,441	102·30
1846	86,388	91·40	1883	415,309	105·02
1847	98,574	99·51	1884	398,942	97·91
1848	103,652	99·88	1885	404,660	96·43
1849	115,672	106·45	1886	404,609	93·66
1850	109,909	96·63	1887	423,599	95·29
1851	118,837	99·87	1888	440,688	96·39
1852	118,011	94·85	1889	480,250	102·18
1853	137,555	105·77	1890	478,425	99·06
1854	136,400	100·40	1891	489,885	98·76
1855	126,428	89·11	1892	495,272	97·26
1856	146,816	99·15	1893	478,432	91·56
1857	150,795	97·61	1894	525,659	98·09
1858	145,752	90·47	1895	551,946	100·46
1859	159,226	94·82	1896	571,546	101·52
1860	183,885	105·11	1897	585,379	101·52
1861	184,390	101·21	1898	613,994	104·01
1862	166,005	87·54	1899	616,313	102·02
1863	176,891	89·66	1900	617,491	99·94
1864	185,162	90·25	1901	633,614	100·30
1865	195,956	91·89	1902	642,647	99·56
1866	220,396	99·47	1903	642,300	97·42
1867	215,901	93·83	1904	647,327	96·17
1868	234,333	98·11	1905	656,620	95·59
1869	238,297	96·17	1906	675,554	96·42
1870	253,265	98·55	1907	687,246	96·21
1871	287,876	108·07	1908	655,364	90·03
1872	288,074	104·38	1909	678,433	91·50
1873	301,656	105·54	1910	686,980	91·00
1874	309,504	104·61	1911	704,200	91·66
1875	321,284	104·95	1912	756,550	96·81
1876	332,764	105·11	1913	768,734	96·76
1877	347,715	106·25			

SOURCE: W. Schlote, op. cit. p. 135.
TREND LINE: $\log Y_c = 1\cdot5149 + 0\cdot0143X - 0\cdot0001X^2$, centred on $X = 0 = 1877$.

Table 126. *Male immigrants into the United States, quarterly, 1869–1913 (seasonally adjusted): original data as percentage of trend*

Quarter	Thousand	Original data as percentage of trend	Thousand	Original data as percentage of trend	Thousand	Original data as percentage of trend	Thousand	Original data as percentage of trend	Thousand	Original data as percentage of trend
	1869	1869	1878	1878	1887	1887	1896	1896	1905	1905
1st	—	—	20·1	41·27	69·0	125·68	65·3	88·12	291·2	243·48
2nd	62·4	121·17	21·9	44·88	87·1	157·50	53·2	71·03	169·6	139·59
3rd	71·9	140·16	28·7	58·81	81·4	146·40	36·0	47·49	151·1	122·45
4th	56·5	110·57	24·8	50·72	75·4	134·64	31·6	41·25	170·8	136·20
	1870	1870	1879	1879	1888	1888	1897	1897	1906	1906
1st	39·7	78·00	22·3	45·60	75·9	134·81	36·5	47·10	286·2	224·47
2nd	60·9	120·12	31·4	64·08	98·3	173·37	32·6	41·58	183·8	141·82
3rd	64·4	127·52	47·7	97·15	72·9	127·89	28·4	35·81	188·0	142·64
4th	38·3	75·99	63·7	129·47	60·8	105·92	33·5	41·77	247·1	184·40
	1871	1871	1880	1880	1889	1889	1898	1898	1907	1907
1st	25·5	50·80	67·8	137·53	55·5	96·02	47·5	58·50	304·1	223·27
2nd	52·0	103·79	90·3	182·79	68·4	117·53	31·6	38·49	220·3	158·95
3rd	63·9	128·06	107·4	216·97	63·7	108·70	38·7	46·57	217·0	153·90
4th	57·3	115·06	96·1	193·75	65·2	110·32	48·8	57·96	255·1	177·89
	1872	1872	1881	1881	1890	1890	1899	1899	1908	1908
1st	45·7	91·95	74·6	150·10	69·7	117·14	57·7	67·72	79·5	54·49
2nd	65·1	131·25	114·7	230·32	76·8	128·00	51·9	60·14	37·8	25·45
3rd	77·2	156·28	117·2	234·40	78·0	129·14	52·0	59·50	55·6	36·77
4th	65·4	132·66	125·5	250·50	83·4	136·95	77·4	87·46	98·1	63·74
	1873	1873	1882	1882	1891	1891	1900	1900	1909	1909
1st	47·4	96·34	117·9	234·39	94·0	153·09	100·0	111·48	260·4	166·28
2nd	75·0	152·75	131·0	259·92	94·4	152·50	78·5	86·45	131·6	82·51
3rd	68·2	138·90	106·7	210·87	91·0	145·83	69·5	75·54	134·8	83·00
4th	51·1	104·29	85·3	167·91	88·3	140·38	69·9	74·92	195·1	117·96
	1874	1874	1883	1883	1892	1892	1901	1901	1910	1910
1st	28·9	59·10	69·4	136·35	103·9	163·62	101·7	107·51	283·5	168·25
2nd	41·9	85·69	93·9	183·76	100·1	156·41	88·1	91·87	164·6	95·86
3rd	49·1	100·61	83·1	161·99	78·2	121·05	77·5	79·73	167·1	95·54
4th	35·2	72·13	83·9	162·91	48·3	74·08	101·4	102·94	173·8	97·53
	1875	1875	1884	1884	1893	1893	1902	1902	1911	1911
1st	29·3	60·16	69·1	133·66	67·6	102·74	164·0	164·16	167·7	92·29
2nd	29·6	60·78	74·1	142·50	96·7	145·63	125·3	123·57	104·5	56·43
3rd	37·5	77·16	67·2	128·74	78·3	116·87	109·0	106·03	102·7	54·40
4th	25·3	52·06	55·5	105·92	41·7	61·69	143·9	137·97	141·9	73·71
	1876	1876	1885	1885	1894	1894	1903	1903	1912	1912
1st	27·4	56·38	42·6	80·83	37·4	54·76	202·1	190·84	180·4	91·90
2nd	24·3	50·00	57·1	107·94	34·3	49·78	161·5	150·37	124·5	62·19
3rd	30·7	63·17	49·2	92·48	33·8	48·56	148·2	135·96	190·4	93·24
4th	21·7	44·65	41·7	77·94	37·4	53·20	159·7	144·26	228·0	109·40
	1877	1877	1886	1886	1895	1895	1904	1904	1913	1913
1st	19·5	40·12	44·2	82·31	34·6	48·66	156·7	139·41	207·8	97·74
2nd	20·9	43·00	57·1	105·74	45·0	62·67	113·0	99·04	193·8	89·35
3rd	24·3	49·90	68·2	125·60	53·1	73·24	126·9	109·49	299·7	135·37
4th	19·0	39·01	70·7	129·49	52·3	71·35	172·3	146·39	267·7	118·45

SOURCE: Based on Jerome, *Migration and Business Cycles*, New York, 1926, p. 245–6.
TREND LINE: $\log \overline{Y}_c = 0.79517 + 0.00361X + 0.00003X^2$, centred on $X = 0 = 1891$, 3rd quarter.

Table 127. *The United States: railroad freight ton-miles, quarterly, 1869–1913 (seasonally adjusted): thousand million ton-miles and original data as percentage of trend*

Quarter	Quarterly value	Original data as percentage of trend	Quarterly value	Original data as percentage of trend	Quarterly value	Original data as percentage of trend	Quarterly value	Original data as percentage of trend	Quarterly value	Original data as percentage of trend
	1869	1869	1878	1878	1887	1887	1896	1896	1905	1905
1st	—	—	7·05	105·22	14·52	101·26	24·24	88·89	46·59	101·28
2nd	2·80	98·25	6·68	97·52	15·10	103·21	23·40	84·45	49·61	106·46
3rd	2·78	95·21	6·94	99·00	15·04	100·87	23·38	83·03	50·28	106·53
4th	2·83	94·33	7·42	103·49	15·53	102·17	23·41	81·80	52·57	109·98
	1870	1870	1879	1879	1888	1888	1897	1897	1906	1906
1st	2·97	96·43	8·04	109·69	15·56	100·39	23·81	81·91	56·31	116·34
2nd	3·17	100·32	7·66	102·13	15·98	101·20	24·60	83·31	54·29	110·77
3rd	3·43	105·86	8·39	109·53	16·51	102·55	26·67	88·90	55·78	112·44
4th	3·42	103·01	9·14	116·58	16·71	101·83	27·32	89·66	56·56	112·60
	1871	1871	1880	1880	1889	1889	1898	1898	1907	1907
1st	3·41	100·00	9·64	120·35	17·59	105·20	28·20	91·11	60·11	118·23
2nd	3·64	104·00	9·75	119·05	17·74	104·17	29·16	92·78	63·28	122·97
3rd	3·78	105·29	9·70	115·89	18·68	107·67	28·63	89·72	62·79	120·56
4th	3·73	101·36	9·93	116·00	18·86	106·67	30·39	93·80	58·79	111·53
	1872	1872	1881	1881	1890	1890	1899	1899	1908	1908
1st	4·03	106·90	9·89	113·03	19·57	108·66	30·20	91·82	53·12	99·61
2nd	4·12	106·46	10·86	121·48	20·19	110·09	31·89	95·48	51·23	94·94
3rd	4·30	108·59	10·96	120·04	20·82	111·46	33·74	99·56	54·00	98·92
4th	4·50	110·84	10·36	111·04	21·04	110·62	34·30	99·71	56·06	101·50
	1873	1873	1882	1882	1891	1891	1900	1900	1909	1909
1st	4·69	112·74	10·96	115·01	21·50	111·05	35·06	100·43	56·28	100·75
2nd	5·05	118·27	10·75	110·37	21·74	110·24	35·52	100·25	57·34	101·47
3rd	5·04	115·33	10·81	108·64	22·77	113·45	35·33	98·28	60·63	106·13
4th	4·92	109·82	10·80	106·30	22·92	112·13	35·47	97·23	62·81	108·71
	1874	1874	1883	1883	1892	1892	1901	1901	1910	1910
1st	5·14	111·98	11·06	106·55	23·28	111·92	37·88	102·38	63·81	109·21
2nd	5·07	107·64	11·04	104·15	23·20	109·59	38·83	103·44	65·63	111·11
3rd	5·07	105·19	11·34	104·81	23·82	110·58	39·07	102·63	63·56	106·43
4th	5·03	101·82	11·73	106·15	23·35	106·52	38·45	99·56	62·80	104·03
	1875	1875	1884	1884	1893	1893	1902	1902	1911	1911
1st	4·92	97·23	11·29	100·09	23·90	107·13	39·47	100·79	62·47	102·39
2nd	5·22	100·77	11·94	103·74	25·24	111·24	40·83	102·82	62·98	102·12
3rd	5·24	98·68	11·71	99·66	22·69	98·31	40·99	101·81	62·73	100·66
4th	5·46	100·55	11·59	96·66	22·10	94·08	42·58	104·31	63·61	101·00
	1876	1876	1885	1885	1894	1894	1903	1903	1912	1912
1st	5·74	103·24	11·79	96·32	20·97	87·81	45·10	108·99	67·05	105·39
2nd	5·61	98·42	11·81	94·56	21·06	86·70	46·06	109·80	66·67	103·72
3rd	5·68	97·43	11·53	90·50	20·32	82·27	45·83	107·81	68·93	106·14
4th	5·89	98·66	12·38	95·23	21·40	85·19	44·33	102·88	74·21	113·13
	1877	1877	1886	1886	1895	1895	1904	1904	1913	1913
1st	5·70	93·29	12·77	96·30	21·43	83·91	44·27	101·40	78·83	118·99
2nd	5·40	86·40	13·44	99·41	22·51	86·68	44·49	100·54	75·14	112·30
3rd	5·56	86·88	13·91	100·87	22·86	86·62	44·90	100·18	73·73	109·13
4th	6·39	97·56	14·10	100·21	24·21	90·23	46·94	103·35	73·43	107·62

SOURCE: *Historical Statistics of the United States, 1789–1945*, Appendices 11 and 12.
TREND LINE: log $Y_c = 1·30262 + 0·00775X - 0·00002X^2$, centred on $X = 0 = 1891$, 3rd quarter.

Table 128. *The United States: pig iron production, monthly, 1898–1907 (seasonally adjusted): original data as percentage of trend*

Month	Daily average (thousands of gross tons)	Original data as percentage of trend	Daily average (thousands of gross tons)	Original data as percentage of trend	Daily average (thousands of gross tons)	Original data as percentage of trend
	1898	1898	1902	1902	1906	1906
Jan.	—	—	46·13	108·26	67·76	111·91
Feb.	31·62	99·40	44·46	103·64	67·14	109·99
Mar.	31·48	98·44	45·60	105·58	68·55	111·43
April	30·83	95·83	47·21	108·55	66·83	107·79
May	30·83	95·30	47·97	109·55	66·68	106·69
June	30·76	94·53	47·86	108·53	66·07	104·86
July	30·76	93·98	47·75	107·55	67·30	105·98
Aug.	31·19	94·74	49·43	110·56	64·12	100·16
Sept.	31·33	94·62	48·64	108·04	65·77	101·91
Oct.	31·77	95·41	47·97	105·82	69·50	106·82
Nov.	32·58	97·25	47·86	104·84	72·11	109·96
Dec.	33·19	98·49	50·23	109·27	73·45	111·09
	1899	1899	1903	1903	1907	1907
Jan.	32·96	97·23	47·53	102·68	72·61	108·91
Feb.	32·06	94·02	49·20	105·53	72·11	107·29
Mar.	32·28	94·08	50·23	106·96	70·47	104·00
April	33·11	95·92	51·40	108·69	71·45	104·60
May	33·96	97·81	53·46	112·26	73·45	106·63
June	35·81	102·52	55·46	115·64	74·82	107·73
July	37·93	107·91	51·17	105·90	75·51	107·83
Aug.	39·17	110·77	52·72	108·34	74·82	105·95
Sept.	39·45	110·88	52·84	107·81	72·28	101·52
Oct.	39·99	111·74	46·03	93·23	73·45	102·30
Nov.	40·83	113·35	34·67	69·72	60·12	83·03
Dec.	41·21	113·71	27·73	55·35	40·64	55·66
	1900	1900	1904	1904		
Jan.	40·83	111·96	29·92	59·28		
Feb.	41·12	112·07	41·30	81·25		
Mar.	40·09	108·59	45·81	89·47		
April	39·36	105·95	50·00	96·94		
May	40·18	107·46	48·08	92·50		
June	40·27	107·02	42·95	82·03		
July	37·58	99·23	37·15	70·43		
Aug.	34·51	90·55	39·26	73·87		
Sept.	32·36	84·38	46·03	85·97		
Oct.	30·48	78·96	46·67	86·51		
Nov.	30·83	79·36	49·43	90·95		
Dec.	33·50	85·68	52·97	96·71		
	1901	1901	1905	1905		
Jan.	36·98	93·95	58·21	105·49		
Feb.	40·09	101·21	56·36	101·37		
Mar.	40·27	100·98	61·38	109·55		
April	40·09	99·90	61·80	109·44		
May	41·50	102·75	61·94	108·86		
June	43·35	106·62	59·70	104·13		
July	45·19	110·38	58·08	100·52		
Aug.	45·50	110·41	61·52	105·63		
Sept.	45·08	108·65	63·97	109·01		
Oct.	44·98	107·71	65·46	110·69		
Nov.	45·50	108·23	66·68	111·86		
Dec.	41·21	97·35	67·14	111·75		

SOURCE: *Historical Statistics of the United States, 1789–1945*, Appendix 10.
TREND LINE: $\log Y_c = 0.665529 + 0.003059X + 0.000005X^2$, centred on $X = 0 =$ January 1903.

Table 129. *Male immigrants to the United States, monthly, 1898–1907*
(seasonally adjusted): original data as percentage of trend

Month	Thousands	Original data as percentage of trend	Thousands	Original data as percentage of trend	Thousands	Original data as percentage of trend
	1898	1898	1902	1902	1906	1906
Jan.	12·54	101·39	35·16	91·35	74·03	104·96
Feb.	11·62	99·06	42·52	108·44	77·24	109·08
Mar.	12·37	102·23	44·28	110·84	71·69	100·45
April	13·44	109·45	43·89	107·86	67·03	93·41
May	11·19	86·95	45·30	109·31	61·50	85·24
June	7·73	57·43	42·61	101·02	65·81	90·76
July	14·81	108·26	41·79	97·37	67·65	92·85
Aug.	13·06	92·62	40·01	91·62	73·07	99·85
Sept.	16·89	116·24	44·52	100·23	77·53	105·48
Oct.	16·03	107·08	46·70	103·41	76·11	103·13
Nov.	16·14	104·74	45·55	99·17	80·80	109·10
Dec.	16·09	101·45	50·63	108·46	89·15	119·95
	1899	1899	1903	1903	1907	1907
Jan.	14·81	90·69	48·32	101·88	83·49	111·98
Feb.	14·57	86·73	55·32	114·84	75·32	100·74
Mar.	14·97	86·63	51·60	105·48	77·70	103·66
April	16·48	92·74	58·61	118·00	68·31	90·90
May	19·62	107·45	56·42	111·90	77·90	103·45
June	18·77	99·95	54·85	107·21	89·57	118·73
July	18·57	96·27	55·10	106·17	81·83	108·30
Aug.	20·98	105·85	56·95	108·19	87·79	116·05
Sept.	20·85	102·46	59·88	112·20	82·40	108·79
Oct.	24·91	119·24	59·04	109·13	83·60	110·36
Nov.	26·44	122·75	54·49	99·38	99·79	131·61
Dec.	25·24	114·68	42·36	76·27	—	—
	1900	1900	1904	1904		
Jan.	24·47	108·37	40·10	71·29		
Feb.	25·60	101·58	35·75	62·76		
Mar.	26·17	110·19	42·44	73·60		
April	26·76	109·94	40·50	69·40		
May	27·30	109·46	39·34	66·63		
June	29·16	114·13	39·23	65·69		
July	30·25	115·59	46·44	76·91		
Aug.	27·36	102·09	50·84	83·28		
Sept.	23·03	83·38	50·15	81·28		
Oct.	24·10	85·86	49·01	78·60		
Nov.	20·73	72·15	57·84	91·84		
Dec.	24·50	83·39	65·54	103·07		
	1901	1901	1905	1905		
Jan.	27·14	90·32	87·39	135·24		
Feb.	30·26	98·50	77·24	119·20		
Mar.	23·92	76·18	69·57	106·39		
April	29·80	92·89	62·53	94·81		
May	33·47	102·14	53·93	81·06		
June	29·08	86·88	63·87	95·34		
July	27·74	81·18	61·75	91·31		
Aug.	28·34	81·27	54·04	79·31		
Sept.	33·78	94·91	59·11	86·12		
Oct.	28·48	78·46	60·42	87·39		
Nov.	35·00	94·54	48·16	69·18		
Dec.	37·93	100·48	60·81	86·77		

SOURCE: Based on Jerome, *Migration and Business Cycles*, p. 246.
TREND LINE: $\log Y_c = 1\cdot6691 + 0\cdot0069865X - 0\cdot000057889X^2$, centred on $X = 0 =$ December 1902.

Table 130. *The United States: patents granted for*
inventions, 1839–1913

Year	No. of patents	Year	No. of patents	Year	No. of patents	Year	No. of patents
1839	404	1858	3,467	1877	12,920	1896	21,867
1840	458	1859	4,165	1878	12,345	1897	22,098
1841	490	1860	4,363	1879	12,133	1898	20,404
1842	488	1861	3,040	1880	12,926	1899	23,296
1843	494	1862	3,221	1881	15,548	1900	24,660
1844	478	1863	3,781	1882	18,135	1901	25,558
1845	475	1864	4,638	1883	21,196	1902	27,136
1846	566	1865	6,099	1884	19,147	1903	31,046
1847	495	1866	8,874	1885	23,331	1904	30,267
1848	584	1867	12,301	1886	21,797	1905	29,784
1849	988	1868	12,544	1887	20,429	1906	31,181
1850	884	1869	12,957	1888	19,585	1907	35,880
1851	757	1870	12,157	1889	23,360	1908	32,757
1852	890	1871	11,687	1890	25,322	1909	36,574
1853	846	1872	12,200	1891	22,328	1910	35,168
1854	1,759	1873	11,616	1892	22,661	1911	32,917
1855	1,892	1874	12,230	1893	22,768	1912	36,231
1856	2,315	1875	13,291	1894	19,875	1913	33,941
1857	2,686	1876	14,172	1895	20,883		

SOURCE: *Historical Statistics of the United States, 1789–1945*, series P 177.

Table 131. *The United States: ratio of capital stock to gross national product in various industrial sectors, 1879–88 to 1919–28*

Section A. Percentage distribution of gross national product
by industrial sector. 1929 prices

Sector	1879–88	1889–98	1899–1908	1909–18	1919–28	Average
1. Agriculture	21·1	18·6	15·6	13·0	10·4	15·7
2. Mining	1·6	2·2	2·8	3·3	3·2	2·6
3. Manufacturing	17·0	19·3	20·0	22·9	22·1	20·3
4. Steam railway, Pullman and express	3·0	4·0	5·0	6·1	5·5	4·7
5. Street railways	0·2	0·5	0·7	0·9	0·8	0·6
6. Telephone	0·03	0·1	0·5	0·8	0·9	0·4
7. Telegraph	0·1	0·2	0·1	0·1	0·2	0·2
8. Electric light and power	0·01	0·1	0·2	0·4	1·0	0·4
9. Other public utilities	1·7	1·8	2·0	1·9	1·2	1·7
10. Residential building	6·6	5·7	6·6	7·2	8·1	6·9
11. All other	48·6	47·6	46·6	43·4	46·5	46·5
12. Total	100·0	100·0	100·0	100·0	100·0	100·0

The data for 1919–28 have been extrapolated by index of the ratio of the physical output index for each industrial sector to the gross national product in 1929 prices.

Note. The figures in this table were kindly supplied by Professor Kuznets, who subsequently published revised estimates, 'Long-term Changes in the National Income of the United States of America since 1870' in *Income and Wealth of the United States: Trends and Structure*, Income and Wealth, Series II. Cambridge, Bowes and Bowes, 1952, pp. 88–131. The major inferences drawn from Table 131 in Chapter x, pp. 163–6, are not contradicted by the published estimates. I take sole responsibility for these inferences.

Section B. Percentage distribution of the value of improvements
and equipment, 1929 prices

Sector	1879–88	1889–98	1899–1908	1909–18	1919–28
1. Agriculture	14·5	11·7	10·8	10·4	10·0
2. Mining	1·4	1·6	1·9	2·0	2·3
3. Manufacturing	7·2	9·4	11·0	11·9	18·0
4. Steam railway, Pullman and express	25·5	23·4	20·0	17·9	15·8
5. Street railways	1·1	2·5	4·5	5·3	3·9
6. Telephone	0·2	0·6	1·2	1·3	1·6
7. Telegraph	0·5	0·5	0·3	0·3	0·3
8. Electric light and power	0·1	0·6	1·6	2·4	3·0
9. Other public utilities	3·2	2·7	2·8	2·8	2·4
10. Residential building	25·4	25·7	25·6	26·1	24·4
11. All other	21·0	21·4	20·2	18·6	18·4
12. Total	100·0	100·0	100·0	100·0	100·0

Derived from the wealth totals in 1929 prices in *National Product since 1869*. The percentage distributions were first established for 1880, 1890, 1900, 1912 and 1922. Then these percentages were averaged as follows:

1880 and 1890 for 1879–88.
1890 and 1900 for 1889–98.
1900 and 1912 for 1899–1908.
1912 was used for 1909–18.
1922 was used for 1919–28.

Section C. Ratio of percentage of improvements and equipment
to percentage of gross national product

Sector	1879–88	1889–98	1899–1908	1909–18	1919–28
1. Agriculture	0·69	0·63	0·69	0·80	0·96
2. Mining	0·87	0·76	0·70	0·63	0·72
3. Manufacturing	0·42	0·49	0·55	0·52	0·81
4. Steam railway, Pullman and express	8·40	5·86	3·99	2·93	2·87
5. Street railways	4·89	5·14	6·31	5·64	4·78
6. Telephone	5·80	7·31	2·46	1·63	1·87
7. Telegraph	3·57	2·59	2·49	2·02	1·64
8. Electric light and power	10·00	6·56	9·21	5·59	2·90
9. Other public utilities	1·85	1·50	1·38	1·48	1·90
10. Residential building	3·85	4·50	3·90	3·61	3·00
11. All other	0·43	0·45	0·43	0·45	0·39

Derived by dividing entries in Section B by corresponding entries in Section A.

Section D. Ratio of improvements and equipment to gross
national product (the latter per year), 1929 prices

Sector	1879–88	1889–98	1899–1908	1909–18	1919–28	Average
1. Total	1·98	2·58	2·56	2·78	2·47	2·67
2. Agriculture	1·37	1·61	1·77	2·22	2·37	1·87
3. Mining	1·71	1·96	1·80	1·74	1·77	1·79
4. Manufacturing	0·83	1·25	1·41	1·45	2·01	1·39
5. Steam railway, Pullman and express	16·62	15·12	10·21	8·15	7·10	11·44
6. Street railways	9·68	13·27	16·15	15·68	11·82	13·32
7. Telephone	11·47	18·87	6·29	4·54	4·61	9·16
8. Telegraph	7·06	6·68	6·17	5·62	4·06	5·92
9. Electric light and power	19·78	16·93	23·56	15·53	7·15	16·59
10. Other public utilities	3·66	3·86	3·53	4·12	4·68	3·97
11. Residential building	7·61	11·62	9·97	10·04	7·42	9·33
12. All other	0·85	1·16	1·11	1·25	0·98	1·07

Line 1. Ratio of improvements and equipment at midpoint (i.e. year ending with 4) to gross national product for decade.

The former is taken for January 1, 1925 (Kuznets, *National Product since 1869*), estimated for January 1934 by adding net producer durables and construction for 1925–33, then extrapolated back from 1934 by subtracting decade totals of net producer durables and net construction.

Lines 2–12. Line 1 multiplied by entries in Section C.

Section E. Changes in ratio (improvements and equipment) to gross national product at constant prices, due to *intra-* and *inter-*sector shifts

	1879–88 to 1889–98	1889–98 to 1899–1908	1899–1908 to 1909–18	1909–18 to 1919–28	Total	Source
1. Total	+0·60	−0·02	+0·22	−0·31	+0·49	Line 1. Section D
2. Due to *intra* movement	+0·53	−0·34	+0·02	−0·27	−0·06	
3. Due to *inter-* sector shifts	+0·07	+0·24	+0·25	+0·06	+0·62	

Line 2. Derived by multiplying the average share of each sector in gross national product (Section A) by the ratio in Section D; adding; then getting differences from decade to decade.

Line 3. Derived by multiplying the average *ratio* of each sector (Section D) by the ratio in Section A; adding; then getting differences from decade to decade.

Table 132. *Statistical material for an index of British building activity per capita, 1830–1947*

Bricks produced per capita in England and Wales (1)		Railway miles added in U.K. per million of population (2)		Parry Lewis index of building per capita in Great Britain (3)		Index of planned building per capita (4)		Insured employed builders per thousand of population (U.K.) (5)	
1830	79·62	1843	3·54	1870	112·9	1911	334·5	1923	14·11
1831	80·98	1844	7·28	1871	114·4	1912	318·9	1924	14·60
1832	68·93	1845	10·85	1872	120·1	1913	345·6	1925	15·55
1833	70·71	1846	21·99	1873	108·4	1914	294·9	1926	16·16
1834	79·46	1847	33·51	1874	123·4	1915	191·4	1927	17·35
1835	91·76	1848	43·47	1875	151·9	1916	137·5	1928	16·06
1836	107.75	1849	33·16	1876	170·8	1917	103·7	1929	16·51
1837	97·85	1850	21·59	1877	159·0	1918	91·3	1930	15·61
1838	93·21	1851	9·82	1878	134·5	1919	322·5	1931	15·19
1839	101·99	1852	16·19	1879	107·1	1920	469·8	1932	13·39
1840	106·78	1853	12·82	1880	100·1	1921	168·9	1933	15·16
1841	89·47	1854	13·21	1881	100·0	1922		1934	16·64
1842	78·93	1855	8·07	1882	94·2	1923	330·9	1935	17·86
1843	71·02	1856	15·16	1883	95·0	1924	395·0	1936	19·17
1844	86·01	1857	13·67	1884	93·6	1925	424·6	1937	19·44
1845	108·90	1858	15·74	1885	85·3	1926	476·4	1938	19·10
1846	120·54	1859	16·07	1886	80·7	1927	445·4	1939	19·24
1847	128·13	1860	14·98	1887	83·9	1928	454·5	1940	14·18
1848	84·33	1861	14·93	1888	81·4	1929	492·5	1941	13·44
1849	83·46	1862	23·51	1889	80·0	1930	490·6	1942	10·97
		1863	26·19	1890	74·4	1931	432·0	1943	8·53
		1864	15·73	1891	74·5	1932	454·3	1944	8·07
		1865	16·69	1892	78·7	1933	570·2	1945	10·33
		1866	18·70	1893	87·5	1934	636·7	1946	17·29
		1867	12·90	1894	88·0	1935	696·0	1947	19·93
		1868	12·40	1895	89·4	1936	745·7		
				1896	104·6	1937	723·7		
				1897	117·9	1938	689·5		
				1898	140·3	1939			
				1899	138·6	1940	608·7		
				1900	125·5	1941	527·9		
				1901	121·0	1942	453·5		
				1902	125·8	1943	352·4		
				1903	127·4	1944	275·9		
				1904	113·7	1945	206·6		
				1905	113·1	1946	449·1		
				1906	98·8	1947	487·4		
				1907	90·9	1948	541·7		
				1908	79·0	1949	561·0		
				1909	77·3	1950	585·0		
				1910	68·2				
				1911	56·9				
				1912	45·7				
				1913	40·5				

SOURCES

(1) H. A. Shannon, 'Bricks—A Trade Index, 1785–1849', *Economica*, new series, vol. 1, no. 3, August 1934, pp. 316–17.

(2) *Statistical Abstract for the United Kingdom*, 1840–54, C. 144, 1870, p. 84, and 1855–69, C. 145, 1870, p. 131.

(3) J. Parry Lewis, *Building Cycles and Britain's Growth*, pp. 316–17.

(4) and (5) *Statistical Abstracts for the United Kingdom* and *Annual Abstracts of Statistics*. See also Appendix 3.

In all cases the figures printed have been derived from those given in the above sources by dividing by the estimated population.

Table 133. *Annual volume of construction per capita in the United States, 1914–48**

Year	Riggleman's index of annual building permits per capita (year ending July 1) (1)	Total new construction expenditure in millions of current dollars (2)	Total new construction expenditure per capita in terms of 1913 dollars (3)
1914	30	—	—
1915	30	2,932	·312
1916	32	3,453	·260
1917	15	4,138	·222
1918	9	4,714	·238
1919	19	5,736	·276
1920	17	6,117	·230
1921	25	5,531	·251
1922	45	7,017	·367
1923	44	8,567	·357
1924	44	9,548	·389
1925	52	10,512	·438
1926	47	11,119	·457
1927	43	11,067	·451
1928	40	10,780	·430
1929	35	9,873	·391
1930	20	8,042	·322
1931	16	5,967	·266
1932	7	3,290	·168
1933	5	2,376	·111
1934	—	2,805	·112
1935	—	3,230	·130
1936	—	4,836	·183
1937	—	5,487	·181
1938	—	5,186	·169
1939	—	6,307	·204
1940	—	7,040	·220
1941	—	10,490	·306
1942	—	13,412	·360
1943	—	7,784	·197
1944	—	4,136	·100
1945	—	4,808	·112
1946	—	10,464	·214
1947	—	14,324	·242
1948	—	18,775	·277

* For 1831–1913 see Table 108.

SOURCES

Column (1). See Table 108.

Column (2). *Historical Statistics of the United States, 1789–1945*, column H 2, and *Statistical Abstract of the United States, 1950*, p. 934.

Column (3). Derived from column (2) by dividing by an index of construction costs (*Historical Statistics*, column H 64) and by the population (*Historical Statistics*, column B 31).

Table 134. *Annual immigration into the United States per 10,000 of population, 1830–1948*

Year		Year		Year	
1830	19·8	1870	98·9	1910	115·1
1831	18·6	1871	80·4	1911	95·1
1832	40·6	1872	99·0	1912	89·2
1833	43·8	1873	109·2	1913	125·7
1834	48·2	1874	72·7	1914	125·3
1835	33·6	1875	51·5	1915	32·9
1836	54·0	1876	37·6	1916	29·9
1837	55·2	1877	30·8	1917	28·9
1838	28·5	1878	29·2	1918	10·7
1839	46·0	1879	36·9	1919	13·5
1840	55·1	1880	92·8	1920	41·0
1841	51·5	1881	135·9	1921	75·6
1842	62·7	1882	156·8	1922	28·6
1843	41·0	1883	117·1	1923	47·5
1844	44·7	1884	95·9	1924	63·2
1845	61·2	1885	71·2	1925	25·8
1846	78·7	1886	58·9	1926	26·3
1847	114·9	1887	84·6	1927	28·5
1848	104·0	1888	92·3	1928	25·7
1849	140·0	1889	73·3	1929	23·2
1850	139·3	1890	73·6	1930	19·8
1851	176·3	1891	88·7	1931	7·9
1852	169·7	1892	89·9	1932	2·9
1853	161·0	1893	66·9	1933	1·8
1854	178·9	1894	42·6	1934	2·3
1855	86·5	1895	37·9	1935	2·7
1856	81·7	1896	49·2	1936	2·8
1857	96·4	1897	32·5	1937	3·9
1858	50·0	1898	31·7	1938	5·2
1859	52·1	1899	42·4	1939	6·3
1860	58·6	1900	60·0	1940	5·4
1861	35·8	1901	64·1	1941	3·9
1862	35·2	1902	83·6	1942	2·1
1863	60·2	1903	108·2	1943	1·8
1864	65·3	1904	100·8	1944	2·1
1865	82·2	1905	124·8	1945	2·7
1866	100·0	1906	131·3	1946	10·8
1867	93·7	1907	150·4	1947	12·2
1868	75·4	1908	90·0	1948	12·1
1869	92·4	1909	84·7		

SOURCE: *Historical Statistics of the United States, 1789–1945,* series B 31 and B 304, and *Statistical Abstract of the United States.*

Table 135. *Volume of imports of foodstuffs into the United Kingdom,* *1841–1913: £ thousand (at constant prices) and original data as percentage* *of trend*

Year	Original data	Original data as percentage of trend	Year	Original data	Original data as percentage of trend
1841	21,244	122·73	1878	135,295	108·29
1842	20,799	112·03	1879	145,967	112·71
1843	16,590	83·40	1880	149,207	111·25
1844	19,887	93·38	1881	142,997	103·04
1845	21,148	92·85	1882	140,709	98·09
1846	25,491	104·73	1883	155,849	105·20
1847	40,141	154·48	1884	142,197	93·02
1848	32,676	117·90	1885	154,666	98·15
1849	39,647	134·25	1886	147,835	91·09
1850	36,999	117·68	1887	157,167	94·12
1851	39,526	118·19	1888	161,087	93·83
1852	33,743	94·95	1889	170,212	96·54
1853	43,157	114·38	1890	177,886	98·32
1854	42,677	106·63	1891	180,163	97·13
1855	37,444	88·28	1892	189,733	99·87
1856	44,582	99·28	1893	186,868	96·12
1857	42,122	88·68	1894	202,496	101·89
1858	45,259	90·16	1895	211,661	104·27
1859	43,333	81·76	1896	220,700	106·54
1860	56,858	101·69	1897	225,198	106·63
1861	63,624	107·97	1898	237,136	110·23
1862	72,534	116·91	1899	245,992	112·36
1863	71,041	108·85	1900	247,690	111·28
1864	64,967	94·71	1901	254,380	112·51
1865	64,524	89·58	1902	249,898	108·91
1866	71,388	94·48	1903	258,226	110·99
1867	73,058	92·25	1904	257,893	109·43
1868	78,119	94·20	1905	251,868	105·60
1869	85,338	98·36	1906	258,022	106·99
1870	83,886	92·51	1907	258,596	106·15
1871	93,889	99·16	1908	250,345	101·82
1872	105,307	106·60	1909	256,860	103·61
1873	110,070	106·90	1910	259,667	103·97
1874	108,673	101·35	1911	267,478	106·41
1875	119,815	107·40	1912	272,212	107·70
1876	124,101	107·02	1913	284,239	111·94
1877	131,431	109·14			

SOURCE: W. Schlote, op. cit. p. 144.

TREND LINE: $\log Y_c = 1·0807 + 0·0162X - 0·0002X^2$, centred on $X = 0 = 1877$.

Table 136. *Net monthly immigration of aliens into the United States,
1919–30 (seasonally adjusted)*

	1919	1920	1921	1922	1923	1924
Jan.	2,449	6,668	69,060	11,485	34,251	39,339
Feb.	− 540	23,749	52,455	4,661	34,043	32,744
Mar.	− 1,785	15,439	42,890	5,820	34,988	27,955
April	− 269	22,851	31,054	4,502	37,617	25,888
May	− 2,366	32,032	46,694	10,614	41,127	23,031
June	− 8,208	42,380	25,727	13,597	43,053	32,750
July	− 10,611	49,207	17,215	36,979	108,010	4,420
Aug.	− 8,936	40,075	11,026	34,606	87,671	15,710
Sept.	− 974	46,857	6,293	34,788	68,467	15,828
Oct.	− 5,454	48,151	8,000	36,721	63,165	14,443
Nov.	− 7,677	47,508	15,751	36,922	74,175	17,918
Dec.	12,050	75,002	4,659	34,779	62,494	18,634
	1925	1926	1927	1928	1929	1930
Jan.	20,636	19,262	20,785	17,917	18,354	15,118
Feb.	21,033	21,011	22,183	20,225	16,375	13,006
Mar.	19,264	23,202	22,826	19,009	15,763	15,018
Apr.	16,531	22,301	22,644	20,560	19,763	14,375
May	15,419	24,185	22,436	17,408	18,114	13,716
June	21,728	19,126	17,628	14,681	19,563	11,803
July	13,682	21,252	19,799	17,968	20,904	11,867
Aug.	15,951	23,483	23,683	19,444	18,443	10,258
Sept.	16,034	23,543	19,199	17,432	18,784	10,425
Oct.	16,438	22,806	19,807	17,554	17,081	6,720
Nov.	17,354	20,645	18,909	15,772	15,956	3,679
Dec.	16,528	19,328	17,899	13,619	17,490	1,335

SOURCE: The original figures are from the annual reports of the United States
Commissioner General of Immigration.

Table 137. The United States: value of construction contracts awarded in various states, monthly, 1921–30

Year		Value of contracts awarded						Estimated value in twenty-seven States		Seasonally adjusted value at constant costs in twenty-seven States	
		In twenty-seven States		In thirty-six States		In thirty-seven States					
		Residential ($ million)	Total ($ million)	Residential ($ million)	Total ($ million)	Residential ($ million)	Total ($ million)	Residential ($ million)	Total ($ million)	Residential (1913) $ million	Total (1913) $ million
		(1)	(2)	(3)	(4)	(5)	(6)	(7)	(8)	(9)	(10)
1921	Jan.	31	112	—	—	—	—	31	112	17	62
	Feb.	36	101	—	—	—	—	36	101	22	58
	Mar.	61	164	—	—	—	—	61	164	23	65
	April	75	221	—	—	—	—	75	221	26	85
	May	83	242	—	—	—	—	83	242	35	100
	June	75	228	—	—	—	—	75	228	31	97
	July	60	212	—	—	—	—	60	212	33	99
	Aug.	80	221	—	—	—	—	80	221	44	110
	Sept.	95	246	—	—	—	—	95	246	55	130
	Oct.	90	222	—	—	—	—	90	222	48	118
	Nov.	90	192	—	—	—	—	90	192	53	129
	Dec.	101	199	—	—	—	—	101	199	62	140
1922	Jan.	76	166	—	—	—	—	76	166	58	127
	Feb.	76	177	—	—	—	—	76	177	56	138
	Mar.	122	294	—	—	—	—	122	294	65	163
	Apr.	132	353	—	—	—	—	132	353	65	176
	May	141	363	—	—	—	—	141	363	77	192
	June	136	343	—	—	—	—	136	343	72	180
	July	109	350	—	—	—	—	109	350	71	197
	Aug.	101	322	—	—	—	—	101	322	62	179
	Sept.	101	271	—	—	—	—	101	271	59	146
	Oct.	111	253	—	—	—	—	111	253	57	131
	Nov.	122	244	—	—	—	—	122	244	63	131
	Dec.	120	215	—	—	—	—	120	215	64	144
1923	Jan.	112	217	123	243	—	—	112	217	75	131
	Feb.	101	230	114	281	—	—	101	230	64	148
	Mar.	164	334	176	371	—	—	164	334	69	154
	April	163	357	175	399	—	—	163	357	62	146
	May	149	374	168	434	—	—	149	374	69	138
	June	129	324	136	371	—	—	124	324	62	150
	July	111	274	124	315	—	—	111	274	49	131
	Aug.	114	253	127	299	—	—	114	253	56	118
	Sept.	102	254	112	289	—	—	102	254	54	110
	Oct.	157	320	173	361	—	—	157	320	50	113
	Nov.	148	289	159	319	—	—	148	289	69	142

Month	1	2	3	4	5	6	7	8	9	10
Mar.	155	—	300	200	—	—	453	—	—	—
April	158	79	426	197	—	—	480	219	426	197
May	141	72	359	165	—	—	419	185	359	165
June	136	67	331	137	—	—	388	161	331	137
July	129	55	290	109	—	—	347	128	290	109
Aug.	136	57	300	133	—	—	354	148	300	133
Sept.	140	66	298	128	—	—	344	144	298	128
Oct.	162	66	345	149	—	—	410	166	345	149
Nov.	185	70	341	178	—	—	380	191	341	178
Dec.	159	84	283	152	—	—	328	167	283	152
1925 Jan.	157	75	258	116	310	133	296	127	—	—
Feb.	163	71	259	122	311	140	299	136	—	—
Mar.	176	73	401	198	491	227	481	221	—	—
April	178	81	473	229	568	262	547	256	—	—
May	179	89	425	207	509	237	496	231	—	—
June	204	90	468	191	561	219	541	209	—	—
July	212	82	458	203	547	232	529	225	—	—
Aug.	239	110	508	236	611	270	590	263	—	—
Sept.	230	122	472	224	566	257	548	250	—	—
Oct.	210	120	442	234	530	268	520	263	—	—
Nov.	213	111	396	215	475	246	465	240	—	—
Dec.	251	102	441	214	529	257	511	250	—	—
1926 Jan.	239	107	384	167	457	191	443	183	—	—
Feb.	218	104	341	205	408	179	392	171	—	—
Mar.	226	124	522	230	624	263	577	258	—	—
April	190	95	478	231	571	265	552	258	—	—
May	193	91	459	214	550	245	521	237	—	—
June	198	93	456	208	548	238	523	225	—	—
July	198	89	432	162	519	185	501	178	—	—
Aug.	232	88	505	195	606	223	574	214	—	—
Sept.	224	99	470	197	562	226	545	220	—	—
Oct.	200	103	430	198	516	227	499	219	—	—
Nov.	219	92	407	200	487	230	474	223	—	—
Dec.	248	92	447	178	537	204	520	199	—	—
1927 Jan.	195	87	320	147	384	168	369	160	—	—
Feb.	206	89	328	143	394	163	381	158	—	—
Mar.	215	85	519	218	621	250	596	240	—	—
April	199	90	504	233	604	267	584	260	—	—
May	195	91	461	192	552	220	531	212	—	—
June	230	84	529	210	632	240	612	233	—	—
July	209	90	445	164	534	187	514	181	—	—
Aug.	216	90	461	182	552	209	535	202	—	—
Sept.	213	94	436	177	522	203	506	197	—	—
Oct.	218	101	457	213	563	244	549	237	—	—
Nov.	215	91	389	188	466	215	444	207	—	—
Dec.	230	92	398	181	477	207	464	202	—	—

Table 137 (continued)

Year		Value of contracts awarded						Estimated value in twenty-seven States		Seasonally adjusted value at constant costs in twenty-seven States	
		In twenty-seven States		In thirty-six States		In thirty-seven States					
		Residential ($ million)	Total ($ million)	Residential ($ million)	Total ($ million)	Residential ($ million)	Total ($ million)	Residential ($ million)	Total ($ million)	Residential (1913 $ million)	Total (1913 $ million)
		(1)	(2)	(3)	(4)	(5)	(6)	(7)	(8)	(9)	(10)
1928	Jan.	—	—	—	—	193	427	168	357	106	225
	Feb.	—	—	—	—	239	465	209	388	127	249
	Mar.	—	—	—	—	275	593	240	495	101	218
	April	—	—	—	—	277	643	242	540	95	215
	May	—	—	—	—	289	668	252	557	109	234
	June	—	—	—	—	258	650	225	542	95	234
	July	—	—	—	—	229	583	200	486	108	223
	Aug.	—	—	—	—	214	517	187	430	95	198
	Sept.	—	—	—	—	203	588	177	490	92	234
	Oct.	—	—	—	—	240	597	209	498	97	232
	Nov.	—	—	—	—	200	471	179	393	83	208
	Dec.	—	—	—	—	178	433	155	361	75	199
1929	Jan.	—	—	—	—	138	410	121	342	74	209
	Feb.	—	—	—	—	129	361	113	302	66	188
	Mar.	—	—	—	—	197	485	172	404	71	174
	April	—	—	—	—	257	642	224	538	89	218
	May	—	—	—	—	192	588	167	490	73	208
	June	—	—	—	—	190	546	166	455	70	196
	July	—	—	—	—	200	652	174	544	95	253
	Aug.	—	—	—	—	146	489	127	398	65	185
	Sept.	—	—	—	—	118	445	103	372	53	177
	Oct.	—	—	—	—	138	446	120	373	56	176
	Nov.	—	—	—	—	114	391	99	326	46	174
	Dec.	—	—	—	—	114	316	99	264	49	148
1930	Jan.	—	—	—	—	67	324	58	271	36	167
	Feb.	—	—	—	—	75	317	65	264	39	169
	Mar.	—	—	—	—	101	456	88	380	36	165

SOURCES: Columns (1)–(6). United States Department of Commerce, *Commerce Year Book*, volumes for 1921–1930, quoting the F. W. Dodge Corporation. Columns (7) and (8). For 1921–24 these are identical with columns (1) and (2). The values for 1921–24 for twenty-seven states were expressed as percentages of the values for thirty-six states. The mean percentage was then used to convert the thirty-six state figures for 1925–27 to twenty-seven state figures. The thirty-seven state figures were similarly converted first to thirty-six state figures and then to twenty-seven state figures. Columns (9) and (10). Columns (7) and (8) were divided by the Engineering News Record index of Building Costs quoted in the *Commerce Year Book*,

Table 138. *Interior demand for gold and gross residential building in the United Kingdom, new building and empty property in London, for various periods 1856–1913*

Year	Interior demand for gold (£ thousands)	Gross residential building in U.K. (£ millions at current prices)	Surveyors' fees for new building in London (£)	Empty property in London (%)
1856	—	9·3	4,936	—
1857	—	8·5	6,729	—
1858	729	9·0	6,964	—
1859	7,724	7·8	8,219	—
1860	1,967	8·0	9,039	—
1861	−3,907	7·9	8,266	—
1862	3,596	10·1	11,138	—
1863	6,716	11·5	13,311	—
1864	2,106	11·1	12,754	—
1865	7,131	9·7	14,433	—
1866	7,500	10·4	16,122	—
1867	5,843	12·1	16,473	—
1868	8,406	13·0	18,344	—
1869	4,069	14·5	14,091	—
1870	5,417	16·5	12,106	—
1871	1,029	17·7	10,487	7·3
1872	558	20·2	10,424	5·9
1873	1,043	19·4	11,054	5·0
1874	8,039	20·9	13,120	4·7
1875	7,317	26·1	14,018	4·3
1876	736	27·8	17,873	3·9
1877	−1,472	26·1	20,523	4·0
1878	3,710	21·4	21,553	4·2
1879	−4,205	16·9	21,608	4·7
1880	−1,398	17·3	25,590	5·2
1881	−3,041	16·1	23,221	5·4
1882	2,687	16·9	22,483	5·8
1883	−759	16·6	20,137	6·9
1884	−222	16·1	20,894	7·7
1885	200	15·0	18,059	7·0
1886	1,442	14·4	16,501	6·6
1887	−1,889	14·9	17,218	6·1
1888	1,809	15·3	17,614	5·9
1889	4,396	15·7	16,406	5·4
1890	3,329	15·6	15,449	5·0
1891	7,980	16·2	14,545	4·8
1892	5,403	16·8	15,066	4·6

Table 138 (*continued*)

Year	Interior demand for gold (£ thousands)	Gross residential building in U.K. (£ millions at current prices)	Surveyors' fees for new building in London (£)	Empty property in London (%)
1893	3,958	17·0	15,917	4·4
1894	4,160	17·9	15,406	4·4
1895	2,788	17·5	15,100	4·2
1896	5,635	21·2	17,487	3·6
1897	4,615	26·6	20,432	3·1
1898	8,873	33·9	19,117	2·9
1899	10,361	35·4	21,947	2·8
1900	10,072	33·6	20,733	3·0
1901	2,975	33·1	21,157	3·1
1902	7,920	34·6	20,103	3·2
1903	2,559	34·4	19,803	3·5
1904	−2,126	29·5	18,614	—
1905	4,332	27·5	19,494	4·7
1906	3,020	29·0	19,986	4·7
1907	4,518	28·0	17,634	5·3
1908	− 29	22·5	17,981	6·0
1909	4,239	21·9	13,591	6·6
1910	4,317	19·7	13,144	5·9
1911	7,256	16·1	14,326	5·3
1912	4,514	13·3	11,403	4·7
1913	9,246	14·0	11,848	3·9

SOURCES

Column (1). R. G. Hawtrey, *A Century of Bank Rate*, London, Longmans Green, 1938, p. 301.

Column (2). C. H. Feinstein's estimate in Mitchell and Deane, *Abstract of British Historical Statistics*, pp. 373–4.

Column (3). The figures give the amount received in fees by London District Surveyors for inspecting new buildings, under the provisions of the London Building Acts. See E. W. Cooney, 'Capital Exports, and Investment in Building in Britain and the U.S.A. 1856–1914', *Economica*, new series, vol. XVI, no. 64, November 1949, p. 354.

Column (4). J. Calvert Spensley, 'Urban Housing Problems', *Journal of the Royal Statistical Society*, vol. LXXXI, pt. II, March 1918, p. 210. The figures represent the percentage of water rates lost through 'Empties, bad debts, etc.'. Spensley states that losses through empties preponderate.

Table 139. *England and Wales, urban regions: houses assessed and not assessed to Inhabited House Duty, by region, 1874–1912.* (*Thousands*)

Year ended 5 April	North West England	Northern England	Midlands	London	Home Counties	South Wales and Mon.	Yorkshire
1875	766·4	266·3	677·9	479·1	370·4	113·1	567·4
1876	788·5	276·3	690·9	485·4	375·5	117·9	584·0
1877	798·9	282·8	699·7	490·9	412·5	121·0	607·8
1878	824·7	289·4	720·6	501·1	385·1	125·9	616·0
1879	849·5	293·5	734·8	513·6	394·2	128·1	630·7
1880	868·1	322·6	740·4	520·7	410·8	132·3	639·2
1881	888·5	315·2	753·1	535·9	424·2	134·3	652·3
1882	905·1	316·8	762·1	543·4	438·2	137·4	660·8
1883	915·1	322·1	778·7	556·6	459·9	139·0	664·2
1884	931·8	326·7	790·6	569·2	475·8	141·8	674·6
1885	945·8	330·9	800·1	572·8	489·5	145·1	681·8
1886	950·1	334·5	811·1	579·9	504·0	150·1	688·1
1887	966·4	339·4	821·7	581·5	515·7	154·5	696·4
1888	979·1	343·3	834·8	591·3	526·4	158·2	706·3
1889	992·2	347·3	844·9	600·8	540·4	162·1	713·7
1890	1010·5	351·9	855·5	613·3	550·2	165·8	725·5
1891	1025·2	356·6	866·6	612·7	559·8	170·0	736·8
1892	1038·8	363·1	878·6	625·0	569·9	175·0	748·8
1893	1053·1	*	*	630·4	*	*	*
1894	*	*	*	636·7	*	*	760·5
1895	1066·0	380·4	912·0	635·8	600·8	192·4	771·5
1896	1083·5	388·2	927·7	641·7	616·7	199·5	783·6
1897	1104·9	396·8	946·9	643·4	635·4	206·0	798·5
1898	1124·1	403·9	962·5	652·1	650·7	210·7	809·6
1899	1137·8	417·7	977·9	669·0	682·6	217·4	828·1
1900	1170·5	428·5	1004·2	673·0	713·9	221·9	845·6
1901	1193·3	438·5	1024·2	681·9	745·0	225·4	865·0
1902	1211·3	450·2	1044·1	689·4	776·0	229·0	881·2
1903	1224·4	459·7	1060·4	700·3	803·5	234·5	892·4
1904	1232·3	461·5	1074·8	711·3	840·5	239·2	910·4
1905	1251·5	471·2	1093·4	725·9	868·4	245·0	925·9
1906	1271·2	480·0	1119·0	738·4	900·7	254·9	941·8
1907	1289·0	489·3	1134·7	742·8	923·0	259·9	955·6
1908	1291·4	495·8	1143·2	744·4	935·9	265·9	957·9
1909	1322·0	505·2	1164·2	751·4	964·4	275·3	974·3
1910	1338·8	516·1	1179·8	755·9	984·2	283·9	992·1
1911	1343·6	513·5	1180·1	759·0	1003·8	289·8	996·4
1912	1359·2	524·2	1194·9	766·8	1022·5	299·4	1009·2

* Missing ledgers, see p. 226.
SOURCE: Inland Revenue ledgers.

Table 140. *England and Wales, urban regions: natural increase and migration of population aged 20–44, 1871–1910. (Thousands)*

Period	North West England	Northern England	Midlands	London*	Home Counties	South Wales and Mon.	Yorkshire	All urban regions
				Natural increase				
1871–75	+70·3	+35·1	+78·1	+46·4	+46·1	+26·4	+60·3	+362·7
1876–80	+88·7	+48·1	+117·5	+75·3	+69·4	+35·2	+71·1	+505·3
1881–85	+96·1	+50·5	+117·0	+73·7	+66·9	+37·5	+82·0	+523·7
1886–90	+113·2	+59·9	+147·2	+109·7	+98·0	+44·5	+94·6	+667·1
1891–95	+150·5	+74·6	+158·8	+106·3	+97·2	+53·1	+115·9	+756·4
1896–1900	+156·6	+77·1	+179·2	+115·0	+128·2	+49·2	+118·8	+824·1
1901–05	+152·4	+79·7	+166·6	+86·5	+119·9	+50·8	+111·2	+767·1
1906–10	+123·0	+76·4	+151·0	+77·1	+116·6	+45·0	+86·3	+675·4

					Migration			
1871–75	+96·6	−0·3	−7·0	+80·7	+9·7	−5·0	+20·9	+195·6
1876–80	+14·5	−0·9	−20·5	+78·3	+9·2	−14·6	+8·5	+74·5
1881–85	+9·5	−10·0	−51·4	+15·0	+50·9	+14·1	−14·2	+12·9
1886–90	+2·1	−11·2	−47·5	+17·7	+28·8	+4·8	−18·2	−23·5
1891–95	+8·0	−11·8	−16·9	−2·9	+88·7	+1·4	−6·3	+60·2
1896–1900	+20·0	−6·4	−1·9	+10·8	+86·6	+1·4	−1·6	+108·9
1901–05	−18·9	−16·9	−27·0	−96·0	+92·4	+36·6	−13·1	−42·9
1906–10	−20·8	−27·6	−51·9	−130·1	+71·6	+35·7	−17·8	−140·9
					Natural increase and migration			
1871–75	+166·9	+34·8	+71·1	+127·1	+55·8	+21·4	+81·2	+558·3
1876–80	+103·2	+47·2	+97·0	+153·6	+78·6	+20·6	+79·6	+579·8
1881–85	+105·6	+40·5	+65·6	+88·7	+117·8	+50·6	+67·8	+536·6
1886–90	+115·3	+48·7	+99·7	+127·4	+126·8	+49·3	+76·4	+643·6
1891–95	+158·5	+62·8	+141·9	+103·4	+185·9	+54·5	+109·6	+816·6
1896–1900	+176·6	+70·7	+177·3	+125·8	+214·8	+50·6	+117·2	+933·0
1901–05	+133·5	+62·8	+139·6	−9·5	+212·3	+87·4	+98·1	+724·2
1906–10	+102·2	+48·8	+99·1	−53·0	+188·2	+80·7	+68·5	+534·5

* Age group 15–44.

SOURCES: Population Censuses, 1871–1911; Registrar General's Decennial Supplements, 1871–1911.

Table 141. *The United States: long swings in immigration, construction, exports and imports (average reference-cycle standings), 1860–1913*

Mid-point of reference-cycle	Immigration (thousands)		Volume of construction		Exports	Imports
	Gross	Net	Index, 1856–97 = 100	Index, 1889–1918 = 100	Per cent of G.N.P.	
	(1)	(2)	(3)	(4)	(5)	(6)
1859·5	122·5	—	54·4	—	—	—
1862	141·4	—	58·5	—	—	—
1864	205·2	—	70·7	—	—	—
1866·5	261·4	—	96·7	—	—	—
1868·5	299·0	—	127·2	—	—	—
1871	385·2	—	148·9	—	6·5	8·2
1874	296·0	232	110·6	—	7·4	7·3
1877·5	354·4	299	83·7	—	7·8	6·5
1881·5	—	397	87·4	—	7·6	6·1
1884·5	—	459	110·0	—	6·6	6·0
1886·5	—	347	136·6	—	6·2	6·1
1888·5	—	349	146·6	—	6·4	6·4
1889·5	—	377	144·0	—	6·7	6·5
1891	—	411	134·0	83·0	7·0	6·4
1892·5	—	356	119·5	77·3	6·9	6·0
1893·5	—	273	112·6	73·1	6·6	6·0
1895	—	146	111·3	71·6	6·9	5·7
1897	—	145	—	71·8	7·6	5·2
1898	—	203	—	71·4	8·0	4·9
1901	—	358	—	79·7	7·3	4·7
1902	—	424	—	84·9	7·1	4·7
1905	—	638	—	118·3	6·6	4·8
1906	—	573	—	124·6	6·6	4·8
1908·5	—	574	—	120·7	6·2	4·8
1909·5	—	510	—	124·2	6·1	4·8
1911·5	—	637	—	129·0	6·3	5·0
1912·5	—	622	—	128·9	6·5	5·1

SOURCES

(1) I. Ferenczi and W. F. Willcox, *International Migrations*, vol. 1, p. 377.

(2) S. Kuznets and E. Rubin, *Immigration and the Foreign Born*, National Bureau of Economic Research, 1954, p. 95.

(3) and (4) M. Abramovitz, *Evidences of Long Swings in Aggregate Construction since the Civil War*, pp. 166–7.

(5) and (6) R. E. Lipsey, *Price and Quantity Trends in the Foreign Trade of the United States*, pp. 430–1.

Table 142. *The United States: population-sensitive capital formation and net foreign claims, 1874–1917: annual changes in successive phases of long swings*

Phase of long swing	Additions to population (millions)	Non-farm gross residential construction	Gross capital expenditure by railways	Total population-sensitive capital formation	Net claims against foreign countries
		000 million dollars in 1929 prices			
Trough to peak 1874–88	+0·23	+0·90	+0·14	+1·01	−0·05
Peak to trough 1888–95	−0·06	−0·32	−0·29	−0·62	+0·64
Trough to peak 1895–1909	+0·34	+0·62	+0·67	+1·29	−0·33
Peak to trough 1909–17	−0·34	−0·80	−0·46	−1·30	+2·67

SOURCE: S. Kuznets, *Capital in the American Economy*, p. 330.

Table 143. *England, Wales and Scotland: annual rates (per 10,000 mean population) of net migration, each inter-censal period 1851–1966*

Period	England	Wales	Scotland
1851–61	− 16	−28	− 101
1861–71	− 7	−47	−44
1871–81	− 5	−35	−28
1881–91	−23	− 11	−58
1891–1901	− 2	− 5	−13
1901–11	− 19	+45	−57
1911–21	− 16	−21	−50
1921–31	+ 3	− 102	−80
1931–39	+24	−72	− 8
1939–46	} + 6 {	+ 1	− 3
1946–51		− 18	−92
1951–61*	+20	− 11	−55
1961–66*	+18	+8	−75

* Excluding movements of armed forces.

SOURCES: Population Censuses, 1851–1961; N. H. Carrier and J. R. Jeffery, *External Migration: a Study of the Available Statistics, 1815–1950*, General Register Office, 1953, p. 14, Table 2; *Registrar General's Quarterly Return for England and Wales* and *for Scotland*, 4th quarter 1968.

Table 144. *Migration balances in coal-mining areas and all areas of England and Wales, 1851–1911.* (*Thousands*)

Decade	Coal-mining areas, net gain or loss by migration		Annual rate of net migration per 10,000 mean population	
	England*	Wales	England	Wales
	(1)	(2)	(3)	(4)
1851–61	+63	+42	−16	−28
1861–71	+82	+9	− 7	−47
1871–81	+63	+10	− 5	−35
1881–91	−30	+86	−23	−11
1891–1901	+18	+40	− 2	−5
1901–11	+35	+126	−19	+45

* The figures published by Cairncross for English colliery areas have had to be revised because the boundaries of his areas were such that they included a great deal which was not primarily coal-mining. When the boundaries are drawn to cover coal-mining areas proper, the migration balance for English colliery areas in 1901–11 changes its sign to +35,000 from the −12,000 shown by Cairncross.
SOURCES:
(1) and (2) T. A. Welton, *England's Recent Progress*; A. K. Cairncross, 'Internal Migration in Victorian England', *Home and Foreign Investment, 1870–1913*.
(3) and (4) Table 143.

Table 145. *England and Wales: net gain or loss by migration in rural and urban areas, decennially, 1871–1911.* (*Thousands*)

Decade	England			Wales		
	Rural	Urban	Total	Rural	Urban	Total
1871–81	−769	+673	−96	−65	+13	−52
1881–91	−731	+132	−599	−106	+88	−18
1891–1901	−596	+551	−45	−57	+48	−9
1901–11	−251	−346	−597	−38	+132	+94

SOURCES: Welton, op. cit.; Cairncross, 'Internal Migration in Victorian England', *Home and Foreign Investment, 1870–1913* (with revisions for English coal-mining areas as in Table 144).

Table 146. *Great Britain: the southward drift, 1931–61. Net gain or loss by migration.* (*Thousands*)

Region	1931–9	1939–51	1951–61
North			
Northern	−149	−60	−86
East and West Ridings	−41	−90	−98
North Western	−59	−70	−124
Wales	−182	+7	−49
Scotland	−32	−247	−255
South			
North Midland	+32	+78	+65
Midland	+100	+88	+61
Eastern	+201	+240	+455
London and South East	+458	−640	−183
Southern	+129	+191	+237
South Western	+36	+236	+78

SOURCES: *Census 1951. England and Wales, Preliminary Report*, p. xv; *Census 1961: England and Wales, Preliminary Report*, p. 7, and *Scotland, Preliminary Report*, p. 8; N. H. Carrier and J. R. Jeffery, *External Migration*, p. 14.

Table 147. *England: the southward drift, 1881–1911. Net gain or loss by migration.* (*Thousands*)

	1881–91	1891–1901	1901–11
North of England			
8 large towns	+21·4	−143·6	−90·0
22 textile towns	+3·7	−40·6	−51·7
14 industrial towns	−88·6	−51·4	−81·1
7 old towns	−17·1	−10·3	+5·4
9 residential towns	+21·7	+59·7	+18·4
South of England			
London	+168·9	+226·5	−231·9
11 industrial towns	−5·9	+25·4*	+6·7
13 old towns	−24·3	+1·5*	−34·7
26 residential towns	+44·8	+83·4*	+129·4
16 military towns	+13·1	+72·5*	+8·5

* Welton, op. cit. pp. 178–85, gives the following figures for net gains by migration, 1891–1900, in individual towns in the South:

Industrial towns		*Old towns*	
Southampton	20,694	Reading	3,856
Swindon	3,459	Gloucester	2,920

Residential towns		*Military towns*	
Bournemouth	10,329	Plymouth	15,838
Brighton	5,201	Portsmouth	13,145
Eastbourne	4,219	Weymouth	6,793
Worthing	4,115	Aldershot	2,895

SOURCE: Cairncross, *Home and Foreign Investment, 1870–1913*, p. 70.

Table 148. *Great Britain: regional migration and growth of manufacturing, 1951–66*

Standard regions	Mid-year employment in manufacturing			Mid-year population 1951	Net civilian migration, 1951–66	
	1953	1966	Percentage change 1953–66		Thousands	Per thousand of 1951 population
	Thousands			Thousands		
South West	333	408	+23	3,247	+198	+60
South East and East Anglia	2,339	2,791	+19	16,604	+662	+40
Wales	276	326	+18	2,589	−16	−6
West Midlands	1,086	1,259	+16	4,426	+92	+21
East Midlands	546	623	+14	2,913	+107	+37
North	406	458	+13	3,130	−111	−36
Yorks. and Humberside	855	897	+6	4,488	−89	−20
Scotland	741	740	—	5,103	−476	−93
North West	1,405	1,364	−3	6,417	−129	−20
Great Britain	7,987	8,866	+11	48,918	+238	+49

SOURCES: *Registrar General's Quarterly Return for England and Wales* and *for Scotland*, 4th quarter 1968; R. S. Howard, *The Movement of Manufacturing Industry in the United Kingdom 1945–1965*, p. 11.

Table 149. *Great Britain: contribution of moves of establishments to changes in regional employment in manufacturing, 1953–66.*
(*Thousands*)

Standard regions	Manufacturing employment			
	Total, mid-1966	Change, 1953–66	End-1966 in inward moves 1952–65	Balance of change, 1953–66
South West	408	+75	28	+47
South East and East Anglia	2,791	+452	39	+413
Wales	326	+50	24	+26
West Midlands	1,259	+173	6	+167
East Midlands	623	+77	18	+59
North	458	+52	27	+25
Yorks. and Humberside	897	+42	16	+26
Scotland	740	−1	50	−51
North West	1,364	−41	68	−109
Great Britain	8,867	+879	56*	+823†

* Employment in establishments moved from abroad. The sum of the regional figures in this column (276 thousand) is total British employment in regional moves.

† Employment change in Britain less employment in establishments moved from abroad. The sum of the regional figures in this column (603 thousand) is the net employment change in Britain excluding employment in establishments moving interregionally.

SOURCE: Howard, *The Movement of Manufacturing Industry*, p. 11.

Table 150. *Great Britain: changes in population and immigration, by region, 1961-6*

Area	Change 1961-6 in				New Commonwealth immigrants per 1000 of 1966 population
	Total population	Total immigrants	New Commonwealth immigrants	Indigenous population*	
		Thousands			
Regions					
South West	+148·7	+17·0	+10·2	+131·7	10·1
South East and East Anglia	+450·4	+227·4	+174·0	+223·0	27·4
Wales	+19·4	+1·5	+2·1	+17·9	3·8
West Midlands	+152·1	+55·3	+49·6	+96·8	22·8
Yorks., Humberside and East Midlands	+200·5	+41·1	+41·3	+159·4	11·4
North	+11·9	+4·7	+3·6	+7·2	4·1
Scotland	-11·1	+4·5	+4·7	-15·6	4·4
North West	+47·9	+30·0	+24·0	+17·9	8·2
Total	+1019·8	+381·5	+309·5	+638·3	16·3
Conurbations					
Greater London	-326·0	+126·0	+124·6	-452·0	47·9
West Midlands	-3·9	+37·4	+37·1	-41·3	35·6
West Yorkshire	+4·6	+19·3	+18·9	-14·7	20·8
Tyneside	-23·1	+1·1	+1·1	-24·2	5·4
S.E. Lancashire	-23·8	+18·7	+15·2	-42·5	12·2
Merseyside	-46·7	+0·1	+1·7	-46·8	6·0
Total	-418·9	+202·6	+198·6	-621·5	32·5

* Population less total immigrants.

SOURCES: *Census 1961: England and Wales, Birthplace and Nationality Tables* and *Scotland, Birthplace and Nationality Tables*; *Sample Census 1966: Great Britain, Summary Tables*; K. Jones and A. D. Smith, *The Economic Impact of Commonwealth Immigration*.

Table 151. *Scientists and engineers, physicians and surgeons admitted to the United States as immigrants, by last permanent residence, fiscal year 1968*

Country or region of last permanent residence	Scientists and engineers				Physicians and surgeons
	Engineers	Natural scientists	Social scientists	Total	
Western Europe					
Austria	59	37	5	101	27
Belgium	50	9	5	64	6
Denmark	93	9	3	105	4
France	153	39	15	207	13
Germany	496	241	32	769	93
Greece	109	27	7	143	34
Ireland	39	15	3	57	21
Italy	80	48	17	145	47
Netherlands	101	45	6	152	18
Norway	132	13	3	148	7
Spain	61	28	6	95	74
Sweden	180	20	5	205	13
Switzerland	172	62	17	251	43
Turkey	47	8	6	61	49
United Kingdom	1,705	462	45	2,212	121
Other	39	11	7	57	2
Total	3,516	1,074	182	4,772	572
Eastern Europe					
Czechoslovakia	22	5	—	27	15
Hungary	5	6	—	11	4
Poland	57	18	13	88	36
Rumania	3	1	1	5	5
Yugoslavia	39	13	9	61	41
Other	6	3	1	10	—
Total	132	46	24	202	101
All Europe	3,648	1,120	206	4,974	673
North and Central America					
Canada	1,447	417	76	1,940	325
Cuba	338	156	31	525	214
Mexico	53	20	8	81	55
Other	203	96	22	321	149
Total	2,041	689	137	2,867	743

Table 151 (continued)

Country or region of last permanent residence	Scientists and engineers				Physicians and surgeons
	Engineers	Natural scientists	Social scientists	Total	
South America					
Argentina	93	49	10	152	95
Bolivia	10	5	1	16	15
Brazil	45	21	7	73	18
Chile	32	7	3	42	16
Columbia	110	26	7	143	116
Equador	33	16	1	50	42
Peru	33	9	3	45	15
Venezuela	35	8	4	47	14
Other	15	11	1	27	10
Total	406	152	37	595	341
Near and Middle East	380	116	26	522	238
Far East					
China	134	54	2	190	6
Hong Kong	130	66	4	200	42
India	944	241	47	1,232	96
Japan	57	43	9	109	23
Philippines	594	151	7	752	639
Taiwan	390	209	27	626	21
Other	248	113	29	390	130
Total	2,497	877	125	3,499	957
All Asia	2,877	993	151	4,021	1,195
Africa	249	94	15	358	87
All other areas	92	62	4	158	21
All countries	9,313	3,110	550	12,973	3,060

NOTE: Figures include professors and instructors.
SOURCE: National Science Foundation, *Reviews of Data on Science Resources*, no. 18, November 1969, p. 7.

Table 152. *The United States: annual additions to professional manpower by American educational institutions and by immigration, 1956 and 1962–7*

Fiscal year	Scientists			Engineers			Physicians		
	Graduates of U.S. institutions	Immigrants		Graduates of U.S. institutions	Immigrants		Graduates of U.S. institutions	Immigrants	
		Number	% of U.S. graduates		Number	% of U.S. graduates		Number	% of U.S. graduates
1956	45,948	1,022	2·2	31,646	2,804	8·9	9,862	1,547	15·7
1962	71,307	1,104	1·5	44,851	2,940	6·6	10,392	1,912	18·4
1963	77,149	1,612	2·1	44,471	4,014	9·0	10,469	2,270	21·7
1964	86,574	1,676	1·9	47,746	3,725	7·8	10,538	2,409	22·9
1965	93,368	1,549	1·6	50,975	3,455	6·8	10,482	2,194	20·9
1966	99,145	1,852	1·9	51,785	4,921	9·5	10,580	2,761	26·1
1967	107,510	2,893	2·6	55,090	8,822	16·0	10,610	3,326	31·4

SOURCES: Government Operations Committee, House of Representatives, 90th Congress, *The Brain Drain into United States of Scientists, Engineers and Physicians*, 1967, p. 3, and *Scientific Brain Drain from Developing Countries*, 1968, pp. 3–4.

Table 153. *The United Kingdom: migration balance of qualified engineers and scientists, 1958–69*

Year	Persons qualified in engineering and technology			Persons qualified in science		
	Emigration	Immigration	Balance	Emigration	Immigration	Balance
1958	2,725	1,785	−940	2,885	3,405	+520
1959	2,525	2,025	−500	2,855	3,935	+1,080
1960	2,530	2,110	−420	2,695	4,100	+1,405
1961	2,430	3,215	+785	3,135	4,035	+900
1962	2,735	3,025	+290	3,100	4,285	+1,185
1963	3,065	2,240	−825	3,490	4,220	+730
1964	3,750	2,355	−1,395	3,880	3,910	+30
1965	4,050	3,125	−925	4,240	4,880	+640
1966	5,255	2,760	−2,495	4,470	4,720	+250
1967	6,180	2,440	−3,740	4,895	4,160	−735
1968	4,945	2,865	−2,080	4,995	4,970	−25
1969*	4,685	2,930	−1,755	4,830	5,020	+190

* Provisional figures.

SOURCE: Department of Trade and Industry, *Persons with Qualifications in Engineering, Technology and Science.*

Table 154. *Great Britain: migration balance of doctors, by country of origin and destination, 1962–4*

Country of origin or destination	Emigrants		Immigrants or returned emigrants		Net gain or loss	
	Born G.B. or Ireland*	Born elsewhere	Born G.B. or Ireland*	Born elsewhere	Born G.B. or Ireland*	Born elsewhere
Ireland*	171†	51	255†	188	+84†	+137
India	44	473	48	709	+4	+236
Pakistan	11	82	9	346	−2	+264
Ceylon	—	40	3	84	+3	+44
Canada	283	97	66	44	−217	−53
Australia	233	304	76	365	−157	+61
New Zealand	65	83	21	103	−44	+20
Other Commonwealth	369	428	315	284	−54	−144
U.S.A.	229	114	102	24	−127	−90
South Africa	32	125	23	117	−9	−8
Other foreign	125	98	93	92	−32	−6
Unknown	86	24	64	21	−22	−3
Total	1,648	1,919	1,075	2,377	−573	+458

* Includes Northern Ireland and Irish Republic.
† Movements between Great Britain and Ireland (North or South) of doctors born in Great Britain or Ireland.
SOURCE: R. Ash and H. D. Mitchell, 'Doctor Migration 1962–1964'.

Table 155. *The United States: immigration of professional manpower and Federal expenditure on industrial Research and Development, 1953–68*

Year	Immigrants in professional, technical and kindred grades		Federal expenditure on industrial R. and D.	
	Numbers	Percentage change	Million dollars	Percentage change
1953	12,783		1,430	
1954	13,817	+ 8	1,750	+22
1955	14,109	+ 2	2,180	+25
1956	18,995	+34	3,328	+53
1957	24,489	+29	4,335	+30
1958	22,480	− 8	4,759	+10
1959	23,287	+ 4	5,635	+18
1960	21,940	− 6	6,081	+ 8
1961	21,455	− 2	6,240	+ 3
1962	23,710	+11	6,434	+ 3
1963	27,930	+18	7,270	+13
1964	28,756	+ 3	7,720	+ 6
1965	28,790	—	7,740	—
1966	30,039	+ 4	8,287	+ 7
1967	41,652	+39	8,400	+ 1
1968	48,753	+17	8,600	+ 2

SOURCES: National Science Foundation, *Science Manpower Bulletin*, no. 8, February 1958, p. 2, *Reviews of Data on Science Resources*, no. 12, January 1968, p. 4, and *Science Resources Studies Highlights*, May 25, 1970, pp. 1–2; U.S. Department of Justice, *Annual Reports of the Immigration and Naturalization Service*, 1953–66, and *Annual indicator of in-migration into United States of aliens in professional and related occupations*, fiscal years 1967 and 1968.

Table 156. *The United States: new entries and alien residents changing status among immigrant scientists and engineers, fiscal years 1965–9*

Fiscal year	New entries	Aliens adjusted to immigrant status			Total immigrant scientists and engineers
		Former students	Other	Total	
1965	4,759	501	85	586	5,345
1966	4,889	1,660	656	2,316	7,205
1967	7,450	3,823	1,250	5,073	12,523
1968	8,836	2,855	1,282	4,137	12,973
1969	6,800	2,700	800	3,500	10,300

SOURCES: National Science Foundation, *Reviews of Data on Science Resources*, no. 13, March 1968, and no. 18, November 1969; *Scientists, Engineers and Physicians from Abroad 1966 and 1967*, 1969; *Science Resources Surveys*, no. 2, February 1970.

Table 157. *United States: net migration rates, sub-regions N3 and CI, 1870–80 to 1940–50*

Decade	Sub-region N3[1]			Sub-region CI[2]		
	Native white Per 1,000 average native white population	Negro Per 1,000 average Negro population	Foreign-born white Per 1,000 average total population	Native white Per 1,000 average native white population	Negro Per 1,000 average Negro population	Foreign-born white Per 1,000 average total population
1870–80	−37	135	45	−65	146	50
1880–90	−20	212	95	−55	91	77
1890–1900	4	382	78	—	195	43
1900–10	−8	272	123	−38	187	60
1910–20	−9	388	43	24	564	41
1920–30	1	485	43	19	524	26
1930–40	−6	169	2	−5	128	−4
1940–50	−33	290	7	−9	407	3

[1] New York, New Jersey and Pennsylvania.
[2] Ohio, Indiana, Illinois, Michigan and Wisconsin.
SOURCE: Hope T. Eldridge and Dorothy S. Thomas, op. cit. pp. 72 and 101.

Table 158. *Occupational distribution of non-white males and females in the United States (outside the South), 1940 and 1960*

Occupational grade	Non-white males in U.S.A. (outside the South)			
	1940 (000)	1960 (000)	1940 (%)	1960 (%)
Total labour force	1,030	2,023		
Unemployed	327	210		
Total employed	702	1,812	100·0	100·0
Professional	21	83	3·1	4·8
Farmers	35	19	5·2	1·1
Managers	27	50	4·0	2·9
Clerical	37	165	5·4	9·4
Craftsmen	48	195	7·1	11·2
Operatives	115	444	16·9	25·5
Private household workers	25	12	3·7	0·7
Service workers	178	269	26·2	15·4
Farm labourers	44	32	6·5	1·8
Other labourers	144	271	21·1	15·6
Not reported	5	203	0·7	11·7

Occupational grade	Non-white females in U.S.A. (outside the South)			
	1940 (000)	1960 (000)	1940 (%)	1960 (%)
Total labour force	501	1,261		
Unemployed	125	124		
Total employed	375	1,137	100·0	100·0
Professional	14	82	3·7	7·2
Farmers	3	2	0·9	0·2
Managers	5	13	1·2	1·2
Clerical	14	180	3·8	15·9
Craftsmen	1	11	0·4	0·9
Operatives	44	206	12·0	18·1
Private household workers	212	259	57·5	22·8
Service workers	59	236	16·1	20·8
Farm labourers	2	5	0·6	0·4
Other labourers	11	12	2·9	1·0
Not reported	3	130	0·8	11·4

SOURCE: C. Horace Hamilton, 'The Negro leaves the South', *Demography*, vol. 1, 1964, pp. 288–91.

LIST OF WORKS CITED

I. Official publications and papers:
    A. Great Britain and Ireland
    B. United States

    C. Other countries
    D. International

II. Books, articles, and other sources.

I. OFFICIAL PUBLICATIONS AND PAPERS

A. GREAT BRITAIN AND IRELAND

(i) Great Britain

General Reports of the Colonial Land and Emigration Commissioners, H.C. papers, annual (1st in 1840 to 15th in 1855).

Report of the Secret Committee of the House of Commons on Commercial Distress, 1848.
Census of Great Britain, 1851: Population Tables, 1854.

General Reports of the Emigration Commissioners, H.C. papers, annual (16th in 1856 to 33rd in 1873).

Census 1861. England and Wales (and *Scotland*): *Population Tables*, 1864 (and similar Tables from Censuses of 1871, 1881, and 1891).

Statistical Abstracts for the United Kingdom, 1840–1938 (published as Command Papers in volumes covering 15 years, C. 144, 1870 to Cmd. 6232, 1940).

Registrar General's Annual Reports, 1871–1911.

Registrar General's Decennial Supplements, 1871, 1881, 1891, and 1901. Inhabited House Duty records, 1875–1910 (in Inland Revenue ledgers, Public Record Office).

Statistical Tables relating to Emigration and Immigration from and into the United Kingdom, with Report to the Board of Trade thereon, H.C. papers, annual, 1877–1913.

Census, 1901. England and Wales and Scotland, Preliminary Report, 1903 (and from Censuses 1911, 1921, 1931, 1951, 1961.)

Annual Abstract of Statistics, Nos. 87 and *91, 1938–49* and *1938–50*, 1951 and 1954.

External Migration: a Study of the Available Statistics 1815–1950, by N. H. Carrier and J. R. Jeffery, General Register Office, 1953.

Commonwealth Immigrants Act, 1962: Control of Immigration Statistics, 1962–3, 1964, 1965, 1966 and *1967*, Cmnd. 2379, 2658, 2979, 3258 and 3594, 1963–8.

Census 1961. England and Wales, Birthplace and Nationality Tables, 1964.

Immigration from the Commonwealth, Cmnd. 2739, 1965.

Census 1961. Scotland, Birthplace and Nationality Tables, 1966.

Sample Census 1966. Great Britain, Summary Tables, 1967.

A Strategy for the South East. A First Report of the South East Economic Planning Council, 1967.

The Brain Drain: Report of the Working Group on Migration, Cmnd. 3417, 1967.

Report of the Royal Commission on Medical Education, Cmnd. 3569, 1968.

The Movement of Manufacturing Industry in the United Kingdom 1945–1965, by R. S. Howard, Board of Trade, 1968.

Registrar General's Quarterly Return for England and Wales and *for Scotland, 4th quarter 1968,* 1969.

Persons with Qualifications in Engineering, Technology and Science 1959 to 1968 (Studies in Technological Manpower no. 3), Department of Trade and Industry, 1971.

Board of Trade Journal (now *Trade and Industry*)

(ii) Ireland

Emigration Statistics of Ireland (Reports and tables issued by the Registrar General for Ireland: from 1851 to 1872 in *Censuses of Ireland,* from 1873 onwards also every year as Command Papers).

Census of Ireland, General Report, 1871–1911.

Eire, *Census of Population 1936, General Report,* Dublin, 1942.

Eire, *Census of Population 1946, Preliminary Report,* Dublin, 1946.

Eire, *Statistical Abstract of Ireland, 1949,* Dublin, 1950.

B. UNITED STATES

Population Census, 1870–1940.

39th Registration Report of the State of Massachusetts, 1880.

Report of the Ford Committee, 1889.

Arrivals of Alien Passengers and Immigrants into the United States from 1820 to 1892, Treasury Department, 1893.

Annual Report of the Superintendent of Immigration, 1894, Treasury Department, 1895.

Annual Reports of the Commissioner General of Immigration, 1898–1932.

Reports of the Industrial Commission, vols. XI and XV, 1901.

Final Report of the Industrial Commission, vol. XIX, 1902.

Monthly Summary of Commerce and Finance of the United States, Treasury Department, 1902–12.

63rd Registration Report of the State of Massachusetts, 1904.

Abstracts of Reports of the Immigration Commission, vol. I. Senate Document no. 747, 61st Congress, 1911–12.

Statistical Review of Immigration, 1820–1910. Reports of the Immigration Commission, vol. III, Senate Document no. 756, 61st Congress, 1911–12.

Immigrants and their Children, by Niles Carpenter, Population Census 1920, Monograph VII, 1927.

Annual Reports of the Secretary of Labor, 1933–40.

Negroes in the United States, 1926–32, Bureau of the Census, 1935.

A Social-Economic Grouping of the Gainful Workers of the United States, 1930, Bureau of the Census, 1938.

A Short Method for Constructing an Abridged Life Table, by L. J. Reed and M. Merrell, Bureau of the Census, Vital Statistics Special Reports, vol. IX, no. 54, 1940.

Annual Reports of the Immigration and Naturalization Service, 1943–.

Comparative Occupation Statistics for the United States, 1870 to 1940, by A. M. Edwards, Bureau of the Census, 1943.

The United States in the World Economy, by Hal B. Lary and Associates, Department of Commerce, 1943 (reprinted 1944 by H.M.S.O., London).

Vital Statistics Rates in the United States, 1900–1940, Department of Commerce, 1943.

Historical Statistics of the United States, 1789–1945, Department of Commerce, 1949.

Science Manpower Bulletin, no. 8, February 1958, National Science Foundation.

Hearings, July 2–August 3, 1964, no. 13, pt. II, Judiciary Committee, House of Representatives, 88th Congress, 1964.

'Characteristics of Foreign Born and Educated Scientists in the United States 1966', by H. G. Grubel (mimeographed paper prepared under National Science Foundation Grant 1678).

Annual Report of the Visa Office, 1967, State Department.

The Brain Drain into United States of Scientists, Engineers and Physicians, Research and Technical Programs Sub-Committee, Government Operations Committee, House of Representatives, 90th Congress, 1967.

Annual indicator of in-migration into United States of aliens in professional and related occupations, fiscal years 1967 and 1968. Immigration and Naturalization Service, Department of Justice, 1968 and 1969.

Reviews of Data on Science Resources, no. 12 January 1968, no. 13 March 1968 and no. 18 November 1969, National Science Foundation.

Scientific Brain Drain from Developing Countries, 23rd report, Government Operations Committee, House of Representatives, 90th Congress, 1968.

Scientists, Engineers and Physicians from Abroad 1966 and 1967, National Science Foundation, 1969.

Science Resources Surveys, no. 2, February 1970, National Science Foundation.

Science Resources Studies Highlights, May 25 and August 14, 1970, National Science Foundation.

Commerce Year Book, Department of Commerce.

Statistical Abstract of the United States, annual, Department of Commerce.

International Effects of United States Economic Policy, Study Paper no. 16, prepared for the Joint Economic Committee by E. M. Bernstein, 87th Congress, 1960.

Characteristics of Professional Workers, Special Report, Census of Population, 1960, Bureau of the Census, 1964.

The Negro Family: the Case for National Action, by D. P. Moynihan, Department of Labor, Office of Policy Planning and Research, 1965.

Socio-economic Status, Special Report, Census of Population, 1960, Bureau of the Census, 1967.

Report of the National Advisory Commission on Civil Disorders, an advance copy published by the New York Times, New York, 1968.

C. OTHER COUNTRIES

(i) Australia

A Statistical Account of Seven Colonies of Australasia, 1901-2, ed. T. A. Coghlan, 1903.

Victorian Year Book, 1905.

Official Year Book of the Commonwealth of Australia, nos. 1–13, 1906–19.

Australian Immigration: Consolidated Statistics, no. 1, 1966.

(ii) Canada

'Long Cycles and Recent Canadian Experience', by D. Daly in *Report of the Royal Commission on Banking and Finance*, appendix vol., 1964.

Immigration and Emigration of Professional and Skilled Manpower during the Post-War Period, by Louis Parai (Special Study no. 1 prepared for the Economic Council of Canada), 1965.

Canadian Immigration Policy, Department of Manpower and Immigration, 1966.

The Migration of Canadian-born between Canada and United States of America 1955 to 1968, by T. J. Samuel, Department of Manpower and Immigration, 1969.

Annual Reports of the Department of Citizenship and Immigration (now Department of Manpower and Immigration).

The Canada Year Book.

(iii) Sweden

Emigrationsutredningen:

Bilaga IX: *Den jordbruksidkande befolkningen i Sverige 1751–1900* (The occupied population in agriculture in Sweden 1751-1900), by N. Wohlin, 1909.

Bilaga IV: *Utvandringsstatistik. Den svenska och europeiska folköknings och omflyttningsstatistiken* (Swedish and European statistics of populations growth and emigration), by G. Sundbärg, 1910.

Bilaga XVIII: *Utalanden av svenska vetenskapsmän* (Statements by Swedish experts), 1910.

Bilaga XIII: *Allmänna ekonomiska data rörande Sverige* (General economic data relating to Sweden) by G. Sundbärg, 1912.

Betänkande (Report of the Royal Commission on Emigration), 1913.

Statistik Årsbok för Sverige, 1950.

Allmän järnvägsstatistik.

D. INTERNATIONAL

Industrialization and Foreign Trade, Geneva, League of Nations, 1945.

Europe's Population in the Interwar Years, by D. Kirk, Geneva, League of Nations, 1946.

Problems of Migration Statistics, New York, United Nations, 1949.

Economic Bulletin for Europe, vol. III, no. 2, second quarter 1951, United Nations Economic Commission for Europe.

International Migration and Economic Development: a trend report and bibliography, by Brinley Thomas, United Nations Educational Scientific and Cultural Organization, Paris, 1961.

II. BOOKS, ARTICLES AND OTHER SOURCES

ABEL-SMITH, B. and GALES, K. *British Doctors at Home and Abroad*, London, Bell, 1964.

ABRAMOVITZ, M. 'The Nature and Significance of Kuznets Cycles', *Economic Development and Cultural Change*, vol. IX, no. 3, April 1961, pp. 225–48.

ABRAMOVITZ, M. *Evidences of Long Swings in Aggregate Construction since the Civil War*, New York, Columbia University Press for National Bureau of Economic Research, 1964.

ABRAMOVITZ, M. 'The Passing of the Kuznets Cycle', *Economica*, New Series, vol. XXXV, no. 140, November 1968, pp. 349–67.

ADAMS, W. (ed.). *The Brain Drain*, New York, Macmillan, 1968.

ADELMAN, I. 'Long Cycles—Fact or Artifact?', *American Economic Review*, vol. LV, no. 3, June 1965, pp. 444–63.

ADLER, J. H. (ed.). *Capital Movements and Economic Development*, from Proceedings of a Conference held by the International Economic Association, London and Basingstoke, Macmillan and New York, St Martin's Press, 1967.

ÅKERMAN, J. *Ekonomisk Teori*, vol. II, *Kausalanalys av det Ekonomiska Skeendet*, Lund, Gleerup, 1944.

ARROW, K. J. and CAPRON, W. M. 'Dynamic Shortages and Price Rises: the Engineer-Scientist Case', *Quarterly Journal of Economics*, vol. LXXIII, no. 2, May 1959, pp. 292–308.

ASH, R. and MITCHELL, H. D. 'Doctor Migration 1962–1964', *British Medical Journal*, March 2, 1968, pp. 569–72.

BARNÉNAS, J. 'International Movement of Public Long-term Capital and Grants, 1951–2'. International Monetary Fund, *Staff Papers*, vol. V, no. 1, February 1956, pp. 108–27.

BARRACLOUGH, G. *An Introduction to Contemporary History*, Harmondsworth, Penguin Books, 1967.

BASTABLE, C. F. 'On Some Disputed Points in the Theory of International Trade', *Economic Journal*, vol. XI no. 42, June 1901, pp. 226–9.

BASTABLE, C. F. *The Theory of International Trade, with some of its Applications to Economic Policy*, 2nd, 3rd and 4th eds., London, Macmillan, 1897, 1900 and 1903.

BEACH, W. E. *British International Gold Movements and Banking Policy, 1881–1913*, Cambridge, Mass., Harvard University Press, 1935.

BECKER, G. S. *Human Capital: A Theoretical and Empirical Analysis with Special Reference to Education*, New York, National Bureau of Economic Research, 1964.

BERNSTEIN, E. M. 'The Post-war Trend Cycle in the United States', Model Roland and Co., *Quarterly Review*, 1963, 1st quarter, pp. 1–10.

BESEN, S. M. 'Education and Productivity in U.S. Manufacturing: Some Cross-Section Evidence', *Journal of Political Economy*, vol. LXXVI, no. 3, May–June 1968, pp. 494–7.

BIRD, R. C., DESAI, M. J., ENZLER, J. J. and TAUBMAN, P. J. 'Kuznets Cycles in Growth Rates: the Meaning', *International Economic Review*, vol. VI, May 1965, pp. 229–39.

BLACKER, C. P. 'Stages in Population Growth', *Eugenics Review*, vol. 39, no. 3, October 1947, pp. 89–94.

BLAUG, M. (ed.). *Economics of Education*, vol. II, Harmondsworth, Penguin Books, 1969.

BLAUG, M., LAYARD, P. R. G. and WOODHALL, M. A. *The Causes of Graduate Unemployment in India*, London, Allen Lane The Penguin Press, 1969.

BLOOMFIELD, A. I. *Monetary Policy under the International Gold Standard: 1880–1914*, New York, Federal Reserve Bank of New York, 1959.

BLOOMFIELD, A. I. *Patterns of Fluctuation in International Investment Before 1914*, Princeton Studies in International Finance no. 21, Department of Economics, Princeton University, 1968.

BORTS, G. H. 'Comments on the papers by Brinley Thomas and Matthew Simon' in J. H. Adler (ed.), *Capital Movements and Economic Development*, q.v., pp. 60–70.

BORTS, G. H. and STEIN, J. L. 'Regional Growth and Maturity in the United States: a Study of Regional Structural Change', *Schweizerische Zeitschrift für Volkswirtschaft und Statistik*, vol. XCVIII, no. 1962, pp. 290–321.

BORTS, G. H. and STEIN, J. L. *Economic Growth in a Free Market*, New York, Columbia University Press, 1964.

BOWLEY, A. L. 'Area and Population' in *The New Survey of London Life and Labour*, vol. I, *Forty Years of Change*, London, P. S. King, 1930.

BOWLEY, A. L. *Wages and Income in the United Kingdom since 1860*, Cambridge University Press, 1937.

BROMWELL, W. J. *History of Immigration to the United States, 1819–1855*, New York, Redfield, 1856.

BROWN, A. J. 'Britain in the World Economy 1870–1914' in J. Saville (ed.) *Studies in the British Economy 1870–1914*, q.v.

BROWN, T. N. *Social Discrimination against the Irish in the United States* (mimeographed), New York, The American Jewish Committee, 1958.

BUCKLEY, K. 'Urban Building and Real Estate Fluctuations in Canada', *Canadian Journal of Economics and Political Science*, vol. XVIII, no. 1, February 1952, pp. 51–62.

BUCKLEY, K. *Capital Formation in Canada 1869–1930*, Toronto University Press, 1955.

BUCKLEY, K. *Population, Labour Force and Economic Growth, 1867–1962*, vol. II, Banff, Alberta, Banff School of Advanced Management, 1964.

BUTLIN, N. G. *Investment in Australian Economic Development, 1861–1900*, Cambridge University Press, 1964.

CAGAN, P. *Determinants and Effects of Changes in the Stock of Money 1875–1960*, New York, Columbia University Press for National Bureau of Economic Research, 1965.

CAIRNCROSS, A. K. 'Internal Migration in Victorian England', *Manchester School*, vol. XVII, no. 1, January 1949, pp. 67–87.

CAIRNCROSS, A. K. *Home and Foreign Investment 1870–1913: Studies in Capital Accumulation*, Cambridge University Press, 1953.

CAIRNES, J. E. 'Fragments on Ireland' (1866) in *Political Essays*, London, Macmillan, 1873.

CAIRNES, J. E. *Some Leading Principles of Political Economy*, London, Macmillan, 1874.

CAMPBELL, BURNHAM O. *Population Change and Building Cycles*, Urbana, Ill., Bureau of Economic and Business Research, University of Illinois, 1966.

CASSEL, G. *Theoretische Sozialökonomie*, 4th ed., Leipzig, Werner Scholl, 1927.

CHICKERING, J. *Immigration into the United States*, Boston, Mass., Little and Brown, 1848.

CLARK, C. 'Investment in Fixed Capital in Great Britain', *London and Cambridge Economic Service Special Memorandum*, no. 38, September 1934.

COALE, A. J. 'The Population of the United States in 1950 classified by Age, Sex and Color—a Revision of Census Figures', *Journal of the American Statistical Association*, vol. L, March 1955, pp. 16–54.

COATS, R. H. 'Statistics Comes of Age', *Canadian Journal of Economic and Political Science*, vol. II, no. 3, August 1936, pp. 269–87.

COATS, R. H. 'Two Good Neighbours: a Study of the Exchange of Populations', Canadian-American Affairs Conference at Queen's University, Kingston, Ont., 1937, *Proceedings*, ed. R. G. Trotter, A. B. Corey and W. W. McLaren, Toronto, Ginn, 1937.

COATS, R. H. and MACLEAN, M. C. *The American Born in Canada*, New Haven, Conn., Yale University Press, 1943.

COMMISSION ON INTERNATIONAL DEVELOPMENT (headed by the Rt. Hon. L. B. Pearson). *Partners in Development*, London, Pall Mall Press, 1969.

COMMITTEE ON INTERNATIONAL MIGRATION OF TALENT. *The International Migration of High-Level Manpower: Its impact on the Development Process*, New York, Praeger, 1970.

CONNELL, K. H. *The Population of Ireland, 1750–1845*, London, Oxford University Press, 1950.

COOMBS, W. *The Wages of Unskilled Labor in Manufacturing Industries in the United States, 1890–1924*, New York, Columbia University Press, 1926.

COONEY, E. W. 'Capital Exports and Investment in Building in Britain and the U.S.A. 1856–1914', *Economica*, new series, vol. XVI, no. 64, November 1949, pp. 347–54.

DAVIS, M. R. 'Critique of Official United States Immigration Statistics', App. II in I. Ferenczi and W. F. Willcox, *Internal Migrations*, vol. II, q.v.

DEDIJER, S. and SVENNINGSON, I. *Brain Drain and Brain Gain. A Bibliography on the Migration of Scientists, Engineers, Doctors and Students*, Lund, Research Policy Program, 1967.

DOUGLAS, P. H. 'Is the New Immigration More Unskilled than the Old?', *Journal of the American Statistical Association*, vol. XVI, no. 125, June 1919, pp. 393–403.

DU BOIS, W. E. B. *The Philadelphia Negro*, New York, Benjamin Blom, 1899, reissued 1967.

DUNNING, J. H. *American Investment in British Manufacturing Industry*, London, Allen and Unwin, 1958.

DYOS, H. J. *Victorian Suburb. A Study of the Growth of Camberwell*, Leicester University Press, 1961.

EASTERLIN, R. A. 'Influences in European Overseas Emigration before World War I', *Economic Development and Cultural Change*, vol. IX, no. 3, April 1961, pp. 331–51.

EASTERLIN, R. A. *Population, Labor Force and Long Swings in Economic Growth: The*

American Experience, New York, Columbia University Press for National Bureau of Economic Research, 1968.

ECKLER, A. R. and ZLOTNICK, J. 'Immigration and the Labor Force', *Annals of the American Academy of Political and Social Science*, vol. CCLXII, March 1949, pp. 92–101.

EDGEWORTH, F. Y. Review of C. F. Bastable, *The Theory of International Trade*, 2nd ed. (q.v.) in *Economic Journal*, vol. VII, no. 27, September 1897, pp. 397–403.

EDGEWORTH, F. Y. 'On a Point in the Theory of International Trade', *Economic Journal*, vol. IX, no. 33, March 1899, pp. 125–8.

EDGEWORTH, F. Y. Review of C. F. Bastable, *The Theory of International Trade*, 3rd ed. (q.v.) in *Economic Journal*, vol. X, no. 39, September 1900, pp. 389–93.

EDGEWORTH, F. Y. 'Disputed Points in the Theory of International Trade', *Economic Journal*, vol. XI, no. 44, December 1901, pp. 582–92.

EDGEWORTH, F. Y. *Papers relating to Political Economy*, vols. I and II, London, Macmillan, 1925.

EDWARDS, A. M. 'Social-economic Groups of the United States', *Journal of the American Statistical Association*, vol. XV, no. 118, June 1917, pp. 643–61.

EDWARDS, A. M. 'A Social-economic Grouping of the Gainful Workers of the United States', *Journal of the American Statistical Association*, vol. XXVIII, no. 184, December 1933, pp. 377–87.

EDWARDS, A. M. 'The White Collar Workers', *Monthly Labor Review*, vol. XXXVIII, no. 3, March 1934, pp. 501–5.

EDWARDS, A. M. 'Composition of the Nation's Labor Force', *Annals of the American Academy of Political and Social Science*, vol. CLXXXIV, March 1936, pp. 10–20.

EDWARDS, A. M. 'The Negro as a Factor in the Nation's Labor Force', *Journal of the American Statistical Association*, vol. XXXI, no. 195, September 1936, pp. 529–40.

EDWARDS, A. M. 'Growth and Significance of the White Collar Class', *American Federationist*, vol. XLV, no. 1, January 1938, pp. 32–4.

ELDRIDGE, H. T. and THOMAS, D. S. *Population Redistribution and Economic Growth, United States 1870–1950*, vol. III, *Demographic Anayses and Interrelations*, Philadelphia, American Philosophical Society, 1964.

ENGINEERS JOINT COUNCIL. 'The Future Supply of Engineers', *Engineering Manpower Bulletin*, no. 6, April 1967.

ENGINEERS JOINT COUNCIL. *Prospects of Engineering and Technology Graduates 1968*, New York, Engineering Manpower Commission, 1968.

ENGINEERS JOINT COUNCIL. *Professional Income of Engineers 1968–69*, New York, Engineering Manpower Commission, 1969.

ENGINEERS JOINT COUNCIL. 'The Future Supply of Engineers 1970–78', *Engineering Manpower Bulletin*, no. 17, September 1970.

FABRICANT, S. *Basic Facts on Productivity Change*, New York, National Bureau of Economic Research, Occasional Paper, no. 63, 1959.

FARLEY, R. *Growth of the Black Population: a Study of Demographic Trends*, Chicago, Markham, 1970.

FEINSTEIN, C. H. 'Home and Foreign Investment 1870–1913' (unpublished thesis, Cambridge University Library, 1959).

FEINSTEIN, C. H. 'Income and Investment in the United Kingdom, 1856–1914', *Economic Journal*, vol. LXXI, no. 282, June 1961, pp. 367–85.

FERENCZI, I. and WILLCOX, W. F. *International Migrations*, New York, National Bureau of Economic Research, vol. I, 1929, vol. II, 1931.

FISHLOW, A. *American Railroads and the Transformation of the Ante-Bellum Economy*, Cambridge, Mass., Harvard University Press, 1965.

FOERSTER, R. F. *The Italian Emigration of Our Times*, Cambridge, Mass., Harvard University Press, 1919.

FOGEL, R. W. and ENGERMAN, S. L. (eds.) *The Reinterpretation of American Economic History*, New York, Harper and Row, 1971.

FORD, A. G. *The Gold Standard 1880–1914: Britain and Argentina*, London, Oxford University Press, 1962.

FORD, A. G. 'Overseas Lending and Internal Fluctuations 1870–1914' in J. Saville (ed.), *Studies in the British Economy 1870–1914*, q.v.

FRIEDMAN, M. and SCHWARTZ, A. J. *A Monetary History of the United States 1867–1960*, New York, Princeton University Press for National Bureau of Economic Research, 1963.

GALLMAN, R. E. 'Gross National Product in the United States, 1834–1909' in National Bureau of Economic Research, *Output, Employment and Productivity in the United States after 1800*, New York, Columbia University Press, 1966.

GISH, O. 'The Royal Commission and the Immigrant Doctor', *The Lancet*, June 29, 1968, p. 1423.

GLASS, D. V. 'A Note on the Under-registration of Births in the Nineteenth Century', *Population Studies*, vol. v, no. 1, July 1951, pp. 70–88.

GLAZER, N. and MOYNIHAN, D. P. *Beyond the Melting Pot: the Negroes, Puerto Ricans, Jews, Italians and Irish of New York City*, Cambridge, Mass., M.I.T. Press, second edition, 1970.

GRILICHES, Z. 'Production Functions in Manufacturing: Some Preliminary Results' in M. Brown (ed.), *The Theory and Empirical Analysis of Production*, New York, Columbia University Press for National Bureau of Economic Research, 1967.

GRILICHES, Z. 'Research Expenditures, Education, and the Aggregate Agricultural Production Function', *American Economic Review*, vol. LIV, no. 6, December 1964, pp. 961–74.

GRUBEL, H. G. and SCOTT, A. D. 'The International Flow of Human Capital', *American Economic Review*, vol. LVI, no. 2, May 1966, pp. 268–74.

GRUBER, W., MEHTA, D. and VERNON, R. 'The R. and D. Factor in International Trade and International Investment of United States Industries', *Journal of Political Economy*, vol. LXXV, no. 1, February 1967, pp. 20–37.

HABAKKUK, H. J. 'Free Trade and Commerical Expansion, 1853–1870' in *Cambridge History of the British Empire*, vol. II, Cambridge University Press, 1940.

HABAKKUK, H. J. 'Fluctuations in House-building in Britain and the United States in the Nineteenth Century', *Journal of Economic History*, vol. XXII, no. 2, June 1962, pp. 198–230.

HABERLER, G. *The Theory of International Trade*, London, Hodge, 1936.

HALL, A. R. 'Some Long-period Effects of the Kinked Age Distribution of the Population of Australia, 1861–1961', *Economic Record*, vol. XXIX, no. 85, March 1963, pp. 43–52.

HALL, A. R. (ed.). *The Export of Capital from Britain 1870–1914*, London, Methuen, 1968.

HAMILTON, C. H. 'The Negro leaves the South', *Demography*, vol. 1, 1964, pp. 273–95.

HANDLIN, O. *Boston's Immigrants, 1790–1865: a Study in Acculturation*, Cambridge, Mass., Harvard University Press, 1941.

HANSEN, M. L. 'The Revolutions of 1848 and German Emigration', *Journal of Economic and Business History*, vol. II, August 1930, pp. 630–58.

HARKNESS, J. P. 'A Spectral-Analytic Test of the Long-Swing Hypothesis in Canada', *Review of Economics and Statistics*, vol. L, no. 4, November 1968, pp. 429–36.

HAUSER, P. (ed.) *Population and World Politics*, Glencoe, Ill., Free Press, 1958.

HAWTREY, R. G. *A Century of Bank Rate*, London, Longmans Green, 1938.

HECKSCHER, E. F. *Mercantilism*, English ed., London, Allen and Unwin, 1934.

HICKMAN, B. G. 'The Post-war Retardation: Another Long Swing in the Rate of Growth?', *American Economic Review*, vol. LIII, no. 2, May 1963, pp. 490–507.

HICKS, J. R. *A Contribution to the Theory of the Trade Cycle*, London, Oxford University Press, 1950.

HICKS, J. R. *A Theory of Economic History*, London, Oxford University Press, 1969.

HIGONNET, R. T. 'Bank Deposits in the United Kingdom 1870–1912', *Quarterly Journal of Economics*, vol. LXXI, no. 3, August 1957, pp. 329–67.

HIRSCHMAN, A. O. *National Power and the Structure of Trade*, Berkeley, Cal., University of California Press, 1945.

HURD, W. B. 'Population Movements in Canada, 1921–31', *Proceedings of the Canadian Political Science Asociation*, 1934.

HURD, W. B. and CAMERON, J. C. 'Population Movements in Canada, 1921–31: Some Further Considerations', *Canadian Journal of Economic and Political Science*, vol. I, no. 2, May 1935.

IMLAH, A. H. *Economic Elements in the Pax Britannica*, Cambridge, Mass., Harvard University Press, 1958.

ISARD, W. 'Transport Development and Building Cycles', *Quarterly Journal of Economics*, vol. LVII, no. 4, November 1942, pp. 90–112.

ISARD, W. 'A Neglected Cycle: the Transport-Building Cycle', *Review of Economic Statistics*, vol. XXIV, no. 4, November 1942, pp. 149–58.

JEFFERYS, J. B. and WALTERS, D. 'National Income and Expenditure of the United Kingdom, 1870–1952' in International Association for Research in Income and Wealth, *Income and Wealth*, series V, London, Bowes and Bowes, 1955.

JENKS, J. W. and LAUCK, W. J. *The Immigration Problem*, New York, Funk and Wagnalls, 1912.

JENKS, L. H. *The Migration of British Capital to 1875*, London, Cape, 1938.

JEROME, H. *Migration and Business Cycles*, New York, National Bureau of Economic Research, 1926.

JOHNSON, H. G. *International Trade and Economic Growth*, London, Allen and Unwin, 1958.

JOHNSON, H. G. 'Some Economic Aspects of Brain Drain', *Pakistan Development Review*, vol. VII, no. 3, Autumn 1967, pp. 379–41 (also in W. Adams (ed.), *The Brain Drain*, q.v.).

JOHNSON, S. C. *A History of Emigration from the United Kingdom to North America, 1763–1912*, London, Routledge, 1913.

JONES, G. T. *Increasing Return: a study of the relation between the size and efficiency of industries with special reference to the history of selected British and American industries, 1850–1910*, Cambridge University Press, 1933.

JONES, K. and SMITH, A. D. *The Economic Impact of Commonwealth Immigration*, Cambridge University Press, for National Institute of Economic and Social Research, 1970.

KALDOR, N. *Causes of the Slow Rate of Economic Growth of the United Kingdom*, Cambridge University Press, 1966.

KALDOR, N. 'Productivity and Growth in Manufacturing Industry: a Reply', *Economica*, vol. XXXV, no. 140, November 1968, pp. 385–91.

KALDOR, N. 'Conflicts in National Economic Objectives' in N. Kaldor (ed.) *Conflicts in Policy Objectives*, Oxford, Basil Blackwell, 1971.

KAPP, F. *Immigration and the Commissioners of Emigration of the State of New York*, New York, The Nation Press, 1870.

KEESING, D. B. 'The Impact of Research and Development on United States Trade', *Journal of Political Economy*, vol. LXXV, no. 1, February 1967, pp. 38–48.

KELLEY, A. C. 'Demographic Change and Economic Growth: Australia 1861–1911', *Explorations in Entrepreneurial History*, second series, vol. V, Spring–Summer 1968, pp. 207–77.

KENDRICK, J. W. *Productivity Trends in the United States*, National Bureau of Economic Research, Princeton University Press, 1961.

KEYNES, J. M. *The General Theory of Employment, Interest and Money*, London, Macmillan, 1936.

KEYNES, LORD, Speech on the International Clearing Union delivered in the House of Lords, 18 May 1943, reprinted in S. E. Harris (ed.), *The New Economics: Keynes' Influence on Theory and Public Policy*, London, Dennis Dobson, 1947, pp. 359–68.

KUZNETS, S. *Secular Movements in Production and Prices*, Boston and New York, Houghton Mifflin, 1930.

KUZNETS, S. *National Income: a Summary of Findings*, New York, National Bureau of Economic Research, 1946.

KUZNETS, S. *National Product since 1869*, New York, National Bureau of Economic Research, 1946.

KUZNETS, S. 'Long-term changes in the national income of the United States of America since 1870' in *Income and Wealth of the United States: Trends and Structure*, Income and Wealth series II, Cambridge, Bowes and Bowes, 1952.

KUZNETS, S. 'Long Swings in the Growth of Population and in Related Economic Variables', *Proceedings of the American Philosophical Society*, vol. CII, no. 1, February 1958, pp. 25–52.

KUZNETS, S. *Capital in the American Economy*, New York, Princeton University Press for National Bureau of Economic Research, 1961.

KUZNETS, S., MILLER, A. R. and EASTERLIN, R. A. *Population Redistribution and Economic Growth. United States 1870–1950*, vol. II, *Analysis of Economic Change*, Philadelphia, American Philosophical Society, 1960.

KUZNETS, S. and RUBIN, E. *Immigration and the Foreign Born*, New York, National Bureau of Economic Research, 1954.

LANGE, O. Review of J. A. Schumpeter, *Business Cycles* (q.v.) in *Review of Economic Statistics*, vol. XXIII, no. 4, November 1941, pp. 190–3.

LAYTON, W. T. and CROWTHER G. *An Introduction to the Study of Prices*, London, Macmillan, 1938.

LEAK, H. and PRIDAY, T. 'Migration from and to the United Kingdom', *Journal of the Royal Statistical Society*, vol. XCVI, pt. II, March 1933, pp. 183–239.

LEBERGOTT, S. 'Labor Force and Employment 1800–1960' in National Bureau of Economic Research, *Output, Employment and Productivity in the United States after 1800*, New York, Columbia University Press, 1966.

LEE, C. H. 'A Stock-Adjustment Analysis of Capital Movements: The United States–Canadian Case', *Journal of Political Economy*, vol. LXXVII, no. 4, pt. I, July–August 1969, pp. 512–23.

LEE, E. S., MILLER, A. R., BRAINERD, C. P. and EASTERLIN, R. A. *Population Redistribution and Economic Growth, United States 1870–1950*, vol. I, *Methodological Considerations and Reference Tables*, Philadelphia, American Philosophical Society, 1957.

LEONTIEF, W. 'Factor proportions and the structure of American trade: further theoretical and empirical analysis', *Review of Economics and Statistics*, vol. XXXVIII, no. 4, November 1956, pp. 386–407.

LEWIS, C. *America's Stake in International Investments*, Washington, Brookings Institution, 1938.

LEWIS, J. PARRY. 'Growth and Inverse Cycles: a Two-Country Model', *Economic Journal*, vol. LXXIV, no. 293, March 1964, pp. 109–18.

LEWIS, J. PARRY. *Building Cycles and Britain's Growth*, London, Macmillan, 1965.

LEWIS, W. A. *Economic Survey 1919–1939*, London, Allen and Unwin, 1949.

LIPSEY, R. E. *Price and Quantity Trends in the Foreign Trade of the United States*, New York, Princeton University Press for National Bureau of Economic Research, 1963.

LONG, C. D., JR. *Building Cycles and the Theory of Investment*, Princeton, N.J., Princeton University Press, 1940.

LUXEMBURG, ROSA. *The Accumulation of Capital*, tr. Agnes Schwarzschild, ed. Joan Robinson, London, Routledge and Kegan Paul, 1951.

MALTHUS, T. R. *An Essay on the Principle of Population as It affects the Future Improvement of Society*, London, 1798.

MARSHALL, A. *Principles of Economics*, 8th ed., London, Macmillan, 1922.

MARTINO, J. P. 'Science and Society in Equilibrium', *Science*, vol. CLXV, August 22, 1969, pp. 769–72.

MARX, K. *Capital*, 4th German ed., 1890, rev. Engels, tr. Eden and Cedar Paul, London, Allen and Unwin, 1928.

MATTHEWS, R. C. O. *The Trade Cycle*, Cambridge University Press, 1959.

MATTILA, J. M. and THOMPSON, W. R. 'Residential-Service Construction: a Study of Induced Investment', *Review of Economics and Statistics*, vol. XXXVIII, no. 4, November 1956, pp. 465–73.

MEIER, A. *Negro Thought in America, 1880–1915*, Ann Arbor, University of Michigan Press, 1963.

MERIVALE, H. *Lectures on Colonization and Colonies, delivered before the University of Oxford in 1839, 1840 and 1841 and reprinted in 1861*, London, Oxford University Press, 1928.

MILL, J. S. *Principles of Political Economy*, 6th ed., London, Longmans, 1909.

MITCHELL, B. R. and DEANE, P. *Abstract of British Historical Statistics*, Cambridge University Press, 1962.

MYRDAL, G. *An American Dilemma: the Negro Problem and Modern Democracy*, vol. I, New York and London, Harper, 1944, reissued 1962.

NELSON, R. R. and PHELPS, E. S. 'Investment in Humans, Technological Diffusion and Economic Growth', *American Economic Review*, vol. LVI, no. 2, May 1966, pp. 69–76.

OHLIN, B. 'Protection and Non-competing Groups', *Weltwirtschaftliches Archiv*, vol. XXXIII, January 1931, pp. 30–45.

O'LEARY, P. J. and LEWIS, W. A. 'Secular Swings in Production and Trade, 1870–1913', *Manchester School*, vol. XXIII, no. 2, May 1955, pp. 113–52.

PATINKIN, D. 'A "Nationalist" Model' in W. Adams (ed.), *The Brain Drain*, q.v.

PEACH, C. *West Indian Migration to Britain: A Social Geography*, London, Oxford University Press for Institute of Race Relations, 1968.

PHINNEY, J. T. 'Gold Production and the Price Level: the Cassel Three Per Cent Estimate', *Quarterly Journal of Economics*, vol. XLVII, no. 3, August 1933, pp. 647–79.

PIGOU, A. C. *Industrial Fluctuations*, London, Macmillan, 1927.

PONSONBY, G. and RUCK, S. K. 'Travel and Mobility' in *The New Survey of London Life*, vol. I, *Forty Years of Change*, London, P. S. King, 1930.

PREST, A. R. 'National Income of the United Kingdom, 1870–1946', *Economic Journal*, vol. LVIII, no. 229, March 1948, pp. 31–62.

RICARDO, D. *Principles of Political Economy and Taxation,* Gonner's ed., London, Bell, 1913.

RIGGLEMAN, J. R. 'Building Cycles in the United States, 1830–1935' (unpublished thesis, Johns Hopkins University Library, Baltimore).

ROBERTSON, D. H. 'New Light on an Old Story', *Economica*, new series, vol. xv, no. 60, November 1948, pp. 294–300.

ROBINSON, JOAN. *An Essay on Marxian Economics*, London, Macmillan, 1942.

ROSE, E. J. B. and ASSOCIATES. *Colour and Citizenship: A Report on British Race Relations*, London, Oxford University Press for Institute of Race Relations, 1969.

ROSTOW, W. W. *British Economy of the Nineteenth Century*, London, Oxford University Press, 1948.

ROUSSEAUX, P. *Les Mouvements de Fond de l'Economie Anglaise, 1800–1913*, Louvain, Institut de Recherches Economiques, 1938.

ROYAL INSTITUTE OF INTERNATIONAL AFFAIRS. *The Problem of International Investment*, London, Oxford University Press, 1937.

SAUL, S. B. 'House Building in England 1890–1914', *Economic History Review*, second series, vol. xv, no. 1, August 1962, pp. 119–37.

SAUL, S. B. 'The Export Economy 1870–1914' in J. Saville (ed.), *Studies in the British Economy 1870–1914*, q.v.

SAVILLE, J. (ed.). *Studies in the British Economy 1870–1914*, Special Number, *Yorkshire Bulletin of Economic and Social Research*, vol. XVII, no. 1, May 1965.

SCHLOTE, W. *Entwicklung und Strukturwandlungen des englischen Aussenhandels von 1700 bis zur Gegenwart*, Jena, 1938.

SCHUMPETER, J. A. *Business Cycles: a Theoretical, Historical and Statistical Analysis of the Capitalist Process*, vols. I and II, New York and London, McGraw Hill, 1939.

SHANNON, F. A. 'The Homestead Act and the Labor Surplus', *American Historical Review*, vol. XLI, no. 4, July 1936.

SHANNON, H. A. 'Bricks—A Trade Index, 1785–1849', *Economica*, new series, vol. I, no. 3, August 1934, pp. 300–18.

SHEPPARD, D. K. *The Growth and Role of U.K. Financial Institutions 1880–1962*, London, Methuen, 1971.

SIDGWICK, H. *The Principles of Political Economy*, London, Macmillan, 1883.

SIGSWORTH, E. M. and BLACKMAN, J. 'The Home Boom of the 1890s' in J. Saville (ed.), *Studies in the British Economy 1870–1914*, q.v.

SIMON, M. 'The United States Balance of Payments, 1861–1900' in National Bureau of Economic Research, *Trends in the American Economy in the Nineteenth Century*, Studies in Income and Wealth, vol. XXIV, Princeton, N.J., Princeton University Press, 1962.

SIMON, M. 'The Pattern of New British Portfolio Foreign Investment, 1865–1914' in J. H. Adler (ed.), *Capital Movements and Economic Development*, q.v.

SMITH, H. N. *Virgin Land*, Cambridge, Mass., Harvard University Press, 1950.

SMITH, K. C. and HORNE, G. F. 'An Index Number of Securities, 1867–1914', *London and Cambridge Economic Service Special Memorandum*, no. 37, June 1934.

SOULE, G. *Prosperity Decade*, London, Pilot Press, 1947.

SPENGLER, J. J. 'Migration within the United States', *The Journal of Heredity*, January 1936.

SPENSLEY, J. C. 'Urban Housing Problems', *Journal of the Royal Statistical Society*, vol. LXXXI, pt. II, March 1918, pp. 161–210.

STAMP, J. C. *British Incomes and Property: the Application of Official Statistics to Economic Problems*, London, P. S. King, 1916.

STOVEL, J. A. *Canada in the World Economy*, Cambridge, Mass., Harvard University Press, 1959.

SUNDBÄRG, G. *Bevölkerungsstatistik Schwedens, 1750–1900*, 2nd ed., Stockholm, Norstedt, 1923.

SUNDT, E. *Om Giftermål i Norge*, Christiania, 1855.

SVENNILSON, I. *Wages in Sweden, 1860–1930*, London, P. S. King, 1935.

SWEEZY, A. 'The Economic Explanation of Fertility Changes in the United States', *Population Studies*, vol. 25, no. 2, July 1971, pp. 255–67.

TAEUBER, K. and A. 'White Migration and Socio-economic Differences between Cities and Suburbs', *American Sociological Review*, vol. xxix, October 1964, pp. 718–29.

TAEUBER, K. and A. 'The Changing Character of Negro Migration', *American Journal of Sociology*, vol. lxx, January 1965, pp. 429–41.

TAUSSIG, F. W. *International Trade*, New York, Macmillan, 1928.

THOMAS, BRINLEY. 'The Migration of Labour into the Glamorganshire Coalfield, 1861–1911', *Economica*, new series, vol. x, no. 30, November 1930, pp. 275–94.

THOMAS, BRINLEY. 'Migration and the Rhythm of Economic Growth, 1830–1913', *Manchester School*, vol. xix, no. 3, September 1951, pp. 215–71.

THOMAS, BRINLEY. 'Migration and International Investment' in B. Thomas (ed.), *The Economics of International Migration*, London, Macmillan, 1958 (reprinted in A. R. Hall (ed.) *The Export of Capital from Britain 1870–1914*, q.v.).

THOMAS, BRINLEY. 'Wales and the Atlantic Economy', *Scottish Journal of Political Economy*, vol. vi, no. 3, November 1959, pp. 169–92.

THOMAS, BRINLEY, 'Recent Trends in American Investment in Western Europe', *The Three Banks Review*, no. 47, September 1960, pp. 3–21.

THOMAS, BRINLEY. 'International Factor Movements and Unequal Rates of Growth', *Manchester School*, vol. xxix, no. 1, January 1961, pp. 7–9.

THOMAS, BRINLEY. 'The Rhythm of Growth in the Atlantic Economy' in H. Hegeland (ed.), *Money, Growth and Methodology, and other Essays in Economics in Honor of Johan Åkerman, March 31, 1961*, Lund, Gleerup, 1961.

THOMAS, BRINLEY. "The Dimensions of British Economic Growth, 1688–1959', *Journal of the Royal Statistical Society*, series A, vol. cxxvii, pt. 1, 1964, pp. 111–23.

THOMAS, BRINLEY. 'Long Swings in Internal Migration and Capital Formation', *Bulletin of the International Statistical Institute* (Proceedings of the 34th Session), vol. xl, bk. 1, 1964, pp. 398–412.

THOMAS, BRINLEY. 'The Historical Record of International Capital Movements to 1913' in J. H. Adler (ed.), *Capital Movements and Economic Development*, q.v.

THOMAS, BRINLEY. 'The International Circulation of Human Capital', *Minerva*, vol. v, no. 4, Summer 1967, pp. 479–506.

THOMAS, BRINLEY. 'The International Circulation of Human Capital: a Reply to Harry G. Johnson', *Minerva*, vol. vi, no. 3, Spring 1968, pp. 423–7.

THOMAS, D. S. *Social and Economic Aspects of Swedish Population Movements, 1750–1933*, New York, Macmillan, 1941.

THOMPSON, W. J. 'The Census of Ireland, 1911', *Journal of the Royal Statistical Society*, vol. lxxvi, pt. 7, June 1913, pp. 635–62.

THOMPSON, W. S. and WHELPTON, P. K. *Population Trends in the United States*, New York and London, McGraw Hill, 1933.

TORRENS, R. *Speech in the House of Commons on the Motion for the Reappointment of a Select Committee for Emigration, February 15, 1827*, London, Longman, Rees, Orme, Brown and Green, 1828.

TORRENS, R. *Colonization of South Australia*, London, Longman, Rees, Orme, Brown and Green, 1835.

TRUESDELL, L. *The Canadian Born in the United States*, New Haven, Conn., Yale University Press, 1943.

TUCKER, G. *Progress of the United States in Population and Wealth in Fifty Years, as exhibited by the Decennial Census from 1790 to 1840*, New York, Press of Hunt's Merchant's Magazine, 1855.

URQUHART, M. C. and BUCKLEY, K. A. H. (eds.). *Historical Statistics of Canada*, Cambridge University Press, 1965.

VANCE, R. B. *Research Memorandum on Population Distribution in the United States*, New York, Social Science Research Council, 1938.

VANCE, R. B. *All These People: the Nation's Human Resources in the South*, Chapel Hill, University of North Carolina Press, 1945.

VERDOORN, P. J. 'Fattori che regolano lo sviluppo della produttività del lavoro', *L'Industria*, vol. I, 1949.

VINER, J. *Canada's Balance of International Indebtedness, 1900–1913*, Cambridge University Press, 1924.

VINER, J. *Studies in the Theory of International Trade*, London, Allen and Unwin, 1937.

VINER, J. 'Clapham on the Bank of England', *Economica*, new series, vol. XII, no. 46, May 1945, pp. 61–8.

WAKEFIELD, E. G. *A Letter from Sydney and Other Writings*, Everyman ed., London, Dent, 1929.

WEBER, B. 'A New Index of Residential Construction, 1838–1950', *Scottish Journal of Political Economy*, vol. II, no. 2, June 1955, pp. 104–32.

WEINER, M. L. and DALLA-CHIESA, R. 'International Movement of Public Long-term Capital and Grants', International Monetary Fund, *Staff Papers*, vol. IV, no. 1, September 1954, pp. 113–78.

WELLS, D. A. *Recent Economic Changes*, New York, Appleton, 1889.

WELTON, T. A. *England's Recent Progress: an Investigation of the Statistics of Migration, Mortality, etc. in the Twenty Years from 1881 to 1901 as indicating tendencies towards the Growth or Decay of Particular Communities*, London, Chapman and Hall, 1911.

WELTON, T. A. 'Note on Urban and Rural Variations according to the English Census of 1911', *Journal of the Royal Statistical Society*, vol. LXXVI, February 1913, pp. 304–17.

WICKSELL, K. *Finanztheoretische Untersuchungen*, Jena, Gustav Fischer, 1896.

WICKSELL, K. 'Frihandel och Utvandring', *Ekonomisk Tidskrift*, vol. XXII, nos. 3–4, 1920, pp. 124–5.

WICKSELL, K. *Lectures on Political Economy*, ed. Lionel Robbins, vol. I, London, Routledge, 1934.

WIDSTAM, T. 'Industriella konjunkturer, skördar och omflyttning', *Statsvetenskaplig Tidskrift*, vol. I, 1934.

WILKINSON, M. 'European Migration to the United States: An Econometric Analysis of Aggregate Labor Supply and Demand' (mimeographed paper presented to the European meeting of the Econometric Society, Brussels, September 1969).

WILLIAMS, J. H. 'The Theory of International Trade Reconsidered', *Economic Journal*, vol. XXXIX, no. 154, June 1929, pp. 195–209.

WILLIAMSON, J. G. *American Growth and the Balance of Payments, 1820–1913*, Chapel Hill, University of North Carolina Press, 1964.

WOOD, G. H. 'Real Wages and the Standard of Comfort since 1850', *Journal of the Royal Statistical Society*, vol. LXXII, pt. 1, March 1909, pp. 91–103.

YOUNG, A. 'Increasing Returns and Economic Progress', *Economic Journal*, vol. XXXVIII, no. 152, December 1928, pp. 527–42.

INDEX OF SUBJECTS

INDEX OF NAMES